36: *British Novelists, 1890-1929: Modernists,* edited by Thomas F. Staley (1985)

37: *American Writers of the Early Republic,* edited by Emory Elliott (1985)

38: *Afro-American Writers After 1955: Dramatists and Prose Writers,* edited by Thadious M. Davis and Trudier Harris (1985)

39: *British Novelists, 1660-1800,* 2 parts, edited by Martin C. Battestin (1985)

40: *Poets of Great Britain and Ireland Since 1960,* 2 parts, edited by Vincent B. Sherry, Jr. (1985)

41: *Afro-American Poets Since 1955,* edited by Trudier Harris and Thadious M. Davis (1985)

42: *American Writers for Children Before 1900,* edited by Glenn E. Estes (1985)

43: *American Newspaper Journalists, 1690-1872,* edited by Perry J. Ashley (1986)

44: *American Screenwriters,* Second Series, edited by Randall Clark, Robert E. Morsberger, and Stephen O. Lesser (1986)

45: *American Poets, 1880-1945,* First Series, edited by Peter Quartermain (1986)

46: *American Literary Publishing Houses, 1900-1980: Trade and Paperback,* edited by Peter Dzwonkoski (1986)

47: *American Historians, 1866-1912,* edited by Clyde N. Wilson (1986)

48: *American Poets, 1880-1945,* Second Series, edited by Peter Quartermain (1986)

49: *American Literary Publishing Houses, 1638-1899,* 2 parts, edited by Peter Dzwonkoski (1986)

50: *Afro-American Writers Before the Harlem Renaissance,* edited by Trudier Harris (1986)

51: *Afro-American Writers from the Harlem Renaissance to 1940,* edited by Trudier Harris (1987)

52: *American Writers for Children Since 1960: Fiction,* edited by Glenn E. Estes (1986)

53: *Canadian Writers Since 1960,* First Series, edited by W. H. New (1986)

54: *American Poets, 1880-1945,* Third Series, 2 parts, edited by Peter Quartermain (1987)

55: *Victorian Prose Writers Before 1867,* edited by William B. Thesing (1987)

56: *German Fiction Writers, 1914-1945,* edited by James Hardin (1987)

57: *Victorian Prose Writers After 1867,* edited by William B. Thesing (1987)

58: *Jacobean and Caroline Dramatists,* edited by Fredson Bowers (1987)

59: *American Literary Critics and Scholars, 1800-1850,* edited by John W. Rathbun and Monica M. Grecu (1987)

60: *Canadian Writers Since 1960,* Second Series, edited by W. H. New (1987)

61: *American Writers for Children Since 1960: Poets, Illustrators, and Nonfiction Authors,* edited by Glenn E. Estes (1987)

62: *Elizabethan Dramatists,* edited by Fredson Bowers (1987)

63: *Modern American Critics, 1920-1955,* edited by Gregory S. Jay (1988)

64: *American Literary Critics and Scholars, 1850-1880,* edited by John W. Rathbun and Monica M. Grecu (1988)

65: *French Novelists, 1900-1930,* edited by Catharine Savage Brosman (1988)

66: *German Fiction Writers, 1885-1913,* 2 parts, edited by James Hardin (1988)

67: *Modern American Critics Since 1955,* edited by Gregory S. Jay (1988)

68: *Canadian Writers, 1920-1959,* First Series, edited by W. H. New (1988)

69: *Contemporary German Fiction Writers,* First Series, edited by Wolfgang D. Elfe and James Hardin (1988)

70: *British Mystery Writers, 1860-1919,* edited by Bernard Benstock and Thomas F. Staley (1988)

(Continued on back endsheet)

Dictionary of Literary Biography • Volume Eighty-one

Austrian Fiction Writers, 1875-1913

Dictionary of Literary Biography • Volume Eighty-one

Austrian Fiction Writers, 1875-1913

Edited by
James Hardin
University of South Carolina

and

Donald G. Daviau
University of California, Riverside

A Bruccoli Clark Layman Book
Gale Research Inc. • Book Tower • Detroit, Michigan 48226

ST. PHILIP'S COLLEGE LIBRARY

Advisory Board for
DICTIONARY OF LITERARY BIOGRAPHY

Louis S. Auchincloss
John Baker
William Cagle
Jane Christensen
Patrick O'Connor
Peter S. Prescott

Matthew J. Bruccoli and Richard Layman, *Editorial Directors*
C. E. Frazer Clark, Jr., *Managing Editor*

Manufactured by Edwards Brothers, Inc.
Ann Arbor, Michigan
Printed in the United States of America

Copyright © 1989
GALE RESEARCH INC.

Contents

Plan of the Series vii
Foreword ix
Acknowledgments xi

Peter Altenberg (1859-1919) 3
   Andrew W. Barker

Leopold von Andrian (1875-1951) 11
   Jens Rieckmann

Raoul Auernheimer (1876-1948) 18
   Donald G. Daviau

Hermann Bahr (1863-1934) 29
   Donald G. Daviau

Richard Beer-Hofmann (1866-1945) 51
   Esther N. Elstun

Max Brod (1884-1968) 61
   Ehrhard Bahr

Franz Theodor Csokor (1885-1969) 71
   Michael Mitchell

Marie Eugenie delle Grazie (1864-1931) ... 78
   Jorun B. Johns

Marie von Ebner-Eschenbach (1830-1916) ... 86
   Jorun B. Johns

Albert Ehrenstein (1886-1950) 95
   Alfred D. White

Franz Karl Ginzkey (1871-1963) 100
   Jürgen Koppensteiner

Albert Paris Gütersloh (1887-1973) 106
   Ludwig Fischer

Enrica von Handel-Mazzetti (1871-1955) ... 113
   Josef Schmidt

Hugo von Hofmannsthal (1874-1929) 119
   Jens Rieckmann

Franz Kafka (1883-1924) 133
   Richard H. Lawson

Alfred Kubin (1877-1959) 169
   Phillip H. Rhein

Ernst Lothar (1890-1974) 177
   Donald G. Daviau

Max Mell (1882-1971) 185
   Jürgen Koppensteiner

Gustav Meyrink (1868-1932) 192
   George C. Schoolfield

Robert Musil (1880-1942) 208
   Michael W. Jennings

Franz Nabl (1883-1974) 224
   Herbert Herzmann

Leo Perutz (1882-1957) 232
   Bettina Kluth Cothran

Rainer Maria Rilke (1875-1926) 244
   George C. Schoolfield

Arthur Schnitzler (1862-1931) 272
   Gerd K. Schneider

Ernst Weiß (1882-1940) 293
   Klaus-Peter Hinze

Franz Werfel (1890-1945) 300
   Lionel B. Steiman

Stefan Zweig (1881-1942) 313
   Ruth V. Gross

Supplementary Reading List 337
Contributors 339
Cumulative Index 343

Plan of the Series

... Almost the most prodigious asset of a country, and perhaps its most precious possession, is its native literary product—when that product is fine and noble and enduring.

Mark Twain*

The advisory board, the editors, and the publisher of the *Dictionary of Literary Biography* are joined in endorsing Mark Twain's declaration. The literature of a nation provides an inexhaustible resource of permanent worth. We intend to make literature and its creators better understood and more accessible to students and the reading public, while satisfying the standards of teachers and scholars.

To meet these requirements, *literary biography* has been construed in terms of the author's achievement. The most important thing about a writer is his writing. Accordingly, the entries in *DLB* are career biographies, tracing the development of the author's canon and the evolution of his reputation.

The purpose of *DLB* is not only to provide reliable information in a convenient format but also to place the figures in the larger perspective of literary history and to offer appraisals of their accomplishments by qualified scholars.

The publication plan for *DLB* resulted from two years of preparation. The project was proposed to Bruccoli Clark by Frederick G. Ruffner, president of the Gale Research Company, in November 1975. After specimen entries were prepared and typeset, an advisory board was formed to refine the entry format and develop the series rationale. In meetings held during 1976, the publisher, series editors, and advisory board approved the scheme for a comprehensive biographical dictionary of persons who contributed to North American literature. Editorial work on the first volume began in January 1977, and it was published in 1978. In order to make *DLB* more than a reference tool and to compile volumes that individually have claim to status as literary history, it was decided to organize volumes by topic, period, or genre. Each of these freestanding volumes provides a biographical-bibliographical guide and overview for a particular area of literature. We are convinced that this organization—as opposed to a single alphabet method—constitutes a valuable innovation in the presentation of reference material. The volume plan necessarily requires many decisions for the placement and treatment of authors who might properly be included in two or three volumes. In some instances a major figure will be included in separate volumes, but with different entries emphasizing the aspect of his career appropriate to each volume. Ernest Hemingway, for example, is represented in *American Writers in Paris, 1920-1939* by an entry focusing on his expatriate apprenticeship; he is also in *American Novelists, 1910-1945* with an entry surveying his entire career. Each volume includes a cumulative index of subject authors and articles. Comprehensive indexes to the entire series are planned.

With volume ten in 1982 it was decided to enlarge the scope of *DLB*. By the end of 1986 twenty-one volumes treating British literature had been published, and volumes for Commonwealth and Modern European literature were in progress. The series has been further augmented by the *DLB Yearbooks* (since 1981) which update published entries and add new entries to keep the *DLB* current with contemporary activity. There have also been *DLB Documentary Series* volumes which provide biographical and critical source materials for figures whose work is judged to have particular interest for students. One of these companion volumes is entirely devoted to Tennessee Williams.

We define literature as the *intellectual commerce of a nation:* not merely as belles lettres but as that ample and complex process by which ideas are generated, shaped, and transmitted. *DLB* entries are not limited to "creative writers" but extend to other figures who in their time and in their way influenced the mind of a people. Thus the series encompasses historians, journalists, publishers, and screenwriters. By this means readers of *DLB* may be aided to perceive litera-

---

*From an unpublished section of Mark Twain's autobiography, copyright © by the Mark Twain Company.

Plan of the Series

ture not as cult scripture in the keeping of intellectual high priests but firmly positioned at the center of a nation's life.

DLB includes the major writers appropriate to each volume and those standing in the ranks immediately behind them. Scholarly and critical counsel has been sought in deciding which minor figures to include and how full their entries should be. Wherever possible, useful references are made to figures who do not warrant separate entries.

Each *DLB* volume has a volume editor responsible for planning the volume, selecting the figures for inclusion, and assigning the entries. Volume editors are also responsible for preparing, where appropriate, appendices surveying the major periodicals and literary and intellectual movements for their volumes, as well as lists of further readings. Work on the series as a whole is coordinated at the Bruccoli Clark Layman editorial center in Columbia, South Carolina, where the editorial staff is responsible for accuracy of the published volumes.

One feature that distinguishes *DLB* is the illustration policy–its concern with the iconography of literature. Just as an author is influenced by his surroundings, so is the reader's understanding of the author enhanced by a knowledge of his environment. Therefore *DLB* volumes include not only drawings, paintings, and photographs of authors, often depicting them at various stages in their careers, but also illustrations of their families and places where they lived. Title pages are regularly reproduced in facsimile along with dust jackets for modern authors. The dust jackets are a special feature of *DLB* because they often document better than anything else the way in which an author's work was perceived in its own time. Specimens of the writers' manuscripts are included when feasible.

Samuel Johnson rightly decreed that "The chief glory of every people arises from its authors." The purpose of the *Dictionary of Literary Biography* is to compile literary history in the surest way available to us–by accurate and comprehensive treatment of the lives and work of those who contributed to it.

The DLB Advisory Board

Foreword

Volume 81 of the *Dictionary of Literary Biography, Austrian Fiction Writers, 1875-1913,* treats two generations of Austrian writers of the twentieth century whose first published works appeared before 1914. Authors whose first works were published after that date will be covered in a subsequent *DLB* volume. The dates that mark each end of the span—the year of publication of Maria von Ebner-Eschenbach's first work and the last year before the outbreak of World War I—naturally do not indicate the period that is covered in the entries; they rather designate the period when these two generations of writers came of age. While any date that might have been chosen as a line of demarcation smacks of the arbitrary—the periodization of literature is always imprecise at best—there is an undeniable break in European history between the years before the outbreak of the war and the period afterward. The break is, of course, reflected in the literature—in its changed themes, techniques, and Weltanschauung. With regard to Austria, which at the end of the war was reduced by the harsh terms of the Versailles Treaty from its former illustrious status as the vast, powerful, and diverse Austro-Hungarian Empire of some fifty million people to a mere "torso," a "state that no one wanted" of less than eight million, the Great War represented a human tragedy of incalculable proportions and a historic watershed.

Several of the writers discussed in this volume were born in parts of that old Austria that ceased to be Austrian at the conclusion of the war: Max Brod, Franz Kafka, Gustav Meyrink, Leo Perutz, Rainer Maria Rilke, and Franz Werfel. All of these writers belonged to the strong German minority that lived in Prague at that time, and all but Rilke further represented the smaller Jewish enclave, a minority within a minority. But despite close ties to the Berlin expressionist movement—the intrepid Brod introduced most of the Prague writers to Berlin literary circles—all of these authors are part of the Austrian literary tradition thematically and stylistically.

The writers in this volume include all of the major figures of the fin de siècle generation: Leopold von Andrian, Hermann Bahr, Richard Beer-Hofmann, Hugo von Hofmannsthal, Kafka, Robert Musil, Rilke, and Arthur Schnitzler. In addition, a representative selection of lesser-known yet significant figures is treated: Peter Altenberg, Raoul Auernheimer, Franz Theodor Csokor, Marie Eugenie delle Grazie, Ebner-Eschenbach, Albert Ehrenstein, Franz Karl Ginzkey, Albert Paris Gütersloh, Enrica von Handel-Mazetti, Alfred Kubin, Ernst Lothar, Max Mell, Franz Nabl, Ernst Weiß, and Stefan Zweig.

We have included not only writers who appear in virtually every literary history—writers of unquestioned literary significance, those who are notable for their influence on contemporary writers and the public, and lesser talents who are especially representative of a given movement or tendency—but also unjustly neglected writers who may have received little attention in English, or, in some cases, even in German. Consequently, some of the most fascinating articles treat obscure figures such as the Prague eccentric Meyrink and his compatriot Perutz, whose works are experiencing something of a rebirth after years of neglect. Likewise, Werfel is currently enjoying a renaissance because of the approaching one-hundredth anniversary of his birth; new biographies have been devoted to him in both German and English.

Although not all of these authors were primarily fiction writers—Hofmannsthal and Rilke are best known as poets and Csokor and Schnitzler as dramatists, for example—the principle followed here, as in the previous *DLB* volumes on German writers, was to include such figures but to concentrate on their fiction works. In such cases the other genres are discussed insofar as they are relevant to the fiction and to the development of the writer in question.

The contributors to this volume attempted to look at their subjects with fresh eyes—to reevaluate their place in the literary canon and to examine their works at first hand, including little-known or "minor" works (the Rilke entry is an excellent example). They also devoted special attention to the primary bibliography of each

Foreword

writer, in some cases discovering that no reliable bibliography existed. The bibliography at the beginning of each entry lists all first editions of the subject's books in chronological order. If a work has been translated into English, the first American and British editions of the translation are listed. The primary bibliography also lists selected periodical publications, works translated by the subject, forewords and afterwords, contributions to collections, and books edited by the subject. As a result of our stress on bibliography, even the specialist will find information in some entries that was heretofore unavailable in English or German reference works.

The editors and contributors have attempted to present the articles in a way that will be understandable and useful. Assuming that many readers will have little or no knowledge of German, the entries include translations of German titles and quotations. German terms not readily understandable to a native speaker of English are also translated. Important secondary literature in both English and German is listed at the end of each entry. The location of letters and other papers (the *Nachlaß*, to use the German term) has been provided in all cases where it is known, since any serious study of the writer in question would have to include a careful evaluation of those materials.

DLB 81: Austrian Fiction Writers, 1875-1913 parallels the coverage of *DLB 66: German Fiction Writers, 1885-1913*. It is part of a series of *DLB* volumes treating German-language literature that also includes *DLB 56: German Fiction Writers, 1914-1945*; *DLB 69: Contemporary German Fiction Writers*, First Series; and *DLB 75: Contemporary German Fiction Writers*, Second Series. Future *DLB* volumes will treat the writers of the "Age of Goethe"; twentieth-century dramatists in Germany, Austria, and Switzerland; and seventeenth-century German writers.

–*James Hardin and*
Donald G. Daviau

Acknowledgments

This book was produced by Bruccoli Clark Layman, Inc. Karen L. Rood is senior editor for the *Dictionary of Literary Biography* series. Philip B. Dematteis was the in-house editor.

Production coordinator is Kimberly Casey. Art supervisor is Susan Todd. Penney L. Haughton is responsible for layout and graphics. Copyediting supervisor is Joan M. Prince. Typesetting supervisor is Kathleen M. Flanagan. William Adams, Laura Ingram, and Michael D. Senecal are editorial associates. The production staff includes Brandy H. Barefoot, Rowena Betts, Charles D. Brower, Joseph M. Bruccoli, Amanda Caulley, Teresa Chaney, Patricia Coate, Mary Colborn, Sarah A. Estes, Brian A. Glassman, Cynthia Hallman, Judith K. Ingle, Kathy S. Merlette, Sheri Beckett Neal, and Virginia Smith. Jean W. Ross is permissions editor.

Walter W. Ross and Jennifer Toth did the library research with the assistance of the reference staff at the Thomas Cooper Library of the University of South Carolina: Daniel Boice, Cathy Eckman, Gary Geer, Cathie Gottlieb, David L. Haggard, Jens Holley, Dennis Isbell, Jackie Kinder, Marcia Martin, Jean Rhyne, Beverly Steele, Ellen Tillett, Carol Tobin, and Virginia Weathers.

The editors would like to extend special thanks to the Austrian Cultural Institute, New York, for its assistance with this volume.

Dictionary of Literary Biography • Volume Eighty-one

Austrian Fiction Writers, 1875-1913

Dictionary of Literary Biography

Peter Altenberg
(9 March 1859-8 January 1919)

Andrew W. Barker
University of Edinburgh

BOOKS: *Wie ich es sehe* (Berlin: Fischer, 1896; revised, 1898; enlarged, 1904); translated by M. Nadir as *As I See It, and Others* (N.p., n.d.);

Ashantee (Berlin: Fischer, 1897);

Was der Tag mir zuträgt: Fünfundfünfzig neue Studien (Berlin: Fischer, 1901); enlarged as *Was der Tag mir züträgt: Fünfundsechzig neue Studien* (Berlin: Fischer, 1902);

Pròdrŏmŏs (Berlin: Fischer, 1906);

Die Auswahl aus meinen Büchern (Berlin: Fischer, 1908);

Märchen des Lebens (Berlin: Fischer, 1908; revised, 1911);

Bilderbögen des kleinen Lebens (Berlin: Reiß, 1909);

Der neue Weg der Genossenschaft deutscher Bühnenangehöriger: Ein Protest in Sachen Herwarth Walden, by Altenberg, Peter Baum, and others (Berlin: Verlag der Druckerei für Bibliophile, 1909);

Neues Altes (Berlin: Fischer, 1911);

Semmering 1912 (Berlin: Fischer, 1913; revised, 1913);

Fechsung (Berlin: Fischer, 1915);

Nachfechsung (Berlin: Fischer, 1916);

Vita ipsa (Berlin: Fischer, 1918);

Mein Lebensabend (Berlin: Fischer, 1919);

Der Nachlaß, edited by Alfred Polgar (Berlin: Fischer, 1925);

Nachlese, edited by Marie Mauthner (Vienna: Lányi, 1930);

Peter Altenberg: Auswahl aus seinen Büchern, edited by Karl Kraus (Vienna: Schroll, 1932);

Alexander King Presents Peter Altenberg's Evocations of Love (New York: Simon & Schuster, 1960);

Peter Altenberg: Reporter der Seele, edited by Gunther Martin (Graz & Vienna: Stiasny, 1960);

Peter Altenberg oder Das Genie ohne Fähigkeiten, edited by Ernst Randak (Graz & Vienna: Stiasny, 1961);

Das Glück der verlorenen Stunden: Auswahl aus dem Werk, edited by Wolfgang Kraus (Munich: Kösel, 1961);

Sonnenuntergang im Prater: Fünfundfünfzig Prosastücke, edited by Hans Dieter Schäfer (Stuttgart: Reclam, 1968);

Das Große Peter Altenberg Buch, edited by Werner J. Schweiger (Vienna & Hamburg: Zsolnay, 1977);

Diogenes in Wien: Aphorismen, Skizzen und Geschichten, edited by Dietrich Simon, 2 volumes (Berlin: Volk und Welt, 1979); published in West Germany as *Peter Altenberg, Ausgewählte Werke in zwei Bänden: Aphorismen, Skizzen und Geschichten* (Munich: Hanser, 1979);

Die Lebensmaschinerie, edited by Elke Erb (Leipzig: Reclam, 1980);

Peter Altenberg: Leben und Werk in Text und Bildern, edited by Hans Christian Kosler (Munich: Matthes & Seitz, 1981);

Gesammelte Werke in fünf Bänden, edited by Schweiger, 2 volumes published (Vienna & Frankfurt am Main: Kösel/Fischer, 1987-).

Peter Altenberg

Bildarchiv der Österreichischen Nationalbibliothek

OTHER: *Adolf Loos zum 60. Geburtstag am 10. Dezember 1930,* contributions by Altenberg (Vienna: Lányi, 1930).

Although Peter Altenberg enjoyed high esteem among writers as diverse as the brothers Mann, Robert Musil, Karl Kraus, Franz Kafka, and Gerhart Hauptmann, he has found little favor with the literary-critical establishment. For more than twenty years, however, this author of delightfully varied and often acute prose poems, vignettes, and short sketches was a central figure in Vienna during a period of cultural efflorescence unparalleled in modern times. Probably the most obviously "impressionistic" of all the creative writers in Austria at the turn of the century, Altenberg attracted a wide readership across the German-speaking lands and had almost all of his books published by the prestigious S. Fischer publishing house in Berlin. Described in the Hamburg newspaper *Die Zeit* (29 March 1985) as "die wahre Eminenz Wiens" (the true eminence of Vienna) and renowned as much for his outrageous life-style and mode of dress as for his literary prowess, Altenberg was one of the many "degenerate" writers whose work was suppressed by the Nazis. Only now, seven decades after his death, are there signs of a positive reassessment of an author who, but for the outbreak of war in 1914, would have been a Nobel laureate.

Born in Vienna in 1859 as Richard Engländer, the eldest son of Moriz Engländer, a wealthy businessman, and Pauline Schweinburg Engländer, Altenberg did not make his literary debut until the mid 1890s. By then he was already a well-known eccentric, haunting both the artistic circles of the Habsburg capital and the less salubrious demimonde of cabaret performers and good-time girls. Like so many other creative figures of the Viennese fin de siècle, Altenberg

Cover for a later edition of Altenberg's first book, a novel about Viennese social life at the turn of the century

was Jewish, though under the influence of his mentor Kraus he became a nominal Christian with the onset of the new century. His background, however, was that of the culturally assimilated Jewish bourgeoisie, whose standards he was vainly expected to emulate. The young Richard Engländer seems to have displayed no early promise as a writer and was spectacularly unsuccessful at cultivating the sort of career likely to appeal to his parents. He attended the Akademisches Gymnasium, which also counted or was later to count Franz Grillparzer, Hugo von Hofmannsthal, Arthur Schnitzler, and Richard Beer-Hofmann among its alumni, and after finally graduating in 1878 he made abortive attempts at the professions of law and medicine and an equally dismal foray into the book trade in Stuttgart. Medical opinion considered him incapable of regular employment because of an oversensitive nervous system; this inability to fulfill the norms of the work ethic led to a lasting rift with his mother, to whom he was attached with perhaps more than normal filial devotion. Altenberg never married, and it is tempting to perceive the beautiful yet estranged mother figure behind the many unsatisfactory affairs and unrequited passions which peppered his life and his writing. In Sigmund Freud's judgment, Altenberg suffered from "aesthetic impotence."

After his failure to establish himself even marginally in regular employment Engländer drifted ever more to the periphery of polite society. By 1902 he was living in a tiny room at the Hotel London, an establishment which was little different from a brothel, on Wallnerstraße. There he stayed for more than a decade, building up a fabled collection of picture postcards and nude pinups with which he covered the walls. (An artistic consequence of significance ensuing from this collecting mania can be found in Alban Berg's "Five Orchestral Pieces after Picture Postcard Texts of Peter Altenberg"; in the opinion of Igor Stravinsky this piece is not only one of the century's most innovative scores but also one of its most perfect. The public uproar at the first performance in March 1913 has gone down in the annals of music history alongside the premiere of *Le Sacre du Printemps*. Outraged listeners screamed for the composer to be committed to the lunatic asylum at Steinhof, where, as it happened, Altenberg himself had been confined since the previous December.)

Of Altenberg's life before his literary breakthrough with *Wie ich es sehe* (translated as *As I See*

*Caricature of Altenberg by Alexander King (*Alexander King Presents Peter Altenberg's Evocations of Love, *1960)*

It, n.d.) in 1896 relatively little is known, although the writer Felix Salten, who was then a journalist in Vienna, remembered him as the representative for a brand of Egyptian cigarettes. In the late 1880s and early 1890s he appears in Schnitzler's diaries and is mentioned in Schnitzler's correspondence with Hofmannsthal and Hermann Bahr. Earlier still Altenberg had enjoyed a friendship with Olga Waissnix, the Semmering hotelier's wife who played a decisive role in Schnitzler's emotional development. She died in 1897, and Altenberg published a poem about her titled "Die Jugendzeit" (Time of Youth) in *Märchen des Lebens* (Life's Fairy Tales, 1908).

According to Altenberg, his entrée as a writer came about almost by accident when Schnitzler chanced upon him in the celebrated avant-garde Café Griensteidl as he was engaged upon the sketch "Lokale Chronik," published in both *Ashantee* (1897) and *Was der Tag mir zuträgt* (What the Day Brings Me, 1901). Thanks to the good agencies of Schnitzler, Beer-Hofmann, Bahr, and Kraus, his literary gifts were recognized and encouraged, and Richard Engländer sloughed off his bourgeois background to reemerge as Peter Altenberg, the Viennese "décadent par excellence." The decision to abandon completely his original identity was symptomatic not only of the new course his life had struck but also of the primacy of the literary persona over the unsatisfactory reality of his life to that point. His choice of the pseudonym went back to a time in 1878 spent with a school friend at Altenberg on the Danube. There he had fallen in love with his friend's thirteen-year-old sister, Bertha Lechner, who was nicknamed Peter. Altenberg always felt attracted to pubescent girls still untainted by the baseness of masculine lust. They figure in *Wie ich es sehe*, as in all of his subsequent works, alongside "femmes fragiles," shop girls, actresses, prostitutes, society women, nannies, parlor maids, and frustrated bourgeois mothers with young children and old husbands. Indeed, in the kaleidoscopic particles of Altenberg's miniature art can be found endless celebrations of the female psyche alongside, in his later works, a fierce misogyny reminiscent of that of his fellow citizen Otto Weininger. Whereas *Wie ich es sehe* conjures up a swath of Viennese and Austrian social life from cashiers to bankers and industrialists—though hardly at all the industrial proletariat, of which Altenberg had scant experience—*Ashantee* deals with a tribe of West African natives whose village life was incongruously re-created in Vienna for the amusement of the populace. Altenberg refused to pander to this condescending voyeurism and attempted instead to reveal the tribe's nobility and uncorrupted dignity. Moriz Engländer, too, was much taken with these gentle "savages," which led someone to remark that he was showing signs of a congenital condition passed down from his son.

In *Was der Tag mir zuträgt* Altenberg returns to the topics of his first book; he includes an autobiographical sketch in which, in generally ironic terms, he sums up his work as being not art but "Extrakte des Lebens" (extracts of life). His eccentricities included views on the need for a new species of man to emerge from the debasement of contemporary life, a "new man" based on Greek ideals of the healthy mind in the healthy body. This goal was to be achieved through strict dietary reform, based on a reliance on easily digested foods, such as pureed vegetables, and a radical reappraisal of male sexual practices.

Pròdrŏmos (1906), in which the impact of Nietzsche is most keenly felt, is Altenberg's manifesto of this new life. Ironically, it came out at a time when he was increasingly suffering from the

Dust jacket for Altenberg's 1897 novel, which deals with a tribe of West African natives whose village life was re-created in Vienna for the amusement of the populace

cumulative physical and mental effects of drugs and alcohol. His impecuniousness was as legendary as his bizarre behavior and clothes, and he lived largely through the largesse of friends and family and through public appeals sponsored by writers such as Kraus and Alfred Kerr. In *Märchen des Lebens*, a grimly ironic title for an often deeply morose book, he recounts inter alia his experiences in one of the assorted asylums he frequented.

During this period he nevertheless managed to complete *Bilderbögen des kleinen Lebens* (Illustrated Broadsheets of the Humble Life, 1909), one of his finest collections and one much ad-

Altenberg in 1907 (Historisches Museum [Museen der Stadt Wien])

mired both by his friend, the great cultural historian Egon Friedell, and by Kraus. Shortly before the architect Adolf Loos secured Altenberg's freedom from the dreaded asylum Steinhof at the end of April 1913, Schnitzler noted in his diary that Altenberg was just as crazy, or just as sane, as he had ever been; he feared, though, and with complete justification, that Altenberg would soon turn to the solace of the bottle again.

On his release Altenberg traveled with Loos and his wife to Venice, where he spent the summer mixing with some of the leading figures of the emergent expressionist movement, such as Ludwig von Ficker and Georg Trakl, as well as Kraus and his publisher Fischer. His happy days there are commemorated in the section "Venedig" (Venice) in the collection *Semmering 1912* (1913). The primary inspiration for this collection was the few relatively carefree summer months he had spent recuperating on the Sem-

mering in 1912. There he had enjoyed a period of relative financial stability thanks to money raised through a newspaper appeal on his behalf and had attempted to come to grips with his alcoholism; by the end of the year, however, he had been in Steinhof. In October 1913 Loos informed Kraus in a letter that the poet was drinking up to eighteen bottles of beer a day.

Altenberg's problems were well advertised both by his friends and by the honesty of his literary self-revelations; in few writers, indeed, can it be harder to determine the boundaries between life and art. He seemed to be in a steep personal decline, yet he remained as popular as ever in Vienna. In 1914, jointly with Schnitzler, he was nominated for the Nobel Prize in literature. The outbreak of war, however, caused the cancellation of the award for that year, and upon its resumption in 1915 it went to Romain Rolland. Altenberg's moment had come and gone, and his decline accelerated in the cruel climate of the Great War. His dependence on drugs and alcohol never abated, and his abode remained a tiny room in the Graben Hotel, alternating with his seat in the Café Central, from which he could watch the world go by. He continued to write, albeit in an increasingly repetitive manner and in a style even more fractured than before. He was obsessed with himself, his digestion, his mortality, and his notions for the reform of humankind. Yet time and again the quirky humor which forms such a refreshing and delightful aspect of his work punctures the gathering gloom, as in these passages from the collection *Fechsung* (Harvest, 1915):

Splitter

Sie ist fast die ganze Hälfte des Jahres so nett zu mir- - -!

Ja, sechs Wochen vor Weihnachten, sechs Wochen vor ihrem Geburtstag, sechs Wochen vor ihrem Namenstag und sechs Wochen vor deinem Besuch in ihrem Seebad. Macht schon ein ganzes halbes Jahr!

(Splinters)

(She's been so nice to me for almost a whole half year- - -!

Well, six weeks before Christmas, six weeks before her birthday, six weeks before her nameday, and six weeks before you visit her at the spa. That makes a whole half year!)

Ein glückliches Paar: Er tut, was sie will - - -und sie tut, was sie will.

Altenberg in 1912

(A happy couple: he does what she wants, and she does what she wants.)

"Was wirst du tun, wenn du mich verlierst?!"
"Dann suche ich mir eine Wertvollere!"
"Da bleibe ich lieber bei dir!"

("What will you do if you lose me?!"
"I'll go find someone better!"
"In that case I'll stay with you!")

Like the majority of Austrian and German writers, Altenberg responded to the outbreak of war with narrow nationalistic fervor; his works published during the hostilities, however, often betray a deep skepticism about such responses to the fighting. He did not embark on an unremitting crusade against the war in the manner of Kraus; he lacked Kraus's stamina, single-mindedness, and capacity for contempt. But he never tried to defend the indefensible, and in "Kriegshymnen" (War Hymns) in *Fechsung*, the first of his wartime collections, he strikes a mordantly satirical tone which must have greatly appealed to Kraus. Along with the vast majority of the civilian population he suffered increasing deprivation as the war dragged on and the long dominion of the Habsburgs crumbled. Altenberg's concern was less, though, with the state and its future than with his chances of seeing his sixtieth birthday. This notion became an obsession as his health collapsed, and his last collections are filled with the premonition of death. In *Vita ipsa* (1918), for example, he pictures his own funeral, the coffin festooned not with wreaths and tributes but with details of donations in lieu of flowers to the Viennese Society for the Prevention of Cruelty to Children.

The end came hard on the heels of the collapse of the empire. At the end of 1918 Altenberg noted in his diary: "The night before last, at 1 A.M. on December 19th, a full glass of wine fell onto my linen and I slept peacefully in the icy wetness with the windows wide open. In the morning the bronchial catarrh of my youth had returned. Sunt certi denique fines!" Altenberg died on 8 January 1919, and his funeral attracted an enormous turnout. Kraus delivered the oration as the poet was laid to rest in a "Grave of Honor" in Vienna's Central Cemetery. The headstone was designed by Loos and bore the simple inscription Altenberg had requested: "Er liebte und sah" (He loved and saw). The writer who had come to regard himself as the archetypically neglected genius, who had pleaded poverty for as long as anyone could remember, is reported to have left a small fortune to a Viennese children's charity. Kraus, Friedell, Polgar, and others strove to preserve Altenberg's writing and his memory, but oblivion soon overcame the work; the memory lives on in Vienna as the epitome of the lovable eccentric. His writing still awaits full critical assessment; yet not only was he widely read in his day (*Wie ich es sehe* had already reached its fifteenth edition at the time of Altenberg's death), but his work also provided inspiration for such diverse writers as Thomas Mann, Rainer Maria Rilke, Schnitzler, Franz Werfel, and Kafka: one might compare, for instance, Altenberg's 1909 sketch "Die Hungerkünstlerin" (The [Female] Hunger Artist), published in *Bilderbögen des kleinen Lebens*, with Kafka's "Ein

Portrait of Altenberg by Oskar Kokoschka

Hungerkünstler" (translated as "The Hunger-Artist," 1938) of 1922.

Altenberg's work is seen as the essence of Viennese impressionism, yet it was also hailed as a precursor of expressionism and has even been seen as leading to the collage techniques of 1960s pop art. Robert Musil pondered whether Altenberg was a great writer and concluded that he sometimes was, though mostly not. Today, however, the basis on which such categorical ranking of authors is made is increasingly called into question, and it is possible that a fuller picture of Altenberg will emerge. He wrote no novels, no stage dramas, and only a handful of conventionally recognizable poems; instead, he created his own miniature forms based on acute perception reproduced in what he dubbed the "Telegrammstil der Seele" (telegram style of the soul). As Musil noted, to read Altenberg's work is an exhausting process, just as reading poetry is tiring. In his books Altenberg has left thousands of fragments which, if viewed individually, may appear slight and inconsequential as well as tediously repetitive. Stepping back from the works, however, one realizes that, intentionally or not, Altenberg has provided a vast mosaic, a composite picture of the life and times of the dying empire just as sensitive, acute, and revealing as anything in the works of those more renowned contemporaries who were so fulsome in their praise of Musil's "Christus mit einem Hornkneifer" (Christ figure in the horn-rimmed lorgnette).

Letters:

Hermann Bahr, "Die Bücher zum wirklichen Leben," in his *Buch der Jugend* (Vienna & Leipzig: Heller, 1908), pp. 144-150;

Das Altenbergbuch, edited by Egon Friedell (Leipzig, Vienna & Zurich: Verlag der Wiener graphischen Werkstätte, 1921);

Egon Friedell: Briefe, edited by Walther Schneider (Vienna & Stuttgart: Prachner, n.d.).

References:

Andrew W. Barker, "Peter Altenberg's Literary Catalysis," in *From Vormärz to Fin de Siècle: Essays in Nineteenth-Century Austrian Literature*, edited by M. G. Ward (Blairgowrie: Lochee, 1986), pp. 91-106;

Barker, " 'Die weiseste Ökonomie bei tiefster Fülle'–Peter Altenberg's *Wie ich es sehe*," in *Studies in Nineteenth-Century Austrian Literature*, edited by B. O. Murdoch and Ward (Glasgow: Scottish Papers in Germanic Studies, 1983), pp. 77-101;

Hans Bisanz, *Peter Altenberg: Mein äußertes Ideal* (Vienna: Brandstaetter, 1987);

Geoffrey Broad, "The Didactic Element in the Works of Peter Altenberg," Ph.D. dissertation, University of Otago, 1980;

Jens M. Fischer, *Fin de Siècle: Kommentar zu einer Epoche* (Munich: Winkler, 1978), pp. 157-168;

Egon Friedell, *Ecce Poeta* (Berlin: Fischer, 1912);

Friedell, "Peter Altenberg: Zu seinem 50. Geburtstag," in Peter Altenberg, *Bilderbögen des kleinen Lebens* (Berlin: Reiß, 1909), pp. 207-218;

Maria Gelsi, *Peter Altenberg: La strategia della rinuncia* (Rome: Edizioni dell'Atene, 1982);

Randolph J. Klawiter, "Peter Altenberg and Das Junge Wien," *Modern Austrian Literature*, 4 (Winter 1968): 1-55;

Irene Köwer, *Peter Altenberg als Autor der literarischen Kleinform* (Frankfurt am Main, Bern, New York & Paris: Lang, 1987);

D. S. Low, "Peter Altenberg: A Case of Neglect," *Trivium*, 4 (1969): 31-42;

Helga Malmberg, *Widerhall des Herzens: Ein Peter Altenberg-Buch* (Munich: Langen & Müller, 1961);

Robert Musil, "Peter Altenberg und die Tänzerin," in his *Gesammelte Werke*, edited by Adolf Frisé (Reinbek: Rowohlt, 1978), VII: 711-715;

Altenberg's grave in Vienna, designed by Adolf Loos (photo by Kurt Gerlach)

Stefan Nienhaus, *Das Prosagedicht im Wien der Jahrhundertwende: Altenberg–Hofmannsthal–Polgar* (Berlin & New York: De Gruyter, 1986);

H. Nunberg and E. Federn, eds., *Minutes of the Vienna Psychoanalytic Society*, translated by Nunberg (New York: International Universities Press, 1967), II: 392;

Hedwig Prohaska, "Peter Altenberg: Versuch einer Monographie," Ph.D. dissertation, University of Vienna, 1948;

Camillo Schaefer, *Peter Altenberg: Ein biographischer Essay* (Vienna: Freibord, 1980);

Barbara Z. Schoenberg, "The Art of Peter Altenberg: Bedside Chronicles of a Dying World," Ph.D. dissertation, University of California, Los Angeles, 1984;

Schoenberg, " 'Woman Defender' and 'Woman Offender': Peter Altenberg & Otto Weininger. Two Literary Stances vis-à-vis Bourgeois Culture in the Viennese 'belle époque,' " *Modern Austrian Literature*, 20, no. 2 (1987): 51-69;

Josephine M. N. Simpson, *Peter Altenberg: A Neglected Writer of the Viennese Jahrhundertwende* (Frankfurt am Main, Bern, New York & Paris: Lang, 1987);

W. Burkhard Spinnen, "Die Seele in der Kritik: Zur Rezeption der literarischen Werke Peter Altenbergs bis 1945," M.A. thesis, University of Münster, 1983;

Peter Wagner, "Peter Altenbergs Prosadichtung: Untersuchungen zur Thematik und Struktur des Frühwerks," Ph.D. dissertation, University of Münster, 1985;

Gisela von Wysocki, *Peter Altenberg: Bilder und Geschichten des befreiten Lebens* (Munich & Vienna: Hanser, 1979).

Papers:
Major holdings of Peter Altenberg's papers are in the Historisches Museum der Stadt Wien and the Bibliothek der Stadt Wien, Vienna, and the Leo Baeck Institute and the Galerie St. Etienne, New York City.

Leopold von Andrian

(9 May 1875-19 November 1951)

Jens Rieckmann
University of Washington

BOOKS: *Hannibal: Romanzen-Cyclus* (Venice: Kirchmeyer & Scozzi, 1888);
Der Garten der Erkenntnis (Berlin: Fischer, 1895); enlarged as *Der Garten der Erkenntnis und die Jugendgedichte* (The Hague: De Zilverdistel, 1913); republished as *Das Fest der Jugend: Des Gartens der Erkenntnis erster Teil, und die Jugendgedichte* (Berlin: Fischer, 1919); enlarged as *Das Fest der Jugend: Des Gartens der Erkenntnis erster Teil, die Jugendgedichte und ein Sonett* (Graz: Schmidt-Dengler, 1948);
Die Ständeordnung des Alls: Rationales Weltbild eines katholischen Dichters (Munich: Kosel & Pustet, 1930);
Österreich im Prisma der Idee: Ein Katechismus der Führenden (Graz: Schmidt-Dengler, 1937);
Leopold Andrian und Die Blätter für die Kunst, edited by Walter H. Perl (Hamburg: Hauswedell, 1960);
Der Garten der Erkenntnis: Mit Dokumenten und zeitgenössichen Stimmen, edited by Perl (Frankfurt am Main: Fischer, 1970);
Frühe Gedichte, edited by Perl (Hamburg: Hauswedell, 1972).

OTHER: "Erinnerungen an meinen Freund," in *Hugo von Hofmannsthal: Die Gestalt des Dichters im Spiegel der Freunde*, edited by Helmut A. Fiechtner (Vienna: Humboldt, 1949), pp. 52-64.

PERIODICAL PUBLICATIONS: "Die Wurzeln des Weltkrieges," *Berliner Tagesblatt*, 5 October 1919, 26 October 1919;
"Das erniedrigte und erhöhte Polen," *Österreichische Rundschau*, 17 (1921): 892-910, 981-994;
"Das große Salzburger Welttheater," *Hochland*, 20 (1922): 177-180;
"Die metaphysische Ständeordnung des Alls: Rationale Grundlagen eines christlichen Weltbildes," *Neue deutsche Beiträge*, 3 (1927): 55-88;
"Meine Tätigkeit als Intendant der Wiener Hoftheater," *Neue Freie Presse*, 28 October 1928, pp. 29-30; 4 November 1928, pp. 33-34; 8 November 1928, pp. 12-13;
"Hofmannsthal und die österreichische Jugend," *Vaterland*, 8 (1934): 130-136;
"Über den Humanismus: Aus den 'Gesprächen dreier Abende,' " *Corona*, 6 (1935-1936): 552-567;
"Vaterland und Vaterlandsvolk," *Neues Wiener Tagblatt*, 7 January 1938;
"Polen, Rußland und die Ukrainer," *Die Ostschweiz: Schweizerisches Tagblatt*, 6 November 1939, 7 November 1939;
"Deutsche und Russen im polnischen Empfinden," *Die Ostschweiz: Schweizerisches Tagblatt*, 10 November 1939, 11 November 1939.

Leopold von Andrian

Shortly after the publication of Leopold von Andrian's short novel *Der Garten der Erkenntnis* (The Garden of Knowledge, 1895), Hermann Bahr, the spokesman for a group of Austrian writers known since 1891 as "Young Vienna," proclaimed that no name in Europe was more famous than Andrian. Before the publication of the novel he had predicted: "Wenn von einem von den modernen Schriftstellern zwei Zeilen leben werden, so sinds welche vom Andrian" (If two lines of any of the modern writers should survive, then they will be lines by Andrian). Bahr's estimation, although exaggerated, was not altogether without merit. Today most critics would agree that, after Hugo von Hofmannsthal, Arthur Schnitzler, and Richard Beer-Hofmann, Andrian was one of the most talented of the Young Viennese writers. Furthermore, Andrian's lifelong preoccupation with Austrian culture as distinct from German culture, which culminated in his *Österreich im Prisma der Idee: Ein Katechismus der Führenden* (Austria in the Prism of the Idea: A Catechism of the Leaders, 1937), assures him a permanent place in Austrian cultural history.

Andrian was born on 9 May 1875 in Berlin; the ardent Austrian patriot tried all his life to keep his place of birth a secret. His father was Ferdinand von Andrian of the noble family of von Andrian-Werburg; his mother, Cäcilie Meyerbeer von Andrian, was the daughter of the Jewish composer Giacomo Meyerbeer. Andrian believed that this German-Jewish, Austrian-Catholic heritage, "die hastige Vermischung zweier sehr avancierter Racen" (the hasty amalgamation of two highly developed races), as he termed it, predestined him to an outsider's existence. In 1885 Andrian was admitted to the exclusive Jesuit boarding school at Kalksburg near Vienna, where, sometime in the next two years, he had the first presentiments of his homosexual orientation. A precocious boy, he read voraciously and started writing poetry when he was ten years old; already he was driven by the ambition to become a great poet, convinced that his fame would raise his family to the most illustrious moment of its history. In 1888 he made his literary debut with a cycle of romances titled *Hannibal*, which he published at his own expense. This epigonic work gave no indication that within a few years Andrian would emerge as one of the most prominent and talented modernist poets of the Young Vienna movement.

Andrian notes in his diary that the transition from epigone to modernist poet occurred shortly after he graduated in 1893 from the prestigious Schottengymnasium in Vienna, and before he enrolled as a law student at the University of Vienna. Reading Paul Bourget's *Mensonges* (1887; translated as *Lies*, 1892) secretly during his Greek and Latin lessons changed his literary direction. From then on he read such prototypical modern writers as Charles Baudelaire, Pierre Loti, Stéphane Mallarmé, Paul Verlaine, Jens Peter Jacobsen, Maurice Maeterlinck, and Oscar Wilde. Perhaps even more significant for his development as a writer was his meeting in the late fall of 1893 with Hofmannsthal, who had already emerged as the most promising of the Young Vienna poets. Their friendship was to last until Hofmannsthal's death in 1929. Even before he made the acquaintance of the nineteen-year-old Hofmannsthal, Andrian had sent one of his poems, "Sie schwieg und sah mit einem Blick mich an" (She was silent and looked at me with a glance) to C. A. Klein, the editor of the *Blätter für die Kunst*. This esoteric journal, founded in 1892 by the German symbolist poet Stefan George, published this and eight other poems by Andrian between 1894 and 1900.

"Sie schwieg und sah mit einem Blick mich an," the best of Andrian's poems to this point in his life, is characterized by what Hofmannsthal admired most in Andrian's poetry: "diese Vergleiche zwischen ganz verschiedenen Sachen ... diese merkwürdigen, wahren, *rätselhaften* Analogien" (these comparisons between two totally different things ... these remarkable, true, and *enigmatic* analogies). In his best poems, such as "Ich bin ein Königskind" (I am a royal prince), "Der Feste Süßigkeit wenn sie zu Ende gehn" (The sweetness of feasts when they end), or "Dann sieht die Seele" (Then the soul sees), Andrian succeeded in transforming moods into metaphors and symbols. Poems, he noted in his diary, should be "hyper-stilisiert, alles Zufällige ist verschwunden" (hyper-stylized, everything accidental [must] vanish), for only then can the poem become a symbol "von großen geheimnisvollen Vorgängen, Zuständen der Seele" (of great and mysterious processes, of states of the soul). Such statements and the poems he wrote between 1893 and 1895 show Andrian's affinities with the symbolist school of poetry.

In 1895 the S. Fischer house published the short novel which was to make Andrian famous, *Der Garten der Erkenntnis*. The book was widely and for the most part favorably reviewed in the leading literary journals; a parody, "Die Geschichte vom müden Fürsten und seinen 100

Stubenmädchen" (The Story of the Tired Prince and His 100 Chambermaids), appeared in 1897, as sure a sign of its fame as Karl Kraus's satiric mention of the "Kindergarten der Unkenntnis" (The Kindergarten of Ignorance) in his polemic pamphlet *Die demolierte Literatur* (Demolished Literature, 1896). Erwin, the protagonist of this miniature Bildungsroman, is a typically modern variant of the quester figure: at the end of his quest for "die Lösung des Geheimnisses vom Leben" (the solution to the secret of life), he dies "ohne erkannt zu haben" (without having gained knowledge).

The wide appeal of the novel can in part be attributed to the sympathy a whole generation felt with the Weltanschauung expressed in it, just as 120 years earlier a whole generation had identified with Goethe's *Die Leiden des jungen Werthers* (1774; translated as *The Sorrows of Werther*, 1779); by 1902 the novel was referred to as the "Wiener Werther-Buch" (Viennese Werther book). The major themes in *Der Garten der Erkenntnis*—narcissism, aestheticism, solipsism, the duality of life, and the crisis of knowledge—struck a responsive chord. They were further developed and explored in much turn-of-the-century Austrian literature, particularly in such seminal works as Hofmannsthal's *Reitergeschichte* (A Tale of the Cavalry, 1899) and "Das Märchen der 672. Nacht" (1905; translated as "A Tale of the Merchant's Son and His Servants," 1969), Beer-Hofmann's *Der Tod Georgs* (Georg's Death, 1900), and Robert Musil's *Die Verwirrungen des Zöglings Törleß* (1906; translated as *Young Törless*, 1955). The success of *Der Garten der Erkenntnis* can also be attributed to its aesthetic qualities: Andrian was the first Austrian writer who largely succeeded in applying symbolist poetic techniques to fiction. The novel is lyrical in character, the language precious and highly stylized. Andrian employs the evocation of objects to convey to the reader the dreamlike states of the soul of his protagonist. Particularly striking are the mysterious, continued metaphors, which derive their effectiveness from the associative pattern they form in the reader's mind. The protagonist's anticipation of his future life as a battle between the church and the world, for example, is expressed in this striking metaphor: "so wie wenn von den Enden der Welt zwei Helden zu kämpfen kommen, der tapferste Held des Morgenlands und der tapferste Held des Abendlands, und sie sich begrüßt haben und mit gesenkten Lanzen und geöffneten Visieren fast des Kampfes vergessen, weil sie einander anschauen" (as if two heroes come from the ends of the world to wage battle, the most courageous hero of the East and the most courageous hero of the West, and having saluted each other they almost forget the battle, their lances lowered, their visors opened, because they gaze at each other). The novel was admired by such diverse writers as Maeterlinck, George, André Gide, Gerhart Hauptmann, Klaus Mann, and Thornton Wilder.

With the exception of the sonnet "Dem Dichter Österreichs" (To Austria's Poet), written on the occasion of Hofmannsthal's fiftieth birthday in 1924, Andrian published no poetry or fiction after 1895. Yet he did not abandon the hope of being a creative writer, and from 1918 on, as his letters to Hofmannsthal, his diaries, and his notebooks make clear, he intended a "retour à l'art." Evidence that he partly realized this goal is a lengthy, unpublished manuscript of an autobiographical novel, "Der Lauf zum Ideal: Des Gartens der Erkenntnis zweiter Teil" (The Path to the Ideal: The Second Part of the Garden of Knowledge).

Much speculation has surrounded Andrian's falling silent as a poet and novelist. The most commonly held view is that he passed through a language crisis—a sudden feeling that words are totally inadequate to express meaning—and that this experience served Hofmannsthal as a model for his "Ein Brief" (1902; translated as "The Letter," 1942). But there is no evidence in Andrian's diaries, notebooks, or letters for this view, nor for the theory that Andrian's crisis as a writer was caused by his sexual orientation. The crisis actually had its roots in the narcissistic Weltanschauung of the twenty-one-year-old Andrian; it was triggered by an "ethisches Erwachen" (ethical awakening) which caused him to reevaluate this Weltanschauung centered "ausschließlich um Ichliebe" (exclusively around love for the self). Andrian's motto from then on was "weg vom Ich" (away from the self); he hoped to achieve this distancing from the self by a "Wille zur Wahrhaftigkeit" (will to objectivity). True knowledge, he was convinced, could be gained only if one perceived the universe within the self and the universe surrounding the self as separate entities, not as mirror images of each other. The "ethical awakening" also meant, however, that Andrian found it impossible to continue writing. The imagination, an indispensable faculty for the artist, had become suspect. Since the imagination, the "herrschende[s] Numen der Kinder- und Jünglingszeit" (dominant numen of child-

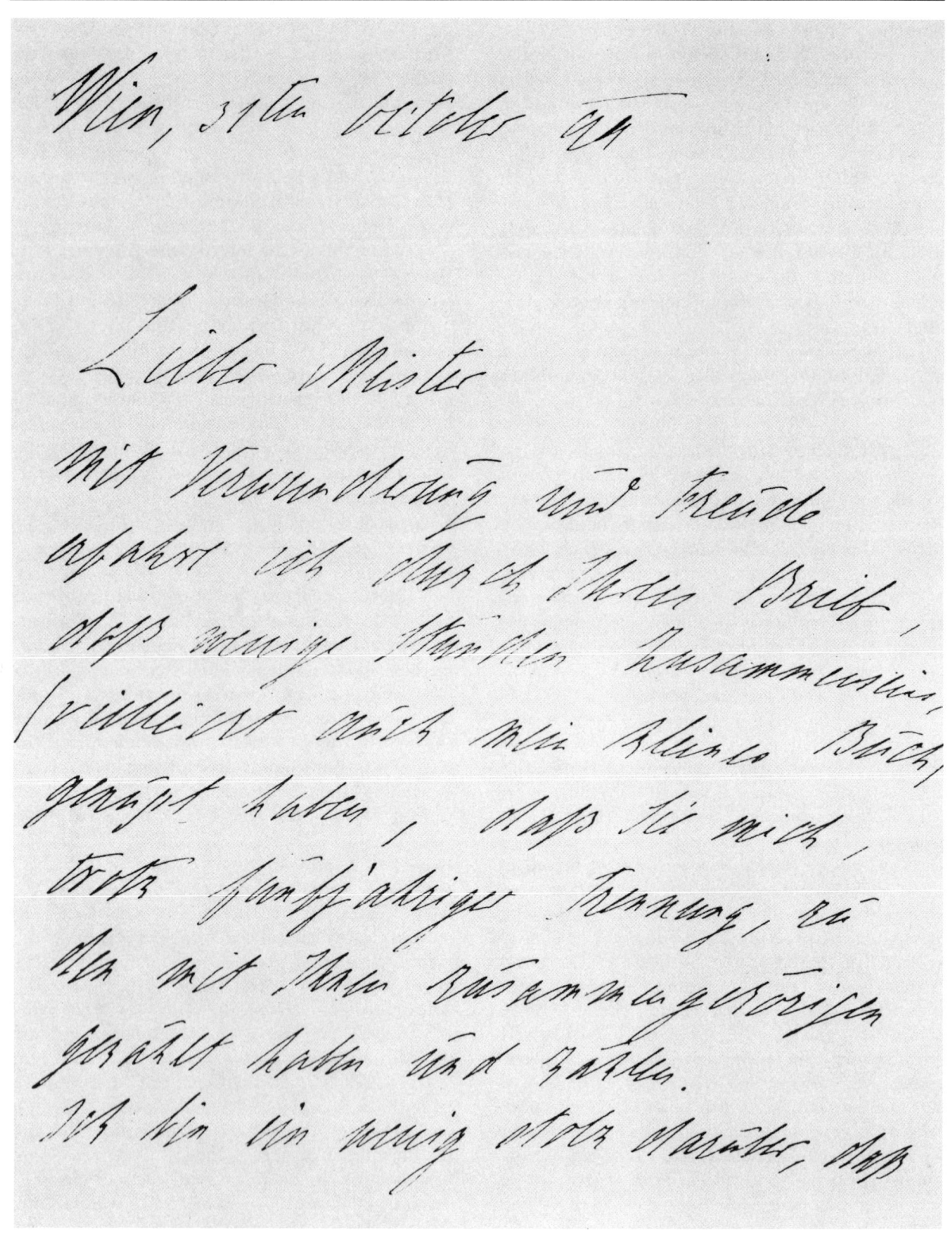

Two-page letter from Andrian to Stefan George dated 31 October 1899 (Walter H. Perl, ed., Leopold Andrian und die Blätter für die Kunst *[1960])*

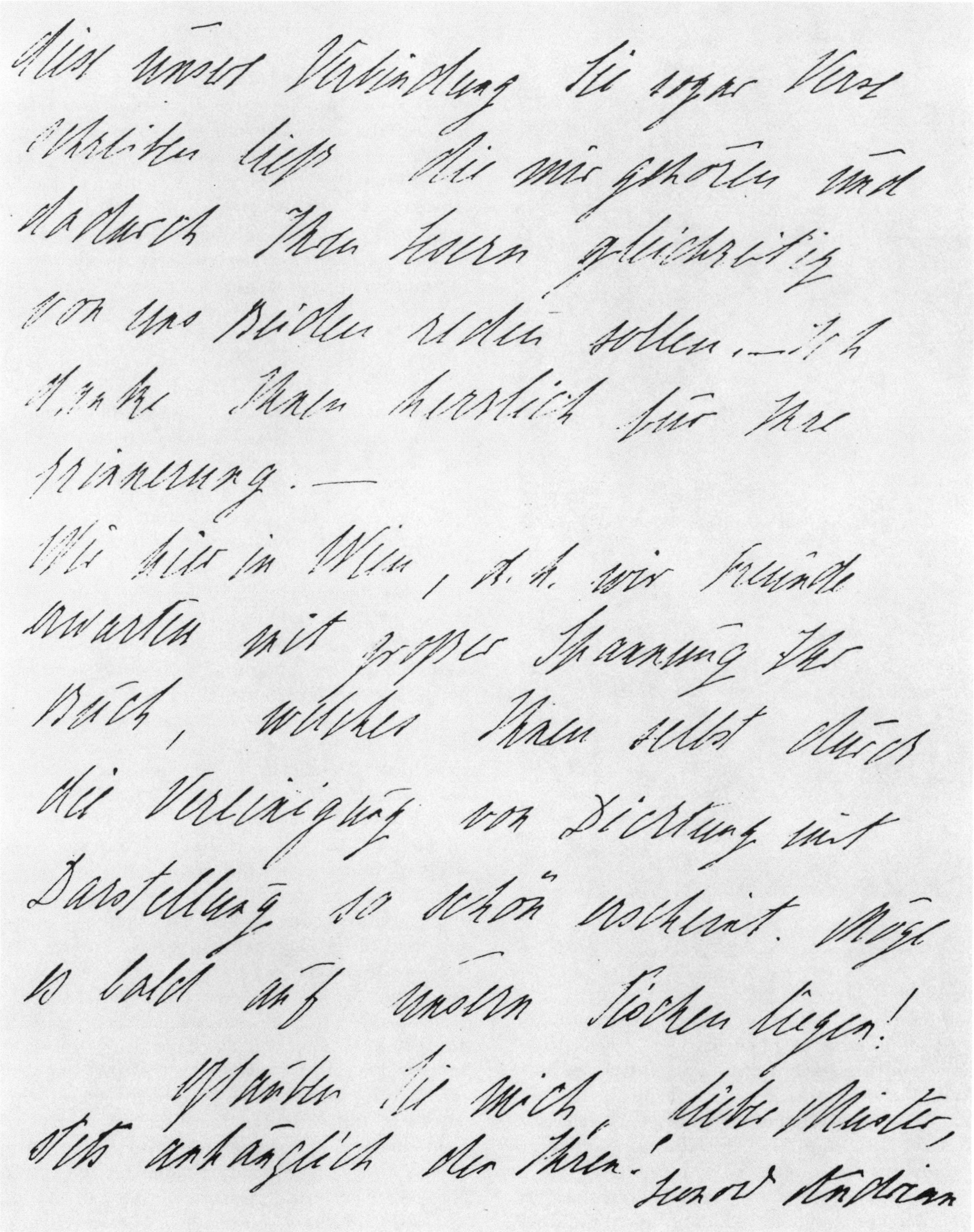

Andrian in 1911 (Bildarchiv der Österreichischen Nationalbibliothek)

hood and youth), had been "dem Ich dienstbar—wird sie in die Krise hineingezogen" (used in the service of the self, it is drawn into the crisis), and Andrian felt that he had to renounce it. To renounce the imagination, however, "involviert Verzicht auf künstler[ische] Produktion" (involves the renunciation of artistic production).

Andrian passed his final examinations in the summer of 1898; in 1899 he received the Doctor of Law degree and entered the Austrian diplomatic service, in which he served with distinction until 1918. In July 1918 he was appointed general director of the Burgtheater in Vienna and also of the Vienna Opera. When the Hapsburg monarchy collapsed four months later he resigned. Despite his short term in office, he achieved significant results: he initiated the appointment of Richard Strauss as director of the Vienna Opera, and from his discussions with Hofmannsthal, Beer-Hofmann, and Max Reinhardt evolved the idea for the Salzburg Festival. After his resignation Andrian became a citizen of Liechtenstein, the last principality in central Europe ruled by a descendant of the Hapsburgs. In 1923 he married Andrée Bourée de Poncay-Wimpffen; the motivations for the marriage were in part financial and in part to conceal his sexual orientation.

In the 1920s Andrian wrote several political articles and engaged in theological, philosophical, and psychological studies. These studies resulted in two works: *Die Ständeordnung des Alls: Rationales Weltbild eines katholischen Dichters* (The Rank Order of the Universe: Rational World View of a Catholic Poet, 1930), an attempt to view the world as a hierarchical order with the Catholic church and the aristocracy at the top of the social pyramid; and the unpublished "De anima et vita Cypriani Morandini," twenty-eight notebooks of aphorisms, psychological observations, and self-analysis. Andrian thought of both works as transitional to a resumption of writing fiction.

By 1933 Andrian felt prepared to begin work on an autobiographical novel, "Der Lauf zum Ideal" (The Path to the Ideal), a sequel to *Der Garten der Erkenntnis*. The major motifs of the earlier novel–Austria, homosexuality, aristocracy, religion, and the self in its totality–were to be revived, although with the significant difference that "sittl[iche] Fragen u. die allgemeinste Sphäre der Erkenntnis, die Realität Gott" (ethical questions and the most general sphere of knowledge, God's reality) were to be given center stage. The novel remained a fragment partly because Andrian decided that he could not deal in it with the theme of homosexuality, and partly because he felt compelled to take part in the struggle against Nazi Germany. His campaign against the sentiment for Anschluß (annexation) found its most eloquent expression in *Österreich im Prisma der Idee* (1937), which can be characterized as his political and cultural testament. The thrust of Andrian's argument is a deeply conservative one, yet he foresaw more clearly than many of his contemporaries the destructive forces inherent in ideologies based on irrationality. When Austria became part of the German Reich in 1938, the book was pulped and Andrian was blacklisted by the Gestapo; he spent the next seven years in exile in Brazil. Andrian returned to Europe in 1946. In the same year his estranged wife, who had remained behind in France, died. In 1949 he married Margaret Ramsay, the sister-in-law of the prime minister of Rhodesia, Sir George Higgins. Andrian died in 1951 in Fribourg, Switzerland, and was buried in Alt-Aussee, Austria, not far from the villa where he had spent much of his childhood and adult life.

Letters:

Hugo von Hofmannsthal, Leopold von Andrian: Briefwechsel, edited by Walter H. Perl (Frankfurt am Main: Fischer, 1968).

References:

Hans Rudolf Klieneberger, "Hofmannsthal and Leopold Andrian," *Modern Language Review,* 80 (July 1985): 619-636;

Walter H. Perl, "Leopold von Andrian, Writer, Statesman, Philosopher," *Books Abroad,* 27 (Winter 1953): 37-38;

Perl, ed., *Leopold Andrian und die Blätter für die Kunst* (Hamburg: Hauswedell, 1960);

Ursula Renner, *Leopold Andrians "Garten der Erkenntnis": Literarisches Paradigma einer Identitätskrise in Wien um 1900* (Frankfurt am Main: Lang, 1981);

Jens Rieckmann, "Narziss und Dionysos: Leopold von Andrians 'Der Garten der Erkenntnis,'" *Modern Austrian Literature,* 16, no. 2 (1983): 65-81;

Gabriella Napoli Rovagnati, *Leopold von Andrian: Poeta dimenticato del fine secolo viennese* (Milan: Cisalpino-Goliardica, 1985);

Hartmut Scheible, "Metaphysik des Fiakers," in his *Literarischer Jugendstil in Wien* (Munich: Artemis, 1984), pp. 32-49;

Carl E. Schorske, "The Transformation of the Garden," in his *Fin-de-Siècle Vienna: Politics and Culture* (New York: Knopf, 1980), pp. 279-321;

Horst Schumacher, *Leopold von Andrian: Werk und Weltbild eines österreichischen Dichters* (Vienna: Bergland, 1967).

Papers:

Leopold von Andrian's diaries and notebooks are at the Deutsches Literaturarchiv, Marbach, West Germany.

Raoul Auernheimer
(15 April 1876-7 January 1948)

Donald G. Daviau
University of California, Riverside

BOOKS: *Talent: Eine Komödie in drei Akten* (Vienna: Buchdruck Reichswehr, 1900);

Rosen, die wir nicht erreichen: Ein Geschichtenband (Vienna: Wiener Verlag, 1901);

Renée: Sieben Kapitel eines Frauenlebens (Vienna: Wiener Verlag, 1902);

Koketterie (Berlin: Bloch, 1902);

Lebemänner: Novelle (Vienna: Wiener Verlag, 1903);

Die Verliebten (Vienna & Berlin: Singer, 1903);

Die Dame mit der Maske (Vienna & Leipzig: Wiener Verlag, 1905)–includes *Die Unverschämte*;

Die große Leidenschaft: Lustspiel in drei Akten (Vienna: Wiener Verlag, 1905);

Die ängstliche Dodo: Novellen (Berlin: Fleischel, 1907);

Der gute König: Lustspiel in drei Akten (Stuttgart & Berlin: Cotta, 1907);

Die man nicht heiratet: Novellen (Berlin: Fleischel, 1908);

Die glücklichste Zeit: Lustspiel in drei Akten (Berlin: Vita, 1909);

Gesellschaft; Mondäne Silhouetten (Berlin: Fleischel, 1910);

Renée und die Männer (Berlin: Flcischel, 1910);

Der gußeiserne Herrgott (Berlin: Fleischel, 1911);

Der Unverschämte: Lustspiel in einem Akt (Berlin: Bloch, 1912);

Das dumme Glück, by Auernheimer and Leo Feld (Berlin: Fischer, 1912);

Das Paar nach der Mode: Wiener Lustspiel in drei Akten (Berlin: Fischer, 1913);

Laurenz Hallers Praterfahrt: Erzählung (Berlin: Fischer, 1913);

Die verbündeten Mächte: Lustspiel aus der Wiener Kongreßzeit in drei Akten (Berlin: Fischer, 1915);

Das wahre Gesicht: Novellen (Berlin: Fleischel, 1916);

Herzen in Schwebe: Novellen (Berlin: Fleischel, 1916);

Der Geheimniskrämer: Novelle (Berlin: Fischer, 1919);

Raoul Auernheimer (Mrs. Clara Auernheimer Fellner)

Das ältere Wien: Schatten und Bilder (Vienna: Tal, 1920);

Maskenball: Novellen im Kostüm (Berlin: Fleischel, 1920);

Lustspielnovellen (Stuttgart: Deutsche Verlags-Anstalt, 1922);

Das Kapital: Roman aus der jüngsten Vergangenheit (Berlin: Ullstein, 1923);

Casanova in Wien (Munich: Drei Masken, 1924);

Die linke und die rechte Hand: Roman (Berlin: Fischer, 1927);

Die Feuerglocke (Berlin: Fischer, 1929);

Evarist und Leander oder Die Damenwahl: Novelle (Leipzig: Staackmann, 1931);

Gewitter auf dem Rigi: Lustspiel in drei Akten (Berlin: Fischer, 1931);

Geist und Gemeinschaft: Zwei Reden (Vienna & Berlin: Zsolnay, 1932);

Der gefährliche Augenblick: Abenteuer und Verwandlungen (Leipzig: Staackmann, 1932);

Gottlieb Weniger dient der Gerechtigkeit: Roman (Leipzig & Vienna: Tal, 1934);

L'Autriche dans le cadre européen, by Auernheimer and others (Paris: Publications de la Conciliation internationale, 1935);

Wien: Bild und Schicksal (Vienna: Lorenz, 1938);

Prince Metternich: Statesman and Lover, translated by James A. Galston (New York: Alliance Book Corp., 1940); German version published as *Metternich: Staatsmann und Kavalier* (Vienna: Ullstein, 1947);

Franz Grillparzer, der Dichter Österreichs: Licht und Dunkel eines Lebens (Vienna: Ullstein, 1948);

Das Wirtshaus zur verlorenen Zeit: Erlebnisse und Bekenntnisse (Vienna: Ullstein, 1948).

OTHER: Theodor Herzl, *Feuilletons,* preface by Auernheimer (Berlin: Harz, 1919);

Paul Géraldy, *Helene: Roman,* translated by Auernheimer (Berlin: Zsolnay, 1924);

"An der Wiege des Burgtheaters," in *Hundertfünfzig Jahre Burgtheater 1776-1926* (Vienna: Krystall, 1926), pp. 42-55;

Die Wienerin im Spiegel der Jahrhunderte, introduced and edited by Auernheimer (Zurich: Amalthea, 1928);

"Stefan Zweig," in *The Torch of Freedom: Twenty Exiles of History,* edited by Emil Ludwig and Henry B. Kranz (New York: Farrar & Rinehart, 1943), pp. 409-426.

PERIODICAL PUBLICATIONS: "In festen Händen," *Die Wage,* 5, no. 31 (1902);

"Die Lügenbrücke," *Die Wage,* 5, no. 46 (1902);

"Karriere," *Die Wage,* 7, no. 19 (1904);

"The Window Cleaner," *International Quarterly* (Spring 1942): 14-16;

"Inside Barbed Wire," *Christian Science Monitor,* 26 September 1942.

Raoul Auernheimer represents a literary type often encountered around the turn of the century in Vienna: a talented author who was primarily a journalist and theater critic but who also wrote novels, short stories, and dramas, some of which reached the level of true literary excellence. He particularly excelled at the feuilleton, a journalistic form devoted to stylistic brilliance rather than depth of meaning, but he tried to raise the level of this form to educate the public. Many of Auernheimer's feuilletons were republished in book form. He was well known as a feuilletonist and critic for the most prestigious Viennese newspaper, the *Neue Freie Presse,* as well as for his psychological novellas, novels, and light comedies, most of which revolve about the theme of playing the game of love. The charm of these works lies in their style and the complexity of their plots. Despite the light tone of his works, Auernheimer was an unusually sensitive observer of Viennese life and foibles, and his works present a breviary of uniquely Viennese situations and types. The comedy and novel of manners were his forte, and in terms of subject matter there is little to distinguish between the dramas and the prose works. Auernheimer was the respected friend of all of the members of the Jung Wien (Young Vienna) group, including Hugo von Hofmannsthal and Arthur Schnitzler, and had he not been forced into exile in 1938, he would probably have continued to pursue a successful career. His name was constantly before the public through his journalistic writings and through the fiction and plays he wrote between 1901 and 1938. His election as the first chairman of the Austrian P.E.N. Club from 1926 to 1927 and later as its vice-president shows his standing among the important writers of his time.

His exile to the United States caused a break in his life that he was unable to overcome. The society that he had studied down to its finest nuances and described in his works had come to an end, and a public faced with the harsh reality of World War II was not interested in the light romantic comedies and stories that were his specialty. He could not change his style or subject matter to conform to the tastes of American readers; as a result, his productivity was severely hampered during the last decade of his life. In 1948, just when it looked as if he might resume his career in Austria, he died. Today his works, with the exception of the novel *Die linke und die rechte Hand* (The Left and the Right Hand, 1927), are out of print, and he is forgotten. For anyone, however, who would like to understand life in upper-middle-class and aristocratic circles in Vienna up to the time of Hitler, there is no better resource than the works of Auernheimer; if they have lost much of their relevance, they have sacrificed none of their readability.

Raoul Othmar Auernheimer was born in Vienna on 15 April 1876 to the businessman Johannes W. Auernheimer, a German from the Nuremberg area, and Charlotte Büchler Auernheimer, who came from a Jewish family of the German-speaking village of Raab in Hungary. Auernheimer's favorite stylistic device was antithesis, and in his autobiography he describes his father and mother as the kind of opposites that only two people who are destined for each other can be. He characterizes his father as having had a pioneering nature and as "a father" but not "a papa," while he describes his mother as a product of civilization and education and "a mama" rather than "a mother." Auernheimer respected his father, from whom he inherited his dedication to hard work; but he loved his mother, from whom he acquired his understanding of and enthusiasm for literature and the theater.

His mixed heritage led Auernheimer to consider himself a genuine child of Vienna. He loved his native city and devoted his life to trying to describe it for his Austrian readers and later for Americans. He attended the gymnasium, the preparatory school for university-bound students, and completed his law degree at the University of Vienna in 1900. Like so many other middle-class young men who wished to pursue literature as a career, he was obligated first to appease his family by having a profession. He completed his legal training by working the obligatory year of apprenticeship in the courts but never practiced law. His legal training, however, may have contributed to the sharp analytical style of his writing. It also provided him with the expertise to use legal problems in the plots of several satirical novellas.

In 1906 Auernheimer married Irene Guttman. The same year his ambition to pursue a career as a writer was given a major boost when he was hired by the *Neue Freie Presse*. He had been recommended by his cousin Theodor Herzl, a virtuoso writer of feuilletons and Paris correspondent for the newspaper, who later became the founder of the Zionist movement. Auernheimer modeled his journalistic style on Herzl's and devoted several essays to his memory; but it is indicative of Auernheimer's general outlook that he presented Herzl only as a writer and completely ignored the political and religious mission to which Herzl devoted his later life. An avoidance of politics was endemic to this generation of Viennese writers, one which they regretted deeply during their later years in concentration camps or in exile.

Vienna at the turn of the century was a city of aesthetes and of materialists. In Auernheimer's opinion these two tendencies amounted to the same thing: he describes aestheticism as materialism with a gold frame. Life in that prosperous, self-indulgent era was devoted to beauty and pleasure; in the hierarchy of the day the artist, the musician, the painter, the dramatist, and the actor formed the ascending rank order of importance. Vienna had long been a city of passionate theatergoers, and at the turn of the century it was enjoying an unprecedented renaissance of the theater. Talent was a means of overcoming the strict class structure of society: a successful writer or artist could find acceptance in social circles that were otherwise closed to him. Under these conditions it was difficult for any young man with a facile pen and a head full of ideas not to write a play; like all of his friends, Auernheimer quickly succumbed to the temptation to become famous.

After publishing his first tales in literary journals such as *Moderne Rundschau* and *Liebelei* under the pseudonyms Raoul Heimer and Raoul Othmar, Auernheimer received his first honorarium in 1899 for a humorous dialogue with song and dance, significantly titled *Talent* (1900), which was successfully performed at the Josefstadt Theater. He later said that these slight early works contained the ingredients that formed the basis of his writings for the next forty years. In thus characterizing his mature works Auernheimer was not displaying false modesty but was revealing his innate honesty; he never overestimated his talent and never referred to himself with the elevated designation *Dichter* (poet) but always with the less prestigious appellation *Schriftsteller* (writer). The word *liebenswürdig* (charming) is used by critics to describe his personality and his oeuvre. He continually rewrote his works to produce the smooth-flowing, highly polished prose that was his pride and hallmark. The chief appeal of his writings lies in their brilliant use of language and imaginative plot twists; their principal weakness is a lack of the depth necessary to transform them from pleasant entertainment into meaningful commentaries on life, from evanescent journalism into enduring literature.

Auernheimer was not a literary innovator; he adopted the manner, technique, and subject matter that were popular in his day. He was an epigone and modeled himself on Schnitzler. Like Hofmannsthal, the leading poet of the time,

Auernheimer preferred the past to the present and felt more at home with the sweet melancholy, playful wit, and lighthearted, mockingly gallant tone of eighteenth-century writing; his style shows little development throughout his career. For the most part his works present variations on the basic theme of flirtation and playing with love. Ultimately it became the tragedy of his career that he continued to write in the same vein even after the world changed radically following World War I.

Auernheimer was forced for financial reasons to combine the careers of creative writer and journalist. He considered the feuilleton, because of the freedom the form provided, the ideal vehicle to bridge the gap between journalism and literature. Auernheimer served as a bylined theater critic for the *Neue Freie Presse* from 1908 to 1933, when he resigned in protest against the pro-Nazi slant of the paper. He produced more than a thousand columns for the paper, including theater and book reviews, cultural commentary, and social criticism. For the most part he wrote about aesthetic matters; even during World War I, echoes of the struggle are only faintly audible in his writings.

Auernheimer's first collection of stories, *Rosen, die wir nicht erreichen* (Roses We Do Not Attain, 1901), contains twelve variations on the theme of love. In the title story a university student finds himself torn between his lower-class mistress and a wealthy, beautiful girl he loves from a distance. Once he completes his degree, he deserts his mistress, rationalizing his behavior with the analogy that gives the story its title: "Rosen, die man uns ins Haus bestellt, einen ganzen Bund auf einmal, sind ja gar keine Rosen. Nur Rosen, die in einem fernen Garten blühen, hinter einer Fliederhecke, die sich im blauen Fond eines vorbeirollenden Wagens schaukeln, am stolzen Busen einer schönen unbekannten Frau funkeln, nur Rosen, die wir nicht erreichen, sind Rosen" (Roses that are delivered to our house an entire bouquet at a time are not roses at all. Only roses that bloom in a distant garden behind a lilac hedge, that sway in the blue vase of a carriage driving by, that sparkle on the proud bosom of a beautiful unknown lady, only roses we do not attain are roses). The overtones of romanticism, with its bittersweet yearning and longing for the unattainable, are evident beyond the eighteenth-century cavalier spirit of flirtation. Also in the manner of romanticism Auernheimer stands above his works with sovereign, good-humored detachment and seems more French than German in his approach. He acknowledges the influence of Guy de Maupassant as well as that of Rudyard Kipling; his fondness for antithesis and surprise endings brings to mind the stories of O. Henry.

For example, in "Das Märchen von der Treue" (The Fairytale of Fidelity), another selection from *Rosen, die wir nicht erreichen,* Auernheimer twists the normal concept of faithfulness inside out. A young man who was counting on the unfaithfulness of women to keep him from becoming seriously involved encounters a faithful woman and can find no excuse not to marry her. Thus he feels that life has treated him worse than his friend, who complains of the faithlessness of his mistress: "Daß einen die Frauen betrügen, kommt in jeder Stunde hundertmal vor, aber daß einem eine das ganze Leben hindurch treu bleibt, in hundert Jahren einmal. Dich hat das Leben enttäuscht, weil du töricht an die Treue geglaubt, aber mich, der ich so klug auf die Untreue gerechnet, hat es vernichtet" (That women deceive a man happens a hundred times every hour, but that one remains faithful to a man all her life only once in a hundred years. Life has disappointed you, because you foolishly believed in fidelity, but it has destroyed me, who so cleverly had counted on infidelity).

Auernheimer described the game of flirtation as played by both men and women. In *Renée: Sieben Kapitel eines Frauenlebens* (Renée: Seven Chapters of a Woman's Life, 1902) he describes the education of a strong-willed girl from youth through maturity, her first affair after marriage, and her decision thereafter to remain faithful to her husband. Portraying women as philanderers was a new departure in the literature of the time, as was showing males as victims rather than as callous seducers. More typical of the period is *Lebemänner* (Men about Town, 1903), which follows in the footsteps of Schnitzler's *Anatol* (1893; translated, 1911). A shallow young man from Prague attempts to emulate the bachelor life he witnesses in Vienna, but he is unsuitable for the game and ends up ruining four lives. The protagonist is too shallow an individual, almost more caricature than character, to allow any possibility for tragic dimensions in the work; he is a deceived deceiver who remains unenlightened.

Although Auernheimer used a light touch and a gentle tone, he was an unusually perceptive observer of Viennese behavior, and his writings form a sympathetic chronicle of Viennese foibles and virtues. His works were primarily intended as entertainment, but several of them, such as "Der Leichenbestätter von Ebenbrunn" (The Mortician of Ebenbrunn) from the collection *Der gußeiserne Herrgott* (The Cast Iron God, 1911), which is worthy of Adalbert Stifter with its bizarre subject matter and eccentric central character; *Laurenz Hallers Praterfahrt* (Laurenz Haller's Drive through the Prater, 1913); *Der Geheimniskrämer* (The Merchant of Secrets, 1919); and *Evarist und Leander oder Die Damenwahl* (Evarist and Leander; or, Ladies' Choice, 1931) can stand beside the better prose writings of the time. These tales surpass Auernheimer's other efforts both technically and thematically and show to best advantage his abilities as a narrative writer. Of these four tales only *Evarist und Leander* is on the light comic level of his typical works, and even here a serious point is made; the other stories end tragically for the central figures, a development which is atypical of Auernheimer's overall production.

In *Evarist und Leander* two friends who are complete opposites in character are in love with the same woman. Evarist employs every conniving trick to win Alegrette after deciding that she will be able to help his career, while the noble Leander loves her deeply without wooing her. Although Alegrette discovers Evarist's true nature, she still chooses him, for, as she explains to Leander: "Darum . . . zieh ich den minder guten Freund dem guten vor. Er ist der bessere Liebhaber; der andere ist der bessere Mensch. Wär ich die himmlische Gerechtigkeit, so könnte ich nicht anders, als mich für ihn entscheiden. Aber ich bin nur eine Frau; und darum entcheide ich mich für Ihren Freund" (Thus . . . I prefer the less good friend to the good one. He is the better lover; the other is a better man. If I were divine justice, I could only decide for you. But I am only a woman, and therefore I am deciding for your friend).

Auernheimer considered "Der Leichenbestätter von Ebenbrunn" one of his best novellas. At the age of seventy-two an innkeeper, who has wearied of this occupation, takes over an undertaking establishment which is up for sale. With careful planning and effective public relations his business flourishes. Prosperity, however, brings ambition for even greater challenges and accomplishments: to climax his career the undertaker yearns to prepare a large funeral for a dignitary. Fate seems to play into his hand, for a

Cover for Auernheimer's 1913 tragicomic tale about how a couple's carriage ride through a Vienna amusement park leads to the ruination of their marriage and the husband's suicide

prince in the vicinity is extremely sick and presumably about to die. In his imagination the undertaker conceives the glorious funeral he will arrange and anticipates the recognition that he will derive from it. To insure that the funeral is offered to him, he bribes the prince's servants. The prince remains alive for a considerable time, costing the undertaker a great deal of money in bribes. One night word arrives that the prince is about to die, and the undertaker rushes to wait outside the house for the news of his death. He paces up and down in a cold rain, only to learn in the morning that the prince has recovered from the crisis. On returning home the undertaker himself falls ill with pneumonia. Now the two men become rivals to see who will die first. A servant finally rushes in and informs the undertaker that the prince has died, but that he did not get the body after all: the prince's wife has returned unexpectedly and insists that he be buried in Vienna. The undertaker uses the preparations that he had made for the prince and has himself buried among his former customers. Auernheimer comments: "So sonderbar spielt manchmal das Leben" (Life sometimes plays such strange tricks). At least the undertaker was spared one final disappointment: the prince's last wish was for a simple funeral, cremation, and burial in the family crypt.

Laurenz Hallers Praterfahrt is another tragicomic tale which provides a good portrait of the customs and character types of an earlier age. Auernheimer signals the tragic ending in the first sentence: "Hallers Unglück war, daß seine Frau Flore einer zu feinen Familie entstammte" (Haller's misfortune was that his wife Flore came from too fine a family). Haller earns a small salary, but with careful management he and his wife are able to sustain themselves. For her thirtieth birthday Flore insists on a carriage ride through the Prater, the large amusement park in Vienna, and despite his misgivings Haller has no choice but to oblige her whim. The repercussions of the ride, which affect every aspect of their lives and lead to Haller's suicide, form the content of this well-conceived and well-executed tale.

Der Geheimniskrämer, another tragicomic tale of the rise and fall of an unfortunate man, is set in Fondo in the territory of Venice in 1866, when this area still belonged to Austria. A pitiful storekeeper by chance comes into possession of a priest's confessional notes which contain the most personal secrets of everyone in town. Because of the townspeople's fear of what he might reveal, the merchant flourishes, his competition goes out of business, and there is even talk of his becoming mayor. But an abortive revolution in which he is not involved leads to his imprisonment, and when he is released the papers have vanished. His fall is rapid. He loses all his customers and soon reverts to his former miserable condition. Furthermore, he is now haunted by an idea that struck him in prison: why was his wife not mentioned in the priest's papers? He discovers that she was having an affair with the priest. One day the store fails to open, and the rumor spreads that he has disappeared, possibly to America. As befits a merchant of secrets, his story ends in mystery.

During World War I Auernheimer published *Das wahre Gesicht* (The True Face, 1916), a collection of novellas that continue the same pattern as the previous ones. Only a few of the stories refer to the war; even in those instances the conflict serves merely as background. "Das Landgut der Fiametta" (The Manor of Fiametta), modeled on Boccaccio's *Decameron,* describes a group of people who seek refuge from the war at a country estate and tell each other stories to pass the time and to illustrate a theoretical discussion of the novella form. "Vetter Maigrün" (Cousin Maigrun), concerning a failure who becomes a hero, is one of the few pieces by Auernheimer that might be classified as propaganda glorifying military feats. Auernheimer was a pacifist and antimilitarist who considered compulsory military service a crime against humanity and criticized writers of stature who popularized the war in their writings or through propaganda releases in the newspapers.

The title *Das wahre Gesicht* reflects the overall theme of these novellas, the revelation of true as opposed to apparent character. A later collection, *Maskenball* (The Masked Ball, 1920), represents a continuation of the same thematic pattern, as does *Lustspielnovellen* (Comic Novellas, 1922). Auernheimer's last major collection of short fiction, *Der gefährliche Augenblick* (The Dangerous Moment, 1932), contains still more variations on the same basic plots.

In the novel *Das Kapital* (The Capital, 1923) Auernheimer shows how the life of a young idealist is ruined by circumstances beyond his control. An unequal contest develops between the entrenched old guard that dominated Austria in the days of the monarchy and the young proletarian Socialists who now expected to rule in the new Republic. With bittersweet mockery Auernheimer shows that nothing fundamental has changed in Austria.

A Socialist party representative, Franz Marks, refuses a bribe from Baron Lundauer in a dispute over the occupancy of rooms at Lundauer's estate. Lundauer decides to teach the arrogant young Socialist a lesson. When Lundauer dies a short time later, Franz is surprised to learn that he has been made heir to his wealth. He intends to decline the money on principle, but circumstances force him to accept it. His life changes radically, as he is subjected to corruption on all sides. Little by little he sinks into debt, and when he becomes hopelessly dependent on the inheritance, a second will is discovered that disinherits him. He is left with enormous debts and no friends, not even within his own party. A codicil to Lundauer's second will offers to pay off all of Marks's debts if the Socialist will utter, as softly as he wishes but audibly, "Es lebe der Kapitalismus" (Long live capitalism). Marks thinks of all he has been through, his indebtedness, the hard life he faces to support a wife and child on his earnings in a candy factory, and says: "Es lebe die Internationale" (Long live the International) followed by "Es lebe der Weltsozialismus" (Long live world socialism). The judge, incensed by this reaction, orders a police search of Marks's home, where nothing more incriminating than a leather-bound copy of *Das Kapital* is found; a gift from Lundauer, the book is the final ironic twist in his scheme to teach Marks a lesson. The idealist is soundly defeated, while the real heir of Baron Lundauer, Baron Freienstein, a spoiled aristocrat without character or principles, will inherit the money, marry a princess, and perpetuate the irresponsible life of the idle rich.

Auernheimer's psychological novel of manners is fast paced, with many clever twists of plot and skillfully drawn psychological portrayals of the characters. It shows that the old customs, the social fabric, and the mentality of the former ruling classes have remained intact.

While *Das Kapital* possesses considerable bite and verges on tragedy despite its light tone, *Die linke und die rechte Hand* (The Left and the Right Hand, 1927) demonstrates that the fall of the monarchy had little impact on the lives of the citizens. The novel contains no discussion of a new revolutionary spirit or of the hardships of the war and offers no insights into such problems of the postwar period as unemployment and inflation. Instead, with great charm and stylistic elegance, Auernheimer treats the same themes of flirtation and love that dominated his writings from the beginning of his career. His three male protagonists have all served in the war, but their experiences have not changed them. Auernheimer was also successful when dealing with the past, as in *Gottlieb Weniger dient der Gerechtigkeit* (Gottlieb Weniger Serves Justice, 1934), a novel set in the 1830s during the reign of Metternich, an age Auernheimer had studied in depth.

Auernheimer scored his greatest literary success with his dramas, which in subject matter and technique differ little from the novellas. All his plays are light comedies treating the themes of love and seduction; they are characterized by sophisticated, witty dialogue and gentle irony. Auernheimer gained experience in writing for the theater with a series of short vignettes, including "Karriere" (Careers, 1904) and *Die Dame mit der Maske* (The Lady with the Mask, 1905), before he wrote *Die große Leidenschaft* (The Grand Passion, 1905), one of his most successful dramatic works. The plot uses a stock situation: a wife, bored with her dull businessman husband, is on the verge of having her first affair when the appearance of a fourth party squares the triangle and makes her more content with her marriage; she is able to call off her planned indiscretion before any harm is done. Although this comedy is the essence of simplicity, it is well constructed and has believable characters and clever dialogue. It ran for hundreds of performances in eight countries.

This play was followed by *Der gute König* (The Good King, 1907), *Die glücklichste Zeit* (The Happiest Time, 1909), *Gesellschaft; Mondäne Silhouetten* (Society; Silhouettes of the Shady World, 1910), *Das dumme Glück* (Dumb Luck, 1912), *Das Paar nach der Mode* (The Fashionable Couple, 1913), *Die verbündeten Mächte* (The Allied Powers, 1915), and *Die Feuerglocke* (The Fire Bell, 1929); but his only other genuine success in the theater was *Casanova in Wien* (Casanova in Vienna, 1924), which was awarded the Volkstheater Prize. This comedy involves the usual antithetical situations and is probably indebted to Schnitzler's *Die Schwestern oder Casanova im Spa* (The Sisters; or, Casanova in the Spa, 1919). Giacomo Casanova has tired of philandering and is ready to marry and settle down to a stable bourgeois life. At the same time his brother, the painter Francesco Casanova, a sedate family man, would like to throw over the traces and emulate his brother's promiscuous life-style. Both learn that the public images they have established over the years make any change of direction impossible.

Another of Auernheimer's theatrical achievements was his adaptation of Molière's comedy *Le Misanthrope* for the German stage. He had discussed the plays of Molière in many reviews and feuilletons, and in recognition of his work on the French playwright he was selected along with the dramatist Anton Wildgans to represent Austria at the Molière tercentenary in Paris in 1922; for his participation he was awarded the Palmes Academiques of the French Academy. On 11 March 1938, the day Hitler's troops marched into Austria to enforce the Anschluß (annexation of Austria by Germany), Auernheimer was in Switzerland celebrating the successful performance of his Molière adaptation.

Auernheimer was as fervently opposed to the Anschluß as he was to Hitler, but he returned to Vienna immediately. He believed that he would be protected by the Nuremberg Laws, which exempted individuals with one German parent from the new harsh regulations against Jews, but he was arrested without charge on 21 March and imprisoned in the Dachau concentration camp. He was released five months later through the intervention of his translator, Prentiss Gilbert, who was the American attaché in Berlin, and the German writer Emil Ludwig. Auernheimer later attributed his arrest to his heedlessness in dedicating his cultural history of Vienna, *Wien: Bild und Schicksal* (Vienna: Portrait and Destiny, 1938), to Chancellor Kurt von Schuschnigg a week before the Anschluß was decreed. Schuschnigg had called for a plebiscite to decide the issue of annexation with Germany and had given an impassioned radio address advising against the union. This speech, which prompted Auernheimer to send a copy of his book to the chancellor with the dedication "unter dem Eindruck Ihrer großen Rede" (under the impact of your grand speech), provoked Hitler to force the cancellation of the vote and march into Austria.

Auernheimer had further attracted the attention of the new authorities because he had signed the P.E.N. Club's 1934 protest against the book burnings in Germany. He had also publicly objected to the German domination of the Viennese Kulturbund, an organization that sponsored prominent speakers, and had voiced his concern over the political trends in Austria in two lectures he delivered before the Kulturbund and then published as *Geist und Gemeinschaft* (Intellect and Community, 1932). This work contains an eloquent defense of the importance of humanistic values. Like his novellas and dramas, which deal almost exclusively with Austrian types in an Austrian milieu, his books of essays, including *Das ältere Wien: Schatten und Bilder* (The Older Vienna: Shadows and Pictures, 1920), reflect his attempt to capture and define the essence of Austrian and particularly of Viennese life.

Auernheimer's arrest virtually ended his career as a writer. Released from Dachau under the condition that he leave the country, he fled via Venice to New York. He arrived virtually penniless, but with the help of Austrian friends who had preceded him into exile and the American writer Dorothy Parker, he and his wife were able to begin their new lives with a minimum of difficulty. For a brief time it appeared as if he would make the transition without any appreciable break in his successful career. During his first six months in New York he completed a book that was published in 1940 in English translation as *Prince Metternich: Statesman and Lover;* the original German version appeared in 1947 as *Metternich: Staatsmann und Kavalier*. The book received favorable reviews in the *New York Times* and the *New York Herald Tribune* and elicited a letter of praise from Thomas Mann, who was then living in Princeton. But Auernheimer was unable to duplicate this initial success, and *Metternich* remains his only significant publication in English. Auernheimer stresses the importance of women for Metternich's career, portraying the romantic and political aspects of his life as standing in a cause-and-effect relationship. This approach is not as successful here as it was to be later in his biography of Franz Grillparzer; for although Metternich's political career was undeniably launched and furthered by various influential women—beginning with his clever and ambitious mother, who arranged his marriage to the wealthy and titled Eleonor Hauwitz, daughter of the Austrian state chancellor—it is debatable how much of Metternich's diplomatic achievement can be attributed to his relationships with women. It is possible, however, to appreciate Auernheimer's development of the two aspects of Metternich's life as parallel developments without accepting the thesis of direct interconnection between them.

The English version includes an introduction, deleted in the German version, in which Auernheimer expresses his views on biography as a literary form. He also stresses the similarities between Napoleon and Hitler, a subject which he also pursued in articles written at this time in an attempt to warn the American public about the Nazi threat. The introduction makes it clear that Auernheimer is advocating the need for a new Metternich to checkmate the excesses of a Napoleonic personality. He recalls Metternich's plan for a European confederation which would ensure the preservation of the balance of power and emphasizes that Metternich's policies contributed to more than five decades of peace in Europe.

Auernheimer portrays Metternich's various love affairs with grace and sophistication. Some of the chapters are self-contained set pieces that could almost stand alone as short stories. Auernheimer is also at his best in capturing the carnival atmosphere that prevailed at the Congress of Vienna in 1815, a setting he had already used in *Die verbündeten Mächte*. But despite its charm, the biography suffers from Auernheimer's inability to get inside the character of his subject; consequently, Metternich remains shadowy and enigmatic. Nor is it made clear why

Raoul Auernheimer and his wife, Irene Auernheimer, in California (Mr. and Mrs. George Peters)

Metternich was so hated that he feared for his life at the hands of the citizenry after he was deposed in 1848; Auernheimer is so anxious to defend Metternich's program for a peaceful Europe that the evils of his repressive political methods are minimized. In Auernheimer's view the goal of keeping Europe from war apparently outweighed every other consideration.

Auernheimer made a further effort to alert America to the danger of Nazism by writing an account of his experiences in Dachau, but he could not find a publisher willing to accept the manuscript. The book was rejected for the rather surprising reason that its description of concentration life was too tame: there were no sensational atrocities, which the publishers felt were necessary to ensure good sales. On 31 January 1940 an excerpt from the manuscript was published in the Parisian journal *Figaro;* a brief excerpt also appeared in the *Christian Science Monitor* for 26 September 1942 under the title "Inside Barbed Wire." Auernheimer also gave free lectures to a variety of organizations under such titles as "Graduate of the Concentration Camp," "Hitler and Napoleon," "The Shadow of Napoleon," "History Repeats in Russia," "How to Live in Wartime," and "To Be a Refugee." None of these speeches was ever published.

To serve the German and Austrian colony in New York, Auernheimer, together with Ernst Lothar, former director of the Josefstadt Theater in Vienna, attempted in 1940 to establish a German-speaking theater in the city. They approached the influential critic Brooks Atkinson for support, but neither he nor any other reviewer had any enthusiasm for the project. Atkinson's pessimistic assessment proved to be correct; although each presentation attracted enthusiastic audiences for three performances, it proved impossible to establish the longer runs that would have made the enterprise financially feasible. As a result the venture was abandoned after celebrating Auernheimer's sixty-fifth birthday with a production of his comedy *Das ältere Fach* (The Part of the Older [unpublished]).

In the summer of 1941 the Auernheimers moved to California, living briefly in Los Angeles and in Berkeley, where their daughter and son-in-law resided, before settling in Oakland. Auernheimer became an American citizen in 1944. He wrote political essays, movie scripts, dramas, biographies, and feuilletons for Swiss, American, and occasionally Argentinian newspapers; except for the feuilletons few of these works were published. Auernheimer's major asset, his attractive style, was lost in English translation, and his subject matter, predominantly attuned to prewar Austrian conditions, had no market in wartime America. Even his timely political articles could not satisfy the requirements of American editors who were unimpressed by Auernheimer's European reputation.

After completing several unproduced movie scripts, including one on Metternich titled "Graduate of Love," Auernheimer offered to write a biography of Franz Grillparzer for Simon and Schuster; but the idea was rejected by the firm's readers on the basis of a sample translated chapter and outline. Nevertheless, Auernheimer proceeded with the book and completed *Franz Grillparzer, der Dichter Österreichs: Licht und Dunkel eines Lebens* (Franz Grillparzer, the Poet of Austria: The Light and Dark Sides of a Life) shortly before his death from a long-standing heart condition on 7 January 1948. This psychological portrait of Grillparzer was published posthumously in Vienna in 1948, as was Auernheimer's autobiography, *Das Wirtshaus zur verlorenen Zeit* (The Inn at the Sign of Lost Time). Another biography, of the socialist Ferdinand Lasalle, failed to find a publisher. At the time of his death Auernheimer was working on a history of the House of Habsburg. He was also preparing a volume of his lyric verse and aphorisms under the title "Was ich sagen wollte" (What I Was about to Say).

Franz Grillparzer, der Dichter Österreichs is not only a tribute to Austria's greatest writer but also Auernheimer's testament of his feelings for his native country and particularly for Vienna. Throughout these pages, in which he attempts to define the essence of Grillparzer's poetic genius as well as to reveal him as a human being, Auernheimer conveys his own thoughts about the country of his birth. The reader leaves this volume with a rich understanding of Grillparzer and to a lesser degree of Auernheimer as well.

Auernheimer attempts to provide a comprehensive psychological portrait of Grillparzer. He particularly excels at delving into Grillparzer's relationships with the key women in his life: Charlotte Paumgartten, Marie Piquot, Katharine Fröhlich, and Maria Daffinger. Auernheimer calls Grillparzer "ein Idealist der Liebe" (an idealist of love), who was powerfully attracted to a succession of women without being able to marry any of them. Part of the tragedy of his life was his poverty: at age sixty-two he lamented that he still could not afford to maintain a family. On the basis of letters, diaries, and Grillparzer's works, as well as his own knowledge of human nature and understanding of the nuances of love, Auernheimer brings the characters in his book to life in a manner rarely achieved in scholarly writing. By showing the role that women played in Grillparzer's life and work, Auernheimer reveals the irreconcilable conflicts within Grillparzer that brought so much suffering to him and to those around him. Part of the problem was Grillparzer's attachment to his art. Individuals were for him only "Figuren einer Komödie" (figures of a comedy). The dramatist always gained the upper hand over the man and never allowed Grillparzer to form a satisfying relationship with anyone.

Auernheimer's one new discovery, which he documents with abundant circumstantial evidence, is that Grillparzer's relationship with Charlotte Paumgartten was not platonic, as earlier scholars had maintained. Auernheimer feels that the truth was missed previously because Grillparzer was considered a classical writer and was not allowed the same freedom as a romantic would have been. In Auernheimer's opinion, Grillparzer was not only a classical writer but a modern one. In addition to his passionate nature and his dedication to writing, Auernheimer stresses Grillparzer's difficult nature and love of truth, a trait which made him a harsh self-critic and equally severe with those about him. Auernheimer's Grillparzer book combines all of his best features as a writer and literary biographer. The book is a rich experience, both for its contents as well as for the fluid, lucid style in which it is written. Proceeding in easy stages, Auernheimer broadens his scope gradually to encompass not only the man but also the period in which he lived.

Likewise, Auernheimer's autobiography provides an overview not only of his life but also of his generation. As a portrait of the time it is comparable to Stefan Zweig's much more famous autobiography, *The World of Yesterday* (1943; German version published as *Die Welt von Gestern*, 1944). The view of Austria runs along parallel lines in both autobiographies, and the two works complement and supplement each other exceptionally well. Auernheimer presents a narrower, more personal view of events than Zweig, whose perspective is more European. Both felt that turn-of-the-century Austria offered special qualities that merited preserving, and both wrote with a strong sense of nostalgia, although neither yearned for a revival of the past. Auernheimer records events in a straightforward chronological manner with a minimum of commentary or interpretation; Zweig, as he often does in his works, interprets the events for the reader. The two men, who were good friends for more than forty years, shared a similar education and literary approach; both wrote for the *Neue Freie Presse;* and both wrote narratives in the psychological manner of Schnitzler. The major differences between them are the greater psychological depth in Zweig's works and Zweig's more pessimistic outlook on life. These two writers, whose lives and careers were so similar, ended in completely different ways, reflecting the antipodal difference in their Weltanschauungen: Zweig, the child of good fortune who seemingly traveled effortlessly through life on wings of success, committed suicide in Brazil in 1942, while Auernheimer, who faced constant rejection during his years in exile, persevered optimistically to the end. Except for the most famous writers, such as Thomas Mann and Bertolt Brecht, the choices of suicide or languishing in penurious obscurity were the only possibilities for many exiled artists during the 1930s and 1940s.

In a 1943 essay in which he tried to provide a psychological explanation for Zweig's act of despair, Auernheimer concluded: "Zweig's real weapon was the martyr's death which he courageously chose. There are two kinds of torchbearers in history: some carry it onward, the others convert their own person into a torch." Perhaps Auernheimer thought of himself as one of those who carried the torch of humanism forward, refusing to relinquish it despite adversity. Although his works describe an era that no longer exists, they retain their readability and interest for their depictions of human nature caught up in the universal game of love. Auernheimer deserves to be remembered as a representative of his generation, both in Austria and in exile, and as an idealist of great integrity whose works are a legacy of his dedication to humanistic values.

Letters:

The Correspondence of Arthur Schnitzler and Raoul Auernheimer with Raoul Auernheimer's Aphorisms, edited by Donald G. Daviau and Jorun B. Johns (Chapel Hill: University of North Carolina Press, 1972);

The Correspondence of Stefan Zweig with Raoul Auernheimer and with Richard Beer-Hofmann, edited by Daviau, Johns, and Jeffrey B. Berlin (Columbia, S.C.: Camden House, 1983).

References:

Ernst Benedikt, "Gedenkwort an Raoul Auernheimer," *Die Presse* (Vienna), 12 January 1948, p. 3;

Donald G. Daviau, "Raoul Auernheimer–In Memoriam," *Modern Austrian Literature,* 3 (Winter 1970): 7-21;

"Dr. Auernheimer, Viennese Author and Playwright," *Baltimore Sun,* 21 March 1941, p. 6;

Lloyd W. Eshleman, "Prince Metternich: Statesman and Lover," *New York Times Book Review,* 8 December 1940, p. 5;

Albert Guerard, "Prince Metternich: Statesman and Lover," *New York Herald Tribune Books,* 17 November 1940, p. 28;

Rudolf Holzer, "Raoul Auernheimer," *Die Presse* (Vienna), 8 January 1948, p. 3;

Hal Johnson, "New American Citizen," *Berkeley Daily Gazette,* 28 December 1944, p. 1;

O. Kleiber, "Raoul Auernheimer," *Baseler National-Zeitung,* 12 January 1948, p. 1;

Ernst Lothar, "Ein wahrer Österreicher: Zum 10. Todestag Raoul Auernheimers," *Die Presse,* 8 January 1958, p. 5;

Edwin Rollett, "Abschied von Auernheimer," *Wiener Zeitung,* 10 January 1948, p. 2;

Karl Rosnovsky, "Erinnerung an das alte Österreich. (Raoul Auernheimer und Stefan Zweig)," Ph.D. dissertation, University of Vienna, 1950;

Paul Stefan, "Österreichisches Theater in New York," *Baseler National-Zeitung,* 16 May 1941, p. 3.

Papers:

Raoul Auernheimer's literary estate is housed for the most part at the Stadtbibliothek (City Library) in Vienna.

Hermann Bahr
(19 July 1863-15 January 1934)

Donald G. Daviau
University of California, Riverside

BOOKS: *Rodbertus' Theorie der Absatzkrisen: Ein Vortrag* (Vienna: Konegen, 1884);
Über Rodbertus: Vortrag (Vienna: Verlag der "Unverfälschten Deutschen Worte," 1884);
Die Einsichtslosigkeit des Herrn Schäffle: Drei Briefe an einen Volksmann als Antwort auf "Die Aussichtslosigkeit der Socialdemokratie" (Zurich: Schabelitz, 1885);
Die neuen Menschen: Ein Schauspiel (Zurich: Schabelitz, 1887);
Henrik Ibsen (Vienna: Verlag der "Deutschen Worte," 1887);
La Marquesa d'Amaëgui: Eine Plauderei (Zurich: Schabelitz, 1888);
Die große Sünde: Ein bürgerliches Trauerspiel (Zurich: Schabelitz, 1889);
Zur Kritik der Moderne: Gesammelte Aufsätze (Zurich: Schabelitz, 1890);
Die gute Schule: Seelenzustände (Berlin: Fischer, 1890);
Fin de siècle (Berlin: Zoberbier, 1890);
Die Mutter (Berlin: Sallis, 1891);
Die Überwindung des Naturalismus: Als zweite Folge von "Zur Kritik der Moderne" (Dresden & Leipzig: Pierson, 1891);
Russische Reise (Dresden & Leipzig: Pierson, 1891);
Die häusliche Frau: Ein Lustspiel (Berlin: Fischer, 1893);
Dora (Berlin: Fischer, 1893);
Neben der Liebe: Wiener Roman (Berlin: Fischer, 1893);
Der Antisemitismus: Ein internationales Interview (Berlin: Fischer, 1893);
Aus der Vorstadt: Volksstück, by Bahr and Carl Karlweiss (Karl Weiss) (Vienna: Konegen, 1893);
Caph (Berlin: Fischer, 1894);
Studien zur Kritik der Moderne (Frankfurt am Main: Rütten & Loening, 1894);
Renaissance: Neue Studien zur Kritik der Moderne (Berlin: Fischer, 1897);
Theater: Ein Wiener Roman (Berlin: Fischer, 1897);
Die Nixe: Drama in vier Akten, nach dem Russischen des Spashinskij (Munich: Rubinverlag, 1898);

Hermann Bahr

Juana: Schauspiel, as Alejandro Lanza (Munich: Rubinverlag, 1898);
Josephine: Ein Spiel (Munich: Rubinverlag, 1898);
Das Tschaperl: Ein Wiener Stück in vier Aufzügen (Berlin: Fischer, 1898);
Der Star: Ein Wiener Stück in vier Akten (Berlin: Fischer, 1899);
Wenn es Euch gefällt: Wiener Revue in drei Bildern und einem Vorspiel, by Bahr and Karlweiss (Vienna: Konegen, 1899);
Wiener Theater, 1892-1898 (Berlin: Fischer, 1899);
Die schöne Frau; Leander (Berlin: Fischer, 1899);
Der Athlet: Schauspiel in drei Akten (Berlin, Cologne & Leipzig: Ahn, 1900);

Wienerinnen: Lustspiel in drei Akten (Berlin: Ahn, 1900);

Secession (Vienna: Wiener Verlag, 1900);

Bildung: Essays (Berlin & Leipzig: Insel, 1900);

Der Apostel: Schauspiel in drei Aufzügen (Munich: Langen, 1901);

Der Franzl: Fünf Bilder eines guten Mannes (Vienna: Wiener Verlag, 1901);

Rede über Klimt (Vienna: Wiener Verlag, 1901);

Der Krampus: Lustspiel in drei Aufzügen (Munich: Langen, 1902);

Wirkung in die Ferne und Anderes (Vienna: Wiener Verlag, 1902);

Premièren: Winter 1900 bis Sommer 1901 (Munich: Langen, 1902);

Rezensionen: Wiener Theater 1901 bis 1903 (Berlin: Fischer, 1903);

Dialog vom Tragischen (Berlin: Fischer, 1904);

Der Meister: Komödie in drei Akten (Berlin: Fischer, 1904); adapted by Benjamin F. Glazer as *The Master* (Philadelphia: Brown, 1918);

Unter Sich: Ein Arme-Leut'-Stück (Vienna: Wiener Verlag, 1904);

Sanna: Schauspiel in fünf Aufzügen (Berlin: Fischer, 1905);

Dialog vom Marsyas (Berlin: Bard, Marquardt, 1905);

Die Andere (Berlin: Fischer, 1906);

Der arme Narr: Schauspiel in einem Akt (Vienna: Konegen, 1906);

Josef Kainz (Vienna: Wiener Verlag, 1906);

Glossen zum Wiener Theater (1903-1906) (Berlin: Fischer, 1907);

Ringelspiel, in drei Akten (Berlin: Fischer, 1907);

Grotesken: Der Klub der Erlöser; Der Faun; Die tiefe Natur (Vienna: Konegen, 1907);

Wien (Stuttgart: Krabbe, 1907);

Die gelbe Nachtigall (Berlin: Fischer, 1907);

Buch der Jugend (Vienna: Heller, 1908);

Die Rahl: Roman (Berlin: Fischer, 1909);

Stimmen des Bluts: Novellen (Berlin: Fischer, 1909);

Tagebuch (Berlin: Cassirer, 1909);

Drut: Roman (Berlin: Fischer, 1909); republished as *Die Hexe Drut: Roman* (Berlin: Sieben Stäbe-Verlags- und Druckereigesellschaft, 1929);

Dalmatinische Reise (Berlin: Fischer, 1909);

Das Konzert: Lustspiel in drei Akten (Berlin: Reiss, 1909); translated by Leo Dietrichstein as *The Concert: A Comedy in Three Acts* (New York: Rosenfield, 1910); German version, edited by Josef Wiehr (New York: Prentice-Hall, 1931);

O Mensch! Roman (Berlin: Fischer, 1910);

Die Kinder: Komödie in drei Akten (Bonn: Ahn, 1911);

Das Tänzchen: Lustspiel in drei Akten (Berlin: Fischer, 1911);

Austriaca (Berlin: Fischer, 1911);

Das Prinzip: Lustspiel (Berlin: Fischer, 1912);

Inventur (Berlin: Fischer, 1912);

Essays (Leipzig: Insel, 1912);

Parsifalschutz ohne Ausnahmegesetz (Berlin: Schuster & Loeffler, 1912);

Bayreuth, by Bahr and Anna Bahr-Mildenburg (Leipzig: Rowohlt, 1912); translated by T. W. Makepeace as *Bayreuth and the Wagner Theater* (London: Unwin, 1912);

Das Phantom: Komödie in drei Akten (Berlin: Fischer, 1913);

Das Hermann Bahr-Buch: Zum 19. Juli 1913 herausgegeben (Berlin: Fischer, 1913);

Erinnerung an Burckhard (Berlin: Fischer, 1913);

Dostojewski: Drei Essays (Munich: Piper, 1914);

Der Querulant: Komödie in vier Akten (Berlin: Fischer, 1914);

Salzburg (Berlin: Bard, 1914); with English translation by G. M. R. Biddulph (Vienna: Agathon Verlag, 1947);

Das Österreichische Wunder; Einladung nach Salzburg (Stuttgart: Die Lese, 1915);

Kriegssegen (Munich: Delphin, 1915);

Der muntere Seifensieder: Schwank aus der deutschen Mobilmachung (Berlin: Fischer, 1915);

Expressionismus (Munich: Delphin, 1916); translated by R. T. Gribble as *Expressionism* (London: Henderson, 1925);

Himmelfahrt: Roman (Berlin: Fischer, 1916);

Rudigier (Kempten & Munich: Kösel, 1917);

Die Stimme: Schauspiel in drei Aufzügen (Berlin: Fischer, 1917);

Um Goethe (Vienna: Urania, 1917);

Schwarzgelb (Berlin: Fischer, 1917);

Vernunft und Wissenschaft (Innsbruck: Tyrolia, 1917);

Der Augenblick: Lustspiel. Nach Goethe (Berlin: Ahn & Simrock, 1917);

1917 (Innsbruck: Tyrolia, 1918);

Adalbert Stifter: Eine Entdeckung (Zurich & Leipzig: Amalthea, 1919);

Tagebuch 1918 (Innsbruck: Tyrolia, 1919);

Die Rotte Korahs: Roman (Berlin & Vienna: Fischer, 1919);

Der Unmensch: Lustspiel in drei Aufzügen (Berlin: Reiss, 1919);

Spielerei: Drei Stücke (Berlin: Ahn & Simrock, 1919);

Tagebuch 1919 (Leipzig: Tal, 1920);

Ehelei: Lustspiel in drei Akten (Berlin: Reiss, 1920);
Burgtheater (Vienna & Berlin: Wiener literarische Anstalt, 1920);
Summula (Leipzig: Insel, 1921);
Bilderbuch (Vienna & Leipzig: Wiener literarische Anstalt, 1921);
Kritik der Gegenwart (Augsburg: Haas & Grabherr, 1922);
Sendung des Künstlers (Leipzig: Insel, 1923);
Selbstbildnis (Berlin: Fischer, 1923);
Schauspielkunst (Leipzig: Dürr & Weber, 1923);
Liebe der Lebenden. Tagebücher 1921-1923, 3 volumes (Hildesheim: Borgmeyer, 1925);
Notizen zur neueren spanischen Literatur (Berlin: Stilke, 1926);
Der Zauberstab: Tagebücher von 1924 bis 1926 (Hildesheim: Borgmeyer, 1927);
Der inwendige Garten: Roman (Hildesheim: Borgmeyer, 1927);
Himmel auf Erden: Ein Zwiegespräch (Munich: Müller, 1928);
Das Labyrinth der Gegenwart (Hildesheim: Borgmeyer, 1929);
Österreich in Ewigkeit: Roman (Hildesheim: Borgmeyer, 1929);
Das junge Österreich (Jerusalem: Verkauf, 1945);
Österreichischer Genius: Grillparzer, Stifter, Feuchtersleben (Vienna: Bellaria, 1947);
Adalbert Stifters Witiko (St. Gallen: Tschudy, n.d.).

Collections: *Mensch, werde wesentlich: Gedanken aus seinen Werken*, edited by Anna Bahr-Mildenburg (Graz: Styria, 1934);
Salzburger Landschaft: Aus Briefen an seine Frau Anna Bahr-Mildenburg und aus seinen Tagebüchern (Innsbruck: Rauch, 1937);
Wirkung in die Ferne: Eine Auswahl der Prosa-Dichtungen (Vienna: Bauer, 1947);
Meister und Meisterbriefe um Hermann Bahr: Aus seinen Entwürfen, Tagebüchern und seinem Briefwechsel mit Richard Strauss, Hugo von Hofmannsthal, Max Reinhardt, Josef Kainz, Eleonore Duse und Anna von Mildenburg, edited by Joseph Gregor (Vienna: Bauer, 1947);
Kulturprofil der Jahrhundertwende: Essays, edited by Heinz Kindermann (Vienna: Bauer, 1962);
Theater der Jahrhundertwende: Kritiken, edited by Kindermann (Vienna: Bauer, 1963);
Sinn hinter der Komödie, edited by Rudolf Holzer (Graz: Stiasny, 1965);
Zur Überwindung des Naturalismus: Theoretische Schriften, 1887-1904, edited by Gotthart Wunberg (Stuttgart: Kohlhammer, 1968);
Hermann Bahr, Prophet der Moderne: Tagebücher 1888-1904, edited by Reinhard Farkas (Vienna: Böhlau, 1987).

OTHER: *Gegen Klimt*, edited by Bahr (Vienna: Eisenstein, 1903);
Briefe von Josef Kainz, edited by Bahr (Vienna: Rikola, 1921);
Martha Berger, *Das Leben einer Frau*, preface by Bahr (Vienna: Rikola, 1925);
Das junge Wien: Österreichische Literatur- und Kunstkritik, edited by Gotthart Wunberg, contributions by Bahr, 2 volumes (Tübingen: Niemeyer, 1976).

Hermann Bahr was one of the protean figures of his generation, virtually omnipresent on the Austrian and German cultural scene through his public readings and lectures, performances of his plays, and his outpouring of writings in a wide variety of forms: dramas, novels, short prose, narrative tales, literary and political essays, theater and book reviews, and, finally, his diary, installments of which he published weekly in the newspaper *Neues Wiener Journal* from 1905 to 1933. He was one of the most prolific authors of his era; his more than one hundred books represent virtually a cultural history of Vienna from the turn of the century until the advent of Hitler in 1933. No other author of his time devoted such attention and effort to revitalizing Austria and helping it make the transition from the stagnation of the late nineteenth century to the progressiveness of the twentieth. After studying in Berlin and Paris and taking an extended trip through France, Spain, and northern Africa in the late 1880s, Bahr returned to Vienna, where he found an abundance of new young writers, artists, architects, and musicians. Throughout the 1890s he was the central figure and catalyst of the "Young Vienna" group, which also included Arthur Schnitzler, Hugo von Hofmannsthal, Richard Beer-Hofmann, Leopold von Andrian, and Felix Salten. He was determined to help orchestrate a great expansion of the arts to achieve a rapprochement of Austria with the rest of Europe and to advance Austrian culture to a level of equality with those of the leading European countries. With total commitment and seemingly inexhaustible energy he pursued his program of modernity until 1906.

Throughout his career Bahr remained in the mainstream of his age, participating influentially in every important trend. In literature he

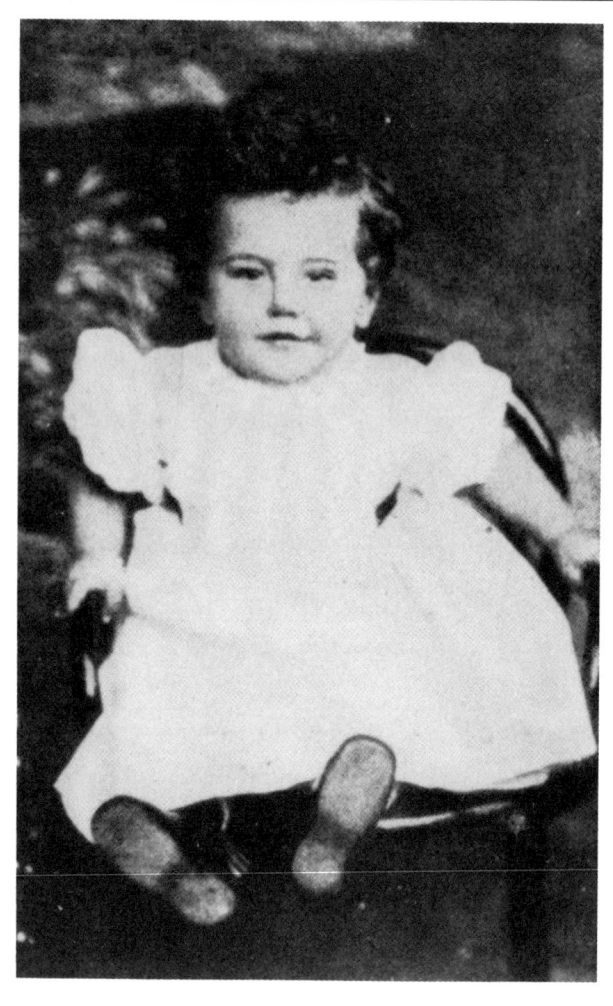

Bahr as a child

began as a naturalist, quickly embraced impressionism, brought the decadent movement from France to Germany and Austria, experimented with expressionism, and finally returned to a traditional classical outlook. In politics he briefly embraced the radical policies of the German National party of Georg Ritter von Schönerer–including its anti-Semitism and its goal of overthrowing the Austrian monarchy–then shifted to a position opposing anti-Semitism and supporting the monarchy. As to religion Bahr was born a Catholic, turned atheist under the influence of Schönerer, proclaimed himself without church affiliation when he married his first wife in 1895, and returned to Catholicism in 1914, attending church every day for the rest of his life.

Because of his frequent changes of direction in his early years, Bahr was dubbed a Verwandlungskünstler (quick-change artist); but his first-hand knowledge of all of these trends enabled him to educate the public to the newest cultural ideas and to a perception of Austria's role in twentieth-century Europe. He was satirically called "die Hebamme der modernen Kunst" (the midwife of modern art); the title is appropriate to describe his contribution to the establishment of a new acting style in the Vienna Burgtheater, new forms in literature, new directions in art and music, and a renewed pride in Austria and its role in Europe.

Nothing in Bahr's small-town, middle-class background would have suggested this kind of future for him. He was born to Alois and Wilhelmine Weidlich Bahr in Linz, then a sleepy provincial town in upper Austria. His father was an attorney and representative to the local assembly, and it was expected that his son would follow him with a career in law and bureaucratic service. Bahr was educated at the Benedictine schools in Linz and Salzburg and in 1881 entered the University of Vienna to study classical philology and law. But he was soon attracted to the new discipline of political economy, joined Schönerer's rabid pan-German political movement, and in 1883 was dismissed from the university for life for a speech which was interpreted as disloyal. He studied in Czernowitz (now Chernovtsy, USSR) in 1883-1884 and in Berlin from 1884 to 1887 without completing a degree. After a year of compulsory military service, he spent the year 1888-1889 in Paris.

He had broken with Schönerer and joined Viktor Adler's socialist movement in 1886, but he became disenchanted with politics because of its petty economic concerns. In Paris he completed the shift from politics to literature, disappointing Adler, who felt that Bahr had great potential for a political career. After traveling in southern France, Spain, and Morocco in 1889, he spent another year in Berlin, where he witnessed the inauguration of naturalism in the theater and the founding of the Freie Bühne (Free Stage) and became acquainted with Gerhart Hauptmann, Arno Holz, and Otto Brahm. He traveled to St. Petersburg, Russia, then returned to Vienna in October 1891 and launched his career as a leading spokesman for "Die Moderne" (modernity). He was a theater critic and feuilletonist for the *Deutsche Zeitung* from 1892 until 1894, when he joined Isidor Singer and Dr. Heinrich Kanner in founding the weekly newspaper *Die Zeit*. The following year he married Rosalie Jokl, a Jewish actress. In 1899 he left *Die Zeit* to become a theater critic for the *Neues Wiener Tagblatt* and also traveled to Italy.

Bahr, circa 1890

Bahr was influential to a large extent through the force of his personality. He was prone to exaggeration and always attempted to dazzle, stimulate, and provoke his audiences—particularly early in his career, when, strongly influenced by Nietzsche, he lived by the motto *"épater les bourgeois"* (shock the middle class). Following Nietzsche, Bahr considered it an essential aspect of modernism to remain a revolutionary, receptive to new ideas and trends. He prided himself on being ahead of his time, a characteristic that earned him the satirical sobriquet "Der Mann von Übermorgen" (the man from the day after tomorrow). But this willingness to change direction frequently was true only until 1906; in that year Bahr, feeling that the Viennese were ungrateful and inhospitable after his fifteen-year cultural campaign, departed to work for two years as a dramaturge and director with Max Reinhardt in Berlin. He returned to Vienna in 1908 as Burgtheater critic for the *Neues Wiener Journal;* but, still not comfortable there, he moved to Salzburg in 1912 with his second wife, the opera singer Anna Mildenburg, whom he had married in 1909 two months after divorcing Jokl. He returned to Vienna in September 1918 as a director of the Burgtheater but left six months later because of internal politics. In 1922 the Bahrs moved to Munich so that Mildenburg could teach at the Academy of the Performing Arts. Bahr died from arteriosclerosis in 1934 and was buried in Salzburg.

During his lifetime Bahr was a controversial, misunderstood, and underrated writer, and he remains so today. Because he was so prolific, failed to polish his writings, could never resist the temptation to overstatement, and changed his ideas frequently in his early years, he was not taken as seriously as his work warranted. His writings offer a valuable and insightful guide through the maze of conflicting currents of an incredibly rich and fascinating period. That Bahr's true importance is still not recognized is perhaps largely due to the inaccessibility of his writings. Because of the policies of the present executor of the Bahr estate, only one of his works, *Der Antisemitismus* (Anti-Semitism, 1893), is currently in print. Eventually, however, his central role will have to be recognized if the cultural situation in fin de siècle Vienna is to be correctly understood.

Bahr followed his own course, unaffected by praise and undeterred by criticism. For example, he withstood the savage onslaught of the writer Karl Kraus, who waged a bitter polemic against him beginning in 1893 and not ending until a year after Bahr's death. (Kraus considered Bahr the leading practitioner of journalistic corruption in Vienna; he also hated Bahr for winning a lawsuit against him in 1901.) Bahr was unconcerned about his reputation in the eyes of posterity; his ambition was to become "ein wirklicher Mensch" (a real person), his highest accolade for any individual. His literary and cultural contribution must be judged on the basis of the aggregate of his many activities, all of which were devoted to helping his contemporaries understand the role of culture as an enrichment and enhancement of life.

To present his view of Austrian life in all its many facets and aspects, Bahr, in emulation of Balzac, embarked on an ambitious series of twelve

The opera singer Anna Mildenburg, Bahr's second wife, whom he married in 1909

novels. The material had been gestating within him, and he wrote in rapid sequence *Die Rahl* (1909), *Drut* (1909), and *O Mensch!* (Oh, Man!, 1910). He continued the series after he left Vienna for Salzburg with *Himmelfahrt* (Ascension, 1916) and *Die Rotte Korahs* (The Band of Korah, 1919). The last two novels, *Der inwendige Garten* (The Inner Garden, 1927) and *Österreich in Ewigkeit* (Austria in Eternity, 1929), which were written in Munich, reveal the increasing difficulty Bahr was experiencing in shaping his ideas as his creative powers faded. Of the twelve projected novels, only these seven were completed; it has not yet been determined whether plans for the remaining novels are included in his literary estate.

The novels were intended as Bahr's analysis of conditions in Austria as he had perceived and experienced them. He also expressed these ideas in essays and theater and book reviews, but he felt that putting them into novelistic form would reach a wider audience. He uses the novel in accordance with his definition of the genre as a "schaffender Spiegel" (creative mirror) that is intended not to reflect reality accurately but to refract it in such a way that its hidden significance is rendered visible. While none of these novels is a great work of literature, as Bahr himself readily admitted, they are eminently readable works even today; they are also informative documents of their time, deserving the attention of anyone interested in Austrian cultural history.

Before he began the Austrian cycle, Bahr essayed the novel form in *Die gute Schule* (The Good School, 1890), *Neben der Liebe* (Next to Love, 1893), and *Theater* (1897). *Die gute Schule* was the residue of his experiences in Paris. He began writing it there on hotel stationery and completed it during his trip through southern France, Spain, and Morocco. The novel is Bahr's attempt to create a German-language counterpart to the breviary of decadence, Joris Karl Huysmans's novel *A Rebours* (1884; translated as *Against the Grain*, 1922). The autobiographical details are only thinly disguised: Bahr transforms his protagonist from a writer into a painter and changes the name of the woman with whom he is involved from Nini to Fifi. The novel of decadence, with its emphasis on states of mind, sensations, and colors, was new to Germany, and *Die gute Schule* caused a minor sensation in Berlin when the work was serialized from April to June 1890 in the journal *Freie Bühne für modernes Leben*. Otto Brahm, editor of the journal and director of the theater Freie Bühne, wrote a favorable review, calling the novel a fin de siècle version of Gottfried Keller's *Der grüne Heinrich* (1854-1855; translated as *Green Henry*, 1960). The subtitle of the novel, *Seelenzustände* (States of Mind), reflects Bahr's early use of inner monologue to present the thoughts of a poor but idealistic Viennese painter living the bohemian life in Paris. A social outsider and aesthete who feels superior to the bourgeois populace, he is driven by the idea of reproducing on canvas the perfect colors that he envisions in his mind's eye; at the same time he wants to capture pure truth. When his efforts to penetrate to the essence of color and truth by ordinary means fail, he invokes the practice current in the decadent literature of the time: he attempts to heighten his sense perception through eroticism which degenerates into sadomasochistic brutality. When even these orgies of lust and cruelty fail to bring the desired artistic breakthrough, the artist sells out to pragmatic, materialistic bourgeois values: if he cannot be a pure artist, he will at least be a financially successful one. "The Good School" in the title is an ironic reference: Goethe had called love the good school that raises man to greater heights, but instead of elevating him as an artist, love has brought Bahr's protagonist to a thoroughly bourgeois existence based on material security and personal comfort. He now wastes most of his time playing cards; his idealistic aesthetic creed of art for art's sake has been abandoned in favor of mass-producing popular paintings, most of which his ex-mistress, who has married a millionaire, buys to support him. Like Huysmans, Bahr depicts a life going "against the grain" from idealism to materialism, rather than following the Goethean formula of man's elevation through love to a higher life.

Die gute Schule shows that Bahr had learned well the literary formula of decadence; at the same time, the cynical, abrupt ending shows that in spite of his mastery of the techniques, Bahr lacked any genuine interest in the principles of decadence. The novel illustrates the decadent aesthetic principle that plot should be subordinate to style and form. As in *A Rebours*, the language is rich in active verbs and descriptive adjectives. While the luxurious style is appropriate to the work's emphasis on the senses of the artist, particularly his visual and olfactory experiences, in 1898 Bahr claimed that he could shorten it by two-thirds if he rewrote it in the manner he had adopted by then. The novel is something of a curiosity today as one of the earliest and best examples of literary decadence in Germany, but it is still quite readable.

As an offshoot of *Die gute Schule* Bahr wrote a series of short prose works to practice further the techniques and themes of decadence; the pieces were collected as *Fin de siècle* (1890). Like the novel, the sketches and vignettes deal with states of mind, aestheticism as a way of life, and erotic sensuality, and feature various sexual perversions. The short tale "Der verständige Herr" (The Reasonable Gentleman), for example, describes an aesthete whose perversity it is to avoid the fulfillment of sex; he is driven to murder a woman who causes him to overcome his principle. In all instances the plot is minimal; it is intended only as a framework within which Bahr can demonstrate his linguistic virtuosity, particularly his skill at describing states of mind and nuances of feeling. The aim of the volume was clearly to shock the bourgeoisie, and Bahr was thrilled when the book was banned and confiscated; the resulting publicity created so much demand for the work that it was reprinted.

Artistically, the book was intended to demonstrate the dictum of Émile Zola that "une phrase bien fait est une bonne action" (a well-made phrase is a good deed). Bahr intended to show that excellence of style could be a moral accomplishment in itself, regardless of subject matter; and he achieved a simplicity and elegance of style in this work that he rarely attained again. As in *Die gute Schule*, the emphasis is on the senses, color, and acoustical and olfactory sensations. And just as in the novel, Bahr could not resist concluding each sketch with a moral or treating his characters satirically; many of the tales end with a surprising twist in the manner of O. Henry. Several of the pieces are intended as social and political criticism. The story "Niklaus, der Verräter" (Niklaus, the Traitor) describes the reaction of Viktor Adler to Bahr's withdrawal from politics.

Other works written during Bahr's decadent period include *Russische Reise* (Russian Trip, 1891), a stylized diary of his trip to St. Petersburg in late 1890 with the actor Emanuel Reicher and the actress Lotte Witt; *Dora* (1893), a collection of three tales–"Dora," "Die Schneiderin" (The Dressmaker), and "Jeanette"; and *Caph* (1894), a collection of prose sketches. All of these works are decadent in that they emphasize states of mind described in elegant style and contain little in the way of plot. *Caph* is the most extreme example of this tendency; the book's motto is taken from Maurice Barrès: "Rien ne vaut que par la forme de dire" (Nothing matters but stylistic form).

Bahr's attempt in *Caph* to transform mundane subject matter into literature through elevated language is, however, a failure. His linguistic brilliance was not enough to overcome the absence of a plot. Most of the selections amount to little more than anecdotes which have neither the interest nor the quality of those in *Fin de siècle*. The volume marks a step forward in the sense that Bahr no longer felt it necessary to rely on the erotic and perverse elements of decadence as a means of enhancing his narratives. But the emphasis on descriptions of thoughts, feelings, and visual and olfactory sensations are still in evidence. Ultimately, *Caph* represents Bahr's attempt to push the decadent formula to its extreme before recognizing its limitations and turning away from it.

In his second novel, *Neben der Liebe*, the overheated, lavishly descriptive style of *Die gute Schule*

Front wrapper for the 1894 collection of sketches that represented Bahr's attempt to push the "decadent" formula of style over plot to its extreme (Deutsches Literaturarchiv, Marbach [S. Fischer-Archiv, Umschlagsammlung Curt Tillman und allgemeiner Bibliotheksbestand])

has been replaced with a cooler one. The contrast is analogous to the shift from oils to pastels: where *Die gute Schule* emphasized the bright colors red and green, in *Neben der Liebe* gray tones predominate to reinforce the monotonous lives of the characters. The novel treats a group of Viennese aesthetes and men-about-town who lead shallow, passive lives without deep feelings or commitments. The plot is a tragic love story played out against a richly ornamented background. Japanese furniture and other indications of the craze for things Japanese at the time are in strong evidence, illustrating how Bahr always included the latest fads in his works. The protagonist, Margit von Rhon, is a married woman whose husband has been away for some time taking a cure for his ill health. Unable to bring herself to surrender to Rudi Lederer, the man she loves, she impulsively spends the night with Strass, a boorish Prussian whom she does not love. She then commits suicide out of self-disgust. She is a sacrifice to strong erotic feelings which she could not suppress and a victim of the moral double standard. The novel, which is largely presented in the form of interior monologue to reveal the complex feelings and thoughts of the protagonist, illustrates Bahr's view that love and erotic desire seldom coincide, a circumstance that causes people to live "next to love" rather than finding fulfillment in a sexually satisfying love. The idea seems outmoded today, but it was widely accepted at the turn of the century, and Bahr treated it in several works. The novel also conveys the naturalistic view that human destiny is determined not by free will but by external powers over which the individual has no control. He later applied this concept to Napoleon's life in the drama *Josephine* (1898).

Bahr's third novel, *Theater*, while not part of his "Austrian cycle," can be regarded as a precursor of *Die Rahl*. *Theater* is a frame novel, with the outer narrative presented in the first person by Bahr. He uses autobiographical details, including his experiences in Berlin, with no attempt to mask them. As in all of his novels, plot is secondary to the study of character. Bahr's narrative strengths lay in creating believable characters and brilliant set pieces; his greatest deficiency, as he himself recognized, was his inability to interweave plot and characters into a unified whole. His novels never achieve the complexity and interpretative ambiguity of great works but invariably end with a clear-cut resolution. This limitation partly results from the tendentious nature of the novels, for Bahr uses them to convey his views on specific areas of Austrian life. He is always clearly recognizable as the author, and the fictional world of the novel never assumes a life of its own. At times there is little difference between Bahr's novels and his essays.

In *Theater* Bahr sought to explore and expose the world of the theater, with which he had become somewhat disenchanted as a result of his close involvement with theater life in Berlin and Vienna. Bahr knew most of the prominent performers of his day, and his theater reviews show how seriously he strove to understand their craft. He was so fascinated by the gallery of theatrical types that although his novels usually only portrayed one or two characters in a rounded manner, here each one is depicted fully. The theater milieu is also described in detail. While the novel exposes the crazy world of the theater and contends that actors should be locked up between performances, it nevertheless views the theater as a valuable institution.

The protagonist is Dr. Maurus Mohr, a man devoted to reason, who writes a play that through sheer luck becomes a hit. Through Mohr, Bahr explores the world of the theater from the vantage point of a neophyte for whom this world is new and exciting. But Mohr's second drama is a failure, and he becomes an object of contempt just as quickly as he was turned into a celebrity. Recognizing that he has no genuine talent, disillusioned with the ephemeral nature of theatrical fame, and rejected by his actress lover, he returns to his understanding wife, Lotte, who unquestioningly takes him back after his lengthy absence in a scene written with great warmth and tact.

Mohr's story is another demonstration of the power of fate, against which human beings are helpless; life is simply a lottery; the nineteenth-century liberal emphasis on rationality and education (Bildung) was misguided. Yet Mohr also echoes Bahr's idea that art should be made a part of everyday life. *Theater* is one of Bahr's best novels because of its author's intimate knowledge of the theater, its excellent characterizations, the quality of the style, and the unity of the plot. Like all of his other novels, however, it lacks the complexity, depth of meaning, and ambiguity that would have made it perennially absorbing and challenging.

The theater is also the subject of the first novel of the Austrian cycle, *Die Rahl*. One of the subthemes of *Theater* is the ability of performers to transform themselves into the characters they are playing; this phenomenon intrigued Bahr, and he wrote about it extensively in his theater reviews. In *Die Rahl* Bahr contrasts the actress Rahl's elevated existence on stage with her empty life when she is not performing. The novel also deals with the deficiencies of the nineteenth-century methods of education. Finally, it shows a change of attitude on Bahr's part toward the aristocracy: previously he had depicted aristocrats as useless holdovers from a bygone age, but he portrays Rahl's husband, a count, as an intelligent, tolerant, and understanding person.

The plot of *Die Rahl*, like those of Bahr's other novels, serves only as a framework for the description of Austrian life and portrayal of character types. The high-school student Franz Heitlinger is infatuated with Rahl, the prima donna

Schloß Burgelstein, Bahr's residence in Salzburg

of the Viennese theater. He waits outside the stage door following her one-hundredth performance as Melitta in Franz Grillparzer's *Sappho;* on impulse she stops her carriage and invites him home for the night. He is transformed by the experience; his fear of the pedantic Professor Samon is replaced by open defiance, causing his expulsion from school. But nothing can intimidate him, since he is the lover of "Die Rahl." His exultation is short-lived, however, for he is informed by the count that Rahl has no intention of seeing him again; the affair was a momentary whim. With the maturity that the experience has brought him, Franz plans to return to school, which he can now face with greater self-assurance. For her part, Rahl will continue to alternate her empty offstage existence with the glorious, exhilarating sense of vitality she has when playing a role.

This view of Rahl's life illustrates Bahr's theory that actors can serve as models to show people how to elevate their existence to a higher level of intensity and meaning. A 1901 visit to Greece and his study of Greek culture impressed Bahr with the importance of reaching beyond oneself, of living at times in states of heightened intensity, even at the cost of subsequent low points. During these periods of depression individuals collect their energies for further bursts of height-

Bahr, circa 1900

ened productivity; it is necessary to lie fallow from time to time to collect one's inner strength to rise to greatness beyond oneself. This ideal also reflects the influence of Nietzsche's attack on mediocrity. (Bahr treated the same theme in his one-act play *Der arme Narr* [The Poor Fool, 1906], which was based loosely on the life of his student friend Hugo Wolf.)

Bahr attempts to describe the workings of Rahl's mind as she assumes the identity of the character she is playing. His conclusion about performers is the same as in *Theater:* that they are empty vessels until given a role to play. The grumbling painter Höfelind, who seems to be modeled on Bahr's friend, the artist Gustav Klimt, describes Rahl's emptiness offstage: he finds it impossible to paint her because she is not present. Instead of the dynamic, charismatic actress seen on stage, the woman posing for him is only a short, overweight person with watery eyes, totally ordinary and uninspiring.

Through Franz's experience in school Bahr exposes the cruelty of the educational system; Bahr and other writers of his generation felt that this system had had a crippling effect on their intellectual growth. The classroom is depicted as a battlefield where Professor Samon imposes conservative values on his students, attempting to break their wills and make them obedient servants of the state. In keeping with what he views as his duty, he refuses to tolerate any spark of originality or freedom of thought. His ideals and attitudes reflect the prevailing educational philosophy; the teacher is as much a victim as the students are. Samon's life is analogous to Rahl's in that he has no existence outside the classroom, just as Rahl loses her identity when she is not on stage. A rule-guided robot, he is the antithesis of what a human being should be. The reform of the educational system, which Bahr saw as a key to improving the quality of life in Austria, is addressed in the essays in his *Buch der Jugend* (Book for Youth, 1908).

Die Rahl contrasts Professor Samon, who would like to marry Franz Heitlinger's widowed mother, with Franz's father, who was the opposite of Samon in character. Franz's father and Samon represent, respectively, individualism and submissiveness, imagination and passivity, originality and sterility, progress and convention, feeling and reason, change and tradition. Bahr repeatedly stressed these contrasts in his subsequent works as he tried to break down the attitude of those who clung to the status quo and feared the new.

The novel also shows how far Bahr had come since his days as a follower of the anti-Semite Schönerer: Franz's friend, the young Jew Adolf Beer, is a positive character with an optimistic view of the future and the new humanity that it will bring. In the friendship of Beer and Franz, Bahr portrays the unity that is needed for progress, thereby introducing another of his major themes: isolation of individuals in Austria as an impediment to improved conditions. Bahr leaves no doubt about his faith in the energy and resolve of the young generation; he fully expects that they will succeed in producing the changes needed to enhance Austrian life. Rahl is used in the novel in a doubly symbolic way as both actress and woman: through her acting she teaches the young people to reach beyond themselves; she also leads and uplifts them in the spirit of Goethe's "eternal feminine" that draws mankind ever onward and upward. The novel concludes as Franz invokes her name as an inspirational symbol of a promising future.

The optimism that characterizes the ending of *Die Rahl* turns to pessimism in *Drut,* a critical examination of the Austrian bureaucracy. Criticism of the bureaucracy was a major topic of Bahr's essays during these years, as in *Wien* (Vienna, 1907), *Buch der Jugend, Tagebuch* (Diary, 1909), *Dalmatinische Reise* (Journey to Dalmatia, 1909), and *Austriaca* (Austrian Matters, 1911). *Drut* is Bahr's fictional presentation of the ideas in the essays. He believed that Austria was controlled by a tightly knit bureaucracy whose purpose was to perpetuate itself rather than to serve the country.

Bahr in 1909 (Bildarchiv der Österreichischen Nationalbibliothek)

An integral part of this bureaucracy was the Hofrat (privy councilor), an office Bahr repeatedly satirized as a menace to the country until he changed his mind in the 1920s. His view of the Hofrat's oppressive hold on the country is reflected in the title *Drut,* which refers to the upper Austrian superstition of the Drut or Trud, a witch who appears during the night and sits on a victim's heart, causing a painful, lingering death by suffocation. To Bahr this figure was the perfect symbol of Austrian bureaucracy. In the dramas *Der Krampus* (1902) and *Sanna* (1905) he shows a Hofrat sitting like a Trud on his own family, suppressing all freedom of spirit and emotion; in *Drut* he portrays bureaucracy as a Trud oppressing and stifling the whole country. Bahr's antipathy to bureaucracy was shared by his upper Austrian countrymen, who were distrustful of all officials and of anything else that emanated from Vienna.

The novel was based on newspaper reports about a young district commissioner from upper Austria who was destroyed by a woman named Drut. In Bahr's story Baron Klemens Furnian, the son of an impoverished nobleman and nephew of the powerful Domherr (Canon) Zingerl, is appointed district commissioner by the calculating Minister Doltsch, who wants to make Klemens one of his protégés. Since Klemens has been trained to obedience by an ambitious father, reminiscent of Professor Samon in his faith in the system and his desire to preserve it, he is well suited for a career as a bureaucrat. His only problem in his new assignment is that he is regarded as an outsider by the upper Austrians and is confronted with mistrust, if not open hostility.

As it does so often in Bahr's works—and, indeed, in the works of all of his contemporary Austrian writers—chance plays a crucial role in the novel. Klemens meets the young Prussian baroness Gertrude Scharrn, nicknamed Drut, who comes from a family of dubious reputation. She attempts to discourage him from pursuing her, but Klemens refuses to heed her advice. When she becomes pregnant and cannot get an abortion, he insists on marrying her. When her papers turn out not to be in order, he uses his official position to force a priest to perform the illegal ceremony. This information is leaked to the press, which exposes Drut's shady past and Klemens's improper use of his authority. Klemens's rivals for Minister Doltsch's favor seize this opportunity to ruin him; even his uncle contributes to his downfall to gain a financial advantage for the church. The minister callously dismisses Klemens, who shoots himself. Drut is arrested on charges of bigamy and is stoned to death by a mob on the way to jail. The townspeople do not consider themselves murderers but feel virtuous for protecting the community. According to Doltsch, they are not bad people, just conservative ones who are unforgiving of any encroachment on their autonomy or breach of their customs. The deaths of Klemens and Drut were tragic, in the minister's view, but the curative powers of nature will soon remove any harmful effects of this aberration from the normal flow of life. With this heavily ironic ending Bahr shows the impossibility of changing the system or even hoping for an occasional exception to its rigid rules.

The novel illustrates the controlling coalition of government and church, the conservatism of the provinces, the quixotic nature of belief in ab-

Front wrapper for Bahr's 1909 collection of essays. The main topic of the book is the Austrian bureaucracy.

solute justice, the system of political protection and connection, and the ruthless competition forced on young administrators trying to curry favor with their superiors. Klemens is trapped between the ambition of his father and the relentless system headed by Minister Doltsch, whose only goal is to survive and who, to keep peace with the church, his rival for power, sacrifices Klemens without a qualm. Survival in the system depends on following the prescribed conservative practices. If one is deflected from this traditional course and attempts to become a real person by breaking through the fetters of rationality to find freedom and love, he will be crushed. At the end of *Die Rahl* the two schoolboys believe that they will be able to change the system; Klemens's fate demonstrates the hopeless idealism of this view.

How to become a real or genuine human being was one of Bahr's basic themes. He repeatedly attacked the artificiality of Austrian life, the role playing that resulted in lonely, isolated, unfulfilled individuals and kept Austrians from working together to create a true sense of nationhood. In the novel *O Mensch!*, which takes its title from the then current expressionist cry for the true human being, Bahr calls for a free, open, universal "natural" religion that proclaims the essential goodness of all people. Like many expressionist works, this novel has no plot; it consists of a series of encounters between various Austrian types. Bahr was so concerned with expressing his idealistic precepts that he lavished all of his attention on the message and little on the form. The result is a succession of monologues in which the characters enunciate their views; there is little interaction between the characters or development of them.

The setting is an upper Austrian estate where the Wagnerian singer Fiechl lives with his sister Annalis. The eccentric Prince Adolar, a misfit trying to find a purpose for his existence, appears from time to time as a symbol of an aristocracy that no longer plays a meaningful role. The most interesting character is the Nußmensch (nut man), an original free spirit, an idealized allegorical figure who serves as Bahr's spokesman for the novel's message: the need for people to show more compassion and humaneness toward each other. The mysterious Nußmensch is the type of independent, genuine, pure-hearted human being that Bahr held up as an ideal in several works of this period. He turns out to be the brother of the mysterious baroness in *Drut,* showing that the attainment of goodness is a matter of individual choice rather than of heredity and environment. In Bahr's view, everyone is capable of finding fulfillment through love of nature and mankind.

To contrast natural to organized religion Bahr has the Nußmensch lecture the local priest on the goodness of man, using the nut as a symbol for the human being: a man is born completely sealed, like a nut in its shell, and has to be opened gradually by life; little by little he emerges from his shell, until he sheds it entirely and stands forth as a beautiful and good human being. According to the Nußmensch, most of the problems in the world result from human beings having forgotten how beautiful they are. This view of universal brotherly love and Bahr's attempt to present his characters stripped of role playing and superficiality mark him as one of the earliest expressionists in Austria.

While the novel's main message is the need for a humanistic religious renaissance, Bahr also continues his analysis of the social situation in Austria. The customary themes of the isolation of Austrians from one another—indeed, their outright hostility to each other, particularly to anyone striving for accomplishment in any area—are strongly in evidence. Bahr, like other writers, constantly criticized the Austrians' treatment of even their greatest creative talents, from Grillparzer to Gustav Mahler. After nearly twenty years of promoting the arts, Bahr himself suffered what he called "das österreichische Schicksal" (the Austrian fate). Disillusioned by the ingratitude shown his good intentions and efforts, he left Vienna for Salzburg in 1912.

O Mensch! was the most poorly received of all of Bahr's novels; and in terms of such aesthetic criteria as characterization, unity, and intensity, it must be judged unsuccessful. It contains flashes of genial inspiration followed by arid stretches and demonstrates that Bahr remained stuck in the early phases of expressionism.

In 1916 Bahr resumed his chronicle of Austria with the autobiographical *Himmelfahrt*, describing his return to the Catholic church in 1914. Whether this novel, which deals with the intellectual's path to religion, was praised or attacked depended on the critic's attitude toward Bahr; attention was focused on the work as exemplifying Bahr's latest phase rather than on the merits of the novel itself. The decline of religious faith under the impact of science and materialism was, in Bahr's view, a major problem of his time. In *Inventur* (Inventory, 1912), a collection of self-reflective essays taking stock of his life at the halfway point, he confronted this problem directly. Now, in his usual fashion, he fictionalizes his personal conflict and its resolution as a means of focusing on a broader issue. He also treated the dilemma of intellectuals caught in the conflict between science and religion in the lengthy essay *Vernunft und Wissenschaft* (Reason and Science, 1917).

Bahr—who certainly knew whereof he spoke—enjoined twentieth-century man to replace the frantic pursuit of trendy "isms" with the solid anchor of religion. In *Himmelfahrt* it is specifically *organized* religion that is advocated. Through his association with clergymen Bahr had learned that the universal natural religion he had espoused in *O Mensch!* is not an adequate substitute for the church. Although he believed that the Catholic church was the proper choice for everyone, his main concern was that everyone have *some* religious affiliation. As usual, Bahr points the gen-

Bahr manuscript (Dichtung und Dichter der Zeit, 1961)

eral direction to follow but leaves the choice of the specific path to the individual.

The protagonist of *Himmelfahrt* is Count Franz Flayn, a thirty-seven-year-old rationalist who has lost touch with his emotions, a painter who has not achieved the level of a real artist, an amateur scientist—in sum, a dilettante who resembles a more active version of the aesthetes of the turn of the century. After years of traveling around the world fruitlessly seeking peace of mind, Flayn returns to Austria psychologically ripe for inner transformation. The trip from the family brewery to the estate over the road called Himmelfahrt symbolically foreshadows the events to come. It is evident from the beginning that Flayn will find the path to faith; the only uncertainty is how long it will take and what will trigger the final transformation.

As in Bahr's earlier novels, there is virtually no plot. Dialogues and essayistic inner monologues present the psychological pressures and changes that push Flayn inexorably toward his conversion. The Domherr enlightens Flayn about the impossibility of the church logically persuading anyone to have faith; that is not the proper role of the church. The church is simply available to those who have made their own decision to accept faith. The path to faith is not difficult; Flayn needs only to ask for grace, and it will be granted to him. But the church cannot provide a rational explanation of how this happens. Flayn continues nevertheless to search for logical reasons for belief. Through his conversations and ruminations he eliminates one avenue of escape after another until he has no choice but to believe. The immediate stimulus for his conversion is the outbreak of World War I. His decision to join the military after the assassination of Archduke Franz Ferdinand, whom he greatly admired, is the act that permits grace to enter his soul. Following a last, lengthy discussion with the Domherr, Flayn is spontaneously moved to enter a small church and confess. In so doing he suddenly feels that the faith he has been seeking for so long has silently and mysteriously taken root within him.

Love also plays a role in Flayn's transformation. Although in his earlier works Bahr usually presented women primarily as sex objects, his love for Anna Mildenburg and his study of Goethe—which resulted in his book of essays *Um Goethe* (1917)—led him to depict women in this novel as inspirational forces capable of leading a man to his higher self: the widow Klara Bucek declines Flayn's offer of marriage, and her religious commitment serves as an example to him.

Another influence on Flayn is the servant Blasl, a mysterious, idealized figure similar to the Nußmensch in *O Mensch!* Blasl has written a series of pamphlets arguing the case for religion. He turns out to be the heir to the Spanish throne, who disappeared and sought to lead an authentic life of Christian poverty. The war revives his sense of duty, and he returns home to fulfill his responsibilities. This unconvincing masquerade contributes little to the novel beyond illustrating the strength of the kind of faith that Bahr was espousing. Blasl is the opposite of the soulless, materialistic, spiritually bankrupt twentieth-century man whom Bahr had attacked since *Inventur*. *Himmelfahrt* repeats the idea Bahr expressed in the essays of *Kriegssegen* (Blessings of War, 1915) that perhaps the war was inflicted on Europe as a test of whether mankind could change its destructive course before the situation became irreversible. Obviously the world had not done so, and thus the moral lesson could only apply to a future era.

One gauge of the seriousness of *Himmelfahrt* as well as of Bahr's other "Austrian" novels is their total lack of pose, skepticism, undermining irony (as in *Die gute Schule*), and any trace of *épater les bourgeois*, qualities which marred his earlier works. He was concerned about what he considered the diseased soul of his generation and wished to contribute to its cure. *Himmelfahrt* is a thoughtful analysis of the universal problem of rationality versus faith that is still relevant today; the novel's limitation is not in choice of theme, at which Bahr usually excelled, but in execution. Like Bahr's other novels, *Himmelfahrt* is linear in construction; it lacks subplots to add complexity and fails to probe deeper levels of meaning. Count Flayn is characterized in considerable detail, but the other characters, many of whom appeared in earlier novels, remain mere spokesmen for various points of view.

Following the war Bahr addressed the issues of anti-Semitism and Zionism in *Die Rotte Korahs*, his longest, most ambitious, most complex, and most profound novel. Bahr exercises his narrative powers to the fullest both to analyze these issues and to capture the essence of the Austrian character. That character, he felt, would guarantee the continued existence of the country even after the population had been reduced from the fifty million of the Austro-Hungarian empire to a "Rumpfstaat" (torso) of seven million. Although the novel again takes a primarily essayistic approach in the form of dialogues or monologues, the powerful themes and the more successful integration of the subplots into a unified whole make it the most satisfying and engrossing of Bahr's novels. It maintains its intensity throughout its more than six hundred pages, and the dialogues sustain a high emotional level. Because of the issues that are treated, *Die Rotte Korahs* transcends its own age and is still relevant today.

A wealthy Jewish entrepreneur named Jason dies and leaves his estate to Count Ferdinand Drzik, whom his will alleges to be his son. The count, a war hero, was raised by aristocratic Austrian parents and was unaware of the identity of his true father. After having grown up thinking of himself as the son of a distinguished Austrian family with a distinguished lineage, Ferdinand must now come to grips with his Jewishness. His initial reaction is to reject the money, but everyone he turns to for advice attempts to dissuade him from such immature behavior; they point out that whether he accepts the money or not, he cannot abolish the fact of his Jewishness, and argue that if he becomes a victim of anti-Semitism, he will be able to combat it better as a wealthy man. He should use the money to support charitable causes rather than let it lapse to the state. Like Count Flayn in *Himmelfahrt*, Ferdinand spends most of the novel having conversations with a variety of people and searching his soul. Finally, he gains the maturity and the understanding to accept his new identity and the inheritance. He will marry his lover Paula, who is pregnant with his child, and move to upper Austria, where he can find the peace of mind and the fullness of life that belong to those with ties to the land. Marriage, family, and homeland were values that Bahr advocated for the rest of his career.

The themes of racial identity and materialism are interrelated in Bahr's attempt to show that the concept of "Betrieb" (high-powered business activity) that he deplored was created by certain Jews at the urging of gentiles. Jason was the embodiment of this drive to generate more and more money for its own sake. As a result, he was disliked even by other Jews but was tolerated by the gentiles because of his usefulness. According to Beer, the Jewish student from *Die Rahl* who reappears here as the military surgeon who saved Ferdinand's life, the history of Europe since the Renaissance shows a pattern of non-Jews imitating and rivaling Jews like Jason in the quest for money. Echoing a theme Bahr first expressed in his booklet *Wien*, Beer says that Europeans must accept the responsibility for this trend toward materialism, for Jews like Jason were exempted from the general harsh treatment of Jews to free them to perform tasks that gentiles did not want to do themselves. Beer calls such a Jew an *Epikores*, a Greek word by which he means a person who has decided to stop being cheated and instead to become the cheater. The *Epikores* will deliver anything for anyone, turning everything he touches into money. He thus makes himself indispensable and is rewarded accordingly, although at the same time he is intensely disliked. In Beer's view, contemporary culture is carried on by such types. Not all Jews are *Epikores*, but the oustanding success of the few has caused an identification of Jewishness with business and the acquisition of money. By tracing this situation to its origins Bahr attempts to show that the sellout to materialism is not a matter of race but of individual choice. *Die Rotte Korahs* is Bahr's strongest statement against anti-Semitism.

Beer represents the antithesis of the *Epikores*. He despises Jews like Jason who he feels sold out their integrity and their people for their own self-interest. His sympathies are with ordinary Jews who have not become financially and socially prominent, who maintain the traditions of the Jewish nation. Beer is convinced that it is the Jewish mission to produce the perfect human being, and he longs for the day when Jews will regain their full identity through the reestablishment of their own homeland in Palestine. In his view, most people do not even know what Jews are really like, because the only ones they meet or read about are of the type belonging to "die Rotte Korahs," a band which Jehovah himself did not know how to handle except by opening up a crack in the earth that swallowed them up with all their property. Beer is a bitter man and a fanatical Zionist, but Ferdinand patiently broadens his perspective and understanding by inviting him on a trip through the "real" Austria that, like the true Jews, goes unrecognized.

Another Jewish type Bahr presents is the converted Jew who is assimilated into Austrian society and has no desire to immigrate to Palestine. These Jews recognize that their people will remain nomads until they have a homeland, but they believe that the Zionists will feel as foreign in Palestine as they do in Austria. The attorney Dr. Raibl, who serves as the spokesman for this point of view, argues that the Jewish homeland need not be in Palestine: Jews should establish roots in the country of their residence. According to Raibl, not only the Jews but Europeans in general have become uprooted and have lost contact with the soil. This contention echoes the theme of Maurice Barrès's *Les Deracinés* (1897), a work that influenced Bahr's thinking on the relationship of individuals to the land and on the feeling of nationhood. Being uprooted and not at home anywhere is a problem for people of all nations in Europe. To combat this trend by setting a personal example, Ferdinand will establish roots for his family in upper Austria.

Bahr consistently denies that race is a determining factor in human behavior. As Ferdinand explains, two brothers can have the same father and mother, but one brother will be a born master and the other a born slave. Members of the aristocracy or of the intellectual elite in different countries feel more akin to each other than they do to lower-class or ignorant individuals in their own nations. Jews are not different from other people, and to regard them as such is irrational. As an example of the anti-Semite, Bahr brings back Franz Heitlinger, who had shown such promise at the end of *Die Rahl* but has now developed into a shallow, opportunist anti-Semite, an Aryan *Epikores*, a member of the materialistic band of Korah. Beer despises his former friend, while Ferdinand, although recognizing Heitlinger's contemptible character, is attracted by his charm. Heitlinger, who is totally devoid of scruples or conscience, has no compunction about asking Ferdinand for a loan to start an anti-Semitic newspaper. Ferdinand underestimates Heitlinger and agrees to lend him the money.

The novel is pervaded by a religious spirit, reflecting Bahr's return to Catholicism. As Bahr felt was true in his own case, Ferdinand notes that a solution to a specific need at a given moment of his life has always been forthcoming, as if by chance. While Bahr had stressed the role of fate or chance in earlier years, he now rejects the idea that man is a pawn of fate. Both Bahr and Ferdinand rationalize the dilemma by interpreting chance as a form of divine guidance. One must have the faith to place oneself with complete trust in the hands of a higher power, and the help that one needs will be provided.

Finally, in *Die Rotte Korahs* Bahr introduces a new theme that became the major one in his later writings: the future of Austria. Like other cultural interpreters and commentators, Bahr had previously emphasized the accomplishments of

Bahr in old age

great artists and leaders; now he discovers that Austria's strength actually resides in its ordinary people. It is through such average individuals, who exemplify the spirit of Adalbert Stifter and Grillparzer, that Austria will fulfill its mission of serving as a political and cultural mediator in Europe. This novel, written in the dark days immediately after World War I, was intended to unite Bahr's countrymen, to restore their national pride, and to instill in them confidence in the future.

After an interlude of eight years, during which he continued to turn out dramas, essays, and his weekly diary installments at a prolific rate, Bahr resumed his novel series in 1927 with *Der inwendige Garten*. The primary theme, the importance of social stability, is clearly an attack on the many factions and paramilitary groups that were formed in Austria in the 1920s. The novel is set in a fictitious upper Austrian village governed by Count Ahamb, who represents and defends the traditional values of old Austria. Through judicious political maneuvering, the count restores order to the village, calming the populace and forestalling a threatened outbreak of civil disobedience.

On a second level the purpose of the novel is to deliver a message on the importance of maintaining agreements, particularly the marriage contract. Divorce is not permissible because the sacredness of marriage rests on its indissolubility; only death can end a marriage. The happiness of the individuals involved is of no importance; only the inviolability of the marriage contract matters. When the count's wife falls in love with his friend, he warns her that he will never give her a divorce. To him it is preferable to allow her to have an affair, as long as she behaves discreetly. The law, in this case the marriage contract, is more important than the individual, for the meaning of every person's life is to serve the law. The count believes that if a couple accepts the impossibility of dissolving their marriage, they will find a solution to their problems. The countess proves the validity of this theory: after reorganizing her "inner garden," she ends her still-platonic attachment to the friend and announces that she is expecting the count's child. This conclusion is reported by the count, leaving the reader to assume that the countess has happily accepted the situation. The novel would have been more convincing if the countess had spoken for herself, but Bahr retained the turn-of-the-century attitude that women's lives were controlled by men, even though his own relationship with Mildenburg did not fit this pattern.

The weak ending of *Der inwendige Garten* is indicative of the shortcomings of the work as a whole; it is the least developed novel of the series. The idea of confronting disorder on both the personal and social levels is not worked out convincingly. The sermonizing of the count, the sketchy plot, and the stereotyped characters diminish the vitality of the novel. Even the countess's love affair is lifeless and without genuine emotion, for it is only reported in rational discussions; the lovers are never shown together. Overall, *Der inwendige Garten* gives the impression less of a novel than of an outline for one. Since it is intended as an idealization, Bahr may have felt less obligated to flesh out the characters and the plot, especially since he believed that he was following the mature Goethe's approach of using abstract figures in his works. But it is more likely that his creative powers were simply waning as his health deteriorated.

The novel serves as a measure of how far Bahr's thinking had changed since 1909, when he had divorced Rosalie Jokl. Eighteen years later Bahr seems to have forgotten the unhappiness that divorce released him from and the fulfillment he had found with Mildenburg. By 1927 he was so immersed in Catholicism that he became dogmatic. Here again Bahr insists, as he had in *Drut,* that the church plays an indispensable role in religion. The rituals are a sign of obedience; any other form of religion is unacceptable to God. Only illness or extraordinary circumstances permit dispensation from the obligation to attend church. As Bahr's spokesman, the count, says: man exists only to serve God, and his happiness lies in God's hand; recognizing this truth is the secret of the art of life.

The value of *Der inwendige Garten* is its insistence on the importance of maintaining form: in one's inner life by arranging one's "inner garden," in one's outer life by exhibiting tact and discretion, in social matters by keeping agreements, and in religion through church affiliation and attendance. Bahr extends this discussion of form to art with a digression on the nature of the novel. A proper novel, he says, is not simply a reflective mirror to reproduce reality as it is, but "ein schaffender Spiegel" (a creative mirror) in the Goethean sense, that is, symbolic art which surmounts reality to illustrate higher truths and produce moral uplift; it should emulate music in banishing reality and transporting its audience to a higher level of feeling. This notion of disregarding the depiction of reality and extracting the essential meaning from the material shows the influence not only of Goethe but also of the classical Greek authors with whom Bahr was much occupied in his later years, as reflected in the essays in *Summula* (1921) and *Sendung des Künstlers* (Mission of the Artist, 1923). Finally, he was influenced by expressionism, as he showed in his book *Expressionismus* (Expressionism, 1916). Bahr believed that expressionism approached life in a more essential way than either naturalism or impressionism; despite his admiration for the technique, however, he was unable to make the transition to expressionism but always remained an impressionist. Bahr's concept of the novel is only stated theoretically; *Der inwendige Garten* does not come close to illustrating his elevated idea of what a novel should be.

Bahr's final novel, *Österreich in Ewigkeit,* conveys its intention through a motto taken from Stendhal's *Le Rouge et le Noir* (1831; translated as *Red and Black,* 1898): "Ah, monsieur, a novel is a mirror that accompanies us on the high road." Again, the mirror in this novel is more reflective than creative, and while the work deals with

Josef Meinrad (Dr. Jura), Alma Seidler (Marie), Inge Konradi (Delfine), and Attila Hörbiger (Heink) in a 1955 Burgtheater production of Bahr's 1909 play Das Konzert *directed by Ulrich Bettac (photo by R. Pittner)*

major issues in a highly inflammatory period—anti-Semitism, Hitler's Brownshirt movement, pacifism, the annexation of Austria by Germany, and the future of Austria—it does so in a sketchy, superficial, highly contrived manner. The princess Uldus, a symbol of old Austria, is preparing to celebrate her ninetieth birthday. She is characterized as a typical upper Austrian: rebellious, tenderhearted, and like Bahr himself, inclined to do the opposite of whatever is suggested. A descendant of one of the oldest families in Austria, she has faith in the future of her country and is unalterably opposed to the annexation of Austria by Germany.

Bahr surrounds the princess with representatives of a cross section of social and political views. The state attorney, whose teenage son is a Nazi, is an old liberal; although he does not agree with his son that Austria's future lies in union with Germany, he has become disenchanted with liberalism and sympathizes with the yearning for a strong leader to save the country from the decline caused by the harsh terms of the Versailles peace treaty. Bahr himself had always been an advocate of strong leaders like Bismarck and Napoleon and lamented that Austria could not find that caliber of leadership. At the same time, he never supported Hitler (although he did admire Mussolini) and could not have endorsed National Socialism because of its anti-Semitism and anti-Catholicism. Nevertheless, he was aware of Hitler's ability to captivate the imagination of fanatical young followers, and Höd Heidel, the young Hitler enthusiast in his novel, is a typical product of his time—rabidly anti-Semitic, dedicated to sports as a means of building his strength and preparing for war, participating in duels to prove his courage, and ignoring school as superfluous to his future purpose. In the contrasting outlooks of father and son Bahr depicted the conflict that would increasingly divide families as 1938, the year of the Anschluß, approached. But on this occasion Bahr's ability to foretell events failed him. Like most people in the 1920s he believed that National Socialism was only a passing fad and that annexation was not a serious threat. Thus, young Heidel is portrayed as more ludicrous than dangerous. His father, who dismisses his son's actions and words as mere signs of immaturity, illustrates the unconcern of the older generation in regard to the young Nazis in their midst.

The princess ridicules the young Nazi's anti-Semitism, telling him that race is not important; it is not what qualities one is born with but what one achieves with one's abilities that matters;

each person creates himself and is his own fate. Clearly, she is here speaking for Bahr. The young man replies that in great individuals like Napoleon it is the element of will that makes the difference. This notion of the fanatical, monomaniacal will is merely stated; Bahr does not elaborate on it. Here he had touched upon one of the key reasons for the rise of the Nazi movement, the concept of the tenacious, focused will, without recognizing its significance. If he had, he might have realized that the movement would not self-destruct after creating some minor disturbances, as many intellectuals believed at the time.

The antithesis of the Hitler youth is Guido Grün, a Jewish war hero who has become a pacifist. When Heidel persecutes him, Grün lays his principles aside, challenges the young Nazi to a duel, and wounds him. They become friends and the Jew educates the young fanatic away from the Nazi program of hatred. The novel exhibits a cheerfully optimistic tone, and the reader is left with the feeling that such a harmonious reconciliation will also occur in the nation at large.

Characters from the preceding works reappear in the novel, all of them repeating the opinions they had enunciated earlier. While this repetition tends to unify the Austrian novels as a series, at the same time it is an indication of how Bahr's powers were fading. He again states his view of art as a creative mirror that does not reproduce what exists in nature but extracts its essence. He also reiterates his idea that Austria will continue to exist because of the characteristics of the average Austrian, who is modest, does not set impossible goals, and thus does not live in a state of dissatisfaction at not having accomplished what cannot be attained. If the Austrians continue to exhibit these characteristics, there will be an "Austria in eternity."

Bahr's own assessment of his strengths as a novelist–that his ability to shape his material was not as great as his gift for conceiving ideas–was accurate. The novels deal with important issues, but he lacked the talent to give them the polished expression that would make them endure. As in all of his writings, he remained interested in a subject until he felt he had mastered it; then he was ready to move on to a new topic. He could not bring himself to devote years to revising a work in the manner of Hugo von Hofmannsthal, Arthur Schnitzler, or Richard Beer-Hofmann. His goal was also different from theirs: while they wrote with an eye on posterity, Bahr was primarily a journalist who wrote for his own satisfaction and for the audiences of his day. He predicted wrongly that three of his dramas, *Der Franzl* (1901), *Sanna*, and *Die Stimme* (The Voice, 1917), would last; instead, it is *Wienerinnen* (Viennese Women, 1900), *Der Krampus*, and *Das Konzert* (The Concert, 1909) that are still performed. His best work, which will endure probably longer than any of his fiction, is his autobiography, *Selbstbildnis* (Self-Portrait, 1923). He did not think that any of his novels would survive; he was well aware of what it would have taken to produce a work of art of enduring quality and was willing to settle for contemporary success. It was his ambition to be the "Praeceptor Germaniae" of his day, to influence his own age, and his novels reflect this intention. They do not reach the standard of the major novels of twentieth-century Austrian and German literature. Bahr's best novels–especially *Die Rotte Korahs*–contain at least some excellently drawn characters, present provocative analyses of major problems, and give the reader an insight into Austrian conditions and institutions at the time they were written. Despite their artistic limitations, all of the novels are still highly readable. Their absence from the book market is not a reflection of their quality but of the legal complexities surrounding the Bahr estate. Their significance lies in their value as cultural documents of their time and in their importance to anyone who wishes to understand the amazingly complex phenomenon of Hermann Bahr.

Letters:

Meister und Meisterbriefe um Hermann Bahr, edited by Joseph Gregor (Vienna: Bauer, 1947);

"Hugo von Hofmannsthal und Hermann Bahr: Zwei Briefe," edited by Rudolf Hirsch, *Phaidros*, 1 (1947): 85-88;

Hermann Bahr: Briefwechsel mit seinem Vater, edited by Adalbert Schmidt (Vienna: Bauer, 1971);

The Letters of Arthur Schnitzler to Hermann Bahr, edited by Donald G. Daviau (Chapel Hill: University of North Carolina Press, 1978);

Dichter und Gelehrter: Hermann Bahr und Josef Redlich in ihren Briefen, 1896-1934, edited by Fritz Fellner (Salzburg: Neugebauer, 1980).

Bibliographies:

Kurt Thomasberger, "Bibliographie der Werke von Hermann Bahr," in *Hermann Bahr: Ein Leben für das europäische Theater*, edited by Heinz Kindermann (Graz & Cologne: Böhlau, 1954), pp. 347-368;

Hermann Nimmervoll, "Materialien zu einer Bibliographie der Zeitschriftenartikel von Hermann Bahr (1883-1910)," *Modern Austrian Literature*, 13, no. 2 (1980): 27-110.

References:

Egon W. Brecker, "Hermann Bahr and the Quest for Culture: A Critique of his Essays," Ph.D. dissertation, University of Wisconsin, Madison, 1978;

Konrad Burdach, "Wissenschaft und Journalismus (Betrachtungen über und für Hermann Bahr)," *Preußische Jahrbücher*, 193 (1923): 17-31;

Frank W. Chandler, "The Austrian Contribution: Schnitzler, Bahr, Schönherr, von Hofmannsthal," in his *Modern Continental Playwrights* (New York & London: Harper, 1931), pp. 345-365;

Emile Chastel, "Hermann Bahr, son oeuvre et son temps," Ph.D. dissertation, University of Paris, 1974;

Herbert Cysarz, "Alt-Österreichs letzte Dichtung, 1890-1914," *Preußische Jahrbücher*, 211 (1928): 32-51;

Donald G. Daviau, "*Dialog vom Marsyas*: Hermann Bahr's Affirmation of Life over Art," *Modern Language Quarterly*, 20 (December 1959): 360-370;

Daviau, "Experiments in Pantomime by the Major Writers of *Jung-Wien*," in *Österreich in amerikanischer Sicht* (New York: Austrian Institute, 1981), pp. 19-26;

Daviau, "The Friendship of Hermann Bahr and Arthur Schnitzler," *Journal of the International Arthur Schnitzler Research Association*, 5 (Spring 1966): 4-37;

Daviau, *Hermann Bahr* (New York: Twayne, 1985);

Daviau, "Hermann Bahr and Decadence," *Modern Austrian Literature*, 10 (June 1977): 53-100;

Daviau, "Hermann Bahr and Gustav Klimt," *German Studies Review*, 3 (February 1980): 27-49;

Daviau, "Hermann Bahr and the Radical Politics of Austria in the 1880s," *German Studies Review*, 5, no. 2 (May 1982): 163-185;

Daviau, "Hermann Bahr and the Secessionist Art Movement in Vienna," in *The Turn of the Century German Literature and Art: 1890-1915*, edited by Gerald Chapple and Hans H. Schulte (Bonn: Bouvier, 1981), pp. 433-462;

Daviau, "Hermann Bahr as Director of the Burgtheater," *German Quarterly*, 32 (January 1959): 11-21;

Daviau, "Hermann Bahr's *Josephine*: A Revisionist View of Napoleon," *Modern Austrian Literature*, 12 (June 1979): 93-111;

Daviau, "Hermann Bahr's Nachlaß," *Journal of the International Arthur Schnitzler Research Association*, 2 (Autumn 1963): 4-27;

Daviau, *Der Mann von Übermorgen: Hermann Bahr (1863-1934)* (Vienna: Österreichischer Bundesverlag, 1984);

Daviau, "The Misconception of Herman Bahr as a Verwandlungskünstler," *German Life and Letters*, 11 (April 1958): 182-192;

Manfred Diersch, "Hermann Bahr: Der Empiriokritizismus als Philosophie des Impressionismus," in his *Empiriokritizismus und Impressionismus* (Berlin: Rütten & Loening, 1973), pp. 46-82;

William A. Drake, "Hermann Bahr," in his *Contemporary European Writers* (New York: Day, 1928), pp. 184-191;

Amelia V. Ende, "Literary Vienna," *Bookman*, 38 (September 1913-February 1914): 141-155;

Otto Michel Hirsch, "Hermann Bahr, der Novellist und Dramatiker," *Xenien*, 2, no. 11 (1909): 279-289;

Hugo von Hofmannsthal, "Die Mutter," in his *Prosa 1* (Frankfurt am Main: Fischer, 1950), pp. 16-23;

Hofmannsthal, "Zum Direktionswechsel im Burgtheater," *Neue Freie Presse*, 5 July 1918, pp. 1-2;

Manfred Jahnichen, "Hermann Bahr und die Tschechen," in *Slavische-Deutsche Wechselbeziehungen in Sprache, Literatur und Kultur*, edited by W. Kraus, J. Belic, and V. I. Borkovskij (Berlin: Akademie, 1969), pp. 363-377;

Heinz Kindermann, ed., *Hermann Bahr: Ein Leben für das europäische Theater* (Graz & Cologne: Böhlau, 1954);

Friedrich Lehner, "Hermann Bahr," *Monatshefte*, 39, no. 1 (1947): 54-62;

Mary M. Macken, "Chronicle: Hermann Bahr, 1865-1934," *Studies: An Irish Quarterly Review*, 23 (March 1934): 144-146;

Macken, "Hermann Bahr: His Personality and his Works," *Studies: An Irish Quarterly Review*, 15 (March 1926): 34-46;

Wilhelm Meridies, *Hermann Bahr als epischer Gestalter und Kritiker der Gegenwart* (Hildesheim: Borgmeyer, 1927);

Meridies, "Hermann Bahrs religiöser Entwicklungsgang," *Das heilige Feuer*, 15 (March 1928): 270-278;

Josef Nadler, "Hermann Bahr und das katholische Österreich," *Die neue Rundschau*, 34 (1923): 490-502;

Nadler, *Literaturgeschichte Österreichs* (Salzburg: Müller, 1951), pp. 397-406, 414-416;

Nadler, "Vom alten zum neuen Europa," *Preußische Jahrbücher*, 193 (1923): 32-51;

Karl Nirschl, *In seinen Menschen ist Österreich: Hermann Bahrs innerer Weg* (Linz: Oberösterreichischer Landesverlag, 1964);

Victor A. Oswald, "The Old Age of Young Vienna," *Germanic Review*, 27 (October 1952): 188-199;

Percival Pollard, "Bahr and Finis," in his *Masks and Minstrels of New Germany* (Boston: Luce, 1911), pp. 290-299;

Christine Zehl Romero, "Die konservative Revolution: Hermann Bahr und Adalbert Stifter," *Germanisch-Romanische Monatsschrift*, 56 (1975): 439-454;

Felix Salten, "Aus den Anfängen: Erinnerungsskizzen," *Jahrbuch deutscher Bibliophilen*, 18-19 (1932-1933): 31-46;

Robert Edward Simmons, "Hermann Bahr as a Literary Critic: An Analysis and Exposition of his Thought," Ph.D. dissertation, Stanford University, 1956;

Joseph Sprengler, "Hermann Bahr–der Weg in seinen Dramen," *Hochland*, 2 (1928): 352-366;

Sprengler, "Hermann Bahr Tagebücher," *Das literarische Echo*, 22 (1919-1920): 262-265;

Peter Wagner, *Der junge Hermann Bahr* (Giessen: Druck der Limburger Vereinsdruckerei, 1937);

Erich Widder, *Hermann Bahr: Sein Weg zum Glauben* (Linz: Oberösterreichischer Landesverlag, 1963).

Papers:

Hermann Bahr's literary estate is in the Theater Collection of the National Library in Vienna.

Richard Beer-Hofmann
(11 July 1866-26 September 1945)

Esther N. Elstun
George Mason University

BOOKS: *Novellen* (Berlin: Freund & Jeckel, 1893);

Der Tod Georgs (Berlin: Fischer, 1900);

Der Graf von Charolais: Ein Trauerspiel (Berlin: Fischer, 1905);

Gedenkrede auf Wolfgang Amadé Mozart (Berlin: Fischer, 1906); translated by Samuel R. Wachtell as "Memorial Oration on Wolfgang Amadeus Mozart," in *Heart of Europe*, edited by Klaus Mann and Hermann Kesten (New York: Bermann-Fischer, 1943), pp. 579-593;

Jaákobs Traum: Ein Vorspiel (Berlin: Fischer, 1918); translated by Ida Bension Wynn as *Jacob's Dream* (New York: Johannespresse, 1946);

Schlaflied für Mirjam (Berlin: Fischer, 1919; New York: Galerie St. Etienne, 1945); translated by Sol Liptzin as "Lullabye for Miriam," *Poet Lore*, 47 (1941): 290;

Der junge David: Sieben Bilder (Berlin: Fischer, 1933);

Vorspiel auf dem Theater zu König David (Vienna: Johannespresse, 1936);

Verse (Stockholm & New York: Bermann-Fischer, 1941);

Aus dem Fragment Paula: Herbstmorgen in Österreich (New York: Johannespresse, 1944);

Paula, ein Fragment, edited by Otto Kallir (New York: Johannespresse, 1949);

Gesammelte Werke (Frankfurt am Main: Fischer, 1963).

OTHER: Ariel Bension, *Die Hochzeit des Todes*, introduction by Beer-Hofmann (Vienna: Tal, 1920);

"Moissi," in *Moissi: Der Mensch und der Künstler in Worten und Bildern*, edited by Hans Böhm (Berlin: Eigenbrödler, 1927), pp. 48-49;

"Herakleitische Paraphrase," in *Aus unbekannten Schriften: Festgabe für Martin Buber zum 50. Geburtstag* (Berlin: Schneider, 1928), p. 29;

Johann Wolfgang von Goethe, *Fest-Aufführung des Faust von Goethe: I. und II. Teil. Mit Benützung des Ur-Faust und des Faust-Nachlasses zur Aufführung an einem Abend eingerichtet,*

Richard Beer-Hofmann (Bildarchiv der Österreichischen Nationalbibliothek)

adapted by Beer-Hofmann (Vienna: Weiner, 1932);

"Pierrot Hypnotiseur," in *Mortifikation und Beschwörung: Zur Veränderung ästhetischer Wahrnehmung in der Moderne am Beispiel des Frühwerks Richard Beer-Hofmanns*, by Rainer Hank (Frankfurt am Main & New York: Lang, 1984), pp. 261-309.

PERIODICAL PUBLICATIONS: "Gesang während des Rauchopfers, aus Entwürfen zu 'Davids Tod' (1908)," *Almanach des Schocken Verlages auf das Jahr 5695* (1934): 33-34;

"Hintergrund," *Österreichische Frauen-Not-Dienst Almanach* (1937): 85;

"Gedichte," *Die Rappen: Jahrbuch des Bermann-Fischer Verlages* (1937): 14-16;

"Das goldene Pferd: Pantomime in sechs Bildern," *Die neue Rundschau*, 66 (1955): 679-726.

Despite the sparseness of his own literary production, Richard Beer-Hofmann was the most influential member of the fin de siècle circle of Austrian writers known as "Young Vienna." His early novel *Der Tod Georgs* (Georg's Death, 1900) is probably the most representative example of literary art nouveau in the German language, and its stream-of-consciousness technique, though familiar to subsequent generations of readers, was still arrestingly innovative at the turn of the century. His influence also stemmed from his work in the theater, much of it in collaboration with the director Max Reinhardt; both as a dramatist and as a director, Beer-Hofmann was extensively involved in efforts to revitalize the theater and free it from what he and others regarded as the dead end of naturalism. And to some extent, finally, his influence can be attributed to his personal charm, his persuasive advocacy of his literary theories, and a reputation for uncompromising artistic integrity best summed up by Hugo von Hofmannsthal, who called Beer-Hofmann "der strengste und unbestechlichste Kritiker, den ich habe" (the sternest and most incorruptible critic I have).

The son of Hermann Beer, an attorney, and Rosa Steckerl Beer, Richard Beer was born in Vienna on 11 July 1866. His mother died within days of his birth, and he was reared by an aunt and uncle, Berta and Alois Hofmann, whose last name was added to his own; the adoption was legally formalized in 1884. By his own account Beer-Hofmann enjoyed a remarkably secure and happy childhood. Anti-Semitism had by no means disappeared, but by the mid 1860s the Jews of imperial Austria had been granted most citizens' rights and were assimilated to a degree that enabled families like the Beers and the Hofmanns to enter the prosperous upper middle class. He spent his early childhood in Brünn (now Brno, Czechoslovakia), where Alois Hofmann owned a textile factory. It was sold in 1880, and the family moved to Vienna, where real estate investments secured their financial future. Beer-Hofmann completed secondary school at Vienna's prestigious Akademisches Gymnasium and in 1883 began the study of law at the University of Vienna. After he received his doctorate in jurisprudence in 1890, the family expected him to join Hermann Beer's law firm, but to their consternation he did not. Like many young Jews of similar background, Beer-Hofmann felt far more powerfully drawn to the arts than to the "respectable" profession for which he had been trained.

Cover of Beer-Hofmann's best-known novel, one of the first in the German language to utilize the stream-of-consciousness technique

Also in 1890 Beer-Hofmann met Arthur Schnitzler. Their acquaintance quickly developed into what was to be a lifelong friendship, probably the firmest and most gratifying in both men's lives. Schnitzler soon introduced Beer-Hofmann to the other members of Young Vienna, who met regularly for animated discussion of artistic topics: Hofmannsthal, Jakob Wassermann, Felix Salten, Peter Altenberg, Paul Goldmann, Alfred Kerr, and Hermann Bahr.

By December 1891 Beer-Hofmann had completed his first work of fiction, "Camelias" (Camellias). Almost totally devoid of external action, the story consists of the reflections of a decadent dandy named Freddy. Infatuated with the beautiful seventeen-year-old Thea, he impulsively decides to marry her. While getting ready for bed, however, he is filled with misgivings provoked by fear of old age, the recollection of friends who had been deceived by young wives, and the reflection in the mirror of his middle-aged face, smeared with cold cream, and his corseted figure. Freddy's fear of disrupting the familiar pattern of his life leads him to give up the idea of marriage. He leaves instructions for his valet to send camellias to his longtime mistress on Sunday, as usual, and goes to bed. Thea, though the reader meets her only in Freddy's thoughts, is clearly meant to bring his decadent qualities into sharper relief by being his opposite in every respect: she is fresh, vigorous, and has a youthful zest for life, while he suffers from acutely sensitive nerves, boredom, narcissism, and a pervasive weariness that paralyzes his will to act. Beer-Hofmann portrays his protagonist's fear of change as yet another decadent quality. The novella's lack of external action, almost total absence of description and exposition, use of interior monologue, and characterization of Freddy all mark it as a work typical of the writers of Young Vienna and of the changes in style and technique that German fiction was beginning to undergo around the turn of the century.

Beer-Hofmann next began work on a four-act pantomime, "Pierrot Hypnotiseur" (1984), which he completed in 1892. Unpublished in his lifetime, it documents that his passion for the theater dates from this early period.

"Das Kind" (The Child), a longer story than "Camelias," was completed in July 1893. Its content is still the familiar fare of "Viennese decadence" but with some important differences. Paul, a young dandy whose affair with the servant girl Juli has produced an unwanted child, learns that the infant has died. Driven by guilt, remorse, and pity for the helpless child, Paul tries unsuccessfully to find the peasant couple with whom Juli had placed it and to locate the child's unmarked grave in the village cemetery. The experience leads him to an awareness of his own selfishness and to some tentative conclusions about life. Death and the transitoriness of human existence are the story's central themes, but they are linked to others that also preoccupied the young Beer-Hofmann: the desire to believe in a universal order that has meaning and purpose despite the suffering and evil in the world, and the use of doubt as a way to faith. These themes were to become recurring motifs in Beer-Hofmann's work; they are developed most fully in his cycle of biblical dramas, Die Historie von König David.

"Das Kind" reflects an artistic independence largely absent from "Camelias," suggesting that Beer-Hofmann had acquired greater confidence in his craftsmanship and instincts as a writer. As before, the prevailing technique is interior monologue, and the descriptive and expository passages are impressionistic in style; but now Beer-Hofmann does not hesitate to use such realistic–indeed, naturalistic–devices as dialect to heighten the effectiveness of a passage or to enhance characterization. He also employs what Ford Madox Ford once called "eccentric chronology": as the story opens Paul is on his way to the meeting with Juli during which she will tell him that the child is dead; only later does the reader find out about their earlier relationship through Paul's recollections. "Das Kind" and "Camelias" were published together in the volume Novellen (Novellas) in 1893.

Five years after the conferral of Beer-Hofmann's law degree, his family was still troubled by his refusal to practice law and his apparent indifference to such middle-class values as thrift, industry, and orderly habits; they were also skeptical of his prospects as a writer. By December 1895, as Beer-Hofmann recounts in Paula, ein Fragment (1949), he had resolved to travel for a year or two, and to try to write on his return only if he still felt an irrepressible urge to do so. This decision suggests that he had doubts of his own about his future as a writer, and letters of Schnitzler and Hofmannsthal to each other and to Beer-Hofmann confirm that his work was not progressing well. Both friends believed that Beer-Hofmann's difficulties stemmed from a lack of self-discipline, but the problem was more complex. Beer-Hofmann had a profound sense of Auserwähltsein (calling) as a writer, but he sometimes experienced it as an excruciating burden. He also aspired to perfection in his use of language, the inevitable result of which was an agonizing dissatisfaction at times with what he had produced. Like his great contemporary Thomas Mann, he also felt intense ambivalence about his chosen profession, regarding the writer on the one hand as uniquely favored and on the other as a deceiver, almost in the criminal sense of a confidence man. In 1895 these feelings caused a crisis of the sort Hofmannsthal was

Richard Beer-Hofmann (photograph from the collection of Jeffrey B. Berlin)

later to describe in "Ein Brief" (1902; translated as "The Letter," 1942), but Beer-Hofmann's resolve to leave Vienna was not carried out because on the day he arrived at it–5 December 1895–he met sixteen-year-old Paula Lissy. When Beer-Hofmann first saw her, she was working in a confectioner's shop. Her mother had recently died, leaving her in the care of two older brothers. Beer-Hofmann courted her despite their strong opposition, for a time concealing the relationship from his own family.

The couple spent the summer of 1897 in Bad Ischl. Paula was expecting their first child. Two weeks after the birth of their daughter Mirjam in September 1897 Beer-Hofmann wrote *Schlaflied für Mirjam* (1919; translated as "Lullabye for Miriam," 1941), the finest of his twenty or so lyric poems. Unlike his other work, it was cast as a whole from the beginning and never underwent the painstaking revision to which he subjected most of his production.

Der Tod Georgs, by contrast, took shape much more slowly: he had begun working on it in 1893. Despite the happiness he had found with Paula, he still suffered periods of debilitating nervousness and depression, during which he found it impossible to work. He began to make better progress on the novel in 1898, perhaps because of the resolution of his personal situation. On 14 May he and Paula were married in Vienna in a Jewish ceremony, with Schnitzler and another lifelong friend, the musician Leo Van Jung, as witnesses; Paula converted from Catholicism to Judaism after the marriage. Their second child, Naemah, was born on 20 December; their third, Gabriel, was born in 1901.

In its language, motifs, and imagery *Der Tod Georgs* is a particularly representative example of literary art nouveau; the German term *Jugendstil* is more descriptive, since it conveys the movement's preoccupation with youth, which, ironically, often found expression in a fear of old age and death. The antithesis of tight, terse prose, the language of *Der Tod Georgs* is filled with symbolism and opulent images in which words often seem like jeweled ornaments. Beer-Hofmann avoided what he called "Allerweltsworte," language distorted or stripped of its power through use in everyday discourse; this effort to revitalize literary language and cleanse it of worn-out effects is one of the notable characteristics of art nouveau writers. Another art nouveau aspect of *Der Tod Georgs* is its image of woman, an ideal of delicate, thin, pale, undeveloped girls' bodies. Equally representative of Jugendstil are the novel's protagonist, a sensitive, high-strung aesthete; its representation of the fantastic, the opulent, and the exotic; its floral and avian imagery; and its pronounced water symbolism.

Der Tod Georgs is one of the earliest works in the German language to use the stream-of-consciousness technique. ("Camelias" and "Das Kind" also used it, but not as extensively and not nearly as well.) The interior monologues are narrated rather than quoted, but the third-person narrator functions entirely anonymously. His lack of intrusion and Beer-Hofmann's liberal use of adverbs, particles, and dashes, which suggest the associative nature of thoughts and strengthen the illusion that they are being directly transmitted, give the novel the same intimacy and immediacy that first-person interior monologue conveys.

The novel's major motifs are woman; death; the relation of the dream to life; and decadence, with its symptoms of narcissism, nervousness, languor, lack of will, and fear of involvement in life. The only external action of any consequence is Georg's sudden death of a heart attack, and even that is important only as the impetus for the wide-ranging recollections and reflections of the protagonist, Paul, whose mind is the locus of almost everything that "happens."

In part 1 Beer-Hofmann uses comparison and contrast to provide the initial characterization of Paul: he longs to be like his friend, the physician Georg–to have his healthy perceptions, strong will, and firm belief in what he wants. Paul appears in part 1 as a young man with fundamentally conflicting desires: he envies Georg's fitness for and involvement in life, but he also wants to remain aloof from the turmoil, pain, and ugliness of life in a spiritual limbo where he can enjoy aesthetic pleasures undisturbed.

The woman motif is represented in part 1 by two variations of a single type: a girl Paul encounters on a nocturnal walk along the river and a fantasy figure, the woman in the clouds. Like Paul, they stand on the periphery of life: the sexuality of the girl by the river is still unawakened, while the woman in the clouds, who is wrapped in a shroud, foreshadows the dying wife of part 2.

The shock effect of part 2 is intense. The reader realizes that the Syrian temple episode is a fantasy but assumes that Paul's marriage and the lingering death of his wife are "real." Only in the closing passages of part 2 does it become clear that it was all a dream which ranged from the "present," in which Paul's "wife" was dying, to antiquity, the scene of orgiastic love-death rites in the Syrian temple. Reflecting on his dream after waking, Paul sees it in several lights. First, it is a form of reality whose impressions and experiences are far more vivid and intense than those of the waking state. In the dream he felt a mysterious unity with all things, past and present, and everything was important; but he is unable to communicate these feelings to others. The dream is Beer-Hofmann's fictional representation of his own language crisis. It also appears as a realm of existence in which the individual enjoys a sovereignty he does not possess in the waking state: "Fremd und sie nie erfassend, war er in die Welt geworfen, in der er im Wachen lebte.... Aber aus ihm geboren war die Welt, in der er träumte; von ihm gesteckt waren die Grenzen ihrer Himmel und ihrer Erden. Allwissend war er in ihr, und alles wußte von ihm" (Like a stranger he had been tossed into the world, in which he lived his waking hours, never understanding it.... But the world in which he dreamed was born of him; he set the boundaries of its heavens and its earth. In it he was omniscient, and all things knew of him). In retrospect Paul recognizes that this sense of control is precisely why he has always preferred his dreams to his waking hours, why he has always feared life and sought to remain aloof from it. The dream is also prophetic: in it Paul experiences everything of importance that will happen to him in the waking state of parts 3 and 4, and the development of his character in these last two parts proceeds along lines established in the dream.

In part 2 the woman motif is represented by the dying wife, and thus it is closely linked to the theme of death. Characterized earlier as unawakened to life, she is now, in the Nietzschean sense, unfit for it: she is childless and dying in young adulthood of an incurable disease. Her thoughts reflect an intense awareness of the preciousness of life and a profound sense of her own aloneness. The preciousness of life also underlies the ancient Syrian love-death rites from his dream. What drives the ritualists to the temple is the desire to dispel the monotony of their days: "wie sie die eingeborenen tiefen Schauer vor dem Tode kannten–die schlummernde Lust des Lebendigseins jubelnd aufwecken" (knowing the innate deep horror of death–to awaken jubilantly the slumbering lust for life). The fear of death and the awareness of the preciousness of life appear as two sides of a single coin.

The themes of part 2 undergo further development in part 3 as Paul accompanies Georg's body to Vienna for burial. His reflections about Georg's compassion and understanding, his power to ease the suffering of his patients, seem to be moving Paul closer to the unity with all life and the sense of a mysterious but purposeful universal order that he had felt in his dream. In wishing that Georg had lived to enjoy a happy old age, however, Paul is struck by the realization that he has never seen old age and happiness together in a human face. All the elderly people he has encountered pass before his mind in a ghastly parade of feebleness, infirmity, and physical deterioration. Comparing these images to Georg's vitality and youthful handsomeness, Paul concludes that his friend should be counted among the fortunate, after all, like the youths of Argos whom the gods favored by granting them an early death.

At the beginning of part 4 Paul is still alone, wrapped in the cocoon of his self-imposed aloofness from life. The two women he encounters on a walk at the Castle Schönbrunn, one of

Beer-Hofmann's residence in Vienna (Mrs. Miriam Beer-Hofmann Lens)

whom bears a striking resemblance to the female figures of part 1 and the dying wife of part 2, set in motion his recollection of the dream and the insights it had brought him. He concludes that the universal order is not only purposeful and unifying but also, in some cosmic sense that transcends human understanding, just. In these final pages, moreover, Paul's affirmation of life and the universal order acquires a new and unexpected dimension: the reader learns that he is a Jew, and his newly won belief is linked to the Jewish tradition.

Der Tod Georgs provides the first unequivocal literary expression of Beer-Hofmann's affirmation of his Jewishness, but there are other indications of Judaism's growing importance to him. At a time when late-nineteenth-century Austrian liberalism had given way to reactionary forces that included virulent anti-Semitism, he and Paula gave their children Old Testament names. (Mirjam Beer-Hofmann recalled an incident that characterizes her father's humor: when an acquaintance questioned Beer-Hofmann's choice of the name Mirjam, he asked, "Well, what should I call her then?" "Why not Elsa?" the acquaintance suggested. "Oh, no," Beer-Hofmann replied, "that's too Jewish for my taste!") A more explicit indication of his growing identification with Judaism was his reaction to Theodor Herzl's *Der Judenstaat* (1896; translated as *A Jewish State*, 1896). In February 1896 Beer-Hofmann wrote to Herzl that he found more appealing than anything *in* the book what stood behind it: "Endlich ein Mensch, der sein Judentum nicht wie eine Last oder wie ein Unglück resigniert trägt, sondern stolz ist, der legitime Erbe uralter Kultur zu sein" (At last a person who does not bear his Jewishness resignedly, like a burden or a calamity, but on the contrary is proud to be the legitimate heir of an ancient culture). Beer-Hofmann never seriously contemplated immigrating to Palestine–he regarded himself as too completely European to be able to transplant himself elsewhere–but he sympathized with Herzl's Zionist movement. Though in his letter to Herzl, Beer-Hofmann refers to Judaism as a *cultural* legacy, it is doubtful that he viewed it as only that, even in his younger years. "Das Kind" already hints of the struggle to believe in a just God, and Jewish ethics and religion, in particular the covenant with God, are at the very core of the David cycle, for which Beer-Hofmann began to lay plans in 1898. It was also his affirmation of the Jewish tradition that enabled him to move beyond the "decadence" and dandyism of his youth.

In 1901 Beer-Hofmann moved to Rodaun. There, as neighbors, he and Hofmannsthal enjoyed a closer association than ever, with frequent opportunities to exchange ideas and share their work in progress. Reminiscing about this period, Beer-Hofmann later recalled that he and Hofmannsthal, reluctant to end a stimulating conversation, often kept walking each other home until far into the night. Beer-Hofmann's five-act verse play *Der Graf von Charolais* (The Count of Charolais, 1905), based loosely on *The Fatal Dowry* (1632) by Philip Massinger and Nathaniel Field, premiered on 23 December 1904 at the Neues Theater in Berlin under the direction of Reinhardt. Beer-Hofmann was awarded the Schiller Prize for the play in 1905.

To commemorate the 150th anniversary of Mozart's birth in 1906, Beer-Hofmann wrote *Gedenkrede auf Wolfgang Amadé Mozart* (1906; translated as "Memorial Oration on Wolfgang Amadeus Mozart," 1943). Its opening paragraphs, a colorful description of the Salzburg region, create a fairy-tale atmosphere. In language that evokes the splendor of eighteenth-century court life, Beer-Hofmann recalls events in Mozart's childhood that were indeed like those of a fairy tale. The tone darkens, however, as he traces the passions and death motif in Mozart's music. Through a comparison of Mozart and Beethoven as representatives of a declining and an ascending age, respectively, he alludes to the ominous changes the future will bring. This passage, which suggests that Beer-Hofmann saw himself, like Mozart, as living at the end of a glittering age and on the threshold of a painful one, gives the conclusion of the piece a prophetic tone.

After 1906, when he moved to Vienna's Cottage Quarter, Beer-Hofmann worked almost exclusively in the theater, both as a dramatist and as a director; he returned to prose fiction only in the last years of his life. The first play in the Historie von König David, *Jaákobs Traum* (translated as *Jacob's Dream*, 1946), was completed in 1915. Beer-Hofmann did not intend to permit the publication or performance of parts of the cycle until the entire work was completed, but the rising tide of anti-Semitism in Austria caused him to change his mind. *Jaákobs Traum* was published in 1918 and had its premiere at Vienna's Burgtheater in 1919. The dominant theme of the play is suffering—the personal suffering that accompanies doubt and the suffering of Israel as a consequence of the covenant. Jaákob does not question God's existence; his spiritual anguish stems from the struggle to fathom the contradictory nature of God. This form of suffering is also represented by the outcast angel Samáel, with whom Jaákob feels a much greater kinship than with the other archangels. Beer-Hofmann's Jaákob begins as the reluctant object of God's election and ends as a proud and free individual who voluntarily enters into the covenant despite the suffering he knows it will mean for him and his people. The serenity Jaákob achieves as a result of this decision is based on trust, on the intuitive sense that God's ways, unfathomable as they may be, are ultimately wise and just. On another level of interpretation, *Jaákobs Traum* can be read as an allegory of the poet and his calling.

In 1921 Beer-Hofmann was awarded the Nestroy Prize for his work in the theater. That year, at Reinhardt's urging, he wrote the pantomime "Das goldene Pferd" (The Golden Horse, 1955). In the decade that followed, Beer-Hofmann's work on the David cycle was frequently interrupted by his increasing involvement in staging and production at Reinhardt's Theater in der Josefstadt, the Salzburg Festspiele, and the Burgtheater. For the centennial of Goethe's death in 1932 he revised and directed a festival production of both parts of *Faust;* Beer-Hofmann's revision remained part of the Burgtheater's standard repertory until the Anschluß (Nazi annexation of Austria) in 1938.

Der junge David (Young David), the second play in the cycle, was completed and published in 1933. Suffering is again an important motif—David struggles with the same doubts that assailed his ancestor Jaákob—but the principal theme is "Treue" (faithfulness). David's vision for his people carries on the tradition established by Jaákob: Israel's destiny under the covenant is to be God's witness and advocate in the world. Within this framework of Jewish history the play presents the love story of David and Maácha; the text offers many indications that Paula Beer-Hofmann was the model for her and that this aspect of the play was a dramatic re-creation of Beer-Hofmann's experience of love. Like *Jaákobs Traum*, finally, *Der junge David* is an allegory of the poet and his calling; David's Auserwähltsein, like the poet's, is both a state of grace and a painful burden.

In 1933 the Hitler regime's first literary blacklist made Beer-Hofmann a forbidden au-

Beer-Hofmann in 1934 (Mr. and Mrs. George Peters)

thor in Germany. In great danger after the Anschluß, he and Paula left their villa in Vienna's Cottage Quarter in the spring of 1938 and lived in hiding while arrangements were completed for their flight from Austria. On the evening of 19 August 1939 they left Vienna en route to the United States via Switzerland. Paula, who had suffered a severe heart attack the preceding winter, collapsed in Zurich and died there on 30 October. Denied permission to remain in Switzerland, Beer-Hofmann went on to New York, where he was joined by Mirjam and Naemah. He lived there for the remainder of his life.

His exile years were devoted to the writing of *Paula, ein Fragment*. Beer-Hofmann was emphatic in his assertion that it was a biographical "Erinnerungsbuch" (book of reminiscences), but it resembles his fiction in the selection and organization of material and in narrative techniques. The foreword ends with a quotation from Dante's *La Vita Nuova* (circa 1293), which suggests how Beer-Hofmann wanted *Paula* to be understood and which also might well be viewed as the underlying theme of his entire oeuvre: "Siehe ein Gott, stärker denn ich; er kommt und wird über mich herrschen!" (Behold a God, stronger than I; He comes and will rule over me!).

Paula consists of a series of fragments organized into five parts of varying lengths in which Beer-Hofmann, functioning as first-person narrator, relates episodes from his and Paula's life. The fragments derive their unity from the fact that he and she are the central figures throughout and, as in *Der Tod Georgs*, from the use of recurring motifs as an organizing principle.

The themes of love and destiny dominate the work. The reader has a powerful sense of destiny at work in the meeting of Beer-Hofmann and Paula, in their love for each other, in their marriage despite great obstacles, and in their life together.

Paula refines the narrative techniques Beer-Hofmann first employed in his early fiction and provides a final representation of important themes that recur in his oeuvre. But the volume is also a historical work in which Beer-Hofmann re-creates a vanished era; it is also a document of exile which attests to the strength and steadfastness of Beer-Hofmann's affirmation of his Jewish-

Josef von Strzygowski, Richard Beer-Hofmann, Mrs. Sol Liptzin, and Sol Liptzin in the Middle East, 1936
(Mrs. Miriam Beer-Hofmann Lens)

ness and to his belief in the ultimate justice of the universal order, despite the suffering and injustice he experienced at the hands of the National Socialists.

Beer-Hofmann gave lectures at Harvard, Yale, Columbia, and Smith College in 1944. He became an American citizen on 14 March 1945, and on 18 May the National Institute of the American Academy of Arts and Letters presented him with its annual Award for Distinguished Achievements. Beer-Hofmann linked the two events in his acceptance speech: "When I came to these shores, I could by no stretch of my imagination foresee that I was to receive again what had been taken from me by tyranny: a home, a working place, a country that was to be mine by choice and by right, and now—this proof of human sympathy, of understanding and recognition. To me–this has come as a lesson in democracy. For: respect for the dignity of man, the basis of democracy, is at the same time the very foundation of any sincere artistic endeavor. A writer's task can never hope to be complete. Yet it was worth trying–if only to learn this lesson. . . ."

Four months later Beer-Hofmann died in New York of pneumonia. He was buried next to his wife in the Friedenberg Cemetery in Zurich.

The place Beer-Hofmann occupies in the history of Austrian literature derives from several aspects of his work. As a writer he was a forerunner of major twentieth-century trends in both the prose and the dramatic genres: *Der Tod Georgs* is one of the earliest stream-of-consciousness novels in world literature and one of the most instructive examples of literary art nouveau in the German language; the passionate intensity of *Der Graf von Charolais* makes it a prelude to the dramas of expressionism; and with his use of epic elements in the David cycle Beer-Hofmann anticipated practices that later became standard features of epic theater. Not only as a playwright but also as a director he contributed significantly to the revitalization of the Austrian theater in such venerable institutions as the Burgtheater and the Salzburg Festspiele.

Letters:

Hugo von Hofmannsthal/Richard Beer-Hofmann Briefwechsel, edited by Eugene Weber (Frankfurt am Main: Fischer, 1972);

Walter Grossman, "Fifteen Letters by Richard Beer-Hofmann," in *Essays in Honor of James Edward Walsh* (Cambridge: The Goethe Institute of Boston and the Houghton Library, 1983), pp. 119-143;

Jeffrey B. Berlin, "The Unpublished Letters of Richard Beer-Hofmann to Hermann Bahr (with the Unpublished Letters between Beer-Hofmann and Theodor Herzl)," in *Identity and Ethos: A Festschrift for Sol Liptzin on the Occasion of His 85th Birthday*, edited by Mark Gelber (New York & Bern: Lang, 1986), pp. 121-144.

Bibliography:

Kathleen Harris and Richard M. Sheirich, "Richard Beer-Hofmann: A Bibliography," *Modern Austrian Literature*, 15, no. 1 (1982): 1-60.

References:

Esther N. Elstun, *Richard Beer-Hofmann: His Life and Work* (University Park & London: Pennsylvania State University Press, 1983);

Elstun, "Richard Beer-Hofmann: The Poet as *Exculpator Dei*," in *Protest—Form—Tradition: Essays on German Exile Literature*, edited by Joseph P. Strelka, Robert Bell, and Eugene Dobson (University: University of Alabama Press, 1979);

Rainer Hank, *Mortifikation und Beschwörung* (Frankfurt am Main: Lang, 1984);

Antje Kleinewefers, *Das Problem der Erwählung bei Richard Beer-Hofmann* (Hildesheim: Olms, 1972);

Sol Liptzin, *Richard Beer-Hofmann* (New York: Bloch, 1936);

Hans-Gerhard Neumann, *Richard Beer-Hofmann: Studien und Materialien zur "Historie von König David"* (Munich: Fink, 1972);

Richard M. Sheirich, "*Frevel* and *der erhöhte Augenblick* in Richard Beer-Hofmann," *Modern Austrian Literature*, 13, no. 2 (1980): 1-16;

Walter Sokel, "Narzißmus und Judentum: Zum Oeuvre Richard Beer-Hofmanns," in *Zeitgenossenschaft: Festschrift für Egon Schwarz zum 65. Geburtstag*, edited by Paul Michael Lützeler, Herbert Lehnert, and Gerhild S. Williams (Frankfurt am Main: Athenäum, 1987), pp. 33-47;

Werner Vordtriede, "Gespräche mit Beer-Hofmann," *Die neue Rundschau*, 63 (1952): 122-151;

Eugene Weber, "The Correspondence of Arthur Schnitzler and Richard Beer-Hofmann," *Modern Austrian Literature*, 6, no. 3/4 (1973): 40-51;

Weber, "Richard Beer-Hofmann: Briefe, Reden, Gedichte aus dem Exil," *Literatur und Kritik*, 10 (1975): 469-479.

Papers:

Beer-Hofmann's literary estate is in the Houghton Library of Harvard University; a collection of Beer-Hofmann family documents, personal papers, and correspondence is in the Leo Baeck Institute, New York City.

Max Brod
(27 May 1884-20 December 1968)

Ehrhard Bahr
University of California, Los Angeles

BOOKS: *Tod den Toten!* (Stuttgart: Juncker, 1906);
Der Weg des Verliebten: Gedichte (Berlin: Juncker, 1907);
Experimente: Vier Geschichten (Berlin: Juncker, 1907);
Schloß Nornepygge: Der Roman des Indifferenten (Berlin: Juncker, 1908);
Die Erziehung zur Hetäre: Ausflüge ins Dunkelrote (Berlin: Juncker, 1909);
Ein tschechisches Dienstmädchen: Kleiner Roman (Berlin: Juncker, 1909);
Tagebuch in Versen (Berlin: Juncker, 1910);
Jüdinnen: Roman (Berlin: Juncker, 1911);
Arnold Beer: Das Schicksal eines Juden. Roman (Berlin: Juncker, 1912);
Der Bräutigam (Berlin: Juncker, 1912);
Abschied von der Jugend: Ein romantisches Lustspiel in 3 Akten (Berlin: Juncker, 1912);
Anschauung und Begriff: Grundzüge eines Systems der Begriffsbildung, by Brod and Felix Weltsch (Leipzig: Wolff, 1913);
Über die Schönheit häßlicher Bilder: Ein Vademecum für Romantiker unserer Zeit (Leipzig: Wolff, 1913);
Die Höhe des Gefühls: Szenen, Verse, Tröstungen (Leipzig: Rowohlt, 1913);
Weiberwirtschaft: Drei Erzählungen (Berlin: Juncker, 1913);
Die Retterin: Schauspiel in 4 Akten (Leipzig: Wolff, 1914);
Tycho Brahes Weg zu Gott: Ein Roman (Munich, Leipzig & Vienna: Wolff, 1915); translated by Felix Warren Crosse as *The Redemption of Tycho Brahe* (New York: Knopf, 1928; London: Knopf, 1928);
Ausgewählte Romane und Novellen, 6 volumes (Leipzig: Wolff, 1915-1919)–includes *Das große Wagnis* as volume 6 (1919);
Die erste Stunde nach dem Tode: Eine Gespenstergeschichte (Leipzig: Wolff, 1916);
Die dritte Phase des Zionismus (Berlin: Verlag der Zukunft, 1917);

Max Brod (photo: Stefan Moses)

Das gelobte Land: Ein Buch der Schmerzen und Hoffnungen (Leipzig: Wolff, 1917);
Die Höhe des Gefühls: Ein Akt (Leipzig: Wolff, 1918);
Eine Königin Esther: Drama in einem Vorspiel und drei Akten (Leipzig: Wolff, 1918);
Die Einsamen (Munich: Wolff, 1919);
Im Kampf um das Judentum (Vienna & Berlin: Löwit, 1920);
Sozialismus im Zionismus (Vienna & Berlin: Löwit, 1920);
Die Fälscher: Schauspiel in vier Akten (Munich: Wolff, 1920);

Heidentum, Christentum, Judentum: Ein Bekenntnisbuch, 2 volumes (Munich: Wolff, 1921); translated by William Wolf as *Paganism, Christianity, Judaism* (University: University of Alabama Press, 1970);

August Nachreiters Attentat (Hannover: Banas & Dette, 1921);

Erlöserin: Ein Hetärengespräch (Berlin: Rowohlt, 1921);

Das Buch der Liebe: Gedichte (Munich: Wolff, 1921);

Adolf Schreiber: Ein Musikerschicksal (Berlin: Welt-Verlag, 1921);

Franzi oder Eine Liebe zweiten Ranges: Ein Roman (Munich: Wolff, 1922);

Leben mit einer Göttin: Roman (Munich: Wolff, 1923);

Sternenhimmel: Musik- und Theatererlebnisse (Prague: Orbis, 1923); enlarged as *Prager Sternenhimmel: Musik- und Theatererlebnisse der zwanziger Jahre* (Vienna & Hamburg: Zsolnay, 1966);

Klarissas halbes Herz: Lustspiel in drei Akten (Munich: Wolff, 1923);

Prozeß Bunterbart: Schauspiel dieser Zeit in 3 Akten (Munich: Wolff, 1924);

Leoš Janáček: Leben und Werk (Vienna: Wiener Philharmonischer Verlag, 1925; revised and enlarged edition, Vienna, Zurich & London: Universal-Edition, 1956);

Zionismus als Weltanschauung, by Brod and Weltsch (Mährisch-Ostrau: Färber, 1925);

Rëubēni, Fürst der Juden: Ein Renaissanceroman (Munich: Wolff, 1925); translated by Hannah Waller as *Reubeni, Prince of the Jews: A Tale of the Renaissance* (New York: Knopf, 1928; London: Knopf, 1929);

David Rëubēni in Portugal (Frankfurt am Main: Kauffmann, 1927);

Die Frau, nach der man sich sehnt: Roman (Berlin: Zsolnay, 1927); translated by Jacob Wittmer Hartmann as *Three Loves* (New York: Knopf, 1929; London: Knopf, 1930);

Die Opuntie: Komödie eines Prominenten, by Brod and Hans Regina Nack (Vienna: Österreichischer Bühnen-Verlag, 1927);

Das Abenteuer des braven Soldaten Schwejk: Komödie nach Jaroslav Haschek, by Brod and Hans Reimann (Vienna: Bühnen-Verlag, 1928);

Zauberreich der Liebe: Roman (Berlin: Zsolnay, 1928); translated by Eric Sutton as *The Kingdom of Love* (London: Secker, 1930);

Lord Byron kommt aus der Mode: Schauspiel in drei Akten (Berlin, Vienna & Leipzig: Zsolnay, 1929);

Liebe im Film, by Brod and Rudolf Thomas (Giessen: Kindt & Bucher, 1930);

Stefan Rott oder Das Jahr der Entscheidung: Roman (Berlin: Zsolnay, 1931);

Die Frau, die nicht enttäuscht: Roman (Amsterdam: De Lange, 1933);

Heinrich Heine (Amsterdam: De Lange, 1934); translated by Joseph Witriol as *Heinrich Heine: The Artist in Revolt* (London: Vallentine, Mitchell, 1956; New York: New York University Press, 1956);

Rassentheorie und Judentum, with an appendix, "Nationalhumanismus" (Prague: Barissia, 1934);

Annerl: Roman (Amsterdam: De Lange, 1936);

Novellen aus Böhmen (Amsterdam: De Lange/Leipzig & Vienna: Tal, 1936);

Franz Kafka: Eine Biographie: Erinnerungen und Dokumente (Prague: Mercy, 1937; New York: Schocken, 1946); translated by G. Humphreys-Roberts as *The Biography of Franz Kafka* (London: Secker & Warburg, 1947); translation republished as *Franz Kafka: A Biography* (New York: Schocken, 1947); German version revised and enlarged (Berlin & Frankfurt am Main: Fischer, 1954); translated by Humphreys-Roberts and Richard Winston as *Franz Kafka: A Biography* (New York: Schocken, 1960);

Abenteuer in Japan: Roman, by Brod and Otto Brod (Amsterdam: De Lange, 1938);

Das Diesseitswunder oder Die jüdische Idee und ihre Verwirklichung (Tel Aviv: Goldstein, 1939);

Der Hügel ruft: Ein kleiner Roman (Tel Aviv: Goldstein, 1942);

Šā'ūl melek Jiśrā'ēl [Saul, King of Israel] (Jerusalem: Hōsā'at Mōd'adīm, 1944);

Diesseits und Jenseits, 2 volumes (Winterthur: Mondial, 1947);

Franz Kafkas Glauben und Lehre; Kafka und Tolstoi: Eine Studie, with an appendix, "Religiöser Humor bei Franz Kafka," by Weltsch (Winterthur: Mondial, 1948);

Galilei in Gefangenschaft: Roman (Winterthur: Mondial, 1948);

Unambo: Roman aus dem jüdisch-arabischen Krieg (Zurich: Steinberg, 1949); translated by Ludwig Lewisohn as *Unambo: A Novel of the War in Israel* (New York: Farrar, Straus & Young, 1952);

Brod (center, standing) and his family on vacation, circa 1900 (Ilse Ester Hoffe)

Die Musik Israels (Tel Aviv: Sefer, 1951); translated by Toni Volcani as *Israel's Music* (Tel Aviv: Sefer, 1951);

Franz Kafka als wegweisende Gestalt (St. Gallen: Tschudy, 1951);

The Master, translated by Heinz Norden (New York: Philosophical Library, 1951); German version published as *Der Meister: Roman* (Gütersloh: Bertelsmann, 1952);

Beinahe ein Vorzugsschüler oder Pièce touchée: Roman eines unauffälligen Menschen (Zurich: Manesse, 1952);

Der Sommer, den man zurückwünscht: Roman aus jungen Jahren (Zurich: Manesse, 1952);

Ein Abenteuer Napoleons und andere Novellen (Zurich: Classen, 1954);

Armer Cicero: Roman (Berlin: Herbig, 1955);

Rebellische Herzen: Roman (Berlin: Herbig, 1957); republished as *Prager Tagblatt: Roman einer Redaktion* (Frankfurt am Main & Hamburg: Fischer, 1968);

Amerika: Komödie in 2 Akten . . . nach dem gleichnamigen Roman von F. K. (Frankfurt am Main: Fischer, 1957);

Mira: Ein Roman um Hofmannsthal (Munich: Kindler, 1958);

Jugend im Nebel (Witten & Berlin: Eckart, 1959);

Verzweiflung und Erlösung im Werk Franz Kafkas (Frankfurt am Main: Fischer, 1959);

Die verbotene Frau, edited by Jörg Mager (Graz & Vienna: Stiasny, 1960);

Streitbares Leben: Autobiographie (Munich: Kindler, 1960); revised and enlarged as *Streitbares Leben, 1884-1968* (Munich: Herbig, 1969);

Gustav Mahler: Beispiel einer deutsch-jüdischen Symbiose. Gedenkrede zum 100. Geburtstag, Herbst 1960 in der Berliner Akademie der Künste (Frankfurt am Main: Ner-Famid-Verlag, 1961);

Die Rosenkoralle: Ein Prager Roman (Witten & Berlin: Eckart, 1961);

Durchbruch ins Wunder: Erzählungen (Rothenburg ob der Tauber: Peter, 1962);

Die verkaufte Braut: Der abenteuerliche Lebensroman des Textdichters Karel Sabina (Munich & Eßlingen: Bechtle, 1962);

Das Schloß: Nach Franz Kafkas gleichnamigem Roman (Frankfurt am Main: Fischer, 1964);

Der Ritter Laberius schafft sich aus der Welt: Novelle (Rothenburg ob der Tauber: Hegereiter, 1964);

Brod as a high school student (Ilse Ester Hoffe)

Johannes Reuchlin und sein Kampf: Eine historische Monographie (Stuttgart, Berlin, Cologne & Mainz: Kohlhammer, 1965);
Gesang einer Giftschlange: Wirrnis und Auflichtung (Munich: Starczewski, 1966);
Der Prager Kreis (Stuttgart, Berlin, Cologne & Mainz: Kohlhammer, 1966);
Das Unzerstörbare (Stuttgart, Berlin, Cologne & Mainz: Kohlhammer, 1968);
Von der Unsterblichkeit der Seele (Stuttgart, Berlin, Cologne & Mainz: Kohlhammer, 1969).

OTHER: Arnošt Dvořák, *Der Volkskönig: Drama in fünf Akten*, translated by Brod (Leipzig: Wolff, 1914);
Caius Valerius Catullus, *Gedichte*, translated by Brod (Munich & Leipzig: Müller, 1914);
Dreibuch: Jüdische Geschichten von Sch. Gorelik, I. L. Perez, Scholem Alejchem, translated from the Yiddish by Mathias Acher, edited by Brod (Berlin, 1916);
Das Lied der Lieder, neu übertragen aus dem Hebräischen, translated by Brod (Munich: Hyperionverlag, 1921);
Franz Kafka, *Der Prozeß: Roman*, edited by Brod (Berlin: Die Schmiede, 1925);
Kafka, *Das Schloß: Roman*, edited by Brod (Munich: Wolff, 1926);
Kafka, *Amerika: Roman*, edited by Brod (Munich: Wolff, 1927); translated by Willa and Edwin Muir as *America* (New York: Schocken, 1946; London: Secker & Warburg, 1949);
Karel Čapek, *Die Sache Makropulos*, translated and adapted by Brod (Vienna & Leipzig, 1927);
Miloš Kareš, *Schwanda der Dudelsackpfeifer: Volksoper in 2 Akten, 5 Bildern*, translated and adapted by Brod, music by Jaromir Weinberger (Vienna & Leipzig: Universal-Edition, 1928);
Leoš Janáček, *Aus einem Totenhaus: Op. posth. Oper in drei Akten, nach F. M. Dostojewskis "Aufzeichnungen aus einem Totenhaus,"* translated by Brod (Vienna: Universal-Edition, 1930);
Kafka, *Beim Bau der Chinesischen Mauer: Ungedruckte Erzählungen und Prosa aus dem Nachlaß*, edited by Brod and Hans Joachim Schoeps (Berlin: Kiepenheuer, 1931);
Kafka, *Gesammelte Schriften*, edited by Brod and Heinz Politzer, 6 volumes (volumes 1-4, Berlin: Schocken, 1935; volumes 5-6, Prague: Mercy, 1936-1937);
Kafka, *Gesammelte Schriften*, edited by Brod, 5 volumes (New York: Schocken, 1946);
Kafka, *The Diaries of Franz Kafka*, translated by Joseph Kresh, Martin Greenberg, and Hannah Arendt, edited by Brod, 2 volumes (New York: Schocken, 1948-1949; London: Secker & Warburg, 1948-1949);
Kafka, *Gesammelte Werke*, edited by Brod, 10 volumes (Frankfurt am Main: Fischer, 1950-1967);
Kafka, *Wedding Preparations in the Country, and Other Posthumous Prose Writings*, translated by Ernst Kaiser and Eithne Wilkins (London: Secker & Warburg, 1954); translation republished as *Dearest Father: Stories and Other Writings* (New York: Schocken, 1954);
Kafka, *Description of a Struggle and The Great Wall of China*, translated by Willa and Edwin Muir and Tania and James Stern, postscript by Brod (New York: Schocken, 1958; London: Secker & Warburg, 1960);
Franz Preissmann, *Jenufa: Oper aus dem mährischen Bauernleben in 3 Akten*, translated by Brod (Vienna: Universal-Edition, 1962);
Jules Laforgue, *Pierrot, der Spaßvogel*, edited by Brod and Franz Blei (Frankfurt am Main: Insel, 1965).

Max Brod's career as a writer of fiction began in 1905 with the novella "Die That" (The Action), published in the journal *Die Gegenwart*, and lasted until his death in 1968. Altogether, his narrative production comprised about 150 titles; yet his reputation as a fiction writer was overshadowed by his fame as Franz Kafka's friend, biographer, interpreter, and editor. By 1948 Brod's biography of Kafka was widely read, but hardly any of his own works of fiction were. This was not always the case. Around 1915, when Kafka had published little, Brod was considered an important representative of early expressionism, if not one of its initiators, and his 1908 novel, *Schloß Nornepygge* (Chateau Nornepygge), was hailed as "the most modern of modern books" by the *Literarisches Zentralblatt*. But when Kafka's fame began to spread during the early 1930s, mostly due to Brod's editorial activities and interpretative efforts on behalf of his deceased friend, Brod's reputation as a writer started to fade. Contributing to Brod's diminished relevance to fiction after 1945 were his preoccupation with the historical novel, which had lost its appeal after World War II; and his narrative techniques, which were considered old-fashioned in comparison to those of Kafka, Ernest Hemingway, William Faulkner, Albert Camus, Georges Bernanos, Jean-Paul Sartre, and Alfred Döblin, who provided the models for the postwar generation of German novelists such as Heinrich Böll, Günter Grass, and Siegfried Lenz. Another factor contributing to his reduced importance may have been Brod's predilection for the erotic or sentimental novel, which made him appear outdated to the young writers in Austria, Germany, and Switzerland after World War II.

Brod's lack of recognition as a creative writer after 1930 is unfair in light of his contributions to the historical novel, the Jewish Zeitroman (novel of the time: a genre dealing with the contemporary German-Jewish milieu), and the Zionist novel. At the age of almost eighty Brod demonstrated great sensitivity to the tribulations of childhood and early adolescence in novels and novellas which preserve the aura of the city of Prague before World War I. Brod's narrative art, as one critic has said, managed to capture that "life which passed like a dream." These late works constitute Brod's greatest and most lasting achievement as a writer of fiction.

Born in Prague, then part of the Austro-Hungarian Empire, on 27 May 1884, Brod came from a German-speaking Jewish family with three-hundred-year-old roots in the city. Adolf Brod, his father, was a banker; Fanny Rosenfeld Brod, his mother, was a high-strung woman who was devoted to her three children's education and welfare. When Brod developed a curvature of the spine (kyphosis) at an early age, his mother moved with him to southern Germany to supervise a cure for his ailment in a special clinic. The treatment was ineffective, and Brod remained afflicted by this deformity for the rest of his life. After high school Brod studied law at the German University of Prague, graduating with a doctor of law degree in 1907. From 1907 to 1924 he was employed by the postal service. In 1913 he married Eva Taussig, the daughter of a Prague wholesale merchant. Active in the Zionist movement since 1910, he was cofounder of the National Council of Jews of Czechoslovakia in 1918. From 1924 to 1929 he served as a member of the press and information office of the Republic of Czechoslovakia. In 1929 he joined the *Prager Tageblatt*, the German-language newspaper of Prague, becoming editor of the theater, literature, and music section.

Brod was the first to recognize Kafka, whom he had met when both were students at the university, as one of the greatest writers of the twentieth century; after Kafka's death in 1924 Brod defied his friend's wish that his manuscripts be burned and arranged for their publication in the 1930s. Brod's biography of Kafka appeared in 1937, followed by several other Kafka studies in subsequent years. Brod also discovered the Prague writer Franz Werfel, whom he helped achieve fame as an expressionist poet, and the Czech writer Jaroslav Hašek, whose *Osudy Dobrého Vojáka Svejka za Světové Války* (1920-1923; translated as *The Good Soldier Schwejk*, 1930) Brod adapted for the stage. He translated the libretti of the Czech composer Leoš Janáček into German and published an introduction to his life and work in 1925. Brod also wrote several philosophical studies, including *Heidentum, Christentum, Judentum* (1921; translated as *Paganism, Christianity, Judaism*, 1970) and *Diesseits und Jenseits* (On This Side and in the Hereafter, 1947). Among his late works were his autobiography, *Streitbares Leben* (Valiant Life, 1960), and *Der Prager Kreis* (The Prague Circle, 1966), his reminiscences of the literary life of Prague.

In 1939 Brod and his wife left Prague before the German army occupied the city. They immigrated to Palestine and settled in Tel Aviv; there Brod worked as a dramaturgical adviser to

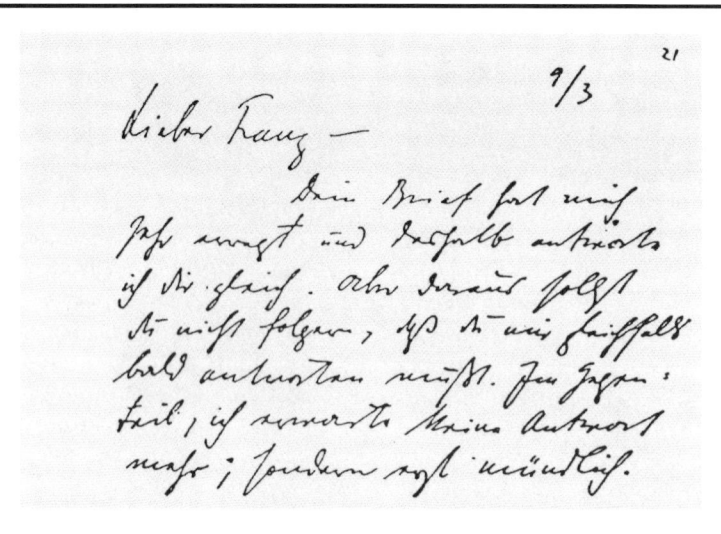

Part of a letter from Brod to Franz Kafka (Berndt W. Wessling, Max Brod: Ein Porträt, *1969)*

the Habimah, which was to become the Israel National Theater. Brod's wife died in 1942. After World War II and the Israeli war of independence Brod resumed his literary productivity with new energy and published ten more novels and approximately the same number of short stories. Between 1949 and 1969 he visited Europe almost every year; after 1954 his visits included West Germany. In 1964 he returned to Prague for the first time to give a speech at a Kafka exhibition. After returning home from a lecture tour in West Germany, Brod died on 20 December 1968.

Brod's fiction can be divided into eight categories: his impressionist beginnings from 1905 to 1908; his expressionist novel, *Schloß Nornepygge*, in 1908; the Jewish Zeitroman, comprising the novels *Jüdinnen* (Jewesses, 1911) and *Arnold Beer: Das Schicksal eines Juden* (Arnold Beer: The Fate of a Jew, 1912); the Zionist novels of 1918 to 1949; the historical novel, beginning with *Tycho Brahes Weg zu Gott* (1915; translated as *The Redemption of Tycho Brahe*, 1928) and ending with *Armer Cicero* (Poor Cicero, 1955); the sentimental novel; the artist novel; and the Prague novel and novella. The only constant in Brod's prose fiction from 1906 to 1968 is the Prague novel and novella; the other five categories after 1908 were simultaneously developed and periodically overlapped each other. For example, *Die Frau, die nicht enttäuscht* (The Woman Who Does Not Disappoint, 1933), one of Brod's most decisive Zionist novels, is also a Prague novel, a sentimental novel, and an artist novel.

At the beginning of his career Brod was influenced by various styles of Viennese fiction such as impressionism and Jugendstil (art nouveau). His early novellas are dominated by the fin de siècle mood that also permeates the works of Arthur Schnitzler and Stefan Zweig. Brod's term for this mood, "Indifferentismus," was coined under the influence of Arthur Schopenhauer's philosophy. The protagonists of Brod's early novellas are either paralyzed in their choice of action or throw themselves blindly into meaningless acts. Their lack of freedom of will amounts to a kind of fatalism which does not allow for the development of ethical standards. In Brod's first novel, *Schloß Nornepygge*, with its subtitle *Der Roman des Indifferenten* (The Novel of the Indifferent Man), ethical indifference is driven to its ultimate extreme: self-destruction. The protagonist's suicide, however, results in a dialectical reversal, inspiring those who struggle for freedom of the will in spite of the prevailing ideology of determinism. This novel constitutes Brod's renunciation of Viennese impressionism and Jugendstil. While *Schloß Nornepygge* was ignored or rejected in Vienna, it was hailed in Berlin as a harbinger of expressionism. Between 1911 and 1919 Brod was closely associated with the leading expressionist circles in Berlin.

The other work indicating Brod's overcoming of "Indifferentismus" is his short novel *Ein tschechisches Dienstmädchen* (A Czech Servant Girl, 1909), the story of an indifferent bookkeeper conducting an unimpassioned love affair with a servant girl. When he is informed of her suicide, he feels compassion for the first time in his life; he is no longer indifferent to the sufferings of other human beings.

Dust jacket for Brod's 1912 novel about a man who comes to terms with his Jewish identity

The next phase in Brod's prose fiction was the Jewish Zeitroman, dealing with conflicts within Jewish society as well as between Jews and Gentiles at the beginning of the twentieth century. *Jüdinnen*, which was much criticized by Brod's friends, including Kafka, deals with the dubious practices employed by Jewish families to marry off their daughters and with self-hatred among the young generation of Jewish men. With his next Zeitroman, *Arnold Beer: Das Schicksal eines Juden*, Brod tried to silence the negative criticism of *Jüdinnen* by having the protagonist come to terms with his Jewish identity after a long and painful struggle. In a concluding statement Brod outlines his plan of writing a cycle of novels representing an ascending line of Jewish types, culminating in the question whether a new type of Jew was possible. Arnold Beer is Brod's first fictional character to find his Jewish heritage an inspiration. Kafka's short story *Das Urteil* (1916; translated as *The Judgment*, 1945) has been interpreted as his response to *Arnold Beer*–albeit a negative response, since Kafka's protagonist fails to emancipate himself from his father and commits suicide.

Brod's Zionism found its first literary expression in *Das große Wagnis* (The Great Dare, 1918), but only indirectly in the implied counter-society to the novel's utopian state–a state which is finally destroyed by its own leaders. A more explicit representation of Zionism is provided by the last two chapters of *Zauberreich der Liebe* (1928; translated as *The Kingdom of Love*, 1930). Although Christof Nowy, the protagonist, does not become a Zionist, he does come to a positive reevaluation of Zionism after a visit to a kibbutz near Haifa.

Brod's first truly Zionist novel is *Die Frau, die nicht enttäuscht*. Julius Spira, a German-Jewish writer from Czechoslovakia, has turned down all offers to deliver lectures on the occasion of the centennial of Goethe's death in 1932, has withdrawn from relief work among miners and peasants in Silesia, and has resigned from his position as an editor for a Munich publishing house to register his protest against the rise of anti-Semitism in Germany. At this moment he meets and falls in love with Carola Weber, a young German woman, who becomes a concert singer to support him while he does research for a book on Platonism in the modern world. The only way for Spira to handle this dilemma is by using what he calls "Distanzliebe" (love at a distance): "*One does love across the abyss. Distance is not denied, but confirmed with extreme clear-sightedness and painfully felt; and yet one does love.*" Spira defends Distanzliebe as a Platonic form of love, a striving for the ideal beyond the world of appearances; he compares it to Goethe's formulation of Spinozian love in *Wilhelm Meisters Lehrjahre* (1795-1796): "If I love you, it's none of your business." Spira conceives of his love for Carola as a parallel to his relationship to Germany. Yet Carola responds to his love–at least for a while–and defends him when he is attacked by Christian bigots, whereas her nation, its tradition, and its literature fail him. Carola finally tires of the vagabond life of an artist and leaves Spira for the bourgeois existence of wife and mother that he could not give her. At this moment of total disappointment Spira turns to Zionism. In a deus ex machina ending a young man from a kibbutz in Eretz, Israel, visits Spira to gain his support for a school for Jewish and Arab children. *Die Frau, die nicht enttäuscht* combines the sentimental love

Brod, circa 1917 (Archiv Dr. Max Brod, Tel Aviv)

story, the Prague novel, and the dilemma of the Jewish writer's relationship to German literature.

Brod's next Zionist novel, *Abenteuer in Japan* (Adventure in Japan, 1938), was coauthored by his brother Otto Brod, who was to die in a German concentration camp in 1944. The protagonist, a Jewish businessman in Paris, is lured to Japan by the promise of a profitable business deal. On his arrival, however, he finds out that the business deal was a ruse; instead, he is invited to arrange for the immigration of all Jews to Japan to form a mystical alliance with Japanese imperialism. Jews and Japanese are to constitute the chosen people of the future. Rejecting this offer by the fanatical leader of a Japanese secret society, the protagonist turns toward the more realistic goals of Zionism. Returning to Paris, he becomes aware of the dangers threatening European Jewry at the outbreak of World War II.

The protagonist of *Der Hügel ruft: Ein kleiner Roman* (The Call of the Hill: A Short Novel, 1942), perhaps Brod's best Zionist novel, is Ruth, a member of a kibbutz and a poet. The hill outside the kibbutz is the central symbol of the novel. The members of the kibbutz do not have enough money to buy the hill, which they need for both agricultural and strategic reasons. Ruth tries to take possession of the hill aesthetically by incorporating it in her poetry. She travels to Prague to raise funds to buy the hill, but her return to Palestine is postponed when she marries a Czech composer. Although she inspires him to compose an opera on the life of the kibbutz titled "The Call of the Hill," with her lyrics as libretto, this artistic achievement cannot serve as an excuse for her desertion of the kibbutz. After the death of her husband Ruth returns to Palestine to discover that the members of the kibbutz have prospered and have bought the hill with their own money. In spite of her failure, the group welcomes Ruth's return. What the kibbutz needs is not her money but her participation. The hill, which had become a fixation for Ruth, is stripped of its obsessive symbolism when she becomes reintegrated into the kibbutz.

Brod's last Zionist novel, *Unambo: Roman aus dem jüdisch-arabischen Krieg* (1949; translated as *Unambo: A Novel of the War in Israel*, 1952), is reminiscent of Thomas Mann's *Doktor Faustus* (1947; translated as *Doctor Faustus*, 1948). Paul Helfin, a film director similar in character to Mann's composer Adrian Leverkühn, is tempted by the Unambo machine, presented to him under mysterious circumstances by a limping devil figure in the no-man's-land between Tel Aviv and Jaffa. The device, which resembles a puppet theater, allows a man to lead two lives: "*Uno*-one; *ambo*-both!" With the aid of this machine Helfin is able to escape the necessity of making a decision about the course of his life. He makes a declaration of neutrality: in one of his lives he is a film director in Tel Aviv, involved in an unsavory love affair; in the other he is a volunteer in the Israeli army, fighting to keep the highway to Jerusalem open. Helfin represents both the generation of European Jews who are skeptical about the future of the new state and the generation of young Israelis who are fighting the war of independence and have no doubts about Zionism. Helfin dies a double death: as a film director in Brazil, after leaving Israel because of charges of espionage; and as a soldier on the highway to Jerusalem, saving the life of his young nephew. But his soldier's death marks a decision, rejecting the devil's pact and delivering him from the evil of neutrality provided by the Unambo machine.

Brod at his desk in Tel Aviv (Ilse Ester Hoffe)

Brod's historical novels, characterized by strong religious overtones, could as well be called religious novels dealing with historical characters. The first three form a trilogy collectively titled "Ein Kampf um Wahrheit" (A Fight for the Truth): *Tycho Brahes Weg zu Gott; Rëubēni, Fürst der Juden* (1925; translated as *Reubeni, Prince of the Jews*, 1928), for which he won the Czechoslovak State Prize; and *Galilei in Gefangenschaft* (Galileo in Prison, 1948), which earned him the Bialik Prize of Israel. The first novel deals with the Danish astronomer Brahe's religious acceptance of his fate as a less gifted forerunner of a true genius, his younger colleague Johannes Kepler. Rëubēni, who seeks to combine Messianism with political exploits for the Jews in medieval Europe, dies imprisoned by the Spanish Inquisition. To protect his daughter from harm at the hands of the Inquisition, Galileo recants his belief in the motion of the earth, hoping that the truth will eventually be discovered. This trilogy was followed by *Der Meister* (1952; translated as *The Master*, 1951), a novel about Jesus, and *Armer Cicero*, about the violent death of the Roman statesman and orator.

As a writer of fiction Brod was most prolific in the genre of the erotic or sentimental novel. The titles of many of these novels seem to have been chosen for their appeal to a mass audience: *Franzi oder Eine Liebe zweiten Ranges* (Franzi; or, A Second-Class Love, 1922), *Die Frau, nach der man sich sehnt* (The Woman for Whom One Longs, 1927; translated as *Three Loves*, 1929), *Zauberreich der Liebe* (1928), and *Annerl* (1936). These novels rely heavily on eroticism. A typical example of this genre is *Die Frau, nach der man sich sehnt*, which was so popular that it was made into a film starring Marlene Dietrich. It is the story of a young Austrian lieutenant who is ruined by his passion for a woman; although she drives him into bankruptcy and exile, he never regrets his days of happiness with her.

In Brod's fiction the erotic novel often overlaps with the artist novel, the protagonist in the latter case being a writer or composer. Typical is *Mira* (1958), about a famous conductor who discovers that Mira, the chambermaid in his Berlin hotel, is an aspiring actress. He falls in love with Mira and dedicates himself to promoting her career at the expense of his own professional life and marriage. But the young woman tires of the vagabond life of an actress. To save their relationship, the conductor introduces Mira to Hugo von Hofmannsthal and Max Reinhardt in Salzburg in an attempt to obtain for her a part in Hofmannsthal's *Jedermann* (1911; translated as *The Play of Everyman*, 1917). His ploy fails; Mira leaves the stage to marry a dentist from Melbourne, while the conductor withdraws into a secular monastery and dedicates his life to contemplation. The story is a variation of one of Brod's favorite themes: the artist couple whose relationship breaks up under the stress of social conventions.

Brod's lasting achievements were in the field of the Prague novel and novella, beginning with *Ein tschechisches Dienstmädchen* of 1909 and continuing with *Stefan Rott oder Das Jahr der Entscheidung* (Stefan Rott; or, The Year of Decision, 1931), *Der Sommer, den man zurückwünscht* (The Summer One Wishes Would Return, 1952), *Beinahe ein Vorzugsschüler oder Pièce touchée* (Almost at the Top of the Class, 1952), *Jugend im Nebel* (Youth in Fog, 1959), and *Die Rosenkoralle* (Pink Coral, 1961). *Stefan Rott*, a Bildungsroman ending with the outbreak of World War I, bears affinities to Hermann Hesse's *Demian* (1919; translated, 1923) and Thomas Mann's *Der Zauberberg* (1924; translated as *The Magic Mountain*, 1927). Brod's protagonist is a high school student torn between Platonism, erotic love, and political activity. Prague serves as a battleground for these conflicts, which suddenly become meaningless with the outbreak of World War I. In *Beinahe ein Vorzugsschüler oder Pièce touchée* the narrator's dream of meeting an old friend from Prague in Tel Aviv leads to the story of their high school days. Although the narrator knows that his friend died at Auschwitz, he furnishes this information to the reader only at the end of the novel. The old city of Prague with its German, Jewish, and Czech heritage is reborn and preserved in Brod's novels and novellas of this genre.

An author not only of fiction but also of poetry, drama, criticism, political and philosophical prose, biography, and autobiography, Brod has been criticized for spreading himself too thin and for publishing many of his books before they had a chance to mature. He was a born storyteller who could not resist the temptation of immediate publication. Yet among his many titles, there are more than a few that deserve attention not only for historical reasons but also for their literary value.

Letters:

Im Streit um Kafka und das Judentum: Max Brod–Hans-Joachim Schoeps Briefwechsel, edited by Julius H. Schoeps (Königstein: Jüdischer Verlag bei Athenäum, 1985).

Bibliography:

Werner Kayser and Horst Gronemeyer, eds., *Max Brod* (Hamburg: Christians, 1972).

References:

Anton Magnus Dorn, *Leiden als Gottesproblem* (Freiburg im Breisgau: Herder, 1981);

Hugo Gold, ed., *Max Brod: Ein Gedenkbuch 1884-1968* (Tel Aviv: Olamenu, 1969);

Ernst Pawel, *The Nightmare of Reason: A Life of Franz Kafka* (New York: Farrar, Straus & Giroux, 1984);

Margarita Pazi, *Max Brod: Werk und Persönlichkeit* (Bonn: Bouvier, 1970);

Pazi, ed., *Untersuchungen zu Max Brods literarischen und philosophischen Schriften* (New York: Lang, 1987);

Charles Susskind, *Janáček and Brod* (New Haven: Yale University Press, 1985);

Robert Weltsch, *Max Brod and His Age* (New York: Leo Baeck Institute, 1970);

Berndt W. Wessling, *Max Brod: Ein Porträt* (Stuttgart: Kohlhammer, 1969).

Papers:

Max Brod's papers are in the private possession of Ilse Ester Hoffe in Tel Aviv.

Franz Theodor Csokor
(6 September 1885-5 January 1969)

Michael Mitchell
University of Stirling

BOOKS: *Die Gewalten: Ein Band Balladen* (Berlin: Juncker, 1912);

Der große Kampf: Ein Mysterienspiel in acht Bildern (Berlin: Fischer, 1915);

Die Sünde wider den Geist (Vienna & Zurich: Amalthea, 1918);

Die rote Straße: Ein dramatisches Werk in 14 Bildern (Weimar: Kiepenheuer, 1918);

Der Dolch und die Wunde: Gedichte (Vienna & Leipzig: Deutschösterreichischer Verlag, 1918);

Der Baum der Erkenntnis: Ein Mythos (Vienna: Amalthea, 1919);

Schuß in's Geschäft (Der Fall Otto Eißler) (Berlin: Die Schmiede, 1924);

Ewiger Aufbruch: Gesammelte Balladen (Leipzig: Wolkenwandererverlag, 1926);

Ballade von der Stadt: Ein dramatisches Fresko (Vienna & Berlin: Zsolnay, 1928);

Gesellschaft der Menschenrechte: Stück um Georg Büchner (Vienna & Berlin: Zsolnay, 1929);

Besetztes Gebiet: Historisches Stück aus der Gegenwart in einem Vorspiel und vier Akten (Vienna: Zsolnay, 1930); translated by Katherine McHugh Lichliter as *Occupied Territory* in her "A Critical Edition and Translation of Franz Theodor Csokor's 'Europäische Trilogie,'" Ph.D. dissertation, Brandeis University, 1979;

Die Weibermühle: Zauberstück in fünf Vorgängen (Vienna & Berlin: Zsolnay, 1932);

Gewesene Menschen: Stück in drei Akten (Vienna & Berlin: Zsolnay, 1932);

Das Thüringer Spiel von den zehn Jungfrauen (Berlin: Volkschaft-Verlag, 1933);

3. November 1918: Ende der Armee Österreich-Ungarns. Drei Akte (Vienna: Zsolnay, 1936); translated by Lichliter as *November 3, 1918* in her "A Critical Edition and Translation of Franz Theodor Csokor's 'Europäische Trilogie,'" Ph.D. dissertation, Brandeis University, 1979;

Über die Schwelle: Erzählungen aus 2 Jahrzehnten (Prague & Vienna: Prasser, 1937);

Franz Theodor Csokor (photo: Fayer, Vienna)

Gottes General: Drama in sieben Stationen (Bilthoven: De Gemeenschap, 1939);

Als Zivilist im polnischen Krieg (Amsterdam: De Lange, 1940); translated by Philip Owens as *As a Civilian in the Polish War* (London: Secker & Warburg, 1940); republished with *Als Zivilist im Balkankrieg* as *Auf fremden Straßen* (Munich: Desch, 1955);

Kalypso: Schauspiel in sieben Vorgängen (Vienna: Published by the author, 1946);

Das schwarze Schiff: Gedichte (Vienna & Jerusalem: Verkauf, 1946; revised, 1947);

Der verlorene Sohn: Tragödie in vier Akten (Vienna: Ullstein, 1947); translated by Lichliter as *The Prodigal Son* in her "A Critical Edition and Translation of Franz Theodor Csokor's 'Europäische Trilogie,'" Ph.D. dissertation, Brandeis University, 1979;

Als Zivilist im Balkankrieg (Vienna: Ullstein, 1947); republished with *Als Zivilist im polnischen*

Krieg as *Auf fremden Straßen* (Munich: Desch, 1955);
Immer ist Anfang: Gedichte von 1912 bis 1952 (Innsbruck: Österreichischer Verlags-Anstalt, 1952);
Olymp und Golgatha: Trilogie einer Weltwende (Hamburg: Zsolnay, 1954)—comprises *Kalypso, Caesars Witwe, Pilatus;*
Der Schlüssel zum Abgrund: Roman einer Zeit (Hamburg & Vienna: Zsolnay, 1955);
Zum 75. Geburtstag Anton Wildgans, by Csokor and Heinrich Drimmel (Vienna: Anton Wildgans Gesellschaft, 1956);
Hebt den Stein ab!: Komödie um die letzten Dinge in drei Akten (Hamburg & Vienna: Zsolnay, 1957);
Der zweite Hahnenschrei: Sechs Erzählungen (Hamburg & Vienna: Zsolnay, 1959);
Treibholz: Stück in drei Akten (Hamburg & Vienna: Zsolnay, 1959);
Du bist gemeint (Graz & Vienna: Stiasny, 1959);
Die Erweckung des Zosimir: Drei Akte (Vienna: Bergland, 1960);
Das Zeichen an der Wand: Stück in drei Akten mit einem Vorspiel und einem Nachspiel (Hamburg & Vienna: Zsolnay, 1962);
Der Mensch und die Macht (Vienna & Hamburg: Zsolnay, 1963)—comprises *Jadwiga, Der tausendjährige Traum, Gesellschaft der Menschenrechte;*
Ein paar Schaufeln Erde: Erzählungen aus fünf Jahrzehnten (Munich & Vienna: Langen/Müller, 1965);
Die Kaiser zwischen den Zeiten: Ein dramatisches Diptychon mit einem Prolog und einem Epilog (Vienna & Hamburg: Zsolnay, 1965);
Alexander: Drama in 9 Bildern (Vienna & Hamburg: Zsolnay, 1969);
Thermidor (Vienna & Munich: Sessler, 1978).

OTHER: Anton Wildgans, *Späte Ernte,* edited by Csokor (Vienna: Globus, 1947);
Die schönsten Erzählungen aus Österreich, introduction by Csokor (Vienna: Desch, 1958);
Ferdinand Bruckner, *Vom Schmerz und von der Vernunft,* edited by Csokor (Graz & Vienna: Stiasny, 1960);
Carl Zuckmayer, *Hinein ins volle Menschenleben,* edited by Csokor (Graz & Vienna: Stiasny, 1961);
Du silberne Dame du: Briefe von und an Lina Loos, edited by Csokor and Leopoldine Rüthner (Vienna & Hamburg: Zsolnay, 1966).

TRANSLATIONS: Nikolai Nikolaevich Evreinov, *Die Kulissen der Seele: Monodrama* (Vienna: Verlag der graphischen Werkstätte, 1920);
Zygmunt Krasiński, *Die ungöttliche Komödie: Dramatisches Gedicht in vier Teilen* (Berlin & Vienna: Zsolnay, 1936).

PERIODICAL PUBLICATIONS: "Blick über mich," *Welt und Wort,* 13 (1958): 301-302;
"Ist der historische Roman noch möglich?," *Wort in der Zeit,* 8, no. 9 (1962): 46-50;
"Büchners 'Woyzeck': Versuch einer Vollendung," *Forum: Österreichische Monatsschrift für kulturelle Freiheit,* 10 (1963): 90-95.

Franz Theodor Csokor was that rare phenomenon, a writer who actually lived out the ideals embodied in his works. His friend Carl Zuckmayer told the story of how, at a party to celebrate one of Zuckmayer's stage successes, a guest who knew neither man assumed for the whole evening that Csokor was the author of the play "because he radiated such happiness." This gift of sharing in the feelings of others is at the heart of Csokor's personality; he had the ability to feel at one with humanity in all its manifestations, not just with those of like mind. All of his characters are depicted with sympathy, even when their actions are condemned. In the story "Letzte Stunde" (Last Hour) in the collection *Der zweite Hahnenschrei* (The Second Crow of the Cock, 1959) the central figure is a liberal writer who bears much resemblance to Csokor; as he faces the firing squad he finds that his life is transformed from a haphazard collection of momentary experiences into a meaningful unity by the idea of "Menschendienst," which literally means service to mankind but with an echo of "Gottesdienst" (divine worship). This service to mankind is just as evident in Csokor's life, in his many friendships with artists and writers, in his constant help and encouragement for younger authors, and, above all, in his unwavering opposition to fascism.

Csokor was born in Vienna in 1885 into a family which was a typically Austro-Hungarian blend of Serbian, Croat, German, Czech, and Hungarian ancestry. His father, Johann Csokor, was a professor of veterinary medicine at the University of Vienna; his mother was Emilie Müller Csokor. Csokor studied art history for a few semesters with Max Dworak before deciding by 1912 to devote himself to writing. He spent two months in St. Petersburg, Russia, in 1913-1914 with a theater group that was performing two of his plays. At the beginning of World War I he joined the infantry, but he was soon transferred to the war archives for medical reasons. During and after the war he was one of the most significant Austrian dramatists of the expressionist movement, his best-known play of that period being *Die rote Straße* (The Red Street, 1918). From 1923 to 1927 he was a dramatic consultant and director at the Raimund-Theater and the Deutsches Volkstheater in Vienna. In the late 1920s and the 1930s, with the radicalization of the political atmosphere, he moved to plays of more immediate political and social relevance, such as his masterpiece, *3. November 1918* (1936; translated as *November 3, 1918*, 1979), which portrays the end of the Austro-Hungarian monarchy and the onset of extreme nationalism in central Europe. His greatest stage success in Austria, it brought him both the Grillparzer Prize and the Burgtheater Ring.

When Hitler invaded Austria in 1938 many noted Austrian authors quickly converted to National Socialism, but the fifty-two-year-old Csokor chose voluntary exile rather than to remain silent in his homeland. His exile took him, often only a step in front of the advancing Germans, to Poland, Romania, Yugoslavia, and, finally, Italy, where he worked for the Allies. He returned to Vienna in 1946. The following year he was the natural choice to become president of the reconstituted Austrian P.E.N. Club, an office he held with dignity through the difficult years of denazification and cold war until his death in 1969. His works after World War II tended to avoid topical social and political issues in favor of more general moral problems. His main work of fiction is a large-scale historical novel, *Der Schlüssel zum Abgrund* (The Key to the Abyss, 1955). Among his awards were the Literature Prize of the City of Vienna in 1925 and 1953 and the Great Austrian State Prize in 1955.

Csokor's earliest stories were published in the collection *Ein paar Schaufeln Erde* (A Few Spadefuls of Earth, 1965). The first two, both written in 1915, form a matching pair with titles and central motifs which echo one another. There is, however, such a contrast in style that one suspects that they may originally have been stylistic exercises. "Die steinerne Frau" (The Stone Lady) treats the theme of death in the manner of the horror stories of E. T. A. Hoffmann or of Csokor's slightly older contemporary, the popular writer Karl Hans Strobl. "Der eherne Jüngling" (The Bronze Youth) deals, much in the manner of the early stories of Hugo von Hofmannsthal, with the theme of art—symbolized by the statue of the title—as a possible substitute for religion or morality. But as the hero, a Roman nobleman, is slaughtered by the barbarians who have broken into his enclosed garden, the statue remains cold and inaccessible, affording him no comfort in his final moment. Another story in the collection, "Der Park, die Tänzerin und das Tier" (The Park, the Dancer and the Beast), written in 1931, is parallel in theme to Thomas Mann's *Der Tod in Venedig* (1912; translated as *Death in Venice*, 1925). In both works the central figures are artists whose lives and art reflect the northern European sense of order and control. For both figures, the experience of the all-pervading sensuality of the south—Italy—is overwhelming. Unlike Mann's Aschenbach, however, Csokor's heroine escapes and returns to the north with her sensibility extended by an increased awareness of the flesh.

These three works are typical of Csokor's short stories in presenting people at a moment of crisis which forces them to confront the meaning of their existence. That this moment is frequently the ultimate one of death is indicated in the titles of two of Csokor's three collections of stories: *Über die Schwelle* (Over the Threshold, 1937) and *Ein paar Schaufeln Erde*. Thus, "Das Zimmer mit drei Betten" (The Room with Three Beds), written in 1936, contrasts three women who lie dying in the same hospital ward. The judgment on their lives that death delivers is different from that of society; at the ultimate moment all social veneer is stripped away, and what is left is what the women have made, or been allowed by society to make, of their humanity. For Csokor the meaning of life is something the individual creates by his own inner activity. The cipher Csokor often uses for this inner activity is *Herz* (heart), a word which appears in the title of one of his last stories, "Jedes Herz hört nur sich" (Each Heart Hears Only Its Own Voice), written in 1962. The story centers on the Empress Elisabeth of Austria and her anarchist assassin in the moments before the assassination. The rigid stratification of society that divides them and motivates his action also creates a parallel between them; each has a heart that has been crushed by the social order. The motif of the heart also appears in the coda to the story, in which Lenin is portrayed as the revolutionary who believes that to change the constricting social order by force he must have the strength to deny his own heart.

Scene from a production of Csokor's 3. November 1918 at the Burgtheater, Vienna, in 1937

Another short story, "Schattenstadt" (Shadowtown), written in 1931, has a characteristically Austrian treatment of the theme of death. It opens with a description of a car journey which reads like a futurist hymn to speed; there is a jolt, after which the journey continues through a town with the symbolic name of Schattenstadt. The narrator now has the sensation of gliding rather than being driven by the rhythm of the machine; gradually he and the reader become aware that this slow journey is a gradual slipping into death and that the jolt was the impact of a fatal accident. The pain of the accident surfaces toward the end of the story; it is assuaged by the arrival of death, which is like a welcoming cave promising comfort and repose. The shadow world between life and death is the subject of another well-known Austrian story of the period, Alexander Lernet-Holenia's *Der Baron Bagge* (1936). Both stories may be contrasted with Ambrose Bierce's "An Occurrence at Owl Creek Bridge" (1890): in the American story the dream sequence is positively oriented toward escape and the future, a future the reader suddenly realizes will never be; the Austrian stories are both characterized by an acceptance of death. Such acceptance is a common theme of Austrian literature from the Baroque period to Hofmannsthal's early poetic dramas.

Csokor's first longer prose work, *Schuß in's Geschäft (Der Fall Otto Eißler)* (A Bullet in the Business [The Case of Otto Eißler], 1924), was a contribution to a series called "Außenseiter der Gesellschaft" (Outsiders of Society) edited by the expressionist poet Rudolf Leonhard, who invited well-known writers to examine the workings of justice in celebrated court cases. Csokor chose what he called a peasant tragedy in a patrician Jewish family: the murder in Vienna the year before of Robert Eißler by his cousin Otto Eißler, after the latter had been excluded from the family business by Robert's sharp, though not illegal, practices. The final third of the book is a critique of various aspects of the trial, but the rest is the work of Csokor the artist rather than social critic. The description of the background of the case in the economic situation of postwar Vienna quickly becomes a vivid re-creation of milieu and character, culminating in a gripping murder scene narrated from the point of view of the murderer. Csokor's view of Otto Eißler as a victim of modern society's obsession with money echoes a central theme of his expressionist plays. *Schuß in's*

Geschäft shows that in Csokor the Austrian novel lost a potentially powerful exponent to the stage.

It may well have been his writing of this tract that suggested to Csokor the idea of a panoramic novel on Vienna which he worked on at the end of the 1920s. It was to have been called "Die Stadt neben der Welt" (The City beside the World), the phrase he uses to characterize Vienna in *Schuß in's Geschäft*. All that has been published of the novel is the opening chapter, a depiction of Vienna as a city, the title suggests, which has shut itself off from the mainstream of the modern world. Novels using Vienna for a nostalgic evocation of the Austrian cultural heritage multiplied in the years following the collapse of the empire; what is unusual about Csokor's plan is his intention to include the working classes as an integral part of his portrait of the city alongside the more traditional representatives of Viennese culture, the aristocracy and the educated middle class. Csokor was aware that to realize this vision formal innovation would be necessary. That he did not intend to write, say, a Viennese version of John Galsworthy's *The Forsyte Saga* (1922) is clear from his description of the work as a "Kollektivroman eines neuen Typus" (collective novel of a new type). The phrase recalls his description of his 1928 play *Ballade von der Stadt* (Ballad of the City) as a "Kollektivdrama" (collective drama) and suggests that he was thinking of reducing the significance of individual character and unified plot in favor of building up a picture of the city through representative types and incidents. The Eißler affair could well have provided one of these incidents.

The historical novel *Der Schlüssel zum Abgrund*, on the reign of the Anabaptists in Münster, Westphalia, in 1534-1535, arose out of his 1933 play on the same subject, *Der tausendjährige Traum* (The Dream of the Millennium, published in *Der Mensch und die Macht* [Man and Power, 1963]). Csokor came across a history of the Münster Anabaptists in 1933 and was struck by the way events in the sixteenth century seemed to prefigure what was then happening in Germany; there was even a burning of books. He finished the play in a few weeks, using Münster as a model through which to treat fascism. His rejection of fascism was clear from the day Hitler became Reichskanzler, and at the meeting of the P.E.N. Congress in Dubrovnik, Croatia, at the end of May 1933 he voted for the resolution condemning the repression of writers by the Nazis. As a result his plays were immediately banned in Germany, where he had had most of his recent successes; he also experienced difficulty in finding theaters willing to perform his plays in Austria. He therefore started to work the Anabaptist material into a novel but did not complete it until after the war.

Anabaptism was the most radical of the movements released in the early sixteenth century by the Reformation. The rejection of infant baptism which gave it its name was the least of its offenses to the establishment. Its belief in personal revelation led to a rejection of ecclesiastical authority; the Münster group also rejected civil authority and attempted to establish a "Kingdom of Sion" on earth by force. All who would not submit were expelled, and a totalitarian regime was set up that introduced polygamy and community of goods. When Münster was shut off from the outside world by a two-year siege, fanaticism reigned unchecked in an orgy of cruelty and licentiousness–that is, if one is to believe contemporary accounts; history is notoriously written by the winning side. Csokor uses the received version as the basis for his play and novel.

The two main characters are Jan Bockelsen, who had himself crowned King of Münster, and the preacher Bernt Rothmann, whom Csokor describes as the "Rosenberg" of the movement (referring to the Nazi ideologist Alfred Rosenberg). In his lowly origins and charismatic attraction for the masses, Bockelsen presents parallels to Hitler. He is also a sensualist who enjoys power and all that it allows him. Characteristic is the scene in which he runs naked through the streets, rousing the population to hysteria as they follow him en masse to the river to be baptized. Rothmann, on the other hand, is a man with a sense of spiritual mission who has lost his faith in God and not found faith in mankind; to conceal this inner void he encourages ever more extreme measures. Less theatrical than Bockelsen, he is the more significant figure: a seeker after God seduced by power into betraying his values.

Csokor's aim in the novel was to give a spiritual portrait of the whole of Europe at that period. The story of Münster is told in an introduction and twelve chapters; interpolated between them are twelve "intermezzi" which present incidents and figures from all over Europe. These figures include both important historical personages– Michelangelo, Ignatius Loyola, Copernicus, Christian II of Denmark, Henry VIII of England–and less exalted but typical figures, including religious refugees in Ragusa (now Dubrovnik), two worldly abbés in Rome, and a poetasters' club in Leyden. These intermezzi take up well over one-third of the book. The events in Münster are referred to by characters in each of the interpolated sections; this is quite natural, given the interest Münster aroused all over Europe, and is done unobtrusively. Less unobtrusive is Csokor's technique of taking part or all of the final sentence of each chapter or intermezzo and using it in the opening sentence of the next section, a practice that becomes mechanical and disturbing in a novel which otherwise keeps authorial intrusions to a minimum.

Csokor is by no means the only writer to have noticed the parallels between Nazi Germany and sixteenth-century Münster; one German historian has called the earlier events a "dress rehearsal for the twentieth century and for Hitler." During the 1930s another German novel, Friedrich Percyval Reck-Malleczewen's *Bockelsen* (1936), was published on the same theme. Both Reck-Malleczewen and Csokor use Münster to portray the disintegration of order into the chaos of mass hysteria, but each depicts the process from a different angle: Reck-Malleczewen's elitist Christianity rejects the modern world, seeing the loss of faith as having fostered the brutal dominion of the masses; Csokor's humanism allows him to understand, if not approve, of all of his characters. The techniques used by the two authors are also diametrically opposed: Reck-Malleczewen's narrator explicitly relates Münster to other revolutionary movements from the Peasant Wars to the Russian Revolution, all of which he condemns; Csokor provides a synchronic view of one particular period of history, prefers direct action and dialogue to interpretation, and allows the reader to make the implied connection between past and present.

Csokor uses the intermezzi to make the Anabaptist rule in Münster the culminating point of a downward slide of history from the light and humanity of the Renaissance to the darkness of conflict and irrationalism. Both ends of this spectrum are evoked through the figure of Michelangelo, as the confident grace of his early sculpture, seen in his *David*, gives way to the tortured figures of the *Last Judgment*, which he conceives as he journeys to Rome after the fall of republican Florence. The novel is not just a veiled presentation of the horrors of Germany under Hitler; the movement from light to darkness also underlies *3. November 1918* and reflects Csokor's vision of the first half of the twentieth century as a decline from order into the irrationality of extreme nationalism.

This pessimistic view is, however, balanced by Csokor's abiding belief in the power of the human heart. Two of the most impressive expressions of that belief are the volumes based on his experiences during the war, *Als Zivilist im polnischen Krieg* (1940; translated as *As a Civilian in the Polish War*, 1940) and *Als Zivilist im Balkankrieg* (As a Civilian in the Balkan War, 1947). It would be misleading to describe these "civilian's-eye" views of the war as autobiographical, because Csokor largely ignores his own adventures in favor of describing the suffering, heroism, guilt, and occasional cruelty he saw around him. The books are the record not of a detached observer but of one who shares in the suffering he sees. The volume on the Balkan war is one of Csokor's most powerful works and deserves to be much more widely known as a document of European humanism.

Most of the stories in Csokor's postwar collection *Der zweite Hahnenschrei* have a political background: the Yugoslav resistance is treated in "Der Verräter" (The Traitor), the Nazi occupation of Poland in "Das Fest des Sardanapal" (The Feast of Sardanapalus), the conflict between the Medici and republican Florence in "Die Angst des Michelangelo" (Michelangelo's Fear), and the discussion by the disciples after the crucifixion whether to continue Christ's work peacefully or by violent resistance to the Romans in the title story. The stories center in the final analysis on individuals, just as Csokor's own credo centers on a belief in the individual rather than in any system. The figure Csokor uses most often as a symbol of suffering humanity is Christ–as man, not as the Son of God–and this figure is evoked by the use of various symbols and motifs in each story. Thus "Letzte Stunde" ends with the firing squad tossing a coin for the writer's clothes; Michelangelo dreams of Christ and Barabbas; the "traitor" in "Der Verräter," who draws the hate of the local population onto himself and away from the Germans so that the latter will have no cause for bloody reprisals, lives in an isolated hut in a garden of olives where he comes to understand the "fear unto death" Christ felt before the crucifixion.

Csokor's works bear witness to the increasing subjection of the individual in the twentieth century to violence and oppression. But they also bear witness, in their affirmation of the values of the human "heart," to his belief in the possibility of a future "world without frontiers"–a belief which was the legacy of his upbringing in the polyglot capital of a multinational empire.

Letters:

Zeuge einer Zeit: Briefe aus dem Exil (Munich & Vienna: Langen/Müller, 1964).

References:

Klaus Amann, *P.E.N.: Politik, Emigration, Nationalismus. Ein österreichischer Schriftstellerclub* (Vienna: Böhlau, 1984);

Jethro Bithell, "Franz Theodor Csokor," *German Life and Letters*, new series 8, no. 1 (1954): 37-44;

Brygida Brandys, "Das dramatische Werk von Franz Theodor Csokor," *Kwartalnik Neofilologiczny*, 28 (1981): 407-427;

Peter Branscombe, "Some Depictions of the First World War in Austrian Drama," in *Studies in Modern Austrian Literature*, edited by Brian O. Murdoch and Mark G. Ward (Glasgow, 1981), pp. 74-86;

Dietmar Goltschnigg, "Csokors Drama, *Gesellschaft der Menschenrechte*," *Jahrbuch des freien deutschen Hochstifts* (1974): 344-361;

Heidrun Graf-Blauhut, *Sprache: Traum und Wirklichkeit. Österreichische Kurzprosa des 20. Jahrhunderts* (Vienna: Braumüller, 1983), pp. 127-129;

Margaret Jacobs, "Franz Theodor Csokor: *Büchners 'Woyzeck'–Versuch einer Vollendung*," *Oxford German Studies*, 1 (1966): 31-52;

Frederick Lehner, "Literatur in Exil: Franz Theodor Csokor," *German Quarterly*, 20 (November 1947): 209-213;

Michael R. Mitchell, " 'Aus der hellen Wohnungen zurück in den Zuchtstall': An Examination of F. T. Csokor's *3. November 1918*," *Modern Austrian Literature*, 16, no. 1 (1978): 95-102;

Paul Wimmer, *Der Dramatiker Franz Theodor Csokor* (Innsbruck: Universitätsverlag Wagner, 1981);

Harry Zohn, "Franz Theodor Csokor's *3. November 1918*," *Modern Austrian Literature*, 11, no. 1 (1978): 95-102;

Carl Zuckmayer, "Rede an einen Freund," *Forum*, 12 (1965): 459-464.

Papers:

Franz Theodor Csokor's papers are in the Vienna City Library.

Marie Eugenie delle Grazie
(14 August 1864-19 February 1931)

Jorun B. Johns
California State University, San Bernardino

BOOKS: *Gedichte* (Herzberg: Simon, 1882; enlarged edition, Leipzig: Breitkopf & Härtel, 1895);
Hermann: Deutsches Heldengedicht in 12 Gesängen (Vienna: Hartleben, 1883);
Die Zigeunerin: Eine Erzählung aus dem ungarischen Heidelande (Vienna: Konegen, 1885);
Saul: Tragödie in 5 Akten (Vienna: Konegen, 1885);
Italienische Vignetten (Leipzig: Breitkopf & Härtel, 1892);
Der Rebell; Bozi: Zwei Erzählungen (Leipzig: Breitkopf & Härtel, 1893);
Robespierre: Ein modernes Epos, 2 volumes (Leipzig: Breitkopf & Härtel, 1894);
Moralische Walpurgisnacht: Ein Satyrspiel vor der Tragödie (Leipzig: Breitkopf & Härtel, 1896);
Schlagende Wetter: Drama in 4 Akten (Leipzig: Breitkopf & Härtel, 1900);
Liebe: Erzählungen (Leipzig: Breitkopf & Härtel, 1902);
Der Schatten: Drama in 3 Akten und einem Vorspiel (Leipzig: Breitkopf & Härtel, 1902);
Zu Spät: Vier Einakter (Leipzig: Breitkopf & Härtel, 1903);
Sämtliche Werke, 9 volumes (Leipzig: Breitkopf & Härtel, 1903-1904);
Narren der Liebe: Lustspiel in vier Akten (Leipzig: Breitkopf & Härtel, 1905);
Ver Sacrum (Leipzig: Breitkopf & Härtel, 1906);
Schwäne am Land: Drama in 3 Akten (Leipzig: Breitkopf & Härtel, 1907);
Vom Wege: Geschichten und Märchen (Leipzig: Breitkopf & Härtel, 1907);
Traumwelt (Leipzig: Breitkopf & Härtel, 1907);
Heilige und Menschen: Roman (Leipzig: Breitkopf & Härtel, 1909);
Vor dem Sturm: Roman (Leipzig: Breitkopf & Härtel, 1910);
Gottesgericht und andere Erzählungen (Leipzig & Berlin: Heilbronn, 1912);
Wunder der Seele: Erzählungen (Leipzig: Breitkopf & Härtel, 1913);
Zwei Witwen (Berlin: Hillger, 1914);
Das Buch des Lebens: Erzählungen und Humoresken (Leipzig: Breitkopf & Härtel, 1914);
Die blonde Frau Fina und andere Erzählungen (Berlin: Hillger, 1915);
Das Buch der Liebe: Roman (Berlin: Ullstein, 1916);
O Jugend! Roman (Berlin: Ullstein, 1917);
Donaukind: Roman (Berlin & Vienna: Ullstein, 1918);
Eines Lebens Sterne: Roman (Berlin: Ullstein, 1919);
Die Seele und der Schmetterling (Leipzig: Reclam, 1919);
Der frühe Lenz (Vienna: Lyra, 1919);
Homo: Roman einer Zeit (Vienna: Wila, 1919);
Die Blumen der Acazia (Berlin: Hillger, 1920);
Der Liebe und des Ruhmes Kränze: Ein Roman auf der Viola d'Amour (Vienna: Wiener Literarische Anstalt, 1920);
Die weißen Schmetterlinge von Clairvaux: Novelle (Freiburg: Herder, 1925);
Unsichtbare Straße: Roman (Freiburg im Breisgau: Herder, 1927);
Titanic: Eine Ozeanphantasie (Elberfeld: Bergland, 1928);
Sommerheide (Elberfeld: Bergland, 1928).

OTHER: "Volkslied," in *Meisternovellen deutscher Frauen*, edited by Ernst Brausewetter, volume 1 (Berlin: Schuster & Loeffler, 1907), pp. 173-192;
"Ernst Haeckel, der Mensch," in *Was wir Ernst Haeckel verdanken: Ein Buch der Verehrung und Dankbarkeit*, edited by Heinrich Schmidt (Leipzig: Unesma, 1914), II: 309-316;
"Matelda," in *Heimlich bluten Herzen: Österreichische Frauennovellen* (Hochdorf & Munich: Pfeiffer, 1926), pp. 1-103.

PERIODICAL PUBLICATIONS: "Selbstbildnis," *Wiener Mode*, 8, no. 24 (1895): 913-914;
"Im Spiegel: Autobiographische Skizzen," *Das literarische Echo*, 3 (1900/1901): 893-895;

"Wilhelm Weigand," *Neue Freie Presse*, 22 September 1901, p. 29;

"Der Sinn meines Dramas 'Der Schatten,'" *Neue Freie Presse*, 15 October 1901, pp. 1-3;

"Geheimrat von Gruber und die Frauenemanzipation," *Neue Freie Presse*, 28 August 1910, pp. 2-4;

"Dogma und Geschlecht: Ein Schlußwort an Herrn Geheimrat v. Gruber," *Neue Freie Presse*, 11 December 1910, pp. 31-34;

"Mieseputz: Ein Schicksal hinter der Front," *Neue Freie Presse*, 24 December 1915;

"Die Gespielin," *Neue Freie Presse*, 1 May 1919, pp. 1-3;

"Von Religion und Kultur," *Das neue Reich*, 4, no. 45 (1922): 887-888;

"Avalon," *Reichspost*, 13 August 1922, pp. 1-2;

"Mein Weg zu Gott," *Das neue Reich*, 4, no. 52 (30 September 1922): 1024-1026;

"Kunst und Credo," *Das neue Reich*, 5, no. 39 (1923): 884;

"Schubertiade," *Der Feuerreiter*, 4, no. 10 (1928): 233-236;

"O Heimat . . . ," *Reichspost*, 11 November 1928;

"Schauen und Schaffen: Romane um Altösterreich," *Schönere Zukunft*, 21 (24 February 1929): 439-440;

"Schauen und Schaffen: Über eigene Bücher," *Schönere Zukunft*, 22 (3 March 1929): 463-464;

Das Buch der Heimat (Temesvar: Deutsche Buchhandlung, 1930);

Die Empörung der Seele (Münster: Helios, 1930);

Die kleine weiße Stadt und andere Kurzgeschichten aus der Banater Heimat (Salzburg: Weißkirchner Ortsgemeinschaft, 1977).

Marie Eugenie delle Grazie's career spanned approximately fifty years, during which she produced work in many literary genres. During the first decade of the twentieth century she was regarded as one of the foremost women writers in the German language and was hailed as the greatest female epic poet; she was not yet forty when the well-known Leipzig firm of Breitkopf und Härtel published a nine-volume collection of her works in 1903-1904. But she proved unable to sustain this early promise, and by the time of her death her reputation had waned considerably. Those who had predicted a great future for her on the basis of the modern spirit in her early writings found little interest in her later mystical-religious works. Today she is usually characterized as a freethinker who turned pious with advancing age and fled to the protection of the Catholic church. Nevertheless, in theme and form her early writings belong to the mainstream of turn-of-the-century Austrian literature, and she ranks as one of the major figures of that generation. Among women writers of that time she is surpassed only by Marie von Ebner-Eschenbach.

The oldest of three children, Marie Eugenie delle Grazie was born on 14 August 1864 in Weißkirchen on the Danube in Hungary (now Bela Crkva) and spent the greater part of her childhood in Bersaska, a small mountain village. Her father, Cäsar delle Grazie, director of coal mines in Drenkowa and of Venetian descent, had at the age of forty-eight married Maria Melzer, a north German twenty years his junior. The difference between her parents was not only one of age. According to delle Grazie, her father was an extremely well-educated, imaginative man with a sense of beauty and an interest in art, whereas her mother was of a more practical turn of mind. Delle Grazie characterizes herself as a nervous and inquisitive child with a tendency toward solitude and fantasy. Her stolid mother did not provide her with much understanding, but her father told her fairy tales and explained many mysteries of nature. Delle Grazie's comfortable and secure youth was first interrupted by the death of her younger sister in 1871 and ended completely in 1872 with the demise of her beloved father.

The family moved to Vienna, where delle Grazie attended a girls' school and, for one year, the teachers' college of St. Anna. She had to interrupt her studies because of a nervous illness, probably caused by the stress of alien surroundings, and aggravated by her mother, who opposed her attempts at poetry. In 1875 she met a person who understood her and tried to guide her as a writer: Laurenz Müllner, the chaplain of St. Leopold. A priest with philosophical and literary interests, Müllner later became professor of Christian philosophy at the University of Vienna. The autobiographical novels *O Jugend!* (Oh Youth!, 1917) and *Eines Lebens Sterne* (Stars of a Life, 1919), which describe a priest counseling and assisting a young girl's literary ambitions, are tributes to Müllner. She also dedicated the collection of stories, *Wunder der Seele* (Wonders of the Soul, 1913), to him, and she concludes the sonnet "An den Ruhm" (To Glory), published in her *Gedichte* (Poems, 1882), with the words "Die Hälfte meines Ruhms sei dir geweiht" (Half of my glory is to be dedicated to you). He believed in her, encouraged her, and criticized her work, and in general gave her the moral support she needed. At his home she met philosophers, artists, and intellectuals, and between 1885 and 1900 a literary circle developed around delle Grazie and Müllner.

Müllner's death in 1911 left delle Grazie with "eine große, unsägliche und unaussprechliche Einsamkeit der Seele" (a great, unspeakable, inexpressible loneliness of the soul). During the summer of 1912, while vacationing in Styria as she had for several years, she had a mystical experience which forced her to return to Vienna. At a Eucharistic congress she was reconverted to the Catholic faith of her youth. Her intellectual disappointment with various scientific theories had prepared her for this change, which she describes in her essay "Mein Weg zu Gott" (My Way to God, 1922). Her subsequent works, until her death in 1931, are infused with the spirit of her regained faith.

Delle Grazie began composing poetry at the age of eight, and some of the verse included in her first collection, *Gedichte,* were written when she was ten and twelve. These early poems already demonstrate remarkable clarity of language. The subject matter is often the conflict between "Geist" (spirit) and "Natur" (nature), the most prominent theme among German-language writers at the turn of the century. Her poems often concern love, sometimes describing quiet happiness but more often rendering the idea that unrequited love results in renunciation and suffering. An atmosphere of resignation dominates, and delle Grazie employs the fashionable pathos of the fin de siècle as well as the idea a flight from oppressive reality to a spiritual realm of form and beauty. In "Oase" (Oasis), for example, beauty is depicted as a shimmering island in the vast expanse of the sea of life where the poet, driven to exhaustion by the world, can find rest.

Later poems continue to treat love, restlessness, lack of peace, melancholy dreams, and loneliness; they also discuss philosophical, scientific, and sociological ideas. Like many of her contemporaries she was influenced by Nietzsche; but in contrast to Nietzsche, delle Grazie intercedes for the poor and those without rights. Some of the poems in *Italienische Vignetten* (Italian Vignettes, 1892) mirror her melancholy disposition and resigned pessimism as she compares her youth to the ruins of the ancient past. But she finds solace in looking at the ocean, which she sees as a reflection of her perception of the unity of all living things.

Her view of nature as the force from which everything comes and to which everything returns is also evident in the descriptions of the Hungarian landscape in her story *Die Zigeunerin* (The Gypsy, 1885), about a gypsy girl who, betrayed in love, takes bloody revenge: "Weit und unabsehbar dehnt sich die Pußta ... in sich selbst verloren, einsam und schwermütig, gleich einem uferlosen Meer in die Ferne strebend, aber dennoch von der wechselnden Kreislinie des Horizontes nach allen Seiten begrenzt, ist sie das verkörperte Bild der menschlichen Sehnsucht, die sich ewig ins Unendliche ergießen will und ewig von den hemmenden Schranken der Endlichkeit umschlossen findet" (Wide and immeasurable stretches the puszta [the Hungarian plain] ... in itself forlorn, lonely, and melancholy, striving into the distance like a boundless sea, yet contained on all sides by the changing lines of the horizon, it is the incarnate picture of human longing which strives eternally toward the infinite and is ever enclosed by the restraining barriers of finiteness).

A different kind of nature description can be found in *Hermann* (1883), one of the nationalistic works inspired by the founding of the German Reich in 1871. This heroic poem in twelve cantos introduces historical personages, evokes the mystique of the German forest with its elves, water nymphs, dwarfs, flowers, and animals, and culminates in an apotheosis of the German spirit and the ideals of freedom, science, and poetry.

Delle Grazie's first drama, *Saul* (1885), was never performed, but it earned her the Grillparzer Prize on the recommendation of Heinrich Laube, the director of the Burgtheater, Austria's leading theater, who was amazed at such maturity, philosophical clarity, and perfection of expression in one so young.

Her blend of talents found its best expression in the work often considered her masterpiece, the epic in iambic pentameter *Robespierre: Ein modernes Epos* (Robespierre: A Modern Epic, 1894). In her autobiographical essay "Mein Lebensweg," published in volume 9 of her collected works, she writes that the spirit and the leaders of the French Revolution had so gripped her imagination that she spent the ten most beautiful years of her life in researching and writing this work. Its basic idea, borrowed from the nineteenth-century French philosopher Hippolyte Taine, is that the French Revolution began as a social rather than a political movement, as a struggle for individual justice, which then developed into a struggle for basic rights. Rousseau's influence is apparent in delle Grazie's contention that in separating human existence from nature man became isolated. Modern culture and civilization are no longer in harmony with nature; the result is nihilism.

In Robespierre she presents the struggle of the idealist against nature's "right of the stronger." He is a dreamer with a utopian vision of the future; he is an advocate for human rights, but his revolt against nature leads to his crimes. The cynic Saint-Just forces the utopian socialist to take the ultimate step by persuading him that victims are necessary in the present for the realization of a better future.

Delle Grazie expresses her own pessimistic views through the fictitious character Lea, who, after great suffering, becomes fatalistic. She feels that there is no hope, and that therefore man should sublimate his wishes and desires and submit to the laws of nature. The same hopelessness turns the priest Claude Fauchet into an advocate of compassion, an attitude which brings him close to the heroes of Dostoyevski's and Rousseau's ideal societies based on the ethics of pity. In the twelfth canto, "Die Mysterien der Menschheit" (The Mysteries of Mankind), which is at the exact center of the epic, Fauchet has a vision of evolutionary creation as proposed by Charles Darwin and Ernst Haeckel.

Robespierre traces the French Revolution from the storming of the Bastille to Danton's death and Robespierre's downfall. Although the author's sympathies clearly lie with the masses, she does not refrain from showing how greed can degrade and dehumanize them. The climactic September murders in the eighteenth canto were found too bloody by some contemporary critics; Hans Hirschstein, who considered the work epoch-making for modern realism, found the depictions of cruelty exaggerated. In general, however, her interpretation of the French Revolution was judged positively. Hans Benzmann considered *Robespierre* "one of the most profound and most beautiful works of art of contemporary literature," and the critic Rudolf von Gottschall compared her language to that of Shakespeare. The leading Viennese newspaper, the *Neue Freie Presse*, wrote that as long as literature existed *Robespierre* would endure.

After the success of *Robespierre* delle Grazie turned to drama. The premiere of the naturalistic play *Schlagende Wetter* (Firedamp, 1900) was held at the Deutsches Volkstheater in Vienna on 27 October 1900. She dedicated the play to the memory of her father; the mine director Baselli, who functions as a mediator between the mine owner and the workers, is based on him. The exploitation of the mine workers by the owner, Fritz Liebmann, is portrayed as an offense against nature. The greedy Liebmann is opposed by Gruber, the only survivor of a catastrophe caused eight years earlier by Liebmann's father. Since then Gruber has been filled with hate, which is not alleviated even when his granddaughter, Marie, marries Liebmann. He refuses every offer of assistance, even though his second granddaughter, Annerl, is dying of consumption in Gruber's humid hut. When Liebmann needs additional coal to fill a contract, he reopens a mine shaft which the superstitious miners had been avoiding. Liebmann enters with the workers to show his good faith; all perish when the firedamp ignites. A parallel between the dangerous conditions in the mine and those in society is suggested: in both there are potentially explosive elements which can ignite if greedy people become exploiters.

Delle Grazie followed this social drama, written in the manner of the early Gerhart Hauptmann, with *Der Schatten* (The Shadow, 1902), a symbolic play which was actually completed in 1897, before *Schlagende Wetter*. Typical of the period, the plot concerns the relationship of art and life. The poet Werner is suddenly filled with regret when he spends a few days in Rome with his friend Klang: he feels that real life has passed him by while he was pursuing his artistic dreams. His envy drives him to slander his friend and to attempt to seduce Klang's mistress; when he fails, he kills her out of fear that she might betray him. When Klang is about to be executed for the girl's murder, Werner's conscience regains control and overcomes the "dark shadow" which had possessed him. The last scene shows Werner back in Rome, writing; the entire incident had been a product of his poetic fantasy. Through the fantasy the poet was able to free himself from the demonic powers which beset the artist more powerfully and dangerously than other people. Dark impulses, an overpowering fantasy life, and the desire to imagine every possibility are characteristic of the poet as well as of the criminal, says delle Grazie, echoing a view of Thomas Mann. This mysterious surplus of energy is harmonized and cultivated in the one, whereas it breaks forth destructively as unbridled atavism in the other.

Der Schatten premiered at the Burgtheater on 28 September 1901 with Josef Kainz, one of Vienna's most celebrated actors, in the leading role. To have a play performed at the Burgtheater was generally acknowledged as a sign of a writer's arrival; *Der Schatten* also received the Bauernfeld Prize. The critics were greatly impressed by the play's depth of thought and its poetic power but felt that it lacked dramatic force; Hugo von Hofmannsthal's lyric dramas received much the same reaction at the time.

Der Schatten shows delle Grazie's interest in delving into the depths of the subconscious in search of "inner truth," a characteristic she shared with such writers as Hofmannsthal, Hermann Bahr, Arthur Schnitzler, and Richard Beer-Hofmann. She was especially interested in dreams, which she considered emblematic of the unconscious and capable of giving information about art and life. Dreams were as real to her as waking reality; in the title story of the collection *Traumwelt* (Dreamworld, 1907), a young widow experiences a dream more real and true than anything she had felt before. Delle Grazie often depicts characters who find that they have acted correctly when they have followed their instincts; like other Viennese writers, she believed that rationality required the supplement of unconscious feeling, fantasy, and dream. She reports that some of her works were conceived in dreams so vivid that she only had to write them down.

The four one-act plays collected under the title *Zu Spät* (Too Late, 1903) were also performed at the Burgtheater. *Vineta* describes the chance encounter of a baroness with a missionary who was formerly a tutor in her home. She had been forced to marry without love and only now, when it is too late, do the two admit their feelings for each other. At the end the missionary goes off to die in China. *Die Mutter* (The Mother) tells of a former actress who gave up her infant daughter to marry a rich man. Now that she is ill she would like to find her child and ask for her forgiveness. It turns out that her companion, who has bitter feelings toward her own mother for abandoning her, is the daughter in question. When the woman dies, the daughter finally relents and cries "mother." In *Donauwellen* (Waves of the Danube) a young pregnant woman who has been deserted by her lover is waiting to meet the man who has been bribed to marry her. During their conversation she realizes the ignominy she had been willing to undergo for her child's sake and decides instead to throw herself into the river.

In contrast to the tragic nature of these plays, the last work in the volume, *Die Sphinx* (The Sphinx), is a comedy. A professor of Egyptology is planning to marry his landlady for the sake of convenience. When he learns that her attractive young niece is leaving the household he quickly escapes, aided by the landlady's nephew, who is concerned about his aunt's inheritance. This truly humorous play was also performed successfully in Berlin, but delle Grazie's next attempt at a comedy, *Narren der Liebe* (Fools of Love, 1905), dealing with the founder of anthroposophy, Rudolf Steiner, found so little critical approval that she returned to more serious subject matter.

Delle Grazie continued to try to find success in the theater with *Ver Sacrum* (1906), a play somewhat reminiscent of Frank Wedekind's *Frühlings Erwachen* (1891; translated as *The Awakening of Spring*, 1909) in its treatment of sexual awakening. The plot concerns a young woman who finds true love after an arranged marriage to an older man. Although the drama lasted for only two performances, it was awarded the Prize of the Wiener Volkstheater.

Despite the award, delle Grazie recognized that her true talent lay in prose, and she completed her first novel, *Heilige und Menschen* (Saints and Humans), in 1907. It was serialized in the *Neue Freie Presse* in 1908 and appeared in book form in 1909. The novel is set in a convent school in Rome, where many of the girls are the illegitimate daughters of wealthy women who want to expiate their sins by having their daughters prepared for the novitiate. The protagonist is Alba Chietti, whose interest in Darwinism brings her into conflict with the dogmatic teachings of the convent. She realizes that to be good does not always coincide with being pious, and she sees that the pious are often so concerned about their own salvation that they lose all human compassion. Most of the nuns are hypocrites who play "die hysterische Komödie der Nächstenliebe" (the hysterical comedy of altruism).

Standing in contrast to the affected piety of some of the nuns is Signor Miller, who turns out to be Ernst Haeckel in disguise. As a scientist he rejects the religion preached in the convent but believes that God exists in nature. Alba comes to the same view while sitting in the grotto at Sorrento during her summer vacation. She intuitively feels connected with all of nature, and she hears a mysterious voice calling to her to throw herself into "der heilige Strom des Lebens" (the holy stream of life). This feeling imbues her with a sense of compassion which is contrasted with the sanctimoniousness of the nuns. Through Alba's brother Flavio, who is being educated by the Jesuits, delle Grazie pleads for a liberalization of the institutionalized Christianity which persecutes those who seek the truth.

Pantheism runs through delle Grazie's oeuvre. In her early poems, personal emotions and theoretical ideas are often permeated by the experience of the wholeness of "mother nature": her view that the conscious, the subconscious, fantasy, and reality are the expression of one all-encompassing force also became the central outlook of Hofmannsthal. The old man in delle Grazie's story "Der goldene Schlüssel" (The Golden Key, published in *Traumwelt*) says "daß alles, was wir Leben nennen, ein einziger großer Zusammenhang ist. Auch dort noch, wo unsere Erkenntnis erlahmt und die Spürkraft unserer Sinne versagt. Und so bin ich fest überzeugt, daß auch Phantasie und Wirklichkeit nur scheinbare Gegensätze sind. Daß es eine Grenze gibt, an der sie geheimnisvoll ineinanderfluten. Und daß an dieser Grenze dasselbe Gesetz waltet, das keine Kraft verloren gehen läßt: ... Diese ewige Dynamik alles Seienden" (that everything we call life is interconnected. Even where our knowledge ends and our senses fail. And so I am convinced that fantasy and reality only seem to be contradictions. That there is a border where they flow together mysteriously. And that this boundary is governed by the same laws which do not allow the loss of any energy: ... The eternal dynamics of all being). In delle Grazie's later works this pantheism takes on a more specifically religious significance.

A book denouncing women's emancipation and stating that all creative accomplishments of women could be eliminated without detriment to history–Max von Gruber's *Mädchenerziehung und Rassenhygiene* (Education of Girls and Racial Hygiene, 1910)–occasioned two articles by delle Grazie in the *Neue Freie Presse* on 28 August and 11 December 1910. In these she expresses her sympathy with the women's movement, although her profession as well as her inclination have kept her removed from the activities of public life. She feels that "die Frau, die jetzt ihre Augen aufschlägt, um dem Manne so unbequem ins Antlitz zu schauen; ihren Mund öffnet, um endlich, endlich auch über sich und ihr innerstes Wesen die Wahrheit zu sagen–erst diese Frau ... ist das *wirkliche* Weib. Das Weib, das sich unter dem Herrenrechte des Mannes, unter dem Kaufzwang des Heiratsmarktes so lange gebeugt, so lange verstellt, so endlos lange selbst erniedrigt hat, bis es eines Tages den Mut fand, die Wahrheit zu sagen: über sich, über den Heiratsmarkt *und* über den Mann" (the woman who now opens her eyes to look directly into the face of man, who finally opens her mouth in order to tell the truth about herself and her innermost being–only this woman ... is the *real* woman. Women who have been repressed for so long under men's laws, who have disguised themselves, and who have humiliated and degraded themselves under the obligation of selling themselves on the marriage market now have found the courage to tell the truth–about themselves, about the marriage market, *and* about men). In her view women should not try to combine motherhood and artistic creativity, because an artist must be totally committed to art; but in all other occupations formerly reserved for males there is no reason why they should not combine the two roles.

The prelude to and beginning of World War I form the background to the novel *O Jugend!*, dealing with several friends who serve as representatives of their generation. One of them, an understanding priest based on Müllner, serves as a mentor to Ina, a young girl who redirects her feelings of love for him into altruistic work for mankind; she becomes a nurse and dies a lonely death in a hospital at the front.

As if to turn away from the bleak reality of the war, in her next two novels, the autobiographical *Donaukind* (Child of the Danube, 1918) and *Eines Lebens Sterne* (The Stars of a Life, 1919), delle Grazie looks back to the childhood and young adulthood of a precocious, imaginative, and proud girl. Nelly is fascinated by nature, especially by the stars, and from her teacher's scientific explanations she learns more about God than from the priest with his Bible and catechism. After her father's death she moves to Vienna, where the stars of her early childhood seem far away and her loneliness increases. At the low point of her young life she meets her second teacher, Laurenz Jilly, the chaplain of St. Leopold, who becomes her mentor. He is convinced of her talent and helps her to conquer her doubts and gain self-confidence to go forth into the world.

During the same period delle Grazie wrote *Homo: Roman einer Zeit* (Homo: Novel of an Era, 1919) to plead with men to live in peace as brothers and to unite the races and nations. The title refers to an orphaned boy from the war-torn city of Homonna; when asked his name, he can only stammer "Homo." He becomes the symbol of true Christian love and causes the cynical scientist Willander, an advocate of a Nietzschean master race, to find his way back to faith in God. In an article about the novel delle Grazie declared her favorite character to be Dietz, a pilot who renounces his love for the beautiful wife of his employer. To put as much distance as possible between himself and the object of his forbidden passion he asks to be transferred to the Palestinian front, and he dies in Jerusalem.

After World War I delle Grazie wanted to show her love for Austria and to express her hope for the revival of her defeated and dismembered homeland. In *Der Liebe und des Ruhmes Kränze: Ein Roman auf der Viola d'Amour* (Wreaths of Love and Glory: A Novel on the Viola d'Amore, 1920), set at the Congress of Vienna from 1815 to 1818, she attempts to re-create that unique period of brilliance, grace, and playful elegance. The action extends from the palaces of the aristocracy to the back rooms of politics, from the alcoves of great ladies to the poor rooms of working-class girls. Intrigues involving the Prince of Ligne, Metternich, and Talleyrand, along with episodes concerning Beethoven and Schubert, illustrate the political and cultural atmosphere of the time. Despite the promising subject, the characters seem somewhat lifeless, and the novel did not receive wide acclaim.

Often considered the best work of delle Grazie's later period, the novella *Die weißen Schmetterlinge von Clairvaux* (The White Butterflies of Clairvaux, 1925) is the tale of a religious conversion in the Middle Ages. The priest Bernard de Clairvaux arrives in Partheney just as a convicted murderer and rapist, the "Wälderschreck" (terror of the woods), is being led to the gallows. Bernard takes the rope from the hangman and throws his tunic over the culprit, signifying asylum. He then requests that the murderer be turned over to him so that he may crucify the man himself. Bernard's actions carry out a dream he had had the preceding night in which God gave him one of a swarm of black butterflies, which he was to turn into a white butterfly. The murderer, on the other hand, had dreamed of a swarm of white butterflies surrounding a monk. Reluctantly, he follows his liberator, and an invisible struggle begins between the two. At the monastery the "terror of the woods" is assigned to tend the cemetery and the flowers. As he digs the graves for the monks he recalls the victims he buried in the forests; his work with the beautiful flowers in the otherwise bleak monastery subdues his brutality. Full of suspicion, defiance, and malice, he lies imprisoned "wie ein Bär im Dickicht seines Ichs" (like a bear in the thicket of his self). He suffers mental torments until he breaks down under the heavy burden of his conscience and repents. That night Bernard lies unconscious, his arms stretched out in the shape of a cross on the floor of his room, while his soul prays: "Laß mich wie du, für ihn am Kreuze leiden" (Let me, as you did, suffer on the cross for him). When the murderer comes to see him, Bernard asks him to pray for him in the chapel. These prayers cause the saints to come to Bernard's room to release him from the spell. When the malefactor observes this miracle, he dies while receiving Bernard's blessing, and Bernard whispers: "Nun ist er doch ein weißer Schmetterling geworden" (Now he has become a white butterfly after all). Sin has been redeemed by repentance through the power of grace.

In a scene where Bernard is to receive the donation of a monastery from the Abbess Ermengarde, Duchess of Bretagne, he is able to meet her with complete equanimity, although he had loved her in his youth, because he has overcome his earthly love by asceticism. He has also shown Ermengarde the way to spiritual love. This scene differs from one in *Heilige und Menschen* in which Mother Renée, who has castigated herself for her secret longing for a priest, is dying, and Alba, out of pity, has called this particular priest to administer the last rites. In the earlier novel the priest is depicted as hard-hearted for refusing any sign of human compassion and understanding, whereas in the later novella Bernard is shown as a saint who has overcome all human emotions.

Dell Grazie's last major novel, *Unsichtbare Straße* (Invisible Road, 1927), also treats a conversion. A convent is desecrated by murder; but this action converts the protagonist, Wald, from class hatred to advocacy of brotherly love, from denying God into believing in Him. He is thus able to overcome his base drives and enter the priesthood. Writing in an age she felt was filled with lies, lasciviousness, envy, and sadism, when mankind walks on the *via triumphalis*, delle Grazie feels that the poet has to walk on the mysterious road of God's providence and intentions, since only poets and prophets have been able to interpret its symbolic signs. The fight between good and evil has to be fought over and over again.

After her return to the Catholic church in 1912 delle Grazie's reputation began to decline. The liberal press, which had printed her stories and had always reviewed her early works, took little notice of her later writings; her relationship with Breitkopf und Härtel, her publishers since 1892, was dissolved; and the author, once hailed as one of the leading literary personalities of her generation, was almost forgotten. Few scholarly works have been written about her. In view of her many and varied literary contributions, Marie Eugenie delle Grazie, who anticipated the major themes and techniques of the leading Viennese writers, deserves greater prominence in Austrian literary history.

Bibliography:
Sigrid Schmid-Bortenschlager and Hanna Schnedl-Bubenicek, eds., *Österreichische Schriftstellerinnen 1880-1938* (Stuttgart: Heinz, 1982), pp. 31-32.

References:
Hans Benzmann, "Marie Eugenie delle Grazie," *Das literarische Echo*, 3 (1900/1901): 888-893;
Hans Hirschstein, *Die französische Revolution im deutschen Drama und Epos nach 1815* (Stuttgart: Metzler, 1912), p. 223;
Hirschstein, "Marie Eugenie delle Grazie: Zum fünfzigsten Geburtstage," *Neue Freie Presse*, 15 August 1914, pp. 10, 11;
Peter Horwath, "Marie Eugenie delle Grazie: Eine geniale Dichterin aus dem Banat," *Donauschwäbische Lehrerblätter*, 21 (June 1975): 21-25;
Josef Jellinek, "Marie Eugenie delle Grazie," *Internationale Litteraturberichte*, 10, no. 15 (1903): 118-119;

Victor Klemperer, "Marie Eugenie delle Grazie," *Die Frau*, 15 (1908): 607-617;
Klemperer, "Österreichische Dichterinnen," *Die Grenzboten*, 71, no. 3 (1917): 551-563;
Rudolph Lothar, "Schlagende Wetter: Erste Aufführung am Deutschen Volkstheater," *Die Wage*, 45 (1900): 299-301;
Marie Mayer-Flaschberger, *Marie Eugenie delle Grazie (1864-1931): Eine österreichische Dichterin der Jahrhundertwende* (Munich: Verlag des Südostdeutschen Kulturwerks, 1984);
Bernhard Münz, *Marie Eugenie delle Grazie als Dichterin und Denkerin* (Vienna & Leipzig: Braumüller, 1902);
Gabriele Reuter, "Die Frau in der deutschen Dichtung," *Der Tag*, 43 (12 February 1901): 5-6;
Robert Seiser, "Aus Rudolf Steiners Wiener Jahren: Marie Eugenie delle Grazie," *Mitteilungen aus der Anthroposophischen Arbeit in Deutschland*, 30, no. 4 (1976): 289-291;
Richard Specht, "Zwei österreichische Dichterinnen," *Moderne Rundschau*, 3 (1 January 1891): 337-340;
Hugo Spitzer, "Literatur über delle Grazie," *Neue Freie Presse*, 7 June 1903;
Rudolf Steiner, "Marie Eugenie delle Grazie," *Das Magazin für Literatur*, 69, no. 37 (1900): 913-919; no. 38 (1900): 937-942;
Alice Wengraf, "Marie Eugenie delle Grazie: Versuch einer zeitgemäßen biographischen Skizze," Ph.D. dissertation, University of Vienna, 1932;
Richard Wengraf, "Der Schatten," *Das literarische Echo*, 4 (1901/1902): 204-206;
Oskar Wilda, "Marie Eugenie delle Grazie," *Nord und Süd* (October 1906): 27-48;
Martha Zenner, "Marie Eugenie delle Grazie," Ph.D. dissertation, University of Vienna, 1932.

Papers:
Marie Eugenie delle Grazie's literary estate is held by the Vienna City Library and the Austrian National Library.

Marie von Ebner-Eschenbach
(13 September 1830-12 March 1916)

Jorun B. Johns
California State University, San Bernardino

BOOKS: *Aus Franzensbad: Sechs Episteln von keinem Propheten,* anonymous (Leipzig: Lorck, 1858);
Maria Stuart in Schottland: Trauerspiel (Vienna: Mayer, 1860);
Die Veilchen: Lustspiel (Vienna: Wallishauser, 1862);
Marie Roland: Trauerspiel (Vienna: Wallishauser, 1867);
Doctor Ritter: Dramatisches Gedicht (Vienna: Jasper, 1869);
Die Prinzessin von Banalien: Ein Märchen (Vienna: Rosner, 1872);
Männertreue: Lustspiel (Vienna: Wallishauser, 1874);
Erzählungen (Stuttgart: Cotta, 1875)–comprises "Ein Spätgeborener," "Chlodwig," "Die erste Beichte," "Die Großmutter," "Ein Edelmann";
Božena: Erzählung (Stuttgart: Cotta, 1876);
Aphorismen (Berlin: Ebhardt, 1880); translated by Mrs. Annis Lee Wister as *Aphorisms* (Philadelphia: Lippincott, 1883); German version enlarged (Berlin: Ebhardt, 1884); enlarged again (Berlin: Paetel, 1890); translated by George Henry Needler as *Aphorisms* (Toronto: Burns & MacEachern, 1959);
Neue Erzählungen (Berlin: Ebhardt, 1881)–comprises "Die Freiherrn von Gemperlein," "Nach dem Tode";
Dorf- und Schloßgeschichten (Berlin: Paetel, 1883)–comprises "Der Kreisphysikus," "Jakob Szela," "Krambambuli," "Die Resel"; (enlarged, 1890)–adds "Die Poesie des Unbewußten: Novellchen in Korrespondenzkarten"; "Krambambuli" translated by A. I. D. Coleman, pp. 417-428, "Der Kreisphysikus" translated by Julia Franklin as "The District Doctor," pp. 345-416, in *The German Classics of the Nineteenth and Twentieth Centuries,* edited by Kuno Francke and William Guild Howard, volume 13 (New York: German Publication Society, 1914);

Marie von Ebner-Eschenbach

Zwei Comtessen (Berlin: Ebhardt, 1885)–comprises "Comtesse Muschi," "Comtesse Paula"; translated by Mrs. Ellen Waugh as *The Two Countesses* (London: Unwin, 1893; New York: Cassell, 1893);
Neue Dorf- und Schloßgeschichten (Berlin: Paetel, 1886)–comprises "Die Unverstandene auf dem Dorfe," "Er läßt die Hand küssen," "Der gute Mond";

Die Unverstandene auf dem Dorfe (Berlin: Paetel, 1886);

Das Gemeindekind: Erzählung, 2 volumes (Berlin: Paetel, 1887); translated by Mary A. Robinson as *The Child of the Parish: A Novel* (New York: Bonner, 1893);

Lotti, die Uhrmacherin: Erzählung (Berlin: Paetel, 1889); edited by George Henry Needler (New York: Holt, 1908);

Miterlebtes: Erzählungen (Berlin: Paetel, 1889)—comprises "Wieder die Alte," "Ihr Traum: Erlebnis eines Malers," "Der Muff," "Die Kapitalistinnen";

Ein kleiner Roman: Erzählung (Berlin: Paetel, 1889);

Unsühnbar: Erzählung (Berlin: Paetel, 1890); translated by Robinson as *Beyond Atonement* (New York: Worthington, 1892);

Margarete (Stuttgart: Cotta, 1891);

Ohne Liebe: Lustspiel in 1 Akt (Berlin: Bloch, 1891);

Drei Novellen (Berlin: Paetel, 1892)—comprises "Oversberg: Aus dem Tagebuch des Volontärs Ferdinand Binder," "Der Nebenbuhler," "Bettelbriefe";

Parabeln, Märchen und Gedichte (Berlin: Paetel, 1892);

Glaubenslos?: Erzählung (Berlin: Paetel, 1893);

Gesammelte Schriften, 10 volumes (Berlin: Paetel, 1893-1910);

Das Schädliche; Die Totenwacht (Berlin: Paetel, 1894);

Rittmeister Brand; Bertram Vogelweid (Berlin: Paetel, 1896);

Am Ende: Scene in einem Aufzug (Berlin: Bloch, 1897);

Alte Schule: Erzählungen (Berlin: Paetel, 1897)—comprises "Ein Verbot," "Der Fink," "Eine Vision," "Schattenleben," "Verschollen: Eine Künstlergeschichte," "Novellenstoffe: Ein Gespräch";

Hirzepinzchen: Ein Märchen (Stuttgart: Union, 1900);

Aus Spätherbsttagen: Erzählungen, 2 volumes (Berlin: Paetel, 1901)—comprises "Der Vorzugsschüler," "Mašlans Frau," "Fräulein Susannens Weihnachtsabend," "Uneröffnet zu verbrennen," "Die Reisegefährten," "Die Spitzin," "In letzter Stunde," "Ein Original," "Die Visite";

Agave (Berlin: Paetel, 1903);

Die arme Kleine: Erzählung (Berlin: Paetel, 1903);

Ein Spätgeborener: Erzählung (Stuttgart: Cotta, 1903);

Uneröffnet zu verbrennen (Berlin: Neelmeyer, 1905);

Die unbesiegbare Macht: Zwei Erzählungen (Berlin: Paetel, 1905)—comprises "Der Erstgeborene," "Ihr Beruf";

Meine Kinderjahre: Biographische Skizzen (Berlin: Paetel, 1906);

Altweibersommer (Berlin: Paetel, 1909; enlarged, 1910);

Genrebilder: Erzählungen (Berlin: Paetel, 1910)—comprises "Ob spät, ob früh," "Im Zauberbann," "Fritzens Ball," "Der Säger," "Unverbesserlich," "Das tägliche Leben";

Stille Welt: Erzählungen (Berlin: Paetel, 1915)—comprises "Der Hofrat: Eine Wiener Geschichte," "Die Sünderin," "Vielleicht," "Erste Trennung," "Die eine Sekunde," "Ein Lied";

Meine Erinnerungen an Grillparzer; Aus einem zeitlosen Tagebuch (Berlin: Paetel, 1916);

Sämtliche Werke, 6 volumes (Berlin: Paetel, 1920);

Letzte Worte: Aus dem Nachlaß, edited by Helene Bucher (Vienna: Rikola, 1923);

Der Nachlaß der Marie von Ebner-Eschenbach, edited by Heinz Rieder (Vienna: Agathonverlag, 1947);

Gesammelte Werke in drei Einzelbänden, edited by Johannes Klein, 3 volumes (Munich: Winkler, 1956-1958);

Weisheit des Herzens, edited by Heinz Rieder (Graz & Vienna: Stiasny, 1958);

Gesammelte Werke, edited by Edgar Gross, 9 volumes (Munich: Nymphenburger Verlagshandlung, 1961);

Das Waldfräulein: Lustspiel in drei Aufzügen, edited by Karl Gladt (Vienna: Belvedere, 1969);

Marie von Ebner-Eschenbach: Kritische Texte und Deutungen, general editor Karl Konrad Polheim, 3 volumes published: *Unsühnbar*, edited by Burkhard Bittrich (Bonn: Bouvier Verlag Herbert Grundmann, 1978); *Božena*, edited by Kurt Binneberg (Bonn: Bouvier Verlag Herbert Grundmann, 1980); *Das Gemeindekind*, edited by Rainer Baasner (Bonn: Bouvier Verlag Herbert Grundmann, 1983);

Seven Stories, translated by Helga H. Harriman (Columbia, S.C.: Camden House, 1986)—includes "Krambambuli," "Jakob Szela," "Countess Muschi," "Countess Paula," "The Wake," "The Finch," "The Travelling Companions";

Tagebücher I, 1862-1869, edited by Polheim and Baasner (Tübingen: Niemeyer, 1988).

Marie von Ebner-Eschenbach continued the short narrative prose tradition of such writers as Gottfried Keller, Conrad Ferdinand Meyer, and Theodor Storm. She is regarded as Austria's greatest nineteenth-century woman writer; her stories and aphorisms have been included in many anthologies and textbooks. But she was generally viewed merely as an aristocrat who afforded readers an impressive and vivid picture of Austrian society before the collapse of the multinational empire. She was considered the gentle advocate of the downtrodden, representing kindness and humanity but incapable of depicting passionate feelings in her works. Her intellectual insights were either overlooked or underestimated. A reevaluation has now begun. A critical edition of her writings is under way, and her work is currently assessed as being much more original and modern both in content and form than had been recognized previously.

Marie von Ebner-Eschenbach was born Baroness Dubsky on 13 September 1830 at Zdislawitz Castle, the estate of her family in Moravia (now part of Czechoslovakia). Her father, Baron and later Count Dubsky, descended from the ancient Bohemian nobility; her mother, Marie Vockel Ebner-Eschenbach, came from a German Protestant family which had settled in Moravia generations earlier. Her mother died shortly after Marie's birth, and she was raised under the care of a maternal grandmother, Czech maids, and French and German governesses. Her father remarried twice and Marie had warm relationships with both of her stepmothers as well as with her half brothers and half sisters. The second stepmother, Xaverine Countess Kolowrat, was especially influential on her development. She gave Marie an edition of the writings of Schiller on her eleventh birthday and in 1847 sent some of her early poems to the most esteemed poet of the time, Franz Grillparzer, even though the family frowned on her ambition to become a writer. Grillparzer felt that the poems demonstrated undeniable talent. Further encouragement came from her cousin Moritz von Ebner-Eschenbach, who advised her to write in German rather than in French. When she was eighteen she and Moritz were married; fifteen years her senior, he was a professor of physics and chemistry at an engineering academy and a prominent military scientist who advanced to the rank of field marshal. The marriage was happy but childless. "Den besten Trost für den Mangel an eigenen Kindern findet man in der Liebe zu denen der anderen" (The best comfort for the lack of one's own children is found in the love for those of others), she wrote in *Rittmeister Brand* (Captain Brand, 1896). The couple spent their winters in Vienna and their summers at Zdislawitz. Moritz von Ebner-Eschenbach died in 1898.

For more than twenty-five years Marie von Ebner-Eschenbach struggled for recognition as a dramatist. She had to contend with opposition from relatives who considered it unseemly for someone of her social position to become a writer and with humiliating rejections from publishers and directors. The five plays that were performed were attacked mercilessly by the critics. After an especially malicious reception in 1873 of her social satire *Das Waldfräulein* (The Forest Nymph, published in 1969), which contained criticism of the shallowness of contemporary aristocratic society, she reluctantly turned away from the theater to concentrate on prose fiction.

She gained her first recognition at the age of forty-five with the story "Ein Spätgeborener" (A Latecomer, 1875), and real success followed in 1879 with the acceptance of "Lotti, die Uhrmacherin" (Lotti the Watchmaker) by the *Deutsche Rundschau*, a prestigious periodical that published many of the well-known German writers of the day. A lasting friendship developed between her and its editor, Julius Rodenberg, whose literary advice she accepted gratefully. After this initial success Ebner-Eschenbach's narratives continued to appear in rapid succession; the years 1880 to 1890 were her most productive. The stories were received enthusiastically by the public and were esteemed by other writers. In 1899 she was the first woman to receive the Medal of Honor for Art and Science. Her seventieth birthday was widely celebrated, and in 1910, the first year that degrees were officially awarded to women, she became the first (and to date the only) woman to be awarded an honorary doctorate from the University of Vienna. During the last two decades of her life she was plagued by ill health, including eye problems, but she continued to work. She lived to see the outbreak of World War I, which caused her tremendous anguish. She died in Vienna on 12 March 1916, a few months before Emperor Franz Joseph I, her exact contemporary, and was buried at her beloved Zdislawitz.

In spite of the honors and recognition accorded her during the last years of her life Ebner-Eschenbach never lost her great modesty, nor did she lessen the demands she placed upon herself. Although as a writer she always receded behind her characters, her personality is reflected in her autobiographical works *Meine Kinderjahre* (My Childhood Years, 1906) and *Meine Erinnerungen an Grillparzer; Aus einem zeitlosen Tagebuch* (My Recollections of Grillparzer; From a Timeless Diary, 1916). Some of her correspondence has been published, as have sections of the diaries she kept from 1867 to her death. The deepest impressions of her stories are made by her sharply contoured, diverse characters, whom she describes with psychological insight, compassion, and humor. Many of her stories, like those in the collections *Dorf- und Schloßgeschichten* (Tales of Village and Manor, 1883) and *Neue Dorf- und Schloßgeschichten* (New Tales of Village and Manor, 1886), deal with the nobility living in their castles and mostly Czech peasants who inhabit the lands surrounding these estates. Although she does not exclude the Viennese bourgeoisie and proletariat from her works, she most often deals with the kinds of people with whom she was most familiar from her childhood days. In juxtaposing the nobility with the exploited peasants and villagers, she takes members of her own class to task for forgetting their obligations and holding to empty social conventions. But she does not issue a blanket condemnation of the nobility because she always sees human beings as individuals; her works contain worthy aristocrats, and she depicts the ruthlessness of the privileged not so much as cruelty as thoughtlessness. But her sympathy is with the weak, the helpless, and the oppressed. Her social consciousness is already apparent in incidents from her childhood as recounted in *Meine Kinderjahre*. She was also free of national, religious, or social prejudices.

As a liberal and a humanist she was a firm believer in education, which plays an important role in her works. In her early epistolary tale *Aus Franzensbad* (From Franzensbad, 1858) and in *Zwei Comtessen* (1885; translated as *The Two Comtesses*, 1893) she pokes fun at the superficial education afforded women of the aristocracy. Countess Paula's father declares that "Eine gelehrte Frau ... das ist die größte von allen Kalamitäten.... Der Kopf der Frau soll in ihrem Herzen sitzen; aus dem Herzen, aus dem Gemüt muß bei der Frau alles kommen" (A learned woman ... is the greatest of calamities.... A woman's head should be found in her heart. She should be all heart and sentiment). Many of Ebner-Eschenbach's aphorisms deal with the lack of education for women: "Man fordere nicht Wahrhaftigkeit von den Frauen, solange man sie in dem Glauben erzieht, ihr vornehmster Lebenszweck sei–zu gefallen" (One should not demand truthfulness from women as long as one brings them up to believe that their foremost aim in life is–to please); "Als eine Frau lesen lernte, trat die Frauenfrage in die Welt" (When one woman learned to read, the question of women's rights came into the world); "Eine gescheite Frau hat Millionen geborener Feinde:–alle dummen Männer" (An intelligent woman has millions of natural enemies:–all stupid men). She sees education less as an acquisition of knowledge than as an attempt to develop the intellectual and ethical powers that lead to inner harmony.

Ebner-Eschenbach's belief in human perfectibility reveals the rationalistic influence on her thinking. Her best-known village tale, *Das Gemeindekind* (1887; translated as *The Child of the Parish*, 1893), is a Bildungsroman in which the outcast Pavel Holub, the son of a murderer, triumphs over heredity and environment to become a useful member of society. The two most important influences in his development are his sister Milada and the schoolteacher Habrecht. Habrecht is one of many good teachers and benign priests who function in Ebner-Eschenbach's work as spiritual guides and role models. There are, however, characters in her stories who do not benefit from education and good influences but persist in their evil ways, as in "Das Schädliche" (The Varmint, 1894) and "Unverbesserlich" (Incorrigible, 1910). Some critics have seen such stories as evidence of the influence of naturalism, with its naturalistic emphasis on the role of heredity. Some of Ebner-Eschenbach's descriptions of misery come close to a naturalistic realism, but she emphasizes ethical questions and does not fall into pessimism. Of the brothers Gemperlein in "Die Freiherren von Gemperlein" (The Barons Gemperlein, 1881) she says: "Sie ehrten in dem Geringsten, ja noch in dem Unverbesserlichen–den Menschen" (They honored in the least of men, even in the incorrigible–the human being), a comment which reflects her own unshakable faith in human nature.

In the rich array of characters drawn with warmth and compassion there are many memorable women who assert themselves despite the vicissitudes of fate. Examples are Anna in "Totenwacht" (1894; translated as "The Wake," 1986), who decides to support herself rather than to accept a marriage in which material security would have to be paid for by oppression; the title charac-

Ebner-Eschenbach circa 1900

ter in "Măslans Frau" (Maslan's Wife), published in *Aus Spätherbsttagen* (From Late Fall Days, 1901); and Ilona in "Der Erstgeborene" (The First-Born, 1905). Other women make sacrifices for the well-being of others, as does Lotti the watchmaker, who releases the man she loves from an engagement and later sells her treasured collection of watches to help him and his wife anonymously. Still others demonstrate strength of character in trying to make up for some failing in the past, as do Božena in *Božena* (1876) and Maria Dornach in *Unsühnbar* (1889; translated as *Beyond Atonement*, 1892), whose attempt at expiating her mistake is accepted by society and the church but not by her own high standards. Other female characters are long-suffering, loyal, and enduring, at times putting up with bad marriages (although Ebner-Eschenbach depicts some marriages in which the wife is an equal partner). Simple women are often shown as the backbone of the family, whereas aristocratic women are judged more severely and sometimes condemned for lack of humaneness, as is the Countess in "Er läßt die Hand küssen" (He Sends Compliments, 1886).

In depicting the psyches of children Ebner-Eschenbach was ahead of her time. In "Die erste Beichte" (First Confession, 1875) she describes her pangs of conscience as a seven-year-old after confession, when she felt that she wanted to die rather than insult God with another sin. Her most subtly drawn character is Pavel Holub in *Das Gemeindekind*, a neglected child whose environment would seem to predestine him to becoming a delinquent but who overcomes almost insurmountable obstacles to gain the respect of his fellow villagers. Here the author demonstrates her independence by going against the prevailing deterministic philosophy of naturalism. Similarly, the foundling Provi Kirchof in "Die Spitzin" (The Pomeranian, 1901) is transformed by witnessing the motherly care and despair of a dying dog, which crawls to him to seek help for her one remaining pup in spite of his former cruel mistreatment of her. The awareness of another creature's suffering awakens in the boy a social conscience and a feeling of responsibility; he decides that caring for a life that has been entrusted to him is more important than following his own interests. He acts out of compassion because "verhungern lassen ist noch etwas ganz anderes als verhungern" (to let someone die of hunger is something different than dying of hunger oneself). In another story a child becomes the victim of his father's ambition: Georg's suicide in "Der Vorzugsschüler" (The Honor Student, 1901) is a deliverance from a life of overwhelming demands. Another victim is Milada, the frail sister of Pavel in *Das Gemeindekind*, who is led to believe that her willingness to sacrifice herself will expiate the guilt of her parents. Many of the children in Ebner-Eschenbach's stories are motherless, as is the girl in *Die arme Kleine* (Poor Little One, 1903), who uses physical weakness to play on the compassion of the people around her. These examples only suggest the variety of the problems touched upon in the author's subtle portrayal of children.

Ebner-Eschenbach's empathy extends to animals, which play a role in tales such as "Der Fink" (1897; translated as "The Finch," 1986). Her most famous animal story and perhaps her most often reprinted tale is "Krambambuli" (1883; translated, 1913), the tragic story of a dog whose fidelity to its first master makes it disloyal to its new one and brings about its destruction. (Ebner-Eschenbach received a silver medal from the International Society for the Prevention of Cruelty to Animals in 1912.)

The moral conflicts confronted by Ebner-Eschenbach's protagonists sometimes change their lives. Dr. Rosenzweig, a cynical hardened materialist and the title figure of "Der Kreisphysikus" (1883; translated as "The District Doctor," 1913), is transformed when he comes to the aid of a Polish aristocrat turned revolutionary during the Galician peasant revolt of 1846-1847. After years of selfless work for others he again meets the agitator and learns that the latter has also changed: he has found that his ideals could not be realized by force and has decided that one has to proceed slowly, helping those in his immediate circle. In Die "Reisegefährten" (1901; translated as "The Travelling Companions," 1986) a doctor tells a stranger on a train about having to face a decision concerning euthanasia. Maria Dornach in *Unsühnbar* decides to admit her dishonor publicly in an attempt to expiate her guilt. Lotti in "Lotti die Uhrmacherin" decides to sacrifice her collection of watches for a weakling, even though she realizes that the sacrifice will be in vain. These characters take the responsibility for their actions; they then accept their fates with resignation, which Ebner-Eschenbach views as an affirmation of their inner freedom. "Eine stolz getragene Niederlage ist auch ein Sieg" (A proudly born defeat is also a victory), she says in one of her aphorisms. This ethical stance is sometimes difficult for observers to understand. The protagonist in "Oversberg" (1892) gave up the woman he loved and who loved him but agreed to remain on her former property as caretaker, friend, and source of moral support for her and her child. He made the decision against his own advantage out of respect for his fellowman. The listeners to his story, who do not see his strength and self-discipline, view his resignation as weakness and his goodness as stupidity. Sometimes a loyal person becomes a victim of circumstances, such as the title figure in "Jakob Szela" (1883), the popular hero of the Galician peasant insurrections, who sacrifices himself for the general good.

Artists in Ebner-Eschenbach's novellas are usually shown as unsuccessful, as in "Ein Spätgeborener," "Bertram Vogelweid" (1896), "Verschollen" (Lost, 1897), and *Agave* (1903). Although they are ironic in tone, these tales show how seriously the author took the role of art and how uncertain she was about her own accomplishments. One of her aphorisms states: "Es gibt eine nähere Verwandtschaft als die zwischen Mutter und Kind: die zwischen dem Künstler und seinem Werk" (There is a relationship closer than that between mother and child: that between the artist and his work).

The gentle humor that is prevalent in Ebner-Eschenbach's work is especially apparent in depictions of eccentric characters. The most outstanding are the barons in "Die Freiherren von Gemperlein," a tale about the love-hate relationship of two brothers who withdraw into worlds of illusion–the liberal into fantasies of the future, the conservative into dreams of the glorious past– as they quarrel about theoretical questions. They only realize how important they are for each other when each is ready to sacrifice his happiness for the other. They are the last of the Gemperleins, so that a certain amount of wistful sadness accompanies the hilarious situations. The kindness and sympathy of the author, apparent in the tone and atmosphere here, can also be seen in "Der Herr Hofrat" (The Privy Councilor, 1915), another odd fellow, whose portrait bears some traits of Grillparzer.

Ebner-Eschenbach's narratives frequently resemble scenes on a stage: they are dominated by dialogue rather than exposition and concentrate on a small number of characters and often on one line of action. For this reason she is more successful with shorter forms than with novels. Her work displays great versatility in form and technique: stories can be in the form of a dialogue, a diary, letters, or even postcards, as in "Die Poesie des Unbewußten" (The Poetry of the Unconscious, 1890). Sometimes she uses a frame story, which adds a new perspective to the main story, as in "Er läßt die Hand küssen," or lets the reader surmise a second untold story, as in "Die Resel" (Resel, 1883); there is a double frame in "Oversberg," in which a diary records a conversation in which the fate of the hero is related and commented upon. Because of their concentration, some of these narratives could be termed short stories, a genre not used by Austrian writers at that time. "Am Ende" (In the End, 1897) takes the form of a scene from a play. Ebner-Eschenbach must be considered one of the great technical virtuosos of her age.

The skepticism one can feel in her narratives comes to the fore in Ebner-Eschenbach's aphorisms, which she began writing early but which were first published in the journal *Die Dioskuren* in 1878. She calls her aphorisms the last link in a long chain of thought, and they deal with all the issues found in her other writings. Since they do not claim to express a closed system, it is natural that one can find contradictory ideas expressed in them.

A major concern in all her writings is man's coming to terms with himself and the reality surrounding him. How can his life be given significance? How can his striving for self-fulfillment be reconciled with the demands of the world around him? Some characters learn to bring their powers into equilibrium with the requirements of reality by recognizing their responsibilities; their inner peace and harmony are brought about by striving for moral perfection. Fulfilling the demands of their consciences often necessitates self-restriction, resignation, pain, and sacrifice. They are prepared to renounce worldly goods because although external circumstances are important, their ultimate concern is to pass the test as an ethical being.

This orientation explains why Ebner-Eschenbach, who was so interested in social problems, did not seek to change the social system: it was not because she was unable to rise above the outlook of her own class but because she wanted those in power to act out of ethical convictions to humanize the existing order. She appealed to their feelings of responsibility and compassion and to their willingness to make personal commitments. If an individual abused his position she did not blame the system but the individual who unscrupulously took advantage of his power; she did not blame the institutions but the people who gave life to them. That is why she remained what one critic called a "conservative revolutionary."

Letters:
"Briefe Grillparzers an die Gräfin Dubsky," edited by Moritz Necker, *Grillparzer-Jahrbuch*, 8 (1898): 214-215;

"Briefe von Franz Grillparzer," edited by Carl Glossy, *Grillparzer-Jahrbuch*, 8 (1898): 256-260;

"Marie von Ebner-Eschenbach und Gustav Frenssen," edited by Anton Bettelheim, *Österreichische Rundschau*, 53 (1917): 175-179;

Der Dichterinnen stiller Garten: Marie von Ebner-Eschenbach und Enrica von Handel-Mazetti. Bilder aus ihrem Leben und ihrer Freundschaft, edited by Johannes Numbauer (Freiburg im Breisgau: Herder, 1918);

"Marie von Ebner-Eschenbach und Gustav Frenssen," *Wiener Biographen-Gänge* (1921): 252-259;

"Ferdinand von Saars und Marie von Ebner-Eschenbachs unbekannte Briefe," edited by Graf O. Seefried, *Neue Freie Presse*, 16 September 1928;

"Aus Briefen an einen Freund: Marie von Ebner-Eschenbach an Hieronymus Lorm," *Deutsche Rundschau*, 249 (1936): 67-74, 212;

"Aus ungedruckten Briefen an Dichter," edited by Heinz Rieder, *Turm*, 2 (1946): 333;

Briefwechsel zwischen Ferdinand von Saar und Marie von Ebner-Eschenbach, edited by Heinz Kindermann (Vienna: Wiener Bibliophilen-Gesellschaft, 1957);

"Aus Raabes Briefwechsel," edited by Karl Hoppe, *Jahrbuch der Raabe-Gesellschaft* (1963): 31-63;

Franz Graf Dubsky, "Aus meinem Briefwechsel mit Marie von Ebner-Eschenbach," *Mährisch-Schlesische Heimat*, 10 (1965): 249-261;

Marie von Ebner-Eschenbach–Dr. Josef Breuer: Ein Briefwechsel, edited by Robert A. Kann (Vienna: Bergland, 1969).

References:
Ingrid Aichinger, "Harmonisierung oder Skepsis? Zum Prosawerk der Marie von Ebner-Eschenbach," *Österreich in Geschichte und Literatur*, 16, no. 9 (1972): 483-495;

Mechtild Alkemade, *Die Lebens- und Weltanschauung der Freifrau Marie von Ebner-Eschenbach: Mit sechs Tafelbeilagen und dem Briefwechsel Heyse und Ebner-Eschenbach* (Graz & Würzburg: Wächter, 1935);

Dee L. Ashliman, "Marie von Ebner-Eschenbach und der deutsche Aphorismus," *Österreich in Geschichte und Literatur*, 18 (1974): 155-156;

Lisa Barck-Herzog, "Hermione Villinger–Marie von Ebner-Eschenbach: Eine Dichterfreundschaft. Nach Briefen von Hermione Villinger dargestellt," *Deutsche Rundschau*, 87 (1961): 845-849;

Anton Bettelheim, *Marie von Ebner-Eschenbach* (Berlin: Paetel, 1900);

Bettelheim, "Marie von Ebner-Eschenbach und Julius Rodenberg," *Deutsche Rundschau*, 46 (April 1920): 6-23;

Bettelheim, "Marie von Ebner-Eschenbach und Louise von François," *Deutsche Rundschau*, 27 (October 1900): 104-119;

Bettelheim, *Marie von Ebner-Eschenbachs Wirken und Vermächtnis* (Leipzig: Quelle & Meyer, 1920);

Heidi Beutin, "Marie von Ebner-Eschenbach, *Bozena* (1876): Die wiedergekehrte 'Fürstin Libussa,'" *Romane und Erzählungen des bürgerli-*

chen Realismus, edited by Horst Denkler (Stuttgart: Reclam, 1980), pp. 246-259;

Wilhelm Bietak, "Marie von Ebner-Eschenbach," Österreich in Geschichte und Literatur, 10, no. 9 (1966): 482-500;

Burkhard Bittrich, ed., Anfänge der sozialen Erzählung in Österreich (Salzburg: Pustet, 1979), pp. 7-18;

Wilhelm Bölsche, "Marie von Ebner-Eschenbach," Deutsche Rundschau, 26 (September 1900): 321-332;

Agathe C. Bramkamp, "Marie von Ebner-Eschenbach and Her Critics," Ph.D. dissertation, Cornell University, 1984;

Felix Braun, "Marie von Ebner-Eschenbach–Ein Lebensbild," in Ebner-Eschenbach, Gesammelte Werke, volume 9 (Munich: Nymphenburger Verlagshandlung, 1961), pp. 215-233;

Herbert Cysarz, "Zur Literatur-und geistesgeschichtlichen Ortsbestimmung der Marie von Ebner-Eschenbach," Sudetenland, 22, no. 2 (1980): 81-90;

Lore Muerdel Dormer, "Tribunal der Ironie: Marie von Ebner-Eschenbachs Erzählung 'Er läßt die Hand küssen," Modern Austrian Literature, 9, no. 2 (1976): 86-97;

Sister M. Rosa Doyle, Catholic Atmosphere in Marie von Ebner-Eschenbach: Its Use as Literary Device (Washington, D.C.: Catholic University of America, 1936);

Franz Graf Dubsky, "Erinnerungen an Marie von Ebner-Eschenbach," Neue Freie Presse, 25 December 1917; pp. 16-17;

Frieda Egger, "Marie von Ebner-Eschenbach und Iwan Turgenjew," Ph.D. dissertation, University of Innsbruck, 1948;

Alfred Ehrentreich, "Marie von Ebner-Eschenbach und Schloß Zdislawitz," Neue Deutsche Hefte, 30 (1983): 553-558;

Erika Fischer, "Marie von Ebner-Eschenbach und ihr Verhältnis zur Frauenfrage," Die Frau, 46 (1939): 343-349;

Gertrud Fussenegger, Marie von Ebner-Eschenbach oder Der gute Mensch von Zdislawitz (Munich: Delp, 1967);

Ingeborg Geserick, "Marie von Ebner-Eschenbach und Ivan Turgenev," Zeitschrift für Slawistik, 3 (1958): 43-64;

Karl Gladt, "Ein Skizzenbuch der Marie von Ebner-Eschenbach," Librarium, 10 (1967): 66-81;

Maria Gögler, Die pädagogischen Anschauungen der Marie von Ebner-Eschenbach (Leipzig: Vieweg, 1931);

Katherine Ramsey Goodman, "German Women and Autobiography in the 19th Century: Louise Aston, Fanny Lewald, Malwida von Meysenburg and Marie von Ebner-Eschenbach," Ph.D. dissertation, University of Wisconsin, 1977;

Kay Goodman, "Die große Kunst, nach innen zu weinen: Autobiographien deutscher Frauen im späten 19. und frühen 20. Jahrhundert," in Die Frau als Heldin und Autorin, edited by Wolfgang Paulsen (Bern & Munich: Francke, 1979), pp. 125-135;

Maria Grundner, "Marie von Ebner-Eschenbach. Wechselbeziehung zwischen Leben, Werk und Umwelt der Dichterin," Ph.D. dissertation, University of Graz, 1971;

Maria Hans, "Die religiöse Weltanschauung der Marie von Ebner-Eschenbach," Ph.D. dissertation, University of Frankfurt am Main, 1934;

Helga H. Harriman, "Introduction," in Seven Stories by Marie von Ebner-Eschenbach, translated by Harriman (Columbia, S.C.: Camden House, 1986), pp. xi-xxxvi;

Harriman, "Marie von Ebner-Eschenbach in Feminist Perspective," Modern Austrian Literature, 18, no. 1 (1985): 27-38;

Ernst Heilborn, "Marie Ebners ethisches Vermächtnis," Die neue Rundschau, 22, no. 1 (1911): 575-578;

Josef Hofmiller, Letzte Versuche (Munich: Nymphenburger Verlagshandlung, 1952);

Brigitte Kayser, "Möglichkeiten und Grenzen individueller Freiheit: Eine Untersuchung zum Werk Marie von Ebner-Eschenbachs," Ph.D. dissertation, University of Frankfurt am Main, 1974;

Viktor Klemperer, "Marie Ebner-Eschenbach und ihre Frauengestalten," Die Frau, 17 (1910): 711-719;

Rudolf Latzke, "Die Ethik der Frau Marie von Ebner-Eschenbach," Die Quelle, 81 (1931): 275-289;

Latzke, "Marie von Ebner-Eschenbach und Iwan Turgenjew," Pädagogischer Führer, 85 (1935): 402-412;

Danuta S. Lloyd, "Dorf and Schloss: The Socio-Political Image of Austria as Reflected in Marie von Ebner-Eschenbach's Works," Modern Austrian Literature, 12, no. 3/4 (1979): 25-44;

Lloyd, "Waifs and Strays: The Youth in Marie von Ebner-Eschenbach's Village Tales," in Views and Reviews of Modern German Litera-

ture: Festschrift for Adolf D. Klarmann, edited by Karl S. Weimar (Munich: Delp, 1974), pp. 39-50;

Lloyd, "A Woman Looks at Man: The Male Psyche as Depicted in the Works of Marie von Ebner-Eschenbach," Ph.D. dissertation, University of Pennsylvania, 1969;

Richard M. Meyer, "Marie von Ebner-Eschenbach: Zum siebzigsten Geburtstage," *Velhagen und Klasings Monatshefte*, 15, no. 1 (1900): 57-60;

Gertraud Motzko, "Die Ständetypen in den Werken der Marie von Ebner-Eschenbach," Ph.D. dissertation, University of Vienna, 1948;

Josef Mühlberger, "Konservative Revolutionärin," *Neue Deutsche Hefte*, 18 (September 1955): 454-459;

Mühlberger, *Marie von Ebner-Eschenbach* (Eger: Verlag der Literarischen Adalbert-Stifter-Gesellschaft, 1930);

Moritz Necker, "Marie von Ebner-Eschenbach: Ein literarisches Charakterbild," *Deutsche Rundschau*, 16 (September 1890): 338-357;

Necker, *Marie von Ebner-Eschenbach: Nach ihren Werken geschildert* (Leipzig & Berlin: Meyer, 1900);

Eileen M. O'Connor, *Marie Ebner* (London: Palmer, 1928);

Karl Konrad Polheim, "Textkritik und Interpretation: Marie von Ebner-Eschenbach und Ferdinand von Saar in wissenschaftlichen Einzelausgaben," *Sprachkunst*, 7 (1976): 127-135;

Gabriele Reuter, *Ebner-Eschenbach* (Berlin: Schuster & Loeffler, 1905);

Karlheinz Rossbacher, "Das Debüt einer Schriftstellerin: Marie von Ebner-Eschenbachs Episteln *Aus Franzensbad* (1858)," in *From Vormärz to Fin de Siècle: Essays in 19th Century Austrian Literature*, edited by Mark G. Ward (Blairgowrie: Lochee, 1986), pp. 57-71;

Rossbacher, "Marie von Ebner-Eschenbach: Zum Verhältnis von Literatur und Sozialgeschichte am Beispiel von 'Krambambuli,' " *Österreich in Geschichte und Literatur*, 24, no. 2 (1980): 87-106;

Erich Schadauer, "Gesellschaft und Kultur Österreichs im Spiegel der Novellen Ferdinands von Saar und Maries von Ebner-Eschenbach," Ph.D. dissertation, University of Vienna, 1949;

Albert Schneider, "Les Aphorismes de Marie von Ebner-Eschenbach," *Études Germaniques*, 26 (1971): 168-193;

Ilse Slama, "Marie Ebner-Eschenbach und das Burgtheater," Ph.D. dissertation, University of Vienna, 1944;

Gerda H. Snapper, "Entfremdung und Isolation in den Prosawerken von Marie von Ebner-Eschenbach," Ph.D. dissertation, University of California, Berkeley, 1982;

Alexandra Unterholzner, "Marie von Ebner-Eschenbach: Eine Analyse der Form und der Rezeption ihres Werkes," Ph.D. dissertation, University of Innsbruck, 1978;

Jiří Veselý, "Ebner-Eschenbach, Saar, David: Tschechische Elemente in ihrem Werk und Leben," *Lenau-Forum*, 1, no. 3/4 (1969): 25-45;

Veselý, "Marie von Ebner-Eschenbach und die tschechische Literatur," *Germanistica Pragensia*, 6 (1972): 91-100;

Veselý, "Tagebücher legen Zeugnis ab: Unbekannte Tagebücher der Marie von Ebner-Eschenbach," *Österreich in Geschichte und Literatur*, 15 (1975): 211-241;

Hans Vogelsang, "Marie von Ebner-Eschenbach als Dichterin des Mitleids," *Wort in der Zeit*, 7, no. 3 (1961): 58-62;

Vogelsang, "Marie von Ebner-Eschenbachs Weltbild und Menschenbild," *Österreich in Geschichte und Literatur*, 10, no. 3 (1966): 122-132;

Heinz Wallach, "Studien zur Persönlichkeit Marie von Ebner-Eschenbachs," Ph.D. dissertation, University of Vienna, 1950;

Oskar Walzel, "Marie von Ebner-Eschenbach," in his *Vom Geistesleben des 18. und 19. Jahrhunderts* (Leipzig: Insel, 1911), pp. 447-487.

Papers:

The major part of Marie von Ebner-Eschenbach's literary estate is at the Vienna City Library. Most of her diaries are at the State Archive in Brno, Czechoslovakia. The Ebner-Eschenbach family archive is in Janovice u Rymarova, Czechoslovakia. Some of her letters are in the Austrian National Library in Vienna and in the Schiller National Museum and the Cotta Archive in Marbach am Neckar, Federal Republic of Germany. Some letters and manuscripts are at the Goethe and Schiller Archive in Weimar, German Democratic Republic.

Albert Ehrenstein
(22 December 1886-8 April 1950)

Alfred D. White
University of Wales College of Cardiff

BOOKS: *Tubutsch* (Vienna & Leipzig: Jahoda & Siegel, 1911; revised edition, Munich: Müller, 1914); translated by Eric Posselt and Eva Zistel (New York: Abramson, 1946);
Der Selbstmord eines Katers (Munich & Leipzig: Müller, 1912); revised as *Bericht aus einem Tollhaus* (Leipzig: Insel, 1919);
Die weiße Zeit (Munich: Müller, 1916 [dated 1914]);
Der Mensch schreit (Leipzig: Wolff, 1916);
Nicht da, nicht dort (Leipzig: Wolff, 1916); revised as *Zaubermärchen* (Berlin: Fischer, 1919);
Die rote Zeit (Berlin: Fischer, 1917);
Eros (Berlin: Fischer, 1918);
Den ermordeten Brüdern (Zurich: Rascher, 1919);
Die Nacht wird (Vienna & Berlin: Genossenschaftsverlag, 1920);
Karl Kraus (Vienna: Genossenschaftsverlag, 1920);
Die Gedichte (Leipzig & Vienna: Strache, 1920);
Wien (Berlin: Rowohlt, 1921);
Dem ewigen Olymp: Novellen und Gedichte (Leipzig: Reclam, 1921);
Briefe an Gott (Leipzig & Vienna: Waldheim, 1922);
Herbst (Berlin: Officina Serpentis, 1923);
Ritter des Todes (Berlin: Rowohlt, 1926);
Menschen und Affen (Berlin: Rowohlt, 1926);
Mein Lied (Berlin: Rowohlt, 1931);
Gedichte und Prosa, edited by Karl Otten (Neuwied am Rhein & Berlin: Luchterhand, 1961);
Ausgewählte Aufsätze, edited by Moshe Yaakov Bengavriêl (Heidelberg: Schneider, 1961);
Wie bin ich vorgespannt den Kohlenwagen meiner Trauer: Gedichte, edited by Jörg Drews (Munich: Edition text + kritik, 1977).

OTHER: *Trauerspiele des Sophokles*, translated by Friedrich Hölderlin, edited by Ehrenstein (Weimar: Kiepenheuer, 1918);
Maria de Zayas y Sotomayor, *Die lehrreichen Erzählungen und Liebesgeschichten*, translated by Clemens Brentano, edited by Ehrenstein (Weimar: Kiepenheuer, 1918);
Kurt Pinthus, ed., *Menschheitsdämmerung: Symphonie jüngster Dichtung*, contributions by Ehrenstein (Berlin: Rowohlt, 1920);
Schi-King: Das Liederbuch Chinas, gesammelt von Kung-fu-tse, translation adapted by Ehrenstein (Vienna: Tal, 1922);
Pe-lo-thien, translation adapted by Ehrenstein (Berlin: Rowohlt, 1923);

Albert Ehrenstein circa 1919 (drawing by Oskar Kokoschka)

Longus, *Daphnis und Chloe*, translated by Friedrich Jacobs, edited by Ehrenstein (Regensburg & Leipzig: Habbel & Naumann, 1924);

China klagt: Nachdichtungen revolutionärer chinesischer Lyrik aus drei Jahrtausenden, translation adapted and edited by Ehrenstein (Berlin: Malik, 1924);

Thomas Schramek, "*Freiherr von Egloffstein*," introduction by Ehrenstein (Berlin: Die Schmiede, 1925);

Lukian: Übersetzungen, translation adapted by Ehrenstein (Berlin: Rowohlt, 1925);

Räuber und Soldaten: Roman frei nach dem Chinesischen, translation adapted by Ehrenstein (Berlin: Ullstein, 1927); translated by Geoffrey Dunlop as *Robbers and Soldiers* (New York: Knopf, 1929; London: Howe, 1929); German version revised and enlarged as *Mörder aus Gerechtigkeit: Romane frei nach dem Chinesischen* (Berlin: Deutsche Buch-Gemeinschaft, 1931);

Edgar Allan Poe, *Die denkwürdigen Erlebnisse Gordon Pyms*, edited by Ehrenstein (Berlin: Deutsche Buch-Gemeinschaft, 1930);

Ich bin der unnütze Dichter, verloren in kranker Welt: Nachdichtungen aus dem Chinesischen, translation adapted by Ehrenstein (Berlin: Friedenauer Presse, 1970).

PERIODICAL PUBLICATIONS: "Wanderers Lied," *Die Fackel*, 18 February 1910, p. 36; "Gottes Tod," *Die weißen Blätter*, 4 (1917): 174; "Ode," *Menschen*, 1 (15 September 1918): 1.

No survey of German expressionist literature fails to mention Albert Ehrenstein, the sharp-tongued yet sensitive author of the lapidary prose sketch *Tubutsch* (1911; translated, 1946) and of some of the most outspoken political and sexual lyrics in German; yet the worthwhile works from his pen are few, and his stature as a writer is doubtful. As a person, though he had some celebrated quarrels, he liked nothing better than to help others: rescuing his friend Oskar Kokoschka from military service on the eastern front, making propaganda for the unknown actress Elisabeth Bergner (the great unhappy love of his life, who inspired many of his poems), and trying to run a writers' cooperative publishing house. In exile in Switzerland and America, often in desperate straits himself, cynical and bitter, he still advised and aided other refugees and writers.

Ehrenstein was born in Vienna on 22 December 1886 to Alexander Ehrenstein, a poor Jewish clerk, and Charlotte Neuer Ehrenstein. He was marked by a physical abnormality (wryneck) and a series of psychological difficulties. He felt that his mother placed great hopes on him but made his life so miserable that he could never fulfill them. A mediocre student, he attempted while still at the Piaristen Gymnasium to establish himself as a writer. He suffered a nervous breakdown in 1906 but went on to the University of Vienna, studied history and philosophy, received his doctorate in 1910, then set out to earn a living as a writer. Karl Kraus helped him make a literary sensation with *Tubutsch* and the poem "Wanderers Lied" (Wanderer's Song, 1910). He lived in Berlin in the thick of early expressionism for some time, then returned to Vienna. He published stories, poems, feuilletons, reviews, and lyrical monologues showing empathy with the suffering and the downtrodden. In 1914, unfit for active service, he was called to serve in the Austrian War Archives but was later demobilized. World War I turned him into an eloquent pacifist and socialist: he blamed arms profiteers for the death of one of his brothers. He published such antiwar poems as he could smuggle past the censorship. In 1915-1916 he worked for publishers in Berlin but soon found it advisable to flee to Switzerland, returning to Berlin in 1918; the failure of the Spartacist risings in January 1919 disappointed him, though he never became a rigid party-line Communist. He fell out of literary fashion as fast as he had come into it: his collected poems of 1920 were printed in 3,600 copies, *Herbst* (Autumn, 1923) in a mere 225. But he was able to collect his works in three imposing volumes: narratives in *Ritter des Todes* (Knights of Death, 1926), essays in *Menschen und Affen* (Men and Apes, 1926), and poetry in *Mein Lied* (My Song, 1931). His essays and poems of the 1920s attack capitalists and moderate socialists and dwell on the theme of oppressed and threatened humanity; he traveled widely in Europe, Asia, and Africa collecting material for these works. An active member of the left-wing Gruppe (Group) 1925, he also became a Buddhist out of respect for all living things. Between 1922 and 1933 he compiled six books of adaptations of Chinese literature, increasingly political in tone; it was mainly this work that kept him in the public eye.

In 1931 he moved to Brissago, Switzerland; in 1933 his books were burned in Berlin. His name did not come before the German public

Illustration by Kokoschka for Ehrenstein's prose sketch Tubutsch

again in his lifetime, though he planned several books and did much work on them. Cut off from his paying readership, he was soon poor. He spent time in the Soviet Union in 1934-1935; in 1941 he moved to New York, where he found few opportunities to publish (his work seemed too esoteric and European) and few friends. He wrote little but some satirical laments on World War II and some fragments of an autobiography. After 1945 he hoped—in vain—that his books would again be published in Germany. Poor and ill, he lost the will to live; he suffered a stroke on the street in 1950 and died without regaining consciousness. The renewed interest in literary expressionism came a decade too late for him: an incomplete edition of his collected works was published in 1961.

Tubutsch, written in 1907, describes a neurotic who minutely observes the grotesque side of Viennese everyday life and peers into frightening existential depths: the hero-narrator's alienation is like that of Rainer Maria Rilke's fictional personage Malte Laurids Brigge, though he lacks Brigge's privileged background. He shows a sense of social pity in telling of the wretched life of the cobbler Peter Kekrewischy, who missed out on a learned vocation because his guardian, a butcher, would not let him attend a university; while Kekrewischy pushes a cripple's wheelchair to earn a little extra money, a less gifted former classmate runs the Vienna observatory. Tubutsch also finds sympathy for underemployed, bored generals and crippled jackdaws, and above all things he pities himself. His neurosis is interpretable by the theories of Alfred Adler, who later became a friend of Ehrenstein's, as an attempt to achieve security and wholeness when feeling insecure and fragmented. Everything Tubutsch does is a cry for attention: he eats in the café in red kid gloves in order to be asked about them, but people think him too mad or too genteel to be spoken to: he has bought the gloves in vain. He declares his religion to be Greek paradox; he sniffs at policemen and plans to write an essay on their preferences in after-shave lotions. But his eccentricities fail to give him the reputation of an eccentric. He is reduced to seeking attention from his bootjack, whom he calls Philipp: they play games in which Philipp is the hard-selling grocer and Tubutsch the shoulder-shrugging customer, or Tubutsch is the sweet baby elephant and Philipp the excited, admiring child. Once ambitious, Tubutsch is now disappointed, sarcastic, bitter, envious, verging on schizophrenia; he serenely defends his asociality, his malevolent sabotage of lovers' harmless occupations on park benches as the only answer to the boredom that arises from his Schopenhauerian pessimism and his intellectual

Title page for Ehrenstein's 1925 volume of translations from the Roman poet Lucan

rejection of all usual human activities. "Das Leben. Was für ein großes Wort! . . . Beschränkt sind die Möglichkeiten, immer aber die großen Worte" (Life. What a big word! . . . The possibilities are limited but always these big words).

Satirical brilliance flashes on the surface of despair in grotesque sketches such as "Kimargouel," published in the volume *Zaubermärchen* (Magic Fairy Tale, 1919), whose hero, a Tubutsch with literary pretensions, travels around the world without the fact being visible from his posthumous works, the explosive poem "Graue Spucke" (Grey Spit), and the apathetic sketch "Vieldüstere Barke" (Much-Gloomy Barque). Another series of stories traces the psychology of the Viennese adolescent, by turns sensitive and egoistic. In "Tai-gin," published in *Der Selbstmord eines Katers* (The Suicide of a Cat, 1912), for example, a dream (actually experienced by Ehrenstein) of unfulfilled love and high drama set in a fairy-tale China is taken by the young hero as a convenient hint from the subconscious that he should throw over the family maid in favor of wooing a girl of higher social status. The psychological and social insights shown here have not been properly appreciated by critics who believe all of Ehrenstein's work to be naively autobiographical. Many of Ehrenstein's poems, less analytic and more subjective than his stories, are brutally frank about his lusts, his longing for a beautiful woman who will understand him, his despair and disillusionment when the beauty turns out to be makeup and the love turns out to be whoring, as in "Warum?" (Why?), published in *Der Mensch schreit* (Man Cries, 1916): "O Schleimgewächs aus Arsch und Puder, / warum zerknie ich mich vor einem Luder?" (O snotty growth of ass and powder, / why do I wear myself out kneeling to a slut?).

Ehrenstein's relatively few antiwar poems of 1914 to 1919 gave him pride of place in the relevant section of the celebrated anthology of German expressionist poetry *Menschheitsdämmerung* (Twilight of Humanity, 1920), a key expressionist document. At first verbose, derivatively apocalyptic, and ironically fatalistic, they quickly develop great satirical force and concentration, as in "Gottes Tod" (God's Death, 1917):

Gott schrie "Hilfe" eine lange Weile.
Nun liegt er längst gefangen, wundverstümmelt,
   totengroß
erschlagen, unbestattet, nackt und bloß
allnächtig im Kriegsberichte: schwarze Zeile.

(God cried 'Help' for a long while.
Now he has long lain captured, wound-mutilated,
   corpse-big,
murdered, unburied, naked and bare
every night in the war report: black type.)

The concept of God's death is part of the poet's attempt to discredit the official ideology of the war– "Gott mit uns" (God [is] with us). In "Ode" (1918) the nations are grotesquely pilloried as vampires "denen der Storch brachte den Krieg" (that the stork brought the war to), arms firms are called bandits, and the shabby role of religion is satirized. The neologism *Barbaropa*, which occurs here and in several other poems, intertwines the notions of barbarism and Europe (*Europa* in German).

Ehrenstein has come to be seen as a minor writer; his earlier work is perceived as slight, and his later efforts were mainly adaptations from the Chinese. He failed to repeat the success of *Tubutsch;* postwar poems on the lines of his wartime ones had a poor reception and still await their real discovery. He embraced a radicalism which considers words no substitute for the barrel of a gun: for him writing is a contemptible compromise between inaction and direct action. But the time is ripe for him to be recognized as a master of depth psychology and of polemical writing in verse and prose.

References:

Gabriel Beck, *Die erzählende Prosa Albert Ehrensteins: Interpretation und Versuch einer literarhistorischen Einordnung* (Freiburg, Switzerland: Universitätsverlag, 1969);

Jörg Drews, "Die Lyrik Albert Ehrensteins: Wandlungen in Thematik und Sprachstil von 1910 bis 1931. Ein Beitrag zur Expressionismus-Forschung," Ph.D. dissertation, University of Munich, 1969;

Karl-Markus Gauss, *Wann endet die Nacht: Über Albert Ehrenstein. Ein Essay* (Zurich: Edition Moderne, 1986);

Hermann Korte, *Der Krieg in der Lyrik des Expressionismus* (Bonn: Bouvier, 1981), pp. 201-218;

Dietrich Krusche, *Kommunikation im Erzähltext*, volume 1: *Analysen* (Munich: Fink, 1978), pp. 51-57;

Uwe Langwitz, *Albert Ehrenstein: Studien zu Leben, Werk und Wirkung eines deutsch-jüdischen Schriftstellers* (Frankfurt am Main & New York: Lang, 1987);

Fritz Martini, "Albert Ehrenstein," in *Expressionismus als Literatur*, edited by Wolfgang Rothe (Berne & Munich: Francke, 1963), pp. 690-707;

Hanni Mittelmann, "Von der Erbärmlichkeit des Exils: Albert Ehrensteins letzte Jahre," *Bulletin des Leo Baek Instituts*, 19, no. 56/57 (1980): 110-134;

Theodor Sapper, *Alle Glocken der Erde: Expressionistische Dichtung aus dem Donauraum* (Vienna: Europa-Verlag, 1974);

Jürgen Serke, *Die verbrannten Dichter*, third edition (Weinheim & Basel: Beltz & Gelberg, 1978), pp. 84-97;

Albert Soergel, *Dichtung und Dichter der Zeit*, 2 volumes (Leipzig: Voigtländer, 1925), II: 322-323, 457-462.

Papers:

Albert Ehrenstein's papers, including his unpublished autobiography and fictional narratives, notebooks, and letters, are in the Jewish National and University Library, Jerusalem.

Franz Karl Ginzkey
(8 September 1871-11 April 1963)

Jürgen Koppensteiner
University of Northern Iowa

BOOKS: *Ergebnisse: Ein Buch Lyrik* (Vienna & Leipzig: Stetter, 1901);

Hatschi Bratschis Luftballon: Eine Dichtung für Kinder (Berlin: Seemann, 1904);

Das heimliche Läuten: Neue Gedichte (Leipzig: Staackmann, 1906);

Jakobus und die Frauen: Eine Jugend (Leipzig: Staackmann, 1908);

Geschichte einer stillen Frau (Leipzig: Staackmann, 1909);

Balladen und neue Lieder (Leipzig: Staackmann, 1910);

Der von der Vogelweide: Roman (Leipzig: Staackmann, 1912);

Der Wiesenzaun: Erzählung (Leipzig: Staackmann, 1913);

Aus der Werkstatt des Lyrikers: Prosaschrift (Vienna: Heller, 1913);

Die Front in Tirol (Berlin: Fischer, 1916);

Der Gaukler von Bologna: Roman (Leipzig: Staackmann, 1916);

Helden: Schilderungen ruhmreicher Taten aus dem Weltkrieg 1914-16 (Vienna & Prague: Schulbücherverlag, 1916);

Befreite Stunde: Neue Gedichte (Leipzig: Staackmann, 1917; enlarged, 1922);

Lieder (Konstanz: Reuß & Itta, 1917);

Die einzige Sünde (Leipzig: Staackmann, 1920);

Der Doppelspiegel: Betrachtungen und Erzählungen (Vienna: Wiener Literarische Anstalt, 1920);

Rositta (Leipzig: Staackmann, 1921);

Vom Gastmahl des Lebens: Ausgewählte Gedichte (Vienna: Österreichische Staatsdruckerei, 1921);

Es war einmal: Alt-Wiener Balladen (Vienna: Munich, 1922);

Gespräch mit Gott, dem Künstler: Vorgesang zu einer epischen Dichtung "Erschaffung Evas" (Vienna: Graphische Lehr- und Versuchsanstalt, 1922);

Von wunderlichen Wegen: Sieben Erzählungen (Leipzig: Staackmann, 1922);

Die Reise nach Komakuku: Geschichten aus seltsamer Jugend (Vienna: Rikola, 1923); republished as

Franz Karl Ginzkey

Zeit und Menschen meiner Jugend (Vienna: Wiener Verlag, 1942);

Balladen aus dem alten Wien (Vienna: Wiener Literarische Anstalt, 1923);

Der Weg zu Oswalda: Eine Erzählung (Leipzig: Staackmann, 1924);

Der seltsame Soldat (Leipzig: Staackmann, 1925);

Der Regenbogen: Ein Buch vom frohgemuten Ich (Dresden & Leipzig: Falken, 1925);

Bunte Welt: Erzählungen, Lieder und Balladen (Vienna: Österreichischer Bundesverlag, 1925);

Der Kater Ypsilon (Leipzig: Staackmann, 1926);

Florians wundersame Reise über die Tapete: Dichtung für Kinder (Vienna: Wiener Verlag, 1928);

Der Gott und die Schauspielerin (Leipzig: Staackmann, 1928);

Der Wundervogel (Leipzig: Staackmann, 1929);

Gespenster auf Hirschberg: Aus der hinterlassenen Handschrift des Majors von Baltram (Leipzig: Staackmann, 1931);

Balladenbuch (Leipzig: Staackmann, 1931);

Magie des Schicksals: Novelle (Leipzig: Staackmann, 1932);

Die Raumrakete: Puppenspiel (Salzburg: Aicher, 1933);

Das Antlitz Salzburgs (Salzburg: Pustet, 1933)—includes English translation, *The Face of Salzburg*, by G. M. Turnell;

Prinz Tunora: Roman (Leipzig: Staackmann/Berlin & Vienna: Zsolnay, 1934);

Salzburg und das Salzkammergut (Bielefeld & Leipzig: Velhagen & Klasing, 1934);

Liselotte und ihr Ritter oder Warum nicht Romantik? (Berlin & Vienna: Zsolnay, 1936);

Sternengast: Neue Gedichte (Berlin & Vienna: Zsolnay, 1937);

Vom tieferen Leben: Auswahl aus den Gedichten (Leipzig: Staackmann, 1938);

Der selige Brunnen: Eine Raphael-Donner-Novelle (Vienna: Zsolnay, 1940);

Meistererzählungen (Berlin & Vienna: Zsolnay, 1940);

Erschaffung der Eva: Ein epischer Gesang (Berlin & Vienna: Zsolnay, 1941);

Schatten im Leben: Drei Erzählungen. Der Gott und die Schauspielerin, Die Frau am See, Frau Doris und das fremde Mädchen (Graz, Vienna & Leipzig: Stocker, 1941);

Mozarts unsterbliche Sendung: Festrede, gehalten zur Mozartwoche des Deutschen Reiches, im Spiegelsaal zu Schönbrunn, am 2. Dezember 1941 (Vienna: Offizin Cyliax Druck, 1942);

Taniwani: Ein fröhliches Fischbuch (Vienna: Amandus-Edition, 1947);

Der Heimatsucher: Ein Leben und eine Sehnsucht (Graz & Vienna: Stocker, 1948);

Das Ginzkeybuch: Eine Auswahl aus den Werken des Dichters, edited by Richard Bamberger (Vienna: Leinmüller, 1948);

Lebenssprüche (Vienna: Österreichischer Bundesverlag, 1951);

Nachdenklicher Tierkreis (Vienna: Kaltschmid, 1951);

Der Träumerhansl (Vienna: Jungbrunnen, 1952);

Seitensprung ins Wunderliche: Grotesk-Gedichte (Vienna: Wiener Bibliophilen-Gesellschaft, 1953);

Lebenserinnerungen (Vienna: Buchgemeinschaft Donauland, 1954);

Der Tanz auf einem Bein: Ein Seitensprung ins Wunderliche (Vienna & Stuttgart: Wancura, 1956);

Ausgewählte Werke in vier Bänden, 4 volumes (Vienna: Kremayr & Scheriau, 1960);

Laute und stille Gassen, edited by Gunther Martin (Graz & Vienna: Stiasny, 1962).

OTHER: Barbra Ring, *Das verlorene Herz: Dem norwegischen Märchenspiel von Barbra Ring nacherzählt*, translated by Ginzkey and Stephanie Ginzkey (Salzburg: Pustet, 1933);

Deutsche Balladen: Eine Auswahl für Schule, Haus und Vortrag, edited by Ginzkey (Leipzig: Reclam, 1940);

Genius Mozart, edited by Ginzkey (Vienna: Gallus, 1949);

Oskar Jellinek, *Gesammelte Novellen*, introduction by Ginzkey (Vienna: Zsolnay, 1950);

Altwiener Balladen, edited by Ginzkey (Vienna: Österreichischer Bundesverlag, 1955).

Once considered the dean of Austrian literature, particularly during the final years of his life, Franz Karl Ginzkey seems to be all but forgotten now. Only children and compilers of school readers have remained loyal to him through the years. Two of Ginzkey's children's books, *Hatschi Bratschis Luftballon* (Hatschi Bratschi's Balloon, 1904) and *Florians wundersame Reise über die Tapete* (Florian's Wonderful Trip up and down the Wallpaper, 1928), are still popular; and his ballads, especially those dealing with the history and folklore of Vienna, have become classics and are reprinted in Austrian schoolbooks.

During his lifetime and within a few years after his death Ginzkey was the subject of several dissertations, but Ginzkey scholarship has long since abated; in fact, he is hardly mentioned in today's standard literary histories. When he is mentioned, it is frequently in connection with those figures of the post-World War I Austrian literary scene who, while promoting the idea of an independent Austria, subscribed to an ideology that contributed to the Nazi takeover of their country. Ginzkey's attitude toward the Nazis was no different from that of many of his contemporaries: he acquiesced in the Anschluß (annexation of Austria by Germany) and supported the regime. Otherwise, however, he stayed out of politics and did not compromise himself to the point where he could not play a useful role in the government's

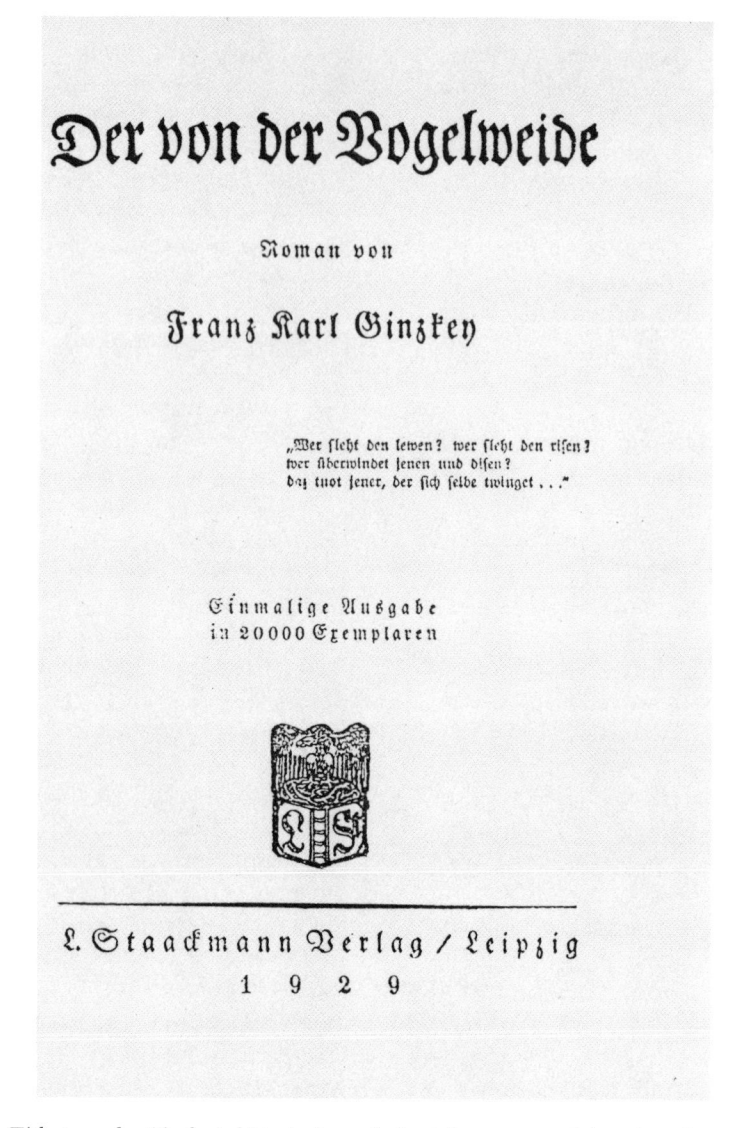

Title page for Ginzkey's historical novel about the greatest of the minnesingers

postwar efforts to establish an Austrian national identity through literature. By then in his seventies, Ginzkey became a link with Austria's glorious past, an exponent of the nation's nostalgia for the lost empire, the respected and revered grand old man among Austria's literati. His country showered upon him all the awards and honors available to its artists; the city of Vienna provided him with an apartment in its first district and buried him in a grave in a special section of the Central Cemetery.

Ginzkey did not become famous overnight, nor did any of his works create a sensation. On the contrary, he matured slowly as a lyric poet, as an author of short fiction, and as a novelist. For almost half a century he was successful in attracting and holding a sizable community of readers and devoted fans throughout Austria and southern Germany.

Ginzkey was born and grew up in Pola (now Pula, Yugoslavia), until 1918 Austria's main naval port. His father, Franz Ginzkey, was the director of the navy's chemical laboratory. Ginzkey's mother, Mathilde Würkner Ginzkey, died when he was one year old, and he was raised for a time by two women in Graz. The elder Ginzkey, however, did not approve of the education his son received there and took him back to Pola, where the boy spent an unhappy childhood and a lonely adolescence in a cultural ghetto. He never established any bonds with his home country; instead, he dreamed up an imaginary Germanic country called "Komakuku," where he planned to travel one day in the hope of finding a true home. He enjoyed his dreamland vicariously through reading books about distant German lands with the dark forests, green pastures, and snow that were lacking in arid Istria.

All of these dreams seemed to evaporate when, following his father's orders, Ginzkey joined the Naval Academy in Fiume (now Rijeka, Yugoslavia). He was dismissed from the academy following a series of small incidents that reflected his growing disillusionment with navy life. His father, lacking means to provide his son with a higher education, decided that he should become an infantry officer, the loss of prestige notwithstanding. Ginzkey obliged again, without much enthusiasm, and graduated from the Infantry Officer's Training School in Triest (now Trieste, Italy) in 1891.

His first post, Salzburg, was a dream come true. The few years Ginzkey spent in Salzburg as a junior officer and aspiring writer left a permanent imprint upon him. His love of all things German found nourishment there: at long last he was able to live in a German environment, to speak German, to inhale German culture. Nevertheless, Ginzkey became increasingly frustrated with military life and tried his best to get a discharge. When, after a few happy years in Salzburg, he was transferred to Pola, his alienation grew; and in 1897 he readily accepted a position at the Vienna Military Institute for Geography. For fifteen years Ginzkey helped draw military maps, work he described as tedious but which he endured out of his conviction that every writer should hold a "real job" in order to be truly independent. He was promoted to first lieutenant in 1898 and became a civil servant in 1899.

Ginzkey's first book, the poetry volume *Ergebnisse* (Results, 1901), caught the attention of Peter Rosegger, one of Austria's most influential writers. Rosegger introduced Ginzkey to his publishing house, the eminent Staackmann Verlag in Leipzig. Ginzkey's second book, *Hatschi Bratschis Luftballon*, published in Berlin in 1904, displays the scurrilous humor characteristic of much of his oeuvre. To this day Hatschi Bratschi, the evil sorcerer who sets out in a balloon to kidnap children, and Kniesebein, the equally evil witch, have not lost their fascination for Austrian children. The publication of Ginzkey's second volume of poetry, *Das heimliche Läuten* (Secret Tolling), by Staackmann in 1906 secured him literary recognition throughout Germany.

Ginzkey's first novel, the highly autobiographical *Jakobus und die Frauen* (Jakobus and the

Title page for Ginzkey's 1913 historical novel about the painter Albrecht Dürer

Women, 1908), is a sentimental love story set in Salzburg. Resembling his creator, 2d Lt. Jakobus Fiedler lacks the martial qualities expected of an army officer. A soft-spoken romantic, Jakobus reads Goethe, writes poetry, prefers solitude to the pleasures of his boisterous comrades, and frequently falls in love. Ginzkey portrays with unconcealed bitterness the "glänzendes Elend" (glorious misery) of the Austrian officer, who often lived an impoverished life behind a facade of elegance. A humiliated Jakobus must give up the woman he loves because of his inability to prove financial security, a prerequisite for any officer who wished to be granted a marriage license. There is little wonder that Ginzkey attacked the strict marriage rules to which Austrian officers were subjected: he had had to wait seven years to marry Stephanie Stoiser in 1900.

Ginzkey owes much of his popularity to his ballads, particularly those about old Vienna. Through the ballads Ginzkey became increasingly interested in historical themes. The major product of what may be labeled his historical phase is the novel *Der von der Vogelweide* (The Man von der Vogelweide, 1912), a medieval love story reminiscent of *Jakobus und die Frauen*. The aging Walther von der Vogelweide, the greatest of the minnesingers, must renounce his love for Gertrudis, the beautiful daughter of an aristocratic lady with whom he was also in love. Walther is destined to remain the lonely artist whose work is not understood by the masses.

By today's standards rather sentimental, even naive, the novel was a big success, encouraging Ginzkey to sever all bonds that still tied him to the army and to become a free-lance writer. In 1912 his request for retirement for medical reasons was granted; the government evidently considered Ginzkey the artist more important than Ginzkey the ex-officer and reluctant civil servant. Only two years later he returned to the army for four more years: during World War I he was a war correspondent, mainly along the Tyrolean front, then was assigned to the war archives in Vienna. One of his subordinates at the archives was Rainer Maria Rilke, the unsoldierlike infantryman who, because of his status as a leading poet, was assigned office duties.

Ginzkey was a prolific writer, leaving an oeuvre of more than fifty titles. Critics consider the novel *Der Gaukler von Bologna* (The Jester of Bologna, 1916), about a girl who is in love with a professor and can get his attention only by dressing as a man and becoming his assistant, one of his best works of fiction. The historical novellas *Der Wiesenzaun* (The Meadow Fence, 1913), featuring Albrecht Dürer, and *Der selige Brunnen* (The Blissful Fountain, 1940), about the sculptor Raphael Donner, also stand out. *Liselotte und ihr Ritter oder Warum nicht Romantik?* (Liselotte and Her Knight; or, Why Not Romanticism?, 1936), on the other hand, is a rather shallow romance. An impoverished aristocratic former officer turned chauffeur falls in love with the daughter of a nouveau riche Viennese. After he pushes out his rival, an arrogant and pompous movie star, the young couple settles in a castle that turns out to be the ancestral seat of the groom.

With increasing age Ginzkey devoted more and more of his writing to his experiences in the imperial Austrian army. These works may be interpreted as Ginzkey's contribution to what Claudio Magris has called the "Habsburg Myth," the idealization by many Austrian writers of the old monarchy. Even so, Ginzkey's autobiographical works

Illustration for Der Wiesenzaun

must be considered the strongest component of his oeuvre. He started writing his memoirs in the 1920s and continued to publish them under various titles for three decades. In *Die Reise nach Komakuku* (The Journey to Komakuku, 1923) and *Der seltsame Soldat* (The Strange Soldier, 1925) Ginzkey portrays the dying monarchy with a mixture of melancholy, nostalgia, and subtle irony. What Ginzkey wrote about this period of Austrian history is likely still to be of interest to readers in the twenty-first century.

Ginzkey received all the recognition a writer could expect in Austria. He became a member of the board of directors of the Salzburg Festival, a position which brought him into contact with the most outstanding artistic personalities of the time, including the writer Stefan Zweig, the director Max Reinhardt, the painter Anton Faistauer (later considered a degenerate artist by Nazi Propaganda Minister Joseph Goebbels), and Austria's leading architect, Clemens Holzmeister. Particularly during the 1930s Ginzkey was part of the cultural establishment of Austria. The University of Vienna conferred an honorary doctorate upon him in 1932, and the Austrian president awarded him the much-coveted title of professor in 1951. He served in the Austrian legislature from 1934 to 1938, making only one speech before the body.

After World War II Ginzkey lived the quiet life of a respected and popular writer, dividing his time between Vienna and Seewalchen on the Attersee. In 1960 the eighty-nine-year-old poet and his wife were the focus of much attention when they celebrated their sixtieth wedding anniversary in Vienna's St. Stephen's Cathedral. Ginzkey died in 1963.

Although he is no longer popular, Ginzkey should not be dismissed. His role as a major figure in Austrian literary circles of the twentieth century has not yet been adequately researched. Whether there will always be a generation for whom Ginzkey still lives, as the editor of his selected works optimistically remarks, remains to be seen.

References:

Roman Herle, "Wo noch Abendsonne liegt: Besuch im Wiener Heim des Dichters Franz Karl Ginzkey," *Die Furche*, no. 52/53 (Christmas 1960): 15-16;

Helene Hofmann, "Franz Karl Ginzkey: Des Dichters Leben und Schaffen," Ph.D. dissertation, University of Vienna, 1923;

Jürgen Koppensteiner, "Die Bedeutung der alten österreichischen Armee für Leben und Werk Franz Karl Ginzkeys," Ph.D. dissertation, University of Graz, 1967;

Koppensteiner, "Franz Karl Ginzkey und die alte österreichische Armee," *Österreich in Geschichte und Literatur*, 5 (1974): 283-290;

Koppensteiner, "Franz Karl Ginzkey: Zum zehnten Todestag des Dichters," *Sudetenland*, 2 (1973): 114-119;

Norbert Langer, "Franz Karl Ginzkey," in his *Dichter aus Österreich* (Vienna: Österreichischer Bundesverlag, 1956), pp. 41-46;

Hertha Richter, "Franz Karl Ginzkey: Sein Leben und seine Weltanschauung," Ph.D dissertation, University of Vienna, 1944;

Werner Röttinger, "In seinen Werken lebt Österreich: Franz Karl Ginzkey zum 85. Geburtstag," *Wiener Zeitung*, 8 September 1956, p. 3.

Papers:

Franz Karl Ginzkey's papers are at the Vienna City Library. In addition to letters, the Austrian National Library in Vienna holds the manuscripts "Der Admiral," "Mein Freund Terribile," "Prinz Tunora," "Wuchergeschichten," and "Wiesensonntag: Gedichte."

Albert Paris Gütersloh
(Albert Conrad Kiehtreiber)
(5 February 1887-16 May 1973)

Ludwig Fischer
Willamette University

BOOKS: *Die tanzende Törin: Ein Roman des Märchens* (Berlin: Baumhauer, 1910; revised edition, Munich: Müller, 1913);

Egon Schiele: Versuch einer Vorrede (Vienna: Gesellschaft für graphische Industrie, 1911);

Die Vision vom Alten und vom Neuen (Hellerau: Hegner, 1921);

Die Rede über Blei oder Der Schriftsteller in der Katholizität (Hellerau: Hegner, 1922);

Innozenz oder Sinn und Fluch der Unschuld (Hellerau: Hegner, 1922);

Der Lügner unter Bürgern (Hellerau: Hegner, 1922); translated by John Nowell as *The Fraud: A Novel* (London: Owen, 1965);

Kain und Abel: Eine Legende (Vienna: Haybach, 1924);

Bekenntnisse eines modernen Malers (Vienna & Leipzig: Zahn & Diamant, 1926);

Der Maler Alexander Gartenberg (Vienna: Haybach, 1928);

Eine sagenhafte Figur: Ein platonischer Roman mit einem Nachwort in usum delphini (Vienna: Luckmann, 1946);

Die Fabeln vom Eros (Vienna: Luckmann, 1947);

Musik zu einem Lebenslauf: Gedichte (Vienna: Bergland, 1957);

Laßt uns den Menschen machen: Erzählungen (Vienna: Luckmann, 1962);

Sonne und Mond: Ein historischer Roman aus der Gegenwart (Munich: Piper, 1962);

Zur Situation der modernen Kunst: Aufsätze und Reden (Vienna, Hannover & Berlin: Forum, 1963);

Gewaltig staunt der Mensch, edited by Heimito von Doderer (Graz & Vienna: Stiasny, 1963);

Der innere Erdteil: Aus den Wörterbüchern (Munich: Piper, 1966);

Zwischen den Zeiten: Texte und Miniaturen, edited by Heribert Hutter (Vienna: Rosenbaum, 1967);

Die Fabel von der Freundschaft: Ein sokratischer Roman (Munich: Piper, 1969);

Albert Paris Gütersloh (Austrian Institute)

Miniaturen zur Schöpfung: Eine kleine Zeitgeschichte (Salzburg: Residenz-Verlag, 1970);

Paradiese der Liebe, edited by Alfred Focke (Vienna: Kremayr & Scheriau, 1972);

Treppe ohne Haus oder Seele oder Leib: Späte Gedichte (Eisenstadt: Edition Roetzer, 1975);

Allegorie und Eros: Texte von und mit Albert Paris Gütersloh, edited by Jeremy Adler (Munich: Piper, 1986);

Die Menschenfreude: Erzählungen, edited by Irmgard Hutter (Munich: Piper, 1987).

OTHER: Franz Blei, *Schriften in Auswahl*, edited by Gütersloh (Munich: Biederstein, 1960);

Wieland Schmied and Hermann Hakel, *Malerei des phantastischen Realismus: Die Wiener Schule*, introduction by Gütersloh (Vienna: Forum, 1964).

PERIODICAL PUBLICATIONS: "Bewertung der Nacht," *Der Ruf*, 4 (May 1913): 1-5;

"Wo steht die Dichtung heute?," *Literatur und Kritik*, 68 (1972): 449-450;

"Kurzgefaßter Prolog zu meinen Schriften," *Literatur und Kritik*, 68 (1972): 450-452;

"Der Roman und die Materiologie," *Literatur und Kritik*, 68 (1972): 452-456;

"Dr. Doderer an seinem Schreibtisch," *Literatur und Kritik*, 80 (1973): 577;

"Tandaradei," *Literatur und Kritik*, 118 (1977): 134-139.

The writer and painter Albert Paris Gütersloh was one of the key figures in the development of Austrian culture during the twentieth century, making major contributions as a teacher, mentor, founder, catalyst, and innovator. Gütersloh was the authority, the theoretician, the academic expert in painting and writing circles. Authors such as Robert Musil, Hermann Broch, and Josef Roth saw him as an equal, and critics of his literary work ranked him with Goethe, Jean Paul, and James Joyce. Gütersloh was indeed a brilliant writer with an encyclopedic knowledge of European culture. His historical awareness, scholarship, and insight were second to those of none of his contemporaries. Gütersloh had the ability to see beyond the immediate situation and could integrate the immense diversity of the cultural movements in his time into a coherent vision. His theoretical contribution to the development of Austrian painting through his advocacy of Fantastic Realism is undisputed. His own paintings, however, found only a limited reception among a relatively small circle of art experts. Similarly, as a writer Gütersloh displays enormous talent and a highly sophisticated style, provides penetrating analyses with startling conclusions, and engages in extremely complex philosophical speculations while at the same time insisting on the concrete reality of each moment; but his works were never widely read. Gütersloh demanded much from his audience; unwilling to simplify or make concessions to the taste and expectations of the literary public, he chose the respect of a few over popular success.

Self-portrait of Gütersloh, 1913 (Historisches Museum der Stadt Wien)

Gütersloh grew up in the world of the old Catholic, aristocratic, multicultural Austria before World War I. The values of the turn of the century provided him with his dominant themes throughout his life: Catholic theology and Christian ethics, the relationship between nobility and bourgeoisie, the conflict between living in middle-class security and pursuing the tenuous path of the true artist.

He was born Albert Conrad Kiehtreiber on 5 February 1887 in Vienna and was educated first at the famous Benedictine boarding school in Melk and then under the direction of Franciscan monks in Bozen in southern Tyrolia. He planned to become a Catholic priest but instead returned to Vienna to take acting and painting lessons. In 1907 his art teacher, Gustav Klimt, recommended him to the director Max Reinhardt in Berlin, where Gütersloh had the opportunity to test his artistic talents as a stage designer. Oscillating between writing and painting, he combined the two interests as the Paris art correspondent for the magazine *Budapester Blätter* from 1911 until 1913. In the latter year he married Emma Berger, a dancer.

After the outbreak of World War I Gütersloh volunteered for medical service at the front but became seriously ill. Through the intervention of his friend, the novelist Robert Musil, he was transferred to the headquarters of the War Information Office, where he met such leading literary figures as Hermann Bahr, Hugo von Hofmannsthal, and Franz Blei. His wife died in 1916 after giving birth to a daughter. Gütersloh married Vera Reichert, another dancer, in 1921. In 1920 and 1921 he was a stage director at the Schauspielhaus in Munich, but his career as a writer and painter began to take priority. For the novel *Der Lügner unter Bürgern* (The Liar among Burghers, 1922; translated as *The Fraud*, 1965) he received the Fontane Prize in 1923. That year he traveled to Rome, where he wrote an autobiography, *Bekenntnisse eines modernen Malers* (Confessions of a Modern Painter, 1926). He lived in Cagnes-sur-Mer in southern France from 1924 until 1929, when he accepted a professorship at the Academy of Applied Arts in Vienna. After the annexation of Austria by Germany in 1938 the Nazis dismissed him from the position because they classified him as a proponent of decadent art. During World War II he was first forced to perform manual labor in an airplane factory and later was assigned to office work. After the war Gütersloh became a professor at the State Academy of Fine Arts in Vienna, serving as rector from 1953 to 1955. In 1952 he was awarded the Austrian State Prize for painting; in 1961 the same honor was bestowed upon him for literature.

Gütersloh, and perhaps with him an era of Austrian culture, died in 1973 in Baden near Vienna. Purity and quality, perfection and individual integrity as criteria for art were much more important to him than success and accessibility. In his eyes the artist is a member of an elite, responsible for expressing his creativity according to his highest ability and with a total commitment to truth. Gütersloh stands in the tradition of German and Austrian writers who do not consider it their task to be easily understandable: the reader has to live up to the artist's vision rather than the artist catering to the reader's tastes and expectations. In the novel *Sonne und Mond* (Sun and Moon, 1962) Gütersloh is quite frank about this attitude: "Who cares about the ordinary person? Do we write or paint for him?" In a speech pre-

Drawing of Gütersloh by F. A. Harta, from the journal Die Aktion, *1914*

sented to the Viennese Academy of Fine Arts in 1948 he asked his audience not to be discouraged by the effort it took to listen to him; they should consider, he said, that a speaker who places high expectations on his audience honors his listeners. More often than not his audience did not feel honored but was simply unable to follow the complexity of his thoughts. The painter Ernst Fuchs remembered Gütersloh's addresses to the International Art Club: "Each of his opening speeches was a widely recognized event. Most of the time we did not understand a single word. It all sounded so educated, what he said. We stood around somewhat embarrassed and were hardly aware that we became a moving force because of his influence." Gütersloh was an untiring seeker of new artistic forms, experimenting with an impressive range of possibilities, rarely hesitating to sacrifice comprehensibility or convention in favor of innovative ideas.

While in matters of form a restless explorer of uncharted territory, Gütersloh adhered to much more traditional views in regard to content. In *Die Rede über Blei* (Speech Concerning Blei, 1922), his manifesto on the writer's role in society, he warned against purely aesthetic approaches to art but also scorned social criticism.

Gütersloh's intellectual roots were the values of a nineteenth-century humanistic education. He opposed the use of art in the service of a political ideology, naive devotion to religious causes, and the rise of twentieth-century rationalism and pragmatism. His complex analyses of modern critical reasoning usually lead to the conclusion that empirical philosophy is unable to penetrate deeply into the mystery of the human experience. Catholicism and its Thomistic philosophy were the major influences on Gütersloh's worldview. In *Bekenntnisse eines modernen Malers* he condemned the lack of spirituality in art and the commercial exploitation of artistic creation and pleaded for an intellectual elite of responsible artists.

Gütersloh's first novel, *Die tanzende Törin* (The Dancing Fool, 1910), shows strong expressionistic influences. Young would-be artists, descendants of wealthy families, try to shed the constrictions of bourgeois life through the uninhibited, passionate pursuit of their desires. The title character, Ruth Herzenstein, the daughter of a Berlin banker, becomes a modern dancer in Vienna and has relationships with various artists. The characters have no clear sense of identity and are thrown from one extravagant adventure and eccentric encounter to the next. Narcissistic indulgences and egocentric aggrandizements are justified by the irrepressible urge to express the feelings of the heart. The trademarks of Gütersloh's fiction—fast-changing scenes, descriptive accuracy, ecstatic monologues, highly lyrical passages alternating with detailed depictions of profane activities, and a disregard for sequences of time and place—are all present in this novel. Gütersloh overwhelms the reader with a kaleidoscope of metaphors moving at a speed that allows no time for the integration and evaluation of the events portrayed. There is an element of visual art in Gütersloh's prose, in that it is more concerned with individual images than with narrative continuity. *Die tanzende Törin* is a self-portrait of the artistic avant-garde in Berlin and Munich before 1918. Gütersloh dedicated the first version of the novel to August Strindberg; he shortened the second version in 1913 and gave it a less dramatic, less mystical ending. In *Die Rede über Blei* Gütersloh affirmed his association with the expressionist movement by saying that the word is expression, not meaning, by which he meant the rules of syntax and semantics should be abandoned in favor of immediacy in the expression of inner feelings. This commitment to the word as a vehicle for the representation of internal states pays little attention to comprehensibility or plausibility, as in this passage from *Die tanzende Törin:* "The blue ceiling of the sky makes the space below so intimate. All conversations can hardly be heard and reach only those who move very close. Nobody tries to push a smile like a huge box through the rows of people. Each smile is oval. Smiling turns the eyes into an oval form, and everything glides along this most personal of all curves."

With *Der Lügner unter Bürgern* Gütersloh turned away from expressionism, calling it a literary vogue of egomania; he defined his novel as a classical-realistic description of a "natural" event. His style did not change toward the classical and realistic in the usual senses of the words, however, but rather into what could be termed a fluid, meandering, baroque factuality. The content of the novel is strongly affected by the growing popularity of psychological theories. Gütersloh became a master at illuminating the intentions, hidden motives, hypocrisy, ambition, jealousy, and pretense underlying human actions. In this novel there is more emphasis on plot and historical context. The story takes place on one evening toward the end of the nineteenth century in Paris. Gütersloh knew the French capital well from many visits, but the city serves only as a distant backdrop to a psychological case study. Rosette Piou, the daughter of a merchant, is leaving the house to attend a formal dance when she finds the aristocratic Thomas Pasteur lying unconscious in the street. The elegant young man is brought into the house and regains consciousness. He is full of gratitude and praise for the charity and compassion of the bourgeois family. He interprets the experience as a sign that his fate is to marry Rosette, but Rosette's mother realizes that Thomas is a confidence man. Before she can warn her daughter, Thomas and Rosette leave the house, but Rosette soon returns in a state of confusion and emotional turmoil. At the end of the novel Rosette leaves the house again and screams that someone is lying in the street. The representatives of the bourgeoisie and the aristocracy are depicted as types, with their characteristic conflicts, prejudices, hopes, and restrictive codes of behavior. The polarity between the social classes remains; the integration of diverging elements toward greater harmony does not take place in Gütersloh's writings.

In the novel *Innozenz oder Sinn und Fluch der Unschuld* (Innozenz; or, The Meaning and the Curse of Innocence, 1922), an allegorical fantasy

Gütersloh in later years (Bildarchiv der Österreichischen Nationalbibliothek)

written in 1914, Gütersloh poses a fundamental existential question: what are the consequences of our disposition both to experience life and yet to remain innocent, to act in the world and at the same time to remain true to ourselves? Gütersloh doubts the competence of human beings to deal with the contradictions and oppositions which every person must live through. Neither celibacy nor sexual passion present a solution. A noble boy raised by hermits visits the girls of the village in his dreams, and they become pregnant in real life. When he falls in love with a nun, the conflict between purity and passion intensifies into a sequence of horrifying mystical events. Gütersloh abandons linear narrative development, brings in the supernatural, paints apocalyptic visions, sets some events in heaven, and moves freely from situation to situation without concern for plausibility, cohesiveness, or context. Gütersloh points out the fallibility of secular interpretations of human experience, but he does not replace the inadequacies of rational thinking with a conciliatory, redemptive, religious trust. He sees the world as being in continuous, unpredictable flux. There is a purpose behind human action, but it remains concealed from the finite mind.

The relationship between God, nature, and man; the attempt to understand the will of God; and the quest for a meaningful human existence are the themes of Gütersloh's novel *Kain und Abel* (1924), illustrated with his own lithographs. The biblical legend becomes a paradoxical parable in Gütersloh's rendition. A world full of error and sin, conflict and betrayal stands in opposition to religious truth. Eve and Cain see God as the mighty ruler, the final authority whose orders must be obeyed, whereas Abel's love of God is an experience of harmony, a presence of God within human beings. Abel claims that God speaks to him; when Cain asks his brother how he, too, can have a relationship with God, Abel admits that he was lying, and Cain kills him. Gütersloh presents a theology in which human beings serve as a vehicle for the divine to experience itself in the realm of the transitory. According to Gütersloh, God develops in man; he says that God jumped on the back of Man to be carried faster and faster through all of His possibilities.

In *Eine sagenhafte Figur* (A Legendary Figure, 1946), written between 1924 and 1929 in Cagnes-sur-Mer, the major theme is the conflict between passionate love, on the one hand, and "pure" love as nonpossessive loyalty and unconditional friendship, on the other. The nobleman Kirill is to wed his stepsister Laura, but she breaks off the engagement out of fear of committing incest (even though they are not related by blood) and develops a hysterical paralysis. When World War I breaks out, Kirill tries to join the army, thinking that his death will cure Laura's paralysis, but he is rejected as unfit for service. His attempt to sacrifice his life for her, however, causes Laura to begin to love him. But in a confusing epilogue Kirill is shown as a bitter and disillusioned painter living alone in Cagnes-sur-Mer. He is unable to escape the norms and restrictions of tradition. Gütersloh's characters find themselves in an intricate web of contradictions from which they cannot escape. The world becomes a "perpetuum mobile," an infinite wheel turning around an unknown center. Every experience is a new and equally valid facet of a life which progresses nowhere. Gütersloh presents reality as an endless series of digressions, disturbed only by human intentions which insist on moving toward a goal. Gütersloh called his form of the novel a "materiology"; in *Albert Paris Gütersloh: Autor und Werk* (1962) the critic Hansjörg Graf defines this narrative mode as one in which "the situation is not developed as a consequence of the character's action, but the protagonists illustrate an insight, as the innocent tragic heroes exemplify the incomprehensible psychology of the gods."

The novel *Sonne und Mond,* on which Gütersloh worked from 1935 until 1962, is his masterpiece. The text is preceded by a sentence from the ancient philosopher of flux, "Ein Haufen auf 's Geratewohl hingeschütteter Dinge ist die schönste Weltordnung" (A pile of things thrown together at random is the most beautiful world order). In keeping with this motto, Gütersloh presents an encyclopedia of digressions, a complex labyrinth of vast dimensions, an immense chaos unfolding over nine hundred pages, through which the reader must find his way without map or guide. Gütersloh gives a single day–27 July 1933–as the narrative present, then sets off on an exploration of the past from the beginning of the thirteenth century to the early 1930s without directly referring to any historical events. No explanations are given, no transitions are provided, no continuing thread connects the individual episodes. A barrage of images, highly sophisticated reflections, profound philosophical speculations, and paradoxical observations leave the reader in a constant state of disorientation. Gütersloh's prose makes no concessions.

The story is told in the first paragraph: Count Lunarin inherits a decrepit old castle from his uncle, Baron Enguerrand, who wanted to force the wandering Lunarin into a more stable life; but Lunarin returns, falls in love with his old girlfriend Bettina, and leaves again, appointing the farmer Adelseher caretaker. Adelseher renovates the castle in Lunarin's absence. After a year Lunarin returns again and presents the castle to Adelseher as a gift but leaves with the caretaker's lover, Melitta. In the course of the novel other characters–there are fifty in all–are introduced and disappear again with an abruptness and arbitrariness rarely found in even the most modern experimental fiction. The central issue in the allegorical novel is the decline of the Austrian monarchy and the rise of the Republic: the question of whether political authority should be based on birth or on ability underlies many of the seemingly unconnected events. Gütersloh is skeptical of the notion of a political system based on democratic consensus and technological progress.

The critics responded to the novel with great admiration for the author's supreme command of language and an equally strong resistance to his complete neglect of narrative structure. The poet Helmut Heißenbuttel, in *Albert Paris Gütersloh: Autor und Werk,* sees the novel as a "radically phenomenological description of man through an intricately allegorical ambiguity." Friedrich Knilli calls Gütersloh's auctorial interruptions "a poetizing desire to transform what could be easily understood into complex, hard-to-understand situations, to change simplicity into universality, and to add superfluous elements to necessities." For Claus Pack the novel consists of "the most circumstantial excesses and digressions ever committed with loving persistence by any author writing in the German language." Replying to his critics, Gütersloh said that it seemed more important to him to show the unfathomable swamp through which we all wade than to point at the firm ground on which we think we stand. Accuracy of detail and depth of insight were more important to Gütersloh than continuity of action and development of character.

Albert Paris Gütersloh played a significant role in the development of twentieth-century Austrian painting and literature as a mentor, guide, and catalyst. In his own creative work he stands out as an innovator, a master of precision in observation, a complex and profound thinker, and one of the most eloquent and erudite critics of the modern rationalistic, materialistic worldview.

Letters:

Briefe an Milena (1932-1970), edited by Reinhard Tötschinger (St. Pölten: Niederösterreichisches Pressehaus, 1980).

Bibliographies:

Hans F. Prokop, "Albert Paris Gütersloh: Bibliographie," *Literatur und Kritik,* 68 (1972): 483-492;

Michael Bielefeld, "Bibliographie zu Albert Paris Gütersloh," in *Kritisches Lexikon zur deutschsprachigen Literatur,* edited by Heinz Ludwig Arnold (Munich: Edition text + kritik, 1978), n.pag.

References:

Kurt Adel, "Güterslohs 'Fabel von der Freundschaft' und die Tradition," *Literatur und Kritik,* 45 (1970): 307-309;

Albert Paris Gütersloh: Autor und Werk (Munich: Piper, 1962);

Ernst Alker, "Albert Paris Gütersloh: Sonne und Mond, Autor und Werk," *Universitas,* 18, no. 11 (1963): 1229-1243;

Otto Basil, "Panorama vom Untergang Kakaniens," *Wort in der Zeit*, 7 (1961): 40-52;

Ludovici Batavia, "Der Roman, der sich selbst liest: Anmerkungen zu Albert Paris Gütersloh," *Die Diagonale*, 1 (1966): 43-47;

Otto F. Beer, "Die letzte große Barockfigur Österreichs: Albert Paris Gütersloh," *Die Zeit*, 25 May 1973;

Henryk Bereza, "Zur polnischen Ausgabe von 'Sonne und Mond,'" *Literatur und Kritik*, 21 (1968): 48-52;

Gunther Bien, "Von Kunst also keine Rede? Zu A. P. Gütersloh, 'Sonne und Mond,'" *text + kritik*, 6 (1964): 25;

Robert Blauhut, "Albert Paris Gütersloh," in his *Österreichische Novellistik des 20. Jahrhunderts* (Vienna & Stuttgart: Braumüller, 1966), pp. 230-236;

Franz Blei, "Kleine Rede auf Gütersloh (1937)," *Agathon*, 47 (1946): 67-73;

Blei, "Paris Gütersloh (zur Malerei)," *Ararat*, 2 (1921): 229-230;

Heimito von Doderer, *Der Fall Gütersloh: Ein Schicksal und seine Bedeutung* (Vienna: Haybach, 1930);

Doderer, "Eine sagenhafte Figur," *magnum*, 12 (1957): 81-82;

Alfred Focke, "Versuch über A. P. Güterslohs Materiologie," *Literatur und Kritik*, 68 (1972): 466-472;

Hans Jürgen Fröhlich, "Albert Paris Gütersloh: 5. Februar in Wien, 16. Mai 1973 in Wien," *Jahresring*, 73-75 (1974): 193-276;

Ernst Fuchs, "Über Gütersloh," *Literatur und Kritik*, 68 (1972): 480-482;

Edwin Hartl, "Gütersloh–den gibt es wirklich," *Wort in der Zeit*, 3 (1963): 36-39;

Heribert Hutter, *Albert Paris Gütersloh* (Vienna: Rosenbaum, 1977);

Friedrich Knilli, "Der Umweg als kürzester Weg," in his *Sprache im technischen Zeitalter* (Stuttgart: Kohlhammer, 1963), pp. 577-580;

Peter Pabisch and Alan Best, "The 'Total Novel': Heimito von Doderer and Albert Paris Gütersloh," in *Modern Austrian Writing*, edited by Best and Hans Wolfschütz (London: Wolff, 1980), pp. 63-78;

Claus Pack, "Paris von Gütersloh," *Die Aktion*, 4, no. 26 (1914): 1229-1230;

Pack, "Parturiunt montes," *Wort und Wahrheit*, 4 (1963): 226-228;

Heinz Rieder, "A. P. Gütersloh, 'Sonne und Mond,'" *Neue deutsche Hefte*, 10 (1964): 133-139;

Rieder, "Jenseits des Romans: Albert Paris Güterslohs 'Sonne und Mond,'" in his *Österreichische Moderne* (Bonn: Bouvier, 1968), pp. 109-117;

Hannes Rieser, "Doderer und Gütersloh: Metaphorik und 'totaler' Roman," Ph.D. dissertation, University of Salzburg, 1968;

Wendelin Schmidt-Dengler, "Die Anfänge des 'Falles Gütersloh,'" *Literatur und Kritik*, 68 (1972): 473-479;

Felix Thurner, *Albert Paris Gütersloh: Studien zu seinem Romanwerk* (Bern: Lang, 1970).

Enrica von Handel-Mazzetti
(10 January 1871-8 April 1955)

Josef Schmidt
McGill University

BOOKS: *Nicht umsonst: Ein Schauspiel in fünf Aufzügen* (Vienna: Norbertus, 1892);

Pegasus im Joch oder Die verwunschenen Telegramme (Vienna: Kirsch, 1895);

In terra pax hominibus bonae voluntatis! Ein Weihnachtsspiel in 3 Aufzügen (Essen: Fredebeul & Koenen, 1899);

Ich kauf' ein Mohrenkind: Ein Weihnachtsspiel in vier Szenen (Berlin: Mecklenburg, 1899);

Die wiedereröffnete Himmelsthür: Ein Osterspiel in 2 Scenen (Essen: Fredebeul & Koenen, 1900);

Meinrad Helmpergers denkwürdiges Jahr: Eine Erzählung (Munich: Allgemeine Verlagsgesellschaft, 1900);

Der König der Glorie: Eine Kommunionerzählung (Limburg: Limburger Vereinsdruckerei, 1901);

Kleine Opfer (Vienna: Buchhandlung des katholischen Schulvereines für Österreich, 1901);

Prinzessin Herzlieb (Limburg: Limburger Vereinsdruck, 1902);

Der Verräter; Fahrlässig getötet (Stuttgart & Munich: Roth, 1902);

Erzählungen I und II, 2 volumes (Neu-Weißensee: Dieter, 1903)–volume 1 comprises "Des braven Fiakers Osterfreude" and "Der Stangelberger Poldi"; volume 2 comprises "'s Engerl" and "Dora";

Ich mag ihn nicht: Eine Erzählung für die Jugend (Neu-Weißensee: Dieter, 1903);

Novellen (Neu-Weißensee: Dieter, 1904);

Als die Franzosen in St. Pölten waren: Eine Klostergeschichte (Neu-Weißensee: Dieter, 1904);

Skizzen aus Österreich: Artstettin, Lambach, Oberkrainerisches (Neu-Weißensee: Dieter, 1904);

Der letzte Wille des Herrn Egler (Neu-Weißensee: Dieter, 1904);

Vom König, den Dracheneiern und der Prinzessin (Munich: Münchener Volksschriftenverlag, 1906);

Jesse und Maria: Ein Roman aus dem Donaulande, 2 volumes (Kempten: Kösel, 1906); translated by George N. Shuster as *Jesse and Maria* (New York: Holt, 1931);

Bildarchiv der Österreichischen Nationalbibliothek

Novellen (Graz: Styria, 1907);

Deutsches Recht: Ein Volkssang aus Stadt Stehr (Kempten: Kösel, 1908); enlarged as *Deutsches Recht und andere Gedichte* (Kempten: Kösel, 1908);

Historische Novellen (Kevelaer: Butzon & Bercker, 1908);

Erzählungen und Skizzen, edited by Johannes Ekkardt (Kevelaer: Thum, 1909);

Sophie Barat: Ein Gedenkblatt zu ihrer Seligsprechungsfeier (Ravensburg: Alber, 1910);

Die arme Margaret: Ein Volksroman aus dem alten Steyr (Kempten: Kösel, 1910);

Imperatori: Fünf Kaiserlieder (Kempten: Kösel, 1910);

Geistige Werdejahre: Dramen, Schwänke und religiöse Spiele aus ihrer literarischen Entwicklungszeit, edited by Eckardt (Ravensburg: Alber, 1911);

Geistige Werdejahre: Neue Folge. Historische Dramen, religiöse Spiele, epische Dichtungen, edited by Ekkardt (Ravensburg: Alber, 1912);

Geschichten: Einige ernste und viele lustige (Klagenfurt: Carinthia, 1912);

Weihnachts- und Krippenspiele, edited by Johann Ranftl (Berlin: Mecklenburg, 1912);

Als unsere großen Dichterinnen noch kleine Mädchen waren (Leipzig: Walther, 1912);

Stephana Schwertner: Ein Steyrer Roman, 3 volumes (Kempten & Munich: Kösel, 1912-1914);

Napoleon II (nach Victor Hugo) und andere Dichtungen, edited by Ranftl (Berlin: Mecklenburg, 1912);

Brüderlein und Schwesterlein: Ein Wiener Roman (Kempten: Kösel, 1913);

Gebet um Beendigung des Völkerkrieges (Salzburg: Lovenz, 1914);

Ritas Briefe, 5 volumes (Saarlouis: Hausen, 1915-1921);

Friedensgebet (Kempten: Kösel & Pustet, 1915);

Die Liebe ist stärker als der Tod: Novelle, bound with Therese Rak, *Fäden der Liebe: Roman* (Neumarkt: Voegl, 1916);

Der Blumenteufel: Bilder aus dem Reservespital Staatsgymnasium in Linz, as Marienkind (Gladbach: Volksvereins-Verlag, 1916);

Unter dem österreichischen Roten Kreuz: Dornbekränztes Heldentum (Regensburg: Kösel & Pustet, 1917);

Ilko Smutniak, der Ulan: Der Roman eines Ruthenen (Kempten: Kösel & Pustet, 1917);

Briefe über einen deutschen Roman (Kempten: Kösel & Pustet, 1917);

Der deutsche Held (Kempten: Kösel & Pustet, 1920); republished as *Karl von Aspern, Österreichs Held* (Linz: Muck, 1953);

Ritas Vermächtnis: Roman (Hochdorf, Switzerland: Verlagsanstalt Buchdruckerei Hochdorf, 1922);

Caritas; Die schönsten Erzählungen: Ein deutsches Jugend- und Volksbuch (Stuttgart: Thienemann, 1922);

Des Christen Wunderschau in der heiligen Nacht: Ein Weihnachtsspiel in 3 Szenen (Berlin: Mecklenburg, 1922);

Das Rosenwunder: Ein deutscher Roman (Kempten & Munich: Kösel & Pustet, 1924);

Deutsche Passion: Ein deutscher Roman (Kempten & Munich: Kösel & Pustet, 1925);

Das Blutzeugnis: Ein deutscher Roman (Kempten & Munich: Kösel & Pustet, 1926);

Seine Tochter (Elberfeld: Bergland, 1926);

Johann Christian Günther (Munich: Kösel & Pustet, 1927);

Frau Maria: Ein Roman aus der Zeit August des Starken, 3 volumes (Munich: Kösel & Pustet, 1929-1931);

Weg in den Herbst (Zurich, Leipzig & Vienna: Amalthea, 1931);

Die Heimat meiner Kunst (Regensburg: Pustet, 1933; enlarged edition, Saarlouis: Hausen, 1934);

Die Waxenbergerin: Ein Roman aus dem Kampfjahr 1683 (Munich: Kösel & Pustet, 1934);

Christiana Kotzebue: Novelle (Paderborn: Schöningh, 1934);

An alle Freunde meiner Kunst: 10. Jänner und 16. Juli 1936 (Linz: Landesarchiv, 1936);

Der edle Baum von Ried (Linz: Published by the author, 1937);

Das heilige Licht: Mein Dank an den mexikanischen Märtyrer P. Miguel Pro (Vienna: Mayer, 1938);

Graf Reichard, der Held vom eisernen Tor: Roman aus dem deutschen Siegesjahr 1691 (Munich: Kösel & Pustet, 1939);

Im stillen Linz (Munich: Kösel & Pustet, 1940);

Der Stangelberger Poldi; Adalbert Stifter: Ein Gang durch die Katakomben Wiens (Vienna: Bernina, 1947);

Günther, der Schlesier (Stuttgart: Brentano, 1949);

Graf Reichard; Held und Heiliger: Roman aus deutschen Siegesjahr 1691 (Vienna: Bernina, 1950);

Renata von Natzmer: Eine Paralleldichtung zu Schillers "Kindsmörderin" (Linz: Kling, 1951);

... Und nie geschah mir das: Die Einleitung zum Romanfragment "Günthers Tod," edited by Kurt Vancsa (Graz: Styria, 1958);

Ein großes Ding ist die Liebe: Magna res est caritas, edited by Vancsa (Graz: Stiasny, 1958).

OTHER: Leopold Arthofer, *Zuchthaus: Aufzeichnungen des Seelsorgers einer Strafanstalt*, edited by Handel-Mazzetti (Munich: Kösel & Pustet, 1932).

Handel-Mazzetti in younger years

Baroness Enrica von Handel-Mazzetti would be a forgotten author of pious historical works had not her novel *Jesse und Maria* (1906; translated as *Jesse and Maria*, 1931) become the focal point in the bitter fight between Integralists and Anti-Modernists, the two camps that dominated political and cultural life in the Catholic regions of the German-speaking countries in the early twentieth century. Handel-Mazzetti tried to steer a middle course between the two movements. Her neoromantic historical novels, dealing with confessional war and reconciliation, marked an important stage in the reintegration of Catholic writers into mainstream German literature, from which the Kulturkampf (conflict between the state and the Catholic church) of 1872 to 1878 had excluded them. Handel-Mazzetti was a popular and respected writer who helped open lines of communication by advocating tolerance.

Handel-Mazzetti was the second child of Irene Cshergeö von Handel-Mazzetti, the widow of Heinrich von Handel-Mazzetti, a captain in the Austro-Hungarian army who died four months before Enrica was born. The parents' families were representative of the ethnic mix of the Austro-Hungarian Empire. The maternal grandmother was a pious Protestant of Dutch origin, while the maternal grandfather was a Hungarian civil servant and a Catholic who believed in the liberal ideas of Joseph II. The paternal grandmother came from a family of Italian civil servants, while the grandfather was a member of the general staff of the Austrian army. Handel-Mazzetti grew up in Vienna, attended the Institut der Englischen Fräulein in St. Pölten in 1886-1887, then returned to Vienna to care for her mother, who died in 1901. After living with an uncle in Steyr from 1905 to 1911, she spent the rest of her life in Linz. She was a popular writer until after World War I, when she became a venerated symbol of a past era.

Handel-Mazzetti was a moderately successful author of pious stories for Catholic magazines and of devotional plays when she attracted the attention of two powerful publications. The Catholic magazine *Die christliche Familie* serialized her *Meinrad Helmpergers denkwürdiges Jahr* (Meinrad Helmperger's Memorable Year; published in book form, 1900) from 1897 to 1899 and her *Brüderlein und Schwesterlein: Ein Wiener Roman* (Brother and Sister: A Viennese Novel; published in book form, 1913) in 1902-1903. The latter, a story about the social conventions that should be observed when a young girl from a good family is married, provided a lively picture of upper- and middle-class Viennese society, with an array of scheming villains and a heroine who preserves her virtue in the midst of moral and religious conflict. In 1905-1906 Carl Muth published *Jesse und Maria* in *Hochland*, a journal that played a leading role in encouraging Catholic writers to join mainstream literature and in developing a discriminating taste among educated Catholics for good literature. These two works were the first of a series of successful historical novels based on actual episodes during the Counter-Reformation in Austria. Handel-Mazzetti did extensive research for the novels; the authentic tone of her dialogue was considered one of the best features of her fiction. Her novels and stories appealed to an audience that enjoyed her folkloristic and thoroughly conservative depictions of society. The writer Peter Rosegger was an early admirer of her writing, and her innovative use of archival materials for authenticity won her the respect of other established writers, such as Marie von Ebner-Eschenbach. It was *Jesse und Maria*, however, that

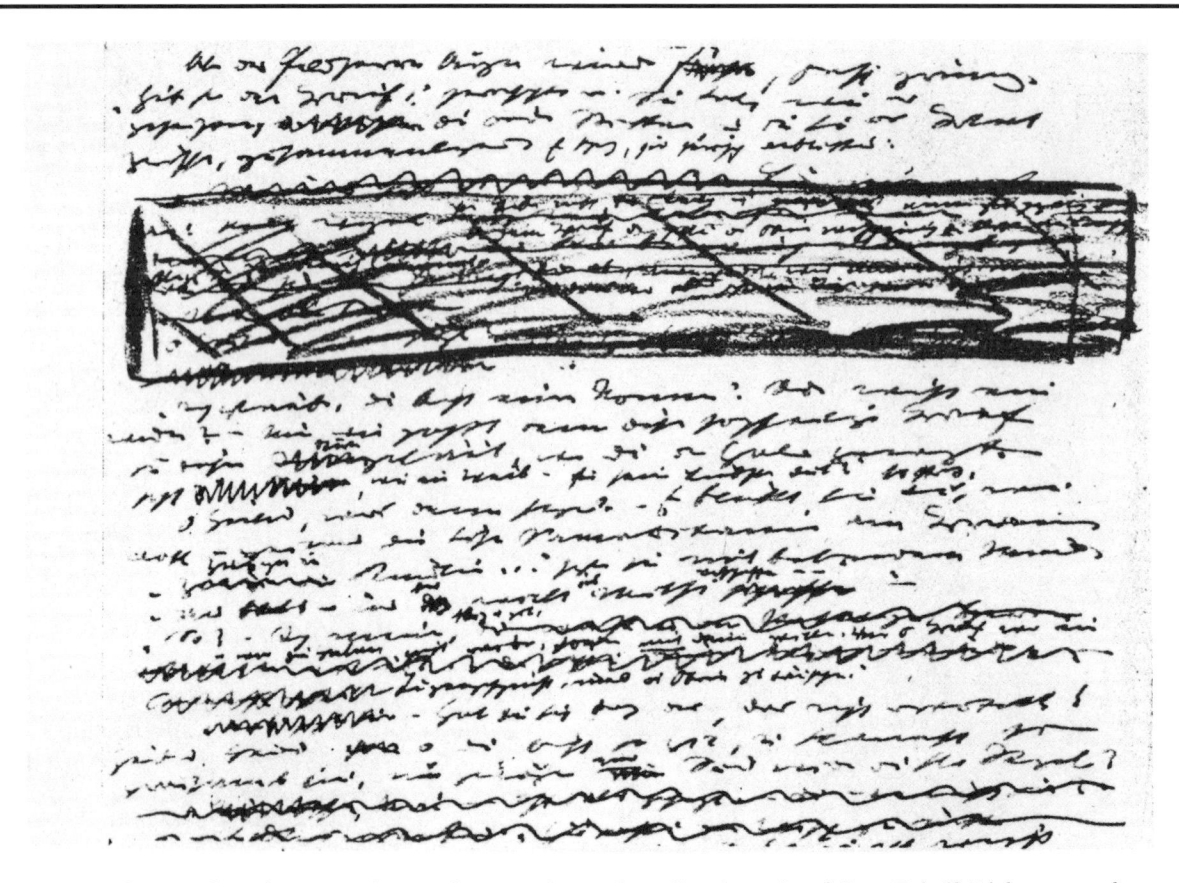

Part of a page from the manuscript for Die Waxenbergerin *(Albert Soergel and Curt Hohoff,* Dichtung und Dichter der Zeit, *1961)*

propelled her from mere success to prominence, for it became the battleground of the controversy between the liberals around Muth and the conservative Anti-Modernists such as Richard von Kralik and the Swiss theologian Caspar Decurtins. The latter made Handel-Mazzetti the prime example of what was wrong in ignoring "les principes catholiques" and condemned the false realism, sensuality, and pseudoreligiosity of *Jesse und Maria* in two articles in the *Monatsschrift für christliche Sozialreform* in 1909 and 1910. Decurtins was particularly incensed by the praise she had won from the leading Modernist religious historian of France, Henri Bremond.

Jesse und Maria has lost much of its appeal for the modern reader. The Catholic forester Schinnagel comes under the influence of a liberal Lutheran nobleman, Jesse von Velderndorffer, who wants Schinnagel to hand over a votive table of St. Mary. The object is to be destroyed because, for the Lutheran, it is the epitome of Catholic superstition. Schinnagel's wife Maria defeats the plan by procuring money and ending her husband's financial dependence on the nobleman. Velderndorffer, who has been denounced by Maria before a church official, is challenged by an inquisitorial commission, acts imprudently, and is beheaded. Maria recognizes that her fanatical religious zeal is sinful and engages in an act of repentance. There is a wide range of minor characters. Handel-Mazzetti uses a neoromantic style borrowed from German writers who used Sir Walter Scott as a model.

Handel-Mazzetti's next successful novel, *Die arme Margaret* (Poor Margaret, 1910), was serialized in the Berlin literary magazine *Deutsche Rundschau*, thus reaching a broad readership for a clearly sectarian work. *Die arme Margaret* is the story of a poor widow who successfully resists the sexual advances of an Austrian army officer and, through her exemplary persistence, converts the whole region back to true Christianity. Conservatives were irked by her sympathetic depiction of Protestants and her inclusion of unattractive features in the portrayal of figures adhering to the "right" faith. The controversy became so intense that Handel-Mazzetti felt obliged to publish a declaration of orthodoxy in the *Allgemeine Rundschau* and many other publications in September 1910.

Handel-Mazzetti

During World War I Handel-Mazzetti visited wounded soldiers in the Linz hospital and published an enormous body of ephemeral patriotic stories, poems, and reflections. She also began detailing the development of Rita, the heroine of *Brüderlein und Schwesterlein,* in a series of novels set in modern times and addressed to an adolescent audience: the five-volume *Ritas Briefe* (Rita's Letters, 1915-1921) and *Ritas Vermächtnis* (Rita's Legacy, 1922). She also returned to the genre of the historical novel: *Der deutsche Held* (The German Hero, 1920) shows the young nobleman Tessenburg as an unworthy hero during the Napoleonic Wars; *Das Rosenwunder* (The Miracle of the Roses, 1924) is a romantic tale of the idealistic revolutionary Karl Ludwig Sand, who assassinated the reactionary playwright and spy August von Kotzebue in 1819; her portrayal in *Johann Christian Günther* (1927) of the baroque poet who died in 1723 suffers from overbearing sentimental descriptions which tone down the robust eroticism of the historical figure. In her later years she became extremely verbose, as can be seen in the trilogy *Frau Maria* (1929-1931). *Graf Reichard der Held vom eisernen Tor* (Count Reichard, the Hero of the Iron Gate, 1939) is an interminable tale of Vienna's crusade against the Turks in the late seventeenth century. An exception to this series of tedious works is *Die Waxenbergerin* (The Woman of Waxenberg, 1934), written to commemorate the 250th anniversary of the great Turkish defeat of 1683. The heroine, a servant who eventually becomes a nun, is painted in fresh and lively colors in a novel that blends history with a picturesque folkloristic background.

She became a firm part of the Catholic literary establishment. There were attempts to nominate her for the Nobel Prize, and even her former enemy Kralik compared her favorably to such "chroniclers of degeneration" as Thomas Mann. Her works were banned by the Nazis.

Until her death a decade after World War II Handel-Mazzetti played the role of the tolerant conservative writer. She once admitted to Ebner-Eschenbach: "Mir liegt, glaube ich, das Moderne nicht" (I think modernity is not for me). She returned a few times to her successful historical formula but never won a new audience; she had become a supplier of thinly veiled devout educational reading material for the "Christian family." She was neither a major writer nor a genius; her merit lies in her opening the doors of religiously segregated literature for the benefit of future writers and audiences. She was a pioneer against her will. An important reason for her return to obscurity is that during her life a host of Austrian writers, including Franz Werfel and Stefan Zweig, elevated her primary genre, the historical novel, to levels of brilliance that she could not remotely attain. But she opened the way for Catholic writers of a more innovative disposition than hers, such as Gertrud von Le Fort, Reinhold Schneider, and Edzard Schaper.

References:

Franz Berger and Kurt Vancza, eds., *Enrica von Handel-Mazzetti: Festschrift zur 75-Jahr-Feier. Der großen Dichterin Oberösterreichs gewidmet von der Landeshauptmannschaft in Oberösterreich und der Landeshauptstadt Linz* (Linz: Buchdruckerei der österreichischen Landeshauptmannschaft, 1946);

Joseph E. Bourgeois, "Ecclesiastical Characters in the Novels of Enrica Handel-Mazzetti," Ph.D. dissertation, University of Cincinnati, 1956;

Bourgeois, "Enrica von Handel-Mazzetti's Tribute to Schiller," *Monatshefte*, 51 (1939): 313-314;

Caspar Decurtins, "Zweiter und dritter Briefe an einen jungen Freund: Monatsschrift für christliche Sozialreform," 31 (1909): 689-703; 32 (1910): 449-469;

Bernhard Doppler, *Katholische Literatur und Literaturpolitik: Enrica von Handel-Mazzetti, eine Fallstudie* (Königstein: Hain, 1980);

Doppler, "Über das Kunstschaffen der Frau: 'Weiblich'–'männlich' in der katholischen Kulturkritik am Beispiel eines unveröffentlichten Essay von Enrica von Handel-Mazzetti," *Adalbert-Stifter-Institut Vierteljahresschrift*, 35 (1986): 191-211;

Moriz Enzinger, "Enrica v. Handel-Mazzetti Gedächtnisschrift zu ihrem 100. Geburtstag," *Adalbert Stifter-Institut Vierteljahreschrift*, 20 (1971): 9-55;

Alcuin Hemmen, "The Concept of Religious Tolerance in the Novels of Enrica von Handel-Mazzetti," Ph.D. dissertation, University of Michigan, 1945;

Eduard Korrodi, *Enrica von Handel-Mazzetti: Die Persönlichkeit und ihr Dichtwerk* (Münster: Alphonsus, 1909);

Paul Siebertz and others, eds., *Enrica von Handel-Mazzettis Persönlichkeit, Werk und Bedeutung* (Munich: Kösel & Pustet, 1930).

Papers:

The Enrica von Handel-Mazzetti Archive of the Adalbert Stifter Institute of Upper Austria, Linz, contains Handel-Mazzetti's papers and personal library.

Hugo von Hofmannsthal

(1 February 1874-15 July 1929)

Jens Rieckmann
University of Washington

BOOKS: *Gestern: Studie in einem Akt, in Reimen,* as Theophil Morren (Vienna: Verlag der "Modernen Rundschau," 1891);

Die Frau im Fenster; Die Hochzeit der Sobeide; Der Abenteurer und die Sängerin: Theater in Versen (Berlin: Fischer, 1899); *Die Hochzeit der Sobeide* translated by Bayard Quincy Morgan as *The Marriage of Sobeide* in *The German Classics of the Nineteenth and Twentieth Centuries,* edited by Kuno Francke and William G. Howard, volume 20 (New York: German Publishing Society, 1914), pp. 234-288;

Der Kaiser und die Hexe (Berlin: Insel, 1900);

Der Thor und der Tod (Berlin: Insel, 1900); translated by Max Blatt as *Death and the Fool* (Boston: Badger, 1913);

Der Tod des Tizian: Ein dramatisches Fragment (Berlin: Insel, 1901); translated by John Heard as *The Death of Titian* (Boston: Four Seas, 1914);

Studie uber die Entwicklung des Dichters Victor Hugo (Vienna: Verlag von Dr. Hugo von Hofmannsthal, 1901); republished as *Victor Hugo* (Berlin: Schuster & Loeffler, 1904); republished as *Versuch über Victor Hugo* (Munich: Bremer Presse, 1925);

Ausgewählte Gedichte (Berlin: Verlag der Blätter für die Kunst, 1903);

Das kleine Welttheater oder Die Glücklichen (Leipzig: Insel, 1903); translated by Walter Rather Eberlein as *The Little Theater of the World* (Aurora, N.Y.: Printed by Victor & Jacob Hammer, 1945);

Elektra: Tragödie in einem Aufzug frei nach Sophokles (Berlin: Fischer, 1904); translated by Arthur Symons as *Electra: A Tragedy in One Act* (New York: Brentano's, 1908);

Unterhaltungen über literarische Gegenstände, edited by Georg Brandes (Berlin: Bard, Marquardt, 1904);

Das gerettete Venedig: Trauerspiel in funf Aufzügen (Berlin: Fischer, 1905); translated by Elisabeth Walker as *Venice Preserved: A Tragedy in Five Acts* (Boston: Badger, 1915);

Das Märchen der 672. Nacht und andere Erzählungen (Vienna & Leipzig: Wiener Verlag, 1905)—comprises "Das Märchen der 672. Nacht," "Reitergeschichte," "Erlebnis des Marschalls von Bassompierre," "Ein Brief"; "Das Märchen der 672. Nacht" partially translated by Alan D. Trethewey as "Tale of the Merchant's Son and His Servants" in his *The Lion Rampant* (Cambridge, Mass., 1969); "Reitergeschichte" translated by Basil Creighton as "Cavalry Patrol" in *Tellers of Tales,* edi-

Hugo von Hofmannsthal

ted by W. Somerset Maugham (New York: Doubleday, Doran, 1939), pp. 860-867; "Ein Brief" translated by Francis C. Golffing as "The Letter," *Rocky Mountain Review*, 6, no. 3/4 (1942): 1, 3, 11-13;

Ödipus und die Sphinx: Tragödie in fünf Aufzügen (Berlin: Fischer, 1906); translated by Gertrude Schoenbohm as *Oedipus and the Sphinx* in *Oedipus: Myth and Drama*, edited by Martin Kalisch and others (New York: Odyssey, 1968);

Kleine Dramen, 2 volumes (Leipzig: Insel, 1906-1907)–comprises in volume 1 *Gestern, Der Tor und der Tod, Der weiße Fächer;* in volume 2 *Das Bergwerk zu Falun, Der Kaiser und die Hexe, Das kleine Welttheater; Der weiße Fächer* partially translated by Maurice Magnus as *The White Fan, Mask: The Journal of the Art of the Theater* (Florence), 1 (February 1909): 232-234;

Die gesammelten Gedichte (Leipzig: Insel, 1907); translated by Charles Wharton Stork as *The Lyrical Poems of Hugo von Hofmannsthal* (New Haven: Yale University Press/London: Milford, 1918);

Die prosaischen Schriften gesammelt, 5 volumes (Berlin: Fischer, 1907);

Vorspiele (Leipzig: Insel, 1908);

Hesperus: Ein Jahrbuch, by Hofmannsthal, Rudolf Alexander Schröder, and Rudolf Borchardt (Leipzig: Insel, 1909);

Cristinas Heimreise: Komödie (Berlin: Fischer, 1910; revised, 1910); translated by Roy Temple House as *Cristina's Journey Home: A Comedy in Three Acts* (Boston: Badger, 1917); German version revised as *Florindo* (Vienna & Hellerau: Avalun, 1923);

Jedermann: Das Spiel vom Sterben des reichen Mannes erneuert (Berlin: Fischer, 1911); edited by Margaret Jacobs (London & Edinburgh: Nelson, 1957); translated by M. E. Tafler as *The Salzburg Everyman: The Play of the Rich Man's Death* (Salzburg: Mora, 1911);

Grete Wiesenthal in Amor und Psyche und Das fremde Mädchen: Szenen (Berlin: Fischer, 1911);

Alkestis: Ein Trauerspiel nach Euripides (Leipzig: Insel, 1911);

Der Rosenkavalier: Komödie für Musik, music by Richard Strauss (Berlin: Fischer, 1911); translated by Kalisch as *The Rose-Bearer* (Berlin & Paris: Fürstner, 1912);

Die Gedichte und kleinen Dramen (Leipzig: Insel, 1911);

Hofmannsthal in 1891, when he was a student at the Akademisches Gymnasium

Ariadne auf Naxos: Oper in einem Aufzuge nebst einem Vorspiel, music by Strauss (Berlin & Paris: Fürstner, 1912); translated by Kalisch as *Ariadne on Naxos: Opera in One Act, with a Prelude* (New York: Boosey & Hawkes, 1924);

Die Wege und die Begegnungen (Bremen: Bremer Presse, 1913);

Josephslegende, by Hofmannsthal and Harry Graf Kessler, music by Strauss (Berlin: Fürstner, 1914); translated by Kalisch as *The Legend of Joseph* (Berlin & Paris: Fürstner, 1914);

Prinz Eugen der edle Ritter: Sein Leben in Bildern, lithographs by Franz Wacik (Vienna: Seidel, 1915);

Der Bürger als Edelmann: Komödie mit Tänzen von Molière. Freie Bühnenarbeitung in drei Aufzügen, music by Strauss (Berlin: Fürstner, 1918);

Rodauner Nachträge, 3 volumes (Vienna: Amalthea, 1918);

Lucidor: Figuren zu einer ungeschriebenen Komödie (Berlin: Reiss, 1919); translated by Kenneth Burke as "Lucidor: Characters for an Unwritten Comedy," *Dial*, 73, no. 2 (1922): 121-132;

Die Frau ohne Schatten: Oper in drei Akten, music by Strauss (Berlin: Fürstner, 1919; London: Boosey & Hawkes, 1964); translated as *The Woman without a Shadow* (London: Decca Records, 1957);

Die Frau ohne Schatten: Erzählung (Berlin: Fischer, 1919);

Der Schwierige: Lustspiel in drei Akten (Berlin: Fischer, 1921); edited by W. E. Yates (Cambridge: University Press, 1966);

Reden und Aufsätze (Leipzig: Insel, 1921);

Gedichte (Leipzig: Insel, 1922);

Das Salzburger große Welttheater (Leipzig: Insel, 1922);

Buch der Freunde (Leipzig: Insel, 1922); enlarged as *Buch der Freunde: Tagebuch-Aufzeichnungen* (Leipzig: Insel, 1929);

Die grüne Flöte: Ballettpantomime, music by Wolfgang Amadeus Mozart (Vienna & Leipzig: Universal-Edition, 1923);

Augenblicke in Griechenland (Regensburg & Leipzig: Habbel & Naumann, 1924);

Der Turm: Ein Trauerspiel in fünf Aufzügen (Munich: Bremer Presse, 1925; revised edition, Berlin: Fischer, 1927);

Die Ruinen von Athen: Ein Festspiel mit Tänzen und Chören, music by Strauss (Berlin: Fürstner, 1925);

Gedichte (Vienna: Johannes-Presse, 1925);

Szenischer Prolog zur Neueröffnung des Josefstädtertheaters (Vienna: Johannes-Presse, 1926);

Früheste Prosastücke (Leipzig: Gesellschaft der Freunde der Deutschen Bücherei, 1926);

Das Schrifttum als geistiger Raum der Nation (Munich: Bremer Presse, 1927);

Drei Erzählungen (Leipzig: Insel, 1927);

Die ägyptische Helena: Oper in zwei Aufzügen, music by Strauss (Berlin: Fürstner, 1928); translated by Kalisch as *Helen in Egypt* (Berlin: Fürstner/New York: Ricordi, 1928);

Loris: Die Prosa des jungen Hugo von Hofmannsthal (Berlin: Fischer, 1930);

Die Berührung der Sphären (Berlin: Fischer, 1931);

Wege und Begegnungen (Leipzig: Reclam, 1931);

Fragment eines Romans (Munich: Privately printed, 1931); enlarged as *Andreas oder Die Vereinigten: Fragmente eines Romanes* (Berlin: Fischer, 1932); translated by Marie D. Hottinger as *Andreas; or, The United: Being Fragments of a Novel* (London: Dent, 1936);

Arabella: Lyrische Komödie, music by Strauss (Berlin: Fürstner, 1933); translated by John Gutman as *Arabella: A Lyrical Comedy in Three Acts* (New York: Boosey & Hawkes, 1955; London: Boosey & Hawkes, 1965);

Semiramis; Die beiden Götter (Munich: Rupprechtpresse, 1933);

Prolog zur Feier von Goethes 50. Geburtstag am Burgtheater zu Wien (Vienna: Officina Vindobonensis, 1934);

Nachlese der Gedichte (Berlin: Fischer, 1934);

Dramatische Entwürfe aus dem Nachlaß (Vienna: Johannes-Presse, 1936);

Beethoven: Rede gehalten an der Beethovenfeier des Lesezirkels Hottingen in Zürich am 10. Dez. 1920, edited by Willi Schuh (Vienna: Reichner, 1938);

Festspiele in Salzburg (Vienna: Bermann-Fischer, 1938);

Gesammelte Werke in Einzelausgaben, edited by Herbert Steiner, 15 volumes (Frankfurt am Main & Stockholm: Fischer, 1945-1959); re-edited by Bernd Schoeller and Rudolf Hirsch as *Gesammelte Werke in zehn Einzelbänden,* 10 volumes (Frankfurt am Main: Fischer, 1979);

Das Theater des Neuen: Eine Ankündigung (Vienna: Edition Komödie in Bindenschildverlag, 1947);

Dem Gedächtnis des Dichters Theodor Storm, in der Handschrift des Dichters, edited by Lothar Hempe (Stuttgart: Hempe, 1951);

Aus dem Jugendwerk Hugo von Hofmannsthal (Loris), edited by Emmy Rosenfeld (Pavia: Editrice viscontia, 1951);

Danae oder Die Vernunftheirat: Szenarium und Notizen, edited by Schuh (Frankfurt am Main: Fischer, 1952);

Selected Writings, volume 1: *Selected Prose,* translated by Mary Hottinger and Tania and James Stern (London: Routledge & Kegan Paul, 1952); volume 2: *Poems and Verse Plays: Bilingual Edition,* edited by Michael Hamburger, translated by John Bednall, Arthur Davidson, and others (London: Routledge & Kegan Paul, 1961; New York: Pantheon, 1961); volume 3: *Selected Plays and Libretti,* edited by Hamburger (New York: Pantheon, 1963; London: Routledge & Kegan Paul, 1964);

Selected Essays, edited by Mary E. Gilbert (Oxford: Blackwell, 1955);

Österreichische Aufsätze und Reden, edited by Helmut A. Fiechtner (Vienna: Bergland, 1956);

Natur und Erkenntnis: Essays (Berlin: Deutsche Buch-Gemeinschaft, 1957);

Hofmannsthal in his Austrian army uniform, 1894. He served one year of active duty, stationed in Moravia.

Ausgewählte Werke, edited by Hirsch, 2 volumes (Berlin & Frankfurt am Main: Fischer, 1957);

Komödie (Graz & Vienna: Stiasny, 1960);

Three Plays, translated by Alfred Schwarz (Detroit: Wayne State University Press, 1966)—comprises *Death and the Fool, Electra, The Tower;*

Four Stories, edited by Jacobs (London: Oxford University Press, 1968);

Das erzählerische Werk (Frankfurt am Main: Fischer, 1969);

Ausgewählte Werke, edited by Eike Middell (Leipzig: Insel, 1975);

Sämtliche Werke: Kritische Ausgabe, edited by Heinz Otto Burger and others, 28 volumes published (Frankfurt am Main: Fischer, 1975-   ).

OTHER: Arthur Schnitzler, *Anatol,* introduction by Hofmannsthal (Berlin: Fischer, 1901); introduction translated by Trevor Blakemore in Schnitzler's *Playing with Love (Liebelei),* translated by P. Morton Shand (London: Gay & Hancock, 1914);

Sophocles, *König Ödipus,* translated by Hofmannsthal (Berlin: Fischer, 1910);

Deutsche Erzähler, edited by Hofmannsthal, 4 volumes (Leipzig: Insel, 1912);

Österreichischer Almanach auf das Jahr 1916, edited by Hofmannsthal (Leipzig: Insel, 1915);

Franz Grillparzer, *Grillparzers politisches Vermächtnis,* edited by Hofmannsthal (Leipzig: Insel, 1915);

Pedro Calderón de la Barca, *Dame Kobold: Lustspiel in drei Aufzügen,* translated by Hofmannsthal (Berlin: Fischer, 1920);

Die Erzählungen aus den Tausendundeinen Nächten, translated by Enno Littmann, introduction by Hofmannsthal, 6 volumes (Leipzig: Insel, 1921-1928);

Griechenland: Baukunst, Landschaft, Volksleben, photographs by Hanns Holdt and others, introduction by Hofmannsthal (Berlin: Wasmuth, 1922); translated by L. Hamilton as *Picturesque Greece: Architecture, Landscape, Life of the People* (New York: Architectural Book Publishing Co., 1922; London: Unwin, 1923);

Deutsches Lesebuch, edited by Hofmannsthal, 2 volumes (Munich: Bremer Presse, 1922-1923; enlarged, 1926);

Deutsche Epigramme, edited by Hofmannsthal (Munich: Bremer Presse, 1923);

Adalbert Stifter, *Der Nachsommer: Eine Erzählung,* afterword by Hofmannsthal (Leipzig: List, 1925);

Johann Christoph Friedrich von Schiller, *Schillers Selbstcharakteristik aus seinen Schriften,* edited by Hofmannsthal (Munich: Bremer Presse, 1926);

Wert und Ehre deutscher Sprache in Zeugnissen, edited by Hofmannsthal (Munich: Bremer Presse, 1927).

Hugo von Hofmannsthal is generally considered the most important Austrian writer of the early twentieth century; among German-speaking writers of this period only Thomas Mann and Franz Kafka have generated more commentary. At the same time, Hofmannsthal's place in the annals of modernism is surrounded by more controversy than are those of Mann and Kafka. Some

Gertrud Schlesinger, whom Hofmannsthal married in 1901

critics think of him as a "genialer Jüngling" (brilliant youth), others belittle him as a "konservativer Ästhet" (conservative aesthete); for some he is a "Götterbote" (messenger of the gods), for others the "Museumsdirektor der Kultur" (director of the museum of culture). He burst onto the literary scene in Vienna in the early 1890s as a precocious and enormously gifted writer of poetry, verse plays, and essays. After 1900 he turned almost exclusively to writing comedies, dramas which were based for the most part on already existing plays, and libretti for operas by Richard Strauss. Those who had seen in the young Hofmannsthal one of the most promising lyric poets ever to have emerged in Austria looked at this shift in interest with misgivings. The German symbolist poet Stefan George, who had published many of Hofmannsthal's poems and verse plays in his esoteric journal *Blätter für die Kunst,* for example, condemned Hofmannsthal's career after 1900 as a betrayal of that early promise, as a development which had led "vom Tempel der Kunst auf die Straße" (out of the temple of art into the street). Even Hermann Bahr, a friend who had been instrumental in propagating the young Hofmannsthal's fame, once remarked facetiously that he could not forgive Hofmannsthal for not having died at the age of twenty.

Thus Hofmannsthal's reputation rests primarily on his poetry, dramas, libretti, and essays. But he also made a significant contribution to modernism with such seminal works of fiction as "Das Märchen der 672. Nacht" (The Fairy Tale of the 672nd Night, 1905; translated as "Tale of the Merchant's Son and His Servants," 1969), "Reitergeschichte" (1905; translated as "Cavalry Patrol," 1939), and, to a lesser extent, "Erlebnis des Marschalls von Bassompierre" (1905; translated as "An Episode in the Life of the Marshal de Bassompierre," 1952), *Die Frau ohne Schatten* (1919; translated as *The Woman without a Shadow,* 1957), and the fragmentary novel *Andreas oder Die Vereinigten* (1932; translated as *Andreas; or, The United,* 1936), written intermittently between 1907 and 1927.

Hugo Laurenz August Hofmann, Edler von Hofmannsthal was born in Vienna on 1 February 1874 to bank director Hugo August von Hofmannsthal and Anna Maria von Hofmannsthal. He entered the Akademisches Gymnasium in Vienna in 1884 after being educated by private tutors. He stood out among his fellow students because of his precocious intellectual achievement, his sensitivity, and his literary ambitions. By the age of eighteen he had read most of the major works of classical, French, English, Russian, Spanish, Italian, and German literature. While still attending the gymnasium he published his first poems; essays on the contemporary writers Paul-Charles-Joseph Bourget, Henri Frédéric Amiel, Maurice Barrès, and Bahr; and the one-act play *Gestern* (Yesterday, 1891). These works appeared under the pseudonyms Loris, Loris Melikow, and Theophil Morren, and it was as Loris that he became famous in the literary circles of Vienna and beyond.

Those who did not know him were convinced that the author of these works must be "zwischen 40 und 50 etwa, in der Reife des Geistes" (approximately between 40 and 50 years

Hofmannsthal in his villa at Rodaun, circa 1904 (Lady Elizabeth von Hofmannsthal and Dr. Rudolf Hirsch)

of age with a mature intellect), as Bahr put it after he read Hofmannsthal's review of his drama *Die Mutter* (The Mother, 1891). What struck Bahr and other Austrian writers, such as Arthur Schnitzler, Richard Beer-Hofmann, and Leopold von Andrian, were the apparent ease of Hofmannsthal's poems and the amazing awareness of the intellectual and cultural problems of his age that informed his essays. Alfred Gold, a fellow student of Hofmannsthal's, best summed up the young Hofmannsthal's image among his contemporaries: "Wenn man vom Hofmannsthal jener frühen Jahre spricht, ist die Gefahr, scheint mir, weniger die, daß man übertreibt, als daß man zu Gewöhnliches von ihm sagt.... Die Wirkung, die von einem Fragment, einem Zeitungsaufsatz von ihm ausging, konnte sich bis zum Magischen steigern" (It seems to me that in talking about the Hofmannsthal of those early years the danger is not so much one of exaggeration as of stating only the all too commonplace.... The resonance which one of his fragments, one of his newspaper essays found could reach magic proportions).

Hofmannsthal thought of himself as the spokesman for his generation. Its consciousness, as he said in an essay on the Italian writer Gabriele d'Annunzio, was represented by a "paar tausend Menschen, in den großen europäischen Städten verstreut" (couple of thousand persons, dispersed in the big European cities). Hofmannsthal identified with this group and discussed its problems in his early essays. His contemporaries agreed with Hofmannsthal's claim that he spoke for his generation: in 1905 he wrote to his friend Edgar Karg von Bebenburg that he had been asked to collect everything "was ich ... vom 16ten bis zum 22ten Jahr gemacht habe" (which I have produced between the ages of 16 and 22) to be published "als das Symbol einer gewissen Generation" (as the symbol of a certain generation).

A leitmotif in these early essays is that of the "Zweiseelenkrankheit" (two-soul sickness) of modern man. In his review of Amiel's *Fragments d'un journal intime* (1883-1884) Hofmannsthal defined modern man as a "Hamletvariation." He saw symptoms of this sickness in his generation's longing for a "verlorene Naivität" (lost naivete), its dilettantism, its oscillation between "Lebensdurst" (thirst for life) and "Lebensangst" (fear of life), its "Abbröckeln des Willens" (crumbling of the will), and its separation of the self into the I "das leidet und [das] Ich, das Leiden zusieht" (which suffers and [the] I which watches itself suffer).

After graduating from the Akademisches Gymnasium in 1892 Hofmannsthal, at the re-

Hofmannsthal in 1929

quest of his father, enrolled as a law student at the University of Vienna. He interrupted his studies in 1894 and served his year of active duty in the Austrian army. Amid the squalor of the small town in Moravia where he was stationed he conceived "Das Märchen der 672. Nacht," which was partly inspired by Andrian's *Der Garten der Erkenntnis* (The Garden of Knowledge, 1895). The story was first published in the newspaper *Die Zeit* in 1895.

Hofmannsthal's beginnings as a writer of fiction can be traced back to 1889, when he wrote what he called a "märchenartiges Feuilleton" (fairy-tale-like feuilleton) titled "Der Geiger von Traunsee" (The Violinist of Traunsee). It is striking that it took Hofmannsthal, who was enormously productive as a lyric poet, essayist, and author of one-act dramas, six years before he proved himself as a writer of fiction with "Das Märchen der 672. Nacht." A look at the "märchenartiges Feuilleton" reveals the reasons for this delay. In this short text, as well as in other fragmentary narratives Hofmannsthal wrote during this period, the lyrical element dominates to such an extent that the narrative element is negligible.

Although Hofmannsthal did not complete a single work of fiction before 1895, his sketches and fragments reveal a progression toward the mastery of narrative form which culminated in "Das Märchen der 672. Nacht." With this work Hofmannsthal realized the ideal he formulated in his diary in 1894: "strenge Ökonomie, suggestive Charakteristik; Bewußtsein des Scheines" (strict economy, suggestive characterization, consciousness of semblance). This ideal, postulated for lyric poetry, he transferred in 1896 to fiction: "Ich glaube, daß ich jetzt wie durch einen Schleier das aufs Wesen gehende Kunstgesetz für die Novelle (oder für eine bestimmte Art der Novelle) ahne, das Kunstgesetz, dessen voller Besitz einem möglich machen muß, eine ganze Prosadichtung durch und durch als Form zu erkennen, wie das lyrische Gedicht" (I believe that I am now beginning to divine as if through a veil the essential law of art for the novella [or for a certain type of novella], the law of art which, possessed completely, must make it possible for one to conceive an entire prose work totally as form, just as the lyric poem).

This consciousness of form manifests itself in "Das Märchen der 672. Nacht" in the bipartite structure of the text. The first, briefer part has an omniscient narrator, while the second part, except for the ending, is narrated from the point of view of the protagonist. The time structure is static in the first part, dynamic in the second part. Whereas the prevailing adjective in the first part is *schön* (beautiful), *häßlich* (ugly) dominates the second part.

The nameless protagonist of "Das Märchen der 672. Nacht"–he is identified only as a merchant's son–seems to be the stereotypical fairy-tale hero: he is young, handsome, and rich. At the age of twenty-five he withdraws from the world, since he neither cares for the companionship of his friends nor is captivated by the beauty of any woman. He lives the life of a recluse, surrounded by the art objects which he has inherited, and dedicates himself to their contemplation. They reveal to him "alle Formen und Farben der Welt" (all forms and colors of the world), and their beauty intoxicates him. Nothing seems to threaten his aesthetic existence, not even the thought of dying; on the contrary, he imagines that his death will be the crowning achievement of his beautiful life. His tranquillity is shared by the four servants he has retained be-

Hofmannsthal's study

cause they are dear to him. But he soon becomes obsessed with the idea that they are constantly watching him and are aware of his "geheimnisvolle, menschliche Unzulänglichkeit" (mysterious, human inadequacy). An increasing fear takes hold of him, a fear of the "Unentrinnbarkeit des Lebens" (inescapability of life), a fear that is directly related to his sense that his servants force him "in einer unfruchtbaren und so ermüdenden Weise an sich selbst zu denken" (to reflect about himself in such a sterile and tiring way).

The tranquillity of his existence is totally destroyed by an anonymous letter accusing his oldest servant of an unspecified but heinous crime. The letter causes the merchant's son great anxiety; it seems to him "als ob man seinen innersten Besitz beleidigt und bedroht hätte" (as though one had insulted and threatened his innermost possession), and he travels to the city to discover the truth of the matter. There he encounters a reality which is at once unfamiliar to him and at the same time "traumhaft bekannt" (known as if from a dream): the labyrinthine cityscape is that of a nightmare which he tries in vain to escape. He finally comes to a barracks courtyard, where soldiers are washing their horses' hooves. Overcome by compassion, the merchant's son searches his pockets for some coins to give to one of the soldiers. Inadvertently he drops a piece of jewelry he had bought in the city; at the same moment he is struck down by a blow from the horse's hoof. He dies shortly thereafter "mit verzerrten Zügen ... und eine[m] fremden, bösen Ausdruck" (with distorted features ... and an alien, malicious expression), denying everything he had ever valued and hating his life because it has led him to his squalid death.

In 1895 Hofmannsthal told his father that he had not "meant" any more by "Das Märchen der 672. Nacht" than is "meant" by any piece of local news in the newspaper. And he once remarked that readers who continuously ask "What does it mean?" reminded him of apes who, seeing their reflection in a mirror, look to see what is hidden behind it. On the other hand, Hofmannsthal in a letter to Richard Beer-Hofmann called the story "ein allegorisches Zeichen" (an allegorical sign), and every reader feels challenged to inquire as to what this sign signifies. At first glance the title seems to contain a clue to this question: but the allusion to the tales of *One Thousand and One Nights* does not contribute to an understanding of the meaning of "Das Märchen der 672. Nacht," since obviously it is not a retelling of Scheherazade's tale of Gharib.

The bipartite structure of the story provides a more meaningful point of departure for critical inquiry. In what way is the death of the merchant's son the necessary corollary of his life? Or, put another way, why did such a beautiful life have to end in such an ugly death? Most critics have answered these questions from a metaphysical perspective: the merchant's son who tried to escape from the realities of life into the realm of a hermetically sealed aesthetic existence is guilty of hubris; life, once spurned, assumes the role of avenger and condemns the aesthete to die. In other words, "Das Märchen der 672. Nacht" expresses the young Hofmannsthal's awareness of the morally dubious nature of aestheticism and his ethical resolve to overcome it by accepting the challenge that life poses. More recently some critics have objected that this reading of the story as a moral tale is too restrictive and have suggested that its density of detail, characteristic of most of Hofmannsthal's prose works, calls for further interpretation. These psychoanalytical, autobiographical, and sociological interpretations have shown new levels of meaning in "Das Märchen der 672. Nacht," which is comparable in its complexity to Kafka's enigmatic tales.

Another product of Hofmannsthal's confrontation with the sordid aspects of life during his active duty in the Austrian army is "Reitergeschichte." The protagonist, Sgt. Anton Lerch, meets a fate similar to that of the merchant's son. His death at the end of the story–he is shot by his commanding officer, Baron Rofrano, for a minor act of insubordination–raises the questions: why did Lerch have to die, and why did he have to die in such a brutal way?

The opening paragraphs of "Reitergeschichte" depict in realistic detail an episode in

Dust jacket for Hofmannsthal's fragmentary novel, written between 1907 and 1927

the Italian nationalist rebellion of 1848. A troop of Austrian cavalry under the command of Baron Rofrano, an Italian nobleman serving in the Austrian army, is fighting the last remnants of the Italian rebels before riding triumphantly into Milan. Among those who distinguish themselves in the skirmishes is Lerch, an Austrian of lower-middle-class origin, who captures "achtzehn Studenten ... wohlerzogene und hübsche junge Leute mit weißen Händen und halblangem Haar" (eighteen students ... well-bred, handsome young men with white hands and long hair). Nothing, however, in these opening paragraphs, prepares the reader for the central role Lerch is to assume in the tale. He is not singled out by the narrator; he and his exploits are only mentioned in a matter-of-fact way along with those of other common soldiers in the unit.

In the closing scene Lerch disobeys Rofrano's command to release a horse he had captured and is shot. The motivation for his act of insubordination is provided by the narrator: "und aus einer ihm selbst völlig unbekannten Tiefe seines Innern stieg ein bestialischer Zorn gegen jenen Menschen da vor ihm auf, der ihm das Pferd wegnehmen wollte, ein so entsetzlicher Zorn über das Gesicht, die Stimme, die Haltung und das ganze Dasein dieses Menschen" (and from depths in him unknown to himself there rose a bestial anger against the man before him who was taking away his horse, a dreadful rage against the face, the voice, the bearing, the whole being of the man). But the narrator is strangely reticent concerning the motivation for Rofrano's action: "Ob aber in dem Rittmeister etwas Ähnliches vorging ... bleibt im Zweifel" (Whether something of the same sort was going on in the captain's mind, too ... we cannot know). The narrator's refusal to explain or even to speculate at this point adds to the enigma and strengthens the impact of the brutal ending.

Whereas the opening and closing scenes are narrated realistically, the central part of the story has an increasingly dreamlike, surrealist quality, which partially carries over into the final scene. Reality in the central part of "Reitergeschichte" is depicted as it is reflected in Lerch's consciousness. This shift is signaled by the replacement of the collective protagonist, the cavalry troop of the opening paragraphs–"so ritt die schöne Schwadron durch Mailand" (thus the splendid squadron rode through Milan)–by Lerch as the perceiver of the subsequent events: "Nicht weit vom letztgenannten Stadttor ... glaubte der Wachtmeister Anton Lerch ein ihm bekanntes weibliches Gesicht zu sehen" (Not far from the [Porta Ticinese] ... it seemed to Sgt. Anton Lerch that he saw a woman's face he knew).

This chance encounter with the woman, whose name is Vuic, and the glimpse Lerch catches in a mirror of an elderly man, possibly Vuic's lover, gradually take possession of his consciousness to such a degree that in the decisive confrontation with Rofrano "war sein Bewußtsein von der ungeheuren Gespanntheit dieses Augenblicks fast gar nicht erfüllt, sondern von vielfältigen Bildern einer fremdartigen Behaglichkeit überschwemmt" (his consciousness was not filled with the huge tension of the moment, but was flooded with visions of an alien comfort). What is happening in the central part of "Reitergeschichte" is the gradual blotting out of Lerch's consciousness by his unconscious desires, the repression of his disciplined military persona by a rebellious, self-centered one.

The sexual attraction he feels toward Vuic transforms itself into a vision of a civilian existence which is a curious mixture of material well-being, brutality, and sexuality, of "eine Existenz in Hausschuhen, den Korb des Säbels durch die linke Tasche des Schlafrockes durchgesteckt" (a life in slippers, the hilt of his saber sticking through the left-hand pocket of his dressing gown). This vision of a petit-bourgeois existence awakens in him "ein Durst nach unerwartetem Erwerb" (a craving for unexpected gains), moving him to break away from his squadron and ride alone through a village in search of "ein ganz außerordentliches Prämium" (an extraordinarily great prize). What he finds instead is life in its most sordid, materialistic, and bestial aspects, a reflection of Lerch's sexual and material desires. The episode culminates in Lerch's encounter with his double, a foreshadowing of his death.

Critics who read the central sequence as the depiction of Lerch's increasing moral degeneration understand the climactic confrontation between Rofrano and Lerch as one between an autonomous power or truth and an anarchistic, instinctive, common, sullied force. Others have objected to such a metaphysical reading and have suggested an interpretation which takes into account the historical setting and the antagonism between the social classes represented by Rofrano and Lerch. On such a reading Rofrano's shooting of Lerch emerges as the excessive reaction of an upper class whose authority is already undermined. Lerch is then seen as a representative of the aspirations of the lower classes, and the depiction of his state of mind in the central part of the story serves to discredit him and his class in the eyes of the reader. The volume of critical response that "Das Märchen der 672. Nacht" and "Reitergeschichte" have engendered and the lack of agreement among critics as to the meaning of either text are testimony to their ambiguity, which, at least in part, can be attributed to the innovative narrative techniques Hofmannsthal employed. The intricate relationship between objective and subjective points of view in both stories and the use of the subjunctive for large parts of them are prototypical examples of the narrative techniques of early modernism.

After the completion of his year of active military duty Hofmannsthal returned to the University of Vienna. Abandoning the study of law for Romance philology, he received the Ph.D. in 1899 with a dissertation on the French pleiad poets. He considered becoming a university teacher, but while writing his Habilitationsschrift (inaugural dissertation) on Victor Hugo he reached the conclusion that such a career would be incompatible with his vocation as a writer. In 1901 he married Gertrud Schlesinger and moved to Rodaun, a small village outside Vienna; he lived there, with frequent intervals of travel, until his death in 1929. He was survived by his wife; a daughter, Christiane; and a son, Raimund; his eldest son, Franz, had committed suicide a couple of days before his father's death.

Although the turn of the century marks Hofmannsthal's increasing preoccupation with the drama, the beginning of his collaboration with Strauss, and his almost complete abandonment of lyric poetry, his interest in prose fiction was an abiding one: in addition to "Erlebnis des Marschalls von Bassompierre" and *Die Frau ohne Schatten* he left many fragments, some published during his lifetime, some after his death. None of these works, however, had such a lasting impact as "Das Märchen der 672. Nacht" and "Reitergeschichte" or were as significant in the development of modernist narrative. *Andreas* might have achieved the same distinction had it not remained a fragment.

"Erlebnis des Marschalls von Bassompierre," characterized by Hofmannsthal in 1919 as a "Schreibübung" (writing exercise), is based on a story from Goethe's novella "Unterhaltungen deutscher Ausgewanderten" (1795; translated as *Recreations of German Emigrants*, 1854), which in turn was a translation of an episode in François de Bassompierre's *Mémoires du Maréchal de Bassompierre contenant l'histoire de sa vie* (1665). In this episode Bassompierre recounts an amorous affair he had at a time when Paris was ravaged by the plague. A married shopkeeper attracts his attention; he approaches her; they spend a night together and agree to meet again. Two nights later he enters the house where their assignation is to take place; instead of the beautiful shopkeeper he finds two corpses. What distinguishes Hofmannsthal's story from the earlier versions is a shift of emphasis from plot to character, particularly that of the shopkeeper. Both her passion and the duality of love and death are expressed by Hofmannsthal in the symbol of fire which organizes the entire novella. The identities of the corpses, the shopkeeper's motivation, and the relationship between the events of the first and second nights all remain a mystery.

After completing "Erlebnis des Marschalls von Bassompierre" Hofmannsthal conceived the idea for a book which was to be titled "Erfundene Gespräche und Briefe" (Imagined Conversations and Letters). Most of the prose works published under this rubric in his collected works are located at the line of demarcation between fiction and essay. The most famous is "Ein Brief" (translated as "The Letter," 1942), published in the magazine *Der Tag* in 1902 and in book form in 1905. In the letter Lord Chandos apologizes to Sir Francis Bacon "wegen des gänzlichen Verzichtes auf literarische Betätigung" (for his complete abandonment of literary activity) which he attributes to a complete loss on his part of "die Fähigkeit ... über irgend etwas zusammenhängend zu denken oder zu sprechen" (the ability ... to think or to speak of anything coherently). The letter is generally considered one of the most poignant and important documents of the language crisis–paradoxically expressed with complete mastery of language–shared by many philosophers and writers at the turn of the century. Since the letter was written at a time when there was a marked transition in Hofmannsthal's development from the lyrical mode to the dramatic, it has often been read as a veiled autobiographical confession. Such a reading, however, is questionable, since the Chandos letter and the other imagined conversations and letters he wrote between 1902 and 1907 reveal the same conscious experimentation with different styles and forms as do his dramatic works during these years.

In 1907 Hofmannsthal embarked on his most ambitious project in fiction, the novel *Andreas*. Stefan Zweig called the eighty completed pages a "Torso des vielleicht schönsten Romans deutscher Sprache" (torso of possibly the most beautiful novel in the German language); the critic Richard Alewyn characterized them as the "schwingungsreichste Prosa, die je in deutscher Sprache geschrieben worden ist" (most vibrant prose that has ever been written in the German language). Hofmannsthal wrote these eighty pages in 1912-1913 and made notes until 1927 for the continuation of the novel.

The fragment belongs to the tradition of the Bildungsroman. Andreas von Ferschengelder is first encountered in Venice in 1778, on the second leg of his Bildungsreise (educational journey). Here he meets two mysterious figures: the Maltese knight Sacramozo and the Countess Maria. According to Hofmannsthal's notes, both of these characters were to play important roles in Andreas's process of maturation. Sacramozo, who is patterned after the mentor figures of earlier Bildungsromane, is a strikingly dual character: a Christian knight and an occult magician, a man of the world and an unworldly mystic. Maria was inspired by Morton Prince's case study of a multiple personality, *The Dissociation of a Personality* (1906). Her personality is split into that of the spiritual Maria, striving for moral perfection, and that of the sensuous Mariquita, devoted exclusively to sensual pleasure. The knight and Maria reflect a latent psychological split in Andreas himself. In one of his notes for the novel Hofmannsthal wrote: "er ist maßlos, einerseits nach dem Sinnlichen, andererseits nach dem Idealen" (on the one hand he is excessively attracted to the sensual, on the other hand to the ideal). This split is explored at great length in a flashback which encompasses half of the eighty completed pages and deals with Andreas's adventures at the Finazzer farm in the Carinthian Alps before his arrival in Venice. At the Finazzers' he is confronted for the first time with the polarities of the ideal and the sensual, symbolized in the figures of the seventeen-year-old Romana Finazzer, with whom he falls in love, and his servant Gotthilff, who rapes one of the Finazzers' maids. The flashback ends in a vision of the ultimate union of the antinomies of the ideal and the sensual.

Andreas's process of maturation, then, as far as can be gathered from the fragment and Hofmannsthal's notes, was to consist of the reintegration of his divided self. Two of the notes in particular point to this theme of the divided self and its reconstitution. One begins with the notation: "Andreas' zwei Hälften, die auseinanderklaffen" (Andreas's two separate halves); a note for the last chapter reads: "Wie Andreas flüchtet und wieder bergauf fährt, ist ihm, als ob zwei Hälften seines Wesens, die auseinandergerissen waren, wieder in eins zusammengingen" (As Andreas is fleeing and is once again going up the mountain, it seems to him that the two parts of his being, which had been torn asunder, were being reunited). *Andreas* thus continues the theme of the search for identity which is central in so many of Hofmannsthal's works. The subtitle of the novel seems to indicate that this search was to be a successful one. Apparently the novel was to end with the resolution of that which Andreas had found most difficult, "zu sich selber zu gelangen" (to arrive at himself); with the healing of Maria's split personality; and with Andreas's reunion with an idealized Romana.

It is curious that this novel, on which Hofmannsthal worked initially with much enthusiasm and which occupied him for so many years, remained a fragment. The novelist Jakob Wassermann was of the opinion that the collapse of the Habsburg world, in which the novel is rooted, made it impossible for Hofmannsthal to continue it; C. J. Burckhardt, a friend of Hofmannsthal's, pointed out that Hofmannsthal devoted all his energies in the last years of his life to the completion of his drama *Der Turm* (1925; revised, 1927; translated as *The Tower*, 1966); and the editor of the fragment and Hofmannsthal's notes concludes that his lack of talent as a novelist and his attempt to integrate ever more figures and themes into the novel doomed it to remain a fragment. Hofmannsthal once spoke of *Andreas* as "diese vielleicht allzu gewagte Arbeit" (this possibly all too daring work), which may indicate that, as Hermann Broch has argued, he could not come to terms with the extremely self-confessional nature of the novel.

Hofmannsthal's last completed work of fiction, the fairy tale *Die Frau ohne Schatten*, was published in 1919. Hofmannsthal was obviously fascinated with the theme of this tale; he had already given it dramatic form in the libretto for the Strauss opera of the same title (1919) which he had completed in 1914. But even while he was working on the libretto he began writing the prose version, convinced that the stricter form of prose was better suited to express the full implications of the theme. The plots of the two versions are almost identical: the daughter of the spirit king Keikobad marries an earthly emperor. If she does not gain a shadow–that is, give birth to a child–within a year, she must return to the unearthly realm whence she came, and the emperor will be turned into stone. To avoid this fate the empress and her nurse travel to a city where they dwell in the house of Barak, the dyer, whose wife is willing to sell her shadow–that is, to renounce childbearing. In the end, however, the empress does not accept the shadow, thus ensuring the happiness of Barak and his wife but risking her own happiness and the life of the emperor. Her ethical decision not to achieve her own happiness through the misfortune of someone else is rewarded: she is granted a shadow and saves the emperor from petrification.

What distinguishes the prose version from the libretto is the elaborate detail in which the characterizations and the complex metaphorical structure are worked out in the tale. Hofmannsthal said that *Die Frau ohne Schatten* represents a "Triumph des Allomatischen. Allegorie des Sozialen" (triumph of the allomatic principle. Social allegory). By the allomatic principle he means a process of mutual change of two or more persons. In *Die Frau ohne Schatten* the empress, the emperor, Barak, and his wife undergo a profound change in their attitudes toward marriage and childbearing as the guarantors of the continuity of life. The reunion of the two couples at the end of the tale symbolizes the reconciliation of the ethical, life-affirming principle represented by the empress and Barak, and the aesthetic, sterile principle represented by the emperor and the dyer's wife.

In a letter to his friend Rudolf Borchardt written in 1917 Hofmannsthal characterized *Die Frau ohne Schatten* as the "schwerste Arbeit die ich je unternommen habe" (most difficult task I have ever undertaken), and indeed one may question whether he was entirely successful in it. The complexity of the tale's symbolism makes it the least accessible of Hofmannsthal's works of fiction, and although one may not want to share the opinion of some critics that the symbolic meanings are superficially arbitrary, *Die Frau ohne Schatten* does not quite achieve the consistency of symbolic structure of "Das Märchen der 672. Nacht" and "Reitergeschichte." Hofmannsthal's potential as a writer of fiction is evident in these early works, which are generally recognized as masterpieces; it is difficult to say why he did not fully realize this potential. Perhaps, as Rolf Tarot has suggested, Hofmannsthal's passion for the theater in the latter part of his career diverted his energy from fiction.

Letters:

Richard Strauss: Briefwechsel wit Hugo von Hofmannsthal (Berlin & Leipzig: Zsolnay, 1926); translated by Paul England as *Correspondence between Richard Strauss and Hugo von Hofmannsthal, 1907-1918* (London: Secker, 1927; New York: Knopf, 1927);

Briefe: 1890-1909, 2 volumes (Berlin: Fischer, 1935);

Briefwechsel zwischen George und Hofmannsthal, edited by Robert Boehringer (Berlin: Bondi, 1938; enlarged edition, Munich: Küpper, 1953);

Briefwechsel: Richard Strauss/Hugo von Hofmannsthal. Gesamtausgabe, edited by Franz and Alice Strauss and Willi Schuh (Zurich: Atlantis, 1952); translated by Hanns Hammelmann and Edward Osers as *A Working Friendship: The Correspondence between Richard Strauss and Hugo von Hofmannsthal* (New York: Random House, 1961);

Hugo von Hofmannsthal/Rudolf Borchardt: Briefwechsel, edited by Marie Luise Borchardt and Herbert Steiner (Frankfurt am Main: Fischer, 1954);

Hugo von Hofmannsthal/Carl Jakob Burckhardt: Briefwechsel, edited by Carl J. Burckhardt (Frankfurt am Main: Fischer, 1956);

Hugo von Hofmannsthal/Arthur Schnitzler: Briefwechsel, edited by Therese Nickl and Heinrich Schnitzler (Frankfurt am Main: Fischer, 1964);

Hugo von Hofmannsthal/Helene von Nostitz: Briefwechsel, edited by Oswalt von Nostitz (Frankfurt am Main: Fischer, 1965);

Hugo von Hofmannsthal/Edgar Karg von Bebenburg: Briefwechsel, edited by Mary E. Gilbert (Frankfurt am Main: Fischer, 1966);

Briefe an Marie Herzfeld, edited by Horst Weber (Heidelberg: Stiehm, 1967);

Hugo von Hofmannsthal/Leopold von Andrian: Briefwechsel, edited by Walter H. Perl (Frankfurt am Main: Fischer, 1968);

Hugo von Hofmannsthal/Harry Graf Kessler: Briefwechsel 1898-1929, edited by Burger (Frankfurt am Main: Insel, 1968);

Hugo von Hofmannsthal/Willy Haas: Ein Briefwechsel, edited by Rolf Italiaander (Berlin: Propyläen, 1968);

Hugo von Hofmannsthal/Josef Redlich: Briefwechsel, edited by Helga Fußgänger (Frankfurt am Main: Fischer, 1971);

Hugo von Hofmannsthal/Anton Wildgans: Briefwechsel, edited by Norbert Altenhofer (Heidelberg: Stiehm, 1971);

Hugo von Hofmannsthal/Richard Beer-Hofmann: Briefwechsel, edited by Eugene Weber (Frankfurt am Main: Fischer, 1972);

Briefwechsel mit Max Rychner; mit Samuel und Hedwig Fischer, Oscar Bie und Moritz Heimann, edited by Claudia Mertz-Rychner (Frankfurt am Main: Fischer, 1973);

Briefwechsel: Hugo von Hofmannsthal/Ottonie Gräfin Degenfeld, edited by Marie Thérèse Miller-Degenfeld and Eugene Weber (Frankfurt am Main: Fischer, 1974); revised as *Briefwechsel mit Ottonie Gräfin Degenfeld und Julie Freifrau von Wendelstadt* (Frankfurt am Main: Fischer, 1986);

Hugo von Hofmannsthal/Rainer Maria Rilke: Briefwechsel, edited by Rudolf Hirsch and Ingeborg Schnack (Frankfurt am Main: Insel, 1978);

Hugo von Hofmannsthal/Max Mell: Briefwechsel, edited by Margret Dietrich and Heinz Kindermann (Heidelberg: Lambert Schneider, 1982);

Ria Schmujlow-Claassen und Hugo von Hofmannsthal: Briefe–Aufsätze–Dokumente, edited by Claudia Albrecht (Marbach: Marbacher Schriften, 1982);

Hugo von Hofmannsthal/Paul Zifferer: Briefwechsel, edited by Burger (Vienna: Verlag der österreichischen Staatsdruckerei, 1983).

Bibliographies:

Horst Weber, *Hugo von Hofmannsthal: Bibliographie. Werke–Briefe–Gespräche–Übersetzungen–Vertonungen* (Berlin & New York: De Gruyter, 1972);

The Hofmannsthal Collection in the Houghton Library: A Descriptive Catalogue of Printed Books (Heidelberg: Stiehm, 1974).

References:

Richard Alewyn, *Über Hugo von Hofmannsthal* (Göttingen: Vandenhoeck & Ruprecht, 1963);

Lowell A. Bangerter, *Hugo von Hofmannsthal* (New York: Ungar, 1977);

Andrew Barker, "The Triumph of Life in Hofmannsthal's 'Märchen der 672. Nacht,'" *Modern Language Review*, 74, no. 2 (1979): 341-348;

Gisa Briese-Neumann, *Ästhet–Dilletant–Narziß* (Frankfurt am Main, Bern & New York: Lang, 1985);

Dorrit Cohn, "'Als Traum erzählt': The Case for a Freudian Reading of Hofmannsthal's 'Märchen der 672. Nacht,'" *Deutsche Vierteljahresschrift*, 54 (1980): 284-305;

Karoly Csuri, *Die frühen Erzählungen Hugo von Hofmannsthals* (Kronberg: Scriptor, 1978);

Donald G. Daviau, "Hugo von Hofmannsthal and the Chandos Letter," *Modern Austrian Literature*, 4 (1971): 28-44;

Volker Durr, "Der Tod des Wachtmeisters Anton Lerch und die Revolution von 1848; zu Hofmannsthals Reitergeschichte," *German Quarterly*, 45 (1972): 33-46;

Mary E. Gilbert, "Some Observations on Hofmannsthal's Two 'Novellen' *Reitergeschichte* and *Das Erlebnis des Marschalls von Bassompierre*," *German Life and Letters*, 11 (1958): 102-111;

Thomas A. Kovach, *Hofmannsthal and Symbolism* (New York, Bern & Frankfurt am Main: Lang, 1985);

Hans Mayer, "Die Frau ohne Schatten," *Jahresringe*, 25 (1978-1979): 221-240;

David Miles, *Hofmannsthal's Novel "Andreas"* (Princeton: Princeton University Press, 1972);

Jens Rieckmann, "Von der menschlichen Unzulänglichkeit: Zu Hofmannsthals 'Das Märchen der 672. Nacht,'" *German Quarterly*, 54 (1981): 298-310;

Ritchie Robertson, "The Dual Structure of Hofmannsthal's 'Reitergeschichte,'" *Forum for Modern Language Studies*, 14 (1978): 316-331;

Carl E. Schorske, "Politics and the Psyche: Schnitzler and Hofmannsthal," in his *Fin-De-Siècle Vienna: Politics and Culture* (New York: Knopf, 1980), pp. 3-22;

Rolf Tarot, "Hugo von Hofmannsthal," in *Handbuch der deutschen Erzählung*, edited by Karl Konrad Polheim (Düsseldorf: Bagel, 1981), pp. 409-420;

Benno von Wiese, "Hugo von Hofmannsthal: 'Reitergeschichte,'" in *Die deutsche Novelle von Goethe bis Kafka*, edited by Wiese (Düsseldorf: Bagel, 1956), pp. 284-303;

Wolf Wucherpfennig, "The 'Young Viennese' and their Fathers: Decadence and the Generation Conflict around 1890," *Journal of Contemporary History*, 17 (1982): 21-49.

Papers:

Some of Hugo von Hofmannsthal's papers are at the Bibliothek des Freien Deutschen Hochstifts, Frankfurt am Main, where a definitive edition of his works is being prepared. Unpublished manuscripts and a comprehensive collection of Hofmannsthal's published writings are at the Houghton Library at Harvard University. Other papers are in the possession of his family or other private collectors.

Franz Kafka
(3 July 1883-3 June 1924)

Richard H. Lawson
University of North Carolina at Chapel Hill

BOOKS: *Betrachtung* (Leipzig: Rowohlt, 1913);

Der Heizer: Ein Fragment (Leipzig: Wolff, 1913);

Die Verwandlung (Leipzig: Wolff, 1915); translated by Eugene Jolas as "Metamorphosis," *Transition* (Paris), no. 25 (Autumn 1936): 27-38; no. 26 (Winter 1937): 53-72; no. 27 (April/May 1938): 79-103; translated by A. L. Lloyd as *The Metamorphosis* (London: Parton, 1937; New York: Vanguard, 1946); German version edited by Marjorie L. Hoover (New York: Norton, 1960; London: Methuen, 1962);

Das Urteil: Eine Geschichte (Leipzig: Wolff, 1916); translated by Jolas as "The Sentence," *Transition* (February 1928): 35-47; translated by Rosa M. Beuscher as "The Judgment," *Quarterly Review of Literature*, 2, no. 3 (1945): 189-198;

In der Strafkolonie (Leipzig: Wolff, 1919); translated by Jolas as "In the Penal Colony," *Partisan Review*, 8 (March 1941): 98-107; (April 1941): 146-158;

Ein Landarzt: Kleine Erzählungen (Munich & Leipzig: Wolff, 1919); translated by Vera Leslie as *The Country Doctor: A Collection of Fourteen Short Stories* (Oxford: Counterpoint, 1945);

Ein Hungerkünstler: Vier Geschichten (Berlin: Die Schmiede, 1924)–"Ein Hungerkünstler" translated by Harry Steinhauer and Helen Jessiman as "The Hunger-Artist," in *Modern German Short Stories*, edited by Steinhauer and Jessiman (New York & London: Oxford University Press, 1938), pp. 203-217; "Eine kleine Frau" translated by Francis C. Golfing as "A Little Woman," *Accent* (Summer 1943): 223-227; "Josefine, die Sängerin, oder das Volk der Mäuse" translated by Clement Greenberg as "Josephine, the Songstress; or, The Mice Nation," *Partisan Review*, 9 (May/June 1942): 213-228;

Der Prozeß: Roman (Berlin: Die Schmiede, 1925); translated by Willa and Edwin Muir as *The Trial* (London: Gollancz, 1937; New York: Knopf, 1937); translation revised, with additional chapters and notes (definitive edition), by E. M. Butler (London: Secker & Warburg, 1956; New York: Knopf, 1957);

Das Schloß: Roman (Munich: Wolff, 1926); translated by Willa and Edwin Muir as *The Castle: A Novel* (London: Secker & Warburg, 1930; New York: Knopf, 1930); translation revised, with additional material (definitive edition), by Eithne Wilkins and Ernst Kaiser (London: Secker & Warburg, 1953; New York: Knopf, 1954);

Franz Kafka

Amerika: Roman (Munich: Wolff, 1927); translated by Willa and Edwin Muir as *America* (London: Routledge, 1938; Norfolk, Conn.: New Directions, 1940);

Beim Bau der chinesischen Mauer: Ungedruckte Erzählungen und Prosa aus dem Nachlaß, edited by Max Brod and Hans Joachim Schoeps (Berlin: Kiepenheuer, 1931); translated by Willa and Edwin Muir as *The Great Wall of China and Other Pieces* (London: Secker & Warburg, 1933);

Gesammelte Schriften, edited by Brod and Heinz Politzer, 6 volumes (volumes 1-4, Berlin: Schocken, 1935; volumes 5-6, Prague: Mercy, 1936-1937); volume 1, *Erzählungen und kleine Prosa* (1935), translated by Kaiser and Wilkins as *In the Penal Settlement: Tales and Short Prose Works* (London: Secker & Warburg, 1973); volume 5, *Beschreibung eines Kampfes: Novellen, Skizzen, Aphorismen aus dem Nachlaß* (1936), translated by Willa and Edwin Muir and Tania and James Stern as *Description of a Struggle and The Great Wall of China* (London: Secker & Warburg, 1960);

Parables in German and English, translated by Willa and Edwin Muir (New York: Schocken, 1947);

The Penal Colony: Stories and Short Pieces, translated by Willa and Edwin Muir and C. Greenberg (New York: Schocken, 1948; London: Secker & Warburg, 1949);

The Diaries of Franz Kafka, edited by Brod, translated by Joseph Kresh, Martin Greenberg, and Hannah Arendt, 2 volumes (New York: Schocken, 1948-1949);

Gesammelte Werke, edited by Brod, 11 volumes (Frankfurt am Main: Fischer, 1950-1974); volume 4, *Briefe an Milena*, edited by Willy Haas, translated by Tania and James Stern as *Letters to Milena* (New York: Farrar & Straus, Schocken/London: Secker & Warburg, 1953); volume 7, *Hochzeitsvorbereitungen auf dem Lande und andere Prosa aus dem Nachlaß*, translated by Kaiser and Wilkins as *Wedding Preparations in the Country, and Other Posthumous Prose Writings* (London: Secker & Warburg, 1954); translation republished as *Dearest Father: Stories and Other Writings* (New York: Schocken, 1954); volume 9, *Briefe 1902-1904*, translated, with additional material, by Richard and Clara Winston, edited by Beverly Colman and other as *Letters to Friends, Family, and Editors* (New York: Schocken/London: Calder, 1977); volume 10, *Briefe an Felice und andere Korrespondenz aus der Verlobungszeit*, edited by Erich Heller and Jürgen Born, translated by James Stern and Elisabeth Duckworth as *Letters to Felice* (New York: Schocken, 1973); volume 11, *Briefe an Ottla und die Familie*, edited by Hartmut Binder and Klaus Wagenbach, translated by Richard and Clara Winston, edited by Nahum N. Glatzer, as *Letters to Ottla and the Family* (New York: Schocken, 1982);

Selected Short Stories, translated by Willa and Edwin Muir (New York: Modern Library, 1952);

Parables and Paradoxes, in German and English, translated by Willa and Edwin Muir (New York: Schocken, 1958);

Erzählungen und Skizzen, edited by Wagenbach (Darmstadt: Moderner Buch-Club, 1959);

Die Erzählungen, edited by Wagenbach (Frankfurt am Main: Fischer, 1961);

Metamorphosis and Other Stories, translated by Willa and Edwin Muir (Harmondsworth, U.K.: Penguin, 1961);

Er: Prosa, edited by Martin Walser (Frankfurt am Main: Suhrkamp, 1963);

Short Stories, edited by J. M. S. Pasley (London: Oxford University Press, 1963);

Der Heizer; In der Strafkolonie; Der Bau, edited by Pasley (Cambridge: Cambridge University Press, 1966);

Sämtliche Erzählungen, edited by Paul Raabe (Frankfurt am Main: Fischer, 1970);

The Complete Stories, edited by Glatzer (New York: Schocken, 1971);

Shorter Works, translated and edited by Malcolm Pasley (London: Secker & Warburg, 1973);

I Am a Memory Come Alive: Autobiographical Writings, edited by Glatzer (New York: Schocken, 1974).

PERIODICAL PUBLICATIONS: "Betrachtung," *Hyperion*, 1, no. 1 (1908): 91-94;

"Gespräch mit dem Beter," *Hyperion*, 1, no. 8 (1909): 126-131;

"Gespräch mit dem Betrunkenen," *Hyperion*, 1, no. 8 (1909): 131-133;

"Brief an den Vater," *Die Neue Rundschau*, 63, no. 2 (1952): 191-231; translated by Ernst Kaiser and Eithne Wilkins as *Letter to His Father/Brief an den Vater* (New York: Schocken, 1953).

Franz Kafka is one of the founders of modern literature. His claim to greatness includes his

Kafka at about ten years of age, with his sisters Valli (left) and Elli (photo: Archiv Klaus Wagenbach)

service in completely collapsing the aesthetic distance that had traditionally separated the writer from the reader. In what is probably his most famous work of fiction, *Die Verwandlung* (1915; translated as "Metamorphosis," 1936-1938), the protagonist, Gregor Samsa, is presented to the reader as a man who has become an insect; Gregor's condition is never suggested to be an illusion or dream (although many critics have commented on its dreamlike qualities). In his shock at the result of Kafka's unmediated aesthetic distance, the reader is led to forgo his usual reflective and explicative function. Kafka has his characters perform that explicative function—hectically, repeatedly, self-contradictorily, and with a new kind of irony that has come to characterize modern literature. Finally, in an age that celebrates the mass, Kafka redirects the focus to the individual. His characters stand for themselves as individuals; in the case of the male protagonists—and almost all of his protagonists are male—they stand for Kafka himself.

Kafka was born on 3 July 1883 in Prague, a large provincial capital of the Austro-Hungarian Empire that was home to many Czechs, some Germans, and a lesser number of German-cultured, German-speaking Jews. His father, Hermann Kafka, of humble rural origin, was a hardworking, hard-driving, successful merchant. His mother tongue was Czech, but he spoke German, correctly seeing the language as an important card to be played in the contest for social and economic mobility and security. Kafka's mother, Julie Löwy Kafka, came from a family with older Prague roots and some degree of wealth. She proved unable to mediate the estrangement between her brusque, domineering husband and her quiet, tyrannized, oversensitive son.

The boy and his three younger sisters were largely cared for by a transient staff of mostly Czech-speaking household servants, for when Julie was not pregnant she helped her husband in his fancy-goods and haberdashery business. At the age of six Kafka began attending the German school, and thereafter he spoke more German than Czech. When he was ten he entered the Altstädter Deutsches Gymnasium, the German preparatory school in Old Town. Kafka, despite his indifferent attitude, was an excellent student. He was conspicuously not one of the gang; while he was not entirely unsociable, he shrank from taking social initiatives.

As a youngster, Kafka, like his father, had no more than the most perfunctory relationship with Judaism. He dutifully memorized what was necessary for his bar mitzvah, but he was already an atheist—as was perhaps to be expected of a youthful fan of the naturalistic drama then in vogue in the German theater in Prague. His interest in drama led him to write scenarios to be acted out by his sisters at home. He also wrote fragments of a novel. Writing early became an issue in the antagonism between Kafka and his father; the latter continued to disdain writing as an unworthy occupation long after Kafka became a published author.

Kafka entered the German Karl-Ferdinand University in Prague in 1901. (The university was divided into a German part and a Czech part.) After enrolling in chemistry and taking one semester of Germanics he switched to law, a field that had his father's blessing because it afforded the prospect of future employment. Kafka began to reach out socially a bit more: among his new friends was Max Brod, who was to be his lifelong friend and literary executor. At this time, too, he

Kafka during his university days, with the waitress Hansi Julie Szokoll and a collie (Briefe an Auguste Hauschner, *1929*)

had a sexual relationship with a young woman and then with an older one.

He received his doctorate in law on 18 June 1907. On 1 October he joined the staff of the Assicurazioni Generali, an insurance office in Prague. As if the overcrowded Kafka residence were not already daunting enough to the budding writer, the Assicurazioni Generali contributed a six-day, fifty-hour week of extremely dull work together with an abrasive environment. Nonetheless, in March 1908 he published his first short prose pieces in the Munich literary magazine *Hyperion*.

In July he received the opportunity to move to the Workers' Accident Insurance Institute for the Kingdom of Bohemia, a semigovernmental agency. Kafka's command of Czech proved useful in the job, which involved the settlement of workmen's compensation claims. The occasional brief trips out of Prague required by the new job were welcome to Kafka; his salary was better; his hours were shorter; and his advancement was gratifying. The din and the harassment from his father at home continued to make writing difficult, but he could have moved out had he resolved to do so.

Early in 1907 he had begun work on a novel titled "Beschreibung eines Kampfes" (1936; translated as "Description of a Struggle," 1960). There were two versions, neither of which was completed. It is a dialogue between the narrator, who is a young artist engaged to be married, and a bachelor; both are obvious projections of Kafka. Among the themes broached, as they hike in and about Prague on a clear, freezing February day, two are of primary interest: the artist suffers psychological discomfort under the spell of his bachelor acquaintance, and the artist casually orders the bachelor to commit suicide.

Within the episodic framework of "Beschreibung eines Kampfes," are two tales that were extracted and, at Brod's urging, published in *Hyperion* in 1909: "Gespräch mit dem Beter" (Conversation with the Supplicant) and "Gespräch mit dem Betrunkenen" (Conversation with the Drunkard). In the former the supplicant is a romantic young man hobbled by self-consciousness in striving to strike up party conversation with a girl. Although he does not know how to do so, the supplicant insists on playing the piano; the girl acts as if he has played excellently. The supplicant dearly wants to believe that he is not awkward, that he is just as graceful as the other guests. His departure from the party is marked by his host's helping him into someone else's topcoat. The central idea of "Gespräch mit dem Betrunkenen" is a cliché, but an amusing one: the presumed benefit to the thinker in learning from the drunkard. Reality and fantasy—vignettes of an imagined Paris—are juxtaposed in both stories. This juxtaposition, along with a striking self-consciousness

Kafka circa 1906 (photo: Archiv Klaus Wagenbach)

and an episodic structure, indicate the direction Kafka's mature fiction was to take.

Coincident with his work on "Beschreibung eines Kampfes"–that is, from 1907 to 1910–Kafka worked on another embryonic novel, "Hochzeitsvorbereitungen auf dem Lande" (1953; translated as "Wedding Preparations in the Country," 1954). In this case there were three uncompleted versions, again written primarily for the benefit of the author himself, although Brod was allowed to read the work in progress. The narrator, Eduard Raban, an exhausted Prague businessman thirty years of age, is a persona of Kafka; the name Raban, Czech for raven, is a cryptogram of Kafka's name, which in the form *kavka* means jackdaw in Czech. Raban, having committed himself to visit his fiancée Betty and her mother in the country, hesitates to undertake the trip. When he does undertake it he is beset by rain, the physical discomfort of the train, awkward conversations with fellow travelers, and a yearning to return to the city. He is uneasy about the darkness; the uncanny atmosphere of the countryside; and the circumstances of his lonely arrival, which is as far as any of the three versions of the story goes.

"Hochzeitsvorbereitungen auf dem Lande" incorporates narrative features that are beginning to emerge as typical of Kafka: a first-person narrator as a persona of the author, an episodic structure, an ambivalent quester on an ambiguous mission, and pervasive irony. Kafka is moving toward a more subtle split projection of his persona; in "Beschreibung eines Kampfes" the artist and the bachelor were separate persons, each representing one side of the author's psyche; in "Hochzeitsvorbereitungen auf dem Lande" the split is implied within the narrator, Raban, who suggests at one point that he is just dispatching his clothed body to the country: most of the time his mind is in a comfortable bed in Prague while his body is suffering the rigors of travel and rurality. As he lies in bed he further splits himself mentally and identifies part of himself with a bug. Pressing his tiny insect legs to his bulging belly he imagines himself whispering instructions to his body, which is standing close by. Raban has not really become an insect, as Gregor Samsa will in *Die Verwandlung;* he is *imagining* that part of him is an insect. But Kafka has traveled at least half of the conceptual distance between the inchoate "Beschreibung eines Kampfes" and the masterpiece that is *Die Verwandlung.*

While writing his drafts of "Hochzeitsvorbereitungen auf dem Lande" and completing several short pieces, Kafka was also writing the first draft of another novel, "Der Verschollene" (He Who Was Lost without Trace). From the point of view of publication history "Der Verschollene" consists of two parts: the first chapter, *Der Heizer* (The Stoker), with which Kafka was satisfied and which was published separately in May 1913; and the entire but never completed novel, as assembled and published by Brod in 1927 as *Amerika* (translated as *America,* 1938). By the time Kafka published *Der Heizer* he abhorred the other five hundred pages. The reason is not difficult to surmise, for in those pages he had employed many of the conventions of nineteenth-century realistic fiction, a mode he rejected wholeheartedly. As a critic, Kafka was extremely hard on himself, but his estimate of *Der Heizer* vis-à-vis *Amerika* is close to the mark–which is not to say that the latter is bad fiction.

Cover for the separate publication of the first chapter of Kafka's Amerika; the rest of the novel, edited by Max Brod, was published posthumously (Ludwig Dietz, Franz Kafka: Die Veroffentlichungen zu seinen Lebzeiten, 1982)

Der Heizer begins in realistic fashion. Karl Rossmann, a fifteen- or sixteen-year-old immigrant, is on the deck of a steamer entering New York harbor. The story becomes increasingly surrealistic when he dashes through an unfamiliar part of the ship on his way back to steerage to retrieve his umbrella. He falls in with a disaffected stoker, and the two make their way to the captain's stateroom. There Karl eloquently, but ineffectively, pleads the stoker's grievance. One of the many dignitaries who have boarded is Karl's long-lost wealthy uncle, who recognizes Karl. Accompanying his uncle to his magnificent home, Karl abandons the stoker's lost cause.

The gap between presumed reality and the actual state of things is so pervasive as to be thematic. It is true that Karl has been expelled from his parents' house in Prague for impregnating a thirty-five-year-old cook. But his parents are not poor, as the narrator early declared; they are well-to-do and inhumane. Uncle Jacob, who rescued Karl because the cook wrote to him, gives out a romanticized version of Karl's seduction by the cook which Karl has to correct. Mostly, however, it is Karl who lacks an accurate perception of reality. His naiveté is profound and stubborn. He accepts his parents' cruelty with an untarnished devotion, fondly imagining how he would rise in their esteem if only they could see him valiantly pleading the cause of justice for the stoker. This point brings up another theme, which is more important for the novel than for the story. The stoker noisily proclaims his Germanness; he is a German fighting the machinations of his Romanian superior. Karl's abrupt and instinctive rapport with the stoker, with whom he would seem to have little in common, lies in the stoker's symbolizing the German world that, for Karl, is forever lost. He has been thrown upon the alien shores of an unknown new world. Just how alien is emphasized by the conspicuous and self-conscious Americanism of his Uncle Jacob. If Karl is an unnested German fledgling, Uncle Jacob is a mature American entrepreneurial raptor in quest of ever more money.

Each of the seven chapters that follow "Der Heizer," as they are arranged by Brod, coincides with an expulsory episode. Karl is brought to one fall after another in an America that remains an enigma to him from beginning to end–even an apparently utopian end in which he precipitately finds acceptance. In addition, there are two incomplete chapters, which Brod places in an appendix; narratively they belong between the penultimate and final chapters.

For a while Karl lives in luxury with Uncle Jacob; Jacob's business friends, Mr. Green and Mr. Pollunder; and the latter's hoydenish daughter, Clara, who attempts to seduce him. In fact it is Karl's unwillingly prolonged–by Clara–stay at the Pollunders that prompts his sudden, apparently capricious expulsion from Jacob's house. Karl is forbidden ever to contact his uncle again. On the streets Karl meets a pair of vagabond machinists, Delamarche and Robinson, who exploit him through much of the novel. Their exploitation results in Karl's expulsion from his employment as an elevator boy at the Hotel Occidental. The pair contrive for Karl to be a slave in a tacky ménage à trois that includes Delamarche's grotesquely fat mistress, Brunelda. Between this exploitation and the final chapter in which Karl discovers unconditional acceptance in the Theater of Oklahoma, there is a narrative gap that is less than completely bridged by the two fragmentary chapters with their indication of Karl's degradation in the filthy and sexually charged Delamarche household and in a shabbily splendid whorehouse where he has some sort of job as a factotum.

Exploitation and expulsion are so often linked with seduction as to make the latter a motif. The very first sentence of the novel informs the reader that the servant girl seduced Karl and had a child by him; this seduction severed him from his previous life and deposited him in America, where the pattern was to be repeated over and over. By no means are all of Karl's subsequent seducers as successful or thorough as Johanna Brummer, the servant girl; most are not, Clara Pollunder among them. Therese Berchtold, a secretary-typist at the Hotel Occidental, is no more than a charmingly innocent flirt who brings Karl a gift apple. But Karl's guilt is, on the whole, simply existential; he does not have to do anything, he does not have to bite into an apple to validate his guilt.

Responding to a recruiting poster of the Oklahoma Theater, which assertedly has a post for every applicant, Karl meets his old friend, Fanny–except that the reader is in the dark about their past friendship, which is not recounted in the published novel. Fanny is already a member of the company, one of hundreds of women dressed as angels, mounted on a tall pedestal, playing trumpets. After the initial reunion, however, Karl never sees Fanny again; he is hired as a technical assistant, and they are posted to different troupes of the Oklahoma Theater. As Karl is on the train headed for Oklahoma the novel breaks off with a description of mountain streams and the chill breath rising from them. Definitive as this imagery may sound as a symbol of death, the reader ought to remember that this is simply where Kafka stopped writing.

The atmosphere of fantasy about the Oklahoma Theater inheres partly in the fact that it is, precisely, a theater, the realm of fantasy, and partly in the reader's perception that it is a very unusual sort of theater: huge, friendly, socially beneficent, open-armed in its hiring policy, and inscrutable. If you want to be an artist, its sign proclaims, come and join us. In this theater even a technical assistant is an artist. Kafka, a highly self-conscious artist holding down a mundane job, may be intimating that fantasy is essential to the salvation of the artist.

Is the reader to imagine that Karl's novel-long probity (even though he does give an alias to the theater interviewer), his naiveté blended with pride, his submissiveness, his slightly ridiculous desire to oblige, are really going to enable him to find redemption for whatever he is guilty of ? This is the gist of the eschatological reading promulgated by Brod and reflected in his editing and subtitling of Kafka's unfinished work. It is a remarkably durable view, especially among Americans attuned to happy endings. There is little in *Amerika* to warrant such a reading, even in the final chapter. In what seems a parodistic finale the chief themes of the preceding chapters are stood on their heads. Where Karl had encountered hostility, now he finds amicability. Where life had consisted of one exploitation after another, from Johanna Brummer forward, now he finds acceptance. Where injustice had everywhere prevailed, now there is sweet justice. And there is the promise, under the benign and expansive wing of the Theater of Oklahoma, of always more amicability, acceptance, and justice.

Now and then it is suggested that *Amerika* is a Bildungsroman, a picaresque novel, or a naturalistic novel of social reform. It is in fact none of these. No additional insight is to be gained by analyzing it as a novel in which the developing hero is formed by his experiences in such a way as to successfully enter and prevail in the middle-class world. For despite the topsy-turvy milieu in which he finds himself in the Oklahoma Theater, Karl himself is unchanged. He seemingly learns nothing, or exceedingly little, from his travails in alien America. He remains a European throughout, with a guileless, immature European's perceptions and expectations. Tellingly, in the last chapter he is still categorized as a European intermediate school pupil.

Nor is Karl the streetwise picaro surviving by playing dirty tricks on the members of bourgeois society. He does not play tricks, others play tricks on him. He does not act upon his environment, he is acted upon by it–and scarcely to his benefit. Karl's social world, it is true, is that common to picaresque novels, where the middle class and the proletarian and petty criminal worlds intersect. But he plays there a role quite the reverse of the picaro's.

Nor is *Amerika* a naturalistic novel of social reform. Somewhat naturalistic it is–much to Kafka's distress; and, from his thoroughly bourgeois perspective, Kafka was indeed sympathetic with the victims of urban industrialization in and

First and last pages of the manuscript of Das Urteil *from Kafka's diary, written during the night of 22-23 September 1912 (Bodleian Library)*

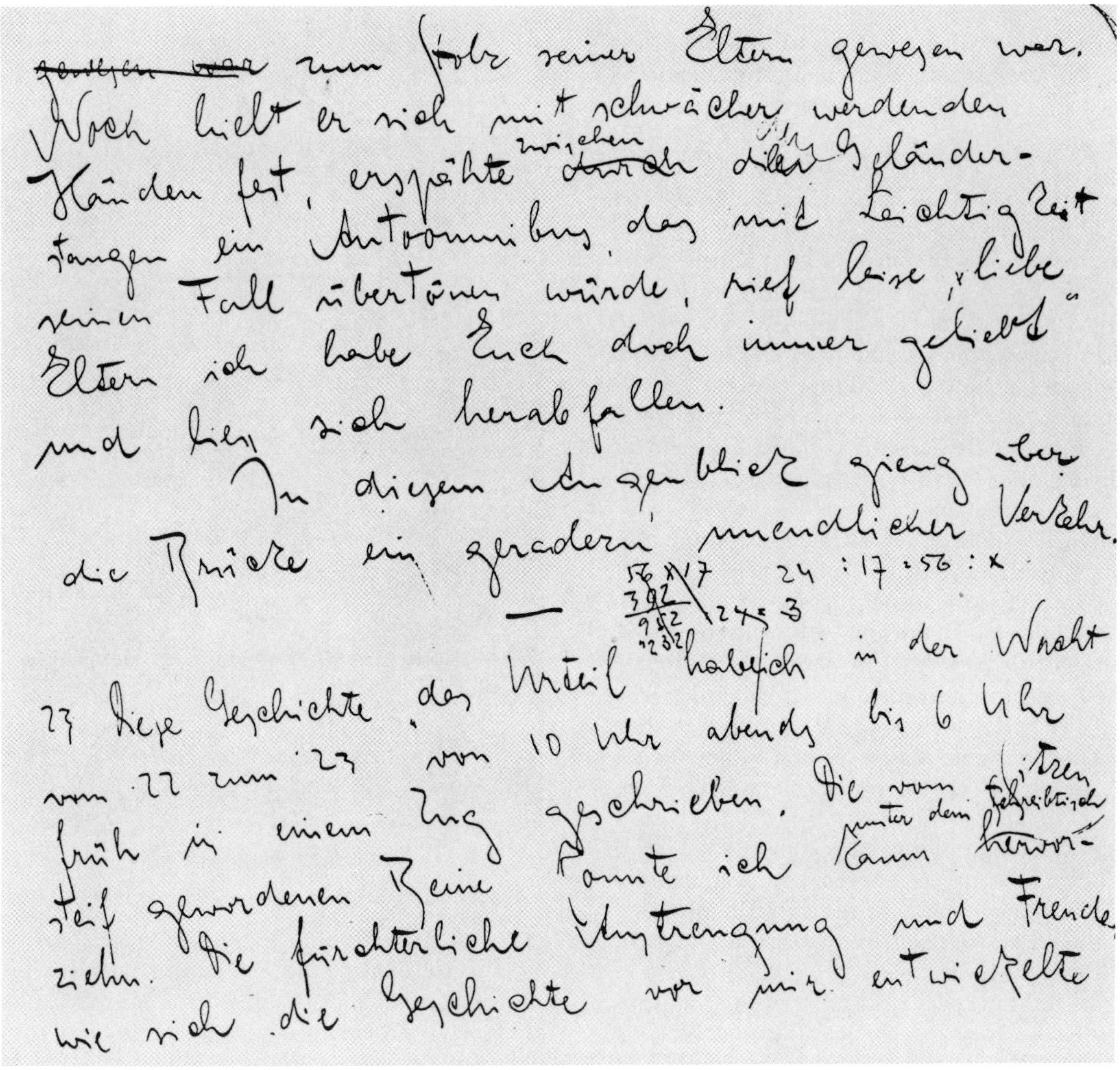

~~gewesen war~~ zum Stolz seiner Eltern gewesen war.
Noch hielt er sich mit schwächer werdenden
Händen fest, erspähte zwischen ~~durch~~ den Geländer-
stangen einen Autoomnibus, der mit Leichtigkeit
seinen Fall übertönen würde, rief leise: „Liebe
Eltern ich habe Euch doch immer geliebt"
und ließ sich herabfallen.

In diesem Augenblick gieng über
die Brücke ein geradezu unendlicher Verkehr.

56 x 17 24 : 17 = 56 : x

—

23 Diese Geschichte „das Urteil" habe ich in der Nacht
vom 22 zum 23 von 10 Uhr abends bis 6 Uhr
früh in einem Zug geschrieben. Die vom Sitzen
steif gewordenen Beine konnte ich kaum unter dem Schreibtisch hervor-
ziehn. Die fürchterliche Anstrengung und Freude,
wie sich die Geschichte vor mir entwickelte

around Prague and insightfully depicted the plight of the exploited. Political and social reform, however, was not the motivating tendency of his art, which has a much more individual basis.

In Prague in May 1910 Kafka discovered with Brod, and was fascinated by, the Polish Yiddish Musical Drama Company of Lemberg (now Lvov, USSR). Another troupe of Yiddish actors, also from Lemberg, played in Prague in the winter of 1911-1912; Kafka attended some twenty performances and became a friend of Jizchok Löwy, one of the actors. These austere Yiddish theaters enabled Kafka to see, in a way that memorizing for his halfhearted bar mitzvah never did, the living and pervasive interrelationships of Jewish tradition and culture.

On 13 August 1912 Kafka met Felice Bauer, who was visiting the Brods from her home in Berlin. Attracted to her to the point of being even more than usually conscious of his supposed awkwardness, he nevertheless soon afterward described with quite unromantic, even unflattering objectivity how she first appeared to him. A short time later he wrote and dedicated to her the novella *Das Urteil* (1916; translated as "The Sentence," 1928), his first masterpiece. Its basis is highly autobiographical, although the theme of the internal conflict inherent in assimilationist Jewry owes something to Brod's 1912 novel *Arnold Beer: Das Schicksal eines Juden* (Arnold Beer: The Fate of a Jew).

In the first part of the twelve-page novella, which Kafka wrote in a single sitting on 22-23 September 1912 between 10:00 P.M. and 6:00 A.M., Georg, a prosperous young businessman, writes a long letter telling a bachelor friend in St. Petersburg (now Leningrad) that he has become engaged to a girl named Frieda Brandenfeld; it is Frieda who has insisted that Georg convey this news. In the course of the letter it is revealed that Georg has taken over the family firm and guided it to dazzling success, relegating his widowed father, with whom he lives, to sterile retirement.

The Westernized reversal of father-son roles—with all that it implies for the traditional hierarchical Jewish family organization—is the meat of the second part of the story. Georg confronts his father in the airless back room and tells the old man that he has written his friend with news of his engagement. The old man at first dismisses the existence of the friend as a joke. But then he is seemingly endowed with a spectacular resurgence of strength and dominance, proclaims that *he* is in touch with the Petersburg friend, whose representative he is and who would be a son after his own heart. Georg is getting married, the old man suggests, because his fiancée lifted her skirts. When Georg retaliates with invective, the father sentences his son to death by drowning. Georg promptly complies by running out and jumping off a nearby bridge, asserting his filial love.

Kafka as a young man

The autobiographical component is amply supported by Kafka's diary entries: Georg is Franz Kafka, Georg's father is Hermann Kafka, Frieda Brandenfeld is Felice Bauer. An Oedipal theme suggests itself: when his mother was still living, Georg seems to have been a dutiful and diligent son. But now that he is engaged–that is, sexually potent–he is also commercially potent: he has displaced his father and permits himself to imagine the father's death. A further thematic possibility besides those of the family dissolution in assimilated Jewry and the dynamics in the Kafka family is that of the lonely artist caught up by mundane responsibilities: Georg, a writer reduced to

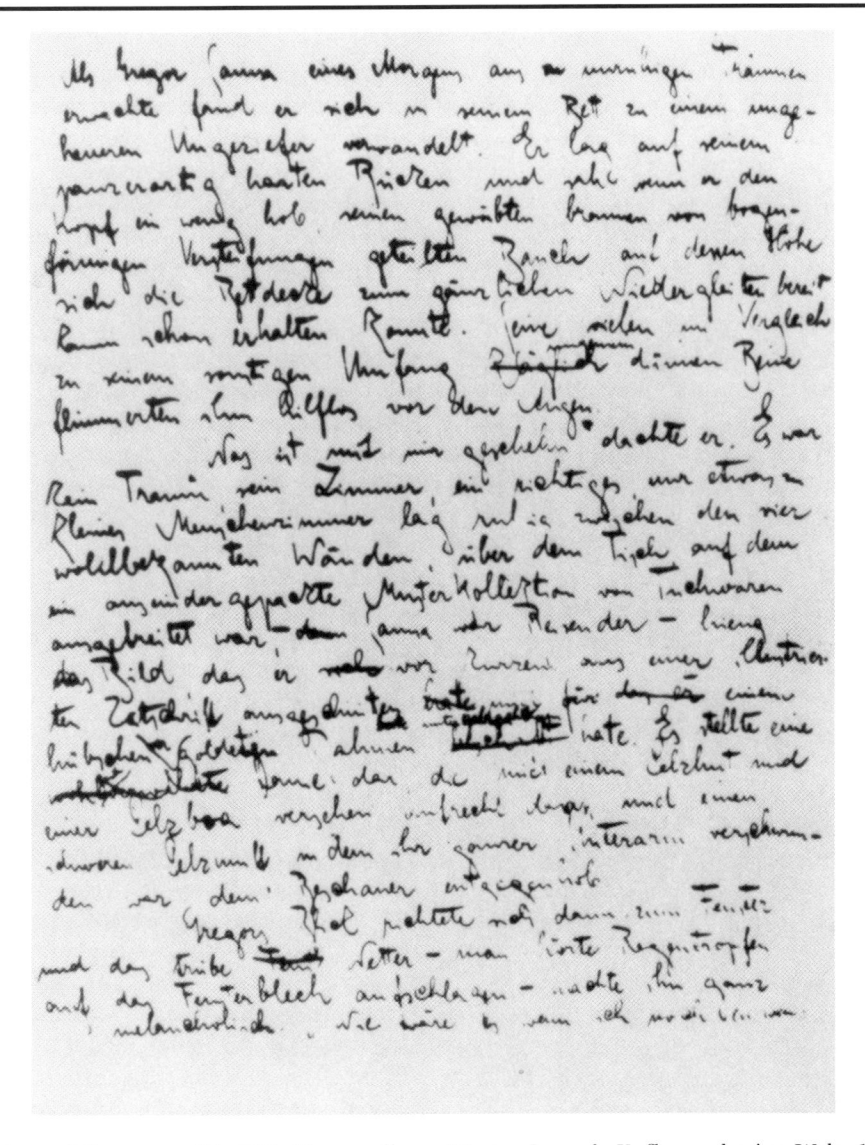

First page of the manuscript of Die Verwandlung *(Gustav Janouch,* Kafka und seine Welt, *1965)*

writing letters, may regard bourgeois marriage as a powerful threat to further writing; thus his unreluctant compliance with his father's judgment of death.

Whichever of the thematic possibilities the reader prefers, he should probably reexamine his natural tendency to identify with Georg, the ostensible victim. In fact, Georg is far from admirable. His manipulativeness is revealed by the letter: he is trying to give the appearance of extending an invitation without really doing so. He also manipulates his father, who is probably fed up with it. His chief concern about Frieda is not related to love and—despite his father's coarse innuendo—perhaps not to sex either, but to the fact that she comes from a prosperous family.

In November and December 1912 Kafka wrote *Die Verwandlung*. The writing took about three weeks; two of them overlapped with extra duties as a substitute superintendent of the family's recently acquired asbestos factory, and of course his duties at the insurance office went on as usual. From this uncongenial mélange of preoccupations came one of the most widely read and discussed works of world literature: a shocking and yet comic tragedy of modern man's isolation, inadequacy, and existential guilt. *Die Verwandlung* represents a substantial advance in technique over *Das Urteil*, and even more over *Amerika*, which still lay incomplete in Kafka's drawer.

While *Amerika* is loose and episodic, never intended by Kafka to be published, *Die Verwandlung* is compact, artistically and formally structured,

Cover, with illustration by Ottomar Starke, for Kafka's story of a man who awakes to find himself transformed into a gigantic insect. Although the date on the cover is 1916, the volume was published in November 1915 (Ludwig Dietz, Franz Kafka: Die Veröffentlichungen zu seinen Lebzeiten, *1982).*

and at least for a short while it had the approbation of its author. After some equivocation Kafka agreed to its publication in *Die Weißen Blätter* and in book form by Kurt Wolff in 1915–although by then he had again changed his mind about its quality: he found the story as a whole to be imperfect and the ending unreadable.

Like the name Raban in "Hochzeitsvorbereitungen auf dem Lande," the surname of the protagonist in *Die Verwandlung*, Gregor Samsa, is a cryptogram of the name Kafka. While Gregor Samsa shares with his fictional predecessor Raban the distinction of turning into an insect, Gregor's metamorphosis is quite different in that it is unwilled, total, and irrevocable. A traveling salesman, Gregor awakens at home one dreary morning after a night of troubled dreams to find himself transformed into a monstrous, beetlelike bug. Unable to go to the tedious job that has provided financial support for his parents and sister, he is held prisoner in a room and subjected to violent persecution by his father and to progressively lessened care and solicitude by his sister. Failing to find satisfaction or nourishment in the fresh food she initially brings him, and gradually taking less interest in sustenance of any sort, alternately ignored and persecuted, he starves and dies, then is swept up and disposed of by the cleaning woman.

Die Verwandlung comprises three Roman-numbered sections, each with its own climax. The first climax occurs when Gregor, having unwisely ventured from his bedroom, is attacked by his father–who, not incidentally, has resumed his role as the family breadwinner. In the second climax Gregor is again driven back to his bedroom; this time his father throws an apple at him which lodges in his back and rots. In the third section, attracted to the living room by his sister's violin playing, Gregor for the last time is driven back to his room, where death comes. After the prompt disposal of his remains his family, buoyant with joy, goes on a spring outing in the country. Although Kafka later found this ending unreadable, it is nonetheless a well-motivated conclusion, lending the story a sense of integrated completeness rarely found in Kafka's previous fiction.

As in *Das Urteil*, the father-son estrangement is thematically fundamental in *Die Verwandlung;* at one point Kafka had the idea of publishing the two novellas together with *Der Heizer* in a single volume to be titled "Söhne" (Sons). In *Die Verwandlung*, however, he achieves a firmer artistic grip on his personal estrangement. Still, the lurking Oedipal component, as well as a counterbalancing sense of humor, are both on view when Gregor is obliged to witness the one scene that he would above all prefer not to see: his mother, stumbling in a mass of hurriedly removed petticoats, hurling herself on his father, with whom she shares perfect sexual congress.

It is not only the father's sexual energy that revives; in the economic sphere his revival is no less marked. From premature retirement he reemerges, coincident with Gregor's transformation, to the fiscal leadership of his beleaguered family, proud in his new role as bank messenger. Even at home he wears the smart uniform of his new calling, with its gold buttons and accumulated grease spots. On resuming the management of the family purse, he finds the latter not to be in such bad shape after all: it contains a reserve

Kafka with his sister Ottla, circa 1914. All three of Kafka's sisters were to die in Nazi concentration camps.

that inexplicably had escaped the collapse of the former family business, and Gregor's long and arduous labors have largely liquidated a family debt to his employer. Restored to his proper petty-bourgeois authority, Samsa senior even feels expansive enough to allow Gregor's bedroom door to be left ajar so that he may have the solace of seeing the family grouped about the lamp-lit table.

Grete is the only Samsa with whom the metamorphosed Gregor has any rapport. Her feelings, however, can survive neither the awful disparity between their personal situations nor her emergence from adolescence. At first she serves Gregor his food conscientiously and does her best to make him comfortable in his new circumstances. She becomes the family expert on Gregor, his representative to their uncomprehending mother and to their antagonistic and revitalized father. But dealing with the unpredictabilities of an insect brother proves too much for the idealistic girl, who at about sixteen years of age undergoes her own metamorphosis into a clear-sighted, practical-minded young woman. She honors the memory of her lost brother, but she no longer objects to the notion of ridding her and her parents' lives of the bug that now dwells in his room.

The climax of Grete's metamorphosis and of Gregor's plight comes when she plays an impromptu violin concert for her parents and the family's three lodgers, all of whom become bored and hostile. On the other hand, Gregor is deeply moved, as if discovering the spiritual nourishment he longed for, and crawls from his room. As a human being he had never had the slightest interest in music, but now, shed of his human materialism, he finds himself propelled toward a mystical union with the music and fantasizes imprisoning his sister and her violin in his room with him forever; his fantasy suggests latent incestuous desire, set free as the music liberates his spiritual desire.

When the lodgers excitedly demand explanations for Gregor's presence and his advance toward the music, the violin recital ends. While the lodgers give notice, Grete rushes into their room and in a flurry of blankets and pillows dexterously makes up their beds. Her violin slips onto the floor with a loud clang, symbolizing her definitive rejection of Gregor. Her whirlwind bedmaking suggests acceptance of her domestic adult function in the real world–the essence of her metamorphosis. It is Grete who has taken to referring to Gregor as "it" and who locks him in his room shortly before the end. The insect's last glance as it is being forced back into its room is at its mother, whom the tumult of the scene has left in a state of exhausted sleep.

While Gregor has metamorphosed and his father and sister have been fundamentally, if less spectacularly, transformed, his mother remains unchanged and somewhat peripheral to the action. Less hostile than the father and with occasional flashes of insight superior to the sister's, she is for the most part unsure of herself, overexcited, subject to asthmatic seizure, all too anxious to indulge her husband–the veritable picture of the harried middle-class housewife.

The reader is not required to grieve for Gregor. Whether before or after his transformation, Gregor is unsuited for the burdensome existence that he was obliged to lead; he is incapable of articulating his desire for a different sustenance, and thus he comes to see that he ought to disappear. With an apple–the fruit of knowledge–stuck in his back, he simply dries up from a not very strongly willed self-starvation of himself. Or maybe his death is not really willed at all but simply an acquiescence. Outside his window dawn is beginning to lighten the world as his head sinks to the floor and he breathes his last. Last-minute illumination from a window or doorway occurs at the moment of expiration of more than one Kafka hero. It is a subject of critical debate whether this light is to be taken as a sign of eschatological hope or is to be taken ironically.

Running parallel with the largely autobiographical theme of the father-son relationship is the theme of losing and then regaining bourgeois status. The reestablishment of the family under the father's dominance is ironically confirmed by the narrator's giving the parents back their proper bourgeois titles: after Gregor's body is certified to be lifeless his parents again become Herr and Frau Samsa rather than father and mother. Shortly thereafter, they note that their daughter Grete is shapely and marriageable; having sacrificed Gregor on the altar of middle-class respectability they are prepared to do the same–only the mechanics are different–to Grete. Everyone, even Grete, is in a good mood as they embark on their Sunday outing. Not only has Gregor departed, but his departure permits more extensive bourgeois self-authentication than the Samsas had ever known.

In 1913 and 1914 Kafka carried on an intense correspondence with Felice Bauer. He was a prolific letter writer and seemed in his element in courting by mail, although he included generous helpings of self-doubt about marriage. He doubted that he could combine the roles of writer and bourgeois husband, and the former was more important to him. He visited Felice three times in 1913, and early in 1914 he went to Berlin to see her again. The two-day visit, however, resulted in even greater doubt and mutual misunderstanding. Yet only four months later, on 12 April, their engagement was officially announced–only to be broken, at Kafka's insistence, on 12 July. His letters and diaries show that in addition to perceiving the incompatibility between writing and the demands of middle-class domesticity, he regarded writing as the means of escaping the intolerabilities of a life so awful that he likened it to an underworld. Kafka's uncertain relationship with Felice during this trying period was mediated by a girlfriend of Felice's, Grete Bloch, who later asserted that Kafka was the father of her son.

Cover for Kafka's novella about an execution machine (Deutsches Literaturarchiv)

In August 1914 the thirty-one-year-old Kafka, having completed the novella *In der Strafkolonie* (1919; translated as "In the Penal Colony," 1941) and begun working on the novel *Der Prozeß* (1925; translated as *The Trial*, 1937), finally moved out of his parents' home. He moved a second time after only a month; nowhere, it seemed, could he escape the distraction of noise and disturbance.

World War I, which broke out in August 1914, seems to have had a remarkably remote effect on Kafka. Owing to his position with the semigovernmental insurance company he was initially exempted from the mobilization. After a trip to war-torn Hungary in 1915 he attempted to enlist in the army but was rejected: in 1914 his incipient tuberculosis had been diagnosed as bronchitis.

In der Strafkolonie is set in a maritime and tropical locale; because it seems to be so much like the formerly notorious French penal colony on Devil's Island, the reader tends to make that identification. Kafka, celebrated otherwise for the absence of distance between the narrative point of view and the events narrated, here interposes a noteworthy distance between the explorer-narrator and the shocking events that he describes. The effect is one of coolness, contrasting effectively with both the tropical heat and the ardor of the executioner and his former superior, the old commandant, for summary judgments of guilt and execution. The judgments are carried out by an officer who presides over a horrible execution machine, which under a new commandant has suffered from a lack of replacement parts and is just barely serviceable. The renowned foreign explorer is witness first to an aborted execution and then to one he could hardly have expected. A simple, animallike soldier has been ordered to awaken every night each hour on the hour to salute his captain's door. At two o'clock one morning he failed to wake up and did not thereafter take kindly to being lashed in the face, nor did he beg the captain's pardon. The judgment pronounced on him is that he shall be killed on the execution machine. He has not been allowed to know the charge against him, to offer a defense, or even to comprehend his sentence. In any case, guilt in Kafka's work is never subject to doubt.

The officer in charge of the execution machine, evidently hoping that a well-impressed foreign dignitary might induce the new commandant to support the renovation and retention of the machine, delivers a long, tendentious explanation while he prepares the machine for the condemned. It is not designed to work quickly. Its victims give up the ghost in twelve hours, during which time their sentence is inscribed into their flesh by the apparatus—the disobedient soldier is to have the legend "Ehre deine Vorgesetzten" (Honor thy Superiors) stitched into his body. Before death, the officer believes, the victims arrive at an insight into their guilt and their sentence—they experience a transfiguration.

In its present, jury-rigged state the apparatus presents a decided contrast to its former efficient operation. In the days of its splendor, under the aggressive sponsorship of the old commandant, huge throngs turned out to witness and be enlightened by its work. Now no one attends; even the new commandant stays away. The decrepitude of the machine is signaled by the loud creaking of a badly worn cogwheel.

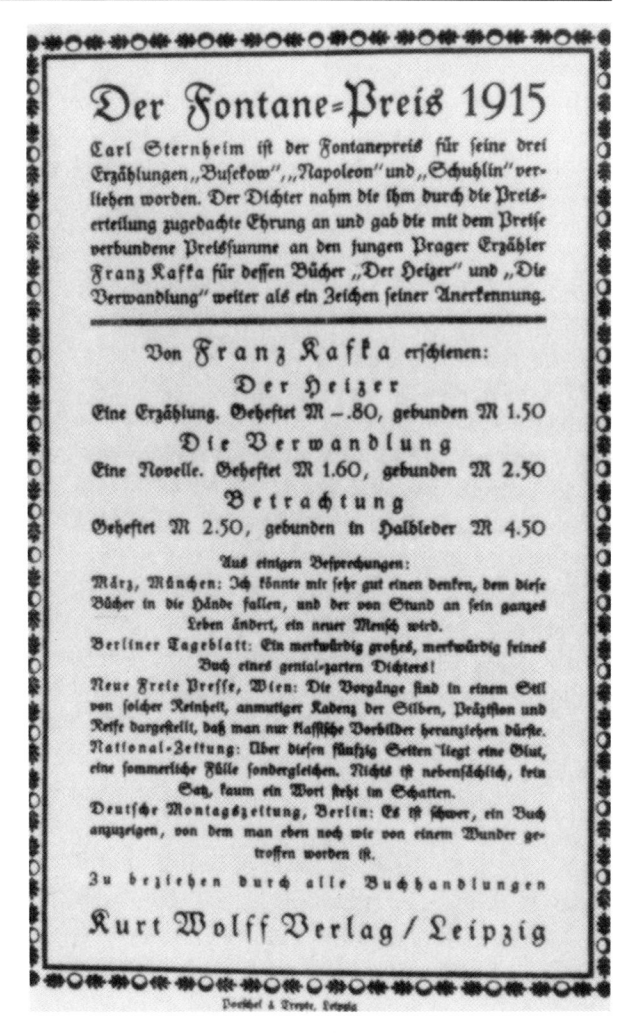

Publisher's announcement, mentioning several of Kafka's works (Deutsches Literaturarchiv)

In spite of the lobbying by the officer, the explorer declines to promise his support of this method of execution before the new commandant. At that, the execution is halted, the condemned man is removed from the apparatus, and the officer takes his place. He cannot reach the starter, but the machine starts itself and even runs for a while without the noise from the worn cogwheel. Soon, however, the gear assembly comes completely apart; the summary sentence of the officer on himself is accomplished in much less than twelve hours. The expression on his corpse suggests no hint of the advertised insight and transfiguration.

The apparently anachronistic status of the officer, an obviously unfavored, even imperiled survivor from the predecessor administration, suggests a Nietzschean theme. This theme requires the reader to perceive the old commandant—who is now dead but whose tombstone prophesies his resurrection and recovery of the old colony–in a positive light, as the representative of a tough and righteous era whose values have been supplanted by a less rigorous, soft order with overtones of feminine weakness and compassion. The new commandant's ladies supply the doomed prisoner with candy before his date with the machine, as well as diverting the commandant from properly exercising his authority. There is a suggestion that the ladies have even softened up the officer in charge of the execution machine, for several ladies' handkerchiefs are to be seen within the neckband of his inappropriately nontropical uniform, helping to soak up the sweat produced by the performance of his office. The work of the machine in making its victims see the light suggests Nietzsche's valuing of pain as a teacher, although the suggestion is free of parodistic implication: the officer's contention that the final expression of the victims reveals transfiguration fails to be verified in his own case.

The story can be interpreted as an analogue to the crucifixion of Christ, with the execution machine standing for the cross. Early critics of Kafka often supported this interpretation, and it has returned to favor despite the obstacle that Kafka was not a Christian. Assertions that Kafka, heir to an assimilationist tradition but increasingly interested in Judaism, flirted with becoming a Christian are quite incorrect. Furthermore, the quite nondivine officer in *In der Strafkolonie* shows no sign of resurrection, and his features fail to reflect the transfiguration that he attributed to the machine's victims in the course of their torture-execution. It is tempting to suggest that the execution of the officer is a parody of the crucifixion; that interpretation seems questionable, however, for the same reason that an exclusively religious interpretation is unlikely: a paucity of sufficient identifying detail.

Kafka's later fiction dispenses with the distanced narrative perspective represented here by the visiting explorer. In the later works there is a closer relationship–even a complete identity–between the narrative point of view and the protagonist. What is sacrificed in narrative tension is replaced by a subtly complex psychology.

Within weeks of terminating his engagement to Felice Bauer in 1914 Kafka had written all but the last chapter of *Der Prozeß*; that chapter was completed in 1916. Kafka gave the manuscript to Brod in 1920. Despite the author's wish that it be destroyed, Brod took it upon himself to have the novel published after Kafka's death.

Brod arranged the unnumbered chapters of the novel according to a sequence based on his memory of Kafka's having read the novel aloud before a group of friends; nonetheless, internal evidence has suggested a different sequence to many critics. (Kafka enjoyed reading *Der Prozeß* to his friends; the first chapter especially gave rise to hearty laughter on the part of author and audience. Conditioned to the mystifying and grotesque elements in Kafka's fiction and to the solemnity that characterizes his Anglo-American reception, one may find it difficult to keep in mind the mirthful first reception of the novel. But there is indeed humor there and elsewhere in Kafka. He had not become enamored of the Yiddish theater for nothing: he knew the comedy of domestic situation, and he was not above using one-liners and burlesque-style skits.)

The novel is fundamentally autobiographical. The hero, Joseph K., shares many characteristics with his author: he is a businessman in Prague whose surname begins with a *K*; further, Joseph K. has just passed his watershed thirtieth birthday as Kafka had just observed his thirty-first. The events of the novel cover one year, and Joseph K. is assassinated on the eve of his thirty-first birthday.

The structure is episodic, hardly less so than that of *Amerika*. Characters frequently disappear, never to return or at most to reappear fleetingly. But *Der Prozeß* is not a detective story with characters and strands to be traced and neatly resolved. The focus of the novel is not the Law that hounds Joseph K. to death but rather Joseph K. himself and his flawed responses to the machinations of the Law.

One morning Joseph K. is arrested without having done anything wrong. He is still in bed in his quarters at Frau Grubach's lodging house when two warders, the lowest rank of Court officials, burst in to arrest him. The warders, Franz and Willem, do not know what he is charged with; they know only that his arrest has been preceded by an adequate investigation and that the Law is not given to frivolous accusation. The officials of the Law, higher officials than the warders, do not go hunting for crime; rather, they are drawn to the guilty. In giving one of the warders his own first name, Kafka calls attention–whether ironically or not–to the compromised authenticity of his "autobiographical" hero, K.

As a high-ranking bank officer Joseph K. knows more than a smattering of law. (In a dis-

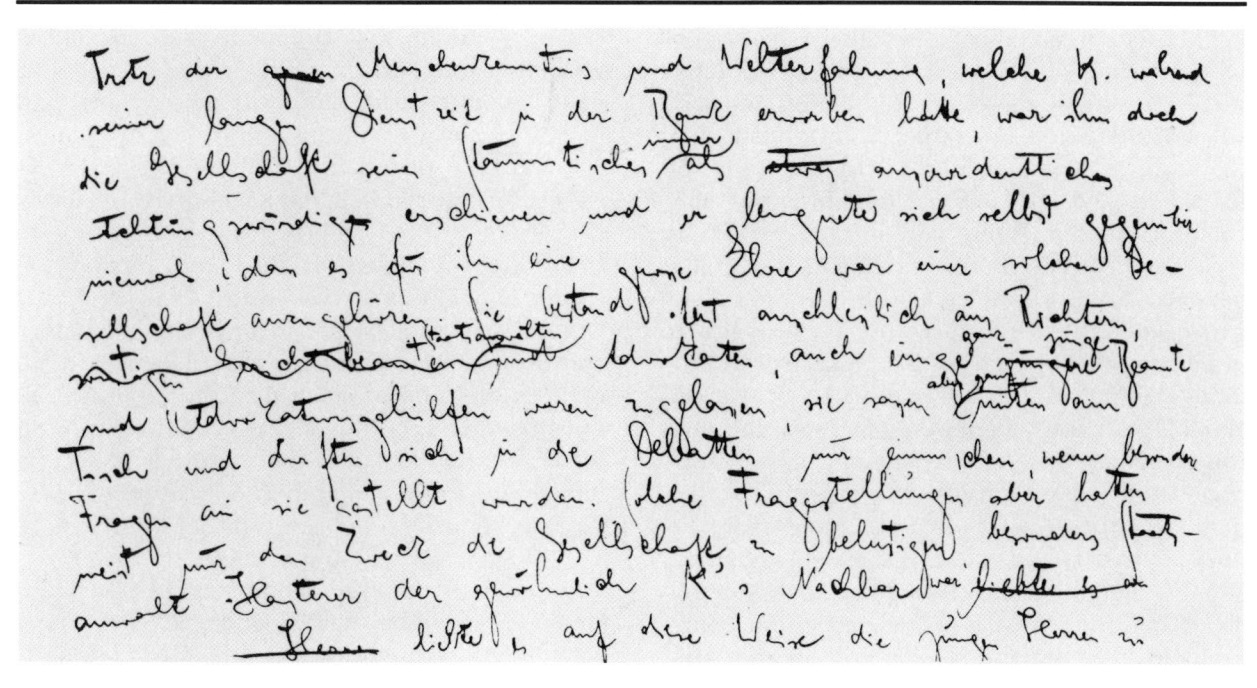

Part of a page from the manuscript of Der Prozeß

carded draft he is shown as a confidant and friend of lawyers and judges. Kafka's deletion of this chapter demonstrates his penchant for economy of narration.) But his arrest so throws him off guard that he fails to use even his mother wit very sensibly: he looks a bit of a fool madly rummaging around after his bicycle license, with the intention of presenting it to the warders as documentation that should lead to the dropping of his case. The warders eat his breakfast, then offer to get a take-out breakfast for him from an apparently–in K.'s haughty view–not very clean coffeehouse across the street.

The arrival of the inspector to afford K. a preliminary hearing right on Frau Grubach's premises does nothing to apprise K. of the charge against him. The inspector recommends that instead of trying so hard to find out what his offense was, he ought to be thinking more about himself. The context of his recommendation tends to reinforce its theme: it is K.'s thirtieth birthday, life's dividing point. As a true adult, K. ought to abandon his argumentative and rationalizing responses and engage in serious contemplation of his self. He may be a wunderkind in the banking business, but in his personal life he is distinctly immature. Doubtless the omniscient Court that has ordered K.'s arrest already knows that K. has given short shrift to his family responsibilities and that his entire emotional life consists of once-a-week appointments to have sex with Elsa, a cabaret waitress.

The hearing itself is a comedy of irregularity, conducted in the bedroom of another of Frau Grubach's tenants, Fräulein Bürstner, who is absent during the day. Fräulein Bürstner's nightstand is pressed into service as a desk. The two bumbling warders are joined by three anemic young men who stand about idly, regard K. gravely, and display an improper curiosity about Fräulein Bürstner's personal photographs. This motley group is witnessed from the window across the way by a curious and salacious old couple.

The reader does not get to know Fräulein Bürstner well, even when, much later in the novel, she appears in person. K. obviously has a crush on her in which gallant friendship and a desire to talk are mixed with lust and jealousy about her being out on a date after 11:00 P.M. She is the fictional persona of Felice Bauer, with whom Kafka had just broken his engagement. Kafka never gives Bürstner's first name; in the published novel she is consistently referred to as Fräulein Bürstner and in the manuscript by the initials F. B.

It is an odd form of arrest under which Joseph K. finds himself. He is not to be hauled away, decrees the inspector; he is not to be hindered from pursuing his ordinary life, including returning to work at the bank as soon as the hearing is over. To accompany him there the inspector has detained the three anemic young men, who, it suddenly dawns on K., are his subordinates at the bank. His earlier failure to identify them can of course be attributed to the shock of his arrest and the unusual circumstances surrounding it. Something additional, however, is reflected here: the hermetic separateness of his personal and professional worlds, the rigid compartmentalization of his perceptions. Flexibility is not among the advantages that K. takes with him in his contest with the Law and the Court. For example, if K.'s disposition were of a less rigid, preconceived cast, he might have derived useful guidance from Frau Grubach's unsophisticated but clear-sighted advice. Freely admitting that she does not understand K.'s arrest, she goes on to assert that there is no need to understand it. K. is unable to accept such a simple suggestion, since Frau Grubach is a stupid woman. Kafka is inviting the reader to ponder who is really stupid, the uncomplicated Frau Grubach or the sophisticated Joseph K.

On receiving a summons to his first formal interrogation, K. is impelled to attend by his desire to find out the identity of his adversary and the nature of the charge against him. While that desire may strike the reader as perfectly normal, the point is that it is not knowledge of his opponent but knowledge of himself that K. needs. The facts that the place of his hearing is in an unlikely tenement district and that the date is on a Sunday, with no hour specified, should give K. pause. But he is resolved to fight; he is strong and determined. Yet a physical toll is exacted from him even on his first confrontation with his adversary, and it will be increased during subsequent encounters. The Court, when he finally finds it, is in the attic room of a tenement, overcrowded with workers on their day off, airless, dirty, and hot. The fetid atmosphere weakens him.

K. makes fine speeches in his defense before the tenement Court, dwelling on the impropriety, the unfairness of the charge against him–whatever that charge might be. In front of the assembly–only somewhat later does he realize that they are all, no matter how shabbily dressed, officials of the Court–K. makes it his tactic to humiliate the examining magistrate. He denounces the warders and the whole organization behind his arrest. When he starts to stalk out, the magistrate informs him that he has flung away all the advantages that an interrogation confers on an accused. Naturally that comment is ironic, but it also has a measure of truth in the case of K., who has overreacted and will do so more and more as his plight worsens and his energy wanes.

Kafka is plainly intent on establishing a social chasm between K. and his adversary. In an earlier version of the novel the Court session is a socialist meeting; even in the final version the reader is not permitted to forget that the Court is a court of proletarians in proletarian territory and that K. is a middle-class striver interloping in that territory. It is probably difficult for an American reader to keep this severe class distinction in focus; but in thematic importance it is second only to K.'s existential guilt and is connected with the latter to it.

Despite Marxist interpretations, Kafka was not concerned to write a novel of social protest, let alone revolution. Rather, and as almost invariably, his concern is with the individual. The constantly reiterated social gulf, even as it stirs K.'s repugnance and discomfort, also feeds his self-satisfaction and props up his self-righteous ego, blinding him to the necessity of forgetting his legal innocence and the traducers thereof and of confessing his existential guilt.

K.'s unbidden second visit to the Court on the following Sunday reiterates the social gulf between him and his tormentors and indicates the attrition of his resistant energy. (The German noun *Prozeß* means process as well as trial.) Touring the upstairs offices of the Court with an usher, K. realizes that the many accused persons waiting in the lobby belong to the same social class as he. When he queries a gray-haired man as to what he is waiting for he receives a confused answer that hardly relates to the question. This response is reminiscent of K.'s own slightly ridiculous confusion on first being arrested, and it anticipates his confusion a moment later at suddenly feeling overwhelmingly tired and faint, wanting only to get out to some fresh air. Just as suddenly, K. becomes passive; unable to either make or find his way, he has to be accompanied to an exit. In his passivity K. hears a voice declaring that even though he is told a hundred times that the way out is right in front of him, he still fails to respond to the information.

The fifth chapter, "Der Prügler" (The Whipper), clarifies the thematic importance of K.'s having failed to recognize his bank subordinates at the scene of his arrest. He is worried that word of his case will be leaked at the bank, that his exalted station as putative successor to the manager-

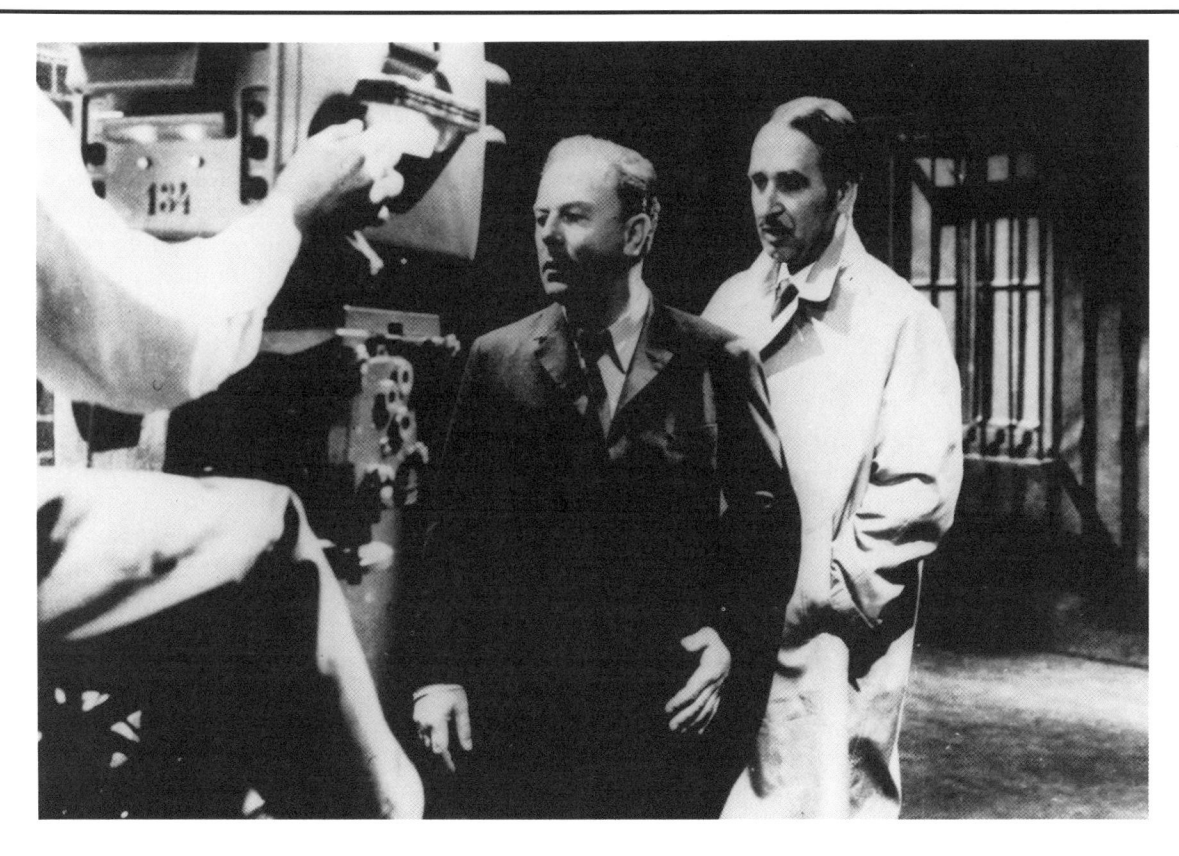

Scene from an operatic version of Der Prozeß, *produced for Austrian television in 1960 (Austrian Cultural Institute)*

ship will be threatened; thus he resorts to subconscious—the nonidentification—as well as conscious stratagems to keep his personal and professional worlds isolated from each other. The maintenance of this separation becomes especially difficult when he hears convulsive sighs issuing from a storage room at the bank. On entering the little-used room he encounters a stranger clad in dark leather beating two other men on their bare backs with a whip. It takes a while before he recognizes the victims as the bumbling warders, Franz and Willem, who had originally placed him under arrest. He had complained to the presiding magistrate about their unprofessional conduct, which is why, the victims shout, they are being whipped. K. honestly declares that he had not asked that they be punished. Forget the excuses, replies the whipper; the punishment is proper and inevitable. That declaration, of course, has a powerful relevance for K.'s own case.

K. has not comprehended that relevance. He is, in any event, less motivated by humane consideration than by the threat to his position posed by the cruel and indecent scene occurring on the bank premises. K.'s attempt to bribe the whipper to stop having proved unsuccessful and the victims' shrieks having become too loud to be ignored, he hurriedly abandons the storage room and assures the two concerned clerks rushing to the scene that the noise is a dog howling in the courtyard. The next day he finds the unsavory tableau in the storage room unchanged, except that the unhappy workers are now completely naked. Distancing himself from the proceedings, he orders the clerks to clean out the room, which he declares is smothered in filth. His order is at odds with his desire to conceal the goings-on in the storage room; perhaps that is why he accedes to the clerks' notion of performing the task the next day. But again, K.'s peremptory cleanup campaign is not so much related to a repugnance toward filth—though he is in fact fastidiously sensitive to dirt—as to an enforcement of the mutual exclusivity between his legal case and his profession. While K. allows himself to imagine that his security remains unbreached, actually the word is out. When his Uncle Karl in the country is informed, he hurries to the aid of his nephew; but K. refuses help from a person he associates with his childhood. The latter is one more walled-off compartment in K.'s psyche.

In spite of the increasing signs, K. is unable to grasp just how serious his plight is. He affects an insouciance quite at variance with what is going on around him. While he fears for his position at the bank enough to take defensive measures, at the same time he underestimates the strength and resourcefulness of his adversaries.

The theme of underestimation dominates chapter 6. K. is by no means enthusiastic about going with his Uncle Karl to consult the lawyer Huld, who was his uncle's classmate (his name, ironically, means grace or mercy in German). Huld, ill though he is, is nevertheless well informed about K.'s case, for he has remained in touch with his colleagues and their professional gossip. More than that, he is at the moment receiving a visit from the chief clerk of the Court that is K.'s nemesis. Uncle Karl joins the discussion, while K. goes off to the study and makes love with Leni, the lawyer's nurse and mistress.

Not only is Leni an exhilarating sexual partner–a fantasized sex object in the manner of many of Kafka's fictional young women–but she is bright and is disposed to use her intelligence in K.'s behalf. From the professional confabulation she has heard that K. is excessively unyielding. She accordingly advises him to confess his guilt. K., having almost willfully damaged his case by making love to his lawyer's mistress, does not believe that a confession might render his case moot. But he does believe that the sick lawyer can do little effective work for his case.

K.'s position at the bank daily becomes more tenuous, dangerous, and complicated. In his growing preoccupation he finds it more and more difficult to clear his mind to serve the needs of the bank's clients. The assistant manager, who is also ambitious for the managership, practically kidnaps K.'s clients. One such client, however, more sympathetic than most, recommends that K. get in touch with a certain Titorelli. Titorelli is not a lawyer, but an artist; yet he has worked for the Court and is well versed in its operations. Such an advocate could prove most useful; even K. is beginning to be aware of his diminishing alertness and vitality, and of the risk entailed thereby. He is helped to this awareness after casually proposing to write Titorelli, a step that, as the helpful client points out to him, could easily prove self-incriminating.

Titorelli's combined studio and living quarters, cramped and stifling, are in a shabby tenement. The painter sympathetically acquaints K. with details of Court procedure, with the kind of justice the Court dispenses, and with the three types of acquittal that are theoretically possible. He volunteers to represent K.'s interests before the Court. Hopeful as all of this sounds, it does not advance K.'s real, though unadmitted interest; it merely facilitates his inquiry into the essence of the Court, whereas he ought to be directing his efforts into self-inquiry. Titorelli is pragmatic where Huld was obscure; where Huld was inconclusive, Titorelli proposes an active defense. He distinguishes between what is written in the Law and the practices he has discovered behind the facade. With good luck, personal connections and influence may prevent a case from achieving formal status before the higher Court. Insusceptible to being shaken from its prior persuasion of guilt, such a higher Court has never been known to issue a decree of definite acquittal. A lower Court is empowered to issue only two decrees: if the defendant and his counsel engage in a concentrated defensive effort they may receive a decree of ostensible acquittal, in which case the charges may be reinstituted at any time; continual but less concentrated defense activity may be answered by a decree of indefinite postponement, with the risks obviously inherent in such a verdict. How much simpler it would be for K. to turn inward and confess his guilt, even though he knows of no offense that he has committed. Titorelli's establishment proves to be adjacent to Court offices–which, he assures K., are in almost every attic. The stifling air in Titorelli's place was the indicator. Even the band of juvenile harlots that besets K. when he emerges is owned by the Court, which indeed owns everything.

Titorelli's instruction impresses K. enough to make him decide to dismiss Huld, and, in the unfinished eighth chapter, he visits the lawyer to inform him that his services are no longer needed. Naturally, Leni is at Huld's, and she assumes cheerfully that K. is going to spend the night with her. But also there is Huld's client Block, whose case has dragged on before the Court for five and a half years–K.'s is at the six-month mark. Block has been reduced to a subhuman figure by the wear and tear of his case, as conducted by Huld and at intervals, with especially sad results, by himself. He is broke, depleted physically and spiritually, and humiliated by Huld, who has converted him into a fawning animal. The last is reflected in a spectacle enacted for K.'s benefit after K. has dismissed the lawyer. This cruel humiliation demonstrates what sort of treatment is reserved for the accused who try to free themselves from the entanglement of Huld's counsel: they are tortured by rumor, subjected to cruel and teasing innuendo, and then despised for their cringing fear. Ironically, it is K.'s despised avuncular connection that saves him from Block's pitiful fate.

The chapter breaks off, to be followed by the chapter "Im Dom" (In the Cathedral), which revolves around the parable "Vor dem Gesetz" (Before the Law). This parable is the key not only to the chapter containing it but to the entire novel. Kafka sets up the parable, which is the only passage in *Der Prozeß* that has a specifically Jewish resonance, with a skill that transcends the episodic nature of the novel. K. is dragooned into serving as guide and quasi-art expert for a visiting Italian client of the bank. He possesses a modest command of Italian and an equally modest layman's knowledge of the artworks displayed in the cathedral, but he is reluctant to commit his time and energies to the project when they are needed to reduce the number of mistakes he is making with ever greater frequency at the bank. Still, his cooperation in serving as companion to the visitor may help compensate for his errors. On top of everything else, he has a severe cold and an even more severe headache. The day is cold, rainy, and dark.

There are further indications that K. is losing his grip. For half of the preceding night he had buried himself in his Italian grammar, laboriously copying, reciting, and memorizing words and phrases that he suppose might be useful on the tour of the cathedral the next day. But now he has forgotten it all; his usually excellent memory has deserted him. To add to K.'s woes the Italian speaks a southern dialect that K. can understand only fragmentarily. Inexplicably K.'s manager understands it well, forcing K. to strain to tune out the Italian's ceaseless babble while he strives to focus on his manager's concise German summaries.

Just before his departure from his office to meet the Italian, K. receives a phone call from Leni. She is calling, she says, to wish him a good morning. When K. mentions his appointment at the cathedral (which, based on what follows, she may already know about), she maintains that "sie" (they) are goading K. He agrees. Superficially, "they" could mean the bank and its manager, attempting to goad K. into improving his professional performance. But K. reconsiders: Leni works for and lives with Huld, who undertakes cases before the Court. "They" could be the Court. More ambiguously, "they" could be both the bank and the Court, between which, for K., the dividing line is shortly to be dissolved.

The Italian fails to keep his appointment to meet K. at the cathedral. K. feels compelled to wait a bit in case the visitor should arrive late. It is raining so hard that he could hardly leave in any case; on the other hand, the urge to get back to the bank gives him no peace. He could be trying to catch up on his work. He begins to examine the finely wrought great pulpit. It is not likely that the reader has imagined K. to be a pious person; and the latter's study of the great pulpit confirms that his interest in religion is small while his interest in art is considerable.

K. is signaled by a verger to a small, cramped pulpit, above which the lamp is on. When a priest ascends the stairs, apparently to give a sermon, although only a couple of people besides K. are present, K. prepares to leave. But he is brought up short when the priest sharply cries his name. It emerges that the priest, who is the prison chaplain and thus an official of the Court, had K. summoned to the cathedral. The mechanism of the summoning is not further explained. What role–if any–did the Italian client play? The reader tends to follow K.'s false concerns by trying to identify his adversary and its modus operandi. But that is not the problem; K. is the problem.

When the priest relays the information that K.'s case before the Court is going badly, K. proclaims his innocence; he is not guilty, it is all a mistake. How can anyone be guilty? After all, we are merely here in this world. The priest declares that that is how guilty men talk. He has other complaints: K. has too much outside help in this case, especially from women. Shrieking, the priest asks if K. cannot see one pace before him. The implication is that K. is forever focusing on the far distance, on irrelevancies such as what the Court is and why it is pursuing him.

Validating the priest's observation that K. is too dependent, K. is quick to imply his dependency on the priest himself, whom he imagines to be more sympathetic than other minions of the Court. You are entertaining a delusion about the Court, replies the priest. To clarify the delusion he tells the parable of the man from the country and the doorkeeper. The man from the country begs the doorkeeper to admit him to the Law. The doorkeeper asserts that at the moment that is impossible; he may be allowed to enter later, but not now. The doorkeeper dares him to try to get in, warning that inside there is a succession of further doorkeepers, each more powerful than the last. The man decides to wait; the doorkeeper provides a stool. Bribing does not work; the doorkeeper accepts the bribes but does not relent. The man grows old, finally senile, waiting. At length the dying old man asks why it is that in all the years no one else had sought admission. The doorkeeper replies that no one else could gain admittance through this door because the door was intended for the man from the country; and it is now going to be closed.

A difficulty with this parable is that, like practically all Kafka parables, it does not explicate the truth but simply offers a metaphor of truth. K., not surprisingly, holds that it inveighs against deception, such as that perpetrated by the doorkeeper; the priest regards it as a summons to penetrate delusion. Neither of these readings, however, comes to grips with the apparently assumed identity between externally imposed deception and inwardly generated delusion. K. blames the doorkeeper for withholding crucial information from the man. The priest denies any contradiction between the doorkeeper's early refusal to allow the man to enter and the information he reveals at the end of the man's days; there would, accordingly, be no deception.

The disputants reach a shaky common ground in the possibility that both the doorkeeper and the man from the country were deluded. But the priest objects that it is not permissible to render a judgment on the doorkeeper, who, as a representative of the Law, is beyond judgment. The priest concludes by saying that one must not look for truth but should accept necessity. K. objects that such a principle merely licenses lying. K. is by now worn down by the stress of work, the preparation for the Italian's visit, the failure of the guest to show up, and finally by the strenuous argument with the aggressive priest; but his desire to leave the cathedral is countervailed by a desire to talk further with the priest. The latter, however, withdraws his apparent friendliness. That K. has not noticed its superficiality before is further evidence of his capacity for delusion. K.'s need for guidance in getting out of the cathedral reminds one of his earlier need for assistance in evacuating the Court's offices. What has happened over the course of the chapter "Im Dom" is the dissolution of the dividing line between K.'s two fundamentally opposed spheres: the bank, the focus of his professional world, and the Court, the focus of his public world.

Following somewhat abruptly after "Im Dom"–Kafka may well have intended to write intervening chapters–is "Das Ende," the final chapter. It is the eve of K.'s thirty-first birthday; thus one year, less a few hours, has elapsed since K. was accosted by the warders in his bed at Frau Grubach's. As with his arrest, K. has no inkling of his execution. True, he is dressed in black, but that is because he is awaiting other visitors–visitors who will arrive to find him gone, marched by his assassins to a quarry at the edge of town. Grotesque, bumbling, fat, and pallid, wearing top hats, his executioners strike K. as resembling tenth-rate actors from a provincial theater. But they have a butcher knife. On the walk that comes to an end at the quarry, K. seems to discern the figure of Fräulein Bürstner approaching the nearby square. K. resolves to keep his composure and to show that he has learned something from his trial. Whether he really saw Fräulein Bürstner is not the point; whether he has experienced an epiphany or undergone gradual change over the year is of thematic importance.

The motif of darkness and occasionally brief and limited light, prevalent in the cathedral, is replicated on K.'s death walk to the quarry–the reader never knows if the quarry was a prearranged destination or if the executioners just became tired at that point. The night is dark, the street is dark, the windows on the other side of the street are dark. The assassins dispute politely with each other who shall plunge the knife into K.'s breast. K. is supposed to do it himself as a redemptive act of autonomy. But redemption is rarely granted a Kafka hero. Finally, one assassin chokes him while the other wields the knife. Just before the knife-thrust K. discerns a flicker of light in a nearby house. It is as if a light were being turned on at the moment the shutters are thrown open and a human figure stretches forward. Whatever the import of the figure–humanity? succor?–no light actually goes on; rather, like the flash of a light, the shutters burst open.

K. has changed only in that his vitality is worn down. For that reason he can be forgiven for his refusal to take the bravura step with the knife that his executioners keep tossing back and forth. The predominant sense to be derived from this scene is not that it takes more heroism not to be a hero–if indeed heroism may be invoked at all in connection with one's own compul-

Kafka and Felice Bauer at the time of their second engagement, July 1917 (photo: Archiv Klaus Wagenbach)

sory suicide–but rather that a macabre comedy is being played about a man's life. The effect is thus one of irony. K.'s eagerness to assert to himself that he has learned something is simply pitiable, and is made more so by his wish that people be left with the correct idea of his change. In other words, he is as concerned with image as with substance. It does come as a surprise that K., who has not previously consulted God, should do so in his final moment. But he invokes God only to lay at His door the responsibility for his own final failure to act: God had failed to leave him sufficient strength for the deed. K. gives up the ghost with his hands raised, fingers spread, in what might or might not be supplication.

Der Prozeß brims with paradoxes, but the most basic one is that K., burdened with existential guilt, is both guilty and innocent. He thus both receives and is denied justice. The ending of the story is closed: he is murdered. Yet it is open if one prefers to think him redeemed. The use of religious categories is encouraged by the finale; on the other hand, the belated proliferation of devotional attitudes suggests irony. The Court is indisputably K.'s adversary. Yet at the same time K. and the Court are members of a symbiotic relationship in which the Court reflects what is going on in K.'s mind but lacks the will or the power to bring K. to look within himself.

Moving, gripping, paradoxical, humorous, and tragic, *Der Prozeß* is not a closely wrought novel. Still, even though Kafka never prepared it for publication, it is more closely structured than *Amerika*. The penultimate chapter that so persuasively anticipates the end may be penultimate only fortuitously, but the obviously final chapter is in fine balance with the opening chapter. The most prominent detail of this balance lies in the two pairs of bumbling Court officials, one pair initiating K.'s misguided relationship with the Court, the other terminating it.

Kafka and Felice Bauer agreed in July 1917 to marry after the war was over and to live in Berlin, but Kafka's incipient tuberculosis was diagnosed as such in September. Resorting to a psychosomatic explanation, he saw his disease as the triumph of evil in the five-year battle for and against Felice. After five months the second engagement went the way of the first. By this time Kafka was on medical leave with pay from his insurance post and living with his youngest and favorite sister, Ottla, and her husband on their farm in Zürau, a village in northwestern Bohemia. There, while blocking out his third novel, *Das Schloß* (1926; translated as *The Castle*, 1930), he wrote a profusion of stories and parables, including "Ein Landarzt" (translated as "The Country Doctor"), "Beim Bau der chinesischen Mauer" (translated as "The Great Wall of China"), "Ein Bericht für eine Akademie" (translated as "A Report for an Academy") and "Der Jäger Gracchus" (1936; translated as "The Hunter Gracchus," 1960). A collection of fourteen stories and sketches was published by Wolff in 1919 under the title *Ein Landarzt: Kleine Erzählungen* (translated as *The Country Doctor: A Collection of Fourteen Short Stories*, 1945). Even so, Kafka was by no means free of his usual concern that his work fell short of his expectations.

On a blizzardy night the country doctor in "Ein Landarzt" receives an urgent summons to make a house call ten miles away. As he laments

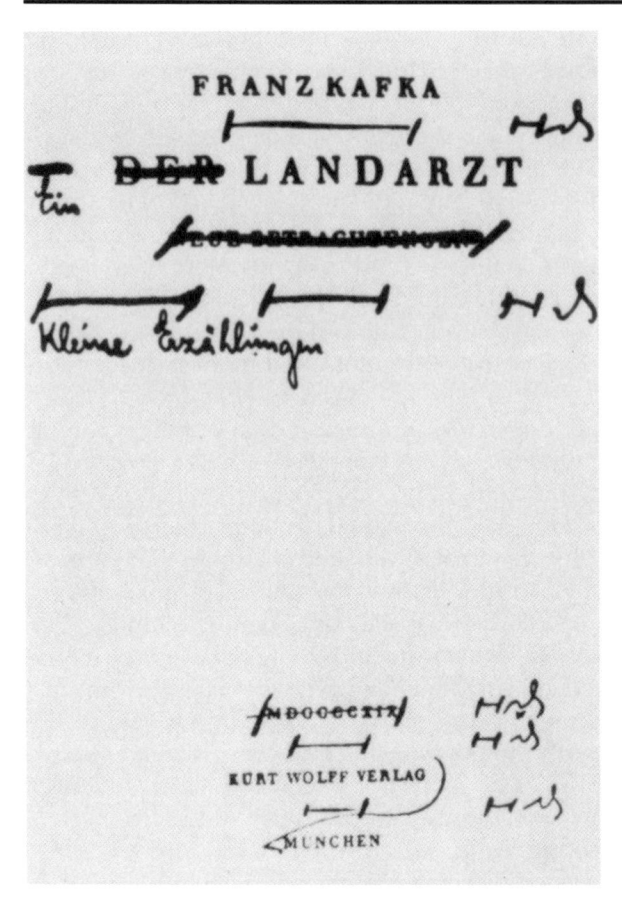

Proof for the title page, with corrections by Kafka, for his 1919 collection of fourteen stories (catalogue of the Kafka Exhibition of the Academy of the Arts, Berlin, 1966)

his lack of transportation–the harsh winter has claimed his horse–two splendid horses and an unknown groom emerge from a supposedly uninhabited pigsty. The doctor drives off to fulfill his duty, while the oafish groom, intent on raping the servant girl Rosa, insists on remaining behind. Speeded by compression of time, as in a dream, the doctor is instantly at the bedside of his patient, a boy who whispers that he desires to die. The doctor at first accuses the boy of malingering, then sees that he has an awful rose-pink wound on his hip, clotted with worms wriggling out toward the light. The doctor falsely assures the boy that his wound is not so bad; in fact, it is incurable. The doctor's supernatural horses peer through the windows, whinnying to remind him that he must return home. Taking curt leave of the young patient's family and friends, he escapes to his sleigh. But the return trip is infinitely labored and slow. He fears that he may never reach home, where he has left poor Rosa to endure the assault of the groom. The night bell to which he had responded was a false alarm, he declares in his desperation–false in that it summoned him to a case beyond his powers: a false era, having abandoned its priests, expects its doctors to save it. Inspired by Kafka's favorite uncle, Siegfried Löwy, who was in fact a country doctor, the doctor is a perplexed Good Samaritan. The quandary in which he finds himself is: shall he save Rosa from the groom or shall he minister to a patient he knows is dying? The groom, indispensable in harnessing the unearthly horses, knows his power, and the doctor cannot neutralize it. He is now prepared, reluctantly, to sacrifice Rosa. If only, he laments, he had been less indifferent over the years that this helpful and pretty girl had lived in his house. He had hardly noticed her, and now. . . . The crisis has stimulated the doctor to a human awareness that had fallen victim to the professional obligations heaped on him by his ungrateful contemporaries. The horns of the doctor's dilemma are joined in the word *rosa* (pink). It is both the girl's name and the color of the patient's wound. The German word, like its English counterpart, also suggests the flower, and, sure enough, the boy's wound is rose-shaped as well as pink. Sexual overtones, heretofore confined to the groom's designs on Rosa, are apparent when, at the boy's house, the boy's family and the village elders strip the doctor naked and put him in bed with the patient, next to the wound. He cannot cure the wound; he is, so to speak, impotent.

"Ein Landarzt" has elicited many Freudian interpretations, most of which point out that the doctor, having ignored Rosa for years, is for all practical purposes impotent with her as well. In any case, the reader is aware that the doctor is beset by failure on every front, a consequence of being obliged to be a shaman as well as a medical man. The most suggestive contribution of Freudian interpretation is in positing the groom as the doctor's long-suppressed id. The dreamlike ambiance, of which the most striking elements are the compression of time and the doctor's final naked flight, also obviously lends itself to Freudian treatment. But Kafka was not writing case histories in "Ein Landarzt" or elsewhere; exhaustive Freudian explication is apt to become mere reductivism. The youngster's flowerlike fatal wound reminds some critics of the wound of King Amfortas in the legend of Parsifal; as such, it would be a mark of the human condition which is beyond the doctor's powers to remedy. Interpretation in Christian terms usually takes its starting point from the wound, which may suggest the wounds of Christ; but redemption is conspicuously absent from the story. The doctor who is perplexed at the start of the story feels betrayed toward the end. He has been betrayed by the groom, maybe by his own id, by the false summons of his night bell, but most of all by his incapacity for coping with new demands that exceed his limited–thus human–competence.

"Beim Bau der chinesischen Mauer" appears at first to have as its theme the social benefit of huge public works. A feared incursion of nomads from the north provides ample reason for erecting the wall. The high command, however, ignoring a fundamental tenet of military defense, has ordered that the wall be built not continuously but in scattered thousand-yard segments. Because each segment requires five years for completion, the wall offers a very porous defense. Even as total completion is proclaimed, word persists that gaps still remain. The subtle Chinese scholar who is the narrator advises against too much diligence in trying to fathom the decrees of the high command, which has, after all, existed for eternity, as has its decision to build the wall. The narrator continues with a discussion of vastness. What is the defense of distant Peking to the people of southeast China? Why should they have to leave their native place to train in unfathomably remote Peking? The people in the remote province hardly know the name of the reigning dynasty, not to speak of that of the emperor. The empire itself is a vague institution; they cannot really conceive of it. Further, the people, rooted in the past and its glories, have allowed themselves to be bypassed by history. The thematic strand that began as one of spatial vastness has evolved into one of time, and it is similar to one of the chief themes of *In der Strafkolonie:* the past is more unrestrained and more vigorous than, and therefore superior to, the present.

The final story in the *Ein Landarzt* collection is "Ein Bericht für eine Akademie." The report, compiled by an ape called Red Peter, chronicles his successful aspiration to become a human being. His transformation commences after his capture on Africa's Gold Coast. In a cage on board ship he perceives that his best interest is served not by escaping and jumping overboard but by learning to imitate the humans around him. Because they are sailors, learning to drink, though revolting to him, is high on his list. He has the wisdom to opt for the vaudeville stage rather than a more commodious cage in a zoo. While being captured, Red Peter received two wounds–one to his cheek, the other to his private parts. In later days, to show visitors where the shot entered, he has the habit of calmly taking down his trousers, knowing even as he does so that what he calls "Windhunde" (windbag commentators) will declare such behavior to be evidence of his still untamed ape nature. Actually, the habit is less a lapse than a provocation. From Red Peter's unhappy assertion that the eye of his ape girlfriend reveals a bewildered, insane look, one may conclude that she, too, has made some progress down the road to becoming human.

Not a part of the *Ein Landarzt* collection is the fragmentary "Der Jäger Gracchus." It is more directly autobiographical than the other stories of the period and thus more reflective of Kafka's state of mind. The name of the hunter appears to be a Latinization of the Italian *gracchio*, which, like the Czech *kavka*, means jackdaw. Gracchus, a German hunter killed in a hunting accident in the Black Forest in the fourth century, was put into a winding sheet and laid in his death boat for transport to the realm of the dead. But the death boat went off course and has been sailing earthly waters with its dead but garrulous passenger for fifteen centuries. Apprised by an advance dove, the mayor of Riva has gone to the harbor to chat with Gracchus. (Riva, by Lake Garda in northern Italy, was a resort town frequently visited by Kafka; he had a brief love affair there in 1913 with an unnamed eighteen-year-old Swiss girl.) All he knows, Gracchus tells the mayor, is that he is forever en route to the other world but never quite attains it. He is a link between men of the present and their forebears–an ineffective link, because no one in the living world is sufficiently interested in the connection to take time to learn about it. And Gracchus is incapable of comprehending the living world. The fundamental incommensurability runs both ways.

In 1918 Kafka contracted influenza, an epidemic of which was then raging worldwide. After three weeks' confinement to bed he obtained further medical leave from his job, during which he convalesced at Schelesen, in the countryside north of Prague.

At Schelesen Kafka met and became engaged to Julie Wohryzek, the keen-witted daughter of a shoemaker and synagogue official in Prague. Kafka's father was outraged that his only son should propose a marital alliance with a socially and economically inferior family. The wedding, scheduled for November 1919, did not take place, for the familiar reason of Kafka's fear that

Postcard from Kafka, who was recuperating from influenza at the Pension Stüdl in Schelesen, December 1918. The circled inscription translates as "Views of my life" (N. N. Glatzer, ed., Letters to Ottla and the Family, *1974)*

marriage would have an adverse effect on his ability to write. Nevertheless, Kafka continued to see Julie well into the inflammatory period of his next romance.

"Brief an den Vater" (1952; translated as *Letter to His Father*, 1953), which Kafka's father never received (either Kafka never sent it or it was intercepted before it reached his father—accounts vary) dates from that troubled November of 1919 when the wedding with Julie Wohryzek failed to occur. It failed to occur because, Kafka says in the letter, for a bourgeois marriage to be successful the man must be forceful, unreflective, healthy, and knowledgeable, all of which he is not. Those are rather the qualities of his father, whereas the son is shy, quiet, bookish, a bit out of place in the bourgeois milieu. Kafka acknowledges his oversensitive fear of his father's noisy, domineering, ridiculing manner, which brought about the loss of whatever filial self-confidence there may have been. In its stead he has only a sense of guilt. It has been an unfair fight: on the one side the defenseless son, on the other a bloodsucking vermin. In spite of the impassioned metaphor, the letter is a rather keen analysis of what went wrong between father and son, with the son's fearfulness readily admitted as a prime ingredient in the bitter brew. "Brief an den Vater" seems to certify the final deterioration of personal contact.

After a somewhat paternal relationship with the much younger Minze Eisner, Kafka's next love affair–typically initiated by letter–was with Milena Jesenská Poláková. She had been the translator of *Der Heizer* into Czech, and Kafka was impressed with the quality of her work. When at length they met he fell madly in love with her. Rendezvous were stormy and passionate. Although Milena's husband physically abused her, she would not leave him. Kafka eventually had to see that, despite the uncustomary ease of his relationship with Milena, it was a love that had nowhere to go. Perhaps it blossomed as it did because he was exempt from the threat of marriage and its feared deleterious effect on his writing.

By 1920 Kafka was almost continually on sick leave. Toward the end of that year, after a creative period that produced several short tales and parables, he was sent to a sanatorium at Matliary in the mountains of Slovakia. Released in September 1921, he returned to his job. In October he was placed on a sick leave of three

Kafka, circa 1922, standing in front of the Prague apartment building where his family lived (photo: Archiv Klaus Wagenbuch)

months. Aware of his deteriorating health, he had already advised Brod that he wanted all of his unpublished work destroyed after his death. In January 1922, at about the time his sick leave expired and its renewal began, he started writing *Das Schloß*.

One inevitably compares its protatonist, K., with the protagonists of *Amerika* and *Der Prozeß*, Karl Rossmann and Joseph K. The K. of *Das Schloß* is more forceful, more aggressive, more consistently tenacious in his quest than the other two. The object of his pursuit is the castle. To be sure, he comes not unbidden: the castle has asked him to come in the capacity of land surveyor. Or has it? Signs are abundant—but far from clear—that he may be an impostor. All the same, he insists on the castle's making good on its presumed offer to him, and he is dogged—if at the same time inwardly uncertain—in his pursuit of his redoubtable target through the maze of its protective bureaucracy.

The circumstances of K.'s arrival near the castle are not propitious. It is evening, it is snowing, he has no surveying equipment, and he is unaccompanied by any assistant such as is essential for land surveying, so that his commitment to surveying is not overwhelmingly convincing. Nor for that matter is his very authenticity: the denotation of his profession, *Landvermesser*, contains not only the suggestion of *messen* (to measure) but also the suggestion of *vermessen* (to strike a presumptuous pose).

Unlike the previous novels, *Das Schloß* does not introduce themes that are never further iterated or developed. Thus, K.'s fatigue on his first evening in the village, where he awaits permission to proceed to the castle, will be often replicated, then become less prominent for a while, to reappear toward the end in full force: K. will be too worn down to take advantage of an opportunity to finally effect a useful connection with the castle.

From the novel's second, terse sentence the reader learns that the village is deep in snow, whereas the castle itself is almost entirely free of snow. That contrast persists: the village seems consistently half-buried in snow. It has always just snowed or is snowing–K. early feels the power of the snow by imprudently getting bogged down in it. Adapting to the all but year-long snow—summer is ephemeral—defines physical existence in the village. Life there is oppressive, whereas the virtually snow-free castle holds out the promise of a better existence.

Not that the castle is a particularly splendid edifice: it is a rambling pile apparently composed of several small buildings. It is not new, but it is not old, either. If it is meant to symbolize God, as some critics have maintained, it is a singularly unprepossessing structure to serve that purpose. It has but one tower, about which fly flocks of crows. It could as well be a symbol of death—that has been critically suggested, too—as of divinity. Days are short; darkness pervasive.

Two fellows named Artur and Jeremias, wearing the uniforms of the castle (which K. does not yet recognize), present themselves as his assistants. K. puts a strange question: are they his old assistants? Surely he would know if they were. They assure him that they are, and he seems to believe them. They say that they have come a long way; in fact, they have come from the castle–which, for K., does turn out to be a terribly long way. Despite tantalizing appearances of cooperation, such as the dispatch of the assistants, the castle is basically characterized by impenetrability. After hearing something like the humming of children's voices on the phone, K. has no difficulty in discerning the "Niemals" (never) pronounced by a castle official with a slight speech defect. The castle appears, however, to evince a further cooperativeness in dispatching Barnabas as a messenger for K.'s use. Barnabas brings K. a letter, signed by a department chief named Klamm, recognizing K.'s appointment as land surveyor. The trouble is that the recognition is ambiguous: K. is left with the options of becoming a village worker with a merely apparent connection with the castle, or an ostensible village worker whose real occupation will be determined by the castle and relayed to him by Barnabas.

He falls in love with Frieda, the barmaid at the Herrenhof–the inn favored by the gentlemen of the castle when on business in the village. Frieda is also the mistress of Klamm. Frieda is gregarious and coquettish; she seems an odd match for the reserved, secretive, imperious Klamm. Indeed, when Klamm calls her from his room near the bar it is difficult to determine whether he desires beer or sex. That perfunctoriness–on both sides–may help make her amenable to an affair with K. The latter's motivation, besides that of amorous attraction, is clear: Frieda can influence Klamm to intercede in K.'s behalf at the castle.

Frieda, like K., is intelligent, ambitious, and energetic; having begun as a stable-girl she was quickly promoted to barmaid and shows promise as a future manager. Instantly in tune with each other, inflamed by a single desire, they sink into an embrace among the puddles of spilled beer on the floor behind the bar and remain so for hours. Kafka's account of their lovemaking has impressed some critics as a lyric description of selfless, unifying love unique in his oeuvre. More likely, however, it is a satire of the sort of European love story rendered obsolete by a novel of modernism like *Das Schloß* itself. Together with the clichés, the locale of this tableau vivant suggests other than idealized love.

During the marathon Klamm calls for Frieda. K., whose chief interest promptly becomes nonerotic, repeats the summons into Frieda's ear as he helpfully refastens her blouse. When Frieda shouts to Klamm that she is with the land surveyor, K. naturally thinks that her role as Klamm's mistress, the role in which she can be of most value to K., will come to an end.

K. is more human–though not necessarily in the most admirable sense–than the heroes of Kafka's other novels. Above all, K. is readier to exploit his fellows. Karl Rossmann in *Amerika* is brought to one fall after another by female seductiveness, but he is in no sense the exploiter; rather the contrary. Joseph K. in *Der Prozeß* is quite willing to abandon his own benefit, dubious as it may be, at the legal conference at the lawyer Huld's for the pleasure of making love with the eager Leni–but again, he does not exploit her. K. does exploit. He may love Frieda, but he loves her the more because she is a conduit to Klamm. On the other hand, he will marry her, even without the opportunity of having a talk with Klamm first.

K.'s tenuous position as ignorant but tolerated outsider is threatened less by his marriage to Frieda than by his socializing with the outcast family of Barnabas. Barnabas himself, it is true, is a castle messenger, but he has insinuated himself into the job, and his family is not thereby relieved from the role of village pariahs. The castle official Sortini once sent a letter to Barnabas's sister, Amalia, by whom, without her doing anything, he had suddenly been smitten at the fire brigade picnic. The letter contained a lewd proposal, which Amalia ignored. By spurning the castle she condemned her family to ruin–not by any dramatic, overt, hostile act, but by the gradual effect of ostracism and deprivation of a livelihood. Now it is clearer why the castle assigned Barnabas as the messenger between itself and K.: the assignment assured that K. would socialize with the pariah family and thus contaminate himself in the eyes of the village. That contamination will scarcely facilitate his quest to penetrate the castle.

K. calls on the mayor, his nominal superior, for enlightenment as to his status. His status, the mayor tells him, is the most insignificant of all petty matters. Further, from an official point of view, his cherished letter of entitlement from Klamm is meaningless; as if to underline that discouraging analysis the mayor's wife folds the letter into a paper boat. Nor do the mayor's voluminous files contain any entry whatsoever under the heading *Landvermesser*. Far from attaining access to the highest reaches of the castle bureaucracy, K. will be lucky to get a part-time job of the lowest rank. And he cannot leave, because he has come from such a long way off, and he is going to marry a local girl.

Momus, Klamm's village secretary, disabuses K. of any remaining grounds for hope. But then comes a second letter from Klamm, lauding K.'s surveying and encouraging continuation of the work. Since K. has performed no surveying at all, his concerns are hardly alleviated. The bureaucracy does offer K. and Frieda a job of sorts: at starvation wages they are signed on as custodians at the schoolhouse, where they are given quarters in one of the two classrooms. This unlikely venue for lovemaking, with classes bursting in on them before they are out of bed, is the castle's way of trivializing sex as a weapon against K. The scene is farce, approaching burlesque, and was perhaps inspired by Kafka's memories of Yiddish theater.

If only, Frieda laments, we had gone off somewhere that first night, then we might always be together. Her only dream has been to have K.'s company, but that has proved an impossible dream. For K. to leave with Frieda, and thus be always in her company without the intrusion of schoolchildren and schoolmasters, is precisely what K. cannot do. He can only stay and try to accomplish his self-imposed mission. Having thus reiterated her love for K. and strongly implied the reason it could not be, Frieda leaves him for Jeremias, an insider like herself.

At this point, in chapter 18, the text of the first edition of *Das Schloß* ends. The rest of chapter 18 and two further chapters, added in the fourth edition, provide, if not an ending, at least a more rounded-off sense of integration. For example, the thematic tiredness of K., lost sight of in the middle chapters, is reintroduced with some effect. K.'s overwhelming fatigue is responsible for the failure of his most promising attempt to establish a connection with the castle. Through Barnabas K. learns that Erlanger, one of Klamm's chief secretaries, wants K. to report to him in room fifteen of the Herrenhof. Except by appointment, all of the Herrenhof but the barroom is off-limits to K. and the villagers. K. is so exhausted that he fails to keep the appointment. Even so, fate makes possible a second chance. His fatigue intensified by the lateness of the hour—Erlanger holds office hours at night—K. is wandering around the Herrenhof at four in the morning in search of an empty bed. Blundering into the room of an insomniac secretary named Bürgel, K. is invited to stay and chat. Bürgel is not one of Klamm's secretaries, so he can help K. in no direct way; but he informs K. that the castle personnel start getting up at about five o'clock, which might be a good time for him to make belated contact with Erlanger.

Meanwhile, Bürgel is genially disposed to talk out his insomnia, with K. as a taciturn audience. Bürgel's admitted ignorance of K.'s case does not prevent him from grandiloquently volunteering to do something that will result in K.'s actually being employed as a surveyor. Sometimes, Bürgel assures him after a tedious bureaucratic discourse, even though a miracle cannot happen it does happen. But K. is too sleepy to follow him.

In the next room Erlanger, kept awake by the noise of Bürgel's unrelenting discourse, gives loud vent to a renewal of the summons to K. Sleepily staggering into the next room K. suffers Erlanger's reproach for his tardiness. Erlanger makes him aware of the futility of his attempts to effect a relationship with the castle. Klamm, he says, may be disturbed by the presence of a new barmaid, Pepi, who was brought in to take Frieda's place when the latter left to join K. That potential disturbance could suffice to dash K.'s hopes forever. Still, K.'s cooperation might yet prove helpful to his aspiration.

Dismissed curtly by Erlanger, and therefore supposedly obliged to promptly vacate the premises of the Herrenhof, K. nonetheless loiters in the corridor. A servant is distributing files from a cart to the castle secretaries in the various rooms. But the servant is angry, some doors hardly open, mistakes are made, one secretary is shouting, a buzzer goes off—all because everyone except K., in his ignorance and fatigue, knows that a trespasser is hanging around in the corridor. So much is his general guilt taken for granted that no one could imagine that he was there by mistake, in perfectly good faith.

After the distribution is apparently concluded a single small piece of paper remains in the file cart. K. cannot escape the suspicion that it is his file. The servant signals his assistant to remain silent about the forthcoming breach of bureaucratic protocol, tears the remaining paper to bits, and puts the pieces into his pocket.

The twentieth and last chapter is devoted primarily to the retrospective story of Pepi, Frieda's replacement as barmaid during her four-day idyll with K. Pepi correctly attributes her installation as barmaid to K.'s influence on Frieda. By the same token, she holds him responsible for her demotion, because his love was insufficient to keep Frieda from returning to the post. In her jealousy, malevolence, and vituperation, Pepi provides the reader with a different view of Frieda, heretofore seen only from the infatuated point of view of K. If one is to credit Pepi, Frieda is no great beauty, nor is she free of character defects. Frieda was a great favorite of the customers, yet she had always to worry about the possibility that they, and Klamm, would grow tired of her. To strengthen her position as barmaid and mistress, Pepi concludes, Frieda needed to provide a spectacle of some sort; she therefore decided to have an affair. K., the stranger, proved the ideal respondent. In other words, Frieda was using K. quite as much as K. was using Frieda.

It has struck many critics that K.'s failure with Frieda presages his failure with the castle. Similarly, if Frieda is unattractive, both physically and as to character, then the castle may be so, too. Neither Frieda nor the castle are what they purport to be, and neither is worth aspiring to; K. should desist. Maybe that is what K. has in mind when he implies that he will join Pepi and the other chambermaids, Emilie and Henriette, in their snug little room in the Herrenhof, where he will be their helper and protector. Yet K., wondering aloud if spring will ever come, seems unlikely to simply relinquish the quest and adopt the peasant life-style of the ever-snowy village in the shadow of the less snowy castle.

There is a recurrent critical urge to equate the castle with God, despite the almost total absence of textual indicators. One wonders if it is the business of God to be granting rights to surveying jobs, especially to such an unrepentant petitioner as K. He would not be a very estimable God, either, to judge from the castle's indifference, pettiness, cruelty, lechery, and fallibility.

Since the castle does not represent God, K.'s quest can scarcely symbolize a religious pilgrimage. Far from contrition or self-knowledge, let alone admission of guilt–in contrast to the guilt-laden protagonists of *Amerika* and *Der Prozeß*–K. comes to demand his rights, not to abjure them. He is a quester, which is by no means the same as a pilgrim. In contrast to a pilgrim's approach, K. is exactly as far from his goal at the end of the novel as at the beginning. Furthermore, the scene is set for another in-house sexual affair, this time with Pepi. The maids' cozy room seems a curious place for a religious pilgrimage to end.

It is all too easy to apply Freudian categories to *Das Schloß*–for example, K. as an Oedipal avenger against the paternal castle. Such efforts may be enlightening or suggestive; any attempt, however–and there have been a few–to impose a Freudian *system* on the novel will leave merely an eviscerated case study, a poor remnant from a

The building in Kierling bei Klosterneuburg, Austria, which formerly housed the sanatorium where Kafka died (photo: Franz Hubmann)

magnificent and ambiguous novel. The reader ought to be able to enjoy and savor those allusive ambiguities without feeling compelled to force them onto the procrustean bed of any single category of reductive criticism.

While writing *Das Schloß*, Kafka continued to write parables, including his perhaps best-known ones, "Gibs auf!" (1936; translated as "Give It Up!," 1960) and "Von den Gleichnissen" (1936; translated as "About Parables," 1960). The purport of the former is summed up in its title. The narrator, lost, appeals to a policeman for directions and is mocked in reply. This is what comes from reposing faith and trust in another; thus the titular admonition to give up the quest. "Von den Gleichnissen" is Kafka's final parable. Its gist is that parables only intend to say that the incomprehensible is incomprehensible, which we already know. This incomprehensibility or inexplicability is a hallmark of the Kafkaesque parable, as opposed to the New Testament parable, which typically concludes with an elucidation to make certain that the hearer gets the point. Familiarity with the latter type probably accounts for the tendency of zealous explicators to force Kafka's parables into the more familiar, but alien, mold.

After June 1922 there were no more renewals of Kafka's sick leaves from the insurance company, and in July he retired on pension. He left Prague to live with his sister Ottla in southern Bohemia for several months and then returned to Prague. Along with work on *Das Schloß* in 1922 he devoted himself to a story called "Ein Hungerkünstler" (translated as "The Hunger-Artist," 1938). In the summer of 1923 he vacationed on the Baltic coast with his sister Elli and her family. There he met Dora Diamant, a young girl of Hasidic roots. Her family background and her competence in Hebrew appealed to Kafka equally with her personal attractiveness. He lived with her in Berlin until the spring of 1924, when she accompanied him to Austria. There he entered Kierling sanatorium near Klosterneuburg. In 1923 and 1924, when able, Kafka worked on three stories that were published posthumously: "Eine kleine Frau" (1924; translated as "A Little Woman," 1943), "Der Bau" (1936; translated as "The Burrow," 1960), and "Josefine, die Sängerin, oder das Volk der Mäuse" (1924; translated as "Josephine, the Songstress; or, The Mice Nation," 1942). After horrible suffering, he died on 3 June 1924 of tuberculosis of the larynx.

The eponymous "hunger artist" is an artist of dubious authenticity, whose art is to starve himself. At the end he dies unnoticed in a pile of dirty straw. His dying reply to the question of why he pursued his unusual–but in nineteenth-century Europe not unique–profession is that he could not find the food he liked; if he had, he would have made no fuss but would have eaten just like anyone else. He fails to disclose what sort of food *would* have appealed to him, an omission that has given rise to the critical suggestion that it is spiritual provender that he is talking about. Add to this speculation the fact that his fasts endure for forty days–thus recalling the temptation of Christ in the wilderness–and the notion grows that the story is a Christian allegory. The problem with this interpretation is that the hunger artist, unlike a hermit in a cave or Christ in the wilderness, was not resisting temptation at all; far from depriving himself of what he wanted, he was, by his lights, indulging his desires in a way unthinkable for an authentic saint. After his sad end, his remains are swept away with the straw and he is replaced in the cage by a sleek and hungry leopard, which draws huge and enthusiastic crowds. The leopard celebrates the joy of life as the hunger artist never had and *that* now attracts the crowds. Thus the theme, as in *In der Strafkolonie* and "Ein Landarzt," has to do with the contrast between former times and the present; in "Ein Hungerkünstler," however, the schema is stood on its head, for it is the present era that is the hardier and the more vigorous. The leopard is by far the healthier act.

"Eine kleine Frau" is a monologue in which a male narrator discusses at somewhat tedious length a highly critical woman and the torment caused him by her gratuitous criticisms. There seems to be no way for him to mute her criticism, which has been going on for years. Their incompatibility is total. In the end he resolves to ignore the little woman as best he can and quietly lead his own life. This fictional little woman is probably a projection of Kafka's unrelenting self-criticism; in any event, there are only occasionally lively narrative passages in the monologue, which is spun out longer than its slight premise can comfortably support. It is conceivable that Kafka's physical exhaustion was taking an artistic toll.

On the other hand, "Der Bau," the next-to-last story Kafka wrote and a monologue of much greater length, does not sag. The species of the fictional burrower Kafka withholds; the burrower no doubt stands for the author. Now past his prime, the burrower in his years of vigor constructed for his protection an elaborate burrow. He does not confine himself to it; he does most of his hunting aboveground. He is tempted to spend the rest of his life on the surface, contemplating the entrance to his burrow. Being aboveground carries risk of confrontation, but being underground does not entirely eliminate danger. For he built his underground works before he adequately comprehended the principles of defense. Sure enough, the burrower returns to his underground castle and perceives a barely audible whistling noise through the earthen walls. At first he dismisses it as unimportant, but the noise does not go away. The burrower wavers between ignoring it and agitatedly weighing methods of confronting it; like Kafka, he is given to neurotic reflection. As the noise changes in volume and quality, he concludes that it must be a large beast digging toward him. The ending of the story is lost. The threat, if one pursues the autobiographical relationship, would be that posed by Kafka's fatal disease. Critics have also detected in "Der Bau" a sexual metaphor–hardly less suggestive

Cover for Kafka's last book to be published during his lifetime (Deutsches Literaturarchiv)

than that in "Ein Landarzt"–which is considerably more apparent in the original German than in translation. Language aside, burrowing is clearly susceptible to interpretation as sexual penetration, especially with so much narrative attention focused on the entrance to the burrow. In conjunction with the sterility of the burrow–the burrower has no mate, no offspring–the sexual metaphor must be taken ironically.

"Josefine, die Sängerin, oder das Volk der Mäuse" is Kafka's last story, written just three months before his death. Like "Eine kleine Frau," it is more a discussion than a narration. The narrator, apparently a fellow mouse of Josefine, is anything but polished: his report is rife with internal qualifications and contradictions, so that it is difficult for the reader to get an accurate perception of Josefine, the idiosyncratic and spurious musical artist, and her relationship with the mouse community. Josefine, for all the glitz of her singing performances, really only makes the whistling sound that all mice make, many of them without even knowing it; and the mouse community for whom she performs lacks a sense of music, for their lives are too fraught with worry, danger, and terror to permit the leisure or the reflectiveness necessary for art. The mice are said to revere Josefine and her singing, yet at times they must be rounded up and coerced into attending her concerts–some given when the mood strikes her, others scheduled in advance, such as the one a day or two ago at which she failed to show up. On previous occasions she has had to be persuaded to perform, but now she has disappeared without a trace. Her habit has been to insist on and feed on the appreciation of her fellow mice even as she disdains it. She gives herself the airs of a prima donna–and yet the question is constantly posed by the narrator: is Josefine an artist at all?

Brod was responsible for the notion that the mouse nation was Kafka's metaphor for the Jewish people. This interpretation probably reflects Brod's Zionist interests more than Kafka's artistic intention, for Kafka causes his narrator to repeatedly deny any historical memory to the mouse people, whereas Jews are singularly rich in historical memory. Marxist interpretation points out that the mass, the community, endures eternally, whereas the individual, represented by Josefine, vanishes. This formulation ignores the final paragraph, which dwells on Josefine's redemption. That redemption will take place in the collective unconscious of the mouse people; she will be forgotten, yet she will have contributed to that collective unconscious.

Perhaps the interpretative line suggested by Kafka's other late stories is the most likely: the problematic authenticity of the artist in an environment not conducive to art. This interpretation makes Josefine a colleague of the hunger artist, of the narrator of "Eine kleine Frau," and of the burrower, all of them personae of the dying and not very hopeful, but still humorously ironic

Kafka's grave in the Jewish Cemetery, Prague (photo: Archiv Klaus Wagenbach)

Kafka. It would not do to suggest that these final stories, conceived and written under the most harrowing personal circumstances, are Kafka's best. But like the best, which signal the beginning of the era of literary modernism, they enlist the reader directly, without mediation, into the work. They embrace deformation, whether physical or spiritual, as an inducement to doubt or to ambiguity; they focus on an individual who is a fictional persona of the author, who is, in turn, not Everyman, and they do all of it with ambiguity and irony that invite, but rarely validate, a single interpretation.

Bibliographies:

Rudolf Hemmerle, *Franz Kafka: Eine Bibliographie* (Munich: Lerche, 1958);

Angel Flores, *A Kafka Bibliography* (New York: Gordian Press, 1976);

Maria Luise Caputo-Mayr and Julius M. Herz, *Franz Kafkas Werke: Eine Bibliographie der Primärliteratur (1908-1980)* (Bern & Munich: Francke, 1982);

Ludwig Dietz, *Franz Kafka: Die Veröffentlichungen zu seinen Lebzeiten (1908-1924): Eine textkritische und kommentierte Bibliographie* (Heidelberg: Stiehm, 1982);

Malcolm Pasley, *Catalogue of the Kafka Centenary Exhibition 1983* (Oxford: Bodleian Library, 1983).

Biographies:

Max Brod, *Kafka: A Biography*, translated by G. Humphreys-Roberts (New York: Schocken, 1947; revised, translated by Humphreys-Roberts and Richard Winston, 1960);

Klaus Wagenbach, *Franz Kafka: Eine Biographie seiner Jugend, 1883-1912* (Bern: Francke, 1958);

Daryl Sharp, *The Secret Raven: Conflict and Transformation in the Life of Franz Kafka* (Toronto: Inner City Books, 1980);

Ronald Hayman, *Kafka: A Biography* (New York: Oxford University Press, 1982);

Joachim Unseld, *Franz Kafka: Ein Schriftstellerleben* (Munich & Vienna: Hanser, 1982);

Rotraut Hackermüller, *Das Leben, das mich stört: Eine Dokumentation zu Kafkas letzten Jahren 1917-1924* (Vienna & Berlin: Medusa, 1984);

Ernest Pawel, *The Nightmare of Reason: A Life of Franz Kafka* (New York: Farrar, Straus & Giroux, 1984);

Klaus Wagenbach, *Franz Kafka: Pictures of a Life*, translated by Arthur S. Wensinger (New York: Pantheon, 1984).

References:

Jürg Johannes Amann, *Das Symbol Kafka: Eine Studie über den Künstler* (Bern & Munich: Francke, 1974);

Günther Anders, *Franz Kafka*, translated by A. Steer and A. K. Thorlby (London: Bowes & Bowes, 1960);

Evelyn W. Asher, *Urteil ohne Richter: Psychische Integration oder Charakterentfaltung im Werke Franz Kafkas* (New York: Lang, 1984);

Evelyn Torton Beck, *Kafka and the Yiddish Theater: Its Impact on His Work* (Madison, Milwaukee & London: University of Wisconsin Press, 1971);

Peter U. Beicken, *Franz Kafka: Eine kritische Einführung in die Forschung* (Frankfurt am Main: Athenaion, 1974);

Beicken, *Franz Kafka. Leben und Werk* (Stuttgart: Klett, 1986);

Friedrich Beißner, *Der Erzähler Franz Kafka* (Stuttgart: Kohlhammer, 1961);

Charles Bernheimer, *Flaubert and Kafka: Studies in Psychopoetic Structure* (New Haven & London: Yale University Press, 1982);

Chris Bezzel, *Kafka-Chronik* (Munich & Vienna: Hanser, 1975);

Hartmut Binder, *Kafka: Der Schaffensprozeß* (Frankfurt am Main: Suhrkamp, 1983);

Binder, *Kafka-Handbuch*, 2 volumes (Stuttgart: Kröner, 1979);

Binder, *Kafka in neuer Sicht* (Stuttgart: Metzler, 1976);

Binder, *Kafka-Kommentar zu den Romanen, Rezensionen, Aphorismen und zum Brief an den Vater* (Munich: Winkler, 1976);

Binder, *Kafka-Kommentar zu sämtlichen Erzählungen* (Munich: Winkler, 1975);

Binder, *Motiv und Gestaltung bei Franz Kafka* (Bonn: Bouvier, 1966);

Jürgen Born, *Franz Kafka: Kritik und Rezeption 1924-1938* (Frankfurt am Main: Fischer, 1983);

Born and others, eds., *Franz Kafka: Kritik und Rezeption zu seinen Lebzeiten* (Frankfurt am Main: Fischer, 1979);

Patrick Bridgwater, *Kafka and Nietzsche* (Bonn: Bouvier, 1974);

Max Brod, *Über Franz Kafka* (Frankfurt am Main: Fischer, 1966);

Brod, *Verzweiflung und Erlösung im Werk Franz Kafkas* (Frankfurt am Main: Fischer, 1959);

Elias Canetti, *Kafka's Other Trial: The Letters to Felice*, translated by Christopher Middleton (New York: Schocken, 1974);

Michel Carrouges, *Kafka versus Kafka*, translated by Emmett Parker (University: University of Alabama Press, 1968);

Peter Cersowsky, *"Mein ganzes Leben ist auf Literatur gerichtet": Franz Kafka im Kontext der literarischen Dekadenz* (Würzburg: Königshausen + Neumann, 1983);

Jules Chaix-Ruy, *Kafka, la peur de l'absurde* (Paris: Centurion, 1968);

Stanley Corngold, *The Commentator's Despair: The Interpretation of Kafka's "Metamorphosis"* (Port Washington, N.Y. & London: Kennikat Press, 1973);

Claude David, ed., *Franz Kafka: Themen und Problemen* (Göttingen: Vandenhoeck & Ruprecht, 1978);

Gilles Deleuze and Félix Guattari, *Kafka: Toward a Minor Literature*, translated by Dana Polan (Minneapolis: University of Minnesota Press, 1986);

Ludwig Dietz, *Franz Kafka* (Stuttgart: Metzler, 1975);

Pavel Eisner, *Franz Kafka and Prague*, translated by Lowry Nelson and René Wellek (New York: Arts, 1950);

Wilhelm Emrich, *Franz Kafka: A Critical Study of His Writings*, translated by Sheema Z. Buehne (New York: Ungar, 1968);

Rose-Marie Ferenczi, *Kafka, subjectivité, histoire et structures* (Paris: Klincksieck, 1975);

Kurt J. Fickert, *Kafka's Doubles* (Bern, Frankfurt am Main & Las Vegas: Lang, 1975);

Karl-Heinz Fingerhut, *Die Funktion der Tierfiguren im Werke Franz Kafkas* (Bonn: Bouvier, 1969);

Brigitte Flach, *Kafkas Erzählungen: Strukturanalyse und Interpretation* (Bonn: Bouvier, 1967);

Angel Flores, ed., *Explain to Me Some Stories of Kafka: Complete Texts with Explanations* (New York: Gordian Press, 1983);

Flores, ed., *The Kafka Debate: New Perspectives for Our Time* (New York: Gordian Press, 1977);

Flores, ed., *The Kafka Problem* (New York: Octagon Books, 1963);

Flores, ed., *The Problem of "The Judgment"* (New York: Gordian Press, 1977);

Flores and Homer Swander, eds., *Franz Kafka Today* (Madison: University of Wisconsin Press, 1964);

A. P. Foulkes, *The Reluctant Pessimist: A Study of Franz Kafka* (The Hague & Paris: Mouton, 1967);

Nahum N. Glatzer, *The Loves of Franz Kafka* (New York: Schocken, 1986);

Eduard Goldstücker, ed., *Franz Kafka aus Prager Sicht* (Berlin: Voltaire, 1965);

Maja Goth, *Franz Kafka et les lettres françaises* (Paris: Corti, 1956);

Ronald Gray, *Franz Kafka* (Cambridge: Cambridge University Press, 1973);

Gray, *Kafka's Castle* (Cambridge: Cambridge University Press, 1956);

Martin Greenberg, *The Terror of Art: Kafka and Modern Literature* (New York & London: Basic Books, 1968);

Karl Erich Grözinger, Stéphane Mosès, and Hans Dieter Zimmermann, eds., *Kafka und das Ju-*

dentum (Frankfurt am Main: Jüdischer Verlag bei Athenäum, 1987);

Jiří Gruša, *Franz Kafka of Prague*, translated by Eric Mosbacher (London: Secker & Warburg, 1983);

Calvin S. Hall and Richard E. Lind, *Dreams, Life, and Literature: A Study of Franz Kafka* (Chapel Hill: University of North Carolina Press, 1970);

Leo Hamalian, comp., *Franz Kafka: A Collection of Criticism* (New York: McGraw-Hill, 1974);

Günter Heintz, *Franz Kafka: Sprachreflexion als dichterische Einbildungskraft* (Würzburg: Königshausen + Neumann, 1983);

Erich Heller, introduction to *The Basic Kafka* (New York: Pocket Books, 1979);

Heller, *Franz Kafka* (New York: Viking, 1975);

Peter Heller, *Dialectics and Nihilism: Essays on Lessing, Nietzsche, Mann, and Kafka* (Amherst: University of Massachusetts Press, 1966);

Klaus Hermsdorf, *Kafka: Weltbild und Roman* (Berlin: Rütten & Loening, 1961);

John Hibberd, *Kafka in Context* (London: Studio Vista, 1975);

Hans Helmut Hiebel, *Die Zeichen des Gesetzes: Recht und Macht bei Franz Kafka* (Munich: Fink, 1983);

Heinz Hillmann, *Franz Kafka: Dichtungstheorie und Dichtungsgestalt* (Bonn: Bouvier, 1964);

Kenneth Hughes, ed. *Franz Kafka: An Anthology of Marxist Criticism*, translated by Hughes (Hanover & London: University Press of New Zealand, 1981);

Adrian Jaffe, *The Process of Kafka's "Trial"* (Lansing: Michigan State University Press, 1967);

Wolfgang Jahn, *Kafkas Roman "Der Verschollene" ("Amerika")* (Stuttgart: Metzler, 1965);

Gustav Janouch, *Conversations with Kafka*, translated by Goronwy Rees (New York: New Directions, 1969);

Harry Järv, *Die Kafka Literatur: Eine Bibliographie* (Malmö & Lund: Bo Cavefors, 1961);

Jean Jofen, *The Jewish Mystic in Kafka* (New York, Bern & Frankfurt am Main: Lang, 1987);

Norbert Kassel, *Das Groteske bei Franz Kafka* (Munich: Fink, 1969);

Lida Kirchberger, *Franz Kafka's Use of Law in Fiction* (New York, Bern & Frankfurt am Main: Lang, 1986);

Jörgen Kobs, *Kafka: Untersuchungen zu Bewußtsein und Sprache seiner Gestalten*, edited by Ursula Brech (Bad Homburg: Athenäum, 1970);

Herbert Kraft, *Mondheimat–Kafka* (Pfullingen: Neske, 1983);

Franz Kuna, *Franz Kafka: Literature as Corrective Punishment* (Bloomington & London: Indiana University Press, 1974; London: Elek, 1974);

Kuna, ed., *On Kafka: Semi-Centenary Perspectives* (New York: Barnes & Noble, 1976);

Richard H. Lawson, *Franz Kafka* (New York: Ungar, 1987);

Mijal Levi, *Kafka and Anarchism* (New York: Revisionist Press, 1972);

René Marill (R. M. Albérès) and Pierre de Boisdeffre, *Kafka: The Torment of Man*, translated by Wade Baskin (New York: Philosophical Library, 1968);

Eric Marson, *Kafka's "Trial": The Case against Josef K.* (St. Lucia: University of Queensland Press, 1975);

Ramón G. Mendoza, *Outside Humanity: A Study of Kafka's Fiction* (Lanham, Md.: University Press of America, 1986);

Weiyan Meng, *Kafka und China* (Munich: Iudicium, 1986);

Modern Austrian Literature, special Kafka issue, 11, no. 3/4 (1978);

Mosaic, special Kafka issue, 3, no. 4 (1970);

Bert Nagel, *Kafka und die Weltliteratur* (Munich: Winkler, 1983);

Ralf R. Nicolai, *Ende oder Anfang: Zur Einheit der Gegensätze in Kafkas "Schloß"* (Munich: Fink, 1977);

Nicolai, *Kafkas Amerika-Roman "Der Verschollene"* (Würzburg: Königshausen + Neumann, 1981);

Margot Norris, *Beasts of the Modern Imagination: Darwin, Nietzsche, Kafka, Ernst, and Lawrence* (Baltimore: Johns Hopkins University Press, 1985);

Charles Osborne, *Kafka* (New York: Barnes & Noble, 1967);

Roy Pascal, *Kafka's Narrators: A Study of His Stories and Sketches* (Cambridge: Cambridge University Press, 1982);

Heinz Politzer, *Franz Kafka: Parable and Paradox* (Ithaca & London: Cornell University Press, 1966);

Elizabeth M. Rajec, *Namen und ihre Bedeutungen im Werke Franz Kafkas* (Bern, Frankfurt am Main & Las Vegas: Lang, 1977);

Phillip H. Rhein, *The Urge to Live: A Comparative Study of Franz Kafka's "Der Prozeß" and Albert Camus' "L'Etranger"* (Chapel Hill: University of North Carolina Press, 1964);

Helmut Richter, *Franz Kafka: Werk und Entwurf* (Berlin: Rütten & Loening, 1962);

Marthe Robert, *Franz Kafka's Loneliness*, translated by Ralph Manheim (London: Faber & Faber, 1982); republished as *As Lonely as Franz Kafka* (New York & London: Harcourt Brace Jovanovich, 1982);

Ritchie Robertson, *Kafka: Judaism, Politics, and Literature* (Oxford: Clarendon Press, 1985);

James Rolleston, *Kafka's Narrative Theater* (University Park & London: Pennsylvania State University Press, 1974);

Rolleston, ed., *Twentieth Century Interpretations of "The Trial"* (Englewood Cliffs, N.J.: Prentice-Hall, 1976);

Richard Sheppard, *On Kafka's "Castle": A Study* (New York: Barnes & Noble, 1973);

Walter H. Sokel, *Franz Kafka* (New York: Columbia University Press, 1966);

Meno Spann, *Franz Kafka* (Boston: Twayne, 1976);

Mark Spilka, *Dickens and Kafka: A Mutual Interpretation* (Bloomington: Indiana University Press, 1963);

J. P. Stern, ed., *The World of Franz Kafka* (New York: Holt, Rinehart & Winston, 1980);

Roman Struc and J. C. Yardley, eds., *Franz Kafka (1883-1983): His Craft and Thought* (Waterloo, Ont.: Wilfrid Laurier University Press, 1986);

Jörg Thalmann, *Wege zu Kafka: Eine Interpretation des Amerikaromans* (Frauenfeld & Stuttgart: Huber, 1966);

Anthony Thorlby, *Kafka: A Study* (London: Heinemann, 1972);

Ruth Tiefenbrun, *Moment of Torment: An Interpretation of Franz Kafka's Short Stories* (Carbondale & Edwardsville: Southern Illinois University Press, 1973);

Alan Udoff, ed., *Kafka and the Contemporary Critical Performance* (Bloomington: Indiana University Press, 1987);

Johannes Urzidil, *There Goes Kafka*, translated by Harold A. Basilius (Detroit: Wayne State University Press, 1968);

Martin Walser, *Versuch über Franz Kafka* (Munich: Hanser, 1961);

Kurt Weinberg, *Kafkas Dichtungen* (Bern & Munich: Francke, 1963);

Melvin Wilk, *The Jewish Presence in T. S. Eliot and Franz Kafka* (Atlanta: Scholars Press, 1986).

Papers:

Most of Kafka's manuscript materials are in the Bodleian Library, Oxford. Two pages of "Der Verschollene" (*Amerika*) are in the Österreichische Nationalbibliothek in Vienna. Most of the "Dorfschullehrer" (Village Schoolmaster–an incomplete tale probably dating from after World War I) papers are in the Deutsches Literaturarchiv in Marbach, West Germany, together with some of Kafka's letters. The letters to Felice Bauer and Milena Jesenská are in the possession of Schocken Books, New York. The manuscript of *Der Prozeß* was purchased at auction at Sotheby's in London for $1.98 million on 17 November 1988 by a West German book dealer reportedly acting on behalf of the German government. He said that the manuscript would be displayed at the Deutsches Literaturarchiv. The price was the highest ever paid for a modern manuscript.

Alfred Kubin
(10 April 1877-20 August 1959)

Phillip H. Rhein
Vanderbilt University

BOOKS: *Fünfzehn Facsimiledrucke nach Kunstblättern* (Munich: Weber, 1903);

Die andere Seite: Ein phantastischer Roman (Munich: Müller, 1909); translated by Denver Lindley as *The Other Side: A Fantastic Novel* (New York: Crown, 1967; London: Gollancz, 1969);

Sansara: Ein Cyklus ohne Ende in einer Auswahl von vierzig Blättern (Munich: Müller, 1911);

Die Blätter mit dem Tod (Berlin: Cassirer, 1918);

Der Prophet Daniel: Eine Folge mit 12 Zeichnungen (Munich: Müller, 1918);

Wilde Tiere (Munich: Hyperionverlag, 1920);

Kritiker: 18 Blätter (Munich: Müller, 1920);

Am Rande des Lebens: Zwanzig Federzeichnungen (Munich: Piper, 1921);

Zeichnungen und Aquarelle (Munich: Recht, 1922);

Von verschiedenen Ebenen (Berlin: Gurlitt, 1922);

Nach Damaskus: Achtzehn Steinzeichnungen (Munich: Müller, 1922);

Fünfzehn Zeichnungen (Munich: Langen, 1923);

Filigrane: Zwanzig Zeichnungen (Munich: Müller, 1923);

20 Bilder zur Bibel (Munich: Piper, 1924);

Rauhnacht: 13 Steinzeichnungen (Berlin: Wegweiser Verlag, 1925);

Der Guckkasten: Bilder und Text (Vienna: Johannes-Presse, 1925);

Dämonen und Nachtgesichte: Mit einer Selbstdarstellung des Künstlers und 130 Bildtafeln (Dresden: Reissner, 1926); revised as *Mein Werk: Dämonen und Nachtgesichte. Bildtafeln mit einer Autobiographie, fortgeführt bis 1931* (Dresden: Reissner, 1931); revised as *Dämonen und Nachtgesichte: Eine Autobiographie*, edited by Ludwig Leiss (Munich: Piper, 1959);

Heimliche Welt (Heidelberg: Merlin, 1927);

Vom Schreibtisch eines Zeichners (Berlin: Riemerschmidt, 1939);

Abenteuer einer Zeichenfeder (Munich: Piper, 1941);

Schemen: 60 Köpfe aus einer verklungenen Zeit (Königsberg: Kanter, 1943);

Die Planeten: Eine Folge (Leipzig: Staackmann, 1943);

Alfred Kubin (Austrian Cultural Institute)

Ein neuer Totentanz (Vienna: Wiener Verlag, 1947);

Ein Bilder-ABC 1933 (Hamburg: Maximilien Gesellschaft, 1948);

Vermischte Blätter: Zwölf Zeichnungen und zehn Graphiken (Berlin: Archivarion, 1950);

Phantasien im Böhmerwald (Vienna: Gurlitt, 1951);

Kollege Großmann: Eine Plauderei mit vier Lithographien (Vienna: Gurlitt, 1951);

Abendrot: 45 unveröffentlichte Zeichnungen mit einer kleinen Plauderei über sich selbst (Munich: Piper, 1952);

Fünfzehn Federzeichnungen (Munich: Gauss, 1959);

Kubin (standing, third from left) with his family in 1902: (left to right) Kubin's sister Roserl; his stepmother; his sister Fritzi; his father, Franz; and his sister Mizzi (Wieland Schmidt, Alfred Kubin, *1969)*

Kubin's Dance of Death, and Other Drawings: 83 Works (New York: Dover, 1973);

Aus meiner Werkstatt: Gesammelte Prosa, edited by Ulrich Riemerschmidt (Munich: Nymphenburger Verlagshandlung, 1973);

Aus meinem Leben: Gesammelte Prosa, edited by Riemerschmidt (Munich: Edition Spangenberg, 1974).

Alfred Kubin produced some of the most exciting graphic and literary art known to the West. He grew up in a world undergoing dramatic technological and intellectual change, and his powerful artistic interpretation of that world sets his achievements apart from other artists of the period. To discover new and fresh images he allowed his imagination to enter the domain of the subconscious and to roam freely through the territory of dream. Through his experience of the subconscious he was able to perceive relationships among all things, a unity that negated the seeming contradictions between the real and the imagined. In both his verbal and his visual art he tried to jar his reader or viewer into an awareness of the subliminal order that he believed integrated all things. Although his works reflect philosophical uncertainties, fears, and nightmares, they are celebrations of a life force Kubin perceived as permeating the multiple facets of existence.

Alfred Leopold Isidor Kubin was born on 10 April 1877 in Leitmeritz, Bohemia, to Friedrich Franz Kubin and Johanna Jenny Kletzl Kubin. His father, a former officer in the Imperial Austrian Army, was a government surveyor; his mother had been a pianist before her marriage. Shortly after Kubin's birth the family moved to Salzburg; they moved again in 1882 to Zell-am-See.

The eleven years between Kubin's mother's death of tuberculosis in May 1887 and his decision to study art in Munich had no direction. He attended the gymnasium in Salzburg, the parish school in Zell-am-See, and the state trade school in Salzburg. In each instance he repeated the same pattern: after initial success, he failed to sustain his interest in academic study. In 1892, no longer knowing what to do with his rebellious son, Franz Kubin arranged for him to work as a photographer's apprentice in Klagenfurt. Although Kubin found the photographs of exotic distant places stimulating to his imagination, he had neither the talent nor the self-discipline to meet the demands of the apprenticeship. In October 1896, distraught because of his inability to

Kubin's desk at Schloß Zwickledt (Wieland Schmidt, Alfred Kubin, *1969)*

focus his life, he attempted suicide with a rusty old pistol, which failed to fire. He joined the army but was discharged for medical reasons three months later, in April 1897. After a year at home, he went to Munich in the spring of 1898.

From 1898 to 1904 Kubin immersed himself in the art world of Munich. After two years of private instruction he enrolled at the Munich Art Academy. He joined various artists' groups and developed close friendships with Maximilian Dauthendey and Hans von Weber. He read Schopenhauer and Nietzsche and studied the art of Francisco de Goya, Henry de Groux, Edvard Munch, James Ensor, Odilon Redon, Max Klinger, and Felicien Rops. He had a one-man show at the Cassirer Gallery in Berlin in 1902. By September 1904 he felt sufficiently secure about his artistic future to marry the widow Hedwig Gründler. They spent the next two years traveling to southern France, Italy, Vienna, and Paris. In 1906 Kubin purchased Schloß Zwickledt, an old manor house near Wernstein am Inn. In the quietude of his beloved home, Kubin led a methodical, largely eremitic existence. Withdrawn from the pressures of urban life, he enjoyed the mysteries of nature while maintaining close contact with major painters and writers of the German-speaking world. He traveled infrequently, but his art became known through exhibitions in Berlin, Munich, Hamburg, Hanover, and Vienna; through his 2,361 illustrations for the books of over 140 authors; and through his own writings.

The centerpiece of Kubin's production is *Die andere Seite* (1909; translated as *The Other Side*, 1967), for it was in the working out of this novel that he found the aesthetic principles that became the foundation of his work. Begun as an adventure story, the novel rapidly seized control of its author. Kubin described the twelve weeks that he spent composing it and the additional four weeks he devoted to illustrating it as a period in which he was whipped on day and night by some inexplicable compulsive urge. The story has a simple plot, yet its meaning is highly complex. The unnamed narrator, a thirty-year-old graphic artist, receives an invitation from a former schoolfriend, Claus Patera, to visit him in Perle (the German word for pearl), the capital city of his so-called Traumreich (dream kingdom). The kingdom has been created by Patera with buildings transported from Europe. Traveling deep into central Asia, the artist and his wife find in Perle a city in which time has been stopped: every-

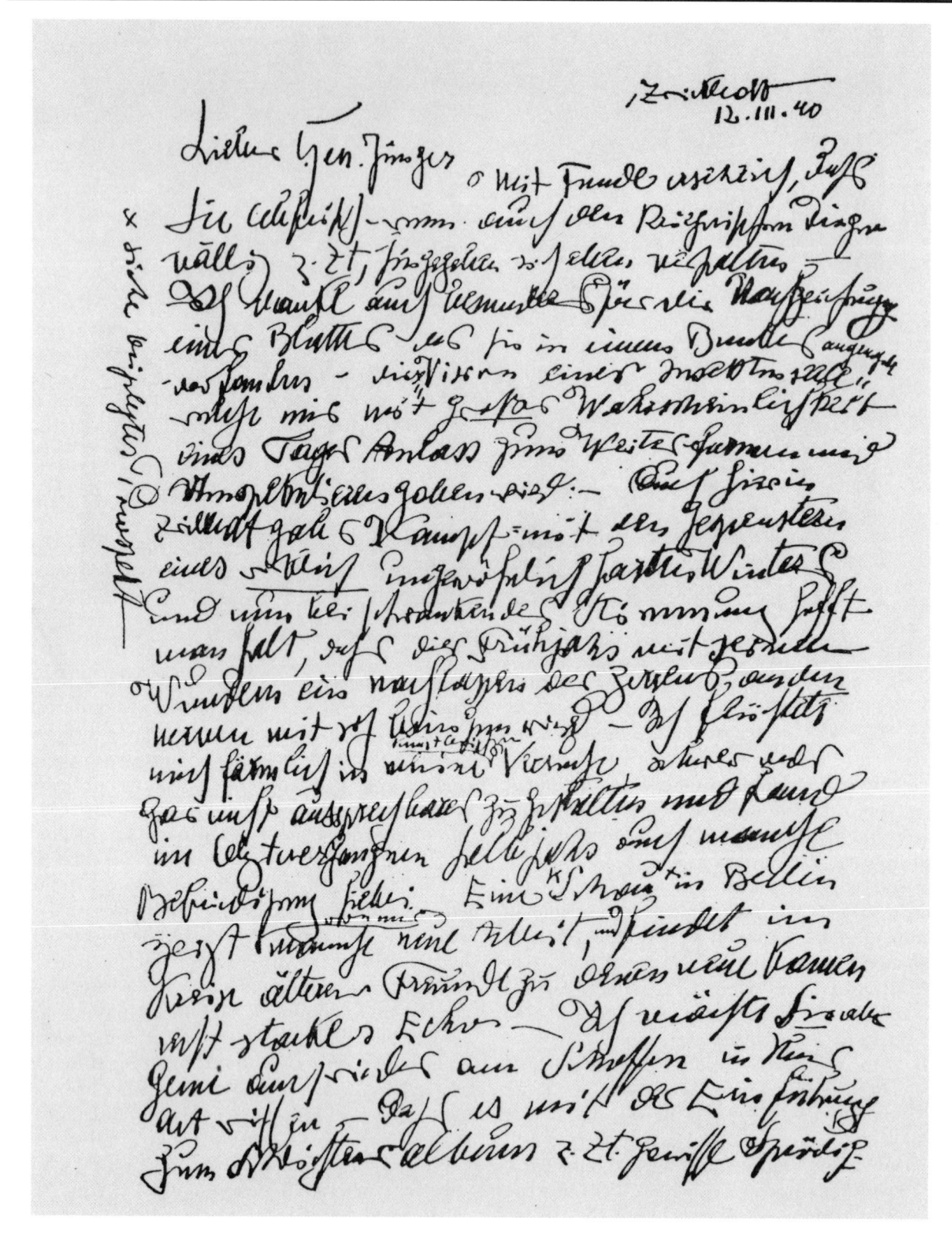

Letter from Kubin to the novelist Ernst Jünger (Eine Begegnung: Ernst Jünger, Alfred Kubin, 1975)

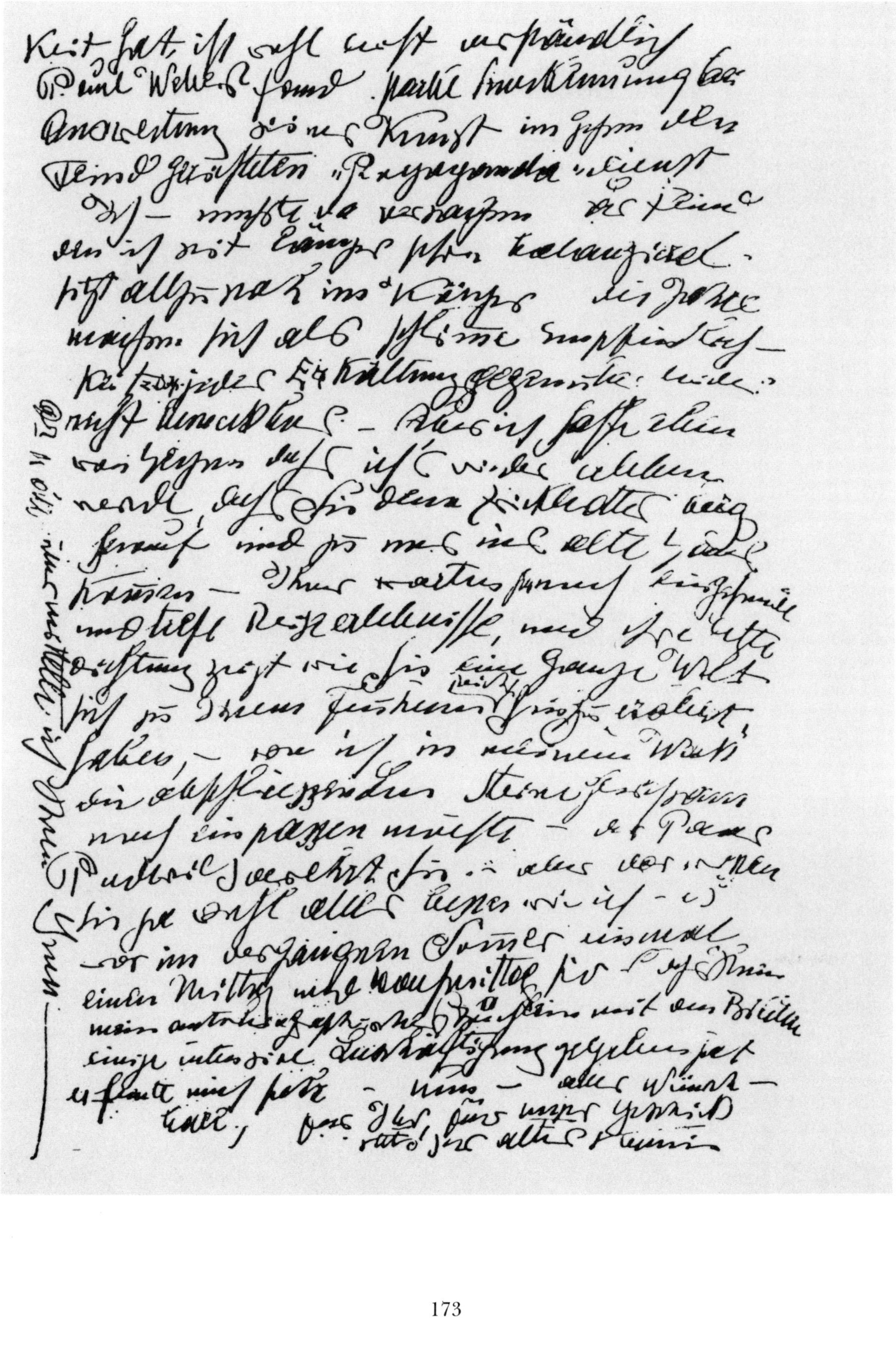

thing predates 1860. Patera remains mysteriously inaccessible to the narrator and his wife as they attempt to understand a series of disturbing events. It becomes clear that the kingdom is doomed to decomposition and putrefaction, both from within and without. An American, the canned-beef king Hercules Bell, has come to Perle to overthrow Patera and open the kingdom to commerce and industry. As the tension between the forces of the past and those of the future increases, the city and its inhabitants physically and psychically deteriorate. The story ends with a cosmic cataclysm that destroys the dream kingdom. Patera dies; Bell escapes; the artist survives to tell his story.

As the reader is carried deeper and deeper into the realm of dream, the "other side" of reality, it becomes clear that he is witnessing the journey of a mind into the depth of its subconscious. The novel is divided into three parts, corresponding to the stages of wakefulness and sleep. In the first part the narrator is invited to the dream kingdom; as in the initial moments of the time between waking and sleep, he drifts in and out of measured clock time and day-to-day materiality. In the second and major portion of the book the narrator is totally immersed in the land of dream, where the laws of logic no longer apply. This is the domain of psychic images that are unknown to the rational, waking consciousness. In the final part the collapse of the dream kingdom is related in a series of graphic and verbal tableaux.

It is twilight when the narrator receives the invitation to the dream kingdom. As he succumbs to the lure of the dream, his contact with material reality gradually gives way to the imaginative world of dream. Before entering the dream kingdom he has to relinquish his binoculars and his camera, underscoring that what he is about to experience only exists in the mind and cannot be perceived or recorded by any means other than the mind. Through this early part of the novel everything is seen in black and gray, often in dimness and shadow, as if to emphasize the absence of the clarity that exists in the ordered world of the conscious mind. Here everything must be experienced and accepted; nothing is to be selected or arranged by an investigative intellect. Gradually the narrator becomes so accustomed to the improbable "daß einem nichts mehr auffiel.... Hier waren Einbildungen einfach Realitäten" (that nothing seemed out of the ordinary.... Here illusions simply were reality). Overcome by

Central illustration by Kubin for his 1909 novel
Die andere Seite

an overwhelming desire to draw, he works intensely and produces his finest drawings.

At this point the narrator perceives life's balance and rhythm; he knows that this balance can only be discovered through an opening of the mind to the powers of an imagination that demands everything at once, "die Sache und ihr Gegenteil" (the thing and its opposite). He realizes that to comprehend the world he needs to understand and partake of both dream and reality.

This revelation of the meaning of existence is immediately followed by a surrealistic description of a bizarre and fantastic dream, in which the narrator stands beside the edge of a river. Clocks with short stubby legs, fish caught out of the air, harmonica music played on a man's eighteen nipples, goose-stepping pigs that vanish into a mouse hole, trains dashing about in a miller's transparent entrails, and a chimpanzee that plants a circular garden of asparaguslike stalks are but a few of the dream's plethora of details.

Kubin in his library at Schloß Zwickledt, 1950 (Wieland Schmied, Alfred Kubin, *1969)*

All are reported without comment, devoid of any personal involvement by the narrator. This switch in the narrator's point of view from active protagonist attempting to transform the dream images into an ordered sequence to passive observer is significant. From this point forward the dream sequence is presented as a series of unrelated tableaux. As in a Kubin drawing, the familiar is transformed into the strange and incomprehensible while the bizarre and unknown are treated realistically.

The narrator on the river's edge learns that there is no need to apply the laws of logic to the illogical. On the contrary, the need is to recognize the validity of the illogical, to step back from the dictates of temporality and submit to the energies of the subconscious and the atemporal. Kubin visually relates the same message in the illustration that accompanies the dream vision. (This illustration, like the passage itself, is in the center of the novel: the text contains fifty-one illustrations, and this one is the twenty-sixth.) The drawing has all of the fantastic elements mentioned in the verbal description of the dream: the man fishing in the air, the clocks with legs, the flying fish, and so on. The narrator is depicted in the lower right-hand corner of the drawing, dressed in top hat and cutaway, obviously distanced from the madness being acted out before him; his position is that of an observer in an art gallery. Clocks lie strewn before the narrator like a bridge from his world into the dream. At this point in the narrative the slow journey away from "the other side" may begin, for the narrator has perceived the ephemeral realm between the conscious and the unconscious, "the thing and its opposite."

By Kubin's admission, all of his work is related to the ideas he developed in *Die andere Seite*. As he aged, his hand became less sure, his line less bold, but his dialogue with life did not end until his death on 20 August 1959. His legacy to the art world is unquestioned. He was a precursor of expressionism and surrealism; yet his greatest bequest may be the power of his art to communicate to ordinary men and women the integration of a universe that embraces "the other side" of existence, the invisible, the fantastic, and the grotesque.

Letters:

Künstlerbriefe 1933-1955: Alfred Kubin, Anton Kolig und Carl Moll an Anton Steinhart, edited by Hans Kutschera (Salzburg & Stuttgart: Das Bergland-Buch, 1964);

Briefe an eine Freundin, edited by Helma de Gironcoli (Vienna: Bergland, 1965);

Die wilde Rast: Alfred Kubin in Waldhäuser. Briefe an Reinhold und Hanne Koeppel, edited by Walter Boll (Munich: Nymphenburger Verlagshandlung, 1972);

Eine Begegnung: Ernst Jünger, Alfred Kubin. Acht Abbildungen nach Zeichnungen und Briefen von Ernst Jünger und Alfred Kubin (Frankfurt am Main: Propylaen, 1975);

Fritz von Herzmanovsky-Orlando, *Der Briefwechsel mit Alfred Kubin, 1903-1952* (Salzburg: Residenz, 1983).

References:

Hans Bisanz, *Alfred Kubin, Zeichner, Schriftsteller und Philosoph* (Munich & Salzburg: Ellermann, 1977);

Kurt Bottcher and Johannes Mittenzwei, *Zwiegespräch: Deutschsprachige Schriftsteller als Maler und Zeichner* (Leipzig: Edition Leipzig, 1980);

Otto Breicha, *Alfred Kubin Weltgeflecht* (Munich: Ellermann, 1978);

Peter Cersowsky, *Phantastische Literatur im ersten Viertel des 20. Jahrhunderts* (Munich: Fink, 1983);

Anneliese Hewig, *Phantastische Wirklichkeit: Interpretationsstudie zu Alfred Kubins Roman "Die andere Seite"* (Munich: Fink, 1967);

Hanne Koeppel, *Freunde, Gäste und andere Leut'* (Passau: Verlag Passavia, 1978);

Alfred Marks, *Der Illustrator Alfred Kubin* (Munich & Vienna: Ellermann, 1977);

Wolfgang Müller-Thalheim, *Erotik und Dämonie im Werk Alfred Kubins* (Munich: Nymphenburger Verlagshandlung, 1970);

Paul Raabe, *Alfred Kubin, 1877/1977* (Munich: Ellermann, 1977);

Raabe, *Alfred Kubin. Leben, Werk, Wirkung* (Hamburg: Rowohlt, 1957);

Phillip H. Rhein, *The Verbal and Visual Art of Alfred Kubin* (Riverside, Calif.: Ariadne Press, 1989);

Wieland Schmied, *Der Zeichner Alfred Kubin* (Salzburg: Residenz, 1967); translated by Jean Steinberg as *Alfred Kubin* (London: Pall Mall Press, 1969; New York: Praeger, 1969);

Wolfgang Schneditz, *Alfred Kubin* (Vienna: Rosenbaum, 1956);

Richard Arthur Schroeder, "Alfred Kubin's *Die andere Seite:* A Study in the Cross-fertilization of Literature and the Graphic Arts," Ph.D. dissertation, Indiana University, 1970.

Papers:

The Kubin Archive in the Lenbachhaus, Munich, contains his publications, first editions of the books he illustrated, writings about him, letters, photographs, films, records, and portraits. Kubin's artistic estate of several thousand drawings and his library are divided between the Albertina in Vienna and the Upper Austrian Museum at Linz. Kubin's home, Schloß Zwickledt, is the property of the Austrian government and is maintained as a museum. The Spangenberg Verlag, Munich, has exclusive rights to Kubin's works.

Ernst Lothar
(25 October 1890-30 October 1974)

Donald G. Daviau
University of California, Riverside

BOOKS: *Der ruhige Hain: Ein Gedichtbuch* (Munich: Piper, 1910);

Die Einsamen: Novellen (Munich: Piper, 1912);

Die Rast: Gedichte (Munich: Piper, 1913);

Italien (Vienna: Kamönenverlag, 1915);

Österreichische Schriften: Weltbürgerliche Betrachtungen zur Gegenwart (Munich: Piper, 1916);

Der Feldherr: Roman (Vienna: Tempsky/Leipzig: Freytag, 1918);

Ich! Ein Theaterstück in vier Akten (Munich: Müller, 1921);

Irrlicht der Welt: Roman (Munich: Müller, 1921);

Irrlicht des Geistes: Roman (Munich: Müller, 1923);

Bekenntnis eines Herzsklaven: Roman (Berlin: Ullstein, 1923); revised as *Der Kampf um das Herz: Roman* (Berlin & Vienna: Zsolnay, 1930);

Licht: Roman (Munich: Müller, 1925);

Triumph des Gefühls: 2 Erzählungen (Vienna: Hartleben, 1925);

Gottes Garten: Ein Buch von Kindern (Vienna: Speidel, 1928); revised as *Kinder: Erste Erlebnisse* (Berlin, Vienna & Leipzig: Zsolnay, 1932);

Drei Tage und eine Nacht: Novelle (Vienna: Speidel, 1928);

Der Hellseher: Roman (Berlin & Vienna: Zsolnay, 1930); translated by Beatrice Ryan as *The Clairvoyant* (London: Secker, 1932; New York: Kinsey, 1932);

Kleine Freundin: Roman einer Zwölfjährigen (Vienna: Zsolnay, 1931); translated by Willa and Edwin Muir as *Little Friend* (New York: Putnam's, 1933; London: Secker, 1933);

Die Mühle der Gerechtigkeit oder Das Recht auf den Tod (Vienna: Zsolnay, 1933); translated by Willa and Edwin Muir as *The Mills of God* (London: Secker, 1935); translation republished as *The Loom of Justice* (New York: Putnam's, 1935);

Eine Frau wie viele oder Das Recht in der Ehe: Roman (Vienna: Zsolnay, 1934);

Ernst Lothar

Romanze F-Dur: Aus dem Tagebuch eines jungen Mädchens (Vienna: Zsolnay, 1935);

Nähe und Ferne: Länder, Leute, Dinge (Brünn, Vienna & Leipzig: Rohrer, 1937);

A Woman Is Witness: A Paris Dairy, translated by Barrows Mussey (Garden City, N.Y.: Doubleday, Doran, 1941; London: Harrap, 1942); German version published as *Die Zeugin: Pariser Tagebuch einer Wienerin* (Vienna: Danubia, 1951);

Beneath Another Sun, translated by Mussey (Garden City, N.Y.: Doubleday, Doran, 1943;

London: Harrap, 1944); German version published as *Unter anderer Sonne: Roman des Südtiroler Schicksals* (Hamburg & Vienna: Zsolnay, 1961);

The Angel with the Trumpet, translated by Elizabeth Reynolds Hapgood (Garden City, N.Y.: Doubleday, Doran, 1944; London: Harrap, 1946); German version published as *Der Engel mit der Posaune: Roman eines Hauses* (Cambridge, Mass.: Schoenhof, 1946; Salzburg: "Das Silberboot," 1949);

The Door Opens, translated by Marion A. Werner (Garden City, N.Y.: Doubleday, Doran, 1945); German version published as *Die Tür geht auf: Notizbuch der Kindheit* (Vienna: Zsolnay, 1950);

Heldenplatz (Cambridge, Mass.: Schoenhof, 1945); translated by James A. Galston as *The Prisoner: A Novel* (Garden City, N.Y.: Doubleday, Doran, 1945);

Die Rückkehr: Roman (Salzburg: "Das Silberboot," 1949); translated as *Return to Vienna* (Garden City, N.Y.: Doubleday, 1949; London: Hodder & Stoughton, 1950);

Verwandlung durch Liebe: Roman (Vienna: Zsolnay, 1951);

Das Weihnachtsgeschenk: Erzählung (Vienna: Zsolnay, 1954);

Die bessere Welt: Reden und Schriften (Hamburg & Vienna: Zsolnay, 1955);

Das Wunder des Überlebens: Erinnerungen und Ergebnisse (Hamburg & Vienna: Zsolnay, 1960);

Ausgewählte Werke, 6 volumes (Hamburg & Vienna: Zsolnay, 1961-1968)—includes as volume 6 *Macht und Ohnmacht des Theaters: Reden, Regeln, Rechenschaft* (Hamburg & Vienna: Zsolnay, 1968).

Title page for the American edition of the English translation of Lothar's Unter anderer Sonne, *a novel about the experiences of a Tyrolean family during the Nazi occupation of Czechoslovakia*

Throughout his life Ernst Lothar remained faithful to a clear set of values, including belief in justice and humanity, the necessity of culture for the improvement of society, the importance of the theater, and, above all, the importance of Austria to the world. He devoted his life as a novelist, short story writer, theater critic, essayist, lyric poet, theater director, government official, and university professor to propagating these views. Even though, as a Jew, he was driven into exile in 1938 after the Anschluß (annexation of Austria by Germany), there is no evidence of any change of outlook in his works. His love of Austria remained dominant throughout his life, and his principles of integrity and honesty never wavered. As a writer in exile he continued to produce workmanlike novels with judiciously chosen topical themes which attracted American and English readers. Lothar was one of the few writers who made the transition to exile successfully, and he no doubt could have continued his career in the United States had he not preferred to return to Austria. His blend of well-drawn characters and elaborate plots involving such universal themes as justice, loyalty, honor, and moral responsibility resulted in his novels being translated into thirteen languages. The major weaknesses that prevented him from reaching the stature of a major novelist are a tendency toward overelaboration and didacticism, a lack of humor, occasional lapses into stereotyped characters and situations, and a tendency toward melodramatic effects. His novels lack the depth and complexity of great works: they proceed in strictly logical fashion and conclude with an unambiguous resolution that leaves no room for the imagination. Despite these limitations his career as a writer and as a theater director distinguishes him as one of the leading literary figures of his day.

Ernst Lothar Müller was born on 25 October 1890 in Brünn, the late-born child of Dr. Joseph L. Müller and Johanna Wohlmuth Müller. His father was a respected lawyer; through his mother's side of the family there were connections with the theater. It was not uncommon for artists and actors to visit their house, and thus from an early age Müller was exposed to the world of art and the theater. Müller had two older brothers: Robert, thirteen years his senior, and Hans, eight years older. Robert Müller became a lawyer and eventually worked as an attorney in his father's government office. Under the pseudonym Hans Müller-Einingen, Hans Müller made a considerable name for himself as the author of more than thirty plays but faded into obscurity during his own lifetime.

Partly because his parents were elderly and his brothers so much older, and partly because he was prone to contagious illnesses that kept other children away, Ernst Müller spent a lonely childhood. He commented that neither of his parents had any great sense of humor, and he apparently never developed one himself. Commentators usually describe his personality as brusque and difficult, yet he also possessed great warmth, sensitivity, and gentleness, evidenced by his books about childhood. He was a complex individual who could command respect from his associates but not love.

He attended the Volksschule in Brünn and a gymnasium in Vienna, where the family moved in 1897. He studied law at the University of Vienna in accordance with the expectation of the family that he would follow his father's profession. While at the university he began to write under the name Ernst Lothar. His early attempts at poetry, *Der ruhige Hain* (The Peaceful Grove, 1910) and *Die Rast* (Repose, 1913), and at prose, *Die Einsamen* (The Lonely, 1912), aroused his father's opposition to the idea of having a second member of the family in the literary profession. The lure of literature and the theater eventually became too strong for Lothar to resist, though he did receive his law degree on 14 June 1914.

With the money from his books and from writing for newspapers and literary magazines he was able to indulge his desire for travel. At the Belgian resort of Westend he met a London-born Viennese girl whom he refers to in his autobiography only as Mary. They were married in Vienna

Title page for the Austrian edition of Lothar's novel tracing the fate of a family through three generations; it became his greatest success both in German and in English translation

in 1914; the marriage later broke up. They had two daughters, Agathe and Hansi, both of whom predeceased their father. In the short-story collection *The Door Opens* (1945; German version published as *Die Tür geht auf*, 1950), Lothar created a poignant memorial to his children. His special understanding of childhood is also evident in the novels *Kleine Freundin* (1931; translated as *Little Friend*, 1933) and *Romanze F-Dur* (Romance in F-Sharp, 1935).

During World War I Lothar spent two and a half years as a lieutenant in the Sixth Imperial Dragoons Regiment before he was declared unfit for service and assigned to duty as assistant state attorney in Wels. In 1916 he wrote a volume of eight essays titled *Österreichische Schriften: Weltbürgerliche Betrachtungen zur Gegenwart* (Austrian Writings: Observations on the Present by a Citizen of the World), a call for tolerance, moderation, mutual understanding and respect. It is a reasoned reminder of civilized values that must be preserved to restore the world after the war. Lothar attacks the generalized hatred on both sides and castigates such patriotic excesses as eliminating "foreign" words from the language. He emphasizes the importance of religion and stresses the strong bond between Austria and Hungary. He later claimed that this book, which was misunderstood as unpatriotic, brought him more enemies than friends. His job as assistant state attorney required him to prosecute as crimes the same kinds of actions that were being rewarded in the military. The necessity of signing a death sentence caused him such a crisis of conscience that he requested, and was granted, his release from the legal service in 1918.

Although his birthplace in Brünn made Lothar technically a citizen of the new Czechoslovakian Republic according to the division of territory after the collapse of the Austro-Hungarian monarchy in 1918, he did not hesitate for a moment in deciding to remain an Austrian citizen. He was thoroughly imbued with the greatness of the Austrian empire and lamented the passing of the monarchy, in which he saw the often-envisioned "United States of Europe" as an accomplished fact. He could not fathom how this nation that exemplified the baroque idea of the fertility of contrasts could cease to exist.

His first novel, *Der Feldherr* (The General, 1918), based on the life of the Austrian commander-in-chief, Conrad von Hötzendorf, was viewed as advocating defeatism and aroused some disfavor. Nevertheless, it enhanced Lothar's reputation as a writer and earned him the Bauernfeld Prize.

While pursuing his literary goals Lothar took an office in the Trade Ministry. Among his contributions to postwar reconstruction was his assistance in bringing the Salzburg festival to realization. Through this project he became acquainted with the famous theater director Max Reinhardt and the poet Hugo von Hofmannsthal. By all accounts Lothar was an efficient and capable official. When he left government service in 1924 to accept a position as a theater critic and feuilletonist with the *Neue Freie Presse*, Lothar, at thirty-four, was the youngest person ever honored with the title of Hofrat (Privy Councillor) for his contributions to Austria.

Lothar took a serious view of the theater, of acting and actors, and of the role of criticism. In his drama criticism as in the other phases of his career Lothar's legal training and logical mind are revealed. His reviews display objectivity of judgment, and his letters reveal that he maintained this sense of unimpeachable impartiality in private.

Following the publication of the trilogy "Macht über alle Menschen" (Power over all People)–*Irrlicht der Welt* (Will-of-the-Wisp of the World, 1921), *Irrlicht des Geistes* (Will-of-the-Wisp of the Spirit, 1923), *Licht* (Light, 1925); the novel *Bekenntnis eines Herzsklaven* (Confession of a Heart-Slave, 1923); and the volume of prose tales *Triumph des Gefühls* (Triumph of Feeling, 1925), Lothar was compared to Jakob Wassermann and Arthur Schnitzler. He continued to produce successful novels, usually based on questions of justice: *Drei Tage und eine Nacht* (Three Days and One Night, 1928), *Der Hellseher* (1930; translated as *The Clairvoyant*, 1932), *Kleine Freundin, Die Mühle der Gerechtigkeit oder Das Recht auf den Tod* (The Mills of Justice; or, The Right to Death, 1933), *Eine Frau wie viele oder Das Recht in der Ehe* (A Woman like Many, or, Justice in Marriage, 1934), *Romanze F-Dur*, and *Nähe und Ferne: Länder, Leute, Dinge* (Near and Far: Continents, People, Things, 1937). Of these works *Die Mühle der Gerechtigkeit*, published in America under the title *The Loom of Justice* (1935) and in England the same year as *The Mills of God*, was especially acclaimed; it was made into an American film titled *A Case of Murder* starring Frederick March. Lothar was stimulated to write the novel by a newspaper account of the deaths of an elderly couple: after a farewell dinner the husband killed his incurably ill wife at her request and then killed himself. In Lothar's version the main character is a rigid judge named Haushofer, whose life has been dedicated to an inflexible application of the law. Faced with the pleas of his terminally ill wife to die so as to escape further suffering, he learns the meaning of a higher humanitarian justice that transcends the written law. (When the book was republished in 1962, Lothar felt obliged to add a preface distancing his idea of mercy killing as an act of love from the practice of euthanasia by the Nazis.)

In 1930 Lothar was considered for appointment as director of the Vienna Burgtheater to replace Franz Herterich; but the position was instead given to Anton Wildgans, who had held it in 1921-1922. When Hermann Röbbeling, who replaced Wildgans in 1932, offered Lothar an opportunity to serve as guest director, Lothar readily accepted. Hofmannsthal had once encouraged Lothar to stage a Franz Grillparzer play, and this idea was brought to fruition in the Burgtheater

Lothar

on 21 October 1932 with a critically and publically acclaimed production of *Ein Bruderzwist in Habsburg* (A Brotherly Quarrel in Habsburg, 1873). This production is generally credited with proving that Grillparzer's works could be theatrically effective, thus inaugurating a Grillparzer renaissance in both Austria and Germany. Lothar staged other Grillparzer productions in the Burgtheater and later in the Theater in der Josefstadt to prove that Grillparzer ranked in Shakespeare's company as a dramatist. Lothar became a hopeless captive of the theater and went on to stage more than one hundred theater productions, including Hofmannsthal's *Jedermann* (1911; translated as *The Salzburg Everyman*, 1911) in Salzburg. His ties to the theater were further enhanced by his marriage to the actress Adrienne Gessner in Vienna on 22 May 1933. In August 1935 Lothar resigned from the *Neue Freie Presse* to replace Max Reinhardt, at Reinhardt's request, as director of the Theater in der Josefstadt.

After the Anschluß on 11 March 1938 and the subsequent occupation of Austria by the Germans, circumstances changed radically for Lothar. Although he had converted to Catholicism, his family was Jewish on both sides. When his management of the theater came under malicious criticism and he witnessed the outbreak of anti-Semitism in the streets of Vienna, he recognized that it was time to leave Austria. He cabled his brother Hans in Switzerland to expect him and made preparations to depart with his daughter Hansi. Adrienne, who was not Jewish and therefore not in immediate danger, would join them later. Efforts were made to prevent Lothar from leaving Austria by taking his passport from him, but it was regained though briefly, along with an exit visa. After a harrowing journey, climaxed by the confiscation of their car at the border by a Nazi patrol, they arrived in Switzerland on 20 March 1938, safe but virtually penniless. Lothar's brother Robert was later deported to Riga and killed by the Nazis.

In Switzerland Lothar realized that his period of exile might be of longer duration than he had first thought–perhaps for life. Consequently, he decided to immigrate to the United States and began to learn English. In June 1938 the family moved to Paris to wait for their visas to enter the United States, experiencing the hardships shared by countless other exiles in France. Lothar had thought that his reputation would smooth the path for him and his family because two of his books had recently been made into popular films: *Little Friend*, directed by Bertolt Viertel in London, and *The Clairvoyant*, with Claude Rains in the title role. But this hope proved to be a vain one. After nine months of waiting in Paris their visas finally were granted, and in April 1939 the Lothars sailed on the *Ile de France* for the United States. In New York they were met by Dr. Franz Horch, Lothar's former colleague at the Theater in der Josefstadt and now a literary agent for European authors, and he helped them get settled in an inexpensive hotel on Lexington Avenue. Although three of his novels, *The Clairvoyant*, *Little Friend*, and *Loom of Justice*, had been published in the United States, Lothar soon learned that they were forgotten and he was unknown. He also discovered, as did almost all exiled writers, that his accomplishments and reputation in Europe were of little interest to Americans.

A visit to Thomas Mann at Princeton was virtually obligatory for all newly arrived exiled writers. Mann suggested that Lothar establish a German-speaking theater in New York. In collaboration with other exiles Lothar initiated this venture in the Therese L. Kaufmann Auditorium on Lexington Avenue on 6 January 1940. He tried to enlist the support of the influential critic Brooks Atkinson, but neither Atkinson nor other critics were interested in reviewing the offerings of a German-speaking theater. Without the publicity that such reviews would have brought, none of the theater's four productions lasted more than one or two performances.

With the failure of the theater Lothar reached the low point of his life in America. Although he had published more than a dozen books, most of which had been translated into several foreign languages, his self-confidence was so eroded that his ability to write was nearly paralyzed. With his money nearly gone, Lothar in desperation applied to a Catholic agency that assisted Catholic emigrants who had made cultural contributions. Instead of receiving any tangible support, he was rebuffed with the admonition that he and his family must not feel too proud to work with their hands. This lesson spurred Lothar not only to write but also to redouble his efforts to master English until he could write well enough to prepare an outline of his new book for an American publisher. Soon the writer Thomas B. Costain, working as an editor for Doubleday, Doran, accepted Lothar's novel *A Woman Is Witness* (1941; German version published as *Die Zeugin*, 1951). Based on an actual diary, the novel is set in Paris in the years 1938 to 1940 and concerns a young Viennese girl, Franzi Durand, who fled Austria just before the Anschluß. She becomes involved with a married French journalist, who eventually becomes her husband. With the outbreak of the war he is called to action and wounded, returning home to die. The Germans occupy Paris, and Franzi joins the Resistance. Her outraged sense of justice and her feelings of frustration drive her to kill an SS officer, for which she is executed. Although the novel seems excessively melodramatic today, at the time it was appropriate to the prevailing mood and particularly to the effort to arouse a war consciousness in the United States. *A Woman Is Witness* appeared to almost uniformly favorable reviews and was made a special selection of the Book League of America, which sold sixty thousand copies.

On the basis of this strong performance Costain immediately asked for a second book, and Lothar proposed a novel set in South Tirol to expose Hitler's false propaganda about protecting the German minorities. *Beneath Another Sun* (1943; German version published as *Unter anderer Sonne*, 1961) became one of Lothar's greatest literary successes in America. He wrote the novel at Colorado College in Colorado Springs, where in 1941 he obtained a position teaching classes in drama and comparative literature and directing student productions. He developed great respect for American students and commented that the best universities in America far surpass their counterparts in Europe.

Lothar wrote the manuscript for *Beneath Another Sun* in longhand and sent the installments to Adrienne in New York; she typed it and forwarded it to Barrows Mussey in Brattleboro, Vermont, for translation into English. The novel traces the fate of a Tirolean family following the German-Italian agreement over South Tirol. When the Memelters, whose ancestors had been residents of the area for hundreds of years, object to their forced Italianization, they are relocated to Czechoslovakia to work in a war factory. The novel is rich in melodramatic twists of plot and ends rather sensationally with a complicated conspiracy to sabotage the Nazi war production. While American critics regarded the novel favorably, they pointed out that it is uneven in quality. The early part of the story, set in South Tirol, is well developed and the characters are fully drawn, while the characters introduced in the second part, set in Czechoslovakia, remain sketchy stereotypes. *Beneath Another Sun* was chosen as a selection of the Literary Guild; for a short time it appeared on the *New York Times* best-seller list, rising to number four in the same week that Franz Werfel's *Song of Bernadette* (1941) ranked seventh.

With the entry of the United States into World War II Lothar returned to New York and joined other leading Austrians in signing a manifesto in the *New York Times* pointing out to Americans that Austria was not at war with the Allies of its own accord, for it had been occupied in 1938 by Germany and robbed of its freedom of action. He devoted himself to creating a favorable image of Austria by giving radio talks and lectures in many cities, usually without fee, under such titles as "Justice for Austria." He argued that because of its forced annexation Austria should receive special treatment after the war.

With two successful novels and a request for a third, along with Adrienne's solid position in the theater, Lothar was able to resign his teaching position. He accompanied his wife on tour while he worked on his novel *The Angel with the Trumpet* (1944; German version published as *Der Engel mit der Posaune*, 1946), which became his greatest success both in English, with one hundred thousand copies sold by 1949, and in German. It was made into a popular German film starring Hedwig Bleibtreu, Helene Thimig, Attila Hörbiger, and Oskar Werner. In 1948 it became the first film to be awarded the Sascha Kolowrat Prize of the Austrian Ministry of Education.

Like its predecessors, *Der Engel mit der Posaune* reveals Lothar's commitment to Austria. The motto, taken from Grillparzer, establishes the tone: "Wüßten die Österreicher besser, was Österreich ist, sie wären bessere Österreicher; wüßte die Welt besser, was Österreich ist, wäre die Welt besser" (If the Austrians knew better what Austria is, they would be better Austrians; if the world knew better what Austria is, the world would be better). Lothar traces the fate of a family through three generations, from the suicide of Crown Prince Rudolf at Mayerling in 1889 to the Anschluß. Like almost all of his novels it is essentially the tale of a woman's heart, and like the other four novels written in America it is intended to help Americans understand Austrians. The reviews were generally favorable, stressing that Lothar knew how to create characters, how to hold them all in focus, and how to keep his story dramatic and entertaining. It is a solid, workmanlike novel but not a true work of art.

While in Colorado Lothar had met a young Viennese prisoner of war; from their conversations he conceived the idea for the novel *Heldenplatz* (1945; translated as *The Prisoner*, 1945). Completed in Connecticut in 1944, it deals with a Hitler youth's moral awakening in a prison camp in the United States and the conflict he faces between justice and expediency. The novel, which was well received by reviewers, continued Lothar's efforts to stimulate discussion of postwar Austrian problems.

Lothar had become a citizen of the United States, having taken out his first papers on 11 August 1939 and his second papers on 19 March 1944, but the necessity of renouncing his allegiance to Austria cost him a great deal of soul-searching. He felt a sense of loyalty and gratitude toward America, but it was not strong enough to overcome his emotional ties to his roots in Vienna. In 1945 he offered to serve the American government in Austria in any capacity and was given an army commission as Theater and Music Officer for Austria. His charge was to promote American theater and American music in Austria and to work for the rehabilitation of artistic life in Austria. He returned to Vienna in May 1946. In addition to his responsibilities as theater and music director of approximately twenty-five theaters in Vienna, Lothar also helped to restore the Salzburg festival. It is generally acknowledged that the rapid revival of theater life in Austria after the war can be attributed largely to his efforts.

In a replay of history, Lothar once again received a petition from the actors of the Burgtheater to become director, and, for the second time, his appointment was blocked in the minister's office. He was also prevented from returning to his post at the Theater in der Josefstadt. At this point Lothar understood that despite the war, much remained unchanged in Austria. Although not the director, Lothar staged several plays at the Burgtheater, as well as at the Akademietheater, between 1948 and 1961. His staging of works by Arthur Schnitzler was particularly acclaimed, and he is credited with initiating a Schnitzler renaissance just as he had done previously for Grillparzer.

Lothar's personal crisis culminated in 1948 when his tour of duty in Vienna ended, and he was ordered to return to the United States. His attempt to extend his stay in Vienna for another year to complete his novel *Die Rückkehr* (1949; translated as *Return to Vienna*, 1949) met resistance from American officials. Although the extension was finally granted, the incident helped resolve the problem of divided loyalties that had plagued Lothar since he had taken his United States citizenship. He went to the American Consulate in Vienna and surrendered the certificates of naturalization for himself and Adrienne.

Lothar treated the problem of divided loyalties in *Die Rückkehr*, which mirrors in thinly veiled terms many of his own experiences. When Felix, a young lawyer, returns to Vienna after the war to straighten out his family's financial affairs, he finds that his former fiancée, whom he had presumed dead, has not only survived but has prospered as an actress by becoming the mistress of Nazi propaganda minister Joseph Goebbels. Felix forgives and marries her although he is engaged to a girl in the United States. His attempt to explain his behavior to a friend enables Lothar to use the situation as a symbolic parallel to his own problem of conflicting allegiances between countries: if the woman you thought dead is alive, you go back to her in spite of all other bonds; if your own country, which has been reported dead, comes to life, you do the same. While reviewers appreciated the abundance of detail about postwar life in Austria, most felt that Lothar was somewhat overtheatrical about his hero's problem of whether to be loyal to his homeland or to America. The novel is unconvincing partly because the characters tend to serve only as stereotyped spokesmen for various points of view.

Reestablished as an Austrian citizen, Lothar continued his activity in the theater and as a critic for the newspaper *Die Presse*. His subsequent works include the novel *Verwandlung durch Liebe* (Transformation through Love, 1951), the story *Das Weihnachtsgeschenk* (The Christmas Present, 1954), the volume of speeches and essays *Die bessere Welt* (The Better World, 1955), his autobiography *Das Wunder des Überlebens* (The Miracle of Survival, 1960), and a volume of theater reviews and essays, *Macht und Ohnmacht des Theaters* (Power and Importance of the Theater, 1968). He received the Literary Prize of the City of Vienna in 1963, the Josef Kainz Medal in 1965, and the Gold Medal of Honor for Special Services to the City of Vienna, also in 1965. He died in 1974.

References:

Otto Basil, "Der Erzähler Ernst Lothar," *Neues Österreich*, 21 August 1949;

Donald G. Daviau and Jorun B. Johns, "Ernst Lothar," in *Deutschsprachige Exilliteratur seit 1933*, volume 2, edited by John M. Spalek and Joseph Strelka (Bern & Munich: Francke, 1989), pp. 520-553;

Oskar Maurus Fontana, "Ernst Lothar: Zum 70. Geburtstag," *Wort in der Zeit*, 6, no. 10 (1960): 8-14;

C. Frank, "Das Theater in der Josefstadt von Lothar bis Steinböck (von 1935 bis 1947)," Ph.D. dissertation, University of Vienna, 1949;

Brigitte Rasser, "Direktion Ernst Lothar. 6. Dezember 1935: 'Ein treuer Diener seines Herrn' von Grillparzer. Bühnenbearbeitung von Ernst Lothar," *Maske und Kothurn*, 10, no. 2 (1964): 162-166;

Harry Zohn, *Wiener Juden in der deutschen Literatur* (Tel Aviv: Olamenu, 1964), pp. 83-88.

Max Mell
(10 November 1882-12 December 1971)

Jürgen Koppensteiner
University of Northern Iowa

BOOKS: *Lateinische Erzählungen* (Vienna & Leipzig: Wiener Verlag, 1904);
Die drei Grazien des Traumes: Fünf Novellen (Leipzig: Insel, 1906);
Jägerhaussage und andere Novellen (Berlin: Paetel, 1910);
Das bekränzte Jahr: Gedichte (Berlin: Juncker, 1911);
Barbara Naderers Viehstand: Eine Novelle (Leipzig: Staackmann, 1914);
Gedichte (Munich: Musarion, 1919);
Hans Hochgedacht und sein Weib (Vienna, Prague & Leipzig: Strache, 1920);
Die Osterfeier: Eine Novelle in Versen (Munich: Musarion, 1921);
Das Wiener Kripperl von 1919 (Vienna: Wiener Literarische Anstalt, 1921);
Alfred Roller (Vienna: Wiener Literarische Anstalt, 1922);
Das Schutzengelspiel (Graz: Moser, 1923);
Das Apostelspiel (Munich: Bremer Presse, 1923); translated by Maude Valerie White as *The Apostle Play* (London: Methuen, 1934);
Morgenwege: Erzählungen und Legenden (Leipzig: Reclam, 1924);
Das Buch von der Kindheit Jesu (Vienna: Rikola, 1924);
Schauspiele (Munich: Bremer Presse, 1927)–comprises *Das Nachfolge Christi-Spiel; Das Apostelspiel; Das Schutzengelspiel;*
Das Nachfolge Christi-Spiel (Munich: Bremer Presse, 1927);
Gedichte, mit Holzschnitten von Switbert Lobisser (Vienna: Speidel, 1929);
Die Sieben gegen Theben: Dramatische Dichtung (Leipzig: Insel, 1932);
Anton Wildgans zum Gedächtnis: Gesprochen bei der Gedenkfeier des Burgtheaters am 8. Mai 1932 (Vienna: Gerold, 1932);
Barbara Naderer: Eine Novelle (Leipzig: Insel, 1933);
Das Spiel von den deutschen Ahnen (Leipzig: Insel, 1935);

Max Mell (Bildarchiv der Österreichische Nationalbibliothek)

Mein Bruder und ich: Den Erinnerungen eines alten Wieners nacherzählt (Munich: Langen-Müller, 1935);
Paradeisspiel in der Steiermark (Salzburg: Pustet, 1936);
Das Donauweibchen: Erzählungen und Märchen (Leipzig: Insel, 1938);
Steirischer Lobgesang (Leipzig: Insel, 1939);
Adalbert Stifter (Leipzig: Insel, 1939);
Verheißungen (Leipzig: Reclam, 1943);
Steirische Heimat (Graz: Leykam, 1943);
Gabe und Dank (Zurich: Scientia, 1949);
Das Vergelt's Gott: Ein Volksmärchen (Vienna: Bernina, 1950);

Mell's house in Vienna

Der Nibelunge Not: Dramatische Dichtung in zwei Teilen (Salzburg: Müller, 1951);

In Zauberkreisen: Werden eines Werkes (Graz: Stiasny, 1951);

Gedichte (Wiesbaden: Insel, 1952);

Verheißungen: Ausgewählte Erzählungen (Einsiedeln, Zurich & Cologne: Benziger, 1954);

Aufblick zum Genius: Drei festliche Reden (Innsbruck: Österreichische Verlagsanstalt, 1955)—comprises "Zur Lage der Kunst"; "Zum Gedenken Schillers"; "Adalbert Stifter";

Jeanne d'Arc: Ein Schauspiel (Wiesbaden: Insel, 1957);

Gesammelte Werke, 4 volumes (Vienna: Amandus, 1962); republished as *Prosa, Dramen, Verse*, 4 volumes (Munich: Langen-Müller, 1962);

Der Garten des Paracelsus: Dramatische Phantasie, edited by Lilli Mell (Graz, Vienna & Cologne: Styria, 1974);

Barbara Naderer und andere Erzählungen, edited by Margret Dietrich (Graz, Vienna & Cologne: Styria, 1976);

Spiegel des Sünders: Drei Erzählungen aus dem Nachlaß (Vienna: Österreichische Akademie der Wissenschaften, 1976);

Der Spiegel der Jahreszeiten: Ausgewählte Gedichte, Wien im Jänner 1905 (Graz: Steiermärkische Landesbibliothek am Joanneum, 1976);

Mächte zwischen den Menschen: Erzählungen, edited by Margret Dietrich (Graz, Vienna & Cologne: Styria, 1978);

Herz, werde groß (Graz: Styria, 1982).

OTHER: *Almanach der Wiener Werkstätte*, edited by Mell (Vienna: Rosenbaum, 1911);

Pope Pius II, *Briefe*, translated by Mell (Jena: Diederichs, 1911);

Österreichische Zeiten und Charaktere: Ausgewählte Bruchstücke aus österreichischen Selbstbiographien, edited by Mell (Vienna: Deutsch-Österreichischer Verlag, 1912);

Österreichische Landschaft im Gedicht, edited by Mell (Vienna: Sesam, 1922);

Ein altes deutsches Weihnachtsspiel, edited by Mell (Vienna: Johannes-Presse, 1924);

Haus- und Volksbuch deutscher Erzählungen, edited by Mell (Leipzig: Staackmann, 1936);

Wolfgang Amadeus Mozart, *Briefe Mozarts*, edited by Mell (Leipzig: Insel, 1937);

Stimme Österreichs: Zeugnisse aus drei Jahrhunderten, edited by Mell (Munich: Langen-Müller, 1938);

Adalbert Stifter, *Gesammelte Werke in sieben Bänden*, introduction by Mell, 7 volumes (Leipzig: Insel, 1939);

Manuscript for a poem by Mell (Albert Soergel and Curt Hohoff, Dichtung und Dichter der Zeit, *1963)*

Scene from the premiere of Mell's Das Schutzengelspiel *at the Burgtheater in Vienna, 1932*

Alpenländisches Märchenbuch: Volksmärchen aus Österreich, compiled by Mell (Vienna: Amandus-Edition, 1946);

Franz Grillparzer, *Österreichischer Lebenslauf,* introduction by Mell (Vienna: Dürer, 1947);

Antoni Edward Odyniec, *Besuch in Weimar: Goethes achtzigster Geburtstag. Briefberichte eines jungen polnischen Dichters,* translated by F. T. Bratranek, edited by Mell (Vienna: Pilgrim, 1949);

Peter Rosegger, *Aus meiner Waldheimat: Eine Auswahl,* afterword by Mell (Stuttgart: Reclam, 1953).

During his lifetime Max Mell was showered with awards and literary prizes, including the Mozart Prize in 1937, the Great Austrian State Prize in 1954, and the Stifter Prize in 1957. Today he would probably be forgotten were it not for *Das Apostelspiel* (1923; translated as *The Apostle Play,* 1934), a religious folk play which is still popular in his native Austria. Mell's short fiction—he did not attempt to publish a novel, although there is evidence that he worked on one—never attracted as much attention as his plays, confirming his conviction that for him drama was the most important genre. He did strive to succeed in the genres of poetry and narrative prose and also wrote many essays, but he always considered drama his true mission. Ironically, early in his career drama was the genre in which Mell was least successful. That situation changed over the years. In 1962, in a ceremony marking Mell's eightieth birthday, Ernst Haeussermann, the director of Vienna's famed Burgtheater, pointed out that Mell's dramatic oeuvre had been performed in the theater in no less than 219 productions—a remarkable record. Mell's last play, *Paracelsus und der Lorbeer* (Paracelsus and the Laurel), premiered in the newly refurbished Schauspielhaus in Graz in 1964. The play, which was published posthumously in 1974 under the title *Der Garten des Paracelsus* (The Garden of Paracelsus), contains the essence of Mell's lifelong philosophy: renunciation of personal aspirations as a precondition for fulfillment. Some critics praised the play lavishly and even compared it to Goethe's *Faust,* but the public reacted with indifference. Mell's time as a playwright seemed to have run out.

Mell was born in 1882 into a family of teachers and army officers from the Sudeten area (now part of Czechoslovakia). His father, Alexander Mell, who was from Prague, attended the Technical University in Graz, Styria. There he met and married Marie Rocek. For a few years Mell's father taught at the teachers' college in Marburg on the Drau (now Maribor, Yugoslavia), but in 1886 he was appointed director of the school for the blind in Vienna. The Mells never severed their ties with Styria: the family owned a summer home in the village of Kirchdorf, north of Graz, which was the author's refuge until the final years of his life. In 1905 Mell received his Ph.D. in German philology and art history from the Uni-

Mell's summer house in Pernegg an der Südbahn, Styria

versity of Vienna. With the exception of a short stint as a journalist for a Vienna literary magazine following World War I, he managed to live the respected yet modest life of a free-lance writer.

In speeches and essays Mell outlined his concept of the role of art as the expression of the divine. He believed that art must be universal, transcending the mundane and all constraints of time; only then can it perform its true mission: to help and to heal. Accordingly, the stories in his early *Lateinische Erzählungen* (Latin Tales, 1904) have little action. Instead, they concentrate on the spiritual development of their characters and discuss the author's aesthetic principles.

Mell soon realized, however, that as an author who wanted to help and to heal he could not afford to ignore the "real world." Between 1908 and 1910 he wrote several novellas in which he dealt with issues such as patriotism, love, and avarice. Some of Mell's "realistic" novellas were published posthumously; most of them, however, for unknown reasons, never saw publication. Only a small selection was incorporated in the four volumes of Mell's collected works (1962), thus depriving contemporary readers of a complete picture of his fiction.

The climax of Mell's realistic phase is the novella *Barbara Naderers Viehstand* (Barbara Naderer's Livestock, 1914), still considered his strongest, most convincing piece of short prose. *Barbara Naderers Viehstand* shows some startling parallels with today's Anti-Heimatliteratur, which portrays rural life without the traditional stereotypical images of tranquillity, harmony, and pretty idylls. Mell may be considered an early forerunner of such Anti-Heimatliteratur writers as Franz Innerhofer, Gernot Wolfgruber, and Hans Haid.

Although he displays a great deal of sympathy for the Styrian villagers in *Barbara Naderers Viehstand*, Mell does not hide their avarice, superstition, hatred, and brutality. There is nothing romantic about life in the country as depicted here. *Barbara Naderers Viehstand* is a captivating story about an impoverished peasant woman's bizarre affection for a cow she acquired in a somewhat deceptive manner. Barbara becomes obsessed with the well-being of the beast, sleeps in the barn with it, and steals hay from the neighbors to feed it properly. Eventually, no longer able to provide for the cow, Barbara is forced to board it with a neighbor, who tries to cheat her out of its calf. Ridiculed by the men of the village and despised by the women, Barbara fights for the survival of her beloved animal but loses the battle. The cow dies, and in an act that reflects her deranged mind Barbara cuts up the carcass and cooks the pieces. Following an Easter tradition, she has them blessed by the priest in the village church; but then she goes home and buries them in a tearful ceremony witnessed accidentally by the priest.

Mell (third from left) at a rehearsal of his Das Apostelspiel *at the Theater in der Josefstadt, Vienna, 1937. (Left to right) Karl Paryla as the "Zweiter Fremder," Attila Hörbiger as the "Erster Fremder," director Paul Kalbeck, Paula Wessely as Magdalen, Alfred Neugebauer as Großvater.*

The ordeal of World War I, in which Mell served as a field officer on the eastern and Italian fronts, reinforced his conviction that art must heal the chaos of contemporary society. Avoiding politics, he limited himself to a "spiritual" approach emphasizing love, tradition, trust in God, and especially devotion to one's Heimat (homeland).

Die Osterfeier (Easter Festival, 1921) is a narrative poem with the combination of dream and reality that is characteristic of Mell's *Das Apostelspiel* as well as his *Das Schutzengelspiel* (Guardian Angel Play, 1923). Both the poem and the plays are full of inspirational elements and are based on the belief in miracles. In *Die Osterfeier* people assume the roles of biblical figures in an Easter festival and find their entire personalities transformed. Similarly, "Die Geschichte vom Gewalttäter" (The Story of the Criminal, 1938) shows the miraculous salvation of an escaped convict following his encounter with a man and a woman and their newborn child, who remind him of the holy family. The story is a variation on the theme of *Das Apostelspiel*, in which two thieves are converted by the faith of a girl who believes them to be the apostles Peter and John.

The volume *Das Donauweibchen* (The Danube Water Nymph, 1938), in which "Die Geschichte vom Gewalttäter" appears, is a collection of stories, fairy tales, and legends set in Vienna. *Steirischer Lobgesang* (Styrian Hymn, 1939), on the other hand, documents Mell's lifelong attachment to "die grüne Steiermark" (green Styria) and, as the title suggests, praises the people and the landscape of this province in the south of Austria. Styrians have always claimed Mell as a native son: he is included in the province's standard literary history, *Literatur von 1945-1976 in der Steiermark* (Literature from Styria, n.d.), and the provincial government honored his one-hundredth birthday in 1982 by sponsoring a major exhibition on his life and work.

Painting of Mell by Lilli Mell, 1957 (Albert Soergel and Curt Hohoff, Dichtung und Dichter der Zeit, *1963)*

After World War II Mell wrote no fiction of any consequence, but many of his earlier works were reprinted in various collections. Like many of his colleagues, Mell was accused of being an opportunist and a collaborator of the Nazi regime that had taken over Austria in 1938, and his work was attacked for being hopelessly antiquated and naive. Mell had welcomed the Anschluß (annexation of Austria by Germany), but as his moving correspondence with his friend Viktor von Geramb, the renowned folklore professor, shows, Mell's hopes for a greater Germany were shattered, and he was so disillusioned that he totally withdrew from public life. After the war Mell steadfastly followed the only mission he felt was left to him: to express beauty in his art. He died in Vienna in 1971 and was buried in a grave provided as an honor by the city.

As a writer of fiction, Mell is a marginal figure in Austrian literature of the twentieth century. While much of his early work does not appeal to the modern reader, some of his work, such as *Barbara Naderers Viehstand*, appears to be quite up-to-date and has lost little of its power over the years. A Mell renaissance is nowhere in sight, but Mell's seriousness and his determination to follow his own path demand respect.

Letters:

Hugo von Hofmannsthal/Max Mell: Briefwechsel, edited by Margret Dietrich and Heinz Kindermann (Heidelberg: Lambert Schneider, 1982);

Christoph Heinrich Binder, ed., "Viktor von Geramb und Max Mell: Aus ihrem Briefwechsel in den Jahren 1938 bis 1945," *Blätter für Heimatkunde,* 59, no. 4 (1985): 121-136.

References:

Hans Bänziger, "'Die Heimat lädt dich ein, sei zu ihr lieb.' Bemerkungen zu Max Mell," *Modern Austrian Literature,* 8, no. 3/4 (1975): 81-99;

Alan Best, "The Austrian Tradition: Continuity and Change," in *Modern Austrian Writing: Literature and Society After 1945,* edited by Best and Hans Wolfschütz (London: Wolff/ Totowa, N.J.: Barnes & Noble, 1980), pp. 23-43;

Christoph Heinrich Binder, *Max Mell: Beiträge zu seinem Leben und Werk* (Graz: Steiermärkische Landesregierung, 1978);

Binder, *Max Mell: 10. XI. 1882 - 12. XII. 1971. Katalog. Ausstellung im Ecksal des Joanneums. 19. XI. - 12. XII. 1982 Graz* (Graz: Steiermärkische Landesbibliothek, 1982);

Margret Dietrich and Heinz Kindermann, eds., *Begegnung mit Max Mell* (Vienna: Böhlau, 1982);

Isolde Emich, *Max Mell: Der Dichter und sein Werk* (Vienna: Amandus, 1957);

Heidrun Graf-Blauhut, *Sprache: Traum und Wirklichkeit. Österreichische Kurzprosa des 20. Jahrhunderts* (Vienna: Braumüller, 1983), pp. 74-78;

Alfred Holzinger, "Große Hoffnungen und langsamer Neubeginn: Tradition und Traditionalismus," in *Literatur von 1945-1976 in der Steiermark* (Graz: Steiermärkische Landesregierung, n.d.), pp. 9-79.

Papers:

Max Mell's papers are owned by the Mell family in Vienna. A small portion of his papers—those pertaining to the province of Styria—are at the Styrian State Library in Graz.

Gustav Meyrink

(19 January 1868-4 December 1932)

George C. Schoolfield
Yale University

BOOKS: *Der heiße Soldat und andere Geschichten* (Munich: Langen, 1903);

Orchideen: Sonderbare Geschichten (Munich: Langen, 1904);

Das Wachsfigurenkabinett: Sonderbare Geschichten (Munich: Langen, 1907);

Jörn Uhl und Hilligenlei: Gustav Meyrink contra Gustav Frenssen. Zwei Parodien (Munich: Langen, 1907);

Der Sanitatsrät: Eine Komödie in drei Akten, by Meyrink and Alexander Roda Roda (Berlin: Schuster & Loeffler, 1912);

Bubi: Ein Lustspiel in zwei Akten, by Meyrink and Roda Roda (Berlin: Schuster & Loeffler, 1912; enlarged, 1913);

Die Sklavin aus Rhodus: Ein Lustspiel in drei Akten, by Meyrink and Roda Roda (Berlin & Leipzig: Schuster & Loeffler, 1912);

Des deutschen Spießers Wunderhorn, 3 volumes (Munich: Langen, 1913);

Der violette Tod und andere Novellen (Leipzig: Reclam, 1913);

Die Uhr: Ein Spiel in zwei Akten, by Meyrink and Roda Roda (Berlin: Schuster & Loeffler, 1913);

Der Kardinal Napellus (Munich: Bachmaier, 1915);

Der Golem: Roman (Munich: Wolff, 1915); translated by Madge Pemberton as *The Golem* (London: Gollancz, 1928; Boston: Houghton Mifflin, 1928);

Fledermäuse: Sieben Geschichten (Leipzig: Wolff, 1916);

Das grüne Gesicht: Roman (Leipzig: Wolff, 1916);

Walpurgisnacht: Phantastischer Roman (Leipzig & Munich: Wolff, 1917);

Gesammelte Werke (Leipzig & Munich: Wolff/Munich: Langen, 1917);

Der Löwe Alois und andere Geschichten (Dachau: Einhorn, 1917);

Der weiße Dominikaner: Aus dem Tagebuch eines Unsichtbaren (Vienna, Berlin, Leipzig & Munich: Rikola, 1921);

An der Grenze des Jenseits (Leipzig: Dürr & Weber, 1923);

Gustav Meyrink (Bildarchiv der Österreichischen Nationalbibliothek)

Meister Leonhard (Munich: Hyperion, 1925);

Die heimtückischen Champignons und andere Geschichten (Berlin: Ullstein, 1925);

Goldmachergeschichten (Berlin: Scherl, 1925);

Der Engel vom westlichen Fenster (Leipzig & Zürich: Grethlein, 1927);

Das Haus zur letzten Latern: Nachgelassenes und Verstreutes, edited by Eduard Frank (Munich & Vienna: Langen-Müller, 1973).

OTHER: "Der heimliche Kaiser," in Otto Julius Bierbaum and others' *Der Roman der Zwölf* (Berlin: Mecklenburg, 1909);

Charles Dickens, *Ausgewählte Romane und Geschichten*, 16 volumes, translated and edited by Meyrink (Munich: Langen, 1909-1914);

Henry Morton Stanley, *Mein Leben,* translated by Meyrink and Achim von Klösterlein (Munich: Die Lese, 1911);

Camille Flammarion, *Rätsel des Seelenlebens,* translated by Meyrink (Stuttgart: Hoffmann, 1919);

Romane und Bücher der Magie, 5 volumes, edited by Meyrink (Vienna, Berlin, Leipzig & Munich: Rikola, 1921-1924);

St. Thomas Aquinas, *Abhandlung über den Stein der Weisen,* edited and translated by Meyrink (Munich: Barth, 1925);

Carl Weisflog, *Das große Los,* edited by Meyrink (Munich: Von Weber, 1925);

George Sylvester Viereck, *Meine ersten 2000 Jahre: Autobiographie des Ewigen Juden,* translated by Meyrink (Leipzig: List, 1925);

Lafcadio Hearn, *Japanische Geistergeschichten,* translated by Meyrink (Leipzig: List, 1925);

Ludwig Bechstein, *Hexengeschichten,* edited by Meyrink (Munich: Barth, 1925);

Rudyard Kipling, *Ausgewählte Werke: Dunkles Indien,* translated by Meyrink (Leipzig: List, 1926);

Ludwig Lewisohn, *Das Erbe in Blut: Roman,* translated by Meyrink (Leipzig: List, 1929).

PERIODICAL PUBLICATIONS: "Gerhart Hauptmanns 'Auf Freiersfüßen im Bischofsberg,'" *März,* 1 (1907): 89-90;

"Selbstbeschreibung," *Der Zwiebelfisch,* 19 (1926): 25-26;

"Mein neuer Roman," *Der Bücherwurm: Monatsschrift für Bücherfreunde,* 12 (1927): 236-238.

A single work of Gustav Meyrink is well known to the English-speaking world, the novel *Der Golem* (1915; translated as *The Golem,* 1928). After the appearance of a translation, Howard P. Lovecraft was moved to praise the book in his *Supernatural Horror in Fiction* (1973), speaking of "its haunting shadowy suggestion of marvels and horrors just beyond reach" and its description, "with singular mastery," of Prague's "ancient ghetto." Meyrink is also repeatedly mentioned in connection with the Golem films of Paul Wegener; the films, however, have little to do with the novel, in which the clay giant given life by the legendary Rabbi Löw plays only a subsidiary role. (Wegener's first film [1914] was based on a 1908 play by Arthur Holitscher; the second, *Der Golem: Wie er in die Welt kam* [The Golem: How He Came into the World, 1920], takes the name of one of its characters, but almost nothing else, from Meyrink's text.)

In France a wave of translations in the 1960s and 1970s won Meyrink a following among devotees of the occult. In Germany the story of Meyrink's reception is more complex. Originally he acquired a small but ardent readership by means of the stories he contributed to the Munich periodical *Simplicissimus;* Erich Mühsam told how young intellectuals eagerly awaited the next number of the magazine: "stand ein neuer Meyrink darin, so war für etliche Abende Diskussionsstoff vorhanden" (if there was a new Meyrink in it, we had material for several evenings of discussion), while Karl Wolfskehl recalled: "Jeder neue 'Meyrink' war ein sehr erwartetes Ereignis und sofort in aller Mund" (Every new "Meyrink" was a keenly anticipated event and immediately discussed by everyone). On the whole, his fans were disappointed when *Der Golem* came out: Hermann Hesse wrote that "Die Romantechnik Meyrinks enthält viel alte Schablone" (The novelistic technique of Meyrink contains a great deal that is old hat), and the satirist Kurt Tucholsky, who had called Meyrink "ein neuer Klassiker" (a new classic), regretfully detected a flagging of artistic power in both *Der Golem* and *Das grüne Gesicht* (The Green Countenance, 1916). Winning a mass audience with *Der Golem,* Meyrink simultaneously became the object of an attack mounted by nationalistic elements in the German press, a wartime reaction against his mocking of "German" values and, perhaps, against the philo-Semitism of the novels. His house at Starnberg in Bavaria was stoned, and the notoriously anti-Semitic, ultraconservative chronicler of German letters Adolf Bartels proclaimed that "Meyrink hat geleugnet Jude zu sein, der literarischen Physiognomie und auch der Tendenz nach ist er es aber zweifellos" (Meyrink has denied that he is a Jew, but, judged by his literary physiognomy and his tendencies, he *is* one, beyond any doubt). The printing of his works was forbidden during Adolf Hitler's "thousand-year empire." More recently, German criticism and the German public have remembered him variously as an heir to E. T. A. Hoffmann and Edgar Allan Poe; as a representative, with Alfred Kubin and H. H. Ewers, of the "magical novel"; and as a cult figure: his novels have been reprinted in a paperback series called "Esoterica." He remains one of the great portrayers of the city of Prague, rivaling Franz Kafka,

Franz Werfel, and the young Rainer Maria Rilke. (Yet Kafka had only a sneer for Meyrink's work, and Rilke, trying to correct what he perceived as the excessive enthusiasm of the Princess Marie von Thurn und Taxis, regarded him as a popular entertainer who had touched "the other side" of human consciousness merely to make a profit from it by vulgar means.)

Meyrink was born Gustav Meyer at the Hotel Blauer Bock in Vienna, the illegitimate child of a highly placed Württemberg official, the Baron Karl Varnbühler von und zu Hemmingen, sixty years old at the time, and the actress Maria Meyer, who, at twenty-five, was on the threshold of a distinguished career; she would become one of the favorite tragediennes of the "mad" Ludwig II of Bavaria, who was falsely rumored to have sired Gustav. The true father shouldered his responsibility by paying for the boy's education; marriage was out of the question. Meyer moved often in his boyhood, changing places in accordance with his mother's engagements: he went to primary school in Munich and began the elite Wilhelmsgymnasium there; he spent the years 1880 and 1881 at the Johanneum in Hamburg, becoming "primus" in his class; he finished his schooling in Prague, first attending the gymnasium and then a commercial academy. He was immediately enchanted by the city; years later he recalled: "Als ich vor 45 Jahren, aus dem nebligen Hamburg vom Lotsen Schicksal in diese seltsame Stadt geführt, schon am ersten Tag eine lange Wanderung durch die mir unbekannten Straßen unternahm, da blendete mich eine helle Sonne, die in sengender Glut über den altertümlichen Häusern brütete–eine Sonne, die so ganz anders schien als der frohe Himmelsglanz, den ich von meiner Kindheit her kannte aus dem hellen, sorglosen Bayern" (When, 45 years ago, led from misty Hamburg by the pilot Fate to this strange city, I undertook a long walk through the unfamiliar streets on the very first day, a brilliant sun, brooding over the archaic houses, and scorching hot, blinded me–a sun altogether different from the serene splendor I remembered from my childhood days in bright and carefree Bavaria). At last, too, he was free of his mother, to whom he must have been an embarrassment and a burden; some of his works contain hints about their unhappy relationship–particularly the story "Meister Leonhard" (1916) and the novels *Walpurgisnacht* (Witches' Sabbath, 1917) and *Der weiße Dominikaner* (The White Dominican, 1921).

As a young lion in the Prague financial world–he founded a bank, Meyer und Morgenstern–as a dandy and lady's man, and as an amateur athlete specializing in rowing, he cut a brave figure. (One of his funniest satires, "Das dicke Wasser," collected in *Orchideen* [Orchids, 1904], has to do with a boastful Viennese crew, accustomed to the "lightness" of the Danube and defeated by the "thick water" of North German Hamburg.) Nevertheless, he was unhappy and in 1890 or 1891 planned suicide, an effort from which he was distracted–or so he reported some twenty years afterwards–by a brochure pushed under the door of the room where he sat, revolver in hand; the pamphlet was called *Über das Leben nach dem Tode* (Concerning Life after Death). This apparent directive from a higher power led him into a variety of religious and occult studies and practices; he became a member of the Prague lodge of the followers of the Russian theosophist Madam Blavatsky, entered into correspondence with the "Supreme Magus of the Societas Rosicruciana," learned yoga, and experimented with hashish. The association with secret societies and with group searches for supernormal phenomena eventually grew abhorrent to him, but his devotion to the several systems of yoga stayed with him until the end of his days.

More mundane troubles kept him aware of the world around him: an unhappy marriage to Aloisia Certl contracted in 1892; a love affair with Philomena Bernt (a cousin of Rilke), whom he was unable legally to make his wife; the appearance of tuberculosis of the spine–cured, he believed, thanks to yoga and not to the physicians of the noted Sanatorium Lahmann in Dresden, where he was a patient in the summer of 1901; a challenge to a duel, also in 1901, delivered to a reserve officer in the Austrian army who had made insulting remarks about his beloved; the rejection of the challenge on the grounds that Meyer was a bastard (actually, he was feared because of his fencing skills); an arrest on charges of embezzlement in January 1902; detention pending trial, and finally his abrupt release, cleared of all charges, in April. (His foes in the military, who felt that he had insulted them as a group, appear to have bribed the corrupt police commissioner Olič; the awful experience of jail is reflected in several of his tales and in *Der Golem*.) The sensational episode received much attention in the Prague press; although he was exonerated, Meyer concluded that his financial career was at an end. In 1904 he moved to Vienna for a brief tenure, from May to December, as editor of the periodical *Der liebe Augustin*. His Prague admirers missed him; the young Max Brod remembered him as resembling an elegant ex-officer, his face arrogant and uncommunicative, a mocking glitter in his large blue eyes; but others observed that he was absolutely without personal vanity. In any event, he was so fascinating that one of his Prague acquaintances, Paul Leppin, used him as the model for the mysterious Herr Nikolaus in the novel *Severins Gang in die Finsternis: Ein Prager Gespensterroman* (Severin's Passage into the Darkness: A Prague Ghost Novel, 1914).

Like many another young man, Brod had become enamored of Meyrink's stories in *Simplicissimus;* the first of these, "Der heiße Soldat" (The Hot Soldier), had appeared on 29 October 1901. Meyrink had toyed with the idea of a literary career at least as early as 1897, when he wrote the sketch "Tiefseefische" (Deep-sea Fish), discovered in 1971 by the Meyrink scholar Manfred Lube: for Meyrink, according to Lube, a "deep-sea fish" is a person whose true life is concealed beneath the surface of his normal activities. This work, a prose poem beginning "Ich glaube jetzt, daß Gustav ein Tiefseefisch ist" (I now believe that Gustav is a deep-sea fish), is not–Meyrink's own marginalia to the contrary–identical with the fragment of the same name published in the sixth volume of his collected works in 1917, a naturalistic tale about a deep-sea fish of a different kind: a society woman from Germany who owns a Prague brothel. At Dresden in the summer of 1901 the writer Oskar A. H. Schmitz–a member of the circle around Stefan George–had encouraged Meyrink in his writing plans, and the submission to *Simplicissimus* had occurred shortly thereafter. (The story that the editor in chief, Ludwig Thoma, found "Der heiße Soldat" in a wastebasket after it was rejected by an underling is apocryphal.) The success of the stories led the publisher Langen to bring out collections of them; the first, *Der heiße Soldat und andere Geschichten* (The Hot Soldier and Other Stories, 1903), was followed by *Orchideen*. Determined to live by his pen, Meyrink obtained a divorce and, on a trip to England, married his longtime mistress Philomena Bernt in 1905. (Meyrink was an admirer of the works of Charles Dickens: between 1909 and 1914 he translated sixteen volumes of Dickens's novels and stories for Langen, rendering the cockney dialogue in Bavarian.) Thinking he was threatened by legal problems or possibly jail in Austria because of his antimilitaristic statements, he decided to settle in Montreux, Switzerland, where a daughter, Sibylle, was born in 1906; Meyrink repaid Montreux by describing the town in the sketch "Ein pessimistisches Reisebild" (A Pessimistic Image of Travel) as a place that should become the site of an 'internationales Wettregnen'(an international raining competition). In 1906 or 1907 he shifted to Munich to be near his publisher and the journal which was his prime showcase. Some of his pieces also appeared in Langen's new periodical *März*, including his descriptions of Montreux and of Prague: "Die Stadt steht nämlich bekanntermaßen auf einem Netz von unterirdischen Gängen (the city stands, you see, as everybody knows, on a network of subterranean passages), one of which connects the German life of Prague with "dem fernen, aber stammverwandten Jerusalem" (distant but kindred Jerusalem). Pro-Jewish though he was, the satirist Meyrink could not let the chance for a painfully clever remark go by. Sometimes his satires grew too complex; such is the case with another of the *März* items, his comment on Gerhart Hauptmann's play *Die Jungfern vom Bischofsberg* (1907; translated as *The Maidens of the Mount*, 1916), which Meyrink wisely never included in any of his books. By 1911 Meyrink was sufficiently secure to buy a villa–he dubbed it "Das Haus zur letzten Latern" (The House at the Last Streetlamp) after a Prague locale–on the shores of Lake Starnberg, both for privacy and for his beloved water sports. (Ludwig II had drowned himself and his attendant psychiatrist in the lake.) He lived at the village of Starnberg for the rest of his life.

Encouraged by the success of the smaller collections–the last was *Das Wachsfigurenkabinett: Sonderbare Geschichten* (The Waxworks: Strange Stories, 1907)–Meyrink and Langen decided to assemble them, along with some other uncollected pieces (including the ones on Montreux and Prague), in three volumes in 1913 under the title *Des deutschen Spießers Wunderhorn* (The German Philistine's Magic Horn), a parodistic allusion to the collection of folksongs made by the romantics Achim von Arnim and Clemens Brentano, *Des Knaben Wunderhorn* (The Boy's Magic Horn, 1806-1808). Praising the new collection, Tucholsky wrote of the range of Meyrink's literary moods: "Wir kennen ja nun die hundert Meyrinks: den lyrischen und den haßenden und den lächelnden und den traurigen und den grinsenden und den schlagenden und den tötenden" (After all, we now know the hundred

Meyrinks: the lyrical one, the one who hates and the smiling one and the melancholy one and the sneering one and the one who strikes [or duels] and the one who slays). Today Meyrink's lethal sneers at the stupid arrogance of scientists, who believe they know all and in fact know nothing, are still readily appreciated. "The Hot Soldier"–the Bohemian bugler Wenzel Zavadil–has such a high body temperature that the objects around him in the Foreign Legion hospital in Indochina begin to char; the visiting professor of medicine, Mostschädel, limply observes that medical matters must be left to physicians. (Mostschädel's name means someone whose brain has been ruined by new wine–Meyrink's comical nomenclature is often heavy-handed.) Zavadil, clad in an old asbestos suit by a helpful Jesuit, disappears into the jungle. A professor of physics, confronted by a car in "Das Automobil," insists that the internal combustion engine is theoretically impossible, lacing his scorn with Latin tags. (One of the nice touches in Meyrink's tale is that the young enthusiast's motor *does* fail in the professor's presence; nothing in the world of phenomena can be depended on–as Meyrink, who boasted that he had owned the first car in Prague, well knew.)

The military gets its comeuppance again and again: in the semiprophetic "Die Eroberung von Sarajewo" (The Conquest of Sarajevo) the Austrian army captures the town, unaware that it has belonged to the Austro-Hungarian Empire for some decades. In "Schöpsglobin" (a title that defies translation: *Schöps* means a castrated male sheep or a simpleton, *-globin* indicates a serum) a fluid, derived first from calves and then from wethers, can be used to give young men "unbekehrbare progressive Patriomanie" (irreversible progressive patriomania). Its "discoverer," Prof. Domitian Dredrebaisel, accompanied by an American named Slyfox, the real maker of the serum, is sent to Borneo to try the stuff on orangutans after trying to enhance its effectiveness by passing it through the circulatory system of a sloth. The orangutans break out of their cages and kill the professor. It might be expected that they will return to freedom; instead–another of Meyrink's surprises–they form themselves into a regiment and, led by the most dull-witted among them, march away. Observing them from his hiding place, Slyfox recalls: "[Es] war mir, als sei ich nicht mehr im Urwalde, sondern ganz, ganz anderswo–in irgendeiner Kaserne Europas" (I felt I was no longer in the forest primeval but somewhere quite, quite different–In some European barracks or other). Other tales take aim at German popular culture: in "Das Wildschwein Veronika" (The Wild Pig Veronika) the reader never knows whether the heroine who achieves phenomenal success in plays and operettas about the sturdy mountain peasantry is a pig or a buxom young woman who yodels. The hypocritical bourgeoisie is humiliated in "Tut sich–macht sich–Prinzess" (That's Fine–That's All Right–Princess): a dignified paterfamilias, on a railroad trip, enjoys the nude snapshots distributed by a boastful dandy until he realizes, when the dandy repeats the words of the title, "eine gedankenlose Redensart von ihr" (a thoughtless turn of speech she has), that one of the bodies, photographed from the neck down, belongs to his daughter Erna. The enormous popularity of the North German pastor and novelist Gustav Frenssen, who captured his audiences with a blend of piety and proto-Nazi racial theories and a strong dose of sexuality, inspired Meyrink's stories "Hilligenlei" and "Jörn Uhl," named after two of Frenssen's books; Meyrink makes capital of Frenssen's phrase, "[sie] offenbarte ihm die Wunder ihres Leibes" ([she] revealed to him the wonders of her body). Such parodies–in which Meyrink shows enormous skill at re-creating dialects on paper–are limited in their appeal by their German frame of reference; his beast fables are more general in their application. A society that pays too much lip service to codes of behavior is the target of "Tschitrakarna, das vornehme Kamel" (Tschitrakarna, the Refined Camel): monocle in eye, the gentlemanly camel forces himself to join the dangerous company of a lion, a panther, a fox, and a raven because he subscribes to Bushido, the Japanese code of valor and chivalry. Growing hungry, the predatory animals decide to eat him, and he submits, slightly misquoting Horace: "Dulce et dignum est pro patria mori" (It is sweet and worthy to die for one's country). The story concludes: ". . . Harry S. Tschitrakarna war nicht mehr. Tja, Bushido ist nicht für Kamele" (. . . Harry S. Tschitrakarna was no more. Well, Bushido is not for camels). The animal stories are few, but they are successful because of their manifold meanings: "Die Geschichte vom Löwen Alois" (The Story of Alois the Lion) tells of a lion brought up by sheep; he gets a glimpse of his true nature but returns to the flock. The tale is patently anticlerical (Dr. Simulans, the sheep-pastor) and antimilitary (Alois wants to become a cadet, not realizing that only sheep are qualified), but the interest for interpreters lies in the tight web of relationships between outsiders and insiders and in the oblique commentary on the dangers and pleasures of fitting in.

Meyrink's full-blown horror stories were once much admired. "Das Wachsfigurenkabinett" includes "magnetic twins" which are actually one person divided into two, "die lebendig gewordene Leiche eines Ertrunkenen" (the corpse of a drowned man come alive) and "ein faustgroßer Kopf mit stechenden Augen" (a head the size of a fist with piercing eyes), all the work of the fiendish Mohammed Daraschekoh. The title of "Das Präparat" (The Specimen) refers to the head and lungs of a young man, kept alive by the same arch-villain. In "Der Albino" a promising young man is smothered in a plaster cast by an albino while friends listen helplessly to his convulsions. Nowadays these stories seem contrived, the material for a television show of the "Twilight Zone" variety. More truly shocking are the tales describing prison experiences, such as "Der Schrecken" (Terror), about a condemned man, and "Das ganze Sein ist flammend Leid" (All Being Is But Fiery Pain), about a released and broken prisoner (the title is taken from Buddhist verses translated by Karl Eugen Neumann). There are stories of disaster–for example, "G. M.," in which George Mackintosh (Gustav Meyrink?) takes revenge on a whole city–and of world destruction: a terrorist plots to flood the seas with oil in "Petroleum, Petroleum," while in "Der violette Tod" (The Violet Death) a single sound, spoken by a lost tribe in Tibet, suffices to reduce any listener to a bright violet cone the shape and size of a thimble; the discovery is carried back to civilization, and in 1950 an ear specialist rules a population consisting of the deaf and dumb (Meyrink insisted that he had made up the story, but its kernel may be found in a newspaper report by Sven Hedin, a Swedish explorer). Journalistic coyness attaches to many of these tales–for example, "Der violette Tod" warns the reader not to pronounce the fearful syllables–yet they contain a strong strain of dark moralism, or simply of contempt for the world as Meyrink found it. A turn to the inward life informs such stories as "Chimäre" (Chimera) and "Der Buddha ist meine Zuflucht" (Buddha Is My Refuge). Stylistically and intellectually these tales presage the would-be "depth" and the sometimes trite pronouncements of Meyrink's novels; the moment of illumination in "Der Buddha ist meine Zuflucht" is described thus: "Wie ein Blitz die Finsternis zerreißt, plötzlich–so war das Licht der Erkenntnis in das Herz des Alten gefallen.... Nicht ist *diese* Welt die wirkliche Welt" (As a bolt of lightning rends the darkness, suddenly–thus the light of knowledge fell into the old man's heart.... *This* world is not the real world).

Der Golem was in gestation for a long time; it seems to have been started as early as 1907 as a common project with Meyrink's friend, the artist Alfred Kubin, who was to do the illustrations. Kubin immediately set to work, but since Meyrink's text moved slowly or not at all, Kubin wrote his own novel to fit his drawings. The result was *Die andere Seite* (1909; translated as *The Other Side*, 1967), a tale of a city called Perle in central Asia, constructed out of bits and pieces of European towns and run by the elusive Claus Patera, a school friend of the narrator. (This classic of fantastic literature has some qualities in common with *Der Golem*, in particular its scurrilous detailing of a moribund Austrian society and its all-pervasive sense of dread.) Meyrink had difficulty in controlling his material; friends were called in for aid, charts were made, sections were eliminated or replaced. Among his confidants were his collaborator in works for the stage, Alexander Roda Roda, and Brod, who is said to have provided Meyrink with information for the cabalistic elements in the novel. Several publishers whom Meyrink approached were uninterested; according to Kurt Wolff, the daring young publisher who at last accepted *Der Golem* for his new firm, the book was offered to him in an unusual fashion: a gentleman of aristocratic appearance, with impeccable manners, turned up in Wolff's Leipzig office and gave him the first chapter of a novel called "Der ewige Jude" (The Wandering Jew), typed from the author's dictation into a "machine" (a rarity in those days, Wolff adds). The visitor wanted a contract granting him not royalties but a flat payment of ten thousand marks. Wolff did not know–or, at any rate, did not mention in his memoirs–that a portion of the novel, "Der Trödler Wassertrum" (The Junkman Wassertrum), had already appeared in the journal *Pan* in 1911. During 1913-1914 the novel, retitled *Der Golem*, was serialized in René Schickele's journal *Die weißen Blätter*. Wolff seems to have been amazed at its subsequent success in book form: "das Buch wurde in Hunderttausenden von Exemplaren verkauft. Es ist trotzdem durchaus kein schlechtes Buch, es ist vielmehr Meyrinks einziger guter Roman" (the book was sold in hunderts of thousands of copies. Nonetheless, it is

Lithographs by Hugo Steiner-Prag for Meyrink's novel Der Golem

by no means a bad book; rather, it is Meyrink's only good novel). Meyrink bitterly resented the circumstance that the profits from his best-seller went to Wolff and not to him.

The popularity of *Der Golem* is understandable: it is at once a detective story, a story about dreams, and a picture of an exotic milieu. In the search of its central figure for self-knowledge it can appeal to both the enthusiast for the occult and the more traditional German reader, brought up on the concept of the classical novel of development, the Entwicklungsroman. Werner Welzig has called attention to Athanasius Pernath's spiritual quest and to the fact that in Hillel, the wise archivist of the Prague synagogue, he has a devoted mentor—Pernath enters into a mystical union with the chaste Mirjam, Hillel's daughter, on the last pages of the novel. (A confusing factor for Meyrink students who see Wegener's 1920 film is that Mirjam is there the name of the flirtatious daughter of Rabbi Löw, who makes the "Golem"—the "Unfinished One"—in an effort to protect the inhabitants of the ghetto from an imperial decree of banishment.) The majority of the novel's action takes place in a dream: the unnamed narrator of the prologue falls asleep while reading a life of Gautama Buddha and becomes the gem-cutter Pernath—long the victim of mental disorders, including amnesia, after an unhappy love experience. Though not a Jew, Pernath resides in the old Prague ghetto. His neighbors are the junk dealer Wassertrum; Wassertrum's depraved yet alluring daughter Rosina; the criminally inclined Loisa, who lusts after Rosina; and Loisa's deaf-mute brother Jaromir. Nearby, Dr. Savioli maintains an apartment for his rendezvous with the married Countess Angelina.

Pernath is quickly drawn into a swirl of events: a stranger brings him a book in which the initial letter of the chapter "Ibbur, die Seelenschwängerung" (Ibbur, the Fecundation of the Soul) has been worn away; he is to repair it, and in the process his own soul will be repaired and purified. Simultaneously, Pernath is made privy to the plots of the half-insane student Charousek against Wassertrum, who is the student's father: years ago, having had his way with Charousek's mother, the vicious Wassertrum put her into a brothel. Wassertrum's legitimate son, the distinguished ophthalmologist Dr. Wassory, has already been driven to suicide by Charousek, aided by Dr. Savioli, who gathered sufficient evidence to denounce Wassory as a charlatan. Wassertrum, avaricious although extremely rich, attempts to blackmail Angelina, to whom Pernath is drawn; he had known her, he recalls, in his childhood; to conceal Angelina's love letters to Savioli from her nemesis, Pernath wanders through the hidden passageways of the ghetto and finds himself trapped in the Golem's dwelling place. He has already recognized his own face in a wooden puppet of the Golem carved by one of his cronies, Vrieslander; another of the minor mentors in the tale, the puppet-master Zwakh, remembers having seen the "monster," supposed to appear every thirty-three years, in his youth. Coming across a pack of Tarot cards in an empty room, Pernath sees on one of them a figure in old-fashioned dress who swells into a "blasigen klumpen" (bubbly lump) and gazes at Pernath "mit [seinem] eigenen Gesicht" (with [his] own face), sitting opposite him until dawn. The Golem is a double that must be overcome—the quest on which Pernath is aided by Hillel. One of the unanswered questions in the book arises in connection with the erotic misadventure that has robbed Pernath of his memory; now and then eroticism overcomes him, as in the passage composed of fantasies about the delectable Angelina snuggled in his arms, then the quiet Mirjam in conversation with him, and finally the naked Rosina dancing in a swallowtail coat. This much is clear: Angelina and Rosina have to vanish before the ethereal union with Mirjam can be achieved.

False clues planted by Wassertrum lead to Pernath's arrest on a charge of murdering a traveling salesman, Karl Zottmann; in prison he is supported by the members of the "Bataillon" (Battalion), a band of thieves and outcasts he had gotten to know in Loisitschek's tavern, to which he was introduced by Zwakh, Vrieslander, and the musician Josua Prokop. An emissary from the Bataillon, briefly Pernath's cellmate, tells him that Wassertrum has been murdered by Loisa and that Angelina and Savioli have run away together; a letter from Charousek informs him that the student has received money from Angelina that Charousek is to use to persuade Jaromir to provide evidence clearing Pernath and proving that Loisa murdered Zottmann. Another cellmate, the rapist and murderer Amadeus Laponder, serves as a medium to let Pernath know that Hillel and Mirjam are still alive (although there are hints that Mirjam has been Laponder's victim); Hillel and Charousek seem to speak to Pernath through Laponder. Freed at last, Pernath sets off in search of Hillel and his daughter and finds that Charousek, robbed of his revenge by Wassertrum's murder, has killed himself on the junk dealer's grave. The ghetto has been razed. Pernath takes rooms in one of the few houses to survive; according to legend, the place has been a refuge of the Golem. Celebrating Christmas alone in his new quarters, Pernath beholds his double, "In einem weißen Mantel. Eine Krone auf dem Kopf" (In a white cloak. A crown on his head); a fire breaks out, and clambering down from the roof on a chimney sweep's rope–suspended between heaven and earth, like the Hanged Man on the Tarot card–he beholds Hillel and Mirjam in a brightly lighted chamber. Then the dream ends. In his explanation of *Der Golem*, Arnold L. Goldsmith says that the Hanged Man is a symbol of "renewal and salvation"; the man on the rope passes through trials of "courage" and "faith" to achieve "a blissful state of freedom from desire." The awakened dreamer, who has picked up the hat of Athanasius Pernath by mistake at mass, begins a search for its owner; he learns that the events he experienced in the dream took place some thirty years before. Loisitschek has become a respectable member of Prague society, and Prince Ferri Athenstädt, the homosexual who once protected the infamous tavern from the police, is now a billiard-marker there. At the café, now a "ziemlich sauberes Lokal" (fairly clean little place), Athenstädt introduces the narrator to a boatman who takes him across the Vltava to Pernath's dwelling, "Das Haus zur letzten Latern," on the Hradčany. Its garden wall is adorned with frescoes "die den Kult des ägyptischen Gottes Osiris darstellen" (depicting the Egyptian cult of the god Osiris), and the garden door is "der Gott selbst: ein Hermaphrodit aus zwei Hälften" (the God himself: a hermaphrodite in two halves). Via an aged servant the narrator returns Pernath's hat; through the door he beholds Pernath and Mirjam, the latter still beautiful and young. They stand on the steps of a "tempelartiges, marmornes Haus" (a templelike marble house), and she leans against Pernath as they gaze at the city below. As Pernath turns toward him, he realizes how much the gem-cutter resembles him: "mir ist, als sähe ich mich im Spiegel, so ähnlich ist sein Gesicht dem Meinigen" (it is as though I saw myself in a mirror, so like his countenance is to mine). The novel concludes: "Dann fallen die Flügel des Tores zu, und ich erkenne nur noch den schimmernden Hermaphroditen" (Then the wings of the door swing shut, and now I can recognize only the shining hermaphrodite)–the image of Osiris.

Whoever attempts to understand the manifold occult and cabalistic allusions in the story of Pernath's (and perhaps the narrator's) purification may share the reaction of Rilke, who wrote of "eine törichte Verkleidung" (a foolish disguise). Whether Meyrink's mystifications are what Rilke suspected or have a deeper meaning, Meyrink proves himself a superior storyteller. Indeed, the book contains tales that can stand on their own, such as the story of Dr. Hulbert's Batallion (recalling the tradition of literature about the Prague underworld begun in the seventeenth century with Niklas Ulenhart's translation and "Pragization" of Cervantes's picaresque novella about Seville, "Rinconete y Cortadillo" (1613), as well as the story of the murderer Babinski which Peter Demetz has included in his 1982 anthology of classic tales from Old Prague, *Alt-Prager Geschichten;* there are, also, the café episodes, Pernath's imprisonment, and the attacks upon Austrian officialdom as personified in Dr. Leisetreter (Dr. Pussyfooter). Another element justifies the claim made by Kurt Pinthus and others that Meyrink is a worthy successor to E. T. A. Hoffmann: the strange good humor and sense of humor with which the exalted and horrible events and moods of the book are described.

In 1916, after the appearance of *Der Golem*, Meyrink published another collection of tales, *Fledermäuse* (Bats); the decline in power noted by Tucholsky is already palpable here. The tale of mother-hatred and of sibling incest, "Meister Leonhard," riveting in its description of the mother and her spirit of unrest in the first pages, goes to pieces as it moves along to séances and secret societies; "Wie Dr. Hiob Paupersum seiner Tochter rote Rosen brachte" (How Dr. Job Paupersum Brought His Daughter Red Roses) drowns in sentimentality; "Meine Qualen und Wonnen im Jenseits" (My Torments and Ecstasies in the Hereafter) takes easy shots at Lutheran pastors and pastors' wives, Catholic intolerance, and Schiller's poetry; "Die vier Mondbrüder" (The Four Moon Brothers) has a cast of evil men who mean to rule the world (mankind, misled by the false light of pedantic reason, will confuse the sun and moon and come to distrust true light); the symbolic giant monkshood of "Der Kardinal Napellus" (The Cardinal Napellus, previously published separately in 1915) seems to have been lifted from Strindberg's *A Dream Play* (1902). Nevertheless, the collection contains some pieces that are essential Meyrink: in "Das Grillenspiel" (The Cricket Game) a European traveler in Tibet witnesses crickets engaged in a blind war to the death; "Der Kommerzienrat Kuno Hinrichsen und der Büsser Lalalaschpat-Rai" (The Councillor of Commerce Kuno Hinrichsen and the Penitent Lalalaschpat-Rai) lets the bluff, hearty, and unscrupulous Hinrichsen pass briefly into the body and soul of a fakir, whose Vedantic teaching "Tat twam asi" (That is you) he then puts to his own brutal ends. The book's single masterpiece, though, is the beast fable "Amadeus Knödlfeder, der unverbesserliche Lämmergeier" (Amadeus Knödlfeder, the Incorrigible Bearded Vulture), the account of a bird that escapes from the Munich zoo and sets up a necktie shop in a little village. Apparently a mildly naughty story for children (who would certainly not learn honesty from the way Amadeus finances his flight), the fable turns, amid the quaintness of Bavarian dialect and customs, into a revelation of mass murder. The private room behind Amadeus's shop is a chamber of horrors: "Ein bestialischer Gestank entströmte der geöffneten Kammer, und wohin sich das Auge wandte: ausgespienes Gewöll, fast bis zur Decke hinauf abgenagte Knochen ... Gebein und Gebein" (A hideous stench streamed out of the opened room, and, wherever one's eye turned: bits of wool spit up, almost all the way to the ceiling ... bones upon bones). At the opening of "Petroleum, Petroleum" Meyrink implied that he possessed the gift of prophecy; the tale of Amadeus might suggest the concentration camps and their Bavarian-Austrian master, with his pose of respectability.

Wolff wrote that he could never convince C.G. Jung that Meyrink's second novel, *Das grüne Gesicht*, was a bad book. That novel has many of the traits and some of the virtues of *Der Golem*. Its main figure, Fortunat Hauberrisser, seeks and eventually finds perfect happiness in a mystical marriage with Eva van Druysen, a girl who, by human reasoning, is dead. A detective plot is again included: a religious fanatic, Klinkherbogk, slays his granddaughter in imitation of the drama of Abraham and Isaac and is murdered in turn by the giant Zulu Usibepu, a circus attraction managed by the Hungarian swindler Zitter Arpad. A Jewish refugee from Russia, Lazarus Eidotter, is accused of the crime but eventually cleared; in one of the best passages of the book Eidotter gives the cool and elegant Spanish Jew Ismael Sephardi an account of the pogrom in which his family was destroyed. The book's "seeker," Hauberrisser, is surrounded, like Pernath, by mentors: Eidotter, Sephardi, the worldly Baron Pfeill, the butterfly collector Jan Swammerdam (Swammerdam's name is identical with that of the seventeenth-century father of microscopy and was also used by Hoffmann to criticize uninspired scientific research in the tale *Meister Floh* [Master Flea, 1822]; Meyrink's Swammerdam is a kindly old man, on whom a single scientific-aesthetic passion has conferred a special purity).

Eva, the daughter of a friend of Sephardi's father, returns the affection of Hauberrisser, whom she meets at the house of Baron Pfeill. It is mutual love at first sight: Hauberrisser is overwhelmed by her wisdom as well as by her complete lack of coquettishness. Unfortunately, she is kidnapped by Usibepu, to whom she is strangely drawn. Meyrink may be accused of the rawest sort of racism, but it should be remembered that the savage is a member of Meyrink's special class of beings, in contact with the "other side" of existence, and is no more culpable than the deluded child-murderer Klinkherbogk. For Meyrink, the truly base creatures are the gentlemen at the pornography shop into which Hauberrisser blunders at the outset of his search for the mysterious Chidher Grün–the possessor of the miraculous "green countenance"–and the well-bred audience in the Amsterdam cabaret where sexual performances are given. It is characteristic of Meyrink that, having briefly revealed an element of carnal lust in his heroine, he drops the matter; Eva is purified much more swiftly than the eroticist Pernath.

The sudden intervention of her double seems to save Eva in the nick of time; but then Eva vanishes and is assumed to be dead by all except Swammerdam and her devoted lover. Hauberrisser searches for her high and low; at last she comes to him in his room, and her words constitute a kind of wedding ceremony. After a night of "wilder, grenzenloser Liebe" (wild, boundless love), described principally by means of a double line of dashes, she dies, and the mighty spirit Chidher Grün appears to the bereaved Hauberrisser in the guise of a rabbi–it is he who has caused the bridal visit of Eva. The next day Hauberrisser is found in his room, kneeling beside the body of a beautiful young woman; Pfeill and Sephardi are horrified by the smile on their friend's face. The clairvoyant Swammerdam insists that Eva is not dead, to the consternation of the rational pair. Surrounded by white roses,

Eva's body is displayed in the nave of the Church of Saint Nicholas; creeping in, Usibepu places the symbol of his Zulu royalty (a white chain made up of the neck vertebrae of the throttled wives of kings) on the bier. Meyrink crowds his stage with the apparatus of several mythologies; at the climax an Egyptian god approaches, accompanied by accessory figures. One of them, with the head of an ibis, bears the Egyptian cross, the symbol of eternal life; the others have the heads of a sparrow hawk and a jackal. They are followed by the Goddess of Truth. Rising up, eyes closed, Eva is led away. Amsterdam decays—a process Meyrink describes brilliantly if not economically; Hauberrisser moves to an ancient house south of the city, reputed to be on the site of a Druid's stone. A prophecy of Eidotter comes true: Amsterdam is destroyed in a terrible hurricane, but from his vantage point, Hauberrisser sees a blooming apple tree in the midst of the tempest and is reminded of Chidher Grün. The dream of paradise is fulfilled when, presaged by a vision of Isis holding a child in her arms, Eva returns; embracing, the lovers gaze out toward the "tote Stadt" (dead city).

Wolff's condemnation of his own publication was correct; the novel—save to admirers of the occult Meyrink—is an artistic catastrophe. Nevertheless, it demonstrates how deep Meyrink's roots were in the literature of the fin de siècle, the phrase a character in Oscar Wilde's *The Picture of Dorian Gray* (1891) glosses as "fin du globe" (end of the world). Meyrink's seedy Amsterdam is a worthy complement to the Dutch Sodom and Gomorrah of Jean Lorrain's late decadent classic, *Monsieur de Bougrelon* (1902). In a review of *Orchideen* Hesse perceived the affinities of Meyrink to *décadence;* on this foundation Meyrink superimposes his vision of a Europe gone to pieces in the wake of World War I. Amsterdam has become the last refuge for the inhabitants of a continent fallen into barbarism. Like other flawed novelists of his time who are too easily put aside as bizarre entertainers—in English literature one thinks of the Frederik Rolfe of *Hadrian the Seventh* (1904) and the Saki (H. H. Munro) of *When William Came* (1913)—Meyrink did have a gift for convincing visions of an imminent European disaster.

The thought of world revolution, if not world destruction, pursues Meyrink in his next narrative, *Walpurgisnacht;* the setting for the Apocalypse is Prague, and the time is again the immediate future. Of all Meyrink's novels this book is

Dust jacket for Meyrink's 1917 novel about an attempted revolution in Prague

the least laden with religious and occult references and puzzles; this relative simplicity has caused it to be neglected by his interpreters. The members of a coterie of "Bohemian-German" aristocrats and officials, living around Hradčany Square and in the citadel, have tried over the years to ignore the "Czech" city; these aged eccentrics meet for dinners and card parties, speak their hopelessly erroneous German (they believe it is quite correct), and despise and fear the Czech majority "unten. In der Welt" (down there. In the world). They are relics, like the desiccated Prague-German families the young Rilke wrote about in "Ein Familienfest" (A Family Celebration, 1898) and *Ewald Tragy* (1929; translated, 1948). The most likable among them is the imperial physician, Thaddäus Flugbeil, nicknamed "der Pinguin" (the Penguin) by the students and street urchins who laugh at his formal clothes and stiff gait; the most unpleasant is the Countess Zahradka, thought to have a hidden treasure, who both aids and humiliates her occasional visitor, the young violinist Ottokar Vondrejc. Ottokar is the adopted son of the museum-keeper at the Daliborka, the "Hunger Tower" on the Hradčany, but in truth the countess's illegitimate son. Exempt from military service because of heart disease, the boy has become involved in a passionate love affair with Polyxena, the countess's niece. Polyxena feels that the spirit of a murderous ancestress has entered her; this eighteenth-century Polyxena had poisoned her husband and, imprisoned in the Daliborka, had painted his picture on the dungeon wall with her own blood before she died. Ottokar has noticed the resemblance between the great-great-grandmother's portrait and the girl: both have the same cruelly lustful expression around their half-open lips, behind which "winzig-kleine blutdürstige Zähne weiß hervorschimmerten" (tiny bloodthirsty teeth shimmered white). A communist revolt is brewing in the city; Polyxena discovers that, against his feeble will, Ottokar has been chosen as a symbolic leader of the mutineers. The revolutionaries (with whom Meyrink patently has no sympathy at all) cover their loose plans for social reform, which boil down to sheer greed, with a patina of Czech patriotism. When the uprising begins Ottokar and Polyxena, who has been captured by the plotters, are married in a mock ceremony in the cathedral; the violinist is proclaimed "Ottokar Borivoj, Kaiser der Welt" (Ottokar Borivoj, Emperor of the World) and given the scepter of Borivoj the First, the heathen prince converted by Archbishop Methodius in the ninth century. Drawn at the head of the mob on a moth-eaten stuffed horse stolen from the palace of Wallenstein, Ottokar is shot by his mother, the countess, whose mansion the revolutionaries mean to plunder. Polyxena is rescued by the Bosnian troops sent from Vienna to put down the rebellion; at the same time, pregnant with Ottokar's child, she is liberated from the spirit of the portrait. The Penguin, having rediscovered the lost love of his youth, the aged prostitute "Bohemian Liesl," escapes from the city, aided by Liesl and his faithful servants. Liesl dies defending the south gate of the Hradčany against the mob; the Penguin, feeling that at last he can fly, is run down by a train (he has always abhorred such modern inventions) bringing the relief forces to Prague.

Thus the book has large elements of the sentimentality from which Meyrink was never free; with the figure of the insane Zrcadlo, "der Spiegel" (the Mirror), a Protean actor sheltered by Liesl, Meyrink introduces his usual mysticism into the novel. The manifold recollections from Bohemian history have a grisly climax: Zrcadlo assumes the form of the Hussite leader Jan Ziska of Tropnov, and in this guise allows himself to be killed and flayed by the revolutionaries so that (as in legend) his skin may serve as a drumhead. According to the recollections of Liesl, Zrcadlo had also transformed himself into Lucifer, and during the march on the citadel Polyxena thinks she sees Lucifer drumming on *his* own skin. At this point the text says that Polyxena's thoughts become confused, a confusion shared by the reader who tries to make out the symbolism of Zrcadlo's several transformations. Nonetheless, the atmosphere of the vernal city awaiting a bloodbath is conjured up wonderfully well; and Meyrink provides two deft characterizations in the silly but brave Penguin and the hapless private detective Stefan Brabetz. *Walpurgisnacht* is a readable book if not read too closely, a display of Meyrink's exceptional narrative talents–which he so often abused.

In *Der weiße Dominikaner* the connection with Prague is broken, unless the white Dominican Raimund de Pennaforte, who gives the book its name and whose redemptive spirit seems to reign in the church of Saint Mary, is from Prague legendry; the unnamed locale has no special features. The book concentrates on the spiritual memoirs of Christopher Taubenschlag, a foundling of a singularly innocent nature. The boy is adopted by the wealthy eccentric Bartholomäus Baron von Jöcher, the town's hereditary lamplighter, a calling that Christopher is trained to assume; the Jöchers, providing light to shine in the darkness, have a lamp, a wick, and a staff in their scutcheon. It is no surprise to learn that Christopher is in fact Jöcher's child by his long-lost wife. The book is a chronicle of the struggles of the pure Christopher against an impure world; he finds an ally and companion in Ophelia, the supposed daughter of the master wood-turner Mutschelknaus. Ophelia's mother is Aglaja, an actress, and her true father the actor and manager Paris; rather than be forced to go on the stage by the theatrical couple, Ophelia drowns herself, leaving behind a suicide note for Christopher in which she promises to meet him in the land of eternal youth. Upon the death of his father Christopher learns much more about his family and its lofty mission, and continues to resist "der Kopf der Medusa" (the Head of Medusa), the alluring evil of the world. The representative of a secret society visits him, telling him that he has been selected as its next leader; in order to achieve this post and aid in conducting mankind from plurality to unity, however, he must swear blind obedience. Christopher sees through the offer and refuses it; the spirit of his father tells him that he has done well–a good deal of old-fashioned political liberalism clung to the unpolitical Meyrink. At the novel's altogether misty finale Christopher is transfigured: "Verbrannt in mir ist das Verwesliche, durch den Tod in eine Flamme des Lebens verwandelt. Aufrecht stehe ich im purpurnen Gewand des Feuers, gegürtet mit der Waffe aus Blutstein" (That which is corruptible in me is burned away, transformed by death into a flame of life. I stand upright in the fire's purple dress, girded about with the weapon of haematite). The language sounds vaguely like Revelations, a fitting close for this most determinedly "Christian" of Meyrink's books; but the last sentence runs: "Gelöst bin ich für immer mit Leichnam und Schwert" (I am freed forever with corpse and sword), which, according to Frank, is Taoist symbolism.

As Meyrink turned away from writing stories, publishers became aware of their commercial value; in 1925 the Ullstein house in Berlin extracted another tale from Meyrink, "Die heimtückischen Champignons" (The Treacherous Mushrooms), which was made the title story of a new collection. Making boisterous fun of harebrained schemes (speculations in mushrooms) and the old Austrian bureaucracy, the story is window dressing meant to lure browsers into the purchase of what otherwise is a selection from *Des deutschen Spießers Wunderhorn*. The same year *Goldmachergeschichten* (Alchemists' Stories) appeared at Scherl's publishing house, also in Berlin; it gave evidence–sometimes bizarre, sometimes learned, sometimes dull–of Meyrink's fascination with alchemy and its mystical ramifications. Meyrink's esoteric interests had wholly gotten the upper hand–he edited, introduced, and partly translated the series *Romane und Bücher der Magie* (Novels and Books of Magic, 1921-1924). At the same time he took on other translating tasks, including the Japanese ghost stories of Lafcadio Hearn and a selection from Rudyard Kipling called *Dunkles Indien* (Dark India); Kipling's curiosity about Indian religions, demonstrated in *Kim* (1901) and elsewhere, appealed to Meyrink.

Meyrink's last novel, *Der Engel vom westlichen Fenster* (The Angel of the West Window, 1927), is far and away the longest of the five. Its authorship is in doubt; the historian Alfred Schmid Noerr claimed that he had participated extensively in the composition of the book, and it is possible that he at least provided much of the historical material. According to Schmid Noerr (who also said he had had a large part in *Goldmachergeschichten*), the project was intended to make money for Meyrink, who was in poor health. (Josef Strelka has proposed a stylistic analysis, following methods developed in Hans Sperber's 1918 study of Meyrink's language, to ascertain the truth of Schmid Noerr's claims.) As a historical novel, it is unique in Meyrink's oeuvre: one of its two major strands is a vita written by the English occultist and alchemist John Dee, who was imprisoned under Bloody Mary and tormented by the infamous Bishop Bonner, variously favored and ignored by Queen Elizabeth, and uncomfortably associated with the alchemist and charlatan Edward Kelly, his companion in Poland and the Prague of Rudolf II. The notebook has fallen into the hands of a German descendant of Dee; like other Meyrink heroes, he searches for an answer to the riddle of his own being. Like Pernath, he is attracted to a trio of women–his first love, the powerful and fickle Elizabeth; the sensual and perhaps supernatural Circassian beauty Assja Chotokalungin; and the pure and intellectually gifted Johanne Fromm–the equivalent figure to Jane Fromont, the devoted wife of John Dee. Near the conclusion the owner of the notebook climbs the Tower of Elspethstein and imagines that he has entered into a union with his first beloved in which the differences between man and woman are erased–a refinement upon the "hermaphroditic" ending of *Der Golem*. The novel has been praised as Meyrink's testament, his *Faust*–it follows the career of a Renaissance seeker for the truth and contains many inlays of "dark song" reminiscent of Goethe's *Chorus mysticus* (Schmid Noerr implied that *he* wrote these verses); yet it may also be put aside as a turgid attempt to attract Meyrink's faithful readership a final time–it is, after all, one more novel about the mystical quest, one more novel set partly in Prague. (The Bohemian sections, with the portraits of Rudolf II and Rabbi Löw, may be intended to emulate Max Brod's novel, *Tycho Brahes Weg zu Gott* [Tycho Brahe's Way to God, 1915; translated as *The Redemption of Tycho Brahe*, 1928], about the Danish astronomer who spent his last days at Rudolf's court.) Marianne Wünsch, however, has argued that *Der Engel vom westlichen Fenster* has a genuine logic and unity of its own and is not an attempt to profit from a tired author's reputation.

Meyrink's finances continued to falter, and in 1928 he was forced to sell his house and rent an apartment some distance from his beloved lake. His son Harro, who had been born in Munich in 1908 and had been partially paralyzed in a skiing accident, committed suicide in July 1932; Meyrink is supposed to have detected a smile of happiness on the dead man's face. Finally, in December of the same year, Meyrink bade farewell to his family, withdrew to his room, and sat, his upper body bare, facing an open window; as he had predicted, he died as the sun rose. His flair for the melodramatic stayed with him to the end and was shared by his widow, from whom this last report came.

An entertaining litterateur himself, Franz Blei called Meyrink an "amüsanter Mystifikateur" (amusing hoaxer); for Jung, Meyrink belonged in the company of world literature's great visionaries. Literary historians have not known quite what to do with him. *Des deutschen Spießers Wunderhorn* has such a variety of themes that it eludes classification, although its best sections, in their brevity, carry on something of the same salubriously destructive work as the earlier novels of Heinrich Mann; Meyrink's flight of outrageous imagination, however, lies outside Mann's range. Literary-historical labels for *Der Golem* seem to contradict one another: it has been interpreted as a belated specimen of the Gothic novel; Jens Malte Fischer calls it is one of the several books about the "dead city" spawned by the decadent mode; several commentators have seen it as an "expressionistic" book, both in its moral imperatives and in the sometimes explosive quality of its language (including its monosyllabic chapter headings, such as "Schlaf" [Sleep], "Not" [Despair], "Trieb" [Urge]). In any event, much of *Des deutschen Spießers Wunderhorn*, *Der Golem*, and *Walpurgisnacht* deserves a place in the canon of early-twentieth-century German literature; yet Meyrink himself would probably prefer that the public read and learn from his esoterica.

References:

Helga Abret, "Frankreich entdeckt Gustav Meyrink," *Sudetenland*, 19 (1977): 101-108;

Abret, " 'Das ganze Sein ist flammend Leid . . .': Karl Eugen Neumann und Gustav Meyrink," *Sudetenland*, 25 (1983): 176-184;

Abret, *Gustav Meyrink conteur* (Bern: Lang, 1976);

Abret, "Gustav Meyrink in Frankreich," *Österreich in Geschichte und Literatur*, 17 (1973): 183-185;

Abret, "Gustav Meyrinks erzählerisches Werk in tschechischer Übersetzung," *Sudetenland*, 20 (1978): 310-315;

Ernst Alker, "Gustav Meyrink," *Schweizerische Rundschau*, 28 (1928): 366-371;

Thomas Anz, *Literatur der Existenz: Literarische Psychopathographie und ihre soziale Bedeutung im Frühexpressionismus* (Stuttgart: Metzler, 1977), pp. 51-59;

Julius Bab, "Gustav Meyrink," *Literarisches Echo*, 20 (1917): 74-79;

John D. Barlow, *German Expressionist Film* (Boston: Twayne, 1982), pp. 70-79;

Adolf Bartels, *Die deutsche Dichtung der Gegenwart: Die Jüngsten* (Leipzig: Haessel, 1921), pp. 101-102;

Kurt Behrsing, "Die Brücke vom Diesseits zum Jenseits," *Begegnung: Zeitschrift für Kultur und Geistesleben*, 13 (1958): 101-102;

Max Brod, *Streitbares Leben* (Munich: Kindler, 1960), pp. 291-305;

William R. van Buskirk, "The Bases of Satire in Gustav Meyrink's Work," Ph.D. dissertation, University of Michigan, 1957;

Richard Burdick Byrne, *Films of Tyranny: Short Analyses of the Cabinet of Dr. Caligari, The Golem, and Nosferatu* (Madison, Wis.: College Print & Typing Co., 1966), pp. 43-96;

Yvonne Caroutch, ed., *Gustav Meyrink* (Paris: Editions de l'Herne, 1976);

Peter Cersowsky, *Phantastische Literatur im ersten Viertel des 20. Jahrhunderts: Untersuchungen zum Strukturwandel des Genres, seinen geistesgeschichtlichen Voraussetzungen und zur Tradition der "schwarzen Romantik" insbesondere bei Gustav Meyrink, Alfred Kubin und Franz Kafka* (Munich: Fink, 1983), pp. 34-63;

Jens Malte Fischer, "Deutschsprachige Phantastik zwischen Décadence und Faschismus," *Phaicon*, 3 (1978): 93-130;

Eduard Frank, *Gustav Meyrink: Werk und Wirkung* (Büdingen: Avalun, 1957);

Frank, "Das Haus zur letzten Latern: Der Visionär Gustav Meyrink," *Sudetenland*, 3 (1961): 17-20;

Frank, "Meyrinkiana: Neue Forschungsergebnisse zur Biographie Gustav Meyrinks," *Sudetenland*, 14 (1972): 97-102;

Frank, "Nachwort," in Meyrink's *Der weiße Dominikaner* (Munich: Langen-Müller, 1978), pp. 259-272;

Frank, "Paul Leppin und Gustav Meyrink: Eine Begegnung im alten Prag," *Sudetenland*, 7 (1965): 20-27;

Frank, "Probleme um Gustav Meyrinks Roman *Der Engel vom westlichen Fenster*," *Sudetenland*, 19 (1977): 258-260;

Frank, "Vom Stand der Gustav-Meyrink-Forschung," *Sudetenland*, 13 (1971): 290-292;

Gerhard Fritsch, "Nachwort," in Meyrink's *Walpurgisnacht* (Munich: Langen-Müller, 1968), pp. 219-227;

Arnold L. Goldsmith, "Gustav Meyrink and the Psychological Gothic," in his *The Golem Remembered, 1909-1980: Variations of a Jewish Legend* (Detroit: Wayne State University Press, 1981), pp. 91-119;

Fritz von Herzmanovsky-Orlando, "Eine Meyrink-Anekdote," in his *Gesammelte Werke* (Munich & Vienna: Langen-Müller, 1957), IV: 60-62;

Bella Jansen, "Über den Okkultismus in Gustav Meyrinks Roman *Der Golem*," *Neophilologus*, 7 (1921-1922): 19-23;

Robert Karle, "Gustav Meyrink und Alfred Kubin," *Sudetenland*, 18 (1976): 175-180;

Arnold Keyserling, *Die Metaphysik des Uhrmachers von Gustav Meyrink* (Vienna: Verlag der Palme, 1966);

Siegfried Kracauer, *From Caligari to Hitler: A Psychological History of the German Film* (Princeton: Princeton University Press, 1947), pp. 31-33, 112-113;

Alfred Kubin, "Vom Schreibtisch eines Zeichners," in *Aus meiner Werkstatt: Gesammelte Prosa*, edited by Ulrich Riemerschmidt (Munich: Nymphenburger Verlagshandlung, 1973), p. 73;

Anton Kuh, "Gustav Meyrink und das deutsche Prag," *Weltbühne*, 28 (1932): 903-906;

Oskar Loerke, "Visionäre Bücher," *Die neue Rundschau*, 27 (1916): 125-127;

Howard P. Lovecraft, *Supernatural Horror in Fiction* (New York: Dover, 1973), p. 51;

Manfred Lube, "Beiträge zur Biographie Gustav Meyrinks und Studien zu seiner Kunsttheorie," Ph.D. dissertation, University of Graz, 1970;

Lube, "Tiefseefische–der erste (und bisher unbekannte) Text von Gustav Meyrink," *Österreich in Geschichte und Literatur*, 15 (1971): 275-281;

Lube, "Zur Entstehungsgeschichte von Gustav Meyrinks Roman *Der Golem*," *Österreich in Geschichte und Literatur*, 15 (1971): 521-541;

Leo Hans Mally, "*Die andere Seite*–der andere *Golem?*," *Sudetenland*, 19 (1977): 256-257;

Florian F. Marzin, *Okkultismus und Phantastik in den Romanen Gustav Meyrinks* (Essen: Blaue Eule, 1986);

Catherine Mathière, *La dramaturgie de Gustav Meyrink* (Paris: Lettres modernes, 1985);

Paul Mayer, *Ernst Rowohlt in Selbstzeugnissen* (Hamburg: Rowohlt, 1967), pp. 41-42;

Erich Mühsam, *Unpolitische Erinnerungen* (Leipzig: Volk und Buch, 1958), pp. 127-129;

Heidemarie Oehm, "Gustav Meyrink: *Der Golem*," in *Spiegel im dunklen Wort: Analysen zur Prosa des frühen 20. Jahrhunderts*, edited by Winfried Freund and Hans Schumacher (Frankfurt am Main: Lang, 1983), pp. 107-203;

Kurt Pinthus, "Zu Gustav Meyrinks Werken," in Meyrink's *Gesammelte Werke* (Leipzig: Wolff, 1917), VI: 329-382;

Hans Arnold Plöhn, "Gustav Meyrink und seine Hamburger Verwandten," *Zeitschrift für niederdeutsche Familienkunde*, 40 (1965): 78-80;

Plöhn, "Zur achtzigsten Wiederkehr des Geburtstages Gustav Meyrinks am 19. Januar 1948," *Der Zwiebelfisch*, 25, no. 8 (1948-1949): 7-9;

Jean-Jacques Pollet, "L'image de Gustav Meyrink dans les lettres allemandes," *Etudes Germaniques*, 32 (1977): 30-39;

Max Pulver, *Erinnerungen an eine europäische Zeit: Begegnung mit Rilke, Kafka, Klee, Meyrink u.a.* (Zurich: Füssli, 1953), pp. 37-39;

Mohammad Qasim, *Gustav Meyrink: Eine monographische Untersuchung* (Stuttgart: Heinz, 1981);

Hans Reimann, *Die dritte Literazzia* (Munich: Pohl, 1954), pp. 224-229;

Reimann, *Mein blaues Wunder: Lebensmosaik eines Humoristen* (Munich: List, 1959), pp. 180-182, 424;

Beate Rosenfeld, *Die Golemsage und ihre Verwertung in der deutschen Literatur* (Breslau: Priebatsch, 1934);

Neil W. Russack, "A Psychological Interpretation of Meyrink's *Der Golem*," in *The Shaman from Elko: Papers in Honor of Joseph L. Henderson on His Seventy-Fifth Birthday*, edited by Gareth Hall and others (San Francisco: Jung Institute, 1978), pp. 157-164;

Siegfried Schödel, "Studien zu den phantastischen Erzählungen Gustav Meyrinks," Ph.D. dissertation, University of Erlangen-Nuremberg, 1965;

Schödel, "Über Gustav Meyrink und die phantastische Literatur," in *Studien zur Trivialliteratur*, edited by H. O. Burger (Frankfurt am Main: Klostermann, 1968), pp. 209-224;

C. G. Scholem, "Die Vorstellung vom Golem in ihren tellurischen und magischen Beziehungen," *Eranos-Jahrbuch*, 22 (1953): 235-290;

Theodor Schwarz, "Die Bedeutung des Phantastisch-Mystischen bei Gustav Meyrink," *Weimarer Beiträge*, 12 (1966): 716-719;

Hermann Sinsheimer, *Gelebt in Paradies: Erinnerungen und Begegnungen* (Munich: Pflaum, 1953), pp. 154-158;

Sinsheimer, "Gustav Meyrinks Weltanschauung: Einleitende Worte zur Feier von Meyrinks 50. Geburtstage im Münchner Schauspielhaus," *Der Zwiebelfisch*, 9, no. 3 (1918): 57-65;

Hans Sperber, *Motiv und Wort bei Gustav Meyrink* (Leipzig: Reisland, 1918);

Hugo Steiner-Prag, "Erinnerungen an Gustav Meyrink anläßlich seines Todes," *Sudetenland*, 20 (1978): 297-299;

Nelly Stéphane, "Un Gothique tardif: *Le Golem* de Gustav Meyrink," *Europe*, 62 (March 1984): 124-133;

Josef Strelka, ed., *Gustav Meyrink: Der Engel vom westlichen Fenster* (Graz, Vienna & Cologne: Stiasny, 1966);

Marga E. Thierfelder, "Das Weltbild in der Dichtung Gustav Meyrinks," Ph.D. dissertation, University of Munich, 1952;

Leonid Tschertkow, "Gustav Meyrink und Leo Perutz in Russland," *Literatur und Kritik*, 95 (1975): 290-297;

Kurt Tucholsky, "Ein neuer Klassiker," "Das grüne Gesicht," in his *Gesammelte Werke*, edited by Mary Gerold-Tucholsky and Fritz J. Raddatz (Reinbek: Rowohlt, 1960), I: 139, 239-241;

Hermann Uhde-Bernays, "Gustav Meyrink," *Berliner Hefte*, 1 (1946): 476-478;

Ludvík Václavek, "Der deutsche magische Roman," *Philologia Pragensia*, 13 (1970): 144-156;

Werner Welzig, *Der deutsche Roman im 20. Jahrhundert* (Stuttgart: Kröner, 1967), pp. 44-46;

Kurt Wolff, "Vom Verlegen im Allgemeinen und von der Frage: Wie kommen Verleger und Autoren zusammen," in *Expressionismus: Aufzeichnungen und Erinnerungen der Zeitgenossen*, edited by Paul Raabe (Olten & Freiburg im Breisgau: Walter, 1965), pp. 286-288;

Karl Wolfskehl, "Meyrink aus meiner Erinnerung," in his *Briefe und Aufsätze* (Hamburg: Claassen, 1966), pp. 200-203;

Thomas Wörtche, *Phantastik und Unschlüssigkeit: Zum strukturellen Kriterium eines Genres. Untersuchungen an Texten von Hans Heinz Ewers und Gustav Meyrink* (Meitingen: Wimmer, 1987);

Marianne Wünsch, "Auf der Suche nach der verlorenen Wirklichkeit: Zur Logik einer fantastischen Welt," in Meyrink's *Der Engel vom westlichen Fenster* (Munich & Vienna: Langen-Müller, 1975), pp. 528-568.

Papers:

Gustav Meyrink's literary remains are in the Bavarian State Library, Munich. Important collections of letters are in the Munich City Library; the Beinecke Library, Yale University (correspondence with Kurt Wolff); and the Austrian National Library, Vienna.

Robert Musil
(6 November 1880-15 April 1942)

Michael W. Jennings
Princeton University

BOOKS: *Die Verwirrungen des Zöglings Törleß* (Vienna: Wiener Verlag, 1906); translated by Ernst Kaiser and Eithne Wilkins as *Young Törless* (London: Secker & Warburg, 1955; New York: Pantheon, 1955);

Vereinigungen: Zwei Erzählungen (Berlin: Fischer, 1911)–comprises "Die Vollendung der Liebe," "Die Versuchung der stillen Veronika";

Die Schwärmer: Schauspiel in drei Aufzügen (Dresden: Sibyllen, 1921); translated by Andrea Simon as *The Enthusiasts* (New York: Performing Arts Journal Publications, 1983);

Die Portugiesin (Berlin: Rowohlt, 1923);

Grigia: Novelle (Potsdam: Müller, 1923);

Vinzenz und die Freundin bedeutender Männer (Berlin: Rowohlt, 1924);

Drei Frauen: Novellen (Berlin: Rowohlt, 1924; enlarged, Reinbek: Rowohlt, 1968);

Rede zur Rilke-Feier in Berlin am 16. Januar 1927 (Berlin: Rowohlt, 1927);

Der Mann ohne Eigenschaften: Roman, 3 volumes (volumes 1 and 2, Berlin: Rowohlt, 1930-1933; volume 3, edited by Martha Musil, Lausanne: Imprimerie Centrale, 1943); translated by Kaiser and Wilkins as *The Man without Qualities*, 3 volumes (London: Secker & Warburg, 1953-1960; New York: Coward-McCann, 1953-1960);

Nachlaß zu Lebzeiten (Zurich: Humanitas, 1936); translated by Peter Wortsman as *Posthumous Papers of a Living Author* (Hygiene, Colo.: Eridanos Press, 1987);

Über die Dummheit (Vienna: Bermann-Fischer, 1937);

Gesammelte Werke in Einzelausgaben, edited by Adolf Frisé, 3 volumes (Hamburg: Rowohlt, 1952-1957);

Das hilflose Europa: Drei Essays (Munich: Piper, 1961);

Aus den Tagebüchern (Berlin: Suhrkamp, 1963);

Tonka, and Other Stories, translated by Wilkins and Kaiser (London: Secker & Warburg, 1965); republished as *Five Women* (New York: Delacorte, 1966)–comprises translations of *Drei Frauen* and *Vereinigungen*;

Theater: Kritisches und Theoretisches (Reinbek: Rowohlt, 1965);

Der deutsche Mensch als Symptom: aus dem Nachlaß, edited by Karl Corino, Elisabeth Albertsen, and Karl Dinklage (Reinbek: Rowohlt, 1967);

Die Amsel: Bilder (Stuttgart: Reclam, 1967);

Photo: Staub

Sämtliche Erzählungen, edited by Frisé (Reinbek: Rowohlt, 1968);

Three Short Stories, edited by Hugh Sacker (London: Oxford University Press, 1970);

Tagebücher, edited by Frisé, 2 volumes (Reinbek: Rowohlt, 1976);

Gesammelte Werke in neun Bänden, edited by Frisé, 9 volumes (Reinbek: Rowohlt, 1978-1981);

Beitrag zur Beurteilung der Lehren Machs, edited by Frisé (Reinbek: Rowohlt, 1980); translated by Kevin Mulligan as *On Mach's Theories* (Washington, D.C.: Catholic University of America Press/Munich: Philosophia, 1983);

Selected Writings, edited by Burton Pike (New York: Continuum, 1986).

PERIODICAL PUBLICATIONS: "Politisches Bekenntnis eines jungen Mannes," *Die Weißen Blätter,* 1, no. 3 (1913): 237-244;

"Anmerkung zu einer Metaphysik," *Die neue Rundschau,* (April 1914);

"Skizze der Erkenntnis des Dichters," *Summa,* 1918;

"Die Nation als Ideal und als Wirklichkeit," *Die neue Rundschau,* (December 1921);

"Symptomen-Theater," *Der neue Merkur,* 6, no. 3 (1922): 179-186; no. 10/12 (1923): 587-594;

"Isis und Osiris," *Die neue Rundschau,* 34, no. 5 (1923): 464;

"Das Fliegenpapier," *Das Tage-Buch,* 4, no. 4 (1923): 122-123;

"Robert Müller," *Das Tage-Buch,* 5, no. 37 (1924): 1300-1304;

"Zur deutschen Literatur: Aus dem Nachruf für Rilke," *Die literarische Welt,* 3, no. 4 (1927): 1;

"Literat und Literatur: Randbemerkungen dazu," *Die neue Rundschau,* 42, no. 9 (1931): 390-412.

Robert Musil belongs to that small group of twentieth-century novelists who strove to capture in fictional form the definitive image of their age. His early works, the novel *Die Verwirrungen des Zöglings Törleß* (The Confusions of Young Törless, 1906; translated as *Young Törless,* 1955) and the novella collection *Vereinigungen* (Unions, 1911; translated in *Tonka, and Other Stories,* 1965), are unsurpassed examples of an innovative, modernist prose style adequate to the representation of complex psychological states. Like his contemporaries James Joyce, Thomas Mann, and Marcel Proust, Musil gradually broadened the scope of his literary investigations to include an entire society. His achievement in some ways parallels that of another contemporary, the painter Wassily Kandinsky: both brought an exceptionally thorough training in philosophy and the physical sciences to the practice of art, and both turned that education to a revolutionary end. Just as Kandinsky opened the way for nonrepresentational painting in the twentieth century, Musil in *Der Mann ohne Eigenschaften* (1930-1943; translated as *The Man without Qualities,* 1953-1960) pointed the modern novel on its path beyond narrative. In this novel Musil emerges as the twentieth century's greatest ironist and one of its premier writers.

Musil's paternal grandfather, Matthias Musil, was born into a peasant family and used his training as a military physician to rise into the bourgeoisie. Musil also had a paternal uncle and several maternal uncles and cousins who became high-ranking staff officers in the imperial army.

His father, Alfred Musil, was trained as an engineer. He worked in Klagenfurt, where Musil was born in 1880; in Komotau, Bohemia; in Steyr, Upper Austria; and achieved appointment as a Professor at the Technical Institute at Brünn (now Brno, Czechoslovakia) in Moravia in 1891. Alfred Musil regarded family life, and in particular attention to Robert, as impediments to his research. The author of a long list of scholarly works and a reliable servant of the emperor, he was elevated to the lower nobility in 1917. Alfred Musil clearly furnished a model for certain prominent characteristics in his son: the exactitude with which he analyzed even the most apparently marginal of his insights and observations and the compulsive necessity to work and to write.

The father's "soft, easily intimidated disposition" was balanced by a mother, Hermine Bergauer Musil, who was passionate, emotional, and often willful. Early in her marriage she entered into a relationship with another engineer, Heinrich Reiter, which was unusual even in the open atmosphere of late imperial Austria. Reiter accompanied the family on their vacations and finally moved in with them in 1900. Musil's writings reflect the family tensions which resulted from this ménage à trois, as well as the atmosphere of illicit eroticism that must have dominated the household.

For the most part Musil distinguished himself both in the classroom and on the athletic field; he was given, though, to lapses into lethargy. When he was about ten he began to reject his parents' values. His father, an advocate of late-nineteenth-century rational positivism, remained basically irreligious and apolitical throughout his life; Musil was critical of what he called an "aufgeklärtes Haus, in dem man nichts glaubt und nichts als Ersatz dafür gibt" (enlightened household, in which no one believes in anything and no one offers anything as a replacement for that belief). His mother's relationship to Reiter became an increasingly bitter source of contention.

His mother solved the problem by convincing Alfred Musil to send Robert to the military academies at Eisenstadt from 1892 to 1894, and at Mährisch-Weisskirchen from 1894 to 1897. Those five years saw an unbroken series of academic successes but also a growing impatience with the intellectual limits of military life. Nevertheless, Musil enrolled in September 1897 in the Technical Military Academy in Vienna, where he intended to study ballistics. In early 1898 he transferred to his father's institution, the Technical Institute in Brünn.

Musil had begun to write in 1897. These sketches, aesthetic pronouncements, reflections on his experiences, and excerpts from his reading were recorded in a series of notebooks, a practice Musil would continue for the rest of his life. Published in full for the first time in 1976, the notebooks comprise over fifteen hundred pages of closely set text.

Musil's initial literary efforts were colored by his reading of Austrian authors such as Peter Altenberg and Richard Schaukal, but also by his enthusiasm for Stéphane Mallarmé, Ralph Waldo Emerson, and, above all, Friedrich Nietzsche. The problem of possibility, the key category of Musil's mature work, derives from his reading of Nietzsche. "Das Charakteristische liegt darin," Musil wrote, "daß er sagt: dies könnte so sein und jenes so. Und darauf könnte man dies und darauf jenes bauen. Kurz: er spricht von lauter Möglichkeiten, lauter Combinationen, ohne eine einzige uns wirklich ausgeführt zu zeigen" (It is characteristic of Nietzsche that he says: this could be so and that could be so. And one could build one thing on one assumption, something else on the latter. In short: he speaks of pure possibilities, pure combinations, without showing us how any single one could really be carried out). Also, the experimental quality of Musil's fiction is the result of a deep reading of Nietzsche's call for new forms of language capable of denoting previously uncharted aspects of human life. Finally, Musil began to grope toward a new conception of the self predicated on Nietzsche's attack on the notion of subjectivity. In his early notebooks Musil stresses the discontinuous, random aspects of human thought and action, anticipating his later notion of a man wholly without salient or defining characteristics.

Musil remarks in the notebooks that no one, including the naturalists, has yet found the form to capture the random, structureless nature of life, while still representing it as beautiful. He styles himself "Monsieur le vivisecteur," a Nietzschean "brain-man" who dissects contemporary culture. Yet this cold modernism is tempered in Musil's early years by a form of the neoromanticism so prevalent in Austria at the turn of the century. Even while thinking of himself as a remorseless vivisectionist, Musil portrays himself at a window, observing the change from day to night. This is the classical romantic figure for a voyage beyond reason into the depths of the unconscious. The notebooks contain excerpts from Eduard von Hartmann's pioneering study of the unconscious, from Ricarda Huch, from Novalis, and from Franz von Baader, one of the central figures in the importation of mystical motifs into German romantic thought.

Musil's fascination with romanticism finally took a different turn from that of other writers of his generation. Whereas for Hugo von Hofmannsthal, for example, the mixture of hermetic symbols derived from French symbolism and German romantic thinking on the possibilities dormant in the unconscious was of primary interest, for Musil it was the more radical fringe of romanticism, the direct line to the German mystical tradition, which was of concern. "Das Ich des Cartesius ist der letzte feste Punkt im erkenntniskritischen Gedankengange, es ist die gewisse augenblickliche Einheit. Das Ich, von dem die Mystiker sprechen, ist das komplexe Ich" (The Cartesian "ego" is the last firm point in the epistemological train of thought, it is the certain, momentary unity. The "I" of which the mystics speak is the complex I). Often portrayed as a dualist who opposed mystical cognition to discursive reason, Musil actually wanted to explore the relations between reason and those aspects of life that are not yet penetrated by reason. Convinced of the importance of mystical experience, Musil tried to discover a rational faculty capable of articulating that experience. His wariness of instrumental reason is characteristic of many of the best minds of his generation, including Mann, Benedetto Croce, Georg Lukàcs, Walter Benjamin, and Ernst Bloch.

The early years of the century were marked for Musil by attempts to break free of his social

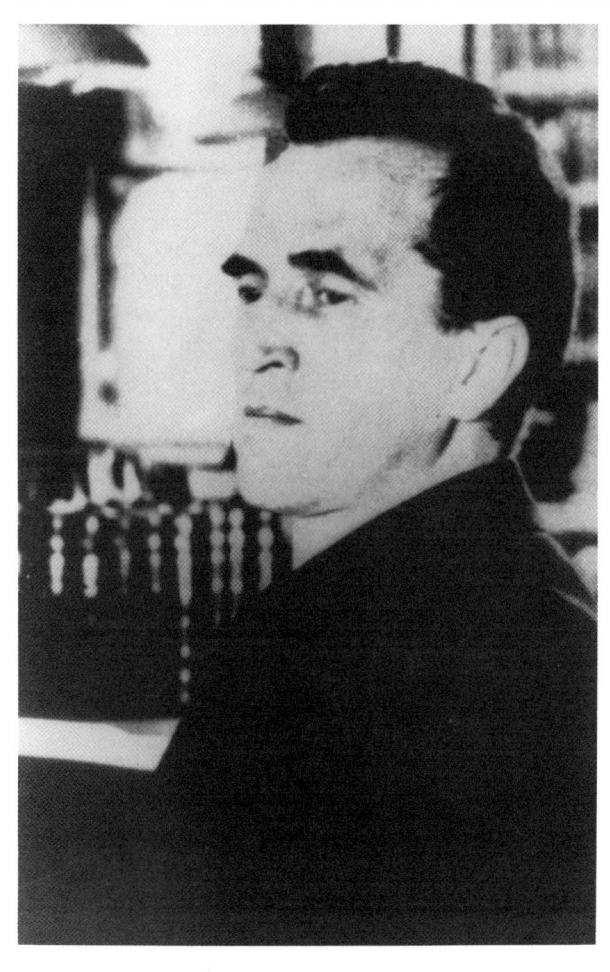

Musil in early years

class. An attempt to become the theater critic of the Brünn socialist paper and the establishment of a long-term relationship with Herma Dietz, a girl of proletarian origins, were steps on Musil's path to the idiosyncratic form of socialism that characterized his later political convictions. A year of compulsory military service in 1901-1902 also left its mark on Musil: he retained throughout the rest of his life something of the posture and dress of the young officer who is also a dandy. The officer's ethos had one other effect: Musil plunged headlong into a series of sexual adventures. One of the key themes of his notebooks from then on was sensuality.

In 1902, with the help of his father, Musil obtained a position as an assistant in one of the leading mechanical engineering laboratories in Europe, that of Julius Carl von Bach at the Technical University in Stuttgart. Ironically, it was there, at the height of his career as an engineer, that Musil made the final turn from science and toward humanism. In the winter of 1902-1903 he formulated a plan to study philosophy and psychology in Berlin. He also began writing a novel.

Die Verwirrungen des Zöglings Törleß, one of the great first novels in German, is nominally a portrait of adolescent life in a military academy. Such "school stories" were a common literary form at the time, with Frank Wedekind's *Frühlings Erwachen* (1891; translated as *The Awakening of Spring*, 1909), Emil Strauß's *Freund Hein* (Friend Hein, 1902), and Hermann Hesse's *Unterm Rad* (Under the Wheel, 1906; translated as *The Prodigy*, 1957) the most obvious comparisons. Yet this generic description hardly does justice to Musil's work. While *Die Verwirrungen des Zöglings Törleß* does depict the coming to adolescent consciousness of the young cadet Törleß, with the attendant painful experiences of awakening sexuality and the struggle for independent critical intelligence, the significance of the concepts and problems with which Törleß struggles far exceed those normally confronted in a novel of puberty.

Sent to an exclusive academy, Törleß enters into a difficult relationship with two classmates, Beineberg and Reiting. The three discover that another, Basini, has stolen from his peers, and they turn this knowledge into a form of brute power over him. Humiliated, subjected to a series of homoerotic episodes, and finally tortured, Basini confesses to the theft in order to escape Beineberg and Reiting. Törleß occupies an ambivalent position in these events. He is frequently present while Basini is being tortured, and he has his own homosexual encounters with him in the absence of Beineberg and Reiting. Yet Törleß remains removed from his fellows and their activities by his confusions, by a pervasive sense that the world before him and the world within himself somehow remain inaccessible to him. "Nein, ich irrte mich nicht, wenn ich von einem zweiten, geheimen, unbeachteten Leben der Dinge sprach! ... Es ist etwas Dunkles in mir, unter allen Gedanken, das ich mit den Gedanken nicht anmessen kann, ein Leben, das sich nicht in Worten ausdrückt und das doch mein Leben ist" (No, I wasn't wrong when I spoke of a second, secret unnoticed life in things! ... There is something dark in me, beneath all thoughts, that I can't measure with thoughts, a life that can't be expressed in words and yet is still my life). When Törleß flees from the academy, he is running less from his role in the Basini affair than the intensity and complexity of his attempt to regulate his thoughts and feelings. He realizes that his two worlds–that which is "hell" (bright) and "täglich" (everyday) and that which is "leidenschaftlich, nackt, vernichtend" (passionate, naked, destructive)–intermingle, that he must search "nach einer Brücke, einem Zusammenhange, einem Vergleich . . . zwischen sich und dem, was wortlos vor seinem Geiste stand" (for a bridge, a context, a comparison–between himself and that which stood wordlessly before his spirit). Much of the book's power stems from the carefully maintained tension between the naturalistic description of milieu and action on the one hand and the variegated portrayal of Törleß's inner life on the other. The novel frequently verges on essayism in its attempts to describe the relations between thought and feeling; the narration spreads out into a morass of description, the formal counterpart to Törleß's reaction to events. Yet the world around Törleß is evoked in a way that is convincing and occasionally frightening.

For all its originality, Musil's novel is a product of its age. The intensive preoccupation with eroticism ties it closely to the work of the psychologist Sigmund Freud, the writer Arthur Schnitzler, and the painters Gustav Klimt and Egon Schiele; and its exploration of the limits of language's ability to give shape to inner states points to the more general "crisis of language" perceived in turn-of-the-century Austria, a crisis best described in Hofmannsthal's "Ein Brief" (1905; translated as "The Letter," 1942). The novel's mixture of innovation and tradition led to an enthusiastic critical response. Alfred Kerr's long review on 21 December 1906 in the Berlin journal *Der Tag* was the first of a long series of positive evaluations. Volker Schlöndorff's 1965 film adaptation attests to the staying power of Musil's first work.

When *Die Verwirrungen des Zöglings Törleß* was published in 1906, Musil had been studying in Berlin for three years under the philosopher and psychologist Carl Stumpf, whose early integration of experimental psychology and phenomenology paved the way for Gestalt psychology.

One of Musil's earliest Berlin acquaintances, Johannes von Allesch, also a student of Stumpf's, proved to be a lifelong friend. Musil also began to move in Berlin's literary circles. Through his contact with Kerr he came to know the writers associated with the journals *Hyperion* and *Die neue Rundschau*. It was also through Kerr that Musil met Martha Marcovaldi.

Martha Heimann Marcovaldi had been raised in an assimilated Jewish family in Berlin, had studied painting with Lovis Corinth, and had attracted considerable attention in the Italian artistic community. When Musil met her in 1907 at the Baltic resort town of Graal, she had been married twice and was separated from her second husband. Seven years older than Musil, Martha was an outspoken feminist and an advocate of sexual freedom. Musil's letters to his parents and to Allesch were soon full of references to Martha as his "married sister."

Musil concluded his studies in 1908 with a dissertation on the Austrian physicist and philosopher Ernst Mach. His interest in Mach centered on Mach's pragmatic, experimental approach to science: in attempting to overcome the Kantian dualism which divides the world into phenomena and noumena and which had dominated nineteenth-century German science, Mach had asserted that only sensations are real; the distinction between mind and body is inappropriate, since neither is anything more than "a relatively stable complex of sensational elements."

More than two years passed between the completion of the dissertation and the publication of Musil's next works, the novellas "Die Vollendung der Liebe" (translated as "The Perfecting of a Love," 1965) and "Die Versuchung der stillen Veronika" (translated as "The Temptation of Quiet Veronika," 1965), which were published together in 1911 under the title *Vereinigungen* (Unions). The long gestation of these short works points to Musil's struggle to discover a formal vocabulary adequate to the expression of his ideas on psychology, one in which the boundary between affectivity and rationality becomes indiscernible. The result was two of the most radically experimental of all modernist texts.

The plots of the novellas consist of little more than the evocation of situations which are in themselves quite banal. In "Die Vollendung der Liebe" a woman travels by train to a distant town and betrays her husband. In "Die Versuchung der stillen Veronika" a woman rejects the advances of the more spiritual of two brothers in favor of his animalistic sibling; ultimately, even this temptation is rejected in favor of an autoeroticism of astonishing intensity. In place of action and even of character, the reader encounters an attempt to make transparent the awakening self-consciousness of the protagonists. The stream of traditional narrative comes to a standstill, to be replaced by a unique combination of figurative language and philosophical reflection on the psyche: "Sie wußte nicht mehr, was sie dachte, nur ganz still faßte sie eine Lust am Alleinsein mit fremden Erlebnissen; es war wie ein Spiel leichtester, unfaßbarster Trübungen und großer, danach tastender, schattenhafter Bewegungen der Seele. Sie suchte sich ihres Mannes zu erinnern, aber sie fand von ihrer fast vergangenen Liebe nur eine wunderliche Vorstellung wie von einem Zimmer mit lange geschlossenen Fenstern" (She no longer knew what she thought; a desire for being alone with alien experiences quietly took hold of her. It was like the play of the lightest, most incomprehensible disturbances and of great, shadowy movements of the soul grasping for them. She tried to remember her husband, but she found of her almost past love only a curious image, like that of a room with long-shut windows). In *Vereinigungen* Musil experiments with the possibilities of the simile, a device which captures the neither/nor, both/and character of certain moments of being. In "Die Vollendung der Liebe" alone Musil employs 337 similes; the combination of this thicket of similes and the static, patient narrative representation of consciousness lends to these novellas a unique, oneiric quality. "Die Versuchung der stillen Veronika" and "Die Vollendung der Liebe" are not easy to read: they have the density and complexity of other classic works of high modernism, qualities reminiscent of Arnold Schönberg's music or Pablo Picasso's cubist canvases.

In 1910, thirty years old and the author of two books, Musil was still being supported by his parents. Contemplating marriage and seeing no possibility of earning a living through literary activity in Berlin, Musil returned with extreme reluctance to Vienna, where his father had obtained for him a position in the library of the Technical Institute. Musil began work in January 1911; he and Martha were married in April, after her divorce became final. What was to have been a brief return home turned into three years of well-paid but exhausting and frustrating employment. The period during which he worked at the library is marked by repeated bouts of illness and by an almost total failure to write; there are almost no notebook entries for the year 1912. Musil's isolation and resentment were exacerbated not only by his work; he also found intellectual life in Vienna stifling. The efflorescence of the arts which Vienna had enjoyed at the turn of the century was on the wane; the important strands of German-language modernism were tied increasingly to Berlin.

Between 1911 and 1921, when his drama *Die Schwärmer* (translated as *The Enthusiasts*, 1983)

Musil as an officer in the Austrian army (Robert Musil Archive, Klagenfurt)

appeared, Musil completed not a single work of imaginative literature. This is not to say that he was not productive: the notebooks again swelled with drafts and materials for an array of later works. In 1913 alone Musil published eleven important essays in the journals *Der lose Vogel* and *Die neue Rundschau*. One of the finest of these, "Über Robert Musils Bücher" (On Robert Musil's Books), offers incisive commentary on his first two books. These essays show Musil moving away from the fascination with decadence and aestheticism that had characterized his early work and, indeed, that of his generation. The relentless introspection of *Die Verwirrungen des Zöglings Törleß* and *Vereinigungen* would be supplanted in years to come by a highly developed sense for the dialectical relationship between the individual and society. In the essay "Moralische Fruchtbarkeit" (Moral Fruitfulness) Musil hints at a new understanding of literature as a tool of moral and not simply psychological analysis. Such essays as "Politisches Bekenntnis eines jungen Mannes" (Political Confession of a Young Man, 1913) and "Europäertum, Krieg, Deutschtum" (European-ness, War, Germanness) point toward Musil's new consciousness of political responsibility. These attempts at political commentary lack the sovereign overview of the European situation, not to mention the ironic, brilliantly satirical voice, that characterizes both his later essays and *Der Mann ohne Eigenschaften,* but they mark Musil's emergence as a writer who would devote enormous time and energy to cultural politics.

Musil visited Berlin whenever possible, and the chance to return for what promised to be an extended stay came in December 1913. Samuel Fischer, the publisher of *Die neue Rundschau,* the leading literary journal of the period, offered Musil a position as editor. An emergent German modernism, with authors such as Mann and Hesse, appeared in its pages alongside the work of established foreign writers such as Hofmannsthal, Oscar Wilde, Maurice Maeterlinck, and Henrik Ibsen. Musil immediately resigned from the Austrian civil service and returned to Berlin. The new position proved short-lived.

A reserve officer since 1911, Musil was called up at the outbreak of World War I in August 1914. He served with distinction, first in command of a company and then as a battalion adjutant, in the southern Tirol. His notebook entries for these years alternate between a sober recounting of the routine of military service and the reworking of individual observations for subsequent use in literary works; the novellas *Grigia* (1923; translated, 1965) and *Die Portugiesin* (1923; translated as "The Lady from Portugal," 1965) are deeply colored by Musil's war experiences. In March 1916 his active service was brought to an end by a stomach ulcer; after six weeks in various hospitals he was reassigned to the headquarters of the southwestern army group in Bozen, Austria.

Musil's new assignment was as editor of the *Soldaten-Zeitung,* the soldiers' newspaper of the southwest front. The "newspaper" had been little more than a newsletter containing a loose and anecdotal collection of reports from the front; under Musil's direction, and at the express wish of the general staff, the publication took shape as a professional and highly sophisticated organ for the dissemination of information and propaganda. Charged primarily with combating irredentism and the spread of nationalist tendencies among the troops of the Austrian Empire, the journal far exceeded this mandate in the prominent position it lent to social and political criticism. Musil's contributions are notable largely for the first appearance of that mode of literature which was to characterize much of his later production: satire. The command to discontinue the paper came in March 1917. Musil was transferred to Adelsberg, near Trieste, and then to Vienna, where he served on the staff of the propaganda journal *Heimat.* He remained an imperial functionary until December 1918, transferring his services to the new Austrian Republic in January 1919. His work in the press section of the Austrian Foreign Office consisted of collecting and indexing newspaper reports relevant to the foreign policy of the new nation. Musil ironically styled himself the "archivist of newspaper cuttings," a vocation which found its way into *Der Mann ohne Eigenschaften.*

The end of the war, the dissolution of the empire, and the creation of the Austrian Republic prompted a series of essays from Musil. "Skizze der Erkenntnis des Dichters" (Sketch of the Poet's Cognition, 1918), "Der Anschluß an Deutschland" (The Union with Germany, 1919), and "Die Nation als Ideal und als Wirklichkeit" (The Nation as Ideal and as Reality, 1921) are political essays only in a limited sense. They deal, to be sure, with the contemporary problems confronting Europe–the peace of Versailles, the establishment of a new identity for Austria, the nature of the state under democracy–but Musil's approach remains that of a humanist primarily concerned with cultural issues. For Musil, the question of European direction remains a radically individual one: what will the new European person be like? Individuals, not collectives and certainly not states, which are for Musil little more than abstract categories invested with brutal power, will determine the shape of the new civilization. Musil described his politics as "conservative anarchy"; he held that the state could only serve as a repressive force, inhibiting the individual's development.

Musil regarded himself as the heir of Emerson and Nietzsche, the advocate of the strong, self-reliant individual; his repeated insistence on the absolute uniqueness of each human, however, points to a Kierkegaardian element in his thinking which is seldom acknowledged. In differentiating the poet from the man of reason Musil points to the ability to recognize the radically individual, the exception to the rule of regularity and law. In "Skizze der Erkenntnis des Dichters" he distinguishes between the "ratioïd" and the "non-ratioïd," that is, the distinction between that which is susceptible to rational understanding due to its regularity and that which eludes rational comprehension because of its endlessly variable and individual character. The poet must above all be sensitive to individual human reactions to the world and to other humans. "Die Aufgabe ist: immer neue Lösungen, Zusammenhänge, Konstellationen, Variable zu entdecken, Prototypen von Geschehensabläufen hinzustellen, lockende Vorbilder, wie man Mensch sein kann, den inneren Menschen *erfinden*" (The task is: always to discover new solutions, contexts, constellations, variables, to suggest prototypes of courses of events, to *invent* the inner man, tempting models of how to be human).

In August 1920 Musil gave up his job in the Foreign Ministry and returned to Berlin, hoping to find an editorial position similar to the one he had occupied so briefly at *Die neue Rundschau* before the war. He met with a total lack of success. Neither Fischer at *Die neue Rundschau* nor any other publisher was in a financial position to enlarge his staff. Musil returned to Vienna in September and assumed a position in the War Ministry, charged with the education and integration of Austrian officers into the ways of a peacetime democratic army. This well-paid job made relatively few demands on his time, making possible a great outpouring of literary production. Musil's position was, however, eliminated for budgetary reasons in December 1922, although his salary was paid until the following summer.

While working at the ministry, Musil also assumed the role of theater critic. The sixty reviews he wrote for the *Prager Presse* between March 1921 and August 1922 and for the Prague magazine *Bohemia* between September and December 1922 constitute one of the most remarkable bodies of theater criticism of the century. The additions to Musil's salary from his literary activity contributed to an unprecedented and never wholly recaptured period of economic security. He was able to buy a large, comfortable apartment at Rasumofskygasse 20 in Vienna's third district.

In the drama *Die Schwärmer*, for which he won the Kleist Prize, and in the novella collection *Drei Frauen* (Three Women, 1924), Musil establishes several of the experimental, prototypical forms of life called for in his essays. He also, for the first time, allows for the interaction of these inventions and a sociopolitical environment.

Like the novellas in *Vereinigungen*, *Die Schwärmer* turns on a banal situation: seduction

*Sketch of Musil by his wife, Martha (*Briefe nach Prag*, edited by Barbara Köpplová and Kurt Krolop, 1971)*

and the breakup of marriage. Anselm, a philosophical seducer, has taken Regine away from her husband, the professor Josef. They have sought refuge in the home of Regine's sister Maria and her husband Thomas. Thomas, the protagonist, is a typical Musil hero, characterized by pure possibility, unpredictability, the refusal to be frozen by concepts or ideals. "Ideale sind toter Idealismus" (Ideals are dead idealism), he says. This same lack of qualities applies to his opponent, Anselm. The two figures are finally differentiated by their language: Thomas emerges as the champion of an intellect intensely, almost morbidly aware of the complexity of human ethical behavior and of the difficulty of finding linguistic forms adequate to express this complexity; Anselm shows himself in his speech to be less fluid than simply unstable, less distanced from the conventions and repression of society than compulsively driven to destroy them. Thomas's language retains a beautifully unfixed quality which stands in stark contrast to the increasingly debased language of the seducer Anselm.

In Josef, Musil caricatures the unthinking bourgeois adherence to moral norms and ideals. Josef is the twentieth-century man of reason who applies tools appropriate to the ratioïd realm to the non-ratioïd sphere of morals. Stringent moral judgments blind him to the complexity and nuance which characterize the relationships in the play. Stader, the detective hired by Josef to unmask Anselm as a fraud and thus to bring Regine back, represents an even more extreme example of the dangers arising from the false application of rationality. A "scientific" detective, Stader believes that the problems of life can be sorted out through the amassing and analysis of factual evidence. The judgmental hubris of Josef and Stader contrasts sharply with Thomas's absolute refusal to judge. Even as Anselm gradually takes Maria away from him, Thomas proves incapable of stopping or condemning him.

Musil's play stands alongside Hofmannsthal's *Der Schwierige* (The Difficult One, 1921) as one of the great German-language comic dramas of the century. Like Hofmannsthal, Musil examines the position of the outsider in a society unwilling to address the changes necessitated by new political, social, and economic conditions, a society content to fall back on the mores and language of the fallen empire. The challenges for theatrical performance of Musil's play are considerable: the almost total absence of action, the extreme subtlety of the language, and the play's resolutely cerebral nature. The first production, in Berlin in 1929, was a bowdlerization, with the play cut in half. Musil, enraged, afterwards stormed through the Berlin streets and could be calmed only as morning approached. The play has since then found its place in the repertory of Germany's and Austria's major theaters.

Although *Drei Frauen* appeared three years later than *Die Schwärmer*, the materials for its three novellas came from Musil's past. "Tonka" makes use of notebook entries from as early as 1903, while sketches for *Grigia* and *Die Portugiesin*—both of which appeared separately in 1923—appear in the notebooks from the war years. The novellas have a common theme: in each, a strong male protagonist discovers in the encounter with the titular female figure what Musil calls "der andere Zustand" (the other condition), the dimension of life which is "beweglich, singulär, irrational" (mobile, singular, irrational). In each case eroticism is the trigger for this turn inward to an epiphanic mystical experience. The three novellas can be seen as Musil's answer to his own challenge, expressed in "Skizze der Erkenntnis des Dichters," to "invent the inner human"; the protagonists represent three radically different experimental instantiations of the "other condition." In search of a firm sense of identity, each of the three emerges instead with a deep sense of the shifting, deeply unsettling character of the self.

The protagonist of *Grigia*, Homo, is an engineer at work in a remote Italian valley whose inhabitants preserve primitive cultural and social practices. Separated from his wife, he satisfies his sexual desires with Grigia, a peasant woman. His encounters with an eroticism both real and imagined open him to a mystical experience: "Er sank zwischen den Bäumen mit den giftgrünen Bärten aufs Knie, breitete die Arme aus, ... und ihm war zu Mut, als hätte man ihm in diesem Augenblick sich selbst aus den Armen genommen. Er fühlte die Hand seiner Geliebten in seiner, ihre Stimme im Ohr, alle Stellen seines Körpers waren wie eben erst berührt, er empfand sich selbst wie eine von einem anderen Körper gebildete Form" (He sank to his knees between the trees with the poison-green beards, spread out his arms, ... and he felt as if someone had at that moment taken him out of his own arms. He felt the hand of his lover in his, her voice in his ear, it was as if every place on his body had just been touched for the first time, he sensed himself as a form shaped by another body). As the subtle negative description of Homo's natural surroundings indicates, though, the preconditions for a productive encounter with the irrational are absent: a parallel is established between the capitalistic exploitation of the valley and its inhabitants on the one hand and Homo's sexual subjugation of Grigia on the other. Homo understands his epiphanic insight as a revelation to him alone, and his messianic pretensions lead him to amorality and to death at the hands of Grigia's husband. In Homo Musil shows that a mere openness to the irrational is insufficient and dangerous.

"Tonka" is a reworking of Musil's relationship with Herma Dietz between 1905 and 1907. The nameless protagonist, a young engineering student, is confronted with apparently insoluble contradiction: the young proletarian woman with whom he lives has contracted a venereal disease and has become pregnant; for either condition he cannot be responsible, yet she insists that she has never betrayed him. The contradiction between the evidence against Tonka, which from a scientific point of view is decisive, and the protagonist's growing conviction of Tonka's deeply rooted simplicity and honesty leads him to call into question the applicability of rational explanations of the world. He discovers, as will Ulrich in *Der Mann ohne Eigenschaften*, that another world exists, "die wir aber nicht bloß im Herzen tragen oder im Kopf, sondern die genau so wirklich draußen steht wie die geltende" (which we don't merely carry in our heart or in our head, but which stands out there exactly as real as the world in force). He is able to transcend, if only temporarily, the rational limits set to knowledge and to perceive something of that "other world" behind appearances. "Wollen, Wissen und Fühlen sind wie ein Knäuel verschlungen; man merkt es erst, wenn man das Fadenende verliert; aber vielleicht kann man anders durch die Welt gehen als am Faden der Wahrheit? In solchen Augenblicken, wo ihn von allen ein Firnis der Kälte trennt, war Tonka mehr als ein Mädchen, da war sie fast eine Sendung" (Volition, knowledge, and feeling are all intertwined like a knot; one notices this only when one has lost the end of the thread; but is it perhaps possible to go through the world other than on the thread of truth? At such moments, when a varnish of coldness separated him from all others, Tonka was more than a girl; then she was almost a revelation). Of all Musil's texts, "Tonka" employs the most radically innovative use of narrative perspective. The point of view is free-floating, attaching itself now to the protagonist, now to a narrator, now to an unidentifiable perspective–though never to Tonka. This feature, together with the jumbled chronology of the novella, evokes in the reader a sense of the epistemological crisis experienced by the protagonist.

The protagonist of *Die Portugiesin* is Lord von Ketten, a medieval robber knight engaged in an endless and draining war with the neighboring bishop. Having won his wife after an assiduous courtship in her native Portugal, von Ketten has spent all but one day and night of each of the succeeding eleven years away from home. The death of the bishop changes this pattern. Von Ketten's sense of the purpose and meaning of his life had been defined by his war with the bishop; the loss of this meaning is symbolized by von Ketten being bitten by a fly and contracting an apparently fatal illness. The pitiful nature of his new existence is brought home to him as a friend of his wife, recently arrived from Portugal, seems gradually to usurp his place. A soothsayer tells von Ketten that he will be cured only if he accomplishes something. One day a small cat, similarly afflicted with a wasting sickness, enters the castle and draws the sympathy of von Ketten, his wife, and the visitor. Unable to watch it suffer further, von Ketten has it killed. In an apparent attempt to avoid the fate of the cat, von Ketten rises from his bed and tries to scale the sheer cliff below the castle–a superhuman task. When he arrives at the top, he finds his strength and will restored to him. He believes that the stranger may be in his wife's room, and intends to kill him. Instead, he finds her sleeping alone and learns that the visitor has departed.

Die Portugiesin mediates between the negative experience of Homo and the largely positive one of the protagonist of "Tonka." The key feature of the central novella is its undecidability. Musil's irony cuts through the lush, exotic quality of the tale, weighing against the unequivocal interpretation of any of its elements, and in particular of the value assigned to von Ketten's encounter with the "other condition." Of all Musil's texts, *Die Portugiesin* conforms most closely to his own demand for fluidity and lack of definition; the novella stubbornly resists assimilation to a unifying interpretation.

Drei Frauen and *Die Schwärmer* appeared to enthusiastic reviews. Musil, who won the Literature Prize of the City of Vienna in 1924, was again a literary celebrity, an important voice not only in Austria but in Weimar Germany as well. Many of his most significant essays appeared in Weimar journals, and his work has affinities with the best Weimar literature, such as Mann's *Der Zauberberg* (1924; translated as *The Magic Mountain*, 1927) and Alfred Döblin's *Berlin Alexanderplatz* (1929; translated as *Alexanderplatz, Berlin*, 1931). Yet Musil's inability to secure a living in Germany and his resulting continued presence in Austria exacerbated his innate tendency to play the role of the passive outside observer who felt that his work was "als ein Fremdes bekämpft, mißverstanden, oder gering geschätzt" (contested, misunderstood, or undervalued as something alien).

In contrast to the war and the period immediately following it, when Musil's engagement with his society and culture were intensive, after 1923 his life became synonymous with the writing of his one great novel. The story of this period is largely that of Musil sitting at his desk in the Rasumofskygasse, wrestling with the enormous amount of material he had assembled for the book. The only significant breaks in this routine were periodic difficulties with Ernst Rowohlt, his Berlin publisher. Rowohlt agreed to pay Musil a monthly stipend against the eventual completion of the great novel, and the late 1920s offered the repeated dance of Musil promising

Musil at his desk in Geneva, March 1941 (photo: Staub)

the first volume, his dissatisfaction with the finished material, his decision to work on, and Rowohlt's threats to suspend his payments. Musil shared with Proust more than the will to complete a definitive work of art: his habit of returning proofs with new text written in every available space recalls Proust's similarly endless marginal scribbling.

The struggle with the novel and his economic circumstances took a terrible toll on Musil. In 1929 he had a nervous breakdown, complicated by nicotine poisoning. His sessions with Hugo Lukács, an Adlerian analyst, apparently had some effect, since the novel began to move forward again. The receipt in autumn 1929 of the Gerhart Hauptmann Prize brought confirmation of his stature, but, owing to the German economic crisis, only a fraction of the monetary award found its way to Musil.

The first volume finally appeared in November 1930 to immediate and unanimous critical acclaim. The widespread recognition that *Der Mann ohne Eigenschaften* was the definitive modern German novel led rapidly to the improvement of Musil's financial and emotional situation. The Robert Musil Society, led by Professor Kurt Glaser, the director of the State Art Library in Berlin, was established in 1931 to provide a stipend to allow Musil to work undisturbed on his novel. Musil and Martha moved to Berlin in November 1931. But residence in Berlin, for all its positive aspects, also led to more direct pressure from Rowohlt; the second volume of the novel was published, with some reservations on the part of the author, in March 1933.

In *Der Mann ohne Eigenschaften* Musil attempted to write the representative novel of his era, an all-encompassing account of the situation of the European intellectual in the new social, political, cultural, scientific, and technological conditions at the end of the war. Although the action of the novel takes place in the years 1912 to 1914 in "Kakanien"–Musil's name for Austria under the monarchy–it is clear that nothing less than the fate of the individual in twentieth-century Europe is the focus. Ulrich, the protagonist, is a representative modern individual whose identity and behavior are in constant flux; he has no defining traits and no permanent core. In contrast to those other great encyclopedic novels of high modernism–Joyce's *Ulysses* (1922), Proust's *A la récherche du temps perdu* (1913-1927; translated as *Remembrance of Things Past*, 1922-1931), and *Der Zauberberg*–Musil's novel conceives this erasure of identity, this lack of definition, as something positive and even difficult to attain. Ulrich comes to the realization that the maintenance of *possibility* outweighs any involvement with, and inevitable fixedness within, the real.

The primary sign of the essential fluidity and lack of definition which characterize Ulrich is the stylistic device of essayism. Ulrich is finally nothing more than a momentary nexus in a larger field made up of the prevalent ideas in Western philosophy, politics, psychology, and literature. Essayism is more than a narrative mode; it is the principle of characterization in the novel. "Ungefähr wie ein Essay in der Folge seiner Abschnitte ein Ding von vielen Seiten nimmt, ohne es ganz zu erfassen,–denn ein ganz erfaßtes Ding verliert mit einem Male seinen Umfang und schmilzt zu einem Begriff ein–glaubte [Ulrich], Welt und eigenes Leben am richtigsten ansehen und behandeln zu können" ([Ulrich] believed it was best to regard and treat the world and one's own life approximately as an essay, which examines, in the sequence of its sections, a thing from many sides, without wholly comprehending it– for a thing wholly comprehended instantly loses its contours and melts into a concept).

Der Mann ohne Eigenschaften remains a fragment. The first volume contains two parts. "Eine Art Einleitung" (A Sort of an Introduction) comprises a brief account of Ulrich's early attempt to become a man of significance by beginning, successively, careers as a soldier, an engineer, and a mathematician. The six-hundred-page second part, "Seinesgleichen Geschieht" (Something Like It Happens), shows that the society is in search of that same identity and definition which had been of such importance to the young Ulrich. This part narrates the foundation and activities of the Parallelaktion (Parallel Action), a committee attempting to organize a celebration of the jubilee of Franz Josef's rule that is conceived as a parallel to the celebration of the German Kaiser's reign. Musil depicts a society which is not so much exhausted as ossified, locked by a rigid structure of beliefs onto a path toward war and defeat. The most prominent figure on this vast stage is Ulrich's opponent, the industrialist Arnheim. Like Anselm in *Die Schwärmer*, Arnheim bears a striking resemblance to the protagonist. Like Ulrich, he is concerned with the balance of "Ratio und Seele" (rationality and soul) in human affairs. Unlike Ulrich, though, Arnheim claims to have found that mystical balance; based loosely upon the industrialist and statesman Walther Rathenau, Arnheim becomes the prophet of a new European order. Ulrich's call for the establishment of a secretariat for "Genauigkeit und Seele" (exactitude and soul) is intended as a rebuttal to Arnheim, as an assertion that these matters admit of no definitive resolution.

Ulrich's infrequent attempts to imbue the Parallelaktion with his own lack of principles are not the only suggested alternatives to the present course of society; Moosbrugger, an apparently insane sex murderer, figures as the window onto another possible form of reality: he exists at "the edge of possibility." But all attempts to open the committee to new courses of action meet with defeat. Having received no response to his call for the creation of the secretariat, Ulrich withdraws from the movement into a liaison with his own sister, Agathe. The novel's second volume, which recounts this relationship, is titled "Ins tausendjährige Reich" (Into the Thousand Year Empire).

Ulrich and Agathe voyage together toward a state–the "other condition"–in which exteriority and interiority might be bridged. The other condition is more than mystical ecstasy; it is a form of self-love open to infinite possibility and variation. Ulrich and Agathe are spiritual Siamese twins in whom the separation between individual identities becomes increasingly blurred. Like Moosbrugger, they journey beyond the border of that which is held to be morally permissible. But their actions are less important than their linguistic attempts to get at the essence of their actions. It is not clear whether the completed novel would have included a portrayal of the consummation of their union.

The meaning of the novel turns on the manner in which the reader constructs the connection between the Parallelaktion and Ulrich and Agathe's love. Both are marked by an intense, always frustrated longing for wholeness and unity. Both are possible modes through which to experience the world, to bridge the gap between feeling and perception. The novel exemplifies Lukács's characterization of the path of the European novel from the nineteenth-century "big world" of society and its complicated net of relationships toward the "small world" of the individ-

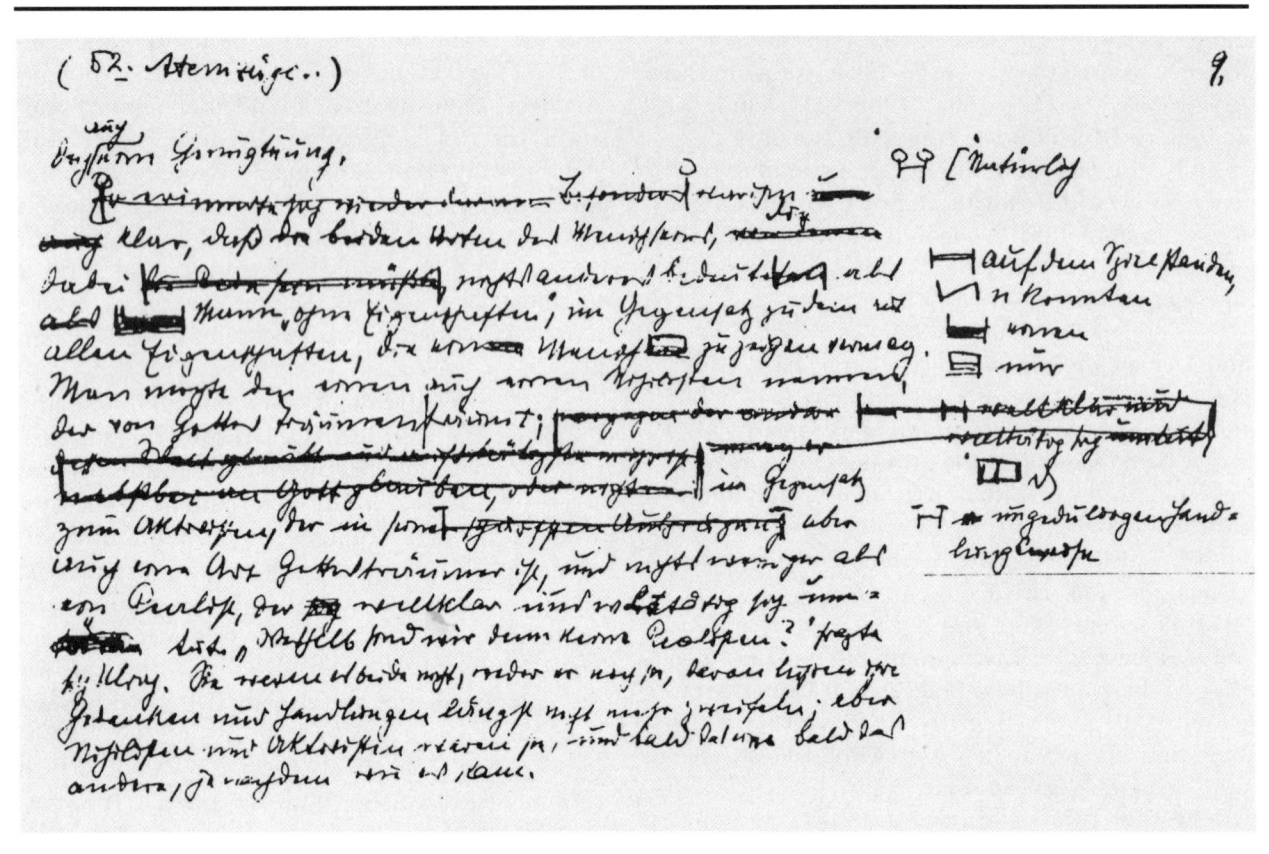

Page from the manuscript for Musil's unfinished novel Der Mann ohne Eigenschaften *(copyright © by Vereinigung Robert-Musil-Archiv, Klagenfurt, 1970)*

ual and his subjectivity, a movement Lukács viewed negatively.

Musil labored in his final years to complete the novel. His papers contain hundreds of pages of fragments and completed chapters which would have gone into the completion of the second volume and into the conclusion, "Eine Art Ende" (A Sort of an Ending). But the resistance to closure evident at every level of the novel–in Ulrich's incompleteness, in the destabilizing effect of the narrator's ironic voice, and in the characteristic eschewal of plot in favor of reflection and analysis–strongly suggest that even a completed *Der Mann ohne Eigenschaften* would have remained radically open. Musil once said that he wanted the novel to end in the middle of a sentence, with a comma.

Hitler's ascent to power in Germany was followed in early summer 1933 by Musil's return to Vienna and to renewed financial worries. The Musil Society ceased to exist, its members either in exile or unable to continue their financial contributions. Voices–among them that of Mann–were immediately raised in support of Musil, and Bruno Fürst was able to form a new Musil Society in Vienna in spring 1934.

In 1935 Musil traveled to Paris to address the International Writers' Congress for the Defense of Culture. His speech met a hostile reception from the largely leftist audience. Somewhat ingenuously, Musil had taken the title of the congress literally and limited himself to the problem of the defense of culture in an age dominated by ideological conflict. He refused to restrict his critique of the dangers of ideology to fascism, and his talk was attacked as an implicit criticism of socialist and communist political activity. Musil's sympathy for socialism could not prevent him from delivering an essentially apolitical speech at a political congress. For him, culture remained the sole repository of hope in the modern world, and any threat to the furtherance of culture was to be scorned. His stance was underlined in 1938 when he turned down an offer by the French Communist Party of a villa on the Riviera.

Soon after his return to Vienna Musil had again been beset with problems with his health

Musil (Landesbildstelle Berlin)

and his psychological state. Dr. Lukács was again able to help him overcome his inhibitions regarding his work, but in 1936 Musil suffered a stroke. Although he recovered to a large extent, he never again felt that his health could support the work he needed to accomplish.

In 1936 appeared Musil's last significant publication, *Nachlaß zu Lebzeiten* (translated as *Posthumous Papers of a Living Author*, 1987), a collection of short pieces most of which had appeared in newspapers and journals. Best known for its inclusion of the novella "Die Amsel" (The Blackbird), *Nachlaß zu Lebzeiten* has been consistently undervalued by Musil's critics and readers. His mastery of the very short prose piece in such texts as "Das Fliegenpapier" (Flypaper) and "Triedere" places him alongside Franz Kafka as the authors who have best opened the short, almost fragmentary sketch to the possibilities of modernity.

In 1937 Musil delivered two of his best-known speeches, "Der Dichter in dieser Zeit" (The Poet in These Times) and *Über die Dummheit* (On Stupidity, 1937), further attempts to define the character of the age and to awaken Europe to the threat posed to its culture. *Über die Dummheit* in particular aroused considerable interest as a definitive characterization of the age; Musil repeated it several times in Vienna, and the Bermann-Fischer Verlag, which had purchased the rights to Musil's works from Rowohlt, published it that same year.

The Anschluß of Austria into the Third Reich occurred in March 1938. That summer, following a visit from a representative of the Propaganda Ministry who requested his services, Musil and Martha quietly left Vienna for Italy, purportedly to restore his health. In September they established themselves in a small hotel in Zurich. Musil continued to labor over the novel, maintaining correspondence with the circle of readers and friends without whose intellectual sustenance he was unable to work, and, as always, seeking financial support. Of Musil's Zurich acquaintances, Pastor Robert LeJeune stands out. LeJeune's aesthetic proclivities and critical insight replaced some of the intellectual and cultural stimulation the Musils had left behind.

Yet the letters and notebooks of the period record Musil's increasing feeling of isolation. Like other German literary figures living in exile, Musil found himself deprived of publishers and readers; his situation was in many ways worse, though, than that of a Mann or a Bertolt Brecht. Musil's readership had in the best of times been limited to a narrow segment of the intelligentsia. Musil moved again after only ten months in Zurich, this time to Geneva, definitively severing his ties to German-language culture. In Geneva he moved four times in two years in search of ideal working conditions for the completion of his novel. In Zurich there had at least been some connection to the community; in Geneva Musil was alone and unknown. He emerged from his retreat only once, for a reading from his works organized by LeJeune in Winterthur. One of the greatest living German-language authors of his age found fifteen listeners awaiting him. One last hope, for immigration to America, was shattered in 1940: Albert Einstein and Mann attempted to persuade the Rockefeller Foundation to grant Musil a stipend, but since he lacked scholarly credentials, nothing could be done.

Martha Musil found her husband on the floor of the bathroom on 15 April 1942, the victim of a massive stroke. Eight friends attended the funeral, after which Musil was cremated. Martha retained his ashes until her departure for America, when she scattered them in the woods near Geneva.

Musil had worked feverishly on his novel to the very end but left behind no indication of how the drafts and completed chapters were to be ordered. Martha published a tentative reconstruction of the continuation of the story of Ulrich and Agathe in 1943. In 1952 Rowohlt published the novel as the first volume of Musil's collected works, edited by Adolf Frisé. This edition, which contains a new ordering of the posthumous material, met with violent criticism from Musil scholars. A third edition, also edited by Frisé, appeared in 1978; it contains a much larger but by no means complete selection from the posthumous papers and still another ordering of the more polished material. A historical-critical edition of Musil's novel remains a desideratum. The uncertain textual status of Musil's masterpiece has not, however, detracted from its acknowledged position as a major monument of twentieth-century European culture; and the very openness of his novel in its final form will continue to remind Musil's readers that he was the author of the possible.

Letters:

Briefe nach Prag, edited by Barbara Köpplová and Kurt Krolop (Reinbek: Rowohlt, 1971);

Briefe, edited by Adolf Frisé and Murray G. Hall, 2 volumes (Reinbek: Rowohlt, 1981).

Bibliographies:

Ulrich Karthaus, "Musil-Forschung und Musil-Deutung: Ein Literaturbericht," *Deutsche Vierteljahrsschrift für Literaturwissenschaft und Geistesgeschichte,* 39 (1965): 441-483;

Jürgen C. Thöming, *Robert-Musil-Bibliographie* (Bad Homburg: Verlag Dr. Max Gehlen, 1968);

Robert L. Roseberry, *Robert Musil: Ein Bericht* (Frankfurt am Main: Fischer Athenäum Taschenbücher, 1974);

Wolfgang Freese, "Zur neueren Musil-Forschung. Ausgaben und Gesamtdarstellungen," *Text und Kritik,* 21/22 (1983): 86-148.

Biography:

David S. Luft, *Robert Musil and the Crisis of European Culture 1880-1942* (Berkeley: University of California Press, 1980).

References:

Helmut Arntzen, *Musil Kommentar sämtlicher zu Lebzeiten erschienener Schriften außer dem Roman "Der Mann ohne Eigenschaften"* (Munich: Winkler, 1980);

Arntzen, *Musil Kommentar zum Roman "Der Mann ohne Eigenschaften"* (Munich: Winkler, 1982);

Dagmar Barnouw, "Skepticism as Literary Mode: David Hume and Robert Musil," *MLN,* 93 (1978): 852-870;

Gerhart Baumann, *Robert Musil: Zur Erkenntnis der Dichtung* (Berne: Franke, 1965);

Wilfried Berghahn, *Robert Musil in Selbstzeugnissen und Bilddokumenten* (Hamburg: Rowohlt, 1963);

Dorrit Cohn, "Psyche and Space in Musil's 'Die Vollendung der Liebe,'" *Germanic Review*, 49 (1974): 154-168;

Karl Corino, "Ödipus oder Orest? Robert Musil und die Psychoanalyse," *Musil-Studien*, 4 (1973): 123-235;

Karl Dinklage, ed., *Robert Musil: Leben, Werk, Wirkung* (Hamburg: Rowohlt, 1960);

Peter Henninger, *Der Buchstabe und der Geist: Unbewußte Determinierung im Schreiben Robert Musils* (Frankfurt am Main: Lang, 1980);

Henninger, "On Literature and Condensation: Robert Musil's Early Novellas," *Glyph*, 5 (1979): 114-132;

Hannah Hickman, *Robert Musil and the Culture of Vienna* (La Salle, Ill.: Open Court, 1984);

Michael Jennings, "Mystical Selfhood, Self-Delusion, Self-Dissolution: Ethical and Narrative Experimentation in Musil's 'Grigia,'" *MAL*, 17, no. 1 (1984): 59-78;

Ernst Kaiser and Eithne Wilkins, *Robert Musil: Eine Einführung in das Werk* (Stuttgart: Kohlhammer, 1962);

Jörg Kühne, *Das Gleichnis: Studien zur inneren Form von Robert Musils Roman "Der Mann ohne Eigenschaften"* (Tübingen: Niemayer, 1968);

Frederick G. Peters, *Robert Musil: Master of the Hovering Life* (New York: Columbia University Press, 1978);

Burton Pike, *Robert Musil: An Introduction to his Work* (Ithaca: Cornell University Press, 1961);

Annie Reniers-Servranckx, *Robert Musil: Konstanz und Entwicklung von Themen, Motiven und Strukturen in den Dichtungen* (Bonn: Bouvier, 1972);

Marie-Louise Roth, *Robert Musil: Ethik und Ästhetik. Zum theoretischen Werk des Dichters* (Munich: List, 1972);

Albrecht Schöne, "Der Gebrauch des Konjunktivs bei Robert Musil," *Euphorion*, 55 (1961): 196-220;

Walter Sokel, "Kleist's Marquise of O., Kierkegaard's Abraham, and Musil's Tonka: Three stages of the Absurd as the Touchstones of Faith," in *Festschrift für Bernhard Blume: Aufsätze zur deutschen und europäischen Literatur*, edited by Egon Schwarz, Hunter G. Hannum, and Edgar Lohner (Göttingen: Vandenhoeck & Ruprecht, 1967), pp. 323-332;

Sokel, "The Problem of Dualism in Hesse's *Demian* and Musil's *Törless*," *MAL*, 9, no. 3/4 (1976): 35-42.

Papers:

The Robert Musil Archive is in Klagenfurt, Austria.

Franz Nabl
(16 July 1883-19 January 1974)

Herbert Herzmann
University College, Dublin

BOOKS: *Noch einmal . . . ! Ein letzter Akt* (Vienna: Das literarische Deutsch-Österreich, 1905);

Weihe, in drei Handlungen (Vienna: Konegen, 1905);

Hans Jäckels erstes Liebesjahr (Berlin: Fleischel, 1908);

Narrentanz: Novellen (Berlin: Fleischel, 1911);

Ödhof: Bilder aus den Kreisen der Familie Arlet, 2 volumes (Berlin: Fleischel, 1911);

Das Grab des Lebendigen: Studie aus dem kleinbürgerlichen Leben (Berlin: Fleischel, 1917); republished as *Die Ortliebschen Frauen: Roman* (Bremen: Schünemann, 1936);

Der Tag der Erkenntnis: Zwei niederösterreichische Erzählungen (Berlin: Fleischel, 1919);

Die Galgenfrist: Eine erfundene und etwas aus der Form geratene Geschichte (Berlin: Fleischel, 1921);

Die Augen und andere Novellen (Vienna: Österreichischer Schulbücherverlag, 1923);

Trieschübel: Eine tragische Begebenheit in drei Aufzügen (Berlin: Volksbühnen Verlags-und Vertriebsgesellschaft, 1925);

Schichtwechsel: Eine Komödie mit Vor- und Nachspiel (Berlin: Österheld, 1928);

Der Schwur des Martin Krist: Erzählung (Hillger: Kürschner, 1931);

Kindernovelle (Tübingen: Wunderlich, 1932; revised edition, Bremen: Schünemann, 1936);

Das Meteor: Erzählungen (Bremen: Schünemann, 1935);

Ein Mann von gestern: Roman (Vienna: Fromme, 1935);

Griff ins Dunkel: Erzählung (Leipzig: List, 1936);

Der Fund: Eine Erzählung (Bremen: Schünemann, 1937);

Die Weihnachten des Dominik Brackel; Pilatus im Credo: Erzählungen (Vienna & Leipzig: Luser, 1938);

Steirische Lebenswanderung (Graz, Vienna & Leipzig: Leykam, 1938);

Spätlese: Gedichte. Gedruckt für meine Freunde (Graz: NS-Gauverlag, 1943);

Franz Nabl (Bildarchiv der Österreichischen Nationalbibliothek)

Kleine Freilichtbühne (Bremen: Schünemann, 1943);

Schmiedeeisen: 47 Bilder, Text (Königstein im Taunus: Der Eiserne Hammer, 1944);

Mein Onkel Barnabas (Graz: Leykam, 1946);

Das ist Graz: Die Landeshauptstadt der Steiermark/ This Is Graz: The Capital of Styria, translation by Walter Puchwein (Graz: Steirische Verlagsanstalt, 1946);

Johannes Krantz: Erzählungen in einem Rahmen (Graz, Salzburg & Vienna: Pustet, 1948; revised edition, Stuttgart: Deutsche Verlagsanstalt, 1958);

Das Rasenstück (Graz: Leykam, 1953);

Österreich (Königstein im Taunus: Langewiesche, 1957);

Der erloschene Stern: Eine Kindheit und Jugend um die Jahrhundertwende (Salzburg: Müller, 1962);

Die zweite Heimat (Graz: Leykam, 1963);

Ausgewählte Werke, 4 volumes (Vienna: Kremayr & Scheriau, 1966);

Spiel mit Blättern: Autobiographische Skizzen (Graz, Vienna & Cologne: Styria, 1973);

Vaterhaus: Roman (Graz, Vienna & Cologne: Styria, 1974);

Meine Wohnstätten (Graz: Leykam, 1975);

Charakter; Der Schwur des Martin Krist; Dokument: Frühe Erzählungen, edited by Peter Handke (Salzburg: Residenz, 1975);

Meistererzählungen (Graz, Vienna & Cologne: Styria, 1978).

OTHER: *Marie von Ebner-Eschenbach: Auswahl aus ihren Werken*, afterword by Nabl (Königstein im Taunus: Langewiesche, 1953).

PERIODICAL PUBLICATIONS: "Mensch und Dichter," *Der Neue Pflug: Monatsschrift der Wiener Urania*, 2, no. 11 (1927);

"Soll Dichten Beruf sein?," *Die Literatur*, 31, no. 3 (1928);

"Gedanken über Ludwig Thoma," *Alpenländische Monatshefte*, 7, no. 3 (1929);

"Gedächtnisworte für Arthur Schnitzler," *Die Literatur*, 34, no. 3 (1931);

"Gerhart Hauptmann und sein Werk: Zum 80. Geburtstag des Dichters," *Tagespost* (Graz), 15 February 1942;

"Theodor Fontane zu seinem 125. Geburtstage," *Tagespost* (Graz), 30 December 1944;

"Der verkehrte Zug," *Austria*, 2, nos. 1-2 (1947);

"Dichtung und Wahrheit," *Austria*, 3, no. 2 (1948);

"Wilhelm Raabe: Zum 40. Todestag," *Steirerblatt* (Graz), 12 September 1950;

"Deutsches Drama und deutsche Erzählung 1900-1930," *Studium Generale*, 24, no. 10/11 (1971): 1271-1333;

"Leben und Werdegang," *Studium Generale*, 24, no. 10/11 (1971): 1373-1376.

Franz Nabl wrote some of his major works at a time when Arthur Schnitzler, Hugo von Hofmannsthal, and Hermann Bahr dominated the Austrian literary scene. In contrast with the impressionism of these contemporaries, he is rooted in the tradition of realism and naturalism. Like Ferdinand von Saar, Nabl sympathized with ways of life that were fast disappearing, and like Adalbert Stifter's characters, his heroes attempt to create an "intact" sphere in order to control the threatening chaotic forces without and within the self. These "idylls," however, show severe cracks and often turn into nightmares. There is an ambiguity in Nabl's work which accounts for part of its fascination: the conflicting forces that constitute the world of his characters–traditional values versus new ways of life, strong father versus weak son, closed family versus the quest of the individual for self-fulfillment–are shown in both their attractive and destructive aspects. The fears and obsessions reflected in Nabl's writings are not purely private ones; on the contrary, they mirror the collective psychological situation of the central European bourgeoisie at a time when the old monarchical order was collapsing and new challenges had to be met.

Nabl's origins lie in Bohemia. His father, Franz, worked as a Forst- und Domänenrat (estate manager) for the Princes Thurn und Taxis in Lautschin (now Loučeň, Czechoslovakia), where Nabl was born in 1883. Nabl's mother was Antonia Untersteiner Nabl. Having accumulated enough money to retire, Franz Nabl Senior moved his family to Vienna in 1886. A year later he bought an estate, Gstettenhof, in Lower Austria near the border with Styria; the young Nabl spent most of his summers there and felt much more at home than he did in the city. The striving of a strong-willed individual for economic independence and self-fulfillment, the effect this struggle has on his dependents, and the erosion of the rural idyll are prominent in Nabl's early novels *Ödhof* (1911) and *Vaterhaus* (Father-House; written in 1914-1915, published in 1974).

In 1905 Nabl married eighteen-year-old Hermengild Lampa. Instead of finishing his doctorate in law at the University of Vienna, he established himself as a free-lance writer in Enzensfeld in Lower Austria. In 1913 he moved to Baden, near Vienna. The Lower Austrian landscape west and south of Vienna provides the setting for many of his novels and novellas. Because of health problems he was exempted from military service during World War I. Like Erich von Groiß in his novel *Ein Mann von gestern* (A Man from Yesterday, 1935) Nabl appears to have felt guilty about this exemption. After the war the money he had inherited from his father dwindled quickly. From 1924 to 1927 Nabl earned a living as feuilleton editor for the *Grazer Tagblatt*, a

Nabl in 1965 (photo: Otto Breicha, Vienna; Bildarchiv der Österreichischen Nationalbibliothek, 1965)

daily newspaper in Graz. The financial success of his play *Trieschübel* (1925) enabled him to give up this position and return to Baden as a free-lance writer. In 1934 Nabl and his wife moved back to Graz.

Originally, Nabl was ambivalent about the "Geborgenheit" (security) offered by autocracy. Experiencing the growing pains of the First Austrian Republic, however, made him more unequivocally benevolent in his treatment of the old order. Like Stefan Zweig and Joseph Roth, he shows great sympathy toward people who do not fit into the modern world in *Trieschübel* and *Ein Mann von gestern*. The novella *Der Fund* (The Found Object, 1937) reveals the author's most reactionary side: the fatal shooting of an evil, opportunistic social democratic newspaper editor by an honorable former Austro-Hungarian officer is clearly condoned by the narrator. The death of Nabl's wife in 1936 probably contributed to his fictional withdrawal from contemporary reality into the relative security of the preindustrial Austrian provinces. His semi-autobiographical apotheosis of the province of Styria, written in memory of his wife, bears witness to this mood. The centerpiece of *Steirische Lebenswanderung* (Styrian Wanderings through Life, 1938) is the chapter "Das Rasenstück" (The Grass Plot), where the writer Johannes Krantz, Nabl's alter ego, explains in Stifter-like fashion how one can find the whole world in little things, even in a section of lawn (Rasenstück). This tendency to turn away from the big world into the confinement of the private sphere was shared by many in the late 1930s, and the book became Nabl's most popular work.

It appears that Nabl had himself fallen victim to certain fascinations whose dangers he had foreseen in his earlier novels and novellas; therefore, it is not altogether surprising that he allowed himself to be used by the National Socialist regime. In 1933 he was among those who left the Austrian P.E.N. Club in protest against a resolution passed in Ragusa condemning the persecution of dissident writers and the burning of books in Germany. The new masters fully approved of *Der Fund*, which was made into a film in 1942 under the title *Die Nacht nach der Oper* (The Night after the Opera Performance). On the other hand, he never became a member of the Nazi party, nor was he among the Austrian writers who in 1939 enthusiastically welcomed the Anschluß (annexation of Austria by Germany) in the notorious *Bekenntnisbuch österreichischer Schriftsteller* (Confession-Book of Austrian Writers).

In 1940 Nabl married Ilse Melzer. He received an honorary doctorate from the University of Graz in 1943, the Prize for Literature of the City of Vienna in 1952, the Great State Prize for Literature in 1957, and the Honorary-Ring from the Province of Styria in 1958. He was made an honorary member of the Austrian P.E.N. Club in 1959, and in 1960 he became a corresponding member of the German Academy for Language and Literature. In 1969 he was given the Austrian Medal of Honor for Science and Art. He died in 1974.

In his first novel, *Hans Jäckels erstes Liebesjahr* (Hans Jäckel's First Year of Love, 1908), Nabl treats the endangering of adolescent development by sexual passions and the predicament of human beings equipped with an insufficiently strong sense of "Lebensberechtigung" (entitlement to live). In *Ödhof*, published three years later, the main theme may be described either as the impact a strong-willed, autocratic individual has on his environment or as the dialectics of self-

Nabl in later years (copyright © by Gery Wolf)

realization and self-destruction. The forty-five-year-old Johannes Arlet realizes his dream of a completely independent life when he acquires a run-down estate, Ödhof (the name means Bleak Farm), from a noble family. His self-realization, however, goes hand in hand with the destruction of the weaker persons surrounding him and with his growing isolation as his few equals–his son's tutor, Dr. Mesner, and his common-law wife, Elisabeth Fuchsthaler–leave him. His main victim is his son Heinz, who is driven to suicide when he realizes that he has no chance of leading his own life. Johannes does not survive his own splendid isolation, either: a silly bet in a country tavern–he cuts off a finger to prove that one can do anything one wants to do–leads to his early death. Nationalist Socialist critics such as Erwin Ackerknecht admired the character's superman qualities, overlooking the fact that his death is the direct result of his exaggerated vitalism.

The little community of Ödhof is a closed society, with the positive and negative features of such a society: security on the one hand, repression on the other. Johannes is viewed from many different perspectives, a technique that reveals various, often conflicting sides of his character: brutality and self-centeredness and yet at the same time a curious benevolence and spontaneity. On another level the novel deals with the conflict between old and new forms of life. The bourgeois Arlet usurps the position as owner of Ödhof, once held by the aristocracy; the fabric of the village community disintegrates under the impact of modern technology and tourism.

Like Heinz Arlet, Paul Deinegger in *Vaterhaus* is a sensitive boy both protected and dominated by a strong father. When his parents' marriage breaks up and their country estate is put up for sale, Paul no longer knows where he belongs. His attempt to find another kind of home through an erotic relationship fails, thus saving him from falling into the trap of a premature marriage. The novel ends with Paul going to Vienna to study law. Painful as the expulsion from the paradise of childhood may be, it offers the protagonist the chance to become an emancipated individual. *Vaterhaus* was planned as the first of a series of novels which were to be grouped together under the title "Menschwerdung" (Becoming a Human Being); World War I and the resulting destruction of the world in which the novel was set led Nabl to abandon this project.

Das Grab des Lebendigen (The Grave of the Living, 1917) is justly considered Nabl's masterpiece. It marks his break from excessive reliance on autobiographical material: *Das Grab des Lebendigen* is based on a newspaper report. Nor is the novel set in the comfortable, upper-middle-class milieu with which he was familiar, as the subtitle *Studie aus dem kleinbürgerlichen Leben* (Study of Petit-Bourgeois Life) reveals. Here Nabl reaches the peak of his narrative powers. Whereas *Ödhof* suffers from overladen imagery and melodramatic effects, *Das Grab des Lebendigen* is written in a sober, matter-of-fact tone that allows the incidents to speak for themselves.

Again there is a microcosmic closed society: a family consisting of father, mother, and three children. The father, Anton Ortlieb, is a petty official; like Johannes Arlet, he is endowed with the "Gefühl einer vollkommenen Lebensberechtigung" (sense of a complete entitlement to live) and succeeds in securing a maximum of independence from the outside world. After the death of this autocrat the oldest daughter, Josefine, runs the family in a dictatorial manner, keeping it together, "protecting" it from all change, subjecting everybody to the "common good." There is little opposition from the mother, as her will had been broken long ago by her husband. The other daughter, Anna, is no match for Josefine; their brother Walter is still too young to count and also suffers from a slight physical deformity. Although Josefine is convinced that the family needs her, the truth is that she needs the family: unattractive and not well educated, she is not likely to marry or to be able to support herself.

The biggest threat to this little world is constituted by Anna's and Walter's shy attempts to meet members of the opposite sex. Josefine interferes by means of psychological manipulation, intrigue, imposing increased isolation from outside influences by moving the family from their city apartment to a house in the country, and ultimately violence: with Anna's help she locks Walter in the cellar to prevent him from meeting a girl. Walter's and Anna's nightmare ends only when the police, informed by suspicious neighbors, storm the house. Josefine hangs herself, and the senile mother dies of a heart attack.

Although Walter is physically liberated thanks to an invasion by outside forces, his inner liberation has already occurred. At the lowest point in his life, when he was imprisoned in the cellar, he felt for the first time free of guilt for the emotions and desires the opposite sex aroused in him. It was at this point that he lost his fear of freedom and that the basis for his "Menschwerdung" was laid.

Nabl has not only dramatically described the consequences of an obsession with "security," "closeness," and the "common good"; he has also exposed the methods which at once create and exploit this obsession. Josefine makes Walter and Anna feel guilty for any wish they may have to lead lives of their own. Significantly, these guilt feelings are intricately tied up with sexual desires. Nabl clearly recognized the link between social and sexual repression which was to form the basis of social theories developed much later–for example, by Wilhelm Reich in *Massenpsychologie des Faschismus* (1933; translated as *The Mass Psychology of Fascism*, 1946). The "idyll" of the Ortliebs, sitting at their round table making music and living only for each other, turns into horror. The harmony between individual and collective can, in the end, be maintained only by reducing the individual to an animal level (locking Walter in the cellar). The novel is prophetic, foreshadowing the terror which was soon to arise from totalitarian political philosophies. The Nazis seem to have understood the latent political message of the novel and insisted that the title be changed. The second edition was brought out in 1936 as *Die Ortliebschen Frauen* (The Ortlieb Women), making the events appear to be more an isolated than an exemplary case.

In 1919 Nabl had two novellas published in one volume. The title story, "Der Tag der Erkenntnis" (The Day of Recognition) had been written in 1913, "Die Augen" (The Eyes) in 1912.

The latter, the story of a lower-class girl who falls in love with a gentleman to whom she is nothing more than a pleasant diversion, is reminiscent of Schnitzler's play *Liebelei* (1896; translated as *Light-O'-Love*, 1912). Yet this novella demonstrates the difference between the two writers: whereas Schnitzler, in his stories and novellas, deliberately blurs the distinction between the narrator's perspective and those of the characters, Nabl remains in the tradition of the realists, using an "objective" narrator. National Socialist critics played the "German" Nabl off against the "Viennese" (that is, Jewish) literary scene of which Schnitzler was a prominent member. The fact is, however, that Nabl greatly admired Schnitzler, whom he had met and with whom he corresponded between 1907 and 1911.

"Der Tag der Erkenntnis" tells of a general practitioner, Dr. Andreas Schiermeyer, who leads a seemingly idyllic life in a small Lower Austrian village. Yet the doctor suffers secretly because his early marriage prevented him from pursuing a glamorous university career. His suppressed discontent surfaces when his friend, a teacher, asks him to persuade the teacher's son to refrain from marrying prematurely and spoiling his promising career as a composer. The son appears to take the doctor's advice, which consists of Schiermeyer's violent outburst against himself; but he is found drowned a few days later. The doctor and the teacher are convinced that he has committed suicide. This catastrophe makes Schiermeyer reconcile himself to his fate: the young man has, so to speak, died in his place. Like Stifter's characters, Dr. Schiermeyer ultimately succeeds in keeping his confined but harmonious world intact. But the price of this kind of happiness becomes shockingly clear. In the discussion between the doctor and the teacher's son it becomes equally clear that greatness and self-fulfillment can often be achieved only at the expense of happiness.

Dr. Schiermeyer turns up as a marginal figure in Nabl's novel *Die Galgenfrist* (The Reprieve, 1921). The theme is a familiar one to Nabl's readers: a well-to-do and well-protected person has to break out of his secure prison in order to achieve true humanity. Felix bears his name, which means "happy," with good reason: inherited money frees him from the necessity of earning a living; he has a beautiful wife of equally sheltered background and no children. Yet it is exactly this freedom from toil and from responsibilities, on the one hand, and the lack of any particular talent, on the other, which make him think of his life as meaning less.

Felix develops a seemingly fatal illness and is treated by Dr. Martiner, assisted by Schiermeyer. Martiner, recognizing the illness to be psychosomatic, tells Felix that he has only a year to live. The fear of death triggers a frantic pursuit of sensuous pleasures that almost destroys Felix's marriage, but in the end he learns to appreciate the value of his life. Dr. Martiner's method is a somewhat drastic precursor of Viktor Frankl's logotherapy, which attempts to cure neurosis and depression by helping the patient discover a meaning in life.

Die Galgenfrist (which was regarded as "unerwünscht" [undesirable] by the Nazis) is divided into five acts, like a play. It has a frame in which the narrator poses as a puppeteer who creates the figures; they then act out their problems independently of him. The experimental character of the novel is indicated by the subtitle: *Eine erfundene und etwas aus der Form geratene Geschichte* (An Invented Story Which Has Got Somewhat Out of Shape). Given this framework, the reader is prepared to accept the doctor's drastic method as credible, although it would hardly be applied in real life.

Like Felix, Baron Trieschübel in the play *Trieschübel* is free from the necessity to fight for survival. He has given up his political office as he feels he does not fit into the new republican era in Austria and has withdrawn to his estate. His crisis comes about when Josefine, a woman of the lower classes with whom he had had an affair some two decades ago, turns up and claims that he is the father of her grown daughter, Elisabeth. Regardless of the consequences to his relationship with a woman of his own class, Trieschübel readily accepts Elisabeth as his daughter because he wants to have a child. Like Felix in *Die Galgenfrist*, Trieschübel desires to be determined rather than to accept the challenge of freedom. But when Josefine, under pressure, retracts her claim, the baron is forced to act. His feelings for the girl change quickly from fatherly to erotic ones, but he feels that it would be unethical for him to abuse his advantage and escapes into suicide. A product of a bygone age, Trieschübel is unable to cope when the traditional norms he has relied on provide him no acceptable solutions. Yet his death brings about a kind of reconciliation between past and present: Elisabeth will inherit Trieschübel's estate.

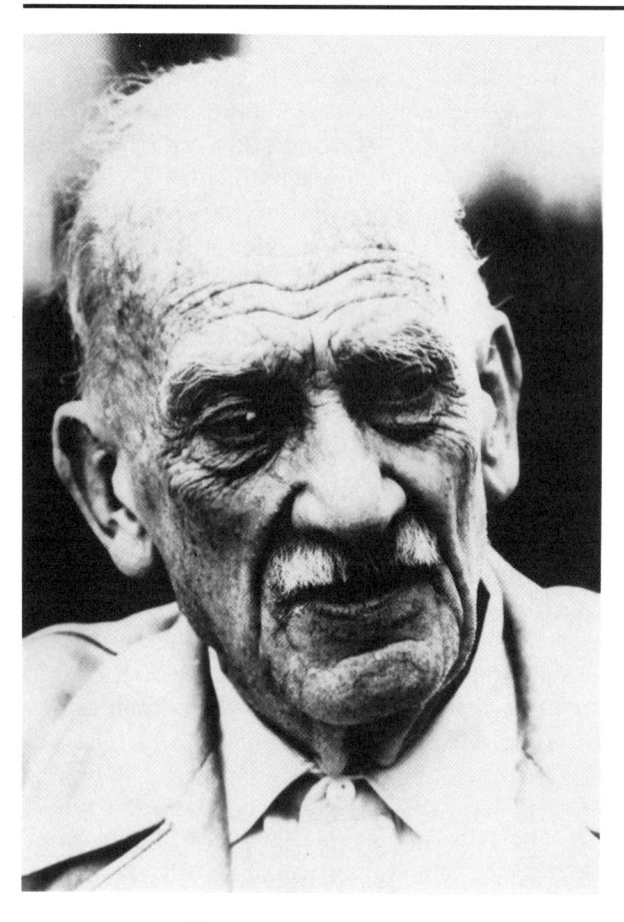

Nabl (copyright © by Gery Wolf)

The conflict between past and modern times is also treated in *Ein Mann von gestern*. In this, his last novel, Nabl skillfully and humorously weaves together many of the themes familiar to his readers: unearned and undeserved comfort and security, personal autonomy threatening to turn into isolation, the dubious attractions of childhood and of past times. The hero, Erich von Groiß, achieves true humanity through a crisis. Like Felix in *Die Galgenfrist*, he is at times painfully aware of the uselessness of his comfortable life. Yet he has succeeded in suppressing guilt feelings about his undeserved luck and has reached the conclusion that there are people who are made for something more than the struggle for survival.

His trial comes when Frau Perkeley, the woman he loves, becomes a widow. Instead of accepting the responsibility of marriage, Groiß decides to revisit the places where he spent his childhood and adolescence. For the forty-eight-year-old Groiß, who is deeply rooted in the time before World War I, this is an attempt to find his own personality. His involvement with Konstanze, a girl in her twenties and the daughter of the couple who had bought his father's country estate, seems to offer him a chance to return to the paradise of the past. It is clear to the reader that Groiß's feelings for Konstanze have more to do with sexual desire than love. He, however, convinces himself that the true motivation behind his proposal to marry her is his wish to offer her a better life. He is somewhat taken aback by the ease with which Konstanze, a child of a new age and not a virgin, is prepared to join him for a holiday in the mountains, but he has no qualms about taking her from her fiancé, Wögerer, a provincial journalist too poor to marry her. Only when he learns that Wögerer is his half-brother, an illegitimate son of his father, is he forced to realize that Wögerer is what, with a little less luck, he himself might have become. He now realizes how undeserved his comfortable life really is. Furthermore, the discovery that his father had an extramarital affair destroys his illusions about the past. He dissolves his engagement with Konstanze and helps Wögerer get a better position. He is now ready to marry Frau Perkeley, a woman close to his own age and, like himself, rooted in the time before the Great War.

After *Ein Mann von gestern* Nabl wrote little fiction. In 1948 he published the collection *Johannes Krantz*, containing six stories written between 1928 and 1935 which had been published under the title *Das Meteor* (The Meteorite) in 1935, plus *Kindernovelle* (Children's Novella, 1932; revised, 1936), *Griff ins Dunkel* (Grasp in the Dark, 1936), and "Der verkehrte Zug" (The Topsy-turvy Train, 1947). The 1958 edition was enlarged by three more stories. The stories are framed by a plot involving Nabl's alter ego, the writer Johannes Krantz, who had already appeared in *Steirische Lebenswanderung*. Krantz falls in love with an astronomer, Frau Dr. Strainz. He never explicitly declares his love to her, sending her his stories instead. Their correspondence discussing the stories and Krantz's relationship with Frau Strainz's dog, which he keeps for her because her husband does not like it, make up the frame. When Frau Strainz, having separated from her husband, meets Krantz again after some years, he does not propose to her; he is unable to overlook the fact that she had married someone who was, in his opinion, not good enough for her.

Krantz is a lonely figure, an outsider not only in the real world but also in the world of literature. He is, like Nabl himself, not read by many. There is no doubt that Nabl suffered from the lack of recognition; his readiness to allow the Nazis to use him for their purposes can partly be explained by his eagerness to reach a larger readership. When, one year before his death, three of Austria's best-known writers–Peter Handke, Alfred Kolleritsch, and Gerhard Roth–paid tribute to him in a television program as the grand old man of Austrian literature, public interest in him was temporarily rekindled. He certainly deserves attention, especially for his early work. No less a figure than Robert Musil highly appreciated *Ödhof*, and in a television documentary broadcast on the centennial of Nabl's birth another giant of Austrian literature, Elias Canetti, called Nabl one of the great Austrian writers.

Letters:
Reinhard Urbach, "Arthur Schnitzler-Franz Nabl: Briefwechsel," *Studium Generale*, 24, no. 10/11 (1971): 1256-1270.

Bibliography:
Franz and Ilse Nabl, "Werkverzeichnis: Franz Nabl," *Studium Generale*, 24, no. 10/11 (1971): 1334-1372.

References:
Erwin Ackerknecht, *Franz Nabl: Der Weg eines deutschen Dichters* (Bremen: Schünemann, 1938);

Ernst Alker, "Franz Nabl," *Wort in der Zeit*, 2 (January 1956): 1-7;

Kurt Bartsch, Gerhard Melzer, and Johann Strutz, eds., *Über Franz Nabl: Aufsätze, Essays, Reden* (Graz, Vienna & Cologne: Styria, 1980);

Ingrid Cella, Afterword to Nabl's *Die Ortliebschen Frauen* (Frankfurt am Main, Berlin & Vienna: Ullstein, 1981), pp. 452-464;

August Closs, "Franz Nabl's Solitary Greatness," *Oxford German Studies*, 7 (1973): 161-165;

Herbert Herzmann, "Erinnerungen an einen Vergessenen: Zum 100. Geburtsjahr des österreichischen Dichters Franz Nabl," *Neue Zürcher Zeitung*, 12/13 (November 1983);

Alfred Holzinger, Afterword to Nabl's *Die zweite Heimat* (Graz: Leykam, 1963), pp. 227-238;

Holzinger, Preface to Nabl's *Ausgewählte Werke* (Vienna: Kremayr & Scheriau, 1966), I: 5-22;

Johannes Langfeldt, "Franz Nabl," *Sudetenland*, 3 (1961): 99-105;

Johann Rieder, "Das epische Schaffen Franz Nabls," Ph.D. dissertation, University of Vienna, 1949;

Studium Generale, special Nabl issue, 24, no. 10/11 (1971).

Papers:
Franz Nabl's literary estate is at the university library, University of Graz.

Leo Perutz
(2 November 1882-25 August 1957)

Bettina Kluth Cothran
Georgia State University

BOOKS: *Die dritte Kugel* (Munich: Langen, 1915);

Das Mangobaumwunder: Eine unglaubwürdige Geschichte, by Perutz and Paul Frank (Munich: Langen, 1916);

Zwischen neun und neun: Roman (Munich: Langen, 1918); translated by Lily Lore as *From Nine to Nine* (New York: Viking, 1926; London: Lane, 1927);

Der Marques de Bolibar: Roman (Munich: Langen, 1920); translated by Graham Rawson as *The Marquis de Bolibar* (London: Lane, 1926; New York: Viking, 1927);

Das Gasthaus zur Kartätsche: Eine Geschichte aus dem alten Österreich (Munich: Musarion, 1920);

Die Geburt des Antichrist (Vienna: Rikola, 1921);

Der Meister des Jüngsten Tages: Roman (Munich: Langen, 1923); translated by Hedwig Singer as *The Master of the Day of Judgment* (London: Mathews & Marrot, 1929; New York: Boni, 1930);

Turlupin: Roman (Munich: Langen, 1924);

Der Kosak und die Nachtigall: Roman, by Perutz and Frank (Munich: Knorr & Hirth, 1927);

Wohin rollst du, Äpfelchen . . . : Roman (Berlin: Ullstein, 1928); translated by Singer as *Where Will You Fall?* (London: Mathews & Marrot, 1930);

Flammen auf San Domingo: Roman nach Victor Hugo's "Bug-Jargal" (Berlin: Maschler, 1929);

Die Reise nach Preßburg: Schauspiel in 3 Akten (9 Bildern) mit einem Vor- und einem Nachspiel (Vienna: Marton, 1930);

Herr, erbarme Dich meiner! Novellen (Vienna: Phaidon, 1930);

St. Petri-Schnee: Roman (Vienna & Leipzig: Zsolnay, 1933); translated by E. B. G. Stamper and E. M. Hodgson as *The Virgin's Brand* (London: Butterworth, 1934);

Der schwedische Reiter: Roman (Vienna: Zsolnay, 1936);

Nachts unter der steinernen Brücke: Ein Roman aus dem alten Prag (Frankfurt am Main: Frankfurter Verlagsanstalt, 1953);

Leo Perutz

Der Judas des Leonardo: Roman (Hamburg & Vienna: Zsolnay, 1959).

OTHER: Victor Hugo, *Das Jahr der Guillotine: Roman*, translated and edited by Perutz and Oswald Levett (Berlin: Ullstein, 1925).

Leo Perutz was a successful writer recognized during his lifetime by an audience that extended far beyond the borders of the Austro-Hungarian Empire, where he was born. Although his oeuvre includes dramas and film scripts, he is best known for his fiction. The success he enjoyed immediately following the publication of his first novel, *Die dritte Kugel* (The Third Bullet) in 1915 continued throughout the 1920s and 1930s; newspapers competed for the privilege of publishing his stories as serialized novels, and several of his works were translated into as many as twenty-one foreign languages. But in 1938, when Hitler's Anschluß (annexation) of Austria forced the Jewish Perutz to flee to Tel Aviv, his career came to an abrupt halt. The absence of a German-speaking audience as well as vastly different conditions made his life as a writer a struggle. After the war, the public's interests and tastes had changed, and Perutz, largely forgotten, had great difficulty finding a publisher for what would be the last novel to be published in his lifetime, *Nachts unter der steinernen Brücke: Ein Roman aus dem alten Prag* (At Night under the Stone Bridge: A Novel of Old Prague, 1953). Despite waning interest in his works, Perutz was convinced of their intrinsic value and believed that they would enjoy a resurgence in the future: "Umso sicherer meine Auferstehung in vierzig Jahren.... Ich glaube daran, daß meine Zeit wiederkommen wird" (The more certain is my resurrection forty years from now.... I am convinced that my time will come again). This prediction, which reflects Perutz's firm belief in a higher power that had predestined him for continued success, has come true. In 1957, the year of Perutz's death, a critic writing for *Die Zeit* stated that "die Literaturgeschichte hat ein Unrecht an Leo Perutz gutzumachen" (literary history needs to redeem Leo Perutz). The increasing attention paid to Perutz's novels in the 1950s and 1960s has culminated in the publication of a new hardback edition of his entire oeuvre by the Zsolnay house beginning with *Der Meister des Jüngsten Tages* (1923; translated as *The Master of the Day of Judgment*, 1929) in 1975 and the republication of selected works in paperback by RORORO and dtv in the 1980s.

Perutz's tension-filled stories commanded an extensive and diverse audience. Among his readers were his friends Ernst Weiß, Egon Erwin Kisch, and Alexander Lernet-Holenia, as well as such other well-known writers as Kurt Tucholsky, Alfred Polgar, and Walter Benjamin. His genius in composition was admired by Ian Fleming and Jorge Luis Borges. Robert Musil saw in Perutz's novels a completely new genre, which he called "journalistische Dichtung" (journalistic fiction). Literary critics, however, denied the rank of high literature to Perutz's novels, claiming that the interest in his works rested on the general popularity of adventure stories in the 1920s. Friedrich Torberg, who called Perutz's genius a "mögliches Resultat eines Fehltrittes von Franz Kafka mit Agatha Christie" (possible result of an illicit union of Franz Kafka with Agatha Christie), aptly defined Perutz's problem: "Für einen Unterhaltungsschriftsteller loteten seine Geschichten zu tief ins Unheimliche, für bloße 'Reißer' erhoben sie zu hohen literarischen Anspruch, für anspruchsvolle Literatur waren sie zu spannend" (For a writer of entertaining literature, his stories plumbed too deeply into the uncanny, for pure "thrillers" they rose to too high literary pretensions, for the highest realm of literature they were too tension-filled). Perutz did nothing to help his image as a writer of serious literature, once advising a young critic that there were subjects more worthy of study than his stories, which in his view were only to be read and enjoyed.

Leopold Perutz was born in Prague on 2 November 1882 into a well-to-do Jewish family. His ancestors—under the name Perez—had left seventeenth-century Spain for Bohemia, where they established themselves as merchants. Perutz's father, Benedikt Perutz, owned a textile plant in Prague until it burned down in 1899. The family relocated to Vienna, where Benedikt Perutz started another successful enterprise. Perutz attended the Erzherzog Rainer-Real-Gymnasium, where he found friends who shared his interest in literature. They formed a literary club called the "Freilicht" (Free Light) and met after school to read and discuss the products of their youthful literary ambitions. Perutz later described their activities: "In einem kleinen Cafe gegenüber der Universität trafen sich zwanzig junge Menschen, um einander ihre lyrischen Gedichte, ihre Novellen, ihre Tragödienentwürfe und ihre 'Bruchstücke aus einem unvollendeten Roman' vorzulesen. Die Gedichte klangen alle, als wären sie von einer Sekretärin Rilkes, die Tragödien kamen von Strindberg her, bei den Novellen hatte Knut Hamsun unfreiwillig Pate gestanden und 'Bruchstücke aus einem Roman' verdankten den eben erschienen *Buddenbrooks* ihr dürftiges Leben" (In a small cafe opposite the university, twenty young people met to read aloud their lyrical poetry, novellas, drafts of tragedies, and "fragments of uncompleted novels." The poems all sounded as if they had been written by one of Rilke's secretaries, the tragedies were descended from Strindberg, for the novellas Knut Hamsun had involuntarily stood godfather, and the "fragments of a novel" thanked their existence, such as it was, to the just-published *Buddenbrooks*).

The other members of the Freilicht became successful doctors, lawyers, and businessmen; Perutz chose mathematics as his vocation. But he lost his table of logarithms on the eve of his mathematics examination. The replacement he obtained from a used-book store contained additional penciled-in information which was not permissible, and Perutz was expelled for cheating. Ineligible to attend the university, Perutz became an actuary. He achieved fame in the insurance field as an astute mathematician, published many articles in professional insurance magazines, and developed the widely used "Perutzsche Ausgleichsformula" (Perutz Equalization Formula). In 1907 Perutz accepted a position with the Assicuranzioni Generali in Trieste, Italy; the same month, Franz Kafka went to work as a temporary assistant with the same company in Prague.

Perutz was reluctant to reveal details about his private life. He rarely granted interviews, and when asked about his development as an artist he replied that it was evident in his books. This modesty, along with the exacting demands he placed on himself, kept him from publishing his first novel until 1915. He labored painstakingly on each of his works, soliciting comments from friends to whom he read them. When Benjamin remarked that Perutz's novels are so tension-filled that one reads them eagerly between stops on a train, Perutz responded that none of his works were written with ease. Behind his engaging writing style lies a carefully designed structure.

All of his novels and stories make use of a narrator who relates the events in retrospect. *Die dritte Kugel* is set in 1547 at the end of the Schmalkadic war, when Charles V and the Catholics defeated the Protestants under Johann Friedrich of Saxony at Mühlberg. An old Spanish soldier tells the story of Count Grumbach of the Rhine to his comrades on a cool autumn night while they sit around the campfire. One of those listening to the tale is the Hauptmann (Captain) Glasäpflein, who, unbeknownst not only to those around him but even to himself, is Count Grumbach; he has no recollection of his former identity. The old Spaniard's tale is set in the time of Cortez's conquest of the Aztec empire. Personal ambitions and old enmities between Catholics and Protestants cause strife among the Spanish troops. Count Grumbach, a staunch defender

Dust jacket for Perutz's first book, a novel set in the sixteenth century at the end of the Schmalkadic war

of Luther's teachings, had been banned from his homeland and had fled with a handful of faithful servants to the wilderness of the New World, where he had become a friend of the Indians. His main opponent is the Prince of Mendoza, who is the exact opposite of the physically formidable, straightforward, and honorable count. Both men love the Indian princess Delila. Grumbach and Mendoza are, in fact, brothers; Grumbach knows of this relationship and changes his course of action several times to spare the life of his brother. Magic forces seem to influence the fates of the protagonists and their followers; the central power is the curse of the three bullets which Grumbach hopes to employ in his cause. According to the soldier from whom they were obtained, the first bullet is to kill the king of the Indians, the second Delila, and the third Grumbach himself. The first two bullets find their marks as the curse demands. Before the Spaniard can finish the tale, he is shot by Grumbach's servant, Melchior Jäcklein. Hauptmann Glasäpflein says: "Und nun hat der Melchior Jäcklein, der Narr, den alten Reiter zu Tod' geschossen, ohne Sinn und Zweck.... Und hat zugleich mein vergangenes Leben getroffen.... Ja, die dritte Kugel hat mich getroffen" (And now Melchior Jäcklein, the fool, shot the old soldier dead, without meaning or purpose.... And shot my past life with him.... Yes, the third bullet did kill me). The brief glimpse of his identity quickly fades away, and Glasäpflein's memories retreat again into distant and indistinct notions. He speculates that he may have read about the strange things floating through his mind long ago in a fairy tale or a novel of knightly valor. To the end, the lines between reality and fate remain blurred. The readers can enjoy the story as a historical novel with elements of the fantastic, can take it as the dream of an old soldier whose mind has been deranged, or can accept the idea that a variety of forces determines one's fate, not all of which are readily accessible to the "enlightened" mind. Perutz juxtaposes objective and subjective time: the reader may have lived through a year of Grumbach's life, or just a few hours.

Perutz joined Infantry Regiment Number Eighty-eight on 16 August 1915. On 4 July 1916 he was shot in the lung at Burkanow, near the Galician front, and was transported to a hospital in Vienna. His life was saved by several operations, but he spent weeks on the brink of death. Unable to return to the front, he was assigned to the war press headquarters in Vienna; other writers also held offices there during the war years, among them Hugo von Hofmannsthal, Rainer Maria Rilke, Robert Musil, and Franz Werfel. At first Perutz was assigned the task of censoring war prisoners' mail; he later worked in the decoding department and was finally sent as a military correspondent to the Ukraine and Romania. From 1917 until the end of the war Perutz's life aside from his duties in the press headquarters was that of a civilian. His evenings were mostly spent in the cafés Herrenhof and Central, where he played his favorite game, tarok, or discussed philosophy, politics, mathematics, and numerology with his friends.

The subjective perception of time is a major element of Perutz's second novel, *Zwischen neun und neun* (1918; translated as *From Nine to Nine*,

Dust jacket for Perutz's 1920 novel set in Spain during the Napoleonic wars

1926). The story depicts a day in the life of the student Stanislaus Demba. His behavior seems odd, even suspect. Together with the elderly shopkeeper the reader wonders why the young man desires home delivery for his cold cuts and slice of bread, or why he sits in his room with the curtains drawn in broad daylight even though he claims to feel perfectly well. He engages in a mad quest for money, which is insufficiently explained by his story that his girlfriend is about to spend her vacation with another young man, and he wants to prevent this by going on vacation with her himself. The bizarre situations which take Demba through the streets and coffeehouses of Vienna strain the reader's patience until, precisely in the middle of the book, the reason for this behavior is explained: he is handcuffed. Demba reveals his situation to his friend Steffi: to supplement his meager income from tutoring the children of wealthy families, he stole several valuable books from the university library and sold them to an antique dealer. The dealer notified the police, who arrested and handcuffed him. He escaped and ran to the attic of his house. When the police forced their way through the door, he jumped out of the window. He lost consciousness after falling to the ground, then ran away. The second half of the novel details Demba's frustrated attempts to gain freedom from the handcuffs and to settle his personal affairs. At the end, Demba is speaking to Steffi in the attic of the house where he is hiding. It is almost nine o'clock in the evening. The police are at the door; Demba jumps out the window; the clock strikes nine. The scene is an exact repeat of the first jump. Demba asks the question which also plagues the reader: "Eine Turmuhr schlägt. Neunmal. Morgens? Abends? Wo bin ich? . . . Zwölf Stunden? Zwölf Sekunden?" (A tower clock is striking. Nine times. Morning? Evening? Where am I? . . . Twelve hours? Twelve seconds?). The police find Demba dead on the ground. What seemed to be the activities of one day were in reality the last seconds of the student's life. In the time of the nine strikes of the clock, Demba relived his life: "Seine Augen lebten. . . . tauchten unter in der brausenden Wirrnis des Daseins, . . . klammerten sich noch einmal an das rastlose Leben des ewig bewegten Tages, . . . kosteten zum letzten Mal von Glück und Schmerz. . . ." (His eyes were alive. . . . immersed themselves once more in the roaring chaos of life, . . . clung again to the restless life of the ever changing days, . . . tasted for the last time happiness and sorrow . . .). The intensity of the story leaves the reader exhausted.

After the psychological novel *Zwischen neun und neun*, which was hailed as a big success on the German book market, Perutz returned to a historical setting with his third novel, *Der Marques de Bolibar* (1920; translated as *The Marquis de Bolibar*, 1926). As in *Die dritte Kugel*, the action takes place during a time of political upheaval. The setting is Spain during the Napoleonic wars; the Spanish are engaged in a battle with the army under Marshal Soults, fortified by regiments of the allied Rheinbund (Rhenish Alliance). Preceding the story is a preface by a fictitious editor of the memoirs of Lieutenant Jochberg, the only survivor of two regiments which were annihilated in the winter of 1812: "Es fällt schwer, daran zu glauben, obgleich in unserer heutigen Zeit Erklärungen mystisch-okkulter Natur, Begriffe wie Selbstmordpsychose oder suggestive Willensübertragung so leicht zur Hand sind. Die

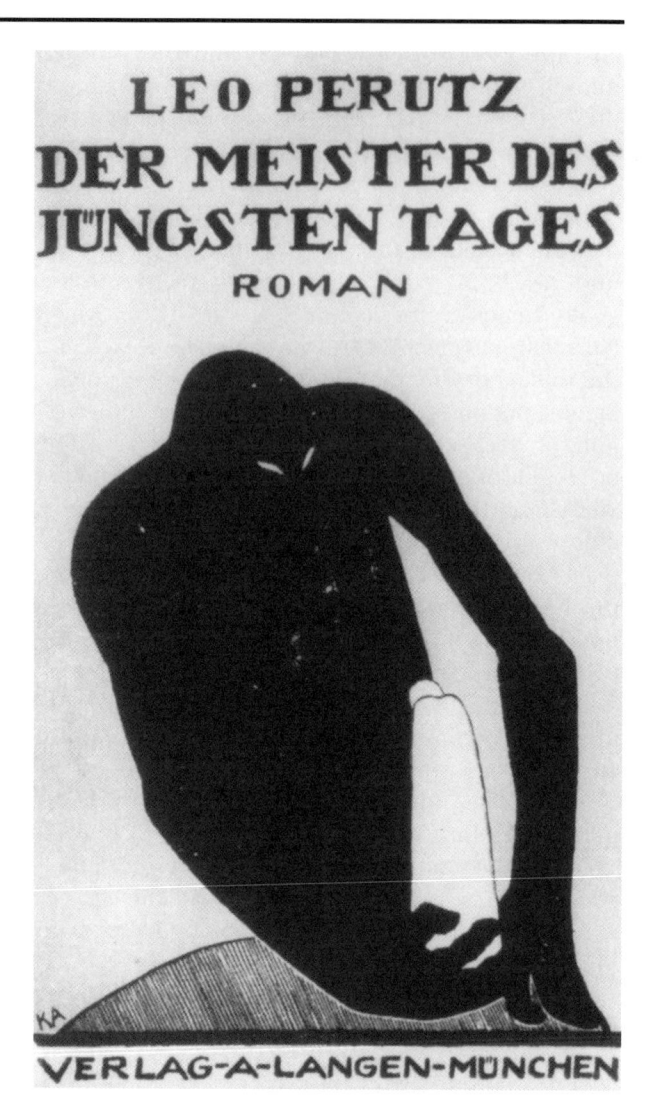

Dust jacket for Perutz's 1923 mystery novel about the apparent suicides of several renowned, but failing, artists

zünftige Geschichtswissenschaft wird denn auch den Wert der Memoiren des Leutnants Jochberg mit Skepsis einschätzen. Sie wird–und ich bin der Letzte, ihr das zu verdenken–seine Darstellung eine allzu romanhafte nennen. Schließlich–wieviel kritische Fähigkeit kann sie auch einem Menschen zusprechen, der überzeugt ist, in Spanien den ewigen Juden getroffen zu haben?" (It is hard to believe, although in our modern times explanations of a mystical-occult nature, concepts such as suicidal psychosis or suggestive will-transferences are so readily available. The proper science of history surely will exercise skepticism when evaluating the memoirs of Lieutenant Jochberg. They will–and I am the last to find fault with this–be called fiction. After all–how much of a critical ability can someone possess who is convinced that he encountered the Wandering Jew in Spain?).

The Marques de Bolibar, an old Spanish noble, is the driving force behind the resistance movement. He is venerated by all, and the peaceful and God-fearing people of the country have united around him to fight off a hated, un-Christian, and insensitive militia. He is able to change his physical appearance so that he is unrecognizable by all but his faithful dog. Mistaken for someone else, he is executed as a common thief. Before his death he commands his officers to swear that they will complete his unfinished task. Only Jochberg, the young officer, understands the meaning of the Marques's prayer, in which he commends the fulfillment of his wish into God's hands. As Jochberg had foreseen, the officers themselves give the signals for the guerrillas to attack. The members of this regiment are killed almost to the last man; Jochberg alone survives. But the Marques's spirit seems to have taken possession of Jochberg to the extent that even his physical appearance has been altered. His thoughts are those of the Marques: "Und es war mir als wäre die Vernichtung des Regiments von Anfang an mein Wille gewesen" (It suddenly seemed to me as if the annihilation of the regiment had been my aim from the beginning).

Perutz uses various elements to heighten the reader's anticipation. One of the most effective is the technique of foreshadowing coming events by either telling the reader what will happen without revealing how it will happen, or by interspersing seemingly insignificant remarks whose full meaning does not become evident until later in the novel. Nature is often a foreboding of evil: snow, wind, and ice reflect the hard luck of the characters. The masterful construction of Perutz's novels was lauded by Egon Erwin Kisch, who compared Perutz to Dumas, and by Kurt Tucholsky, who praised Perutz's books as ideal "zum Schmökern" (for curling up and just reading).

Der Meister des Jüngsten Tages, which one reviewer called an "exciting mystery-murder story, a choice product of the famous Viennese author's culture and imagination," depicts a series of apparent suicides which shock the Viennese upper class. The victims are artists whose creative powers are no longer adequate. The narrator of the story is Baron von Yosch, a wealthy Austrian cavalry officer. Von Yosch had had an affair with the wife of one of the victims, the aging actor Eugene Bischoff, prior to her marriage. Did

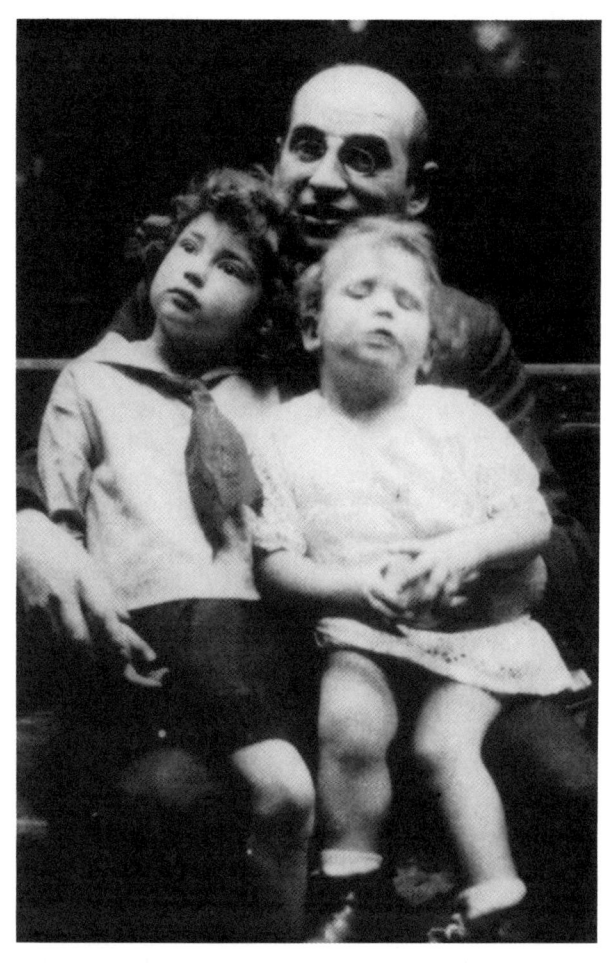

Perutz in 1925 with his daughters Michaela and Lore

Bischoff really commit suicide? Was he driven to take his own life or simply murdered? Baron von Yosch feels forced to solve the mystery. A bizarre turn of events finally reveals the culprit: a book from the Florence of the Medicis. It relates the story of an artist who was persuaded to drink a magic potion that would supposedly restore his artistic vision; instead, the potion left him insane, and he spent the last days of his life in a monastery painting the terrible vision he had of the day of judgment. The painting was characterized by a particularly vivid color called "Drommetenrot" (trumpet-red) a word that alludes to the trumpets of Judgment Day and the redness of the fires of hell. The book, with the recipe for the potion, was discovered by a painter, then by Bischoff, then by an artistic pharmacist, and finally by von Yosch, none of whom could resist the temptation to revive his flagging inspiration. All of them committed suicide except von Yosch, who at the last minute is dissuaded by his friends from shooting himself. The events demonstrate that we all carry our own day of judgment within us. In an epilogue, one of von Yosch's fellow officers calls the incredible story a feeble attempt by von Yosch to hide the fact that he killed Bischoff out of jealousy. The reader is left to judge for himself.

Critics have pointed to the "pragerische Färbung ... Hang zum Unheimlichen und Dämonischen" (the Prague mood ... propensity for the sinister and demonic) of this novel and have compared Perutz to Kafka and Gustav Meyrink, other Prague Jewish writers who wrote in German. The topic of personal identity is central to Meyrink's novel *Der Golem* (1915; translated as *The Golem*, 1928), in which one person relives part of another's life by simply wearing that person's hat. The themes of subjective versus objective time, a fascination with the mystic powers of the occult, a love for historical settings, an interest in Jewish culture, and the use of a frame story are shared by the two authors. Perutz, however, did not want to be likened to Meyrink, insisting that he wrote more in the manner of E. T. A. Hoffmann. The fate of Perutz's protagonists, like that of Hoffmann's, is influenced by intangible powers outside the rational realm. As is true for his literary idol, music and mystical qualities also hold a special place in Perutz's work. Music frequently serves as an agent to conjure up memories and dreams. Perutz also seems to believe–like the romantics–that music is the key to a higher realm and that people with an affinity to the arts in general are sensitive to a world which lies beyond the grasp of those obsessed with material things.

In the novels *Turlupin* (1924) and *Wohin rollst du, Äpfelchen* ... (1928; translated as *Where Will You Fall?*, 1930), set respectively in seventeenth-century France and during the Bolshevik revolution in Russia, events follow a predetermined course, leading to an inevitable end that defies common sense. Thus, the lowly peruke maker Turlupin assumes the false identity of a French noble and causes Cardinal Richelieu's well-laid plans to topple the established order to fail miserably. In *Wohin rollst du, Äpfelchen* ... Vittorin's desire to revenge himself on a former prison guard who insulted him causes the senseless deaths of many people, including the Menshevik leader who might have saved Russia from Bolshevik domination. Entire regiments of soldiers who have helped Vittorin's cause are sacrificed for the sake of his goal. The absurdity of this train of events is underscored by the fact that the insult Vittorin suffered was insignificant; nevertheless, it takes on supernatural dimensions in his mind, and this fact, coupled with his extreme determination, enables him to overcome all obstacles between himself and the old and now harmless sergeant who is living in Vienna just three blocks from where Vittorin started his vengeful search. In the course of his destructive life Vittorin sacrifices his personal happiness: his fiancée finds more promising suitors, and the founder of a large industrial conglomerate loses interest in his services. A Jewish proverb proclaims: "Der Mensch denkt, Gott lacht" (Man thinks, God laughs); there appears to be no logic in what a higher being does. Perutz imbues his readers with a profound respect for the limitations of the human mind.

In 1928 Ida Weil Perutz, the writer's wife of ten years and the love of his youth, died while giving birth to their third child. In his despair, Perutz resorted to spiritualists in an attempt to make contact with her; he then threw himself into several love affairs with beautiful young women of means whom he tried to impress, at times through extreme measures. He even went so far as to serenade a young lady who bemoaned the lack of chivalry in the postwar world: while horrified bystanders looked on, Perutz climbed up the facade of the hotel to her second-story balcony. Perutz was known for feats of strength, and although the war left him with reduced lung capacity, he later became an avid waterskier.

In *Flammen auf San Domingo* (Flames on San Domingo, 1929) the hero's wife is killed in a slave revolt shortly after their marriage. His love and property lost, he seeks an honorable death in war. The collection *Herr, erbarme Dich meiner!* (Lord, Have Mercy on Me!, 1930) contains reprints of the novellas *Das Gasthaus zur Kartätsche* (The Inn of the Grapeshot, 1920) and *Die Geburt des Antichrist* (The Birth of the Antichrist, 1921), as well as new material such as "Dienstag, 12. Oktober 1916" (Tuesday, 12 October 1916) and the title story. All the novellas employ elements characteristic of Perutz's novels: they are told by a narrator and make use of devices to build tension, such as foretelling certain aspects of the outcome.

In *St. Petri-Schnee* (Saint Peter-Snow, 1933; translated as *The Virgin's Brand*, 1934) Perutz takes up a pressing theme doubtless suggested by the tactics of Hitler: mass seduction by a single-minded man. The setting is a hospital where Dr.

Dust jacket for Perutz's 1953 novel set in Prague during the reign of Rudolph II

Amberg, the narrator, is recovering from an almost fatal head injury. According to the official account, Amberg was struck by an automobile; but his own recollection is quite different. The young physician had come to Morwede, the small town where he now lies in the hospital, due to a series of strange coincidences. In search of a permanent position, he had chanced upon a newspaper advertisement in which the name Baron Melchin caught his attention. Amberg's father, a renowned historian who had died when Amberg was a young boy, had been a friend of the baron. Melchin, also an avid historian, sees himself as the instrument through which divine rule will be reestablished. His search for a catalyst for a renewed religious fervor–without which the claim to a God-given rule would be without base–leads to a chemical substance known as "St. Petri-Schnee." He seeks to refine and produce this chemical with the help of a young woman doctor,

Kallisto Tsanaris, known as Bibiche. She is no stranger to Dr. Amberg: years before, they had worked in the same institute in Berlin, where she was the object of his admiration and desire. Bibiche had left the institute suddenly and without explanation; Amberg had searched for her in vain, finally giving up hope of ever seeing her again. But their paths crossed in Osnabrück, where she was driving the green Cadillac the doctors now claim ran over him. In his astonishment, he missed the opportunity to get her attention. During his stay in Morwede, he and Bibiche spend a blissful night together.

Other events had foreshadowed the future before his arrival in Morwede. While strolling through Osnabrück he had felt himself directed by an unknown power to an obscure antique shop in a distant corner of the old town. Looking at the objects in the shop window, he saw two things which he realizes later were related to his own future: a booklet titled *Warum verschwindet der Gottesglaube aus der Welt?* (Why Is Belief in God Vanishing from the World?) and an old marble bust of a man of unusual and noble features. These features are those of the Hofenstauffen kings and of the boy Federico, whom the baron has adopted as his son. The baron, it turns out, wants to put his son on the restored throne of the Holy Roman Empire. Although Amberg cooperates only halfheartedly in the baron's scheme, he is nevertheless pulled into the cataclysmic series of events that culminates in a communist revolution by the peasants. Storming the castle, the frenzied crowds kill the baron and severely wound Amberg. Law and order are quickly restored, however, and the baron's followers are removed from the scene. The authorities want to cover up this failed coup, and thus Amberg, presumed to be without memory because of his injuries, is given a new past that conforms to the official version of history. There are official explanations for everything: Bibiche is now the chief resident's wife, who supposedly returned to him after months of separation.

Another plausible solution could be that the entire Morwede episode is a figment of Amberg's imagination. Perhaps he retained bits and pieces from his past which simply merged in his subconscious with impressions he received in the hospital. One clue supporting this explanation is the frequent reference to the color blue, which signifies the realm of dream and fantasy. Federico has "große, blaue Augen, die wie Irisblumen waren" (large blue eyes like the bloom of an iris). Bibiche

Perutz, 1957, at his summer residence in St. Wolfgang on the Wolfgangssee

works in a house with blue shutters and wears a "kornblumenblaues Kleid" (a cornflower-blue dress). Should the reader evaluate the likelihood of Amberg's story according to the principles he held prior to the Morwede experience: "Ich neige nicht dazu, das Übersinnliche zur Deutung einfacher Vorfälle heranzuziehen ... ich halte mich an die realen Tatsachen" (I do not agree with evaluating simple happenings by transcendental standards ... I stick to the facts)? Or should one believe his claims about the clairvoyant incidents he experienced in Morwede? Waking from his coma, Amberg says: "Ich war ein namenloses Etwas, ein unpersönliches Wesen, das die Begriffe 'Vergangenheit' und 'Zukunft' nicht kannte" (I was a nameless thing, an impersonal being that did not know the concepts of "past" and "future"). His recollection of the past returns slowly and in fragments. His first memory is of the night he spent with Bibiche, when he felt that she was his forever. He says: "Was man im Traum besitzt, kann einem keine Welt von Feinden nehmen" (What one owns in a dream, no world of foes can take away). Thus, in the final analysis, one is faced with the romantic solution: reality is not what one may think it is but what one *feels* it is. The truth of the moment transcends time and space.

In 1935 Perutz married Grete Humburger, the daughter of a grocery wholesaler. Twenty-two years younger than her husband, she was frequently mistaken for his daughter.

The hero of Perutz's novel *Der schwedische Reiter* (The Swedish Soldier, 1936) is known only by his nickname, "Hahnenschnapper" (Chicken-thief). The four chapter headings reveal the identities he assumes in the course of the novel: "Der Dieb" (The Thief), "Der Gottesräuber" (The Robber of God), "Der schwedische Reiter," and "Der Namenlose" (The Nameless One). The story is once again set in times of upheaval: Sweden is fighting against Russia in the Nordic War at the beginning of the eighteenth century. In the course of the fighting, two unlikely companions are fleeing the authorities: a common thief and the young nobleman Christian von Tornefeld, who has deserted from the Swedish army. In the course of their association, the thief finds out enough about Tornefeld's life to enable him to assume Tornefeld's identity. He tricks Tornefeld into surrendering his most treasured possession, a Bible which once belonged to the seventeenth-century Swedish king, Gustavus Adolphus, by promising to deliver it to the current king. He also tricks Tornefeld into taking his place at the "cursed steel mills of the bishop," as they are known to the people. The mill is a last refuge for all scoundrels who have nowhere else to go and more often than not a place from which they never return. The millworkers are driven by brutal overseers. Leading Tornefeld away, the three emissaries from the mill remark that the thief, now running away as fast as his feet will carry him, will have to serve his time after a short reprieve.

In the second chapter the thief is a Robin Hood of sorts, the head of a band of thieves who steal church treasures and distribute them to the poor. Common sense and a concern for those in need lead to his success as Tornefeld's impostor at the estate of his wealthy uncle. Falling in love with Tornefeld's bride, he convinces her that he is the long-awaited soldier who had finally come home to save the estate, which is almost completely ruined. He proves himself to be an exemplary husband and manager. His happiness is complete when his daughter Christina is born. After seven years, however, some members of the robber gang reappear. Fearing that they will expose his real identity, he decides to leave his wife and daughter and join the Swedish army. On his way he encounters the real Tornefeld, who miraculously survived the brutal mill and is now strong and fearless. The thief returns the Bible to him, thereby finally fulfilling his promise. Identities are exchanged again: Tornefeld rides off to war, where he becomes famous for his brave deeds; the thief expiates his sins in the mills of the bishop.

The story is introduced by a preface in which Christina recalls her childhood. After her father departed, he reappeared at her window each night for brief visits. Christina believes that these appearances were the result of a spell she had placed on him. One day, news came that Tornefeld had died on the field of honor; that night, her father failed to appear. Christina's mother asked the girl to pray for her father's soul; instead, she prayed for the soul of a poor stranger who was passing by their house at the moment. At the end of the novel, it is revealed that the thief, Christina's real father, had escaped from the bishop's mills but, in so doing, had been injured and died. His last wish was that his daughter should pray for his soul, and this wish was granted.

After the Anschluß Perutz, sharing feelings of isolation with other writers in exile, settled in Tel Aviv. He did not join any literary groups and even refused to contribute to magazines dedicated to exile literature. When he was invited to contribute a story to *Aufbau*, a magazine published in New York, he reacted with disgust: "Für mich ist nämlich der *Aufbau* ein Brechmittel" (I feel like vomiting when I hear about *Aufbau*). He labored to complete his two last novels in Tel Aviv. "Die Erde des winzigen Piniengartens ist bedeckt mit erst zerrissenen und dann zerknüllten Blättern" (The soil of the tiny garden with stone-pines is covered with pages first torn and then crumpled up), he complained in a letter.

A close connection between the life of the spirit and that of the flesh is depicted in the last of Perutz's novels to appear in his lifetime, *Nachts unter der steinernen Brücke*. Several novellas, each complete in itself, form the story set in Prague during the time of Rudolph II. As in his other works, Perutz foreshadows at the beginning of the book the events to come. In three lapidary sentences the reader learns that on the same night the pestilence ceased its furious reign in the Josefstadt, the Jewish quarter; Esther, the beautiful wife of Mordechai Meisl, died; and Rudolph II woke from his dreams with a fearful scream. The following thirteen chapters relate the story behind these events. The narrator, Jakob Meisl, a medical student, is a distant relative of the legendary Mordechai Meisl; he was also, according to the epilogue, Perutz's mathematics tutor. At what was to be his last tutoring session, Jakob Meisl showed Perutz Mordechai Meisl's last will and testament; it bequeathed his personal belongings to his closest relatives but did not mention his legendary wealth because he had spent it all building houses, synagogues, and other improvements in the Josefstadt. That same day Perutz witnessed the demolition of the Josefstadt in an urban renewal project. Together with the younger Meisl he watched the houses crumble, the wind dispersing the dust in the air.

In the main part of the novel, Rudolph II lays eyes on the beautiful Esther one day while riding through the Jewish quarter. Unable to forget her, he summons Rabbi Loew and demands that the girl become his. Rabbi Loew recognizes from the emperor's description that the girl is the wife

Perutz in his home in Tel Aviv

of Mordechai Meisl and explains to the king that the eternal laws of marriage make the fulfillment of his wish impossible. In a fit of rage, Rudolph declares that he will take revenge on all Jews in his realm if the rabbi does not deliver Esther to him. The rabbi, well versed in the mysteries of the cabala, devises a solution: he plants a rosebush and a rosemary bush close together under the Charles Bridge, the stone bridge of the novel's title. Each night, as the wind blows the blossoms of the two plants against each other, the emperor and Esther are together in their dreams. The rabbi's solution, however, enrages God, who sends the plague into the Jewish quarter as punishment. Only after the rabbi throws the rosemary bush into the river is the curse lifted.

Before embarking on what was to be his last trip to his summer residence in St. Wolfgang on the Wolfgangsee in Austria, Perutz finished the novel he had been writing concurrently with the Prague novel for the past several years. *Der Judas des Leonardo* (The Judas of Leonardo), which appeared posthumously in 1959, could be considered Perutz's final statement on the emerging personality that was to dominate all others in modern times: the man who judges everything according to its price. The archetype of this mercantile mentality is Judas Iscariot. Joachim Behaim, a young Bohemian merchant, is such a man. After concluding a profitable sale of two horses to the count of Milan, he stays in the city ostensibly to settle an old debt with Boccetta, a miser whose love of money is so great that he allows his daughter to go begging. The true reason for his delaying his departure is that he has fallen in love with Nicoletta, the most beautiful girl he has ever seen; he does not know that she is Boccetta's daughter. He admits to himself that his feelings for this girl are different from those he had for the other women in his life, whom he had merely used for his own pleasure and then discarded. Women had always been another possession like the things he bought and sold. Nicoletta is the opposite of her father: full of life, compassionate, and, as it turns out, passionate in her love for Behaim. She even betrays her duty as a daughter and steals money from her father to follow the man she loves. Behaim, however, is undeserving of this devotion, for when he realizes that Nicoletta is the daughter of his despised opponent, his pride causes him to betray her. True to his unemotional business sense, he even gives Nicoletta a receipt for the seventeen ducats she had stolen from her father for him.

Others, particularly artists such as the poet Mancino, the painter d'Oggione, and the wood carver Simoni, recognize that Behaim reveres only money and would deal with anything, including the blood of Christ, if it would be profitable for him. In the end, however, higher values win out over Behaim's merchant mentality. Leonardo da Vinci is working on the *Last Supper*. The completion of the painting has been delayed because Leonardo has not been able to find a model for Judas; when he sees Behaim he recognizes his Judas. Years later, when Behaim returns to Milan, he notices that people point their fingers at him, make the sign of the cross, or stare blankly at him. Only when he sees the *Last Supper* does he discover the cause of his notoriety: "Judas hat sich den Judas angesehen" (Judas looked at Judas).

What remains closed to the philistine, whose soul is blinded by the power of temporal things, is open to the artist. Perutz does not distinguish between the arts or even the character of the artists: both Mancino, governed by feeling, and Leonardo, governed by reflection, have an unerring sense of true values. Those with an aesthetic nature, represented here in almost Schillerean terms as the naive and the sentimental in their approach to art, are united by values that transcend the order of this world. In Leonardo's words: "Ich diene keinem Herzog und keinem Fürsten.... Ich diene allein meiner Leidenschaft des Schauens, des Erkennens, des Ordnens und des Gestaltens, und ich gehöre meinem Werk" (I serve no duke and no prince.... I serve only my passion of viewing, of recognizing, of ordering and of shaping, and I belong to my work).

Leonardo's credo might have been Perutz's own: no matter where he had his home, he belonged to his art. What stands out most prominently about this unjustly neglected writer is his endlessly creative and fantastic imagination. The things around him took on a life and a meaning apparent only to his own artistic eye. The Tel Aviv house of the Perutz family was not just an "Arab style" home but an enchanted one; the cistern behind the house, he was sure was the one in which John the Baptist was held captive; for him, the ruins of the old bakery next door came to life each night with boisterous fighting, ending in the small hours of the morning with loud cries for help and the murder of the baker.

On the night of 25 August 1957 Perutz had a heart attack in the house of his friend Alexander Lernet-Holenia in Bad Ischl, Austria. He is buried in the cemetery at Bad Ischl.

References:

Jeremy Adler, "Voices in a Metaphysical Madhouse," *Times Literary Supplement*, 7-13 October 1988, p. 1121;

Otto Beer, "Ein Fehltritt von Kafka mit Agatha Christie," *Tagesspiegel*, 6 July 1975, p. 37;

Beer, "Freischütz in Mexiko," *Tagesspiegel*, 22 October 1978, p. 53;

Beer, "Von Goldmachern und Sterndeutern," *Tagesspiegel*, 26 October 1975, p. 47;

Peter Engel and Hans-Harald Müller, eds., "'... ein guter Freund und Kamerad täte mir oft hier sehr wohl': Ernst Weiß' Briefe an Leo Perutz," *Modern Austrian Literature*, 21, no. 1 (1988): 27-59;

K. H. Kramberg, "Wiener Phantasiestücke: Der Geschichtenmacher Leo Perutz," *Süddeutsche Zeitung*, 12 July 1975, p. 80;

Hans-Harald Müller, "Leo Perutz–Eine biographische Skizze," *Exil*, 6, no. 2 (1986): 5-17;

Dietrich Neuhaus, *Erinnerungen und Schrecken: Die Einheit von Geschichte, Phantastik und Mathematik im Werk Leo Perutz'* (Frankfurt am Main; Lang, 1984);

Peter Panter (Kurt Tucholsky), "Die Geburt des Antichrist," *Die Weltbühne*, no. 2 (1922): 179-180;

C. F. S., "A Mystery," *The Friend* (6 December 1929): 1120;

Andreas Sattler, "Zu lange vernachlässigt: Österreichische Erzähler und große Literatur," *Die Zeit*, 26 December 1957, p. 9;

Jürgen Serke, *Böhmische Dörfer: Wanderungen durch eine verlassene literarische Landschaft* (Vienna & Hamburg: Zsolnay, 1987);

F. T., "Leo Perutz (1882-1957), Ein Romancier aus Österreich: Zum Gedenken an Leo Perutz," *Forum*, 4 (1957): 332;

Friedrich Torberg, "Wenn der Boden schwankt," *Die Welt*, 3 April 1975, p. iii;

Leonid Tschertkow, "Gustav Meyrink und Leo Perutz in Rußland," *Literatur und Kritik*, 10 (1975): 290-295;

Gert Ueding, "Triebkraft ist die Furcht: Gelegenheit, den Romancier Leo Perutz wiederzuentdecken," *Frankfurter Allgemeine Zeitung*, 24 May 1975, p. 93;

Ulrich Weinzierl, "Frohnatur und manche Leiche: *Die dritte Kugel* von Leo Perutz," *Frankfurter Allgemeine Zeitung*, 7 November 1978, p. 24.

Papers:

Leo Perutz's papers are at the Deutsche Bibliothek in Frankfurt am Main.

Rainer Maria Rilke
(4 December 1875-29 December 1926)

George C. Schoolfield
Yale University

BOOKS: *Leben und Lieder: Bilder und Tagebuchblätter* (Strassburg & Leipzig: Kattentidt, 1894);
Wegwarten (Prague: Selbstverlag, 1896);
Larenopfer (Prague: Dominicus, 1896);
Todtentänze: Zwielicht-Skizzen aus unseren Tagen (Prague: Löwit & Lamberg, 1896);
Im Frühfrost: Ein Stück Dämmerung. Drei Vorgänge (Vienna: Theaterverlag O. F. Eirich, 1897);
Traumgekrönt: Neue Gedichte (Leipzig: Friesenhahn, 1897);
Advent (Leipzig: Friesenhahn, 1898);
Ohne Gegenwart: Drama in zwei Akten (Berlin: Entsch, 1898);
Am Leben hin: Novellen und Skizzen (Stuttgart: Bonz, 1898);
Zwei Prager Geschichten (Stuttgart: Bonz, 1899);
Mir zur Feier: Gedichte (Berlin: Meyer, 1899); republished as *Die frühen Gedichte* (Leipzig: Insel, 1909; New York: Ungar, 1943);
Vom lieben Gott und Anderes: An Große für Kinder erzählt (Berlin & Leipzig: Schuster & Loeffler, 1900); republished as *Geschichten vom lieben Gott* (Leipzig: Insel, 1904; New York: Ungar, 1942); translated by Nora Purtscher-Wydenbruck and M. D. Herter Norton as *Stories of God* (London: Sidgwick & Jackson, 1932; New York: Norton, 1932);
Zur Einweihung der Kunsthalle am 15. Februar 1902: Festspielszene (Bremen, 1902);
Die Letzten (Berlin: Juncker, 1902);
Das tägliche Leben: Drama in zwei Akten (Munich: Langen, 1902);
Das Buch der Bilder (Berlin: Juncker, 1902; enlarged, 1906; New York: Ungar, 1943);
Worpswede: Fritz Mackensen, Otto Modersohn, Fritz Overbeck, Hans am Ende, Heinrich Vogeler (Bielefeld & Leipzig: Velhagen & Klasing, 1903);
Auguste Rodin (Berlin: Bard, 1903); translated by Jesse Lemont and Hans Trausil (New York: Sunwise Turn, 1919); translation republished as *Rodin* (London: Grey Walls Press, 1946);

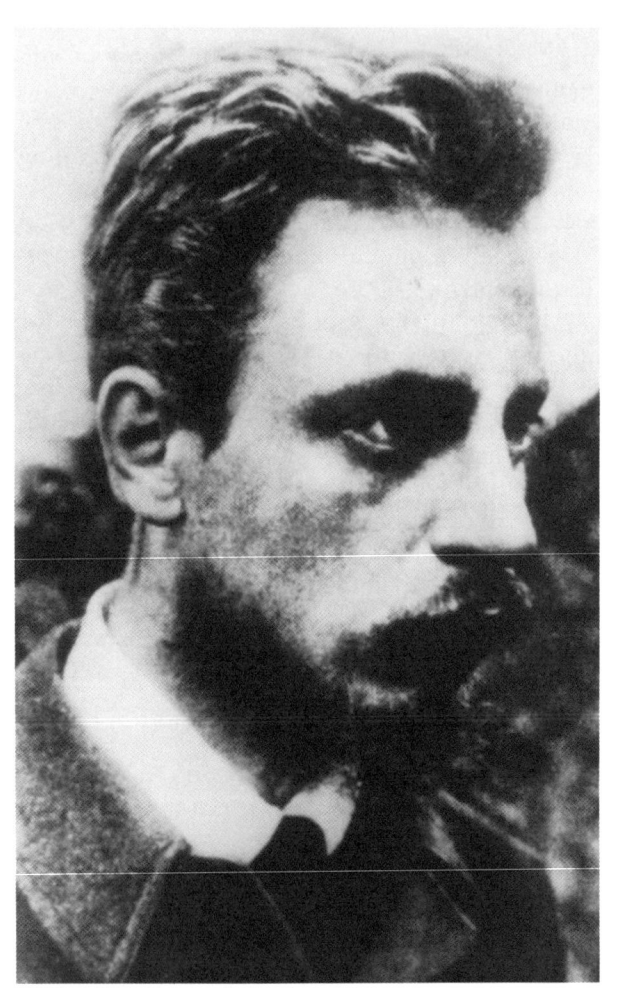

Rainer Maria Rilke

Das Stunden-Buch enthaltend die drei Bücher: Vom mönchischen Leben; Von der Pilgerschaft; Von der Armuth und vom Tode (Leipzig: Insel, 1905); translated by A. L. Peck as *The Book of Hours; Comprising the Three Books: Of the Monastic Life, Of Pilgrimage, Of Poverty and Death* (London: Hogarth Press, 1961);
Die Weise von Liebe und Tod des Cornets Christoph Rilke (Berlin: Juncker, 1906); translated by B. J. Morse as *The Story of the Love and Death of the Cornet Christopher Rilke* (Osnabrück,

1927); translated by Herter Norton as *The Tale of the Love and Death of Cornet Christopher Rilke* (New York: Norton, 1932);

Neue Gedichte, 2 volumes (Leipzig: Insel, 1907-1908); translated by J. B. Leishman as *New Poems* (London: Hogarth Press, 1964; New York: New Directions, 1964);

Requiem (Leipzig: Insel, 1909);

Die Aufzeichnungen des Malte Laurids Brigge (Leipzig: Insel, 1910); translated by John Linton as *The Notebook of Malte Laurids Brigge* (London: Hogarth Press, 1930); translation republished as *The Journal of My Other Self* (New York: Norton, 1930);

Erste Gedichte (Leipzig: Insel, 1913; New York: Ungar, 1947);

Das Marien-Leben (Leipzig: Insel, 1913); translated by R. G. L. Barrett as *The Life of the Virgin Mary* (Würzburg: Triltsch, 1921); translated by C. F. MacIntyre as *The Life of the Virgin Mary* (Berkeley & Los Angeles: University of California Press, 1947); translated by Stephen Spender as *The Life of the Virgin Mary* (London: Vision Press, 1951; New York: Philosophical Library, 1951);

Poems, translated by Lemont (New York: Wright, 1918);

Aus der Frühzeit Rainer Maria Rilkes: Vers, Prosa, Drama (1894-1899), edited by Fritz Adolf Hünich (Leipzig: Bibliophilenabend, 1921);

Mitsou: Quarante images par Baltusz (Erlenbach-Zurich & Leipzig: Rotapfel, 1921);

Puppen (Munich: Hyperion, 1921);

Die Sonette an Orpheus: Geschrieben als ein Grab-Mal für Wera Ouckama Knoop (Leipzig: Insel, 1923; New York: Ungar, 1945); translated by Leishman as *Sonnets to Orpheus, Written as a Monument for Wera Ouckama Knoop* (London: Hogarth Press, 1936); translated by Norton as *Sonnets to Orpheus* (New York: Norton, 1942);

Duineser Elegien (Leipzig: Insel, 1923; New York: Ungar, 1944); translated by V. Sackville-West and Edward Sackville-West as *Duineser Elegien: Elegies from the Castle of Duino* (London: Hogarth Press, 1931); translated by Leishman and Spender as *Duino Elegies* (New York: Norton, 1939; London: Hogarth Press, 1939);

Vergers suivi des Quatrains Valaisans (Paris: Éditions de la Nouvelle Revue Française, 1926); translated by Alfred Poulin as *Orchards* (Port Townsend, Wash.: Graywolf Press, 1982);

Les Fenêtres: Dix poèmes (Paris: Officina Sanctandreana, 1927); translated by Poulin as "The Windows" in *The Roses and the Windows* (Port Townsend, Wash.: Graywolf Press, 1979);

Les Roses (Bussum: Stols, 1927); translated by Poulin as "The Roses" in *The Roses and the Windows* (Port Townsend, Wash.: Graywolf Press, 1979);

Gesammelte Werke, 6 volumes (Leipzig: Insel, 1927);

Erzählungen und Skizzen aus der Frühzeit (Leipzig: Insel, 1928);

Ewald Tragy: Erzählung (Munich: Heller, 1929; New York: Johannespresse, 1944); translated by Lola Gruenthal as *Ewald Tragy* (London: Vision, 1958; New York: Twayne, 1958);

Verse und Prosa aus dem Nachlaß (Leipzig: Gesellschaft der Freunde der Deutschen Bücherei, 1929);

Gesammelte Gedichte, 4 volumes (Leipzig: Insel, 1930-1933);

Über den jungen Dichter (Hamburg, 1931);

Gedichte, edited by Katharina Kippenberg (Leipzig: Insel, 1931; New York: Ungar, 1947);

Rainer Maria Rilke auf Capri: Gespräche, edited by Leopold von Schlözer (Dresden: Jess, 1931);

Späte Gedichte (Leipzig: Insel, 1934);

Bücher, Theater, Kunst, edited by Richard von Mises (Vienna: Jahoda & Siegel, 1934);

Der ausgewählten Gedichte anderer Teil, edited by Kippenberg (Leipzig: Insel, 1935);

Ausgewählte Werke, edited by Ruth Sieber-Rilke, Carl Sieber, and Ernst Zinn, 2 volumes (Leipzig: Insel, 1938);

Translations from the Poetry of Rainer Maria Rilke, translated by Herter Norton (New York: Norton, 1938);

Fifty Selected Poems with English Translations, translated by C. F. MacIntyre (Berkeley: University of California Press, 1940);

Selected Poems, translated by Leishman (London: Hogarth Press, 1941);

Tagebücher aus der Frühzeit, edited by Sieber-Rilke and Sieber (Leipzig: Insel, 1942);

Briefe, Verse und Prosa aus dem Jahre 1896, edited by Mises, 2 volumes (New York: Johannespresse, 1946);

Thirty-one Poems, translated by Ludwig Lewisohn (New York: Ackerman, 1946);

Freundschaft mit Rainer Maria Rilke: Begegnungen, Gespräche, Briefe und Aufzeichnungen mitgeteilt durch Elga Maria Nevar (Bümpliz: Züst, 1946);

Five Prose Pieces, translated by Carl Niemeyer (Cummington, Mass.: Cummington Press, 1947);

Gedichte, edited by Hermann Kunisch (Göttingen: Vandenhoeck & Ruprecht, 1947);

Gedichte in französischer Sprache, edited by Thankmar von Münchhausen (Wiesbaden: Insel, 1949);

Aus Rainer Maria Rilkes Nachlaß, 4 volumes (Wiesbaden: Insel, 1950); volume 1, *Aus dem Nachlaß des Grafen C. W.,* translated by Leishman as *From the Remains of Count C. W.* (London: Hogarth Press, 1952);

Werke: Auswahl in zwei Bänden (Leipzig: Insel, 1953);

Gedichte 1906-1926: Sammlung der verstreuten und nachgelassenen Gedichte aus den mittleren und späteren Jahren, edited by Zinn (Wiesbaden: Insel, 1953); translated, with additions, by Leishman as *Poems 1906 to 1926* (Norfolk, Conn.: Laughlin, 1957; London: Hogarth Press, 1957);

Selected Works, translated by G. Craig Houston and Leishman, 2 volumes (London: Hogarth Press, 1954; New York: New Directions, 1960);

Sämtliche Werke, edited by Zinn, 6 volumes (Wiesbaden & Frankfurt am Main: Insel, 1955-1966);

Angel Songs/Engellieder, translated by Rhoda Coghill (Dublin: Dolmen Press, 1958);

Die Turnstunde und andere Novellen, edited by Fritz Fröhling (Freiburg im Breisgau: Hyperion, 1959);

Poems, edited by G. W. McKay (London: Oxford University Press, 1965);

Werke in drei Bänden, 3 volumes (Frankfurt am Main: Insel, 1966);

Gedichte: Eine Auswahl (Stuttgart: Reclam, 1966);

Visions of Christ: A Posthumous Cycle of Poems, translated by Aaron Kramer, edited by Siegfried Mandel (Boulder: University of Colorado Press, 1967);

Das Testament, edited by Zinn (Frankfurt am Main: Insel, 1975);

Holding Out: Poems, translated by Rika Lesser (Omaha, Neb.: Abbatoir Editions, 1975);

Possibility of Being: A Selection of Poems, translated by Leishman (New York: New Directions, 1977);

Werke: In 3 Bänden, edited by Horst Nalewski, 3 volumes (Leipzig: Insel, 1978);

Nine Plays, translated by Klaus Phillips and John Locke (New York: Ungar, 1979);

I Am Too Alone in the World: Ten Poems, translated by Robert Bly (New York: Silver Hands Press, 1980);

Selected Poems of Rainer Maria Rilke, translated by Bly (New York: Harper & Row, 1981);

Requiem for a Woman, and Selected Lyric Poems, translated by Andy Gaus (Putney, Vt.: Threshold Books, 1981);

An Unofficial Rilke: Poems 1912-1926, edited and translated by Michael Hamburger (London: Anvil Press, 1981);

Selected Poetry, edited and translated by Stephen Mitchell (New York: Random House, 1982);

Selected Poems, translated by A. E. Flemming (St. Petersburg, Fla.: Golden Smith, 1983);

The Unknown Rilke: Selected Poems, translated by Franz Wright (Oberlin, Ohio: Oberlin College, 1983);

Between Roots: Selected Poems, translated by Rika Lesser (Princeton: Princeton University Press, 1986).

TRANSLATIONS: Elizabeth Barrett Browning, *Sonette nach dem Portugiesischen* (Leipzig: Insel, 1908);

Maurice de Guérin, *Der Kentaur* (Leipzig: Insel, 1911);

Die Liebe der Magdalena: Ein französischer Sermon, gezogen durch den Abbé Joseph Bonnet aus dem Ms. Q I 14 der Kaiserlichen Bibliothek zu St. Petersburg (Leipzig: Insel, 1912);

Marianna Alcoforado, *Portugiesische Briefe* (Leipzig: Insel, 1913);

André Gide, *Die Rückkehr des verlorenen Sohnes* (Leipzig: Insel, 1914);

Die vierundzwanzig Sonette der Louise Labé, Lyoneserin, 1555 (Leipzig: Insel, 1918);

Paul Valéry, *Gedichte* (Leipzig: Insel, 1925);

Valéry, *Eupalinos oder Über die Architektur* (Leipzig: Insel, 1927);

Übertragungen (Leipzig: Insel, 1927);

Dichtungen des Michelangelo (Leipzig: Insel, 1936);

Gedichte aus fremden Sprachen (New York: Ungar, 1947);

Maurice Maeterlinck, *Die sieben Jungfrauen von Orlamünde* (Liege: Editions Dynamo, 1967).

PERIODICAL PUBLICATIONS: "Die goldene Kiste," *Unterhaltungs-Blatt der Nürnberger Stadt-Zeitung,* 2 February 1895, pp. 19-20;

"Eine Tote," *Deutsches Abendblatt* (Prague), 22-24 January 1896;

"Ihr Opfer," *Sommer-Beilage der "Politik"* (Prague) (28 June 1896);

"Der Apostel," *Die Musen*, 4 (1896): 24-28;

"Heiliger Frühling: Skizze," *Jugend*, 2, no. 19 (1897): 303-306;

"Leise Begleitung," *Das neue Jahrhundert*, 1, no. 4 (1898): 119-123;

"Masken," *Ver sacrum*, 1, no. 4 (1898): 12-13;

"Teufelsspuk," *Simplicissimus*, 3, no. 50 (1899): 395;

"Das Lachen des Pán Mráz," *Simplicissimus*, 4, no. 22 (1899): 170;

"Wladimir, der Wolkenmaler," *Revue franco-allemande*, 1 (1899): 378-380;

"Die Turnstunde," *Die Zukunft*, 10, no. 18 (1902): 211-214;

"Der Totengräber," *Österreichisches Novellenbuch*, 2 (1903): 59-81.

Rainer Maria Rilke is one of the major poets of twentieth-century literature. In the collections with which his early verse culminates, *Das Buch der Bilder* (The Book of Pictures, 1902; revised and augmented, 1906) and *Das Stunden-Buch* (1905; translated as *The Book of Hours*, 1961), he appears as a creator or discoverer of legends—his own and history's—and, particularly in the latter work, as a special brand of mystic. With the poems of his middle years, *Neue Gedichte* (1907-1908; translated as *New Poems*, 1964), he is an expert instructor in the art of "seeing," as well as a guide through Europe's cultural sites just before the onslaught of general war and, subsequently, mass tourism. Because of statements in *Duineser Elegien* (1923; translated as *Elegies from the Castle of Duino*, 1931) and *Die Sonette an Orpheus* (1923; translated as *Sonnets to Orpheus*, 1936) on the limitations and possibilities of the human condition, he has become something of a teacher and consoler to readers aware of the fragility and the potential of man. Long the prey of cultists and often obscure exegetes and regarded as the bearer of a "message" or "messages," he has more recently been seen as a brilliant verse tactician whose visions may be more original in their manner of perception than in their philosophical core. His novel *Die Aufzeichnungen des Malte Laurids Brigge* (1910; translated as *The Notebook of Malte Laurids Brigge*, 1930) was initially received as a belated product of European decadence or as an autobiographical document (neither opinion is wholly off the mark); later it was identified as a striking example of the "crisis of subjectivity and its influences on the traditional possibilities of narration," in Judith Ryan's formulation. Of all Rilke's works, the large body of stories he wrote has received the least attention; as a mature artist he himself grew condescending when he occasionally mentioned them in his letters—in striking contrast to *Die Aufzeichnungen des Malte Laurids Brigge*, which he continued to praise and explicate until his death. These tales and sketches, some seventy of them, fall into the beginning of his career, before the changes that took place in his life and production in the years from 1902 to 1905.

Rilke's attitudes toward Prague, where he was born René Karl Wilhelm Johann Josef Maria Rilke in 1875, were mixed, as were those toward his parents. His father, Josef, was a former warrant officer in the Austrian army who at the time of Rilke's birth was a railroad official—a job perhaps owed to the influence of Josef's well-to-do elder brother, Jaroslav. His mother, Sophie (Phia) Entz Rilke, homely and socially ambitious, was the daughter of a perfume manufacturer. Rilke was their only child; a daughter, born before him, had survived only a few days. The parents were divorced before Rilke's childhood was past. The epistolary evidence indicates that Rilke was devoted to his father, who was simple, gregarious, and a lady's man, but saw rather little of him, and that he nearly detested his mother; yet it was the latter who encouraged his literary ambitions. The complexity of his feelings for his mother may be indicated in his early verse and stories by the appearance of a dream mother, lovely and even desirable; his reaction to Phia's bigoted Roman Catholicism, the faith in which he was reared, is reflected both in the ambiguous allusions to a Roman Catholic world in his early verse and *Das Marien-Leben* (1913; translated as *The Life of the Virgin Mary*, 1921) and in his much-proclaimed dislike of Christianity. Rilke's snobbery, which led him to cling obstinately to a family saga of age-old nobility, was encouraged by the genealogical researches of his uncle Jaroslav and by his mother's pretensions and prejudices; Phia Rilke was distinguished by her sense of extraordinary refinement and by her contempt for Jews and Czech speakers. Both the Rilkes and the Entzes were "Prague Germans," aware that they were up against an ever more aggressive Slavic majority in a city where German speakers were confronted, as the century wore on, by the rapid weakening of their social and political position.

At ten, after an elementary education, much interrupted by real or fancied illness, with the Piarist Brothers, Rilke was sent to the military school at Sankt Pölten in Lower Austria; save for summer vacations he remained there until 1890, when he was transferred to the military upper school at Mährisch-Weißkirchen in Moravia. The abrupt change from the cosseted existence at home to regimented boarding-school life cannot have been pleasant, even though his teachers encouraged him to read his poems aloud to his fellow students. As a young man Rilke planned to free himself from "jenes böse und bange Jahrfünf" (that evil and frightened half-decade) by writing a military-school novel, and in a letter of 1920 he made an extremely harsh reply to Major-General von Sedlakowitz, his German teacher at Sankt Pölten, who had written to congratulate him on his fame: "Als ich in besonneneren Jahren ... Dostojewskis Memoiren aus einem Toten-Hause zuerst in die Hände bekam, da wollte es mir scheinen, daß ich in alle Schrecknisse und Verzweifelungen des Bagno seit meinem zehnten Jahre eingelassen gewesen sei" (When, in years of greater reflection ... I first got hold of Dostoyevski's *Memoirs from the House of the Dead*, it seemed to me that I had been exposed to all the terrors and despairs of the prison camp from my tenth year on). After not quite a full year at the second school, from which he emerged, he told Sedlakowitz, "ein Erschöpfter, körperlich und geistig Mißbrauchter" (exhausted, abused in body and soul), he was discharged for reasons of health and went back to Prague—only to show off by wearing his cadet's uniform and bragging about a future return to the colors. His uncle Jaroslav then sent him to a commercial academy at Linz, an experience about which he later wrote that investigations were pointless, since he had not been himself at the time. Recent research indicates that he was a would-be bon vivant who persuaded a children's nurse to run away with him to a hotel in Vienna.

In 1892 Jaroslav agreed to finance private instruction leading to the qualifying examination at Prague's German Charles-Ferdinand University, so that one day Rilke could take over his uncle's law firm. Not that Jaroslav was at all confident about the boy's future: "Renés Phantasie ist ein Erbteil seiner Mutter und durch ihren Einfluß, von Hause aus krankhaft angeregt, durch unsystematisches Lesen allerhand Bücher überheizt—[ist] seine Eitelkeit durch vorzeitiges Lob erregt" (René's imagination is an inheritance from his mother, abnormally excited through her influence from the very beginning, overheated by the unsystematic reading of all sorts of books—his vanity has been aroused by premature praise). Tutorial instruction was congenial to Rilke's temperament; by 1895 he was ready to matriculate. He was already avidly seeking an audience—his unbearably sentimental first book, *Leben und Lieder* (Life and Songs), had come out in 1894, dedicated to Valerie David-Rhonfeld, the niece of the Czech poet Julius Zeyer (Valerie had financed the book's publication). The twenty-one artificially simple poems of *Wegwarten* (Wild Chicory) appeared in January 1896. At the end of the summer of 1896 he moved to Munich, ostensibly for art history studies but with an eye to the cultural and publishing opportunities afforded by the Bavarian capital, which was then Berlin's equal as an artistic center. By this time he had considerably better proof of his lyric talent to display: *Larenopfer* (Offering to the Lares, 1896), with its tributes to Prague, was followed by *Traumgekrönt* (Crowned with Dreams, 1897), containing some turgid but striking erotic poems, and he was already a busy contributor to popular journals.

Some of Rilke's Munich acquaintanceships were plainly meant to further his career—for example, that with the dramatist Max Halbe. (Rilke's naturalistic drama *Im Frühfrost* [1897; translated as *Early Frost* in *Nine Plays*, 1979] was produced in Prague in July 1897 with the young Max Reinhardt in the role of the weak father.) Others were more important: the novelist Jakob Wassermann introduced him to the works of the Danish author who became his vade mecum, Jens Peter Jacobsen. Another young friend, Nathan Sulzberger from New York, provided him with a second major object of cultural devotion: in March 1897, at Sulzberger's invitation, he visited Venice for the first time. He spent an April vacation on Lake Constance with "the mad countess," Franziska zu Reventlow, who was pregnant with another man's child; and in May 1897 he met Lou Andreas-Salomé, fifteen years his senior, the author and former friend of Nietzsche, and the wife (in name only, it would seem) of the Iranian scholar Friedrich Carl Andreas. The summer Lou and Rilke spent at Wolfratshausen in the Bavarian Alps wrought remarkable changes in him: he altered his name from René to Rainer, his handwriting became firmer and clearer, and he gathered his passionate love poetry to Lou into the manuscript collection "Dir zur Feier" (In Celebration of You), which, at her request, he did not publish. (The title, transmuted into *Mir zur Feier* [In Celebration of Me], was used for a book of

Rilke (left) and Lou Andreas-Salomé (bottom, right) at the home of the poet Spiridon Drozhzhin in Novinki on their second trip to Russia in 1900

verse in 1899.) Some of these poems, estimated to have been about one hundred in number, were subsumed into published collections; others survived only in manuscript; others were destroyed. How long Lou and Rainer remained lovers is not known, but Rilke followed her and her husband to Berlin in the autumn of 1897.

The Prussian capital remained Rilke's home until the new century. His stay there was interrupted by trips that were to be of major importance for his poetic development: a springtime journey to Italy in 1898 (his verse play *Die weiße Fürstin* [published in *Mir zur Feier;* translated as *The White Princess* in *Nine Plays,* 1979] grew out of a stay at Viareggio); an excursion to Russia from April to June 1899 in the company of the Andreases; and a second and much more carefully prepared Russian trip from May to August 1900, again with Lou but without her husband. Rilke—who had learned Russian easily and quickly on the basis of his school training in Czech—visited the peasant poet Spiridon Drozhzhin and had an uncomfortable interview with Leo Tolstoy at his estate, Yasnaya Polyana. The Russian experience under the tutelage of Lou, a native of Saint Petersburg, provided him with new poetic material: following a fad of the time, he professed a mystic love for the great land in the east; he read its literature carefully and used Russian themes in the poems in *Das Buch der Bilder* and *Das Stunden-Buch,* in his tales, and in *Die Aufzeichnungen des Malte Laurids Brigge.* During a late summer stay with the artist Heinrich Vogeler in the artists' colony at Worpswede, near Bremen, after his return from Russia, he wore a Russian peasant's blouse and a large Greek cross. In Worpswede, thus attired, he met the painter and sculptress Paula Becker and the sculptress Clara Westhoff. Rejected by Paula, he turned his affection to her statuesque friend. On 28 April 1901 Rilke and Clara were married.

The affair with Lou had been broken off, but their years together had been enormously productive for Rilke. Some of the poems in *Advent* (1898) are from the Wolfratshausen summer; Rilke came to regard *Mir zur Feier* as the first of his "admissible" books; his career as a dramatist had been encouraged by the publication of *Ohne Gegenwart* (1898; translated as *Not Present* in *Nine Plays,* 1979), with its Maeterlinckian suggestions of ineffable fears, but it concluded disastrously with *Das tägliche Leben* (1902; translated as *Everyday Life* in *Nine Plays,* 1979), a play written in 1900 about a painter caught between two loves. Produced at the Residenz Theater in Berlin in December 1901, it was greeted with laughter: Rilke resolved never to try the stage again.

The writing of stories had occupied much of Rilke's time: a first collection, *Am Leben hin* (Along Life's Course), had appeared in 1898. The book contains eleven tales, six of which can be identified as having been finished at Wolfratshausen during the summer with Lou. Some of the tales suffer from the mawkishness that beset Rilke during his early years, whether he was writing poems, plays, or narratives. In "Greise" (Old Men) a little girl brings a flower to her grandfather as he sits on a park bench. Other old men watch; one of them, Pepi, spits contemptuously as his companion, Christoph, picks up some stray blossoms from the street and carries them back to the poorhouse. Yet Pepi puts a glass of water on the windowsill of their room, waiting in the darkest corner for Christoph to place the scruffy bouquet in it. In "Das Christkind" (The Christ Child) a little girl, mistreated by her stepmother, takes the money her father has slipped to her as a Christmas gift, buys some paper ornaments, and adorns a young fir tree with them; then she lies down in the forest to die, imagining that she is in her mother's lap. Here Rilke ventures into a maudlin realm long since cultivated by certain nineteenth-century masters; in fact, he identifies one of them: in Elisabeth's dying dreams, "Die Mutter [war] schön, wie die Fee im Märchen von Andersen" (The mother [was] beautiful, like the fairy in the tale of Andersen). In "Weißes Glück" (White Happiness) a tubercular girl tells her sad life story to another traveler, a man hoping for erotic adventure at a railroad station in the middle of the night. A blind girl has a beautiful voice but will live out her life unloved in "Die Stimme" (The Voice). Gypsies fight over a girl, and the stronger, Král, slays the boyish flute player in "Kismet."

With such stories, save for his awareness of language and a certain psychological refinement, Rilke does not rise much above the level of, say, another popular writer from Prague, Ossip Schubin (pseudonym of Aloisia Kirschner, 1854-1934). Yet there are flashes of a brilliant satiric gift in the depiction of a moribund Prague-German family in "Das Familienfest" (The Family Festival) and "Sterbetag" (Death Day), and evidence of a keen insight into human relations in "Das Geheimnis" (The Secret), about the romantic dreams of two old maids, and "Die Flucht" (The Flight), about a schoolboy's plans for an escapade with a young girl and his failure—not hers—to carry through with them. In "Alle in Einer" (All in One Woman) Rilke shows a penchant for the shocking and the horrible which he shared with other Prague writers such as Gustav Meyrink and Paul Leppin: tormented by passion, a lame woodcarver makes one image after another of the same girl, until he ends by hacking at his own hands. The concluding story, "Einig" (United), has autobiographical tones: a son with artistic ambitions has returned home ill to his pious mother. It is spoiled by a contrived happy ending—each learns that the other has been sending money to the family's estranged father—but it offers a nice specimen for students of the Ibsen craze in Germany around the turn of the century: like Oswald in Henrik Ibsen's *Ghosts* (1881), Gerhard says that he is a "wurmfaule Frucht" (worm-eaten fruit), recalling Oswald's famous description of himself as "*vermoulu*"), and claims that his illness has been bestowed upon him by his father.

Zwei Prager Geschichten (Two Prague Stories, 1899) was composed at Berlin-Schmargendorf in 1897-1898. The foreword says: "Dieses Buch ist lauter Vergangenheit. Heimat und Kindheit—beide längst fern—sind sein Hintergrund" (This book is nothing but the past. Homeland and childhood—both far removed, long since—are its background). The two lengthy stories, however, have little to do with the Prague Rilke had known; rather, they take place in Czech milieus and are expressions of Rilke's brief flaring-up of interest in Czech nationalism (other evidence is to be found in *Larenopfer*). No doubt Rilke was also aware of the interest of German publishers and their public in Prague's semi-exotic world: Karl Hans Strobl (1877-1946), for example, launched his long career as a popular author by writing about the city and the tensions between its language groups. "König Bohusch" (King Bohusch) uses Prague's Czech-speaking artistic circles as a contrasting background for two outsiders who are far more energetic and tormented than the ineffectual aesthetes, actors, and dandies of the city's cafés: the student Rezek, detesting both German speakers and the Austrian government, organizes a terrorist band; Bohusch, a hunchback, loves his "Mütterchen" (little mother), Prague, and dreams of an affair with the prostitute Frantischka. Familiar with the city's nooks and crannies, the self-important Bohusch shows Rezek a hiding place for the latter's group; simultaneously, he falls into fantasies of his own power. The police capture all the plotters save Rezek, who kills the poor, addled Bohusch because he suspects him of betraying the gang to the authorities. In fact, it was Frantischka who did so; her high-minded sister, Carla, is a member of Rezek's group. Based on actual events in the Prague of Rilke's youth, the story is an attempt to provide a dispassionate view of what, for Rilke, was an alien world, however close at hand.

More loosely constructed, "Die Geschwister" (The Siblings) looks sympathetically at a Czech family that has moved to the capital from the countryside. The son, Zdenko, is at the university; the mother does washing for the arrogant German speakers, Colonel and Mrs. Meering von Meerhelm, the depiction of whom may be the most convincing part of the story. Zdenko takes up with the radical circles around Rezek, who is carried over from "König Bohusch," but dies of illness before he can be forced to participate in their activities. The daughter, Louisa, has aroused the interest of Rezek but falls in love with Ernst Land, a young Bohemian-German who rents the late Zdenko's room and stays on after the death of Louisa's mother. By the end it is plain that the Czech and the German, the representatives of two hostile camps, will marry. The simple plot is drawn out by allusions to Bohemia's history, especially to the legends surrounding Julius Caesar, the vicious illegitimate son of Rudolf II who was said to have driven a girl to her death as he attempted to rape her during a masked ball at Krummau Castle. Rilke describes the Daliborka, the "hunger tower" on the Hradčany, later to serve as the setting for the love and conspiratorial scenes in Gustav Meyrink's *Walpurgisnacht* (1917). These tidbits are not just window dressing but are used by Rilke in an attempt at psychological portraiture. Louisa mingles the tale of Julius Caesar with her impressions of Rezek: "Und sie konnte ihm nicht wehren, daß er auch in ihre Träume wuchs und endlich eines wurde mit dem dunklen Prinzen des alten Maskentraumes und nun für sie nicht mehr Rezek sondern Julius Cäsar hieß" (And she could not prevent him from entering into her dreams and finally becoming one with the dark prince of the old dream of the masked ball, and now for her he was no longer Rezek but Julius Caesar). When Zdenko, Rezek, and Louisa visit the Daliborka, the obsessive thought returns, and she imagines herself naked, fleeing before the advances of Julius Caesar. Her rescue from these fantasies by the calm presence of Land may indicate that Rilke naively thought his Czech compatriots could be saved from the destructive allure of a Rezek by good-natured German liberalism.

Plainly, Rilke is fascinated by sexuality; but he often shies away from addressing it directly. (One of the most linguistically tortuous and emotionally tormented poems in the whole of his work is "Das Bett" [The Bed] in *Neue Gedichte*.) It is surprising that in the title tale of his third story collection, *Die Letzten* (The Last, 1902), written in 1898-1899 under Lou's aegis, he can be as frank as he is in discussing a taboo theme: mother-son incest. (*Die Letzten* was the first of Rilke's books to be published by the Dane Axel Juncker, who shared, Rilke believed, his own interest in the physical make-up of books: a "quiet" text merited "quiet" and elegant printing and binding.) The first story, "Im Gespräch" (In Conversation), records the talk of a group of artists in the salon of the Princess Helena Pavlovna at Venice. The speakers each have roles to play: the German painter is clumsy and loud, the gentleman from Vienna (a city Rilke, from provincial Prague, especially disliked) speaks with empty elegance, the Frenchman Count Saint-Quentin is still and polite, and the Pole Kasimir is the mouthpiece for Rilke's theories of artistic creation: "'Kunst ist Kindheit nämlich. Kunst heißt, nicht wissen, daß die Welt schon *ist,* und eine machen. Nicht zerstören, was man vorfindet, sondern einfach nichts Fertiges finden'" ("Art is childhood, you see. Art means not knowing that the world already *is*, and making [one]. Not destroying what one finds but rather simply not finding something finished"). Turning to the princess, Kasimir quotes her: "'Man muß, sagen Sie, dort muß man anfangen, wo Gott abließ, wo er müde wurde'" ("One must, you say, one must begin there where God left off, where He became tired"). At the end, having almost found a kindred soul, the Pole leaves, "wie einer der nicht wiederkommen wird an einen lieben Ort" (like someone who will not return to a beloved place).

A sensitive man is the central figure in the next story, "Der Liebende" (The Lover); the fragile Ernst Bang (his last name may allude to the adjective *bang* [anxious, afraid] or the Danish writer Herman Bang, whose works Rilke deeply admired) talks with his friend, the vigorous Hermann Holzer–like Král in "Kismet," Holzer shuts out the light with his "seinem schwarzen Rücken" (black silhouette; in Král's case it was "breite schwere Schultern" [broad, heavy shoulders]).

Bang is in love with Helene, whom Holzer is going to marry; after many pauses (Rilke was captivated by Maeterlinck's use of silences onstage), Bang summons the courage to tell Holzer that the latter will destroy Helene with his clumsy affection: " 'Nimm mir's nicht übel, Hermann, aber ... du ... zerbrichst ... sie.... ' Pause" ("Don't take it amiss, Hermann, but ... you ... will shatter her...." Pause). The difficult conversation drifts along; affable and even respectful, Holzer asks what Bang thinks he should do. " 'Sprich, die ganze Kultur steht hinter dir, bedenke' " ("Speak up—remember, the whole culture stands behind you"). The struggle may be not so much between two lovers of the same woman as between the subtle heir to an ancient tradition and the bluff bearer of contemporary strength: Holzer is a peasant's son and has his father's qualities—"Sowas Grades, Eichenes" (something straightforward, oaken). The juxtaposition of the two types is a common one in the fin de siècle, with its sense of the ending of an old Europe and the beginning of a less nuanced world. Helene enters, learns of the conversation, and weeps; taking her on his lap, Holzer tries to console her as she turns pale. The melodrama is obvious: she will stay with Holzer, but both she and Ernst know how sad her fate will be. Rilke's sympathy, however, is not wholly on the side of Bang and Helene; regarding himself as the spokesman of beleaguered refinement, he still looks with some admiration and envy at what is young and fresh and vigorous.

As Rezek turns up both in "König Bohusch" and "Die Geschwister," so an apparent relative of Hermann Holzer appears as the third person in the title story, "Die Letzten." Marie Holzer's grandfather was a peasant; more self-aware than Hermann, she has a sense of being "jünger in der Kultur" (younger in culture) than the members of the impoverished noble family to which she has become attached. She is engaged to Harald Malcorn, whom she met at a gathering of social reformers where he was the impassioned speaker. Now she and Harald's mother await his return from another speaking engagement amid the Malcorns' "Dinge" (things—a word to which Rilke attaches much significance), the great age of which Marie respects and yet cannot quite comprehend. Almost maternally concerned for little Frau Malcorn's well-being, Marie nonetheless senses a rival in the widow, and their competition for Harald comes to the surface in a long stichomythia. Returning home exhausted and ill, Harald decides to abandon his agitator's calling: he breaks with Marie and places himself in his mother's care.

In the story's second part the convalescent Harald and his mother talk of going to an uncle's estate, Skal; but the plan is dropped, in part because of a family curse: the death of a family member has always been presaged by the appearance of a "dame blanche," Frau Walpurga, at the castles the family once owned, and most frequently at Skal. Harald tells his mother about his misty notions of becoming an artist; after recalling circumstances that point to Frau Malcorn's having had a lover long ago and to his own role as a childish and unwitting surrogate for the lover, and after recalling his reaction to his father (" 'Er hatte einen dichten weißen Bart. Er war alt' " ["He had a heavy white beard. He was old"]), Harald entices his mother into adorning herself like a bride: together they will celebrate a festival of beauty. Frau Malcorn reappears in a white dress, and Harald collapses; hitherto the room has been illuminated only by moonlight, but now someone lights a light, and the reader sees a terrifying tableau: "Harald sitzt entstellt in den Kissen, den Kopf noch vorgestreckt, mit herabhängenden Händen. Und vor ihm steht Frau Malcorn, welk, in Atlas, mit Handschuhen. Und sie sehen sich mit fremdem Entsetzen in die toten Augen" (Harald sits distorted in his cushions, his head still stretched forward, with his hands hanging down. And Frau Malcorn stands before him, withered, in satin, with her gloves. And they gaze into one another's dead eyes with strange horror).

"Die Letzten" is a grotesque and fascinating melange of themes: the "last of the line," unable to create the art that might have been born of his sensitivity; the mother who is led into a fatal attempt to recover her lost youth; the well-meaning outsider, "healthier" than the inhabitants of the old world to which she is drawn. The literary echoes are many: Ibsen's *Ghosts*, Maeterlinck (the numerous pauses, the subtle anxiety), Jacobsen (Frau Malcorn's *nom d'amour* is Edel, reminiscent of Edele Lyhne, the aunt of whom the adolescent Niels Lyhne becomes enamored in the novel *Niels Lyhne* [1880; translated, 1919]), the Gothic tale. What were Rilke's intentions with the story, which comes dangerously close to unintentional comedy with its "white lady" and its family curse? Did he mean to write a *conte cruel* to vie with the most exaggerated specimens of contemporary decadent literature? The decadent apparatus is plainly on display: the ancient family, incestuous eroticism, a shocking close. Did he intend to plumb the depths of an erotic mother-son relationship of whose existence he was aware in his own case (the psychiatrist Erich Simenauer thinks so) and then mix these personal problems with his theories on the creation of art? Does the story (as Egon Schwarz believes) show the young Rilke's swerve away from the social concerns with which he had flirted to the aesthetic vision of life he subsequently and adamantly maintained? "Die Letzten" is one of Rilke's most tantalizing works, a bizarre conclusion to his early fiction.

In the years between the start of his career in Prague and his removal from Berlin-Schmargendorf and the ambience of Lou in February 1901, Rilke wrote some thirty other tales and sketches: some of these appeared in journals; others were never printed during his lifetime. Exaggerated and often banal effects are common: in a painful specimen of naturalism, "Die Näherin" (The Seamstress, first published in volume 4 of Rilke's *Sämtliche Werke* [Collected Works] in 1961), the narrator is seduced by a lonely and physically unattractive woman; in the lachrymose "Die goldene Kiste" (The Golden Chest, 1895) little Willy admires a golden chest in an undertaker's window, and his dying words express his desire to be laid to rest in it; a beautiful girl is the victim of brain damage in "Eine Tote" (A Dead Girl, 1896); a wife kills herself so that her husband can devote himself fully to his art in "Ihr Opfer" (Her Sacrifice, 1896); a tubercular girl is used and then forgotten, after her death, by a robust male in "Heiliger Frühling" (Holy Spring, 1897); the young bride of a jovial and hearty older man falls in love with her husband's willowy and melancholy son in "Das Lachen des Pán Mráz (The Laughter of Pán Mráz, 1899); the story of the masked ball at Krummau Castle from "Die Geschwister" is retold in "Masken" (Masks, 1898); a mother loves her son too well in "Leise Begleitung" (Soft Accompaniment, 1898) and vicariously experiences his disappointment in a love affair with a girl of his own age as she sits beside her unfeeling husband. There are stunted figures: the emotionally frigid man searching for an "event" in "Das Ereignis" (The Event, published in *Todtentänze* [Dances of Death, 1896]); the doctrinaire Nietzschean in "Der Apostel" (The Apostle, 1896); the dreamy would-be artist in "Wladimir, der Wolkenmaler" (Wladimir the Cloud-Painter, 1899)–in "Die Letzten," Harald planned to paint clouds, a subject quickly transmuted into his mother, clad in her white dress. Attempts are made at comedy: in "Teufelsspuk" (Devilment, 1899) the new owners of the estate of Gross-Rohozec are terrified by what they think is the castle ghost, but it is merely the former owner, a nobleman, who–slightly intoxicated–has groped his way back to his family's previous possessions. The story might seem to have anti-Semitic overtones, since the buyers of the castle are Jewish and Rilke implies that they are somehow ennobled by their midnight contact with nobility. "Teufelsspuk" was printed in the Munich journal *Simplicissimus* and intended for inclusion in a new volume of novellas Rilke outlined for the publisher Bonz in the summer of 1899; nothing came of the project.

Some of Rilke's best tales are autobiographical. One of the stories unpublished during his lifetime is "Pierre Dumont" (first published in Carl Sieber's biography *René Rilke*, 1932), about a boy parting from his mother at the military school's gate. Another is *Ewald Tragy* (written, 1898; published, 1929; translated, 1958), a long story in two parts about a watershed in the life of a young man. The first half consists of the cruel yet somehow affectionate depiction of his last dinner with the members of his Prague family (made up mainly of desiccated oldsters and eccentrics) and his difficult relation with his father, the bestower of uncomprehending love; in the second, Ewald moves away to the loneliness and freedom of Munich. "Die Turnstunde" (The Exercise Hour), published in *Die Zukunft* in 1902, pays painfully accurate attention to the petty obscenities and large emotional deformations of adolescence. Little Krix tells Jerome, Rilke's alter ego, that he has beheld the body of Gruber, a boy who had died during gymnastics: " 'Ich hab ihn gesehen,' flüstert er atemlos und preßt Jeromes Arm und ein Lachen ist innen in ihm und rüttelt ihn hin und her. Er kann kaum weiter: 'Ganz nackt ist er und eingefallen und ganz lang. Und an den Fußsohlen ist er versiegelt. . . .' Und dann kichert er, spitz und kitzlich, kichert und beißt sich in den Ärmel Jeromes hinein" ("I have seen him," he whispers breathlessly and presses Jerome's arm and a laughter is within him and shakes him back and forth. He can scarcely continue: "He's all naked and collapsed and very long. And there are wax seals on the soles of his feet. . . ." And then he giggles, in a sharp, tickling way, giggles and bites into Jerome's sleeve).

"Die Turnstunde" was written only four days before Rilke essayed another descent into physical and psychological horror in "Frau Blahas Magd" (Frau Blaha's Maid); like "Die Turnstunde," it was first set down in Rilke's diary in the autumn of 1899 at Berlin-Schmargendorf, but it remained in manuscript. An early Rilke biographer, Eliza M. Butler, called it a "truly ghastly tale," while a more sympathetic commentator, Wolfgang Leppmann, has characterized it as "one of the most impressive short stories we have from his hand." Annuschka, a simple-minded country girl leading a wretched life as kitchen help in Prague, gives birth to a child, throttles it with her apron, and puts the corpse away at the bottom of her trunk. Then she buys a puppet theater she has seen in a toy-store window: "Jetzt hatte Annuschka etwas für das Alleinsein" (Now Annuschka had something for her loneliness). Neighbor children cluster around the theater; Annuschka tells them she also has a very large doll. They want to see it, but when she comes back "mit dem großen Blauen" (with the large blue thing) they become frightened and run away. Annuschka wrecks her theater, and "als die Küche schon ganz dunkel war, ging sie herum und spaltete allen Puppen die Köpfe, auch der großen blauen" (when the kitchen was quite dark, she went around and split the heads of all the puppets, and of the large blue one too). Annuschka has found refuge in an imaginary world; then, at the intrusion of reality, she destroys it. More successfully than in "King Bohusch," Rilke demonstrates what he imagines goes on in a limited or disturbed mind.

Other stories from the diary seem almost compulsively to seek after gruesome effects: the title character in "Der Grabgärtner" (The Grave-Gardener) transforms a cemetery into a garden in full bloom; he has come from the outside world to take the place of the old gravedigger, who has died. During an outbreak of the plague the townspeople, believing that the stranger has caused the epidemic, try to murder him; they succeed in slaying Gita, the mayor's daughter, whom the gravedigger loves. He kills the leader of the mob and goes off into the night, "Man weiß nicht, wohin" (One knows not whither). The story's emphasis is not on the beauty and order the gravedigger has brought to the realm of death, but on mass hysteria and mass horror; Rilke was probably trying to emulate Jacobsen's story "Pesten i Bergamo" (The Plague in Bergamo, 1881; translated as "Death in Bergamo," 1971). Philippe Jullian has called attention to the popularity in late-nineteenth-century art of what may be called necrophiliac scenes, with a superabundance of beautiful dead or dying bodies, as in Jean Delville's *Les Trésors de Sathan* (The Treasures of Satan, 1895) and Aristide Sartorio's *Diana d'Efeso e gli schiavi* (Diana of Ephesus and the Slaves, 1899): "eroticism and death have been blended with great skill." In the Rilke story, revised and published as "Der Totengräber" (The Gravedigger) in *Österreichisches Novellenbuch* (1903), the same public taste is fully met: "Der Wagen ist über und über mit Leichen beladen. Und der rote Pippo hat Genossen gefunden, die ihm helfen. Und sie greifen blind und gierig hinein in den Überfluß und zerren einen heraus, der sich zu wehren scheint.... Der Fremde schafft ruhig weiter. Bis ihm der Körper eines jungen Mädchens, nackt und blutig, mit mißhandeltem Haar, vor die Füße fällt" (The wagon is laden with corpses, pile upon pile. And the red-haired Pippo has found comrades who help him. And they reach blindly and greedily into this abundance, and pull out someone who seems to fend them off.... The stranger keeps calmly at his work. Until the body of a young girl, naked and bloody, with ill-treated hair, falls at his feet).

In the same autumn of 1899–as Rilke claimed, "in einer stürmischen Herbstnacht" (in a stormy autumn night)–he composed the initial version of the work that, in his lifetime, would make his name familiar to a broad public. It was called "Aus einer Chronik–der Cornet (1664)" (From a Chronicle–the Cornet [1664]); a revision made in Sweden in 1904 became "Die Weise von Liebe und Tod des Cornets Otto Rilke" (The Lay of the Love and Death of the Cornet Otto Rilke) and was published the same year in August Sauer's Prague journal *Deutsche Arbeit*. The final version, with the hero's name changed to Christoph, was published by Juncker in 1906; in 1912 it was the introductory number in Anton Kippenberg's series of inexpensive but handsome little books, "Die Inselbücherei," and made its way into thousands of romantically inclined hearts. In twenty-six brief poems in prose (reduced from twenty-nine in the first version and twenty-eight in the second) it gives an account of the last days of a noble officer from Saxony, eighteen years old, during an Austrian campaign against the Turks in western Hungary. Rilke had found a reference to this supposed ancestor in the genealogical materials assembled by his uncle Jaroslav; when he sent the manuscript of "Aus einer Chronik–der Cornet (1664)" to Clara Westhoff, he told her

Page from the manuscript for Rilke's verse collection Das Stunden-Buch *(1905) (Wolfgang Leppmann,* Rilke, *1981)*

that it was "eine Dichtung ... die einen Vorfahren mit Glanz umgiebt. Lesen Sie sie an einem Ihrer schönen Abende im weißen Kleid" (a poetic work that surrounds a forebear with splendor. Read it, on one of your beautiful evenings, in your white dress). The boy rides over the dusty plain; makes friends with a French marquis; sits by the campfire; observes the rough life of the bivouac; is presented to the commander, Johann von Sporck (of whom a portrait had hung in the military school at Sankt Pölten); and frees a girl tied nude to a tree–she seems to laugh when her bonds are cut, and the boy is horrified: "Und er sitzt schon zu Ross/und jagt in die Nacht. Blutige Schnüre fest in der Faust" (And he is already mounted on his steed/and gallops into the night. Bloody cords held tight in his grip). The cornet writes to his mother; sees his first dead man, a peasant; senses that the enemy is near. The company comes to a castle, and the officers are feted–another of Rilke's festivals of beauty. Dressed in white silk (reminiscent of the dress uniform worn by Austrian officers in Viennese operettas), the virgin youth meets the lady of the castle, and shortly, "nackt wie ein Heiliger. Hell und schlank" (naked as a saint. Bright and slim), he spends a night of love with her. "Er fragt nicht: 'Dein Gemahl?' Sie fragt nicht: 'Dein Namen?'... Sie werden sich hundert neue Namen geben..." (He does not ask: "Your husband?" She does not ask: "Your name?" ... They will give one another a hundred new names ...). The Turks attack, and the troop rides out to meet them; the cornet, whose task is to bear the flag, is not present. But he appears in the nick of time, finds the banner–"auf seinen Armen trägt er die Fahne wie eine weiße, bewußtlose Frau" (he carries the flag in his arms, like a woman, white and unconscious)—and gallops into the midst of the foes; "die sechzehn runden Säbel, die auf ihn zuspringen, Strahl um Strahl, sind ein Fest./Eine lachende Wasserkunst" (the sixteen curved sabers that leap at him, beam upon beam, are a festival./A laughing fountain). The next spring, a courier brings the news of his death to his mother. That the tiny book captured a large readership is quite understandable: the impelling rhythms of its prose, the colorful settings, the theatrically simple situations, the amalgamation of eroticism and early heroic death were irresistible. That Rilke's view of war was hopelessly false, and a throwback to the worst extravagances of romanticism, is another matter.

A second book that also found a devoted audience, *Vom lieben Gott und Anderes* (Concerning Dear God and Other Matters), had also gotten under way in the busy autumn of 1899. These playfully "pious" tales were quickly delivered to the Insel publishing house, administered by Schuster & Loeffler in Berlin, and appeared just in time for the Christmas trade of 1900; a new edition, *Geschichten vom lieben Gott* (translated as *Stories of God*, 1932), came out in 1904, with a dedication to the Swedish feminist and pedagogical writer Ellen Key. The stories have held a prominent place among the "standard" items by the young Rilke, but the Rilke scholar Eudo C. Mason dismissed them as a reproduction of "much of the religious doctrine of *Das Stunden-Buch* in prose, in the form of whimsical little tales told to children by a lame cobbler." Professor Mason's statement might be refined to say that the stories reproduce in particular the message of the first part of *Das Stunden-Buch*, "Das Buch von mönchischen Leben" (The Book of Monkish Life), which Rilke also wrote in the early autumn of 1899. God is in a state of becoming, perceived by artists and repeatedly created in their works, or God is the mystery from which art emanates: "Du Dunkelheit, aus der ich stamme" (You darkness, out of which I come), as *Das Stunden-Buch* proclaims. Mason's indifference toward *Geschichten vom lieben Gott* is evidenced by his unwonted inaccuracy; the tales are told to several listeners—a neighbor lady, a visiting stranger, a priggish male schoolteacher, District Commissioner Baum, and an artistically inclined young man, as well as the lame cobbler Ewald.

Oddly, the gentle book delights in making fun of the establishment; amid the often sugary trappings and language a sense of rebellion can be detected. In the first tale, "Das Märchen von den Händen Gottes" (The Tale of the Hands of God), the Lord's hands let humankind loose from heaven before the Maker has had a chance to inspect His work; in "Der fremde Mann" (The Strange Man) God's right hand, long since out of favor with God, is cut off by Saint Paul and sent to earth in human form; in "Warum der liebe Gott will, daß es arme Leute gibt" (Why Dear God Wants There To Be Poor People) the shocked schoolteacher is informed that the poor are closest to the truth and so are like artists. (In *Das Stunden-Buch* Rilke coined the phrase that has garnered him some scorn from socially aware readers: "Denn Armuth ist ein großer Glanz aus Innen" [For poverty is a great shining from within].) The pompous Baum, with his bourgeois view of a "romantic" Venice, is told in "Eine Szene aus dem Ghetto von Venedig" (A Scene from the Venetian Ghetto) about the precarious lot of the Jews in that splendid city, and about the vision of one of them, old Melchisedech, whose daughter has just had a child by a Christian. The narrator wonders what Melchisedech has seen: "'Hat er das Meer gesehen oder Gott, den Ewigen, in seiner Glorie?'" ("Has he beheld the sea or God, the Eternal Being, in His glory?"), to which Baum confidently replies: "'Das Meer wahrscheinlich ... es *ist* ja auch ein Eindruck'" ("The sea, probably ... after all, *that's* an impression too"). As these examples show, the tales suffer from excessive archness; in "Wie der Fingerhut dazu kam, der liebe Gott zu sein" (How the Thimble Came To Be Dear God), the all too clear message is that God is to be found in the least significant of objects—as obvious a point as that made in "Ein Verein aus einem dringenden Bedürfnis heraus" (A Club Created To Meet a Pressing Need), a long-winded formulaic narrative directed against artistic organizations.

The best of the stories are the three devoted to Russian themes, "Wie der Verrat nach Russland kam" (How Treachery Came to Russia), "Wie der alte Timofei singend starb" (How Old Timofei Died Singing), and "Das Lied von der Gerechtigkeit" (The Song of Justice). They are all told to the receptive Ewald and illustrate that Russia is a land that borders on God, a land of true reverence. The opportunity of making a thrust at dry scholarly authority is not allowed to slip by: the tales are based on *byliny* and *skazki*, epic folk songs and folktales long hidden away by learned men. According to the narrator, the tales have died out among the Russian people, and it seems to be his intention to bring them to life again. The first of the trio tells how a simple peasant demands from the czar not gold but truth and integrity (one more example of the poverty–and poverty of spirit in the biblical sense–that Rilke so admired); the second hopes for a continuation of the ancient line of folksingers and their songs, "darin die Worte wie Ikone sind und gar nicht zu vergleichen mit den gewöhnlichen Worten" (in which the words are like icons and not at all to be compared with ordinary words), even though such a continuation requires the singer to abandon his wife and child; the third is a historical tale from western Russia, in which a blind singer inspires his listeners to throw off the yoke of the Polish lords and the greed of the Jews.

There are also three tales from Italy: the Venetian ghetto story; a tribute to Michelangelo, "Von Einem, der die Steine belauscht" (Concerning Someone Who Eavesdropped on Stones); and another legend on the nature of true poverty, "Der Bettler und das stolze Fräulein" (The Beggar and the Proud Maiden), in which a Florentine noble disguises himself as a beggar and asks the prideful Beatrice to let him kiss the dusty hem of her garment. She is afraid of the strange beggar, but gives him a sack of gold. The experience transforms him: he remains in his beggar's rags, gives away all his possessions, and goes off barefoot into the countryside. Hearing the story, the teacher concludes that it is a tale of how a profligate becomes an eccentric tramp; the narrator rejoins that he has become a saint; and when the children hear the tale, they assert, "zum Ärger des Herrn Lehrer, auch in *ihr* käme der liebe Gott vor" (to the annoyance of the teacher, that dear God appeared in *this* story too). Like "Der Bettler und das stolze Fräulein," "Ein Märchen vom Tode" (A Tale about Death), with its glorification of "der alten schönen Gebärde des breiten Gebetes" (the beautiful old gesture of broad prayer), offers an example of the author's belief in the efficacy of a great or brave gesture that transforms its maker. Having begun with a double prologue set in heaven–the two tales about the hands of God–the collection harks back at its end to Rilke's more realistic stories with "Eine Geschichte, dem Dunkel erzählt" (A Story Told to the Darkness). Klara Söllner defies society's norms by divorcing her husband, a state official, and embarking on an affair with an artist; she rears their love child by herself. The narrator, twitting a narrow-minded public one last time, claims that nothing in the tale is unfit for children's ears; in fact, it reflects the scandalous independence of Rilke's friend, Franziska zu Reventlow.

Klara generously encourages her lover to leave her in pursuit of his art; Rilke himself was settling down to a life of considerably less freedom than he had known before. The young couple took up residence in Westerwede, near Worpswede; Rilke did reviews for a Bremen newspaper and larger periodicals and prepared *Die Letzten* and *Das Buch der Bilder* for publication. On 12 December 1901, their only child, Ruth (named after the heroine of a novel by Lou), was born. Home life could not long appeal to Rilke, and he began to conceive new plans. As a result of his Jacobsen enthusiasm, further readings of the Nordic works that were phenomenally popular in Germany at the time, and his association with Juncker, his interest in the north grew. Spending a month in the early summer of 1902 at Castle Haseldorf in Holstein as a guest of the poetaster Prince Emil von Schönaich-Carolath, he found in the archives sources that had to do with the great Danish-German Reventlow family: "Diese Wochen hier haben doch ihren Sinn, auch wenn sie nur im Lesen einiger Bücher bestehen" (These weeks here have their meaning after all, even though they consist only of the reading of some books). Simultaneously, he wrote a review of the Swedish reformer Ellen Key's *Barnets arhundrade* (1900; translated into German as *Das Jahrhundert des Kindes*, 1902; translated into English as *The Century of the Child*, 1909), with its recommendation for greater openness in the education of children; the review led to a correspondence with Key and, in time, to an invitation to the north.

But Rilke's immediate plan, the composition of a book about Auguste Rodin, led him to Paris in August 1902. The autumn weeks in the metropolis were difficult for him and formed the basis for several episodes in *Die Aufzeichnungen des Malte Laurids Brigge*; leaving Ruth in her parents' care, Clara also traveled to Paris to study with Rodin, but maintained a residence separate from her husband's so that each would have greater freedom. Rilke's production at the time was varied; he had completed his book on the Worpswede painters and the north German landscape in which they worked before he set out for Haseldorf; the Rodin book was written in Paris during November and December 1902 and was published in 1903; the second part of *Das Stunden-Buch*, "Das Buch von der Pilgerschaft" (The

Rilke with his wife, the sculptress Clara Westhoff Rilke, in 1906

Book of Pilgrimage), had been completed at Westerwede in 1901; and in Paris he wrote verses that would be included in the augmented edition of *Das Buch der Bilder,* as well as "Der Panther" (The Panther), destined to become one of his best-known poems and the earliest of the items included in *Neue Gedichte.* A springtime trip to Viareggio in 1903 gave him the third part of *Das Stunden-Buch,* the upsetting mixture of eroticism and thoughts about death called "Das Buch von der Armuth und vom Tode" (The Book of Poverty and Death).

After a summer in Germany, the Rilkes set out in September 1903 for Rome; the poet's reaction to the city was one of discomfort. He found himself yearning for the north, and he sent pathetic letters to Key about the failure of the Roman winter and spring to be "real." In February 1904 Rilke made the first sketches for a novel about a young Dane in Paris: "An einem Herbstabende eines dieser letzten Jahre besuchte Malte Laurids Brigge, ziemlich unerwartet, einen von den wenigen Bekannten, die er in Paris besaß" (On an autumn evening of one of these last years Malte Laurids Brigge, rather unexpectedly, visited one of the few acquaintances he had in Paris). Malte tells his listener of a dinner interrupted by a ghostly apparition, an experience he had had when he was twelve or thirteen during a visit to his maternal grandfather's estate, Urnekloster, in the company of his father. The story would become one of the Danish episodes in the novel.

By the most skillful sort of hinting, Rilke arranged a Scandinavian stay from June to December 1904 to collect material for the book. The trip was spent largely with the artist and writer Ernst Norlind and Norlind's fiancée at a chateau, Borgeby, in south Sweden, and then at the home of an industrialist, James Gibson, at Jonsered near Gothenburg. The Gibsons were friends of Key, and a Sunday at the farmhouse of Key's brother, Mac Key (like the Gibsons, the family was of Scottish origin), in late November 1904 inspired another episode in *Die Aufzeichnungen des Malte Laurids Brigge,* the visit to the manor house of the Schulins, the center of which has been burned out. There, young Malte learns about fear. For a while Rilke toyed with the idea of preparing monographs on Jacobsen and on the Danish painter Vilhelm Hammershøj, but dropped both projects. He had learned to read Danish but could not speak it, and Copenhagen, which had initially charmed him as he passed through it, had come to seem ominous to him. He left Denmark on 8 December 1904 and never returned to the north; meeting a young Danish woman, Inga Junghanns, in Munich during the war, he rejoiced to think that the book about Malte would be returned to its "original language" in her translation. But Paris remained his true home, if so peripatetic a soul as Rilke may be said to have had a home.

In many ways 1905 marked a turning point in Rilke's career, just as the liaison with Lou had been the turning point in his personal development. Anton Kippenberg took over the Insel firm; in Kippenberg Rilke discovered a skillful and usually generous manager of his literary fortunes and personal finances. His employment as Rodin's secretary began in September; it would end abruptly, in a dreadful scene, in May 1906.

He made his first public appearances in Germany, reading from his works with a fire that was in contrast to his frail figure and exquisitely gloved hands. And, in part through the agency of the Rhenish banker Karl von der Heydt, he began to make the acquaintance of the noble ladies who would offer him so much solace and so many refuges. The relationship with Clara, whom he had to "keep at bay," in Miss Butler's malicious phrase, grew ever more tenuous, and Rilke developed the talent for swift wooing that would make the Princess Marie von Thurn und Taxis (happily married and, save intellectually, not one of his conquests) tell him that Don Juan was an innocent babe in comparison to him. Clara and Ruth briefly joined him on a trip to Belgium, sponsored by von der Heydt, late in the summer of 1906; but he much preferred to travel alone. Perhaps the first of his extramarital romances was with the Venetian Mimi Romanelli, whom he met at the pension of her brother in the autumn of 1907. He was the guest of Frau Alice Faehndrich at the Villa Discopoli on Capri in the winter and spring of 1906-1907 and again in the winter and spring of 1908; there he was surrounded by admiring ladies, among them the young and beautiful Countess Manon zu Solms-Laubach, for whom he wrote the poem "Migliera" (published in volume 2 of his *Sämtliche Werke*, 1956). With Frau Faehndrich, before her death in 1908, he translated Elizabeth Barrett Browning's *Sonnets from the Portuguese*. Some of the poems from the Capri days found their way into *Neue Gedichte;* the first part, dedicated to the von der Heydts, appeared in 1907, the second, dedicated "À mon grand ami Auguste Rodin," in 1908. The quarrel with the master had been patched up; Rilke remained grateful to Rodin for having taught him the doctrine of work: "Il faut travailler toujours, rien que travailler" (One must work always, nothing but work).

Capri was not the main growing ground for the *Neue Gedichte;* that was Paris, to which Rilke became more attached the more he was able to transform its beauties and horrors into literature. An apartment at the Hôtel Biron in the Rue de Varenne became Rilke's pied-à-terre in August 1908; Rodin liked the Louis-Quatorze mansion so much that he immediately moved his own Parisian studio there. In 1910, on a trip to Leipzig during which he stayed in the tower room of the Kippenbergs' home, Rilke looked after the final stages of *Die Aufzeichnungen des Malte Laurids Brigge*. The production of the slender book emptied him, he liked to declare, and no other major work came from his hand during the next twelve years, although the production of this so-called barren period includes some of his best verse.

Die Aufzeichnungen des Malte Laurids Brigge consists of seventy-one entries divided into two parts, with a break after entry thirty-nine. It has often been conjectured that the model for Malte was the Norwegian poet Sigbjørn Obstfelder (1866-1900), a devotee of Jacobsen who had lived for some time in Paris; his fragmentary novel *En prests dagbok* (1900; translated into German as *Tagebuch eines Priesters*, 1901; translated into English as *A Priest's Diary*, 1987), and a collection of his other prose, which Rilke reviewed in 1904, had come out in German translation. Much about Obstfelder does not fit, however, the picture of Malte in Rilke's novel: Obstfelder was of modest parentage, an engineer by calling, and had lived and had a nervous breakdown in the American Middle West; the aristocratic Malte–the last of his line–is fetched rather from Rilke's reading of Bang and his own musings about himself and his fancied background. The age of Rilke in February 1904, when the first sketches were made, is that of Malte as he looks back on his life as a man of letters: "Ich bin achtundzwanzig, und es ist so gut wie nichts geschehen. Wiederholen wir: ich habe eine Studie über Carpaccio geschrieben, die schlecht ist, ein Drama, das 'Ehe' heißt und etwas Falsches mit zweideutigen Mitteln beweisen will, und Verse. Ach, aber mit Versen ist so wenig getan, wenn man sie früh schreibt" (I am twenty-eight, and as good as nothing has happened. Let's repeat: I have written a study about Carpaccio, which is poor, a drama, called "Marriage," that tries to prove something false with ambiguous means, and verses. Oh, but how little is accomplished with verses when one writes them early in life). Rilke appears to have imagined that Malte was emotionally destroyed by the Parisian experience; he says in a letter of May 1906, after having heard the "inappropriate" laughter of a French audience at a performance of Ibsen's *Wild Duck:* "Und wieder begriff ich Malte Laurids Brigge und sein Nordischsein und sein Zugrundegehen an Paris. Wie sah und empfand und erlitt er es" (And once more I understood Malte Laurids Brigge and his Nordicness and his destruction by Paris. How he saw and felt and suffered it). Malte is undergoing a severe crisis: entry number twenty describes his visit to the Salpêtrière Hospital, apparently for electrotherapy. (That Rilke sometimes feared that he would

Rilke at his desk in the Hôtel Biron, Paris, in 1908 (Archiv des Insel Verlags, Frankfurt am Main)

go insane is indicated by the "last will and testament" he sent to Nanny Wunderly-Volkart on 27 October 1925.)

The substance of the first part of *Die Aufzeichnungen des Malte Laurids Brigge*, on the one hand, is Malte's awareness of Paris: of "die Existenz des Entsetzlichen in jedem Bestandteil der Luft" (the existence of the horrible in every particle of the air)–the factory-like dying in the city's hospitals, the terrible street noises, the sordidness exposed on every side, coupled with the joy he feels while visiting an antiquarian bookseller's booth by the Seine, reading the poetry of Francis Jammes in the Bibliothéque Nationale, or viewing the tapestry "La dame à la licorne" in the Musée de Cluny. But intermingled with Parisian episodes are memories of his childhood in Denmark–a childhood of dramatic and terrifying scenes: the death of his paternal grandfather at Ulsgaard; ghost stories connected with Urnekloster, the maternal seat; hallucinations, such as a hand emerging from the wall, that he had while recovering from fever; his tender "Maman," his reserved father, and his maternal aunt Abelone, whom he loves in some never clearly defined way. He wishes he could show her the tapestries in the Parisian museum: "Ich bilde mir ein, du bist da" (I imagine that you are here). The kernel of the Parisian sections is Rilke's own observations, which he often put down in letters; save for quotations from Baudelaire's *Spleen de Paris* and the Book of Job, the Parisian material draws little on literary sources. The Danish components are more mixed, with strong echoes of the description of Danish estate life in the novels of Bang and Jacobsen and of Rilke's own childhood. Upon its appearance *Die Aufzeichnungen des Malte Laurids Brigge* was often treated by critics as another novel about the "decadent hero"–the scion of the old family, disheartened, quiveringly sensitive, and suffering from an inability to act, yet admiring those beings– such as a man with Saint Vitus' dance trying to sustain his dignity by a tremendous act of will–who are undefeated. The book is also one of the several works of German fiction from the time that display a strong "Nordic" side.

The second and more difficult part of the novel again employs the main figures from the Danish past: Maman reappears, appreciating the careful work of anonymous lace-makers; young Malte visits the neighboring estate of the Schulins

Notebook pages containing a draft of a passage for Die Aufzeichnungen des Malte Laurids Brigge *written in Paris in the winter of 1908 (Rilke-Archiv der Schweizerischen Landesbibliothek, Bern)*

(based on the Key farm); birthdays are celebrated. A mature Malte returns to Copenhagen ("Ulsgaard war nicht mehr in unserm Besitz" [Ulsgaard was no longer in our possession]); witnesses the perforation of his dead father's heart lest he be buried alive; and ponders the death of Denmark's great baroque king, Christian IV, an account of which his father kept in his wallet. Among the Scandinavian figures, Abelone is the most important: taking dictation from her aged father, Count Brahe, for whom the past is part of the present; introducing young Malte to one of the great "loving women," Bettina Brentano, who outdid Goethe, Malte claims, in the sheer strength of her emotion. Memories of Abelone come to Malte when he hears a Danish woman sing about "besitzlose Liebe" (possessionless love) and its splendors in a Venetian salon: " 'weil ich dich niemals anhielt, halt ich dich fest' " ("since I never detained you, I hold you fast"); other salutes to splendid women–the Portuguese nun Heloise, Louise Labé, Sappho, and others–who know that "mit der Vereinigung nichts gemein sein kann als ein Zuwachs an Einsamkeit" (with union nothing can be meant save an increase in loneliness) prepare for this last quasi-appearance by Abelone. Thus far it is relatively easy to follow Rilke's arguments on love; save in the artistry of the presentation, not much difference exists between the selfless Klara Söllner of the last story of *Geschichten vom lieben Gott* and the singer of the song in Venice. It is harder to grasp, however, what Rilke means when he speaks of Abelone's yearning to take everything that was transitive out of her love, to make it objectless loving, "absolutely, in complete loneliness," in Eudo C. Mason's words.

The horrors of Paris are still with the diarist: Malte–"Ich lerne sehen" (I am learning to see) is the way he describes his most imperative task–cannot shut his eyes to a girl who stands "mit ihrem dürren, verkümmerten Stück" (with her stunted, withered stump) of an arm or to a blind newspaper vendor. The fear of death is still overriding, not only in the story of the postmortem operation on Malte's father but even in the comical tale of Nikolaj Kusmitsch, Malte's neighbor in Petersburg, who, realizing how much time he had in his account (he assumed he would live another fifty years or so), resolved to use it sparingly. The Kusmitsch tale leads into stories about a mother who comes to console her disturbed son and about the rebelliousness of objects, followed by glosses on the dangers of loneliness and an intense and horrifying rehearsal of the temptations of Saint Anthony.

Other narratives are baffling, especially the stories recalled from the little green book Malte owned as a boy about the end of the false Dmitri, Grischa Otrepjow; the death of Charles the Bold of Burgundy; the mad Charles VI of France; John XXII, the Avignon pope; and the terrible fourteenth century, "Die Zeit, in der der Kuss zweier, die sich versöhnten, nur das Zeichen für die Mörder war, die herumstanden" (The time in which the kiss of reconciliation between two men was merely the signal for the murderers standing nearby). This awful reflection comes to Malte after he has remembered a trauma of his childhood, a time of similar insecurity, in which he thought himself pursued by another of those large and threatening male figures, like Král and Holzer of the early stories. Perhaps the historical exempla are meant to illustrate Rilke's thoughts on the human will, a will that is variously jeopardized or fails: just before the pistol shot that ends Grischa Otrepjow's life, the pretender experiences "noch einmal Wille und Macht . . . alles zu sein" (once more the will and power . . . to be everything). The will also sustains Eleonora Duse, to whom tribute is paid after a sideswipe at contemporary theater, but here the artist's will has made her overrun—magnificently and frighteningly—the limits of the art in which she must perform. Much of the second part of *Die Aufzeichnungen des Malte Laurids Brigge* could be presented as a statement, as oblique as the first part's is direct, on the strange heroism of the exceptional human who exceeds, or attempts to exceed, his own limitations, forever standing alone. The original ending of the novel, criticizing Tolstoy, who had abandoned his art and was beset by fears of death ("Es war kein Zimmer in diesem Haus, in dem er sich nicht gefürchtet hatte, zu sterben" [There was no room in this house in which he had not feared he would die]), was supplanted by the story of the Prodigal Son, retold as "die Legende dessen . . . der nicht geliebt werden wollte" (the legend of him . . . who did not wish to be loved)—a representation, as Joseph-François Angelloz thought, of Rilke's long search for the freedom that would enable him to apply his artistic will to the fullest. The final lines are cryptic: "Er war jetzt furchtbar schwer zu lieben, und er fühlte, daß nur Einer dazu imstande sei. Der aber wollte noch nicht" (He was now terribly difficult to love, and he felt that there was only One who was capable of it. He, however, did not yet want to). Mason suggests that this is a "hyperbolic way" of implying that there is no plane, "human or superhuman," on which the problem of love can be solved for one who, like the Prodigal Son, is "governed by a daemonic dread of his sacrosanct, isolated selfhood being encroached upon through the love of any other human being."

Die Aufzeichnungen des Malte Laurids Brigge is at once a profoundly satisfying and unsatisfying book. It presents in unforgettable language the tribulations of a sensitive being in an overwhelmingly beautiful and ugly world—the omnipresence of fear; the search for small joys ("Was so ein kleiner Mond alles vermag" [How much such a little moon can do]); the residual terrors of childhood, never to be overcome; the problems of loving; the profits and torments of being alone. Formally, the novel seems less daunting than it did to readers of the past; Rilke advertises his intention of writing a nonlinear novel: "Daß man erzählte, wirklich erzählte, das muß vor meiner Zeit gewesen sein" (That people told stories, really told stories, that must have been before my time). Just the same, in many episodes—the banquet at Urnekloster, the death of the chamberlain Brigge, the visit to the Schulins, the death of Charles of Burgundy—Rilke proved himself a master of the short story, in which he had served such a long apprenticeship. As Wolfgang Leppmann points out, the reader can become "frustrated": he is asked to know the obscure historical facts Rilke had stored away in the corners of his mind or culled directly from other texts; he may find some of the doctrines advanced (for example, intransitive love) hard to grasp, let alone embrace. What may be overlooked, in grappling with *Die Aufzeichnungen des Malte Laurids Brigge*, is that it is, after all, a feigned diary and also incomplete: Rilke told Lou Andreas-Salomé that he had ended it out of exhaustion. Furthermore, it is a personal document: Rilke made fun of Ellen Key for having identified Malte with him, yet she was by no means inaccurate in her naiveté. In Paris for his last visit, he would write to Nanny Wunderly-Volkart: "Je m'effraie comme, autrefois, Malte s'est effrayé . . ." (I am terrified, as, formerly, Malte was terrified . . .). In his letters, he could never let Malte go.

Rilke

The post-*Malte* time was marked by flurries of frantic travel: to North Africa in the autumn of 1910; to Egypt in the spring of the next year with the mysterious Jenny Oltersdorf, about whom Rilke remained forever close-mouthed; to Castle Duino, near Trieste, a holding of the Thurn und Taxis clan, in 1911-1912 (here the "angel" of the *Duineser Elegien* is supposed to have spoken to him, inspiring the work that would not be complete until 1922); to Venice again, to spend much of the remainder of 1912-1913; to Spain in the winter of 1912-1913; and, in the summer of 1913, to Göttingen for a visit with Lou Andreas-Salomé. He spent October 1913 to late February 1914 in Paris and was in Munich when World War I broke out in August 1914. (The singer of the deeds of the cornet greeted the conflict with enthusiastic verse he soon regretted.) If the itinerary of these years is long, so is the list of feminine friends: the motherly and excitable Marie von Thurn und Taxis; the haughty Helene von Nostitz; the vivacious Sidonie Nádherný von Borutin, whom Rilke dissuaded from marrying the satirist Karl Kraus. On the passionate side, there was the simple Parisienne Marthe Hennebert, for a time Rilke's "ward"; and the pianist Magda von Hattingberg, or "Benvenuta," for both of whom he pondered a divorce from Clara. He could not do without the blue-blooded friends or the ones who became objects of his desire—such as the "douce perturbatrice," the phrase he bestowed on Marthe in one of the French poems he wrote more and more frequently.

The war years kept him far away from his Parisian books and papers, some of which were irretrievably lost, others saved through the good offices of his friend André Gide, whose *Le Retour de l'enfant prodigue* he had translated into German in 1913-1914. His principal residence was Munich, and his principal companion for a while was the painter Lulu Albert-Lasard. A rising tide of mainly erotic poetry in 1915 was interrupted by a draft call to the Austrian army at Christmas. He spent a wretched few weeks in basic training and was saved by powerful friends, including Princess Marie, who effected his transfer to the dull safety of the War Archive and comfortable quarters in Hietzing's Park-Hotel. Rilke continued to complain about his enforced residence in detestable Vienna and was released from service in June. The rest of the war went by in a kind of convalescence—mostly in Munich, but the summer of 1917 included a stay on an estate in Westphalia, and the autumn of the same year a stay in Berlin. There he saw both Walther Rathenau and Marianne Mitford (née Friedländer-Fuld), whose exceptionally wealthy family owned an estate in the vicinity of the capital: she received one of the first copies of his 1918 translation of the sonnets of the Lyonnaise poetess of the Renaissance, Louise Labé, whom he had ranked among the great lovers in *Die Aufzeichnungen des Malte Laurids Brigge*. Back in Munich, he lived first at the Hotel Continental and then in an apartment in the artists' quarter of Schwabing; observing the "Munich revolution," vaguely sympathizing with Kurt Eisner's idealistic socialism, and giving shelter for a night to the fugitive author Ernst Toller, Rilke was briefly suspected of leftist sympathies by the victorious "White" forces that took over the city on 1 May 1919. At the same time, he enjoyed the innocent attentions of Elya Maria Nevar, a young actress, and the less innocent ones of the would-be femme fatale Claire Studer ("Liliane"), shortly to

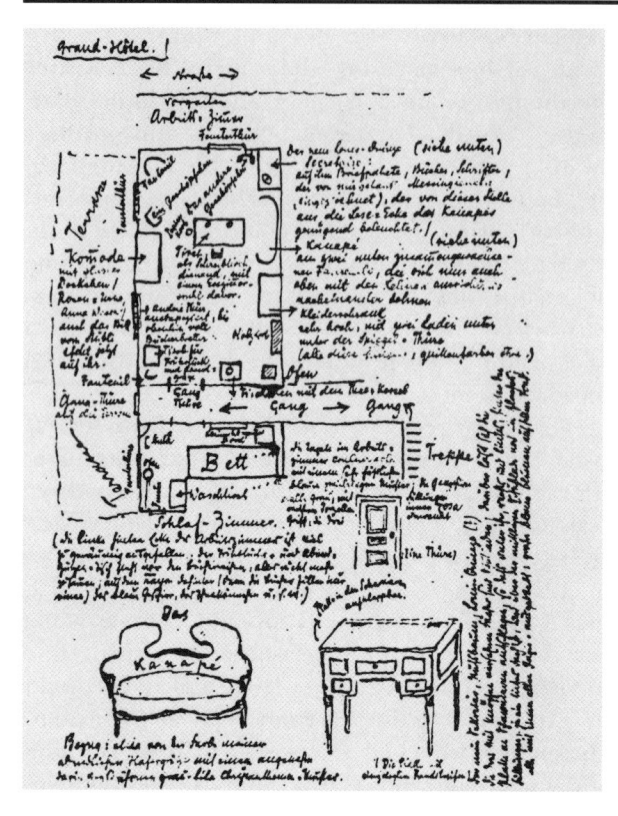

Sketch by Rilke of his room in a pension in Locarno, 1920 (Rilke-Archiv der Schweizerischen Landesbibliothek, Bern)

become the mistress and then the wife of the expressionist poet and editor Iwan Goll.

Casting about for a refuge from postwar Germany's turbulence, Rilke was invited to undertake a reading tour in Switzerland. Once he had made fun of Switzerland and its scenic "Übertreibungen" (exaggerations), its "anspruchsvolle" (pretentious) lakes and mountains; now he was glad to cross the border. Some of his Swiss sanctuaries were much less satisfactory than he had hoped: at Schönenberg, near Basel, a summer home of the Burckhardt family, where he lived from March until May 1920, he liked neither the house's grounds nor its feeble stoves; at Castle Berg am Irchel, near Zurich, placed at his disposal by a Colonel Ziegler for the winter of 1920-1921, he was bothered by children at play and the noise of a sawmill—but at Berg there also appeared to him, he said, the phantom who dictated the double cycle of poems *Aus dem Nachlaß des Grafen C. W.* (1950; translated as *From the Remains of Count C. W.*, 1952). He quickly found new friends; the most important was "Nike," Nanny Wunderly-Volkart, the witty and self-controlled wife of the industrialist Hans Wunderly. Through her Rilke discovered and had rented for him a little tower at Muzot, near Sierre, in the canton of Valais; there—as literary histories never tire of repeating—he finished the *Duineser Elegien* and received the "additional gift" of *Die Sonette an Orpheus* in February 1922. (It is plain, though, that he knew the storm of inspiration was coming: he had some difficulty in persuading the great love of the first Swiss years, "Merline" or Baladine Klossowska, that he needed to be alone, cared for only by his competent housekeeper, Frida Baumgartner.)

Rilke announced the completion of his task with justifiable pride; the afterglow of accomplishment permeates his letters during the remainder of 1922. A sense of aging also came over him, however: his daughter married, and in 1923 he became a grandfather. (The birth of Ruth herself, he had told a friend years before, had given him a similar sense of "l'immense tristesse de ma propre futilité" [the immense sadness of my own futility].) His health declined: he spent time at a half-resort, half-hospital at Schöneck on the Lake of Lucerne, and then repeatedly at the sanatorium of Valmont above the Lake of Geneva. Rilke had always had a weakness for the restful weeks at a sanatorium or spa—for the sake of his nerves, he liked to say—and they brought useful and interesting contacts: in 1905 at the sanatorium "Weisser Hirsch" near Dresden he had met Countess Luise Schwerin, who had put him in touch with the von der Heydt and Faehndrich circles. Nevertheless, he had become hesitant about the efficacy of physicians in dealing with his ills, real or fancied, and regarded sleep as the great cure-all. The year 1924 opened and closed with stays at Valmont. From January to August 1925 he had his final sojourn in Paris—he was lionized during his stay there, but perhaps the most sincere of his many admirers was the Alsatian Maurice Betz, who was at work on a translation of *Die Aufzeichnungen des Malte Laurids Brigge*. By December he was back at Valmont, staying until May 1926. His last works were his translations of Paul Valéry's poetry and prose and three small volumes of his own French verse. Carl J. Burckhardt, a Swiss diplomat who possessed a keen eye for Rilke's weaknesses, recalled that Rilke did not understand how reserved and even condescending Valéry was toward the "German" poet who late in his career tried his hand at French. Rilke appears to have sought Valéry's company, chatting with him a last time in September 1926 at Anthy on the French side of Lake Geneva. A special issue of *Les Cahiers du Mois*, "Reconnaissance à

Rilke with the great love of his early years in Switzerland, the painter Baladine Klossowska ("Merline") (Rainer-Maria-Rilke-Archiv, Gernsbach, West Germany)

Rilke," edited by the faithful Betz, had appeared at Paris in the summer of 1926–its opening a restrained salute from Valéry's own hand.

Also in September 1926 the critic Edmond Jaloux introduced Rilke to Nimet Eloui Bey, an Egyptian beauty of Circassian background. When Rilke was still viewed as the devoted and sensitive admirer of women but not an erotic adventurer, Jaloux's account of this "last friendship" seemed the perfect finale for the poet's romantic life; gathering white roses for her, Rilke pricked his hand, and the injury became infected, a harbinger of the final onslaught of his illness. It is now known that the Egyptian was but one of the women and girls who surrounded and attracted him almost to the end: the eighteen-year-old Austrian Erika Mitterer, who carried on a correspondence in poems with him from 1924 to 1926; the Russian poetess Marina Tsvetayeva, who wanted to visit and consume him; the pretty Lalli Horstmann, a friend of Marianne Mitford; the Dutch singer Beppy Veder; and the actress Elisabeth Bergner were among the many. What may be more significant about the "last friendship" with Nimet Eloui Bey, though, is that she wanted to meet the author of *Die Aufzeichnungen des Malte Laurids Brigge,* which she had just read in Betz's translation–the book of his that lay closest to his own heart.

Rilke returned to Valmont in November 1926. On 29 December he died of leukemia.

Letters:

Briefe an Auguste Rodin (Leipzig: Insel, 1928);

Briefe aus den Jahren 1902 bis 1906, edited by Ruth Sieber-Rilke and Carl Sieber (Leipzig: Insel, 1929);

Briefe an einen jungen Dichter (Leipzig: Insel, 1929); translated by M. D. Herter Norton as *Letters to a Young Poet* (New York: Norton, 1934); translated by K. W. Maurer as *Letters to a Young Poet* (London: Langley, 1943);

Briefe an eine junge Frau (Leipzig: Insel, 1930); translated by Maurer as *Letters to a Young Woman* (London: Langley, 1945);

Briefe aus den Jahren 1906 bis 1907, edited by Sieber-Rilke and Sieber (Leipzig: Insel, 1930);

Briefe und Tagebücher aus der Frühzeit, edited by Sieber-Rilke and Sieber (Leipzig: Insel, 1931);

Drawing of Rilke by Emil Orlik (Bildarchiv der Österreichischen Nationalbibliothek)

Briefe aus den Jahren 1907 bis 1914, edited by Sieber-Rilke and Sieber (Leipzig: Insel, 1933);

Über Gott: Zwei Briefe (Leipzig: Insel, 1933);

Briefe an seinen Verleger 1906 bis 1926, edited by Sieber-Rilke and Sieber (Leipzig: Insel, 1934);

Briefe aus Muzot 1921 bis 1926, edited by Sieber-Rilke and Sieber (Leipzig: Insel, 1935);

Gesammelte Briefe, edited by Sieber-Rilke and Sieber, 6 volumes (Leipzig: Insel, 1936-1939);

Lettres à une Amie Vénitienne (Milan: Hoepli/Leipzig: Asmus, 1941);

Briefe an eine Freundin, edited by Herbert Steiner (Aurora, N.Y.: Wells College Press, 1944);

Briefe (Olten: Oltener Bücherfreunde, 1945);

Briefe an Baronesse von Oe, edited by Richard von Mises (New York: Johannespresse, 1945);

Letters of Rainer Maria Rilke, translated by Jane Bannard Greene and Herter Norton, 2 volumes (New York: Norton, 1945-1948);

Briefe an eine Reisegefährtin: Eine Begegnung mit Rainer Maria Rilke (Vienna: Ibach, 1947);

Briefe an das Ehepaar S. Fischer, edited by Hedwig Fischer (Zurich: Classen, 1947);

La dernière amitié de Rainer Maria Rilke: Lettres inédites de Rilke à Madame Eloui Bey, edited by Edmond Jaloux (Paris: Laffont, 1949); translated by William H. Kennedy as *Rainer Maria Rilke: His Last Friendship. Unpublished Letters to Mrs. Eloui Bey* (New York: Philosophical Library, 1952);

"*So laß ich mich zu träumen gehen*" (Gmunden & Bad Ischl: Mader, 1949); translated by Heinz Norden as *Letters to Benvenuta* (New York: Philosophical Library, 1951; London: Hogarth Press, 1953);

Briefe an seinen Verleger, edited by Sieber-Rilke and Sieber, 2 volumes (Wiesbaden: Insel, 1949);

Briefe, edited by Sieber-Rilke and Karl Altheim, 2 volumes (Wiesbaden: Insel, 1950);

Die Briefe an Gräfin Sizzo, 1921 bis 1926 (Wiesbaden: Insel, 1950); enlarged edition, edited by Ingeborg Schnack (Frankfurt am Main: Insel, 1977);

Briefwechsel in Gedichten mit Erika Mitterer 1924 bis 1926 (Wiesbaden: Insel, 1950); translated by N. K. Cruickshank as *Correspondence in Verse with Erika Mitterer* (London: Hogarth Press, 1953);

Lettres françaises à Merline 1919-1922 (Paris: Edition du Seuil, 1950); translated by Violet M. Macdonald as *Letters to Merline, 1919-1922* (London: Methuen, 1951);

Rainer Maria Rilke/Marie von Thurn und Taxis: Briefwechsel, edited by Ernst Zinn, 2 volumes (Zurich: Niehans & Rokitansky, 1951); translated by Nora Wydenbruck as *The Letters of Rainer Maria Rilke and Princess Marie von Thurn and Taxis* (London: Hogarth Press, 1958; Norfolk, Conn.: New Directions, 1958);

Rainer Maria Rilke/Lou Andreas-Salomé, Briefwechsel, edited by Ernst Pfeiffer (Zurich: Niehans/Wiesbaden: Insel, 1952; revised and enlarged edition, Frankfurt am Main: Insel, 1975);

Rainer Maria Rilke/André Gide: Correspondance 1909-1926, edited by Renée Lang (Paris: Corrêa, 1952);

Briefe über Cézanne, edited by Clara Rilke (Wiesbaden: Insel, 1952); translated by Joel Agee as *Letters on Cézanne* (New York: Fromm, 1986);

Die Briefe an Frau Gudi Nölke aus Rilkes Schweizer Jahren, edited by Paul Obermüller (Wiesbaden:

Insel, 1953); translated by Macdonald as *Letters to Frau Gudi Nölke during His Life in Switzerland* (London: Hogarth Press, 1955);
Rainer Maria Rilke/Katharina Kippenberg: Briefwechsel, edited by Bettina von Bomhard (Wiesbaden: Insel, 1954);
Briefwechsel mit Benvenuta, edited by Kurt Leonhard (Esslingen: Bechtle, 1954); translated by Agee as *Rilke and Benvenuta: An Intimate Correspondence* (New York: Fromm, 1987);
Rainer Maria Rilke et Merline: Correspondance 1920-1926, edited by Dieter Basserman (Zurich: Niehans, 1954);
Lettres milanaises 1921-1926, edited by Lang (Paris: Plon, 1956);
Rainer Maria Rilke/Inga Junghanns: Briefwechsel, edited by Wolfgang Herwig (Wiesbaden: Insel, 1959);
Selected Letters, edited by Harry T. Moore (Garden City, N.Y.: Doubleday, 1960);
Briefe an Sidonie Nádherný von Borutin, edited by Bernhard Blume (Frankfurt am Main: Insel, 1973);
Über Dichtung und Kunst, edited by Hartmut Engelhardt (Frankfurt am Main: Suhrkamp, 1974);
Rainer Maria Rilke/Helene von Nostitz: Briefwechsel, edited by Oswalt von Nostitz (Frankfurt am Main: Insel, 1976);
Briefe an Nanny Wunderly-Volkart, edited by Niklaus Bigler and Rätus Luck, 2 volumes (Frankfurt am Main: Insel, 1977);
Lettres autour d'un jardin (Paris: La Delirante, 1977);
Hugo von Hofmannsthal/Rainer Maria Rilke: Briefwechsel, edited by Rudolf Hirsch and Ingeborg Schnack (Frankfurt am Main: Suhrkamp, 1978);
Briefe an Axel Juncker, edited by Renate Scharffenberg (Frankfurt am Main: Insel, 1979);
Briefwechsel mit Rolf Freiherrn von Ungern-Sternberg, edited by Konrad Kratzsch (Leipzig: Insel Verlag Anton Kippenberg, 1980);
Rainer Maria Rilke/Anita Forrer: Briefwechsel, edited by Magda Kérényi (Frankfurt am Main: Leipzig, 1982);
Rainer Maria Rilke/Marina Zwetajewa/Boris Pasternak: Briefwechsel, edited by Jewgenij Pasternak, Jelena Pasternak, and Konstantin M. Asadowskij (Frankfurt am Main: Insel, 1983); translated by Margaret Wettlin and Walter Arndt as *Letters Summer 1926* (New York: Harcourt Brace Jovanovich, 1985);
Rainer Maria Rilke: Briefe an Ernst Norlind, edited by Paul Åström (Partille: Paul Åströms Forlag, 1986);
Rilke und Rußland: Briefe, Erinnerungen, Gedichte, edited by Konstantin Asadowski, Russian texts translated by Ulrike Hirschberg (Frankfurt am Main: Insel, 1986);
Rainer Maria Rilke: Briefwechsel mit Regina Ullmann und Ellen Delp, edited by Walter Simon (Frankfurt am Main: Insel, 1987);
Rainer Maria Rilke/Stefan Zweig: Briefe und Dokumente, edited by Donald Prater (Frankfurt am Main: Insel, 1987).

Bibliographies:
Fritz Adolf Hünich, *Rilke-Bibliographie: Erster Teil: Das Werk des Lebenden* (Leipzig: Insel, 1935);
Walter Ritzer, *Rainer Maria Rilke: Bibliographie* (Vienna: Kerry, 1951);
Paul Obermüller, Herbert Steiner, and Ernst Zinn, eds., *Katalog der Rilke-Sammlung Richard von Mises* (Frankfurt am Main: Insel, 1966).

Biographies:
Carl Sieber, *René Rilke: Die Jugend Rainer Maria Rilkes* (Leipzig: Insel, 1932);
Sophie Brutzer, *Rilkes russische Reisen* (Königsberg: Klutke, 1934);
Eliza M. Butler, *Rainer Maria Rilke* (Cambridge: Cambridge University Press/New York: Macmillan, 1941);
Maurice Zermatten, *Les Années valaisannes de Rilke* (Lausanne: Rouge, 1941); translated by Waltrud Kappeler as *Der Ruf der Stille: Rilkes Walliser Jahre* (Zurich: Rascher, 1954);
F. W. van Heerikhuizen, *Rainer Maria Rilke: Leven en werk* (Bussum: Kroonder, 1946); translated by Fernand G. Renier and Anne Cliff as *Rainer Maria Rilke: His Life and Work* (London: Routledge & Kegan Paul, 1952; New York: Philosophical Library, 1952);
Werner Kohlschmidt, *Rainer Maria Rilke* (Lübeck: Wildner, 1948);
Nora Wydenbruck, *Rilke: Man and Poet* (London: Lehmann, 1949);
Joseph-François Angelloz, *Rilke* (Paris: Mercure de France, 1952); translated by Alfred Kuoni as *Rainer Maria Rilke: Leben und Werk* (Munich: Nymphenburger Verlagsbuchhandlung, 1955);
J. R. von Salis, *Rainer Maria Rilkes Schweizer Jahre: Ein Beitrag zur Biographie von Rilkes Spätzeit* (Frauenfeld: Huber, 1952); translated by

N. K. Cruickshank as *Rainer Maria Rilke: The Years in Switzerland* (London: Hogarth Press, 1964; Berkeley & Los Angeles: University of California Press, 1964);

Peter Demetz, *René Rilkes Prager Jahre* (Düsseldorf: Diederichs, 1953);

Erich Simenauer, *Rainer Maria Rilke: Legende und Mythos* (Bern: Haupt, 1953);

Else Buddeberg, *Rainer Maria Rilke: Eine innere Biographie* (Stuttgart: Metzler, 1955);

Ingeborg Schnack, *Rilkes Leben und Werk im Bild* (Wiesbaden: Insel, 1956);

Heinrich Weigand Petzet, *Das Bildnis des Dichters: Paula Becker-Modersohn und Rainer Maria Rilke. Eine Begegnung* (Frankfurt am Main: Societätsverlag, 1957);

Hans Egon Holthusen, *Rainer Maria Rilke in Selbstzeugnissen und Bilddokumenten* (Hamburg: Rowohlt, 1958);

H. F. Peters, *Rainer Maria Rilke: The Masks and the Man* (Seattle: University of Washington Press, 1960);

Eudo C. Mason, *Rainer Maria Rilke* (Edinburgh & London: Oliver & Boyd, 1963);

Mason, *Rainer Maria Rilke: Sein Leben und sein Werk* (Göttingen: Vandenhoeck & Ruprecht, 1964);

George C. Schoolfield, *Rilke's Last Year* (Lawrence: University of Kansas Libraries, 1969);

Leonid Čertkov, *Rilke in Russland: Auf Grund neuer Materialien* (Vienna: Österreichische Akademie der Wissenschaften, 1975);

Schnack, *Rainer Maria Rilke: Chronik seines Lebens und seines Werkes*, 2 volumes (Frankfurt am Main: Insel, 1975);

Joachim W. Storck, ed., *Rainer Maria Rilke, 1875-1975: Katalog der Ausstellung des Deutschen Literaturarchivs im Schiller-Nationalmuseum Marbach* (Stuttgart: Klett, 1975);

Zermatten, *Les dernières années de Rainer Maria Rilke* (Fribourg: Le Cassetin, 1975); translated by Arthur Fibicher as *Rilkes letzte Lebensjahre* (Fribourg: Le Cassetin, 1975);

Horst Nalewski, *Rainer Maria Rilke* (Leipzig: VEB Bibliographisches Institut, 1981);

Wolfgang Leppmann, *Rilke: Sein Leben, seine Welt, sein Werk* (Bern & Munich: Scherz, 1981); translated by Leppmann, Russell S. Stockman, and Richard Exner as *Rilke: A Life* (New York: Fromm, 1984);

J. F. Hendry, *The Sacred Threshold: A Life of Rainer Maria Rilke* (Manchester, U.K.: Carcanet Press, 1983);

Richard Pettit, *Rainer Maria Rilke in und nach Worpswede* (Worpswede: Worpsweder Verlag, 1983);

Donald Prater, *A Ringing Glass: The Life of Rainer Maria Rilke* (Oxford & New York: Oxford University Press, 1986).

References:

Hans Aarsleff, "Rilke, Herman Bang, and Malte," in *Proceedings of the IVth Congress of the International Comparative Literature Association* (The Hague: Mouton, 1966), pp. 628-636;

Renate Adler, "Some Technical Problems in Translations of Rilke's *Notebooks of Malte Laurids Brigge*," *Die neueren Sprachen*, new series 12 (1963): 622-628;

Lou Andreas-Salomé, *Rainer Maria Rilke* (Leipzig: Insel, 1928);

Lydia Baer, "Rilke and Jens Peter Jacobsen," *PMLA*, 54 (1939): 900-932, 1133-1180;

Frank Baron, ed., *Rilke and the Visual Arts* (Lawrence, Kans.: Coronado, 1982);

Baron, Ernst S. Dick, and Warren R. Maurer, eds., *Rilke: The Alchemy of Alienation* (Lawrence, Kan.: Regents Press, 1981);

K. A. J. Batterby, *Rilke and France: A Study in Poetic Development* (London: Oxford University Press, 1966);

Marga Bauer, *Rainer Maria Rilke und Frankreich* (Bern: Haupt, 1931);

Ruth Bauer, "Rainer Maria Rilke: 'Der Bettler und das stolze Fräulein,'" in her *Interpretationen moderner Prosa: Anläßlich der Fortbildungstagung für Deutsch-und Geschichtslehrer* (Frankfurt, Berlin, Bonn & Munich: Diesterweg, 1968), pp. 55-63;

Hans Berendt, "Rainer Maria Rilke: Zu den *Aufzeichnungen des Malte Laurids Brigge*," *Mitteilungen der literaturhistorischen Gesellschaft Bonn*, 6 (1911): 75-104;

Maurice Betz, *Rilke à Paris et Les cahiers de Malte Laurids Brigge* (Paris: Émile-Paul, 1941); translated and enlarged by Willi Reich as *Rilke in Paris* (Zurich: Arche, 1948);

Betz, *Rilke vivant* (Paris: Émile-Paul, 1937); enlarged and translated by Reich as *Rilke in Frankreich: Erinnerungen, Briefe, Dokumente* (Vienna, Leipzig & Zurich: Reichner, 1938);

Elaine Boney, "Love's Door to Death in Rilke's *Cornet* and Other Works," *Modern Austrian Literature*, 10, no. 1 (1977): 18-30;

Hans H. Borcherdt, "Das Problem des 'Verlorenen Sohnes' bei Rilke," in *Worte und Werte:*

Festschrift für Bruno Markwardt (Berlin: De Gruyter, 1961), pp. 24-33;

Brigitte L. Bradley, *Zu Rilkes Malte Laurids Brigge* (Bern & Munich: Francke, 1980);

Bradley, "Rilke's *Geschichten vom lieben Gott:* The Narrator's Stance toward the Bourgeoisie," *Modern Austrian Literature*, 15 (1982): 1-24;

Patricia Pollock Brodsky, "The Military School: A Shared Source in Rilke and Musil," *Modern Language Studies*, 10 (1979-1980): 88-93;

Brodsky, *Russia in the Works of Rainer Maria Rilke* (Detroit: Wayne State University Press, 1984);

Brodsky, "The Russian Source of Rilke's 'Wie der Verrat nach Russland kam,'" *Germanic Review*, 5 (Spring 1979): 72-77;

Russell E. Brown, *Index zu Rainer Maria Rilkes Die Aufzeichnungen des Malte Laurids Brigge* (Frankfurt am Main: Athenäum, 1971);

Timothy J. Casey, *Rainer Maria Rilke: A Centenary Essay* (London: Macmillan, 1976);

Robert J. Clements, "Rainer Maria Rilke, Michelangelo and the *Geschichten vom lieben Gott*," *Comparative Literature*, 6 (1954): 218-231; reprinted in *Studies in Germanic Languages and Literatures Presented to Ernst A. G. Rose*, edited by Robert A Fowkes and Volkmar Sander (New York: New York University Press, 1967), pp. 57-70;

Charles Dédéyan, *Rilke et la France*, 4 volumes (Paris: Société d'édition d'enseignement supérieur, 1961);

Kirk Dethlefsen, "'Die Turnstunde': Rilkes Beitrag zu einer neuen Schule des Sehens," *Seminar*, 18 (1982): 236-260;

Eva Fauconneau Defresne, "Wirklichkeitserfahrung und Bewusstseinsentwicklung in Rilkes *Malte Laurids Brigge* und Sartres *La Nausée*," *Arcadia*, 17 (1982): 258-273;

Reidar Ekner, "Rilke, Obstfelder och *Die Aufzeichnungen des Malte Laurids Brigge*," in his *En sällsam gemenskap: Litteraturhistoriska essäer* (Stockholm: Norstedts, 1967), pp. 152-171;

Hartmut Engelhardt, ed., *Materialien zu Rainer Maria Rilkes 'Die Aufzeichnungen des Malte Laurids Brigge'* (Frankfurt am Main: Suhrkamp, 1974);

F. K. Feigel, "*Rilkes Geschichten vom lieben Gott*," *Pforte: Monatsschrift für Kultur*, 6 (1954-1955): 228-245;

Diana Festa-McCormick, "Rilke's *Notebooks:* Paris and the Phantoms of the Past," in her *The City as Catalyst* (Rutherford, Madison & Teaneck, N.J.: Fairleigh Dickinson University Press, 1979), pp. 69-88;

Heinrich Gerhard Franz, "Wandlungen des Menschenbildes in Rainer Maria Rilkes *Die Aufzeichnungen des Malte Laurids Brigge*–Parallelen zur gleichzeitigen Malerei," in *Marginalien zur poetischen Welt: Festschrift für Robert Mühlher*, edited by Alois Eder, Hellmuth Himmel, and Alfred Kracher (Berlin: Duncker & Humblot, 1971), pp. 341-367;

Ulrich Fülleborn, "Form und Sinn der *Aufzeichnungen des Malte Laurids Brigge:* Rilkes Prosabuch und der moderne Roman," in *Unterscheidung und Bewahrung: Festschrift für Hermann Kunisch* (Berlin: De Gruyter, 1961), pp. 147-169;

Henry F. Fullenwider, *Rilke and His Reviewers: An Annotated Bibliography* (Lawrence: University of Kansas Libraries, 1978);

Rüdiger Görner, "Über die Fiktion des Täglichen: Das Diaristische moderner Literatur," in his *Das Tagebuch: Eine Einführung* (Munich & Zurich: Artemis, 1985), pp. 98-122;

Diego Hanns Goetz, *Der unsterbliche verlorene Sohn* (Vienna: Amandus, 1949);

Hartmann Goertz, *Frankreich und das Erlebnis der Form im Werke Rainer Maria Rilkes* (Stuttgart: Metzler, 1932);

Thomas Elwood Hart, "Simile by Structure in Rilke's *Geschichten vom lieben Gott*," *Modern Austrian Literature*, 15, no. 3/4 (1982): 25-69;

Hildburg Herbst, "*Die Weise von Liebe und Tod des Cornets Christoph Rilke:* Ein Vergleich der Urfassung mit dem endgültigen Text," *German Quarterly*, 50 (January 1977): 21-31;

Ernst Fedor Hoffmann, "Zum dichterischen Verfahren in Rilkes 'Aufzeichnungen des Malte Laurids Brigge,'" *Deutsche Vierteljahresschrift für Literaturwissenschaft und Geistesgeschichte*, 42 (1968): 202-230;

Hermann von Jan, *Rilkes Aufzeichnungen des Malte Laurids Brigge* (Leipzig: Weber, 1938);

Rudolf Jancke, "Rilke und Kierkegaard," *Deutsche Vierteljahresschrift für Literaturwissenschaft und Geistesgeschichte*, 39 (1938): 314-329;

Klaus W. Jonas, "Die Rilke-Kritik 1950-1966," *Insel Almanach auf das Jahr 1967* (Frankfurt am Main: Insel, 1967), pp. 94-121;

Philippe Jullian, *Dreamers of Decadence: Symbolist Painters of the 1890s* (New York & Washington, D.C.: Praeger, 1971);

Wolfgang Kayser, "Eine unbekannte Prosaskizze von Rainer Maria Rilke," *Trivium*, 5 (1947): 81-88;

Byong-Ock Kim, *Rilkes Militärschulerlebnis und das Problem des verlorenen Sohnes* (Bonn: Bouvier, 1973);

Johannes Klein, "Die Struktur von Rilkes *Malte*," *Wirkendes Wort*, 2 (1951-1952): 93-103;

H. R. Klieneberger, "Romanticism and Modernism in Rilke's *Die Aufzeichnungen des Malte Laurids Brigge*," *Modern Language Review*, 74 (April 1979): 361-367;

Karl Klutz, "Rilke-Bibliographie des Jubiläumsjahres 1975," *Blätter der Rilke-Gesellschaft*, 5 (1978): 63-79;

Klutz, "Rilke-Bibliographie für das Jahr 1976," *Blätter der Rilke-Gesellschaft*, 6 (1979): 62-85;

Klutz, "Rilke-Bibliographie für die Jahre 1977 und 1978," *Blätter der Rilke-Gesellschaft*, 7-8 (1980-1981): 143-168;

Klutz, "Rilke-Bibliographie für das Jahr 1979," *Blätter der Rilke-Gesellschaft*, 9 (1982): 128-151;

Klutz, "Rilke-Bibliographie für die Jahre 1980 und 1981," *Blätter der Rilke-Gesellschaft*, 10 (1983): 124-159;

Klutz, "Rilke-Bibliographie für das Jahr 1982," *Blätter der Rilke-Gesellschaft*, 11-12 (1984-1985): 137-164;

Klutz, "Rilke-Bibliographie für das Jahr 1983," *Blätter der Rilke-Gesellschaft*, 13 (1986): 155-175;

Klutz, "Rilke-Bibliographie für das Jahr 1984," *Blätter der Rilke-Gesellschaft*, 14 (1987): 201-217;

Werner Kohlschmidt, "Rilke und Kierkegaard," in his *Entzweite Welt: Studien zum Menschenbild in der neueren Dichtung* (Gladbeck: Freizeiten, 1953), pp. 88-97;

Kohlschmidt, "Rilke und Obstfelder," in *Die Wissenschaft von deutscher Sprache und Dichtung: Methoden, Probleme, Aufgaben: Festschrift für Friedrich Maurer* (Stuttgart: Klett, 1963), pp. 458-477;

Kohlschmidt, ed., *Rilke: Interpretationen* (Lahr: Schauenburg, 1948);

Wilhelm Loock, *Rainer Maria Rilke: Die Aufzeichnungen des Malte Laurids Brigge* (Munich: Oldenbourg, 1971);

Claire Lucques, "La Chanson d'amour et de mort du cornette Christophe Rilke: Est-elle une exception d'art populaire dans l'œuvre de Rainer Maria Rilke?," in her *L'Absence ardente: Visages de Rilke* (Troyes: La Renaissance, 1977), pp. 19-31;

Lucques, "La Poétique de *Malte Laurids Brigge*," *Blätter der Rilke-Gesellschaft*, 9 (1982): 22-32;

Børge Gedsø Madsen, "Influences from J. P. Jacobsen and Sigbjørn Obstfelder on Rainer Maria Rilke's *Die Aufzeichnungen des Malte Laurids Brigge*," *Scandinavian Studies*, 26 (August 1954): 105-114;

Lorna Martens, "Reliable Narration: Rainer Maria Rilke's *Die Aufzeichnungen des Malte Laurids Brigge*," in her *The Diary Novel* (London & New York: Cambridge University Press, 1985), pp. 156-172;

Fritz Martini, "Die Aufzeichnungen des Malte Laurids Brigge," in his *Das Wagnis der Sprache: Interpretationen deutscher Prosa von Nietzsche bis Benn* (Stuttgart: Klett, 1954), pp. 137-175;

Eudo C. Mason, "Rilkes Humor," in *Deutsche Weltliteratur von Goethe bis Ingeborg Bachmann: Festschrift für J. Alan Pfeffer*, edited by Klaus W. Jonas (Tübingen: Niemeyer, 1972), pp. 216-244;

Gert Mattenklott, "Die Zeit der anderen Auslegung der 'Aufzeichnungen des Malte Laurids Brigge von Rilke,'" in *Methodische Praxis der Literaturwissenschaft: Modelle der Interpretation*, edited by Dieter Kimpel and Beate Pinkerneil (Kronberg im Taunus: Scriptor, 1975), pp. 117-157;

Josef Mayrhöfer, "Motivegeschichtliche Untersuchungungen zu Rainer Maria Rilkes 'Cornet,'" *Blätter der Rilke-Gesellschaft*, 2 (1975): 59-74;

Veronika Merz, "Die Gottesidee in Rilkes *Aufzeichnungen des Malte Laurids Brigge*," *Jahrbuch der deutschen Schillergesellschaft*, 26 (1982): 262-295;

Armand Nivelle, "Sense et structure des 'Cahiers de Malte Laurids Brigge,'" *Revue d'Esthétique*, 12 (1959): 5-32;

Idris Parry, "Malte's Hand," *German Life and Letters*, new series 11 (1957): 1-12;

Wolfgang Paul, "R. M. Rilkes 'Die Weise von Liebe und Tod des Cornets Christoph Rilke' und die Schlacht von Mogersdorf," *Neue deutsche Hefte*, 11 (1964): 84-95;

Guenther C. Rimbach, "Zum Begriff der Aquivalenz im Werke Rilkes und zur Entsprechung zwischen den Künsten in der Poetik der Moderne," *Modern Austrian Literature*, 15, no. 3/4 (1982): 127-143;

Hugo Rokyta, *Das Schloß im "Cornet" von Rainer Maria Rilke* (Vienna: Bergland, 1966);

Inca Rumold, *Die Verwandlung des Ekels: Zur Funktion der Kunst in Rilkes "Malte Laurids Brigge" und Sartres "La Nausée"* (Bonn: Bouvier, 1979);

Judith Ryan, " 'Hypothetisches Erzählen': Zur Funktion von Phantasie und Einbildung in Rilkes 'Malte Laurids Brigge,' " *Jahrbuch der deutschen Schillergesellschaft*, 15 (1971): 341-374;

Dieter Saalmann, *Rainer Maria Rilkes "Die Aufzeichnungen des Malte Laurids Brigge": Ein Würfelwerf nach dem Absoluten: Poetologische Aspekte* (Bonn: Bouvier, 1975);

Clementina di San Lazzaro, " 'Die Aufzeichnungen des Malte Laurids Brigge' von R. M. Rilke im Vergleich mit Jacobsens 'Niels Lyhne' und A. Gides 'Nourritures Terrestres,' " *Germanisch-romanische Monatsschrift*, 29 (1941): 106-117;

Wolfgang Schneditz, *Rilkes letzte Landschaft* (Salzburg: Pallas, 1951);

George C. Schoolfield, "A Bad Story of Young Rilke," in *From Vormärz to Fin de Siècle: Essays in Nineteenth Century Austrian Literature*, edited by Mark G. Ward (Blairgownie: Lochee Publications, 1986), pp. 107-132;

Schoolfield, "Rilke's Ibsen," *Scandinavian Studies*, 51 (Autumn 1979): 460-501;

Walter Seifert, *Das epische Werk Rainer Maria Rilkes* (Bonn: Bouvier, 1969);

Walter Simon, "Philologische Untersuchungen zu Rainer Maria Rilkes 'Cornet,' " *Blätter der Rilke-Gesellschaft*, 2 (1975): 26-58;

Simon, ed., *Rainer Maria Rilke: Die Weise von Liebe und Tod. Texte und Dokumente* (Frankfurt am Main: Suhrkamp, 1974);

William Small, *Rilke-Kommentar zu den Aufzeichnungen des Malte Laurids Brigge* (Chapel Hill: University of North Carolina Press, 1983);

Walter H. Sokel, "Zwischen Existenz und Weltinnenraum: Zum Prozess der Ent-Ichung in Malte Laurids Brigge," in *Probleme des Erzählens in der Weltliteratur: Festschrift für Käte Hamburger*, edited by Fritz Martini (Stuttgart: Klett, 1971), pp. 212-233;

Ingeborg H. Solbrig and Joachim W. Storck, eds., *Rilke heute: Beziehungen und Wirkungen* (Frankfurt am Main: Suhrkamp, 1975);

August Stahl, *Rilke Kommentar: Zu den Aufzeichnungen des Malte Laurids Brigge, zur erzählerischen Prosa, zu den essayistischen Schriften und zum dramatischen Werk* (Munich: Winkler, 1979);

Steffen Steffensen, *Rilke und Skandinavien: Zwei Vorträge* (Copenhagen: Munksgaard, 1958);

Steffensen, "Rilkes Malte Laurids Brigges optegnelser: En førlober for den moderne roman," in *Romanproblemer: Teorier og analyser: Festskrift til Hans Sørensen*, edited by Merete Gerlach-Nielsen, Hans Hertel, and Morten Nøjgaard (Odense: Universitetsforlaget, 1968), pp. 254-263;

Anthony R. Stevens, *Rilkes Malte Laurids Brigge: Strukturanalyse des erzählerischen Bewusstseins* (Bern & Frankfurt am Main: Lang, 1974);

Gottfried Stix, "Das Geheimnis der Rose: Zu Rainer Maria Rilkes *Geschichten vom lieben Gott*," *Literatur und Kritik*, 123 (1978): 171-180;

Ferenc Szasz, "Der Jugendstil als Weltanschauung am Beispiel Raines Maria Rilkes," *Blätter der Rilke-Gesellschaft*, 14 (1987): 11-20;

Marie von Thurn und Taxis-Hohenlohe, *Erinnerungen an Rainer Maria Rilke* (Munich, Berlin & Zurich: Oldenbourg, 1932);

Hermann Uyttersprot, "Rilkes Weise von Liebe und Tod," *Nieuw Vlaams Tijdschrift*, 20 (1966): 2-21;

Alfred Vogt, "Ärztliche Betrachtung über 'Die Aufzeichnungen des Malte Laurids Brigge' von Rilke," *Deutsche Medizinische Zeitschrift*, 64 (1938): 457-459;

Karl E. Webb, *Rainer Maria Rilke und Jugendstil: Affinities, Influences, Adaptations* (Chapel Hill: University of North Carolina Press, 1978);

Felix Wittner, "Rilkes Cornet," *PMLA*, 44 (1929): 911-924;

Helmut Wocke, *Rilke und Italien* (Giessen: Von Münchow, 1940);

Wayne Wonderley, "An Analysis of Rilke's Novella 'Die Turnstunde,' " *Perspectives on Contemporary Literature*, 2 (1976): 134-139;

Eva C. Wunderlich, "Slavonic Traces in Rilke's *Geschichten vom lieben Gott*," *Germanic Review*, 22 (1947): 287-297;

R. Zellweger, *Genèse et Fortune du "Cornette" de Rilke* (Neuchâtel: A la Baconnière, 1971);

Werner Zimmermann, "Rainer Maria Rilke: 'Der Bettler und das stolze Fräulein,' " in his *Deutsche Prosadichtung der Gegenwart* (Düsseldorf: Schwann, 1956), I: 145-154.

Papers:

Principal collections of Rainer Maria Rilke's papers are at the Rilke-Archiv, Gernsbach; the Rilke-Archiv of the Schweizerische Landesbibliothek, Bern; and the Deutsches Literaturarchiv, Marbach, West Germany.

Arthur Schnitzler
(15 May 1862-21 October 1931)

Gerd K. Schneider
Syracuse University

BOOKS: *Anatol: Mit einer Einleitung von Loris* (Berlin: Bibliographisches Bureau, 1893); translated by Grace Isabel Colbron as *Anatol*, in *Anatol; Living Hours; The Green Cockatoo* (New York: Boni & Liveright, 1917), pp. 1-97;

Das Märchen: Schauspiel in drei Aufzügen (Dresden & Leipzig: Pierson, 1894; revised edition, Berlin: Fischer, 1902);

Sterben: Novelle (Berlin: Fischer, 1895); translated by Harry Zohn as "Dying," in *The Little Comedy and Other Stories* (New York: Ungar, 1977), pp. 147-234;

Liebelei: Schauspiel in drei Akten (Berlin: Fischer, 1896); translated by Bayard Quincy Morgan as *Light-O'-Love: A Drama in Three Acts* (Chicago: Dramatic Publishing Co., 1912);

Die Frau des Weisen: Novelletten (Berlin: Fischer, 1898);

Freiwild: Schauspiel in drei Akten (Berlin: Fischer, 1898); translated by Paul H. Grummann as *Free Game* (Boston: Badger, 1913);

Der grüne Kakadu; Paracelsus; Die Gefährtin: Drei Einakter (Berlin: Fischer, 1899); translated by Horace B. Samuel as *The Green Cockatoo and Other Plays* (Chicago: McClurg, 1913)—comprises *The Green Cockatoo: Grotesque in One Act, The Mate, Paracelsus*;

Das Vermächtnis: Schauspiel in drei Akten (Berlin: Fischer, 1899); translated by Mary L. Stephenson as *The Legacy: Drama in Three Acts, Poet Lore*, 22 (July-August 1911): 241-308;

Der Schleier der Beatrice: Schauspiel in fünf Akten (Berlin: Fischer, 1901);

Leutnant Gustl: Novelle (Berlin: Fischer, 1901); translated by Richard L. Simon as *None But the Brave* (New York: Simon & Schuster, 1926);

Frau Bertha Garlan: Novelle (Berlin: Fischer, 1901); translated by Agnes Jacques as *Bertha Garlan* (Boston: Badger, 1913); translated by J. H. Wisdom and Marr Murray as *Bertha Garlan: A Novel* (London: Goschen, 1914);

Arthur Schnitzler (Austrian Cultural Institute)

Lebendige Stunden: Vier Einakter (Berlin: Fischer, 1902); *Die Frau mit dem Dolche: Schauspiel in einem Akt*, pp. 37-70, translated by Grummann as *Living Hours: Four One-Act Plays* (Boston: Badger, 1913);

Reigen: Zehn Dialoge geschrieben Winter 1896/97 (Vienna & Leipzig: Wiener Verlag, 1903); translated by L. D. Edwards and F. L. Glaser as *Hands Around: A Cycle of Ten Dialogues* (New York: Privately printed, 1920); translated by Eric Bentley as *La Ronde*, in *Arthur Schnitzler: Plays and Stories*, edited by Egon Schwarz (New York: Continuum, 1982), pp. 53-116; translated by Charles Osborne as *The Round Dance*, in *The Round Dance and*

Other Plays (Manchester, U.K.: Carcanet New Press, 1982);

Der Einsame Weg: Schauspiel in fünf Akten (Berlin: Fischer, 1904); translated by Edwin Björkman as *The Lonely Way* (Boston: Little, Brown, 1904);

Die griechische Tänzerin: Novellen (Vienna & Leipzig: Wiener Verlag, 1905);

Marionetten: Drei Einakter (Berlin: Fischer, 1906);

Der Ruf des Lebens: Schauspiel in drei Akten (Berlin: Fischer, 1906);

Zwischenspiel: Komödie in drei Akten (Berlin: Fischer, 1906); translated by Björkman as *Intermezzo: A Comedy in Three Acts*, in *The Lonely Way; Intermezzo; Countess Mizzie: Three Plays* (New York: Kennerley, 1915), pp. 139-259;

Dämmerseelen: Novellen (Berlin: Fischer, 1907);

Der Weg ins Freie: Roman (Berlin: Fischer, 1908); translated by Samuel as *The Road to the Open* (New York: Knopf, 1932; London: Allen & Unwin, 1932);

Der tapfere Kassian: Singspiel in einem Aufzug, music by Oscar Straus (Leipzig & Vienna: Doblinger, 1909);

Der junge Medardus: Dramatische Historie in einem Vorspiel und fünf Aufzügen (Berlin: Fischer, 1910);

Der Schleier der Pierrette: Pantomime in drei Bildern, music by Ernst von Dohnanyi (Vienna & Leipzig: Doblinger, 1910);

Das weite Land: Tragikomödie in fünf Akten (Berlin: Fischer, 1911); translated by Edward Woticky and Alexander Caro as *The Vast Domain: A Tragi-Comedy in Five Acts*, Poet Lore, 324 (September 1923): 317-407; translated by Tom Stoppard as *Undiscovered Country* (Boston & London: Faber & Faber, 1980);

Masken und Wunder: Novellen (Berlin: Fischer, 1912);

Professor Bernhardi: Komödie in fünf Akten (Berlin: Fischer, 1912); translated by Hetty Landstone as *Professor Bernhardi: A Comedy in Five Acts* (London: Faber & Gwyer, 1927); translated by Mrs. Emil Pohli as *Professor Bernhardi*, in *A Golden Treasury of Jewish Literature*, edited by Leo W. Schwarz (New York & Toronto: Farrar & Rinehart, 1937), pp. 468-504;

Frau Beate und ihr Sohn: Novelle (Berlin: Fischer, 1913); translated by Jacques as *Beatrice: A Novel* (New York: Simon & Schuster, 1926);

Gesammelte Werke in zwei Abteilungen, 7 volumes (Berlin: Fischer, 1913-1914);

Komödie der Worte: Drei Einakter (Berlin: Fischer, 1915); translated, with additions, by Pierre Loving as *Comedies of Words and Other Plays* (Cincinnati: Stewart & Kidd, 1917);

Fink und Fliederbusch: Komödie in drei Akten (Berlin: Fischer, 1917);

Doktor Gräsler, Badearzt: Erzählung (Berlin: Fischer, 1917); translated by E. C. Slade as *Dr. Graesler* (New York: Seltzer, 1923; London: Chapman & Hall, 1924);

Casanovas Heimfahrt: Novelle (Berlin: Fischer, 1918); translated by Eden and Cedar Paul as *Casanova's Homecoming* (New York: Seltzer, 1922; London: Brentano's, 1923);

Die Schwestern oder Casanova in Spa: Ein Lustspiel in Versen. Drei Akte in einem (Berlin: Fischer, 1919);

Komödie der Verführung: in drei Akten (Berlin: Fischer, 1924);

Fräulein Else: Novelle (Berlin, Vienna & Leipzig: Zsolnay, 1924); translated by Robert A. Simon as *Fräulein Else: A Novel* (New York: Simon & Schuster, 1925); translated by F. H. Lyon as *Fräulein Else* (London: Philpot, 1925);

Die Frau des Richters: Novelle (Berlin: Propyläen, 1925); translated by Peter Bauland as "The Judge's Wife," in *The Little Comedy and Other Stories*, pp. 85-145;

Traumnovelle (Berlin: Fischer, 1926); translated by Otto P. Schinnerer as *Rhapsody: A Dream Novel* (New York: Simon & Schuster, 1927; London: Constable, 1928);

Der Gang zum Weiher: Dramatische Dichtung in fünf Aufzügen (Berlin: Fischer, 1926);

Spiel im Morgengrauen: Novelle (Berlin: Fischer, 1927); translated by William A. Drake as *Daybreak* (New York: Simon & Schuster, 1927);

Buch der Sprüche und Bedenken: Aphorismen und Betrachtungen (Vienna: Phaidon, 1927); partially translated by Dorothy Alden as "Aphorisms: From an Unpublished Book 'Proverbs and Reflections,'" *Plain Talk*, 2 (May 1928): 590; 3 (October 1928): 419; (December 1928): 733; partially translated by Frederick Ungar as *Practical Wisdom: A Treasury of Aphorisms and Reflections from the German*, edited by Ungar (New York: Ungar, 1977);

Der Geist im Wort und der Geist in der Tat: Vorläufige Bemerkungen zu zwei Diagrammen (Berlin: Fischer, 1927); translated by Robert O. Weiss as *The Mind in Words and Action: Preliminary*

Remarks Concerning Two Diagrams (New York: Ungar, 1972);

Therese: Chronik eines Frauenlebens (Berlin: Fischer, 1928); translated by Drake as *Therese: The Chronicle of a Woman's Life* (New York: Simon & Schuster, 1928);

Im Spiel der Sommerlüfte: in drei Aufzügen (Berlin: Fischer, 1930);

Flucht in die Finsternis: Novelle (Berlin: Fischer, 1931); translated by Drake as *Flight into Darkness: A Novel* (New York: Simon & Schuster, 1931);

Anatols Größenwahn: Ein Akt (Berlin: Fischer, 1932);

Die Gleitenden: Ein Akt (Berlin: Fischer, 1932);

Die kleine Komödie: Frühe Novellen (Berlin: Fischer, 1932);

Die Mörderin: Tragische Posse in einem Akt (Berlin: Fischer, 1932);

Abenteurernovelle (Vienna: Bermann-Fischer, 1937);

Über Krieg und Frieden (Stockholm: Bermann-Fischer, 1939); translated by Weiss as *Some Day Peace Will Return: Notes on Peace and War* (New York: Ungar, 1972);

Gesammelte Werke: Die Erzählenden Schriften, 2 volumes (Frankfurt am Main: Fischer, 1961-1962);

Gesammelte Werke: Die Dramatischen Werke, 2 volumes (Frankfurt am Main: Fischer, 1962);

Das Wort: Tragikomödie in fünf Akten. Aus dem Nachlaß, edited by Kurt Bergel (Frankfurt am Main: Fischer, 1966);

Aphorismen und Betrachtungen, edited by Weiss (Frankfurt am Main: Fischer, 1967);

Jugend in Wien: Eine Autobiographie, edited by Therese Nickl and Heinrich Schnitzler (Vienna, Munich & Zurich: Molden, 1968); translated by Catherine Hutter as *My Youth in Vienna* (New York & San Francisco: Holt, Rinehart & Winston, 1970);

Frühe Gedichte, edited by Herbert Lederer (Berlin: Propyläen, 1969);

Zug der Schatten: Drama in 9 Bildern. Aus dem Nachlaß, edited by Françoise Derré (Frankfurt am Main: Fischer, 1970);

Meisterdramen (Frankfurt am Main: Fischer, 1971);

Meistererzählungen (Frankfurt am Main: Fischer, 1975);

Ritterlichkeit: Fragment. Aus dem Nachlaß, edited by R. Schlein (Bonn: Bouvier, 1975);

Entworfenes und Verworfenes: Aus dem Nachlaß, edited by Reinhard Urbach (Frankfurt am Main: Fischer, 1977);

Gesammelte Werke in Einzelausgaben, 15 volumes (Frankfurt am Main: Fischer, 1977-1979);

Tagebuch 1909-1912, edited by Werner Welzig and others (Vienna: Verlag der Österreichischen Akademie der Wissenschaften, 1981);

Tagebuch 1913-1916, edited by Welzig and others (Vienna: Verlag der Österreichischen Akademie der Wissenschaften, 1983);

Tagebuch 1917-1919, edited by Welzig and others (Vienna: Verlag der Österreichischen Akademie der Wissenschaften, 1985);

Tagebuch 1879-1892, edited by Welzig and others (Vienna: Verlag der Österreichischen Akademie der Wissenschaften, 1987);

Beziehungen und Einsamkeiten: Aphorismen, edited by Clemens Eich (Frankfurt am Main: Fischer, 1987).

PERIODICAL PUBLICATIONS: "Er wartet auf den vazierenden Gott," *Deutsche Wochenschrift*, 4 (12 December 1886): 644;

"Amerika," *An der schönen blauen Donau*, 4, no. 1 (1889): 197; translated by Franzi Ascher as "America," *Decision*, 3 (January/February 1942): 35-36;

"Mein Freund Ypsilon: Aus den Papieren eines Arztes," *An der schönen blauen Donau*, 4, no. 2 (1889): 25-28;

"Der Andere: Aus dem Tagebuch eines Hinterbliebenen," *An der schönen blauen Donau*, 4, no. 21 (1889): 490-492;

Alkandis Lied: Dramatisches Gedicht in einem Aufzug, *An der schönen blauen Donau*, 5, no. 17 (1890): 398-400; no. 18 (1890): 424-426;

"Reichtum," *Moderne Rundschau*, 3 (1 September 1891): 385-391; (15 September 1891): 417-423; 4 (1 October 1891): 1-7; (15 October 1891): 34-40; translated by Helene Scher as "Riches," in *The Little Comedy and Other Stories* (New York: Ungar, 1977), pp. 37-73;

"Der Sohn: Aus den Papieren eines Arztes," *Freie Bühne für den Entwicklungskampf der Zeit*, 3 (January 1892): 89-94; translated by Peggy Stamon as "The Son," in *The Little Comedy and Other Stories*, pp. 75-83;

"Blumen," *Wiener Neue Revue*, 5 (1 August 1894): 151-157; translated by Frederick Eisemann as "Flowers," in *Viennese Idylls* (Boston: Luce, 1913), pp. 1-18; translated by Elsie M.

Lang as "Flowers," in *Beatrice and Other Stories* (London: Laurie, 1926), pp. 121-136;

"Der Witwer," *Wiener Allgemeine Zeitung*, 25 December 1894, pp. 3-4; translated by Paul F. Dvorak as "The Widower," in *Illusion and Reality: Plays and Stories by Arthur Schnitzler* (New York, Bern & Frankfurt am Main: Lang, 1986), pp. 129-138;

"Die drei Elixiere," *Moderner Musen-Almanach auf das Jahr 1894: Ein Jahrbuch deutscher Kunst*, 2 (1894): 44-49;

"Die kleine Komödie," *Neue Deutsche Rundschau*, 6 (August 1895): 779-798; translated by George Edward Reynolds as "The Little Comedy," in *The Little Comedy and Other Stories*, pp. 1-36;

"Ein Abschied," *Neue Deutsche Rundschau*, 7 (February 1896): 115-124;

"Die überspannte Person," *Simplicissimus*, 1 (18 April 1896): 3, 6; translated by Dvorak as "The High-Strung Woman," in *Illusion and Reality: Plays and Stories of Arthur Schnitzler*, pp. 63-68;

"Die Frau des Weisen," *Die Zeit*, 2 January 1897, pp. 15-16; 9 January 1897, pp. 31-32; 16 January 1897, pp. 47-48; translated by Eisemann as "The Sage's Wife," in *Viennese Idylls*, pp. 19-52; translated by Lang as "The Wife of the Wise Man," in *Beatrice and Other Stories*, pp. 163-188;

Halbzwei: Ein Akt, *Die Gesellschaft*, 13 (April 1897): 42-49; translated by Dvorak as *One-Thirty*, in *Illusion and Reality: Plays and Stories of Arthur Schnitzler*, pp. 69-76;

"Die Toten schweigen," *Cosmopolis*, 8 (October 1897): 193-211; translated by Courtland H. Young as "The Dead are Silent," in *Short Story Classics: Foreign*, edited by William Patten (New York: Collier, 1907), III: 953-977;

"Der Ehrentag," *Die Romanwelt*, 5, no. 16 (1897): 507-516; translated by Agnes Jacques as "The Hour of Fame," in *Beatrice and Other Stories*, pp. 189-220; translated by Jacques as "The Jest," in *Rejections of 1927*, edited by Charles H. Baker (Garden City, N.Y.: Doubleday, Doran, 1928), pp. 171-194;

"Um eine Stunde," *Neue Freie Presse*, 24 December 1899, p. 29;

"Der blinde Gieronymo und sein Bruder," *Die Zeit*, 22 December 1900, pp. 190-191; 29 December 1900, pp. 207-208; 5 January 1901, pp. 15-16; 12 January 1901, pp. 31-32; translated by Eisemann as "Blind Geronimo and His Brother," in *Viennese Idylls*, pp. 53-106;

Lebendige Stunden: Schauspiel in einem Akt, *Neue Deutsche Rundschau*, 12 (December 1901): 1297-1306; translated by Helen Tracy Porter as *Living Hours: A Play in One Act*, *Poet Lore*, 17 (Spring 1906): 36-45; translated by Colin Clements and Alice Ernst as *Living Hours*, *Stratford Journal*, 4 (March 1919): 155-166;

Sylvesternacht, *Jugend*, 1, no. 8 (1901): 118-119, 121-122; translated by Dvorak as *New Year's Eve*, in *Illusion and Reality: Plays and Stories of Arthur Schnitzler*, pp. 77-85;

"Andreas Thameyers letzter Brief," *Die Zeit*, 26 July 1902; translated by Eisemann as "Andreas Thameyer's Last Letter," in *Viennese Idylls*, pp. 107-120;

"Die Griechische Tänzerin," *Die Zeit*, 28 September 1902; translated by Pierre Loving as "The Greek Dancer," *Dial*, 71 (September 1921): 253-264;

"Exzentrik," *Jugend*, 2, no. 30 (1902): 492-493, 495-496;

"Dämmerseele," *Neue Freie Presse*, 18 May 1902, pp. 31-33; translated by Eric Sutton as "The Stranger," in *Little Novels* (New York: Simon & Schuster, 1929), pp. 39-54;

Der Puppenspieler: Studie in einem Aufzug, *Neue Freie Presse*, 31 May 1903;

"Die Grüne Krawatte," *Neues Wiener Journal* (25 October 1903);

"Das Schicksal des Freiherrn von Leisenbogh," *Neue Rundschau*, 15 (July 1904): 829-842; translated by Kenneth Burke as "The Fate of the Baron von Leisenbogh," *Dial*, 75 (December 1923): 565-582;

Der tapfere Cassian: Puppenspiel in einem Akt, *Neue Rundschau*, 15, no. 2 (1904): 227-247; translated by Adam L. Gowans as *Gallant Cassian: A Puppet Play in One Act* (London & Glasgow: Gowans & Gray, 1914); translated by Moritz A. Jagendorf as "Gallant Cassian: A Puppet Play," *Poet Lore*, 33 (December 1922): 507-520;

"Das neue Lied: Erzählung," *Neue Freie Presse*, 23 April 1905, pp. 31-34; translated by Burke as "The New Song," *Dial*, 79 (November 1925): 355-369;

Zum großen Wurstel: Burleske in einem Akt, *Die Zeit*, 23 April 1905;

"Die Weissagung," *Neue Freie Presse*, 24 December 1905, pp. 31-38; translated by Marie Bush as "The Prophecy," in *Selected Austrian Short Stories*, edited by Bush (London: Milford,

1928), pp. 246-279; translated by Sutton as "The Prophecy," in *Little Novels*, pp. 79-118;

"Die Geschichte eines Genies," *Arena*, 2 (March 1907): 1290-1292;

"Der tote Gabriel: Novelle," *Neue Freie Presse*, 19 May 1907, pp. 31-35; translated by Sutton as "Dead Gabriel," in *Little Novels*, pp. 195-217;

"Der Tod des Junggesellen: Novelle," *Österreichische Rundschau*, 15 (1 April 1908): 19-26; translated by Sutton as "The Death of a Bachelor," in *Little Novels*, pp. 259-279;

Die Verwandlungen des Pierrot: Pantomime in einem Vorspiel und sechs Bildern, *Die Zeit*, 19 April 1908;

Komtesse Mizzi oder der Familientag: Komödie in einem Akt, *Neue Freie Presse*, 19 April 1908, pp. 31-35; translated by Edwin Björkman as *Countess Mizzie* (Boston: Little, Brown, 1907);

"Der Mörder: Novelle," *Neue Freie Presse*, 4 June 1911, pp. 31-38; translated by O. F. Theis as "The Murderer," in *The Shepherd's Pipe and Other Stories* (New York: Brown, 1922), pp. 81-120;

"Die dreifache Warnung," *Die Zeit*, 4 June 1911; translated by Barrett H. Clark as "The Triple Warning," in *Great Stories of the World: A Collection of Complete Short Stories from the Literatures of All Periods and Countries*, edited by Clark and Maxim Lieber (New York: McBride, 1925), pp. 284-285;

"Die Hirtenflöte: Novelle," *Neue Rundschau*, 22 (September 1911): 1249-1273; translated by Theis as "The Shepherd's Pipe," in *The Shepherd's Pipe and Other Stories*, pp. 15-80;

"Das Tagebuch der Redegonda: Novellette," *Süddeutsche Monatshefte*, 9 (October 1911): 1-7; translated by Sutton as "Redegonda's Diary," in *Little Novels*, pp. 181-192;

"Wohltaten, still und rein gegeben," *Neues Wiener Tagblatt*, 25 December 1931, pp. 27-28; translated as "Charity's Reward," *Living Age*, 342 (March 1932): 48-52;

"Welch eine Melodie," *Neue Rundschau*, 43 (1932): 659-663;

"Der Sekundant," *Vossische Zeitung* (1-4 January 1932); translated by Dvorak as "The Second," in *Illusion and Reality: Plays and Stories of Arthur Schnitzler*, pp. 199-216;

"Der letzte Brief eines Literaten: Novelle," *Neue Rundschau*, 43 (January 1932): 14-37; translated by Dvorak as "The Last Letter of an Artist," in *Illusion and Reality: Plays and Stories by Arthur Schnitzler*, pp. 177-198;

"Die Nächste," *Neue Freie Presse*, 27 March 1932, pp. 33-39;

"Der Empfindsame: Eine Burleske," *Neue Rundschau*, 43 (May 1932): 663-669;

"Ein Erfolg," *Neue Rundschau*, 43 (May 1932): 669-678;

"Der Fürst im Hause," *Wiener Arbeiter Zeitung* (15 May 1932);

"Frühlingsnacht im Seziersaal: Phantasie," *Jahrbuch Deutscher Bibliophilen und Literaturfreunde*, 18-19 (1932-1933): 86-91;

"Boxeraufstand: Fragment. Entwurf zu einer Novelle," *Neue Rundschau*, 68, no. 1 (1957): 84-87;

"Über Psychoanalyse," edited by Reinhard Urbach, *Protokolle*, 2 (1976): 277-284.

Schnitzler (center) with his brother, Julius, and his sister, Gisela

Arthur Schnitzler was born on 15 May 1862 in Vienna, the first child of Johann Schnitzler, a laryngologist, and Louise Markbreiter Schnitzler, a physician's daughter. Johann Schnitzler, who wrote for the *Wiener Medizinische Presse* and in

1887 founded the *Internationale Klinische Rundschau*, was also one of the twelve founders of the Allgemeine Wiener Poliklinik (General Viennese Polyclinic), which he headed until his death in 1893. Johann Schnitzler did not have much impact on his son's literary work, which he did not fully understand and of which he occasionally disapproved. The family was Jewish, but not orthodox, and Jewishness became for Arthur Schnitzler only a question of race, not one of religious commitment. His lengthy novel *Der Weg ins Freie* (1908; translated as *The Road to the Open*, 1932) contains many discussions on Jewish problems; a comment made by Heinrich Bermann, a character in this work, seems to reflect Schnitzler's view: "Was ist Ihnen Ihr 'Heitmatland' Palästina? Ein geographischer Begriff. Was bedeutet Ihnen 'der Glaube Ihrer Väter'? Eine Sammlung von Gebräuchen, die sie längst nicht mehr halten und von denen Ihnen die meisten gerade so lächerlich und abgeschmackt vorkommen, als mir" ("What does your 'homeland' Palestine mean to you? A geographical concept. What meaning does 'the belief of your forefathers' have for you? A collection of customs to which they have not adhered for a long time and most of which appear as ridiculous and tasteless to you as to me").

In 1879 Schnitzler graduated with distinction from the Viennese Akademisches Gymnasium, and, following his father's wish, he enrolled in the School of Medicine of the University of Vienna. His heart, however, was in writing. His time was spent primarily in cafés or coffeehouses, which were the typical meeting places for young people of his social class. These cafés were also frequented by artists or would-be artists in need of like-minded people and of an audience interested in new ideas and approaches to literature. In 1885 Schnitzler completed his studies and became a doctor of medicine, working in residence at the General Hospital in Vienna until 1888. In 1886 he met Olga Waisnix, who was married and the mother of three sons. Her husband was the owner of the renowned Thalhof in Reichenau, where Schnitzler and his family occasionally spent a few weeks during their summer vacations. Schnitzler and Olga Waisnix fell in love; their relationship remained platonic, however, owing to Olga's scruples and to her fear of disclosure, which, according to the customs of the time, would surely have led to a duel. Olga recognized Schnitzler's poetic talent; she strengthened his belief in his creativity and encouraged him to write and submit his work to a publisher. Schnitzler did so in 1886, and a few aphorisms and a short story, "Er wartet auf den vazierenden Gott (He Is Waiting for the Vacationing God), were printed. In the same year he became an assistant in his father's clinic; in 1887 he took over as editor of the *Internationale Klinische Rundschau*, a position he held until 1894. He contributed as many as twenty-five articles to the magazine, most of them book reviews.

Between 1888 and 1891 Schnitzler worked on *Anatol* (1893; translated, 1917), a cycle of seven one-act plays held together by Anatol, a young bachelor who discusses his views on women and other personal subjects with his friend Max. Each play in the cycle adds a new facet to his character; although kind and affable, he is basically superficial. Anatol is a "melancholischer Liebhaber" (melancholy lover) who prefers to hang on to his illusions rather than be disappointed by the facts. In the first play, *Die Frage an das Schicksal* (The Question of Fate; translated as *Ask No Questions and You'll Hear No Stories*), Anatol has the opportunity to ask his girlfriend Cora, whom he has hypnotized, whether she really loves him. He does not have the courage to do so, rationalizing his decision by doubting whether the real truth can ever be known. In the second play, *Weihnachtseinkäufe* (translated as *A Christmas Present*), Anatol meets Gabriele, a married high-society lady. She suggests a present for Cora, who, in contrast to Gabriele, is naive enough to love someone unconditionally. Anatol's feelings for Cora are nurtured not only by her devotion to him but also by her inability to use big words and to make promises and eternal vows.

Plays from the *Anatol* cycle were staged separately between 1893 and 1901; in December 1903 Otto Brahm produced five of the plays at the Berlin Lessing Theater and at the Vienna Deutsches Volkstheater. After 1910 the *Anatol* cycle was played more often, and today it is part of the repertoires of major theaters around the world. The reception of *Anatol* in the United States was positive, especially the 1912 premiere with John Barrymore; later, as Stephanie Hammer reports, "the play came increasingly to be dealt with as either a curio or a farce."

Between 1890 and 1891 Schnitzler finished his first full-length play, *Das Märchen* (The Fairy Tale, 1894), based on his relationship with the actress Mizi Glümer. She was passed on to him as a sixteen-year-old by his acquaintance Theodor Friedman, with whom he sometimes exchanged

Schnitzler circa 1890

girls once they lost their charm or novelty. Schnitzler was Mizi's third affair and thus she was considered a fallen woman who could not expect to be treated as a lady in a society that cherished appearance more than essence. Schnitzler, however, fell in love with her. Their affair was characterized by passion and extreme jealousy and proved to be an emotional roller coaster, but it was primarily Mizi who helped him to mature and become more productive. In 1925, having learned of her death, Schnitzler noted in his diary: "Am (7?) Juli 1889 lernte ich sie kennen, keinem Wesen verdankt mein Dichtertum so viel wie ihr. Keine hat mich geliebt wie sie (besonders nach ihrem 'Betrug')" (On (7?) July 1889 I made her acquaintance. My writing is indebted to her as to no one else. No one has loved me as she [especially after her "betrayal"]). Schnitzler thought of marrying her but rejected the idea for two reasons he recorded in his diary: "sie heiraten kann ich nicht. Es ist materiell unmöglich, und ich gesteh' es, in Wien mit ihr als mit meiner Frau zu leben bin ich noch zu feig.–Ich brauch das nicht näher auszuführen–es steht alles schon im Märchen" (I cannot marry her. It is impossible for material reasons, and I confess that I am still too much of a coward to live in Vienna with her as my wife.–I don't have to explain this further–everything is already contained in *Das Märchen*).

In *Das Märchen* the actress Fanny Theren has had two lovers before she meets Fedor Denner, who does not seem to be a slave to the rigid rules of society. Denner talks about the "fairy tale of the fallen woman," and his revolutionary words give Fanny new hope. Denner, however, is too weak to shake off the chains of convention, and he leaves her. Fedor's words at the end show the conflict Schnitzler suffered in his relationship with Mizi, a conflict not only between reason and emotion but also between emotional states: "und es gibt keinen Kuß keusch genug–und keine Umarmung glühend genug, und keine Liebe ewig genug, um die alten Küsse und die alte Liebe auszulöschen. Was war, ist!–Das ist der tiefe Sinn des Geschehenen" (and there is no kiss chaste enough–and no embrace scorching enough, and no love eternal enough, to extinguish the old kisses and the old love. What was, is!– that is the deeper significance of events). In his diary entry of 31 December 1922 Schnitzler wrote: "Was war, ist, das ist der tiefere Sinn des Geschehenen,–noch heute das Motto meines innern Lebens" (what was, is, that is the deeper significance of events,–today still the motto of my inner life).

The three versions of the play show Schnitzler's dissatisfaction with any one solution and his aversion to any one-sided dogma. As Sol Liptzin points out, "The apparent contradictions often encountered in Schnitzler's works result from his anxiety to view each problem from various angles.... After he has treated a problem from one angle and offered an apparently successful solution to it, he is tempted to revert to the same problem from another angle and to demonstrate the absurdity of the very same solution."

Schnitzler wrote several short stories between 1889 and 1892; the best known is *Sterben* (1895; translated as "Dying," 1977), which he began in February 1892 and finished five months later. It is a realistic portrayal of a young man, ironically called Felix (the happy one), who learns that he is soon to die. He does not want to die alone, so he is happy when his girlfriend Marie informs him that she intends to share his fate. During the weeks that follow deterioration sets in, not only in Felix's physical appearance but also in Marie's love for him. At the end she disassociates herself from him and follows her instinct to live. The story, sometimes referred to as an "Anti-Tristan," shows Schnitzler's mastery of clinical observation and his doubt about "eternal" promises.

In 1893 *Das Märchen* premiered at the Deutsches Volkstheater with the well-known actress Adele Sandrock as Fanny Theren; it was withdrawn after the second performance. The Viennese audience could not yet accept the daring thesis that a woman's value and honor were independent of the number of lovers she had had.

Schnitzler's breakthrough came in 1894, when *Liebelei* (1896; translated as *Light-O'-Love*, 1912) was performed. This play was based on Schnitzler's love affair with Marie Reinhard. Fritz has an affair with a married woman and is killed by the woman's husband in a duel. One irony is that he is no longer in love with the woman but, according to the social convention of his time, has to duel with the betrayed husband. The other irony is that Fritz had just met Christine, a so-called süßes Mädel (sweet girl) who is ignorant of her lover's other affair. Equally ironic is Christine's label *süßes Mädel*, a type Reinhard Urbach describes "as a loving and frivolous young thing from the outskirts who, during the flower of her youth, seeks pleasurable experience with the young men of better social class and then, in maturity, marries a workman–a good man." This definition much better fits Christine's friend Mizi, who, knowing the rules of the game, has an affair with Fritz's friend Theodor. When Christine learns of her lover's death, she feels betrayed and runs away. Christine's action is not motivated by Fritz's death; as J. P. Stern points out in his introduction to *Liebelei*: "The tragic conclusion lies not in Fritz's death in the duel, but in Christine's realization that she meant nothing to him: that *nothing* meant anything to him: and that she gave herself, all she was, to this nothing. The tragic conclusion lies in her realization of an absolute betrayal." Michaela L. Perlmann agrees with this verdict: "Im Duell mit dem Gatten der verheirateten Geliebten stirbt Fritz und zerstört damit das Selbstgefühl der schwächeren Partnerin, die sich um ihre Illusion von der wahren Liebe betrogen sieht" (Fritz dies in the duel with the husband of his married mistress, and thus he destroys the self-assurance of his weaker partner, who sees herself betrayed in her illusion of true love).

Liebelei premiered on 9 October 1895 with Adele Sandrock as Christine. A scandal was anticipated because Mizi and Christine daringly visit the apartment of a young man; the premiere, however, was a success, as were subsequent perfor-

Schnitzler's son, Heinrich Schnitzler, as Theodor and Maria Paudler as Mizzi in a scene from a 1925 production of Liebelei *at the Schillertheater, Berlin*

mances in the Deutsches Theater in Berlin, with Brahm directing. Successful performances were also staged in New York in 1905 under the title *Flirtation;* the American title was changed in 1907 to *The Reckoning*. More recent performances in the United States have not received the same acclaim; a possible explanation is suggested by Hammer: "*Liebelei* is generally not hedonistic, erotic, and amoral, that is to say, not European, not Austrian, and especially not Viennese enough to satisfy an American audience, which both craves and fears the artistic presentation of continental degenerateness. Sadly it seems that *Liebelei* must await the magic of Stoppardization in order to win the attention which it deserves on the U.S. stage."

Criticism of society is also the subject of Schnitzler's next play, *Freiwild* (1898; translated as *Free Game*, 1913). The title refers to actresses in summer theaters who were considered "free game" for officers stationed in nearby garrisons. Anna Riedel refuses to obey these rules because she is in love with Paul Rönner. Lieutenant Karinsky offends Anna and is slapped by Paul. Karinsky challenges Paul to a duel, which Paul declines as a matter of principle; to save his honor, Karinsky shoots him down. The tragic figure is Anna; when she is told to leave, her final word is "Wohin?" (Where to?). She has lost the man she loved, and she cannot go back to the theater after the scandal. Schnitzler's concern was not so much the duel itself but the obligation to fight a duel. Schnitzler also criticized such social pressure in *Das weite Land* (1911; translated as *The Vast Domain*, 1923) and the fragment *Ritterlichkeit* (Chivalry, 1975). The absurdity of having to fight a duel can be clearly seen in his comedy *Fink und Fliederbusch* (1917), in which a journalist writes under two different names for opposing newspapers, changing his point of view according to the philosophy of the paper. The situation climaxes when his personas attack each other's viewpoints so vehemently that he has to challenge himself to a duel.

Probably the most controversial play Schnitzler ever wrote was *Reigen* (Round Dance, 1903; translated as *Hands Around*, 1920, and *La Ronde*, 1982). This "dance" is executed by ten couples, consisting of ten persons, doubly linked by sex. The cycle begins with a streetwalker and a soldier; in scene 2 the soldier makes love to a parlormaid; in scene 3 the parlormaid sleeps with a young gentleman, then the gentleman with a married woman, the married woman with her husband, the husband with a "süßes Mädel," the süßes Mädel with a poet, the poet with an actress, the actress with a count, and the count with the prostitute from the beginning. This play is not only about sex but about language: the characters carefully use language to achieve their goals; the language moves from the vernacular in the first two scenes to a highly elaborated code in the last episodes. The play was written in the winter of 1896-1897 and privately printed in 1900 with a preface expressing Schnitzler's intention not to publish the play because of possible misinterpretations.

Schnitzler was right in his pessimistic prediction. The first performances–scenes four to six were staged in Munich on 25 June 1903; the entire work was performed for the first time on 13 October 1912 in Budapest–received reviews which were based less on the artistic merits of the play than on the Jewish background of its author. Hermann Bahr, trying to rescue the work and its author, scheduled a public reading of *Reigen*; but the government objected, probably not on moral grounds as much as from fear of anti-Semitic demonstrations. The book version was confiscated by the prosecuting attorney's office in Berlin on 16 March 1904, and its sale was banned throughout Germany. This prohibition, however, did not deter various groups from giving performances of the work. After the German government lifted the ban, *Reigen* premiered on 23 December 1920 in Berlin and on 1 February 1921 in Vienna. Neither performance fared well. In Berlin nationalistic and anti-Semitic groups demonstrated during the performance of 22 February 1921. The director and the actors were prosecuted in a trial which lasted from 5 November to 18 November.

The transcript of this trial shows clearly the unstable situation in the Weimar Republic. Some comments indicate a genuine concern for the moral safety of young people who might be led into thinking that love is nothing but the pursuit of sexual satisfaction; other comments, however, reveal anti-Semitic sentiments. Pointing to the Jewish director and the Jewish author, the witnesses accused the Jews of demoralizing the German people, especially the young. Racial invectives came from Nazi groups and other right-wing organizations. "Für die Verteidigung kommt es darauf an, festzustellen, daß es sich gar nicht um einen Kampf gegen den *Reigen* handelt, sondern um einen Kampf gegen die Juden, daß man den *Reigen* nur benutzt hat, um in dieser Form eine antisemitische Aktion ins Werk zu setzen" (For the defense it is important to state that this trial is indeed not a battle against *Reigen* but one against the Jews, that *Reigen* was only used in order to bring about an anti-Semitic action). The trial ended with the acquittal of the defendants, but Schnitzler decided to withdraw the play in Germany and Austria. It was not until 1982 that *Reigen* could be seen again in those countries.

Reigen was not easily accepted in America, either. Translated into English by F. L. Glaser and L. D. Edwards as *Hands Around* in 1920, it was banned in New York State at the instigation of John S. Sumner, secretary of the New York Society for the Suppression of Vice. In 1929 charges were brought against a New York bookstore owner who had *Reigen* in stock; the case was dismissed with the following ruling: "Although the theme of the book is admittedly the quite universal literary theme of men and women, the author deals with it in a cold and analytical, one might even say scientific, manner that precludes any sala-

Robert Forster-Larrina as the count and Blanche Dergan as the actress in a 1920 production of Schnitzler's Reigen *at the Kleines Schauspielhaus in Berlin*

cious interpretation. A careful scrutiny reveals not a single line, not a single word, that might be regarded as obscene, lewd, lascivious, filthy, indecent, or disgusting within the meaning of the statute." The French movie version of *Reigen*, titled *La Ronde* (1950) and directed by Max Ophuls, was banned in New York State; the United States Supreme Court, however, overturned the ban in 1954.

Personal tragedies in 1897–Olga Waisnix died and Marie Reinhard's child was stillborn–influenced Schnitzler in the writing of *Das Vermächtnis* (1899; translated as *The Legacy*, 1911), in which a dying man asks his family to accept his girlfriend and child into their home. The family agrees, but favors the child over the mother. When the child dies, the mother leaves the house because she feels unwelcome. The play premiered in Berlin in 1898, directed by Brahm. Although it was initially a success, it ran for only two weeks. The same happened in Vienna: it premiered in the Burgtheater on 30 November 1898 to good initial response; but the interest of the Viennese audience waned, and *Das Vermächtnis* was canceled after only ten performances.

In 1899 Schnitzler met the young actress Olga Gussmann, whom he married in 1903, the year after the birth of their son Heinrich. Also in 1899 the Burgtheater premiered three of his one-act plays: *Der grüne Kakadu* (1899; translated as *The Green Cockatoo*, 1913), *Die Gefährtin* (1899; translated as *The Mate*, 1913), and *Paracelsus* (1899; translated, 1913). The common element running through all of these plays is the blending of illusion and reality which becomes not only for the audience but for the characters as well. In *Der grüne Kakadu* the time is 14 July 1789, the eve of the outbreak of the French Revolution. In a tavern called Der grüne Kakadu extemporaneous plays are performed for members of the aristocracy. The actors make every attempt to present their illusion as reality; the audience is titillated by the thought that these exchanges could be true, even though it knows that they are not. What the audience does not realize is that the events acted out onstage will actually take place a little later on the streets of Paris, with some of the actors taking part in the real revolution. Illusion and truth are so finely interwoven that it is almost impossible to separate them. As William H. Rey comments: "Die bunte Fülle des Lebens–ist sie nicht nur gefälliger Schein, ausgebreitet über dem Abgrund des Todes? Die Wirklichkeit–ist sie nicht nur ein Traum, ein Spiel, ein Erzeugnis unserer Phantasie? Und wenn dem so ist, tritt dann nicht eine verwirrende Vertauschung der Gegensatzpole ein, so daß das Wirkliche zum Unwirklichen und das Unwirkliche zum Wirklichen wird? Eine klare Abgrenzung ist unter diesen Umständen kaum noch möglich" (The many-colored fullness of life–isn't it only a pleasing illusion, spread over the abyss of death? Reality–isn't it only a dream, a game, a product of our fantasy? And if this is so, does not then a confusing exchange of the opposite poles set in, so that the unreal becomes the real and vice versa? A clear demarcation under these circumstances is almost impossible). Adding to the confusion is that *Der grüne Kakadu* consists of three overlapping circles; as Robert Nelson remarks: "The frame or invisible play is the revolution taking place outside; the play within a play is all that we see going on in the tavern; the play within a play within a play is the 'entertainment' which Prosper offers his customers...." In this mixture of reality and illusion all revolutionary efforts seem questionable: if actors are supporters of the revolution, then the revolutionaries are also actors, and the proclaimed political values thus appear in a doubtful light.

The juxtaposition of reality and unreality is also found in the verse drama *Paracelsus*, performed along with *Der grüne Kakadu* at the Deutsches Theater in Berlin in 1899. Paracelsus, the great illusionist, returns to Basel and visits Justinia, his former lover. She is now married to Cyprian, who is absolutely sure of Justinia's love. His certainty is shaken after Paracelsus hypnotizes Justinia and suggests to her that she is infatuated with a young nobleman. Awakened from the trance, Justinia asks her husband's forgiveness. Paracelsus hypnotizes her again and tells her to forget the event. When Justinia awakens the second time, she admits that she is in fact attracted to the young nobleman, but is also in love with her husband. As Martin Swales points out: "At the beginning Cyprian arrogantly asserts total possession of Justinia. As a result of Paracelsus' hypnotic arts, however, he comes to realize that he can never possess Justinia fully–there will always be memories, desires, longings in her heart of which he is not the object. But this is not to say that Justinia is incapable of fidelity; Paracelsus' hypnotism also reveals that she is happy with Cyprian and that she, at the deepest level of her being, does desire to remain faithful to him. Paracelsus' intervention does not destroy Cyprian's and Justinia's marriage. It puts it on a footing that is in one sense more precarious, because both partners are now aware of the possibility of desires and intentions that are in conflict with the marriage; and yet, in another sense, their marriage is more secure in that they *know* that moral certainty in relationships can only be partial, and that this partial certainty is yet a value by which man can live." The difficulty in distinguishing between inner and outer reality is expressed in *Paracelsus* in the often-quoted lines:

> Es fließen ineinander Traum und Wachen,
> Wahrheit und Lüge. Sicherheit ist nirgends.
> Wir wissen nichts von andern, nichts von uns;
> Wir spielen immer, wer es weiß, ist klug.
> (There flow together dream and waking time,
> Truth and deception. Certainty is nowhere.
> Nothing we know of others, of ourselves no more;
> We always play–and wise is he who knows.)

The theme of the nature of illusion and reality is also the basis of *Die Gefährtin*. Professor Pilgram knows that his wife, Eveline, who has just died, had an affair with his young assistant. Pilgram accepted this affair because he felt guilty about marrying someone much younger than himself. Pilgram is a man who, as he proudly announces, cannot be surprised: "Fur mich gibt es keine Überraschungen und Entdeckungen" (For me, there are no surprises and discoveries). He is wrong: he finds out that Eveline's lover was having a simultaneous affair with another woman whom he intends to marry and, worst of all, that Eveline had known of this double game all along. She had accepted this arrangement because it had provided her with emotional fulfillment she had not found in her marriage to Pilgram, whose work was more important to him than his wife. It becomes apparent that Pilgram did not know Eveline at all; as another character, Olga, points out: "wie unendlich fern von Ihnen diese Frau gelebt hat–die zufällig in diesem Hause gestorben ist" (how infinitely remote from you this woman lived–who, by coincidence, died in this house). At the end Pilgram is relieved; he smiles "wie befreit" (as if liberated), realizing that his wife's affair means that he no longer has to feel guilty.

The mixture of reality and illusion, of play and seriousness, dream and waking life points to a unity which lies outside time and space. Such a unity Schnitzler saw as an Urkraft (a primordial power) which unifies all seemingly polar elements. He believed that it was possible, under certain conditions, for the individual to transcend the limitations of time and space and to be part of this elemental power. The individual then experiences a feeling of simultaneity. This feeling occurs especially in music and in dreams.

Schnitzler shows this mystical experience in the novella *Fräulein Else* (1924; translated 1925), written in the form of an interior monologue. Else is pressured by her mother to ask the rich art dealer Dorsday for a large amount of money to help her father pay back money he borrowed from a trust fund and lost on the stock market. Dorsday promises to help on the condition that he be allowed to see Else naked for a few minutes. Else is in a state of great confusion–she wants to help her father, but her strong sense of decency forbids her succumbing to Dorsday's wish. At the same time, her sensuality is as strong as her modesty, and her love for her father includes resentment because his gambling placed

Schnitzler (photo in possession of Heinrich Schnitzler)

her in this situation in the first place. Else has nobody to whom she can turn; Schnitzler stresses her existential loneliness in several passages. After an inner struggle, she goes to the hotel vestibule where Dorsday is sitting and shows herself in the nude to him and all the other guests. Afterward, she collapses and is carried to her room, where she takes an overdose of sleeping tablets. Before she dies, she experiences a musical vision which changes the motif of loneliness and anxiety to one of togetherness and cosmic harmony: "Ich habe ja Angst so allein.... Wo seid Ihr denn? ... Was ist denn das? Ein ganzer Chor? Und Orgel auch? Ich singe mit, was ist es denn für ein Lied? Alle singen mit. Die Wälder auch und die Berge und die Sterne. Noch nie habe ich etwas so Schönes gesehen. Gib mir die Hand, Papa. Wir fliegen zusammen. So schön ist die Welt, wenn man fliegen kann" (I am afraid so alone.... Where are you? ... What is this now? A complete choir? And also an organ? I am singing along, what kind of song is it? All are singing along. The forests, too, and the mountains and the stars. I have never seen anything so beautiful. Father, give me your hand. We will fly together. The world is so beautiful if one can fly). Else is in harmony with the cosmos, and out of this feeling of union she can forgive her father.

The verse drama *Der Schleier der Beatrice* (The Veil of Beatrice, 1901) is frequently cited to show that Schnitzler anticipated Freud's theory of the interpretation of dreams. The title character is a beautiful young woman who lives in Bologna during the Renaissance. Beatrice has just met the poet Filippo Loschi, and Loschi has fallen in love with her. When she tells him of a dream in which she has seen herself married to the duke, he condemns her. Later the dream comes true: Beatrice meets the duke and marries him. Then both discover the body of Loschi, who has taken his own life. Freudian dream analysis would point out that Beatrice had previously seen the duke, to whom she was unconsciously attracted. Beatrice is longing for a union of Loschi, the man of reflection, and the duke, the man of action. She also longs for death, which she regards as a transition to another existence.

Leutnant Gustl (1901; translated as *None But the Brave*, 1926), called by Swales "unquestionably the towering masterpiece of Schnitzler's prose narrative production," is written entirely in the form of an interior monologue. In a cloakroom after a concert Gustl gets into an argument with a baker who insults him and grabs his sword. Dishonored, Gustl must, according to the military code, commit suicide or quit the army. He wanders through Vienna; close to midnight he wishes that the baker would die of a stroke. When Gustl learns that this event has actually happened, a burden is removed from him. The entire experience is forgotten, along with the conviction that it was his duty to commit suicide. He returns to his aggressive nature and looks forward to a duel he knows he will win. Schnitzler's criticism of Gustl, who can be considered representative not only of Austria's army officers but of a military mentality just waiting for the outbreak of war, cost him his commission as lieutenant in the reserve. J. P. Stern, in the introduction to his edition of *Liebelei, Leutnant Gustl, Die letzten Masken* (1966), characterizes Gustl as "a typical product of his military environment–that is, he is perfectly adjusted to it. In every one of his reactions and half-thoughts, urges, desires, fears, he conforms to and is protected by the military code, the social convention to which he conforms, and the convention is nothing more than a systematic manner of gratifying those desires and urges with the least possible bother, and of protecting him as best may be from his fears.... Gustl emerges as a recognizable type, as the portrait of a man in whom a number of historically significant qualities are combined in so powerful and concentrated a fashion that he becomes representative of a whole mode of life ... the temper not only of a young Austrian lieutenant but of Europe in 1914 is encompassed." *Leutnant Gustl*, based on an experience Schnitzler's acquaintance Felix Salten had had in the foyer of the Musikvereinssaal in Vienna, not only caused one of the literary scandals of the year but led to strong anti-Semitic attacks such as this verse published in the Viennese periodical *Kikeriki* on 25 July 1901:

> Leutnant Gustl, der vom Schnitzler
> Als ein Feigling hingestellt,
> Der nicht Mut noch Ehre kennet
> Und als Kneifer sich gefällt:
> War der etwa nicht ein Jude,
> Wie es Schnitzler ist und bleibt?
> Und wenn ja, warum dann klagen,
> Daß ein Jud' "nen Jud" beschreibt?
>
> (Lieutenant Gustl, who by Schnitzler
> Is presented as a coward,
> Bare of courage and of honor
> And who shows himself a shirker:
> Was he not himself a Jew,
> Just as Schnitzler is and will be?
> And if so, then why complain,
> If one Jew describes another?)

In the one-act play *Die Frau mit dem Dolche* (1902; translated as *The Lady with the Dagger*, 1904) Pauline, who is married, and Leonhard, who desires her, look at a painting by an unknown Renaissance artist. Pauline points out to Leonhard that the two figures on the canvas resemble the two of them and mentions that her ancestors had come from Florence. She also says that she feels she has led a previous existence. When the bells start to ring noon, the scene on the canvas comes to life for Pauline: Paola, married to the painter Remigio, has spent the night with Lionardo. The lover boasts of the affair, but Paola makes it clear to him that a nighttime adventure does not count: "Zusammen wach sein, das allein bedeutet" (To be awake together, that alone is important). Because Lionardo brags of his adventure in front of the returned husband, Paola kills him with a dagger, and this scene is painted by Remigio. When the bells stop, Pauline returns to reality and, still in a dreamlike state, asks Leonhard: "Kommt alles wieder, was wir einst erlebt–Muß es wiederkommen?" (Does everything return that we have experienced–Must it return?). Because she is convinced of the inevitability of her fate, she will become Leonhard's lover.

Another work with a mystical basis is "Die Weissagung" (1905; translated as "The Prophecy," 1928), in which Marco Polo prophesies that a colonel who insulted him will die soon. This and another prophesied event both occur. Freud remarked about this story: "Bei uns bleibt ein Gefühl von Unbefriedigung, eine Art Groll über die versuchte Täuschung, wie ich sie besonders deutlich nach der Lektüre von Schnitzler's Erzählung *Die Weissagung* und ähnlichen mit dem Wunderbaren liebäugelnden Produkten verspürt habe" (A feeling of dissatisfaction remains with us, a kind of resentment about the attempted deception, such as I have felt, especially after having read Schnitzler's *Die Weissagung* and similar products which flirt with the supernatural).

Schnitzler's parable "Die dreifache Warnung" (1911; translated as "The Triple Warning," 1925) usually serves as the basis for a discussion of his views on free will versus determinism. A young hiker hears a voice warning him not to proceed unless he wants to commit a murder. Walking on, he hears the voice a second time, warning him not to cross a meadow unless he wants to bring disaster to his country. The youth heeds neither this warning nor a third one, to stop unless he is prepared to die. When he reaches the mountaintop, he accuses the voice of having erred. The voice now informs him of the consequences of his actions: when he crossed a meadow, he made a butterfly change its direction to the emperor's palace; it will lay an egg from which will hatch a caterpillar which will frighten the pregnant queen so that her unborn child will die. As a result, the emperor's evil brother will succeed to the throne and cause the destruction of the country. The last warning will also be fulfilled because the young man will perish on his way down from the mountaintop during the night. The youth curses the voice, which defines itself as "die Kraft, die am Anfang aller Tage war und weiter wirkt unaufhaltsam in die Ewigkeit durch alles Geschehen" (the power which was at the beginning of time and which is active in all eternity through all events). If this is true, the young man claims, then the power knew the outcome of all actions, and its warning was in vain. Were not the results of his actions, and the actions themselves, determined ahead of time? According to Rey, the youth comes to the wrong conclusion because he forgets that the same power which is outside him is also within him: "sein Wille ist nichts anderes als eine individuelle Erscheinungsform der gleichen Lebensmacht und daher zur Mit-wirkung im großen Spiel der Kräfte bestimmt" (his will is nothing else but an individual manifestation of the same vital force and therefore destined to partake in the huge play of forces). The young man had the choice to act or not to act, but once he had decided on a specific action, it had inevitable consequences.

In *Das weite Land*, which premiered in 1911, Friedrich Hofreiter accuses his wife, Genia, of fidelity! The consequence of his wife's moral character was that his friend, who wanted to have an affair with her, was driven to suicide. Hofreiter's resentment against his wife is strengthened by his own infidelity. When Genia finally enters into an affair with the young Lieutenant Otto, Hofreiter is relieved; but at the same time he invokes the social convention and kills Otto in a duel. The title is explained in the central statement of the play: "Sollt' es Ihnen noch nicht aufgefallen sein, was für komplizierte Subjekte wir Menschen im Grunde sind? So vieles hat zugleich Raum in uns–! Liebe und Trug . . . Treue und Treulosigkeit . . . Anbetung für die eine und Verlangen nach einer andern oder nach mehreren. Wir versuchen wohl Ordnung in uns zu schaffen, so gut es geht, aber diese Ordnung ist doch nur etwas Künstliches. . . . Das Natürliche . . . ist das Chaos. Ja . . . , die Seele . . . ist ein weites Land, wie ein Dichter es einmal ausdrückte . . ." (Shouldn't you have observed what complex subjects we humans basically are? We can accommodate so many things at the same time–! Love and deception . . . faithfulness and infidelity . . . worship for one and desire for another one or others. We try to create order in us, as best we can, but this order is, to be sure, only something artificial. . . . The natural state . . . is chaos. Yes, . . . the soul . . . is a vast domain, as a poet once expressed it).

In his autobiography, *Jugend in Wien* (1968; translated as *My Youth in Vienna*, 1970), Schnitzler refers to *Das weite Land* and remarks: "Gefühl und Verstand schlafen wohl unter einem Dach, aber im übrigen führen sie in der menschlichen Seele ihren völlig getrennten Haushalt" (Feelings and understanding may sleep under the same roof, but they run their own completely separate households in the human soul). It would be wrong, though, to identify Schnitzler fully with

Ernst Deutsch (left) as Bernhardi and Kurt Buecheler as Pfarrer in a 1955 production of Schnitzler's Professor Bernhardi *at the Theater am Kurfürstendamm in Berlin*

this statement; there are some convictions which, in his view, are not subject to perspectivism. A case in point is *Professor Bernhardi* (1912; translated, 1927). Bernhardi is the director of the Elisabethinum Clinic in Vienna. A young woman patient is dying but is unaware of the fact. Since she is feeling euphoric, Bernhardi refuses to let her see a priest called in by the Catholic nurse. The nurse then informs the patient of her real condition, thus thwarting Bernhardi's attempt to make death easier for her. Because Bernhardi is a highly successful Jewish physician, the incident stirs up anti-Semitic prejudices which are fueled by the Catholic church. Bernhardi defends his action by declaring that it is his professional duty to reduce suffering and pain in any way he can. At the same time he fights against the opportunistic attacks of his colleagues, who hide their egotistical motives behind the masks of church and state ideology. Bernhardi's conviction and courage are also found in the figure of the priest, who has an unshakable belief in his mission. Schnitzler shows that understanding and a feeling of mutual tolerance are possible between opponents who are true to themselves and their callings.

Schnitzler's criticism of the prevailing attitudes in his society, especially of anti-Semitism, led the Austrian censorship to bar performance of the play in 1913. It was only after the collapse of the monarchy in 1918 that the work was allowed to be staged. Since then it has been performed many times in Europe and the United States, and many critics consider it to be one of the finest works Schnitzler ever created.

Schnitzler was a pacifist; the horrors of war are described realistically in his pamphlet *Über Krieg und Frieden* (1939; translated as *Some Day Peace Will Return*, 1972), written in 1915 during World War I: "Kriegsgreuel: Ein wehrloser Verwundeter wurde auf dem Schlachtfeld geblendet, verstümmelt, von einem Feind natürlich. Ich weiß noch Ärgeres zu erzählen: ein Dutzend Soldaten saßen in einem Schützengraben, ein Schrapnell kam, der eine wurde blind, dem anderen wurde der Bauch aufgeschlitzt, dem dritten der Kehlkopf zerfetzt, dem vierten das ganze Gesicht weggerissen, dem fünften zwei Arme und ein Bein zerschmettert und so weiter. Die nicht gleich tot waren, lagen stundenlang da in Durst, Martern, Höllenschmerzen, Todesangst. Auch sie waren wehrlos gewesen, vollkommen wehrlos. Es gab keine Möglichkeit, sich gegen das Schrapnell zu verteidigen. Auch davonlaufen durften sie nicht, dann wären sie mit Recht wegen Feigheit erschossen worden. Die Wehrpflicht hatte sie wehrlos gemacht" (War atrocity: a defenseless wounded man was blinded and mutilated on the battlefield–by an enemy, of course. I can tell a worse tale. A dozen soldiers were sitting in a trench when a shrapnel struck. One was blinded, another had his abdomen slit open, the third had his larynx shredded, the entire face of the fourth was torn off, the fifth had both arms and a leg shattered, and so forth. Those who were not immediately killed lay there for hours suffering thirst, torments, hellish pain, the fear of death. They too had been defenseless, completely defenseless. There was no possibility of defending themselves against the shrapnel. Also, they could not run off, for had they done so, they would have been shot for cowardice, justifiably. The obligation to defend their country had rendered them defenseless).

In 1918 Schnitzler published *Casanovas Heimfahrt* (translated as *Casanova's Homecoming*, 1922), showing a morally disintegrated, aging adventurer, and in 1919 *Die Schwestern oder Casanova in Spa: Ein Lustspiel in Versen* (The Sisters; or, Casanova in Spa: A Comedy in Verse), which presents Casanova at the peak of his career as a respected diplomat, a famous mathematician, an eminent philosopher, a widely read author, and, above all, an admired amorous adventurer. *Casanovas Heimfahrt* is of greater interest than the comedy because it deals with aging, a problem Schnitzler addressed in various works. Schnitzler's concerns about the aging process are documented in his diaries. As early as 8 April 1900 he noted: "Frühlingsmorgen. Die Melancholie des Alterns. Ich weinte sehr" (Morning in springtime. The melancholy of getting old. I cried a lot). On 23 April he wrote: "Ich habe eine wachsende Angst vor dem Altwerden, ein ungeheures Bedürfnis nach Zärtlichkeit, Geliebt, Angebetet, Bewundertwerden. Nur das befreit mich zuweilen von meinem Angstgefühle" (I have a growing fear of becoming old, an immense need for tenderness, to be loved, adored, admired. Only this relieves me occasionally of my feelings of anxiety). And on 27 April he recorded his thoughts on old age in an entry which has special significance for *Casanovas Heimfahrt*: "Es gibt nur *ein* Erlebnis–das heißt Altern. Alles andere ist Abenteuer" (There is only *one* experience–that is: getting old. Everything else is adventure). In the novella Casanova is fifty-three, Schnitzler's own age at the time of writing in 1915: "In seinem dreiundfünfzigsten Lebensjahre, als Casanova längst nicht mehr von der Abenteuerlust seiner Jugend, sondern von der Ruhelosigkeit nahenden Alters durch die Welt gejagt wurde, fühlte er in seiner Seele das Heimweh nach seiner Vaterstadt Venedig so heftig anwachsen, daß er sie, gleich einem Vogel, der aus luftigen Höhen zum Sterben nach abwärts steigt, in eng und immer enger werdenden Kreisen zu umziehen begann" (In his fifty-third year, when Casanova was no longer driven through the world by the adventurousness of youth but by the restlessness of approaching old age, he felt grow in his soul an intense homesickness for Venice, the city of his birth; and so, like a bird that slowly descends from the lofty heights to die, he began to approach the city in ever-narrowing circles). The metaphor of the slowly descending bird in its death flight indicates that Casanova's days are numbered. His main concern now is to return to the city of his youth, the city he loved and was forced to leave because of his political convictions, which were at variance with those of the Supreme Council. While waiting for the letter informing him whether the Council will allow him to return, he accepts an invitation from an old benefactor to visit him and his wife Amalia, who was one of Casanova's former mistresses.

At the estate of his benefactor he meets Marcolina, who, he realizes, is the person he had sought all through his life. She has expert knowledge in philosophy, art, science, and mathematics, and she is ravishingly beautiful. Casanova's passion is inflamed; from now on his only thought is to win her favor. He could have Amalia, who implores him: " 'Du bist nicht alt. Für mich kannst du es niemals werden. In deinen Armen hab' ich meine erste Seligkeit genossen...' " ("You are not old. For me you cannot be an old man. In your arms I had my first taste of bliss..."). Casanova, however, is realistic enough to see the signs of advancing old age and almost takes delight in pointing them out to Amalia: " 'Sieh mich doch an, Amalia! Die Runzeln meiner Stirn.... Die Falten meines Halses! Und die tiefe Rinne da von den Augen den Schläfen zu! Und hier ... ja, hier in der Ecke fehlt mir der Zahn,'–er riß den Mund grinsend auf. 'Und diese Hände, Amalia! Sieh sie doch an! Finger wie Krallen ... kleine gelbe Flecken auf den Nägeln.... Und die Adern da– blau und geschwollen–Greisenhände, Amalia!' " ("Look well, Amalia! The wrinkles on my forehead.... The loose folds of my neck! And the crow's-feet around my eyes. And, here ... yes, here I have lost one of my eyeteeth,"–he opened his mouth in a grin. "And these hands, Amalia! Look at them! Fingers like claws ... little yellow spots on the fingernails.... And the veins–blue and swollen–the hands of an old man, Amalia!").

Great disappointment comes for Casanova when he sees Marcolina with Lieutenant Lorenzi, who is described as a young Casanova; he has similar looks and the same life-style as the great Venetian adventurer. One night Casanova sees Lorenzi leave Marcolina's chamber. His rage is increased by a letter from the Council informing him that he can return to Venice provided that he agrees to spy for the state. In this state of mind he rapes Teresina, Amalia's thirteen-year-old daughter, who has come to summon him to dinner. The same evening Casanova wins at cards, and Lorenzi, the big loser, agrees to exchange places with Casanova so that the old adventurer can spend the night with Marcolina. Casanova enters Marcolina's chamber in the dark and takes Lorenzi's place. Marcolina, deceived, experiences a bliss which can be described as a mystical union: "An Marcolinens seufzendem Vergehen, an den Tränen der Seligkeit, die er ihr von den Wangen küßte, an der immer wieder erneuten Glut, mit der sie seine Zärtlichkeit empfing, erkannte er bald, daß sie seine Entzückungen teilte. die ihm als höhere, ja von neuer, andrer Art erschienen, als er jemals genossen. Lust ward zur Andacht ... " (From Marcolina's sigh of surrender, from the tears of happiness which he kissed from her cheeks, from the ever-renewed warmth with which she received his caresses, he felt sure that she shared his rapture; and to him this rapture seemed more intense than he had ever experienced, seemed to possess a new and strange reality. Pleasure became worship ...). In the morning Marcolina discovers the betrayal, and in her terrified eyes Casanova reads "das Wort, das ihm von allen das furchtbarste war, da es sein endgültiges Urteil sprach: Alter Mann" (the word which to him was the most dreadful of all words, since it passed the final judgment upon him: old man). Leaving her room, he is confronted by Lorenzi, who challenges him to a duel. Casanova kills Lorenzi, but in the end it is questionable who has actually won: Lorenzi does not have to suffer the fate of Casanova, who will spend the rest of his life as a spy for the authorities he had detested in his younger days.

In the United States *Casanova's Homecoming* was considered obscene, and a seven-year legal battle followed its publication. Instrumental in banning the work was Sumner of the New York Society for the Suppression of Vice, who later brought charges of obscenity against *Reigen*. Sumner lost both cases in 1930. *Casanova's Homecoming* was cleared of the charge of obscenity in a ruling that said "that the book must be measured by living standards of our own time, not by those of the Mid-Victorian era" and called Schnitzler "one of the world's greatest writers and ... *Casanova's Homecoming* ... an incontestable contribution to literature."

At the beginning of *Traumnovelle* (1926; translated as *Rhapsody: A Dream Novel*, 1927), which is considered one of Schnitzler's best works, the physician Fridolin and his wife Albertine talk about the previous night's experiences at a fancy-dress ball. Memories of unfulfilled erotic opportunities as well as mutual mistrust are awakened. This mistrust can only be eliminated if both go through the zone of temptation. Fridolin has such an experience at a party,

Schnitzler in later years (Walter Firner, Berlin)

and Albertine lives out her desires in a dream which parallels Fridolin's adventures in detail. Fridolin and Albertine learn that they are susceptible to erotic temptations, but that their sexual drives are only one side of their human nature; equally important is the moral component which is present in both of their adventures. According to Dorrit Cohn (in Erika Nielsen, ed., *Focus on Vienna 1900* [1982]), both partners fulfill their unconscious wishes: "the erotic wish for an infinitely protracted sexual arousal by a partner who is simultaneously the familiar mate and a total stranger; and the destructive wish for that same partner's self-sacrificial death. What makes Fridolin's experience dream-like–and not merely bizarre or horrific–is that it matches his secret desires no less exactly than Albertine's dream matches hers. Freed from the censuring precepts of conscience for the duration of a night, Fridolin literally lives his dream. It is as though Schnitzler had meant to demonstrate by a kind of limit case Schopenhauer's thesis that life and dream are cut from the same cloth."

In 1929 a collection of Schnitzler's fiction was published in the United States under the title *Little Novels;* it contained "The Fate of the Baron," "The Stranger," "The Prophecy," "Redegonda's Diary," "The Murderer," and "The Death of a Bachelor." The review in the *New Statesman* of 21 September 1929 said: "All these stories are told with a grace and delicacy that relieve them of the horror without depriving them of force.... In his stories Herr Schnitzler does not produce the gaiety of *Anatol*. Ten stories give us four suicides, two deaths in duels, two other sudden deaths, and a murder. But one ends, under the force of the author's persuasiveness, by believing with him that it does not much matter. For Herr Schnitzler is one of the most persuasive writers alive, and the mood into which he most often seeks to persuade us is this of attentive and interested detachment."

Schnitzler's pessimism and disillusionment were partly rooted in his health problems; in his later years he complained of frequent headaches and an increasingly severe ear ailment. He was also despondent over the suicide of his daughter Lily on 26 July 1928 in Venice. His diary entry for 15 September 1928 says: "Tolle Sehnsucht nach Lily.–Die Hoffnungslosigkeit in Hinsicht auf O[lga Schnitzlers] Wesen. Die triste Situation C[lara Katharina] P[ollaczeks], die finanz. Aussichtslosigkeit–die Unfähigkeit zu arbeiten–man müßte jünger sein, um all das zu ertragen" (Mad longing for Lily.–The hopelessness with regard to O[lga Schnitzler's] nature. The sad situation concerning C[lara Katharina] P[ollaczek], the lack of financ. prospects–the inability to work–one has to be younger to endure all this).

Schnitzler had met Clara Pollaczek (then known as Clara Loeb) in 1896; they had broken up soon afterward, and each had married someone else. Only after Schnitzler's divorce in 1921 and the death of Clara Pollaczek's husband did they see each other again, and they continued their relationship, which was marked by Pollaczek's jealousy, from 1923 until Schnitzler's death. One of Schnitzler's last diary entries, dated 21 June 1931, points to the tension between them: "Um 9 kam C.P.... endlich sagte sie: sie gehe auf alles ein, d.h. sie wird nichts dagegen haben, wenn ich Frauen empfange, so viel ich wolle, aber Aufrichtigkeit etc.... Ich war ziemlich todt, als sie, auch ziemlich todt, ging. Ich fühle mich innerlich in mancher Hinsicht schuldig, u[nd] bin es doch nicht" (At 9 C.P. came.... finally she said: she would accept everything, that is, she would have no objections if I receive women, as many as I wanted, but honesty etc.... I was rather beat when she left, and she was, too. I feel guilty in some respects, but in other ways not).

It was during this difficult period that Schnitzler decided to publish his novella *Flucht in die Finsternis* (translated as *Flight into Darkness*, 1931), which he had written in 1913 and revised in 1915, 1916, and 1917. *Flucht in die Finsternis* was printed in May 1931 in the *Vossische Zeitung*; the book version appeared one day before Schnitzler's death in October. The novella concerns two brothers: Otto, a psychiatrist, and Robert, whose mind is deteriorating. Years earlier Robert had asked Otto to kill him in a painless fashion if madness were ever to befall him, and Otto had reluctantly agreed. Robert cannot forget the promise and interprets his brother's every action as threatening. In the final scene Otto visits Robert in a hotel room to assure him of his love and devotion. But Robert misunderstands the situation. In Otto's "Augen war Angst, Mitleid und Liebe ohne Maß. Doch dem Bruder bedeutete der feuchte Glanz dieses Blickes Tücke, Drohung und Tod. Otto wieder, von dem Ausdruck des Grauens in des Bruders Antliz im tiefsten erschüttert, beherrschte sich nicht länger, trat ganz nah an ihn heran, um ihn zu umarmen und ihn durch die rückhaltlose innigste Gebärde seiner brüderlichen Zärtlichkeit zu versichern. Robert aber, des Bruders kühle Hand an seinem Halse fühlend, zweifelte nun nicht mehr, daß der gefürchtete, daß der Augenblick der höchsten, der entsetzlichsten Gefahr gekommen sei, gegen die in jeder Weise sich zu wehren durch menschliche und göttliche Gesetze erlaubt, ja geboten war" (eyes were anxiety, sympathy, and love unbounded. But the twinkling moisture in those eyes meant to his brother malice, menace, and death. Otto, shaken to the depths by the expression of terror in his brother's face, could restrain himself no longer. He went up quite close to him, to embrace him and reassure him with the most tender, unreserved gestures of his brotherly affection. But Robert, feeling his brother's cool hands at his neck, could not doubt that the long-dreaded moment of supreme and unspeakable danger had come. He was permitted, commanded by all laws, human and divine, to defend himself as he could). Robert shoots Otto, who dies instantly; three days later Robert is found dead.

The tragicomedy *Das Wort* (The Word, 1966) remained a fragment although Schnitzler worked on it for thirty years, until his death. One of the central figures in *Das Wort* is the Literat (poetmaster) Anastasius Treuenhof, a Literat being the negative counterpart of the poet. What sets them apart from one another is their attitudes toward the word: while for the poet word and action are one and while he is guided by ethical considerations, the Literat is a sensationalist who is motivated by egotistical drives and opportunism. Treuenhof himself characterizes this type, whom Schnitzler criticized in many of his plays, as follows: "Sie werden an ihre Sargdeckel klopfen und den Totengräber um Papier und Bleistift bitten, um die Sensationen während des Begräbnisses aufzuzeichnen" (They will knock on their coffin lid and ask the undertaker for paper and pencil in order to record the sensations during their burial). The editor of the play, Kurt Bergel, sees its central problem as "die Verantwortung, die der Gebrauch der Sprache dem Menschen auferlegt" (the responsibility which the use of language imposes on man). Treuenhof is responsible for the death of a young man who is driven to suicide by Treuenhof's words. In an exchange between Treuenhof and Hofrat (Councillor) Winkler in the last act, the difference between the Literat and the human being becomes clear:

Treuenhof: Worte sind nichts.
Winkler: Worte sind alles. Wir haben ja nichts anderes.
(Treuenhof: Words are nothing.
Winkler: Words are everything. We have nothing else.)

Winkler's attitude toward the word is also Schnitzler's: words are important and one has to be careful in their usage. In many of his aphorisms Schnitzler points to the ethical, aesthetic, and psychological issues inherent in language. Words, as well as actions, have consequences, and sometimes the result is different from what one expects.

Schnitzler wrote at a specific time for a specific audience. The era was that of the Austro-Hungarian monarchy; the audience was the educated bourgeoisie of Vienna and Berlin. Schnitzler's work does not deal with the period after the end of World War I, which destroyed the culture he knew. But Schnitzler also transcends his time, as Frederick Ungar stresses in his foreword to the collection *The Little Comedy:*

"His work has the validity of what is eternally human. Even though the world he captured with such charm and refinement has long since disappeared, Schnitzler's characters are still very much alive; they are true and original. And this is so because the questions he posed are timeless, as are the topics of his stories and plays–the lure of love, man's transitoriness, the incomprehensibility of fate. Nothing has gone stale–his work still speaks to us today."

Letters:

Briefwechsel mit Otto Brahm, edited by Otto Seidlin (Berlin: Gesellschaft für Theatergeschichte, 1953);

Sigmund Freud, "Briefe an Arthur Schnitzler," *Die neue Rundschau*, 66 (1955): 95-106;

Briefwechsel Georg Brandes und Arthur Schnitzler: Ein Briefwechsel, edited by Kurt Bergel (Bern: Francke, 1956);

Heinrich Schnitzler, "Briefwechsel Arthur Schnitzler und Rainer Maria Rilke," *Wort und Wahrheit*, 13, no. 4 (1958): 283-298;

"Unveröffentlichte Briefe Schnitzlers an Brahm," *Kleine Schriften der Gesellschaft für Theatergeschichte*, 16 (1958): 44-45;

Briefwechsel Hugo von Hofmannsthal-Arthur Schnitzler, edited by Therese Nickl and Heinrich Schnitzler (Frankfurt am Main: Fischer, 1964);

"Briefe an Josef Körner," *Literatur und Kritik*, 2, no. 12 (1967): 79-87;

"Karl Kraus und Arthur Schnitzler: Eine Dokumentation," edited by Reinhard Urbach, *Literatur und Kritik* (1970): 513-530;

Schnitzler and Olga Waisnix, *Liebe, die starb vor der Zeit: Ein Briefwechsel*, edited by Nickl and Heinrich Schnitzler (Vienna, Munich & Zurich: Molden, 1970);

"Briefwechsel Arthur Schnitzler-Franz Nabl," edited by Urbach, *Studium Generale*, 24 (1971): 1256-1270;

Briefwechsel Arthur Schnitzlers mit Max Reinhardt und dessen Mitarbeitern, edited by Renate Wagner (Salzburg: Müller, 1971);

The Correspondence of Arthur Schnitzler and Raoul Auernheimer with Raoul Auernheimer's Aphorisms, edited by Donald G. Daviau and Jorun B. Johns (Chapel Hill: University of North Carolina Press, 1972);

"The Correspondence of Arthur Schnitzler and Richard Beer-Hofmann," edited by Eugene Weber, *Modern Austrian Literature*, 6, no. 3/4 (1973): 40-51;

"Briefe: Arthur Schnitzler-Thomas Mann," edited by Hertha Krotkoff, *Modern Austrian Literature*, 7, no. 1/2 (1974): 1-33;

"Briefwechsel Richard Schaukal-Arthur Schnitzler," edited by Urbach, *Modern Austrian Literature*, 8, no. 3/4 (1975): 15-42;

"Vier unveröffentlichte Briefe Arthur Schnitzlers an den Psychoanalytiker Theodor Reik," edited by Bernd Urban, *Modern Austrian Literature*, 8, no. 3/4 (1975): 236-247;

Adele Sandrock und Arthur Schnitzler: Geschichte einer Liebe in Briefen, Bildern und Dokumenten, edited by Wagner (Vienna: Amalthea, 1975);

"Briefwechsel Fritz von Unruhs mit Arthur Schnitzler," edited by Ulrich K. Goldsmith, *Modern Austrian Literature*, 10, no. 3/4 (1977): 69-127;

"Arthur Schnitzler an Marie Reinhard (1896)," edited by Nickl and Urbach, *Modern Austrian Literature*, 10, no. 3/4 (1977): 23-68;

The Letters of Arthur Schnitzler to Hermann Bahr, edited by Daviau (Chapel Hill: University of North Carolina Press, 1978);

Briefe 1875-1912, edited by Nickl and Schnitzler (Frankfurt am Main: Fischer, 1981);

Briefe 1913-1931, edited by Peter Michael Braunwarth, Richard Miklin, and others (Frankfurt am Main: Fischer, 1984);

Briefe und Tagebücher: Hedy Kempny-Arthur Schnitzler. Das Mädchen mit den dreizehn Seelen (Reinbek: ro-ro-ro, 1984).

Bibliographies:

Richard H. Allen, *An Annotated Arthur Schnitzler Bibliography: Editions and Criticism in German, French and English* (Chapel Hill: University of North Carolina Press, 1965);

Jeffrey B. Berlin, *An Annotated Arthur Schnitzler Bibliography* (Munich: Fink, 1978).

References:

Friedbert Aspetsberger, "'Drei Akte in einem.' Zum Formtrieb von Schnitzlers Drama," *Zeitschrift für Deutsche Philologie*, 85 (1966): 285-308;

Joseph W. Bailey, "Arthur Schnitzler's Dramatic Work," *Texas Review*, 5, no. 4 (1920): 294-307;

Gerhart Baumann, *Arthur Schnitzler: Die Welt von gestern eines Dichters von morgen* (Frankfurt am Main: Athenäum, 1965);

Frederick J. Behariell, "Arthur Schnitzler's Range of Theme," *Monatshefte für deutschen Unterricht*, 43, no. 7 (1951): 301-311;

G. J. Carr and G. J. Eda Sagarra, eds., *Fin-de Siècle Vienna* (Dublin: Trinity College, 1985);

Giuseppe Farese, ed., *Akten des Internationalen Symposiums 'Arthur Schnitzler und seine Zeit'* (Bern, Frankfurt am Main & New York: Lang, 1985);

Alfred Fritsche, *Dekadenz im Werk Arthur Schnitzlers* (Bern: Herbert Lang/Frankfurt am Main: Peter Lang, 1974);

Barbara Gutt, *Emanzipation bei Arthur Schnitzler* (Berlin: Spiess, 1978);

Stephanie Hammer, "Fear and Attraction: *Anatol* and *Liebelei* Productions in the United States," *Modern Austrian Literature*, 19, no. 3/4 (1986): 63-74;

Michael Imboden, *Die surreale Komponente im erzählerischen Werk Arthur Schnitzlers* (Bern & Frankfurt am Main: Lang, 1971);

Rolf-Peter Janz and Klaus Laermann, *Arthur Schnitzler: Zur Diagnose des Wiener Bürgertums im Fin de Siècle* (Stuttgart: Metzler, 1977);

Gottfried Just, *Ironie und Sentimentalität in den erzählenden Dichtungen Arthur Schnitzlers* (Berlin: Schmidt, 1968);

Julius Kapp, *Arthur Schnitzler* (Leipzig: Xenien Verlag, 1912);

Klaus Kilian, *Die Komödien Arthur Schnitzlers. Sozialer Rollenzwang und kritische Ethik* (Düsseldorf: Bertelsmann, 1972);

Josef Koerner, *Arthur Schnitzlers Gestalten und Probleme* (Vienna: Amalthea, 1921);

Hans Landsberg, *Arthur Schnitzler* (Berlin: Gose & Tetzlaff, 1904);

Herbert Lederer, "Arthur Schnitzler's Typology: An Excursion into Philosophy," *PMLA*, 78 (1963): 94-406;

Hans-Ulrich Lindken, *Arthur Schnitzler: Aspekte und Akzente. Materialien zu Leben und Werk* (Frankfurt am Main & Bern: Lang, 1984);

Lindken, *Interpretationen zu Arthur Schnitzler: Drei Erzählungen [Spiel im Morgengrauen; Der blinde Geronimo und sein Bruder; Leutnant Gustl]* (Munich: Oldenbourg, 1970);

Sol Liptzin, *Arthur Schnitzler* (New York: Prentice-Hall, 1932);

Christa Melchinger, *Illusion und Wirklichkeit im dramatischen Werk Arthur Schnitzlers* (Heidelberg: Winter, 1968);

Gerhard Naumann and Jutta Müller, *Der Nachlaß Arthur Schnitzlers: Verzeichnis des im Schnitzler-Archiv der Universität Freiburg i. B. befindlichen Materials* (Munich: Fink, 1969);

Wolfgang Nehring, "Schnitzler, Freud's Alter Ego," *Modern Austrian Literature*, 10, no. 3/4 (1977): 179-194;

Robert James Nelson, *Play within a Play: The Dramatist's Conception of His Art from Shakespeare to Anouilh* (New Haven: Yale University Press, 1958), p. 118;

Erika Nielsen, ed., *Focus on Vienna 1900: Change and Continuity in Literature, Music, Art and Intellectual History* (Munich: Fink, 1982);

Ernst L. Offermanns, *Arthur Schnitzler: Das Komödienwerk als Kritik des Impressionismus* (Munich: Fink, 1973);

Michaela L. Perlmann, *Arthur Schnitzler* (Stuttgart: Metzler, 1987);

Heinz Politzer, "Arthur Schnitzler: Poetry of Psychology," *Modern Language Notes*, 78, no. 4 (1963): 353-372;

Herbert W. Reichert and Herbert Salinger, eds., *Studies in Arthur Schnitzler: Centennial Commemorative Volume* (Chapel Hill: University of North Carolina Press, 1963);

Theodor Reik, *Arthur Schnitzler als Psycholog* (Minden: Bruns, 1913);

William H. Rey, "Arthur Schnitzler," in *Deutsche Dichter der Moderne*, edited by Benno von Wiese, revised edition (Berlin: Schmidt, 1969), pp. 237-257;

Rey, *Arthur Schnitzler: Die späte Prosa als Gipfel seines Schaffens* (Berlin: Schmidt, 1968);

Heinz Rieder, *Das dramatische Werk* (Vienna: Bergland, 1973);

Felix Salten, "Arthur Schnitzler," in his *Gestalten und Erscheinungen* (Berlin: Fischer, 1913), pp. 49-63;

Hartmut Scheible, *Arthur Schnitzler in Selbstzeugnissen und Bilddokumenten* (Reinbek: Rowohlt, 1976);

Scheible, "Arthur Schnitzler–Figur-Situation-Gestalt," *Neue Rundschau*, 92, no. 2 (1981): 67-89;

Scheible, *Arthur Schnitzler und die Aufklärung* (Munich: Fink, 1977);

Scheible, ed., *Arthur Schnitzler in neuer Sicht* (Munich: Fink, 1981);

Otto P. Schinnerer, "The Early Works of Arthur Schnitzler," *Germanic Review*, 4 (1929): 153-197;

Schinnerer, "The Literary Apprenticeship of Arthur Schnitzler," *Germanic Review*, 5 (1930): 58-82;

Schinnerer, "Schnitzler and the Military Censorship: Unpublished Correspondence," *Germanic Review*, 5 (1940): 238-246;

Gerd K. Schneider, "The Reception of Arthur Schnitzler's *Reigen* in the Old Country and the New World: A Study in Cultural Differences," *Modern Austrian Literature*, 19, no. 3/4 (1986): 75-89;

Schneider, "Ton- und Schriftsprache in Schnitzlers *Fräulein Else* und Schumanns *Carnaval*," *Modern Austrian Literature*, 2, no. 3 (1969): 17-20;

Heinrich Schnitzler, Christian Brandstätter, and Reinhard Urbach, eds., *Arthur Schnitzler: Sein Leben, sein Werk, seine Zeit* (Frankfurt am Main: Fischer, 1981);

Olga Schnitzler, *Spiegelbild der Freundschaft* (Salzburg: Residenz, 1962);

Carl E. Schorske, "Politics and the Psyche: Schnitzler and Hofmannsthal," in his *Fin-De-Siècle Vienna. Politics and Culture* (New York: Random House, 1981), pp. 3-23;

Schorske, "Schnitzler und Hofmannsthal: Politik und Psyche im Wien des *Fin de Siècle*," *Wort und Wahrheit*, 16 (1962): 367-381;

Herbert Seidler, "Die Forschung zu Arthur Schnitzler seit 1945," *Zeitschrift für Deutsche Philologie*, 95 (1976): 576-595;

Oskar Seidlin, "In Memoriam Arthur Schnitzler: May 15, 1862-Oct. 21, 1931," *American-German Review*, 28, no. 4 (1962): 4-6;

Richard Specht, *Arthur Schnitzler: Der Dichter und sein Werk. Eine Studie* (Berlin: Fischer, 1922);

Martin Swales, *Arthur Schnitzler: A Critical Study* (Oxford: Clarendon Press, 1971);

Petrus W. Tax and Richard H. Lawson, eds., *Arthur Schnitzler and His Age: Intellectual and Artistic Currents* (Bonn: Bouvier, 1984);

Reinhard Urbach, *Arthur Schnitzler* (Velber: Friedrich, 1968); translated by Donald G. Daviau (New York: Ungar, 1973); German version revised (Munich: Deutscher Taschenbuch Verlag, 1977);

Urbach, *Schnitzler-Kommentar: Zu den erzählenden Schriften und dramatischen Werken* (Munich: Winkler, 1974);

George S. Viereck, "The World of Arthur Schnitzler," *Modern Austrian Literature*, 5, no. 3/4 (1972): 7-17;

Marc Weiner, *Arthur Schnitzler and the Crisis of Musical Culture* (Heidelberg: Winter, 1986);

Robert O. Weiss, "Arthur Schnitzler's Literary and Philosophical Development," *Journal of the American Arthur Schnitzler Research Association*, 2, no. 1 (1963): 4-20;

Harry Zohn, "Schnitzler and the Challenge of Zionism," *Journal of the American Arthur Schnitzler Research Association*, 1, no. 4/5 (1962): 5-7.

Papers:

The Schnitzler Archive is in the Schiller-Nationalmuseum, Marbach am Neckar, West Germany.

Ernst Weiß
(28 August 1882-15 June 1940)

Klaus-Peter Hinze
Cleveland State University

BOOKS: *Die Galeere: Roman* (Berlin: Fischer, 1913; revised 1919);
Der Kampf: Roman (Berlin: Fischer, 1916; revised as *Franziska: Roman* (Berlin: Fischer, 1919);
Tiere in Ketten: Roman (Berlin: Fischer, 1918);
Mensch gegen Mensch: Roman (Munich: Müller, 1919);
Das Versöhnungsfest: Eine Dichtung in vier Kreisen (Munich: Müller, 1920);
Tanja: Drama in Drei Akten (Berlin: Fischer, 1920);
Stern der Dämonen: Roman (Munich: Müller, 1921);
Nahar: Roman (Munich: Wolff, 1922);
Die Feuerprobe: Roman (Berlin: Die Schmiede, 1923; revised edition, Berlin: Propyläen, 1929);
Atua: Drei Erzählungen (Munich: Wolff, 1923);
Olympia: Tragikomödie (Berlin: Die Schmiede, 1923);
Hodin (Berlin: Tillgner, 1923);
Daniel: Erzählung (Berlin: Die Schmiede, 1924);
Der Fall Vukobrankovics (Berlin: Die Schmiede, 1924);
Männer in der Nacht: Roman (Berlin: Propyläen, 1925);
Boëtius von Orlamünde: Roman (Berlin: Fischer, 1928); republished as *Der Aristokrat Boëtius von Orlamunde: Roman* (Hamburg: Claassen, 1966);
Dämonenzug: Fünf Erzählungen (Berlin: Ullstein, 1928);
Das Unverlierbare (Berlin: Rowohlt, 1928);
Georg Letham, Arzt und Mörder: Roman (Vienna: Zsolnay, 1931);
Der Gefängnisarzt oder Die Vaterlosen: Roman (Leipzig: Kittl, 1934);
Der arme Verschwender: Roman (Amsterdam: Querido, 1936);
Der Verführer: Roman (Zurich: Humanitas, 1938);
Ich, der Augenzeuge: Roman (Icking: Kreisselmeier, 1963); translated by Ella R. W. McKee as *The Eyewitness* (Boston: Houghton Mifflin, 1977; London: Proteus, 1978);

Ernst Weiß (Archiv des Suhrkamp Verlags, Frankfurt am Main)

Der Zweite Augenzeuge, edited by K. P. Hinze (Wiesbaden: Steiner, 1978);
Gesammelte Werke, edited by P. Engel and V. Michels, 16 volumes (Frankfurt am Main: Suhrkamp, 1982).

OTHER: Theodore Dreiser, *Das Buch über mich selbst (Jahre des Kampfes)*, translated by Weiß (Berlin: Zsolnay, 1932).

The novelist and medical doctor Ernst Weiß enjoyed a high reputation before Hitler came to power; he was considered "ein Romancier von europäischem Rang" (a novelist of European rank) whose works were mentioned together with those of Franz Kafka, Joseph Roth, Alfred Ehrenstein, Stefan Zweig, and even Thomas Mann. He died an exile in Paris in 1940, and almost all his manuscripts, letters, and diaries were lost during the turbulent years of World War II. The uncertain fate of his literary estate was partly responsible for the fact that his large oeuvre remained almost forgotten for over thirty years after the war. While his fifteen novels, his short stories, and his essays have been rediscovered and reedited and included in the 1982 sixteen-volume Suhrkamp edition of his collected works, his two dramas and a volume of poetry remain unavailable, and his name is still missing from most literary histories.

Weiß was born into a progressive Jewish family in Brünn (now Brno, Czechoslovakia), then the capital of the Austrian province of Moravia. He was the second of four children of a successful textile merchant who died when Weiß was four years old. Even as a young man he was still searching for a father figure and role model among his teachers and older colleagues; many of his novels' protagonists who bear strong autobiographical features develop an exaggerated, almost pathological relationship to their "beloved" fathers. Weiß's mother was a strong, intelligent, and artistically inclined woman who furthered the boy's creative talents. Weiß's two brothers studied the law, with his older brother becoming a professor of law at Prague's Karl-Ferdinand University. Weiß and his younger sister chose the medical profession.

Weiß studied at the universities of Prague and Vienna. In Prague he found a circle of friends, including Kafka, with similar interests. In Vienna he was fascinated by the new school of psychoanalysis, although he was never a student of Sigmund Freud, as has often been suggested. He was mainly interested in the analysis of dreams and the use of hypnosis in the treatment of mental disturbances. Both of these topics play an integral part in the works of Arthur Schnitzler, whom Albert Ehrenstein called Weiß's "literarischer Taufpate" (literary godfather). In 1908 Weiß received his medical doctorate from the University of Vienna, after which he specialized in surgery. During his internship he served as assistant to some of the most famous surgeons in Europe: in Bern in 1910 he assisted Theodor Kocher, who had received the Nobel Prize in 1909 for his research on the physiology, pathology, and surgery of the thyroid gland; later in the same year he was the assistant of August Bier at the Charité hospital in Berlin; and in 1911 he returned to Vienna, where he worked under Julius Schnitzler at the Wiedener Hospital. It was especially Kocher whom he chose as his father figure, and many doctor characters in Weiß's novels are based on him. Kocher's requirement that his assistants write clear and concise medical reports and structured case histories is reflected in the scientific style and clear structure in Weiß's earliest and latest novels.

In Berlin toward the end of 1910, Weiß wrote the novel *Die Galeere* (The Galley, 1913) "in knapp vier Wochen" (in less than four weeks), but he could not find a publisher for it. Exhausted from working daily for twelve and more hours at Wiedener Hospital in Vienna, he contracted a mild case of tuberculosis but had no money for treatment in a sanatorium. Friends helped him to get the position of ship's doctor on board the M.S. *Austria*, and he sailed to Japan, China, and India in 1912-1913. His experiences in the Orient and Pacific islands later found expression in several of his stories and novels.

Before leaving Europe he had received acceptance letters for his *Die Galeere* from four of the most prestigious publishing houses in Germany. He chose S. Fischer, and upon his return in 1913 he found the novel published to favorable reviews. The hero of *Die Galeere* is a successful young physicist who experiments with the newly discovered X-rays, becomes ill from exposure to radioactivity, and commits suicide. He is a self-possessed, egotistical scientist, incapable of forming close human relationships. Weiß's critics and colleagues saw this hero as symptomatic of an egocentric yet highly talented generation.

Because of this literary success Weiß decided to give up the strenuous medical profession and try to earn a living as a writer. Around 1913 he met the beautiful and gifted seventeen-year-old Johanna Bleschke; she became his protégée and lover for many years and remained a good friend until her death of cancer in 1936. At his suggestion she adopted the Jewish-sounding pseudonym Rahel Sanzara, under which she became famous as a dancer, expressionist actress, and novelist.

Dust jacket for Weiß's first novel, about a scientist who becomes ill from exposure to X-rays

Dust jacket, designed by Renée Sintenis, for Weiß's 1928 novel about a young aristocrat who becomes a factory worker

Dust jacket for Weiß's novel about a psychiatrist, one of whose patients is based on Adolf Hilter

Like many young artists from Vienna and Prague, Weiß was attracted by the lively metropolis of Berlin. He settled there but often visited his friends in Prague, especially Kafka. In his second novel, *Der Kampf* (The Struggle, 1916), renamed *Franziska* in a second version (1919), a highly talented pianist is betrayed by her weak lover and then devotes her life to art.

Weiß corrected the galley proofs for the novel during a vacation with Sanzara and Kafka at a Danish seaside resort in the summer of 1914. The Danish idyl was cut short by the outbreak of World War I in August. Although Weiß could have remained in Scandinavia, he immediately returned to Austria and served as a military doctor on the eastern front until the end of the war.

In many lyrical poems written during the war Weiß, following the fashion of other contemporary expressionist poets, created the image of a "Gegen-Gott" (Anti-God) who was either asleep or enjoyed the suffering of mankind. These poems, published in both conservative and avantgarde journals, became known as his "Gegen-Gott-Lyrik." They were collected in 1920 as *Das Versöhnungsfest* (The Festival of Reconciliation).

During the war he also finished two novels which he had begun before 1914. *Tiere in Ketten* (Animals in Chains, 1918) is a story of the powerful love-hate relationship of the prostitute Olga and her pimp Michalek, a dishonorably discharged officer of the imperial army; it can be interpreted as an allegory of the moral decay of prewar Austrian society, similar to Roth's *Radetzkymarsch* (1932; translated as *Radetzky March*, 1933). The largely autobiographical *Mensch gegen Mensch* (Man against Man, 1919) traces young Alfred's educational path from the day of his high school graduation through his studies in medical school to his service on the eastern front and ends as a scathing indictment of war.

At the end of 1918 Weiß returned to Prague, where his drama *Tanja* (1920) was performed the following year. He had written this starkly expressionistic play for Rahel Sanzara, who played the title role at the play's premiere. Both author and actress were celebrated in the Czech capital, and their fame spread throughout the German-speaking countries. A second production in Vienna, however, with Ida Roland as Tanja, was a disaster. Weiß was deeply hurt by the harshly personal, even anti-Semitic attacks of the critics.

In 1920 Weiß moved back to Berlin, and the following thirteen years were to be the most productive epoch of his life. He published an average of one book per year with the most prestigious houses; was a regular contributor of reviews and cultural essays to several leading newspapers and journals; and gave public readings, lectures, and radio talks. In short, he became a highly respected member of the literary establishment.

In 1922 his expressionistic novel *Nahar*, a continuation of *Tiere in Ketten*, appeared. Olga is reincarnated as a tigress in the jungles of India. She experiences a life of fulfillment as a loved daughter, mate, and mother, until she is caught in man's traps and dies in his cages.

The following year Weiß published the novel *Die Feuerprobe* (Test by Fire), which, more than any of his other works, shows Kafka's influence. The narrator lives through a nightmare of guilt and persecution, half in a nauseating reality, half in a visionary world of self-destruction.

For many years Weiß regularly visited murder trials; he was a fascinated student of psychopathology. *Hodin* (1923), the story of a matricide, and *Der Fall Vukobrankovics* (The Vukobrankovics Case, 1924), an analytical case study of a compulsive murderess, testify to his interest in the minds of criminals. His colorful legend *Daniel*, dealing with the birth, adolescence, and divine calling of the Old Testament prophet in Nebuchadnezzar's Babylon, was also published in 1924.

Although Weiß's literary career had begun with novels written in a clear, sober, almost scientific language, he had fallen prey to the shrieking, stammering style of expressionism during and after the war. It was Thomas Mann who criticized Weiß most effectively and argued the necessity of making a decision either to write novels or to continue as an expressionist writer. Consequently, during the 1920s he rewrote several of his expressionistic novels in the disciplined and objective style of his earliest works; the charm of the original versions, however, was lost in the process.

Newly conceived novels were much more successful. Weiß became a master of the techniques of Neue Sachlichkeit (New Objectivity) with *Männer in der Nacht* (Men in the Night, 1925). In the novel Honoré de Balzac visits his friend, the lawyer Peytel, in the prison where Peytel is to be executed the next morning for a double murder. The novel is an intimate psychological study of both Balzac and the murderer. Stefan Zweig

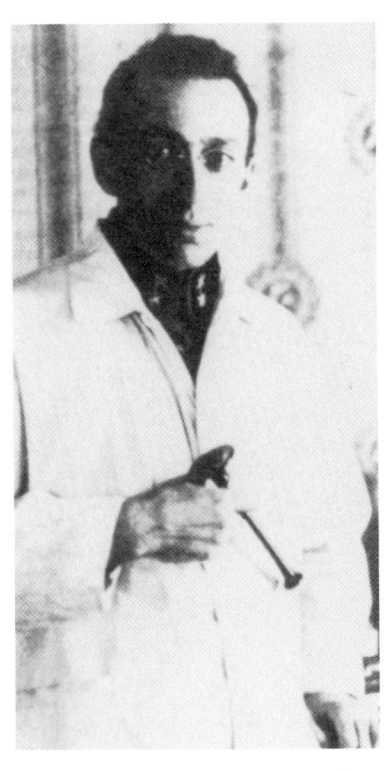

Weiß as a military doctor during World War I

Weiß in uniform

Weiß in the 1930s

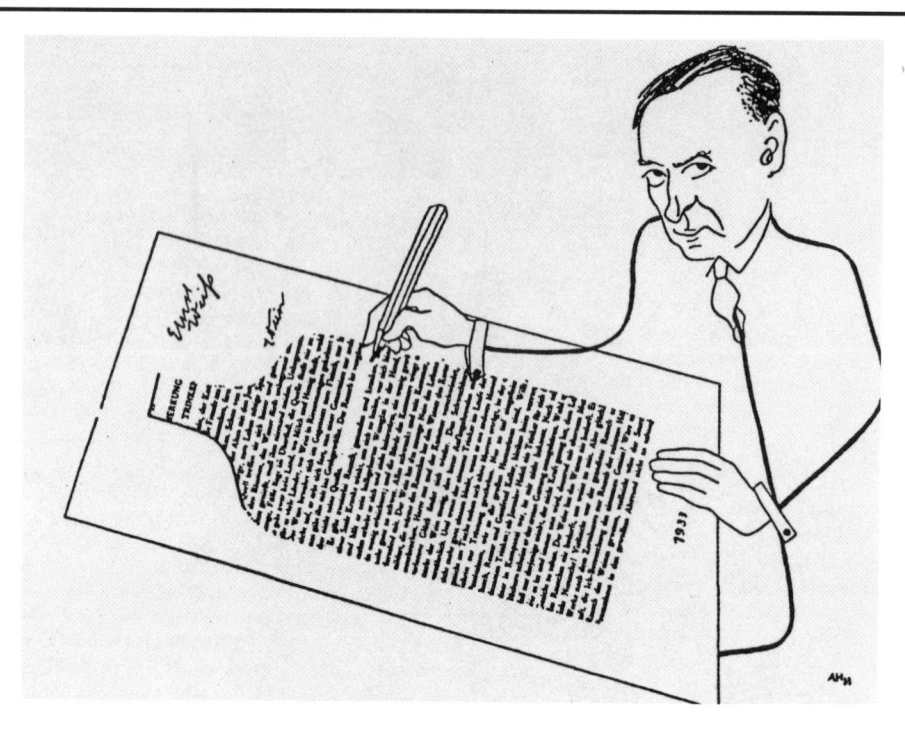

Caricature of Weiß by Adolf Hoffmeister

called the work Weiß's "Durchbruch" (breakthrough) to the new objective writing technique.

In 1928 his most pleasant and optimistic novel, *Boëtius von Orlamünde*, appeared. Boëtius, a member of an old aristocratic family, decides that he can no longer claim the social prestige inherent in his position because he fails to live up to his own expectations of a leader. He decides to become a simple unskilled worker in a huge factory. The novel represents Weiß's farewell to the prewar world, for which he retained a nostalgic love. For this work Weiß won the Silver Medal for Prose Fiction at the 1928 Olympic Games in Amsterdam, and German president Paul von Hindenburg congratulated him in person.

Georg Letham, Arzt und Mörder (Georg Letham, Doctor and Murderer, 1931) was the first of four novels whose heroes were doctors. Letham (the name is an anagram for Hamlet) feels betrayed when his beloved father refuses to help him after Letham murders his rich elderly wife. Letham is condemned for life to the penal colony Cayenne; there he becomes a benefactor of mankind, developing a serum against yellow fever but remaining anonymous.

When Hitler came to power in 1933 Weiß returned to Prague, where he cared for his dying mother. During this period he suffered from deep depression and isolated himself from his friends and acquaintances, but he finished a novel he had begun in 1923. *Der Gefängnisarzt oder Die Vaterlosen* (The Prison Doctor; or, The Fatherless, 1934), set in postwar Germany, is about a generation that manages without the guidance of fathers; the focus is on a family in Silesia. The oldest son, the prison doctor, cannot be a substitute father for his brother and sister in spite of his love for them. The book contains Weiß's most outspoken criticism of fascism, but, ironically, it was openly sold in Nazi Germany.

After his mother's death early in 1934 Weiß moved to Paris, which he had briefly visited the previous summer. Many of his exiled colleagues had settled there. Although he worked as never before, the income from his books did not cover his living expenses. His colleagues helped him intermittently; finally, through the good offices of Mann and Zweig, Weiß was awarded a monthly stipend of thirty dollars from the American Guild for German Cultural Freedom in 1938. Weiß suffered from painful ulcers, but he continued to write contributions for journals and newspapers; and he finished three more novels, his most mature works.

The narrator of *Der arme Verschwender* (The Poor Spendthrift, 1936), a psychiatrist, begins his pseudobiography with a confession: "Das Schreiben war immer eine verbotene Freude für mich" (writing has always been a forbidden joy to me), and then tells the story of his life from the decaying Hapsburg monarchy through World War I and the postwar decade. In a subplot, the psychiatrist cures his school friend Pericles of progressive hysterical paralysis; afterwards Pericles develops into a fanatical demagogue reminiscent of Hitler. Mann called the novel "ein Werk von bewundernswerter künstlerischer Diskretion und melancholischer Tiefe" (a work of admirable artistic discretion and melancholic depth).

Der Verführer (The Seducer, 1938) takes place in prewar Austria. The narrator has a close relationship with his charming father, who dies "viel zu früh" (much too early); the son's goal is to become like his father. The novel ends with the outbreak of World War I.

During his visit to Paris in 1933 Weiß had met Dr. Edmund Forster, a psychiatrist who had cured a certain Private First Class A. H.–Adolph Hitler–of hysterical blindness in November 1918. Forster had shown the case history to Weiß, who had used it in the story of Pericles in *Der arme Verschwender*. When the American Guild announced a literary contest for the best novel by an exiled writer, Weiß wrote *Ich, der Augenzeuge* (translated as *The Eyewitness*, 1977), a thinly fictionalized account of the case, within a few weeks. During the next six months he revised it but did not win the prize. While the manuscript of the final version was lost together with his other manuscripts, the first version survived. Published in 1963, it has been translated into many languages.

Weiß was working on a new project, an optimistic, even humorous novel titled "Sered," when German troops marched into Paris in June 1940. Tired of a life which had been a continuous flight from persecution during the past ten years, he committed suicide.

Interviews:
"Ernst Weiß über seine *Tanja*," *Wiener Mittagspost*, 23 December 1919, p. 2;

"Interview: Balzac als Romanfigur," *Berliner Börsen-Courier*, 7 August 1925, pp. 1-7.

Bibliographies:
Klaus-Peter Hinze, *Ernst Weiß: Bibliographie der Primär- und Sekundärliteratur* (Hamburg: Verlag der "Weiß-Blätter," 1977);

Peter Engel, "Weiß-Bibliographie," *Weiß-Blätter*, 3 (May 1985): 32-33.

References:
Willi Bredel, "Ernst Weiß, Arzt und Dichter," *Heute und Morgen* (1947): 455-457;

Bredel, "Ein Hoffender ohne Hoffnung," *Aufbau*, 5 (1949);

Jan Chytil, "Zum Werk von Ernst Weiß," in his *Weltfreunde* (Prague: Frazensis, 1967), pp. 271-278;

Albert Ehrenstein, "Ernst Weiß," *Berliner Tageblatt*, 11 July 1925;

Peter Engel, "Ernst Weiß–eine Skizze von Leben und Werk," *Text + Kritik*, 76 (October 1982): 13-19;

Engel, ed., *Ernst Weiß* (Frankfurt am Main: Suhrkamp, 1982);

Klaus-Peter Hinze, "Postscript," in *The Eyewitness*, by Ernst Weiß (Boston: Houghton Mifflin, 1977), pp. 201-206;

Hinze, "Vorwort," in *Ich, Der Augenzeuge*, by Weiß (Munich: Heyne, 1978), pp. 5-15;

Hinze, ed., *Ernst Weiß, der zweite Augenzeuge* (Wiesbaden: Steiner, 1978);

Hermann Kesten, "Ernst Weiß," in his *Meine Freunde, die Poeten* (Vienna & Munich: Donau, 1953);

Dieter Lattmann, "Posthume Wiederkehr–Ernst Weiß, Arzt und Schriftsteller," in his *Zwischenrufe und andere Texte* (Munich: Kindler, 1967), pp. 120-146;

Margarita Pazi, *Fünf Autoren des Prager Kreises* (Würzburg: Lang, 1977);

Text + Kritik, special Weiß issue, 76 (1982);

Wolfgang Wendler, "Ernst Weiß," in his *Expressionismus als Literatur* (Bern: Francke, 1969), pp. 656-668;

Eduard Wondrak, *Einiges über den Arzt und Schriftsteller Ernst Weiß ...* (Munich: Kreißelmeier, 1968).

Papers:
Ernst Weiß's letters to Rahel Sanzara are at the Deutsches Literaturachiv, Marbach, Federal Republic of Germany; his letters to Stefan Zweig are at Reed Library, Fredonia, New York; his letters to Martin Buber are at the Jewish National and University Library, Jerusalem; and his letters to Thomas Mann are at the Eidgenössiche Technische Hochschule, Zurich.

Franz Werfel
(10 September 1890-26 August 1945)

Lionel B. Steiman
University of Manitoba

BOOKS: *Der Weltfreund: Erste Gedichte* (Leipzig: Juncker, 1911);
Wir Sind: Neue Gedichte (Leipzig: Wolff, 1913);
Die Versuchung: Ein Gespräch des Dichters mit dem Erzengel und Luzifer (Leipzig: Wolff, 1913);
Einander: Oden, Lieder, Gestalten (Leipzig: Wolff, 1915);
Gesänge aus den drei Reichen: Ausgewählte Gedichte (Leipzig: Wolff, 1917);
Der Gerichtstag, in fünf Büchern (Leipzig: Wolff, 1919);
Der Dschin: Ein Märchen; Gedichte aus Der Gerichtstag; Blasphemie eines Irren; Fragmente (Vienna: Genossenschaftsverlag, 1919);
Der Besuch aus dem Elysium: Romantisches Drama in einem Aufzug (Munich: Wolff, 1920);
Nicht der Mörder, der Ermordete ist schuldig: Eine Novelle (Munich: Wolff, 1920);
Spiegelmensch: Magische Trilogie (Munich: Wolff, 1920);
Spielhof: Eine Phantasie (Munich: Wolff, 1920);
Bockgesang: In fünf Akten (Munich: Wolff, 1921); translated by Ruth Langner as *Goat Song (Bockgesang): A Drama in Five Acts* (Garden City: Doubleday, Page, 1926);
Arien (Munich: Wolff, 1921);
Schweiger: Ein Trauerspiel in drei Akten (Munich: Wolff, 1922);
Beschwörungen (Munich: Wolff, 1923);
Verdi: Roman der Oper (Vienna: Zsolnay, 1924); translated by Helen Jessiman as *Verdi: A Novel of the Opera* (New York: Simon & Schuster, 1925; London: Jarrolds, 1926);
Juarez und Maximilian: Dramatische Historie in 3 Phasen und 13 Bildern (Vienna: Zsolnay, 1924); translated by Langner as *Juarez and Maximilian: A Dramatic History in Three Phases and Thirteen Pictures* (New York: Simon & Schuster, 1926);
Paulus unter den Juden: Dramatische Legende in sechs Bildern (Berlin: Zsolnay, 1926); translated by Paul P. Levertoff as *Paul among the Jews (A Tragedy)* (London: Diocesan House, 1928; Milwaukee: Morehouse, 1928);

Austrian Cultural Institute

Der Tod des Kleinbürgers: Novelle (Vienna: Zsolnay, 1927); translated by Clifton Fadiman and William A. Drake as *The Man Who Conquered Death* (New York: Simon & Schuster, 1927); translation republished as *The Death of a Poor Man* (London: Benn, 1927);
Geheimnis eines Menschen: Novellen (Berlin: Zsolnay, 1927) —comprises "Die Entfremdung"; "Geheimnis eines Menschen"; "Die Hoteltreppe"; "Das Trauerhaus";
Neue Gedichte (Vienna: Zsolnay, 1928);

Werfel (center) with the writers Walter Hasenclever (left) and Kurt Pinthus in Leipzig in 1912 (Deutsches Literaturarchiv, Marbach)

Der Abituriententag: Die Geschichte einer Jugendschuld (Vienna: Zsolnay, 1928); translated by Whittaker Chambers as *Class Reunion* (New York: Simon & Schuster, 1929);

Barbara oder Die Frömmigkeit (Vienna: Zsolnay, 1929); translated by Geoffrey Dunlop as *The Pure in Heart* (New York: Simon & Schuster, 1931); translation republished as *The Hidden Child* (London: Jarrolds, 1931);

Das Reich Gottes in Böhmen: Tragödie eines Führers (Vienna: Zsolnay, 1930);

Realismus und Innerlichkeit (Vienna: Zsolnay, 1931);

Kleine Verhältnisse: Novelle (Vienna: Zsolnay, 1931);

Die Geschwister von Neapel: Roman (Vienna: Zsolnay, 1931); translated by Dorothy F. Tait-Price as *The Pascarella Family: A Novel* (New York: Simon & Schuster, 1932; London: Jarrolds, 1932);

Können wir ohne Gottesglauben leben? (Vienna: Zsolnay, 1932);

Die vierzig Tage des Musa Dagh, 2 volumes (Vienna: Zsolnay, 1933); translated by Dunlop as *The Forty Days of Musa Dagh* (New York: Viking Press, 1934); translation republished as *The Forty Days* (London: Jarrolds, 1934);

Der Weg der Verheißung: Ein Bibelspiel (Vienna: Zsolnay, 1935); translated by Ludwig Lewisohn as *The Eternal Road: A Drama in Four Parts* (New York: Viking Press, 1936);

Schlaf und Erwachen: Neue Gedichte (Vienna: Zsolnay, 1935);

In einer Nacht: Ein Schauspiel (Vienna: Zsolnay, 1937);

Höret die Stimme (Vienna: Zsolnay, 1937); translated by Moray Firth as *Hearken unto the Voice* (New York: Viking Press, 1938);

Twilight of a World, translated by H. T. Lowe-Porter (New York: Viking Press, 1937);—comprises "Essay Upon the Meaning of Imperial Austria"; "Poor People" ("Kleine Verhältnisse"); "Not the Murderer" ("Nicht der Mörder, Der Ermordete ist schuldig"); "The House of Mourning" ("Das Trauerhaus"); "Estrangement" ("Die Entfremdung"); "The Staircase" ("Die Hoteltreppe"); "Saverio's Secret" ("Geheimnis eines Menschen"); "The Man Who Conquered Death"; "Class Reunion";

Von der reinsten Glückseligkeit des Menschen (Stockholm: Bermann-Fischer, 1938);

Der veruntreute Himmel: Die Geschichte einer Magd (Stockholm: Bermann-Fischer, 1939); translated by Firth as *Embezzled Heaven* (New

Woodcut by Ludwig von Hofmann for Die Troerinnen, *Werfel's adaptation of Euripides'* The Trojan Women

York: Viking Press, 1940; London: Hamilton, 1940):

Gedichte aus dreißig Jahren (Stockholm: Bermann-Fischer, 1939);

Eine blaßblaue Frauenschrift (Buenos Aires: Editorial Estrellas, 1941);

Das Lied von Bernadette (Stockholm: Bermann-Fischer, 1941; London: Hamilton, 1941); translated by Lewisohn as *The Song of Bernadette* (New York: Viking Press, 1942; London: Book Club, 1945);

Die wahre Geschichte vom wiederhergestellten Kreuz (Los Angeles: Pazifische Presse, 1942);

Jacobowsky und der Oberst: Komödie einer Tragödie in drei Akten (Stockholm: Bermann-Fischer, 1944); translated by Gustave O. Arlt as *Jacobowsky and the Colonel: Comedy of a Tragedy in Three Acts* (New York: Viking Press, 1944); German version, edited by Arlt (New York: Crofts, 1945);

Between Heaven and Earth, translated by Maxim Newmark (New York: Philosophical Library, 1944); German version published as *Zwischen oben und unten* (Stockholm: Bermann-Fischer, 1946);

Poems, translated by Edith Abercrombie Snow (Princeton: Princeton University Press, 1945);

Stern der Ungeborenen: Ein Reiseroman (Stockholm: Bermann-Fischer, 1946); translated by Arlt as *Star of the Unborn* (New York: Viking Press, 1946);

Gedichte aus den Jahren 1908-1945, edited by Ernst Gottlieb and Felix Guggenheim (Frankfurt am Main: Fischer, 1946; Los Angeles: Pazifische Presse, 1946);

Gesammelte Werke, edited by Adolf D. Klarmann, 8 volumes (volume 1, Stockholm: Bermann-Fischer, 1948; volumes 2-7, Frankfurt am Main: Fischer, 1948-1974; volume 8, Munich & Vienna: Langen-Müller, 1975);

Cella oder Die Überwinder (Frankfurt am Main: Fischer, 1982);

Das Franz Werfel Buch, edited by Peter Stephan Jungk (Frankfurt am Main: Fischer, 1986).

OTHER: Euripides, *Die Troerinnen (Troades)*, adapted by Werfel (Leipzig & Munich: Wolff, 1915);

Giuseppe Verdi, *Briefe*, translated by Paul Stefan, edited by Werfel (Vienna: Zsolnay, 1926); translated by Edward Downes as *Verdi: The Man in His Letters* (New York: Fischer, 1942);

Verdi and F. M. Piave, *Simone Boccanegra: Lyrische Tragödie in einem Vorspiel und drei Akten*, translated by Werfel (Leipzig & New York: Ricordi, 1929);

Verdi and Piave, *Die Macht des Schicksals: Oper in einem Vorspiel und drei Akten* (Mailand: Ricordi, 1950).

PERIODICAL PUBLICATIONS: "Die christliche Sendung," *Die Neue Rundschau*, 28 (January 1917): 92-105;

"Begegnungen mit Rilke," *Das Tagebuch*, 8, no. 4 (1927): 140-144.

Franz Werfel belonged to the "Prague Circle" of German Jewish writers whose most famous member was Franz Kafka. Werfel attained fame easily and at an early age: before World War I he was the leading poet of early expressionism; after the war, in Vienna, he produced a stream of plays, stories, and novels which made him rival Stefan Zweig as the most widely read German Jewish writer in Europe. In exile his popularity rose to even greater heights. Although his literary stature remains below those of Kafka, Hermann Broch, and Robert Musil, Werfel's oeuvre offers a more accessible portrayal of their common world. It is an evocative and sympathetic portrayal marked by the peculiar passions and loyalties of a man who insisted that he was at once a Jew and a believer in Christ.

Born in Prague in 1890, Werfel was the first-born child and only son of Rudolf Werfel, a glove manufacturer, and Albine Kussi Werfel. Through infancy, childhood, and youth he enjoyed the advantages of wealth and status. His father's business and his mother's social concerns left Babi, the family's Czech nursery maid, in charge of Werfel. She began taking him to Mass with her when he was four; her religion and affection had such a profound impact on him that his oeuvre became a celebration of Roman Catholicism, and its female heroines became embodiments of her quiet, loving acceptance of life, a quality Werfel called "Frömmigkeit" (piety). His contact with the Jewish faith was, by contrast, formal and dutiful, laden with the guilt and anxiety Werfel felt all his life in relation to his father, whom he survived by only four years. The synagogue was mysterious and forbidding, while the Catholic church, with its open, all-accepting embrace, met the emotional needs and appealed to the developing aesthetic instincts of the precocious adolescent.

In his youth Werfel went to school and frequented cafés with other members of the Prague Circle of German Jewish writers; he was a close friend of Max Brod and Franz Blei, and his personality and early verse made a favorable impression on Kafka. He enrolled at the German Karl Ferdinand University, but his true interests were literature and the opera. In the fall of 1910 Werfel's father sent him to Hamburg to prepare for a career in business. Meanwhile, Brod was arranging for the publication of Werfel's first collection of verse, *Der Weltfreund* (The Philanthropist, 1911). The book established the reputation of the cherubic twenty-year-old almost overnight; it is still regarded as among his best works and one of the key texts of early expressionism.

The best-known lines from *Der Weltfreund*, "Mein einziger Wunsch ist Dir, O Mensch, verwandt zu sein!" (My one and only wish, O Man, is to be thy brother!) express Werfel's need to transcend societal barriers and embrace all mankind. Other expressionists sought to achieve this goal through political activism, but Werfel believed that one could not be true to one's muse while engaging in partisan politics.

What moved Werfel to attack literary "activists" was their criticism of *Die Troerinnen* (1915), his adaptation of Euripides' *The Trojan Women*, which was produced in 1916. In response, he muted the pacifism of his initial version and moved it even further from the Greek original by increasing the Christian emphasis. In open letters he elaborated his condemnation of political action as a legitimate avenue for the creative artist, and he publicly proclaimed his faith in Christianity and outlined his peculiar vision of it in the article "Die christliche Sendung" (The Christian Mission, 1917). For Werfel, Christianity was hedonistic rather than ascetic: a sensually self-affirming celebration of humanity, it had social and ethical goals identical to those of the political activists and was capable of achieving those goals without violence.

Military service during World War I scarcely interfered with Werfel's literary and polemical writing. He was never close to the actual fighting. In 1917 he was transferred from his communications post in the east to join other literary figures in the military press office in Vienna. On a propaganda mission to Switzerland and again in Vi-

Drawing of Werfel by L. Meidner

enna at the war's end he violated his anti-activist creed by engaging in leftist political agitation, possibly an implicit confession that his social conscience was satisfied by neither his art nor his faith but probably the result of his dramatic instincts. In any case, the entry of the staunchly conservative Alma Mahler–the widow of the composer Gustav Mahler and wife of the architect Walter Gropius–into his life marked the end of his political adventures.

Alma left Gropius, and she and Werfel settled in Vienna. In 1920 appeared Werfel's first important work of fiction, the short novel *Nicht der Mörder, der Ermordete ist schuldig* (Not the Murderer, the Victim Is Guilty; translated as "Not the Murderer," 1937). As in many of Werfel's stories, the material is based on an actual incident, in this case one which occurred in Vienna's famous Wurstelprater amusement park. The expressionist theme of father-son conflict is treated within a larger framework of patriarchal power, that of the Habsburg monarchy, which, together with its supporting institutions, is made the personification of authority per se. For Werfel, as for Kafka and others of the Prague Circle, the problem of all authority is rooted in the patriarchal relation.

Nicht der Mörder, der Ermordete ist schuldig was followed by the dramatic verse trilogy *Spiegelmensch* (Mirrorman, 1920), which enjoyed a brief success because of the vogue of expressionist theater. It is a plotless review of the Faustian motif of "two souls within the human breast," with a bewildering series of images, settings, and elements of music and dance which made it difficult to stage and easy to dismiss as derivative because of its obvious parallels with other treatments of the Faust theme. But it developed a motif which Werfel continued in subsequent dramatic efforts: political activism as an expression of egomania disguised as messianism. In *Bockgesang* (1921; translated as *Goat Song*, 1926), Werfel's first drama in prose, the son of a prostitute grows to adulthood filled with resentment, becomes a rebel, and leads his followers to destruction. *Schweiger* (1922), the last play of Werfel's expressionist period, exposes nihilism behind the idealistic mask of a political messiah. The attempts of the protagonists of *Juarez und Maximilian* (1924) and of *Das Reich Gottes in Böhmen* (The Kingdom of God in Bohemia, 1930) to establish utopian societies both end in disaster.

Verdi: Roman der Oper (1924; translated as *Verdi: A Novel of the Opera*, 1925) was Werfel's first full-length novel and his greatest success of the

Werfel, Alma Mahler-Gropius, and her daughter Manon Gropius in Venice, 1920 (Lionel B. Steiman, Franz Werfel: The Faith of an Exile. From Prague to Beverly Hills, *1985)*

postwar decade. In the judgment of Walter Sokel, *Verdi* closed the era of expressionism. It explores the relation between artistic inspiration and the creative process as embodied in two great rivals of genius; Giuseppe Verdi and Richard Wagner–the ethical artist and the egocentric one, the Latin and the Germanic. Werfel depicts Verdi as pure melody and Wagner as abstract structure; Verdi is humanity in all its fullness, Wagner is disembodied intellect and dissatisfied soul. In addition to historical and cultural themes there are projections of characters and conflicts from Werfel's own life. He harbored a burden of guilt for conceiving a child with Alma while she was still married to Gropius, a guilt he discharged by glorifying virginity, maternal love, and woman's love while denigrating the male as a pleasure-seeking egotist. In *Verdi* such a character conceives a child with a woman nine years his senior; Alma was eleven years older than Werfel.

Werfel's *Verdi* was almost the only book Kafka, suffering in a sanatorium near Vienna, could bring himself to read during his last days. Some reviewers objected to the elements of fictional romance in the book, but there was unanimous admiration for the knowledge of music it displayed, and some acclaimed the author as an important new authority on Verdi. In 1926 Werfel published an edition of Verdi's letters; his adaptation of the composer's *La forza del destino* was posthumously published in 1950. In 1926 Werfel was made a member of the newly founded literary section of the Prussian Academy of the Arts and was awarded the Grillparzer Prize for *Juarez und Maximilian*, whose recent outstanding stage success owed as much to Max Reinhardt's innovative direction and Werfel's insistence on historical authenticity in costuming as it did to its story of the ill-fated Habsburg candidate for the throne of Mexico and its anti-activist lecture against political utopianism.

Werfel led an idyllic life in the 1920s, working in resort hotels on the Italian Riviera; in Capri, Locarno, and Ischl; as well as in Alma Mahler's summer home on the Semmering, south of Vienna, and in her townhouse in Venice. A visit to Palestine in 1925 resulted the following year in the play *Paulus unter den Juden* (translated as *Paul among the Jews*, 1928), which focuses on the historical moment when Christianity definitively parted from Judaism. Palestine had awakened in Werfel an acute sense of the inner conflict he suffered for his attachment to both faiths. He suffered further when he was accused of presumption in attempting to write of the origins of Christianity. The play had only limited success at the time, but it was one of Werfel's few plays to be performed in Germany after 1945.

Werfel's most successful short stories first appeared after the mid 1920s. In them he put to more effective use the elements of local color and character which figure in his dramas. Because the stories are not burdened with long-winded, tendentious dialogue and lack the polemical intent of the plays, they re-create more convincingly the world of old Austria. In *Der Tod des Kleinbürgers* (1927; translated as *The Man Who Conquered Death*, 1927), which was filmed for West German television in 1974, the quintessential Viennese petit bourgeois Karl Fiala, mortally ill, summons the strength to hold death off long enough to pay up his insurance policy. The treatment of youthful guilt in *Der Abituriententag* (1928; translated as *Class Reunion*, 1929) reveals

Werfel in 1920 (Bildarchiv der Österreichischen Nationalbibliothek)

traces of its author's early life in Prague; the protagonist, Franz Adler, bears distinct resemblances to Werfel. In "Das Trauerhaus" (1927; translated as The House of Mourning, 1937) a bordello is a microcosm of the monarchy in its twilight years. The proprietor, personnel, and patrons embody the vices, foibles, ideals, and illusions of the larger world outside.

In the summer of 1929 Werfel and Alma Mahler were married; in the fall of that year appeared Werfel's most ambitious prose work to date, *Barbara oder Die Frömmigkeit* (Barbara; or, Piety; translated as *The Pure in Heart* and *The Hidden Child*, 1931). The two events were related. One of the reasons Alma was reluctant to marry Werfel and hesitated to do so long after her divorce from Gropius would have made it possible was that she still suspected him of left-wing sympathies. *Barbara* removed any remaining doubt about Werfel's attitude toward politics and society. The activists conjuring new worlds in the cafés of Vienna as the monarchy crumbled in the last days of the war range from the vicious and cynical to the inept and ridiculous. The novel's real hero is a spiritual presence who scarcely figures in the action at all: Barbara, the childhood nurse of Ferdinand, the novel's ostensible hero. The memory of her love and simple faith accompany this orphaned son of an infantry colonel on his odyssey of self-discovery, which takes him through seminary, war, revolution, and all sorts of intellectual and religious seeking, until his final withdrawal to live out his life as a ship's doctor on a luxury liner. His companion throughout is Alfred Engländer, a wealthy young Jew whose ambition of bringing about the reunification of Christianity and Judaism results in his mental and emotional collapse and illustrates the folly of intellectual hubris. While Engländer goes berserk, Ferdinand is sustained by the totally unintellectual power of Barbara's "Frömmigkeit," the quiet, loving acceptance of all of life in its manifold totality. The work is a conservative polemic against activism and marked its author's final departure from his early belief in the social utility of human brotherhood to the increasingly private concerns of religious faith.

Zsolnay, Werfel's publisher from 1924 until the Nazi takeover of Austria fourteen years later, authorized an initial printing of fifty thousand copies of *Barbara oder Die Frömmigkeit*. The success of *Verdi* and the short stories, together with an opinion survey ranking Werfel higher in popularity than Gerhart Hauptmann, had encouraged hopes that were not fulfilled. The novel's title was misleading, and its eight hundred pages displayed Werfel's weaknesses as well as his strengths as a writer. Moving passages of intense action and powerfully evocative characterization were followed by preachy didacticism and melodrama. Werfel was unable to discipline his writing in any genre other than verse or the short story.

Barbara aroused controversy more for its content than for its literary quality, for it portrayed Werfel's friends and erstwhile companions in revolution in a most unflattering light. The left-wing journalist Egon Erwin Kisch, when asked if he planned to sue Werfel for defamation of character for depicting him as the cynical opportunist Ronald Weiß, replied that he did not; Werfel had not misrepresented the actions and events of the time, Kisch said, and had reproduced conversations "with the exactness of a gramophone." Some reviewers found the novel's message of quiet spiritualism the very thing needed for a culture in crisis; others considered it reactionary or irrelevant.

Werfel conceived the purpose of his next novel as that of fulfilling the task of art, which was to render in human terms an appropriate

Werfel circa 1927 (Lionel B. Steiman, Franz Werfel: The Faith of an Exile. From Prague to Beverly Hills, *1985)*

image of God's world. *Die Geschwister von Neapel* (The Siblings of Naples, 1931; translated as *The Pascarella Family*, 1932) centers around the widowed banker Domenico Pascarella and his seven children. The strict patriarch experiences the gradual rupture of family ties and domestic discipline as the fascist state penetrates the closed family circle. A treacherous partner brings Pascarella close to bankruptcy and imprisonment, but he is saved from the apparently hopeless situation by his daughter's English suitor. The depiction of Mussolini's fascism, which Werfel came to know well through his yearly sojourns in Italy, expresses his increasing preoccupation with the problem of power. In no other work is Werfel's affinity for music so evident: the novel is replete with musical analogies.

The book's European success moved Werfel to contemplate a sequel, but he abandoned the idea when political developments restricted his market largely to America, where *The Pascarella Family* enjoyed little popularity. In lectures in Vienna in 1931 and 1932, reprinted in *Zwischen oben und unten* (1946; translated as *Between Heaven and Earth*, 1944), he defined the basic evil of the time as "radical realism." It was responsible for the two dangerous ersatz religions of Nazism and Communism, and it was behind the rampant materialism of both the United States and the Soviet Union. Werfel saw no fundamental difference between the two powers: both had rejected metaphysical values to chase the idol of material comfort, their only difference being that the United States already enjoyed what the Soviets still wanted. Werfel's solution to the current malaise was a return to "metaphysical" values and a genuinely spiritual belief in God. He was applauded by the center and the right, but the left did not miss the opportunity to comment sarcastically on the connection between Werfel's "metaphysical" line and his upper-class friends and lifestyle.

Toward the end of 1933 Zsolnay published *Die vierzig Tage des Musa Dagh* (translated as *The Forty Days of Musa Dagh*, 1934), Werfel's two-volume epic of the fate of an Armenian community in Turkey during World War I, when the Ottoman state pursued a policy of extermination resulting in the deaths of over a million Armenians. Werfel's interest in the tragedy had been spurred in 1929 at the sight of half-starved Armenian orphans working in a factory in Damascus. Following research in Armenian, German, and French sources and over a hundred secondary works, he completed the writing in the spring of 1933. The protagonist is Gabriel Bagradian, an Armenian assimilated into European culture who is visiting his ancestral home at the outbreak of the war. The novel describes Bagradian's organization of the defense of his besieged community on a mountain; his rediscovery of his Armenian identity at the cost of estrangement from his European wife; the death of their son in service to his father's cause; the ultimate rescue of the beleaguered community by Anglo-French forces; and Bagradian's self-sacrifice. Werfel altered facts in order to emphasize Biblical analogies; for example, he put the length of the siege at forty days instead of the fifty-three or thirty-six days indicated in the sources he consulted, thus establishing parallels with the forty days of the Flood, of Moses' fast on Mt. Sinai, and Christ's forty days in the wilderness. The resonance of Calvary in the death scene of Bagradian's son struck

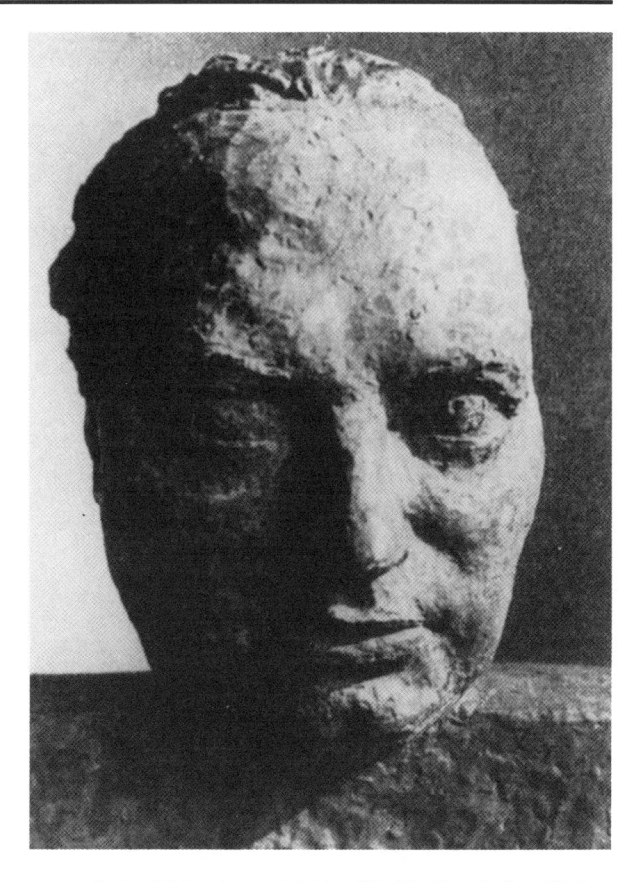

Bust of Werfel by Anna Mahler-Werfel (S. Fischer Verlag, Frankfurt am Main)

some readers as presumptuous. Other parallels emerged later: the reluctance of the Armenian community to believe the extent of the threat until it was too late; the indifference of the major powers to the plight of the Armenians; the courteous and detached efficiency with which high-ranking officials issued the order of genocide, with the brutalities of execution carried out by lower-ranking thugs. It was assumed that Werfel had written the book with the contemporary threat to European Jewry in mind and intended it as a warning, but he later gave conflicting answers when questioned on the point. In fact, the book was finished before the gravity of the danger to the Jews was clear, and it is likely that Werfel wrote it without that threat consciously in mind. It was for that reason a better book.

It displays, however, the weaknesses which mar all Werfel's longer prose works, weaknesses only magnified in English: an aloof and omniscient tone, ideological moralizing, and prolixity. Scenes of brilliant dramatic intuition are followed by endlessly detailed bits of melodrama, a contradiction in craft which Lionel Abel (in the *Nation*,

12 December 1934) related to a contradiction in Werfel's purpose. Instead of coming to terms with the problem of modern nationalism, Werfel had merely pitted a form of it he favored, the mystical nationalism of the Armenians, against a form he regarded as evil, the mechanical nationalism of the Turks. But George Schulz-Behrend (in *Germanic Review*, 1951) concluded, after analyzing Werfel's use of historical source materials in *Die vierzig Tage des Musa Dagh*, that the book was a "solidly based work of art, one of the great novels of the first half of the twentieth century."

Banned in Germany because of pressures from the Turkish embassy, by July 1935 the novel had been translated into twenty-four languages (although the English translator deleted over three hundred passages unfavorable to the Turks or laudatory to the Armenians). It was a Book-of-the-Month Club choice in 1935, and in four months total American sales reached 125,000. A major Hollywood studio acquired the film rights but abandoned production plans in response to State Department pressure. Another attempt to turn the book into a movie was launched by Israeli producers in the late 1970s but did not come to fruition.

In 1935 Werfel took up Reinhardt's suggestion that he write a play with a biblical theme in response to the events in Germany. *Der Weg der Verheißung* (1935; translated as *The Eternal Road*, 1936) was first performed on 7 January 1937 in the Manhattan Opera House in New York, with music by Kurt Weill. It impressed some critics as a genuine portrayal of Jewish personalities, but others pointed out that all of the sympathetic characters were either non-Jews or lacked "typically Jewish" traits. Werfel's depictions of Abraham haggling with God for the preservation of Sodom and Joseph's brothers restrained from fratricide only by their greed were true to the Bible but also appeared to follow anti-Semitic stereotypes.

Werfel had a marked preference for retiring, scholarly, "spiritual" Jews, and in his next work, *Höret die Stimme* (1937; translated as *Hearken unto the Voice*, 1938), he made even more explicit his view that the destruction of Israel was a consequence of the Jews' rejection of spiritual substance for material show. The prophet Jeremiah holds up the "religion of the heart" against the formalism of the temple as the devotion most pleasing to God, and his final message to his defeated people is that God's judgment was executed so that they might reverse their priorities and rise again.

The annexation of Austria by Germany in March 1938 found Werfel on Capri; from there he went immediately into exile in France. The beginning of exile coincided with the onset of a serious heart ailment, but exile and illness spurred Werfel's productivity. In Paris he completed *Der veruntreute Himmel* (1939; translated as *Embezzled Heaven*, 1940), the story of a simple Czech woman who spends her life savings in a vain attempt to secure heaven. Teta finds her way to genuine faith only after discovering her Christian broker's fraud. She is assisted on her new path by a Jewish convert to Catholicism who organizes pilgrimages to the Vatican. Teta's simple piety marks her as a typical Werfel heroine, inspired by his nursemaid and modeled on Alma's house cook, whose story he heard in a Paris café in the spring of 1938.

The German exile house of Bermann-Fischer published the book in Stockholm, and Viking brought out an English translation in New York the following year. Werfel had told Alma that a big American success was their only hope. He had been greatly disappointed when the Book-of-the-Month Club rejected *Hearken unto the Voice*, which suggested a limited market for religious novels in the United States. But *Embezzled Heaven* was lauded in the press, with *Time* magazine (25 November 1940) comparing Werfel favorably with the greatest storytellers of all literature; the novel was a Book-of-the-Month Club selection in 1940.

Der veruntreute Himmel is a fascinating tale full of unlikely but entertaining twists. Although the heroine's combination of piety, gullibility, and opportunism was offensive to some Catholics, New York archbishop Francis Spellman read the book "with interest," received the author and his wife in New York, and remained on friendly terms with them. A Jesuit reviewer claimed that even a Catholic could not have written a more Catholic book, but other Catholics criticized the author for tailoring their religion to suit his purposes.

One of Werfel's finest pieces of writing is the novel fragment *Cella oder Die Überwinder* (Cella; or, The Conqueror), included in volume 3 of his collected works (1948) and only published as a separate title in 1982. Written in the fall of 1938, it depicts the fate of Vienna's Jews during the Nazi takeover earlier that year. Werfel put the work aside after six months, saying that it had been overtaken by events. An Austrian Jew, Bodenheim, joins a group of inept conspirators at-

Werfel and his wife, Alma, at their home in California (Lionel B. Steiman, Franz Werfel: The Faith of An Exile. From Prague to Beverly Hills, 1985)

tempting a monarchist restoration to head off a Nazi takeover. The pathetic outcome of their scheme reflects Werfel's view that there is no political solution to the Jewish plight. While Bodenheim's political activities occupy the foreground, his gifted daughter Cella is being prepared for a grand benefit concert symbolizing the cultural solution in which Jews like Bodenheim had for so long placed their hope. But Werfel refused to toy with reality by contriving a triumph for Cella, who flees with her mother to Paris, leaving Bodenheim to face the Nazis in Vienna. The novel is a sympathetic but unsparingly authentic portrayal of Viennese society during a shameful period of its history. Watching Jewish citizens forced to scrub the street, the reader enters the psyches of victim, tormentor, and impassive onlooker alike. Nowhere else did Werfel express more effectively or more sadly his conviction that the Jews could not escape their tragic destiny.

When the Germans invaded France in the spring of 1940 the Werfels took flight; the *New York Post* erroneously reported on 16 July that Werfel had been shot by the Nazis. During a three-week respite in Lourdes, Werfel became engrossed in the story of Bernadette Soubirous, the girl whose vision of a "lady" in 1858 led to decades of controversy until her ultimate beatification. He saw in Bernadette a simple soul whose faith was like that of Babi, Barbara, and Teta. He vowed that if he reached the safety of America he would set all other work aside and would "sing the song" of Bernadette. Within five months after reaching the United States in October 1940, Werfel fulfilled his vow, and *Das Lied von Bernadette* (1941; translated as *The Song of Bernadette*, 1942) became his greatest commercial success. The American edition sold five hundred thousand copies in the first eight months; it was the Book-of-the-Month Club choice for June 1942, an Academy Award-winning movie in 1943, and was still selling ten thousand copies a month in 1944.

The story pits the simple piety of a poor innocent girl against the self-satisfied materialism and intellectual arrogance of nineteenth-century European civilization. Bernadette's teacher, the aristocratic Sister Vauzous, is made to suffer mental and spiritual anguish for her envy and doubt. The poet Lafite, the epitome of enlightened scientific skepticism, finally abandons his years of arrogant aloofness to fall on his knees at the shrine erected on the site of Bernadette's vision of "the lady." Werfel's own self-satisfaction was evident

Werfel in the final days of his life (Lionel B. Steiman, Franz Werfel: The Faith of an Exile. From Prague to Beverly Hills, *1985)*

as he portrayed the pompous representatives of state, science, and all authority as ultimately powerless against the faith of a child. American readers were entranced, but critics found Werfel's characterization of nineteenth-century thinkers inaccurate and tendentious. In reply to the claim that he was himself above believing in the simple pieties his book celebrated, Werfel reaffirmed his conviction that it was "a jubilant hymn to the supernatural." During the last years of his life he was something of a Roman Catholic celebrity, but he often insisted that he would always remain a Jew.

At his hotel in Lourdes Werfel had met a Jewish refugee from Poland; later, in America, he told the man's strange tale to Reinhardt. The director urged him to turn it into a play. Thus was born *Jacobowsky und der Oberst* (1944; translated as *Jacobowsky and the Colonel*, 1944), the most performed of all Werfel's dramatic works. A Polish colonel and a Jewish businessman, opposites in every respect, make common cause in an odyssey whose goal is to escape the Germans while pursuing the object of their affections, Marianne. Behind the succession of unlikely twists of plot Werfel plays out an allegory on the Last Judgment and his vision of the Jews as witnesses for Christ. Werfel's belief in the interdependence of Judaism and Christianity was illustrated by the Jewish businessman and the Polish aristocrat who contribute to each other's salvation not by forswearing their respective Jewishness and anti-Semitism but by being themselves.

The play was performed in New York in the spring of 1944; but the adaptation by S. N. Behrman had taken most of the tragedy out of a work Werfel had subtitled *Komödie einer Tragödie* (Comedy of a Tragedy) and had deleted material that Americans might have found offensive or incomprehensible, such as an encounter between St. Francis and the Eternal Jew and speeches implicating the United States in the current plight of European Jews. Werfel was deeply disappointed in the adaptation, and the months of haggling with writers, agents, and lawyers further drained the already ailing author.

The original play was performed in Göteborg and Basel in the fall of 1944 and enjoyed regular performances in Germany and Austria in the postwar years; it was a hit at the Vienna Festival of 1983. In 1958 a Hollywood motion picture based on Behrman's adaptation appeared as *Me and the Colonel*, starring Danny Kaye as Jacobowsky and Curt Jurgens as the colonel. An opera adapted by Giselher Klebes was performed in Hamburg in 1965 and even more successfully in 1982. Jerry Herman's 1978 Broadway musical *The Grand Tour* was adapted from a book based on Behrman's adaptation.

Werfel wrote his last work in a race with death, with physician and translator at his side in the bungalow of his Santa Barbara retreat. The posthumously published *Stern der Ungeborenen* (1946; translated as *Star of the Unborn*, 1946) is a confession and a testament, a roman à clef that is historically accurate and rich in biographical material. Werfel's boyhood friend Willy Haas, who thought Werfel had forgotten him, found reproduced verbatim in the book lengthy conversations he had had with the author during their youth in Prague. The work is also an antiutopian fantasy in which the protagonist, "FW," returns to discover what the world is one hundred thousand years in the future. Guided by "BH"

(Haas) as his Virgil, FW discovers that there is no work, illness, or distinctions of class; all the physical and material problems humanity had known have been overcome in the most ingenious manner in the "Astromental Era." But moral problems have not been overcome, and *Stern der Ungeborenen* is an extended polemic against the nihilism and "radical realism" Werfel had opposed all his life. FW recounts to the Grand Bishop the suffering he had witnessed on earth–the thousands of rickety slum children, their youth wasted by tuberculosis, syphilis, and moral nihilism, growing up with no choice other than to become wretched wage slaves or whores and gangsters. But it is for the politically active opponents of such evils that FW reserves his bitterest words. A conceited clique "motivated by the consuming ambition to outdo each other in absurdity," they are incarnate in the astromental world as grotesquely vain barnyard animals, immobilized between sterile intellectualism and impotent sensuality and relegated to the "Jungle," a region which owes its existence to the persistence of man's darker impulses. Werfel's solution is still Roman Catholicism: FW undergoes exorcism of every pernicious idea from Voltaire to Freud, commends himself to the ministrations of the Grand Bishop, and surrenders himself in serenity to the Catholic credo.

The novel was neither a critical nor a popular success, though it was held in high regard by scholars such as Adolf D. Klarmann. Eric Bentley wrote scathingly of it in the *New Republic*, and even a friendly reviewer in the *Saturday Review of Literature* (2 March 1946) confessed that despite its magnificent and poetic passages the book was "as cold and bloodless as outer space." Even Thomas Mann, who in the 1930s had called Werfel the most talented writer of his generation, concluded that *Stern der Ungeborenen* could not be considered an artistic success, and other admirers also admitted that the novel did not "work." Briefly in print in 1976 as a Bantam paperback, it is not among the few of Werfel's titles still available in English. Werfel was himself ambivalent about the book; in a letter to Brod he called it "monstrous mixture of philosophy and entertainment," and only days before his death on 26 August 1945 he handed the completed manuscript to a friend with the words, "I could have made a nice life for myself, but instead I slaved."

There is still a wonderful purity in Werfel's poetry, but much of it is full of rhetorical excesses embarrassing to contemporary sensibilities. It is in his novels and stories, in their richly evocative portrayal of the world of old Austria, that Werfel's lasting achievement lies. The passage of time has rendered the philosophical ballast in his work less irritating, while the best of his writing retains the quiet and absorbing power that once enthralled millions of readers.

Biographies:

Lore B. Foltin, *Franz Werfel* (Stuttgart: Metzler, 1972);

Lionel B. Steiman, *Franz Werfel: The Faith of an Exile. From Prague to Beverly Hills* (Waterloo, Ontario: Wilfrid Laurier University Press, 1985);

Peter Stephan Jungk, *Franz Werfel: Eine Lebensgeschichte* (Frankfurt am Main: Fischer, 1987).

References:

Gustave O. Arlt, "Franz Werfel and America," *Modern Language Forum*, 36 (March-June 1951): 1-7;

Eric Bentley, "Franz Werfel's Open Secret," *New Republic*, 114 (18 February 1946): 259-260;

Werner Braselmann, *Franz Werfel* (Wuppertal-Barmen: Müller, 1960);

Irwin Edman, "What Price Mysticism?," *Saturday Review of Literature*, 27 (18 November 1944): 9-11;

Lore B. Foltin, ed., *Franz Werfel 1890-1945* (Pittsburgh: University of Pittsburgh Press, 1961);

Foltin and John M. Spalek, "Franz Werfel's Essays: A Survey," *German Quarterly*, 42 (March 1969): 172-203;

Willy Haas, *Die literarische Welt: Erinnerungen* (Munich: List, 1958);

Lothar Huber, ed., *Franz Werfel: An Austrian Writer Reassessed* (Oxford & New York: Berg, 1988);

Adolf D. Klarmann, "Franz Werfel's Eschatology and Cosmogony," *Modern Language Quarterly*, 7 (December 1946): 385-410;

Henry A. Lea, "The Failure of Political Activism in Werfel's Plays," *Symposium*, 22 (Winter 1968): 319-334;

Alma Mahler-Werfel, *Mein Leben* (Frankfurt am Main: Fischer, 1960);

Mahler-Werfel and E. B. Ashton, *And the Bridge is Love* (New York: Harcourt, Brace, 1958);

Heinz Politzer, "Prague and the Origins of Rainer Maria Rilke, Franz Kafka, and Franz

Werfel," *Modern Language Quarterly*, 16 (March 1955): 49-62;

James Rolleston, "The Usable Future: Franz Werfel's *Star of the Unborn* as Exile Literature," in *Protest-Form-Tradition: Essays on German Exile Literature*, edited by Joseph P. Strelka, Robert F. Bell, and Eugene Dobson (University: University of Alabama Press, 1979);

Harry Slochower, "Franz Werfel and Alfred Döblin: The Problem of Individualism in *Barbara* and in *Berlin Alexanderplatz*," *Journal of English and Germanic Philology*, 33 (1934): 103-112;

Slochower, "Franz Werfel and Sholom Asch: The Yearning for Status," *Accent*, 5/6 (1944-1946): 73-82;

Jeremy Smith, *Religious feeling and religious commitment in Faulkner, Dostoyevsky, Werfel, and Bernanos* (New York: Garland, 1988);

Walter Sokel, *The Writer in Extremis: Expressionism in Twentieth-Century German Literature* (Stanford: Stanford University Press, 1959);

John M. Spalek and Robert Bell, eds., *Exile: The Writers' Experience* (Chapel Hill: University of North Carolina Press, 1982), pp. 300-310;

Richard Specht, *Franz Werfel: Versuch einer Zeitspiegelung* (Berlin: Zsolnay, 1926);

Israel Stamm, "Religious Experience in Werfel's *Barbara oder die Frömmigkeit*," *PMLA*, 54 (1939): 332-347;

C. E. Williams, *The Broken Eagle: The Politics of Austrian Literature from Empire to Anschluss* (London: Elek, 1974), pp. 60-90;

Leopold Zahn, *Franz Werfel* (Berlin: Colloquium, 1966).

Papers:

Some of Franz Werfel's letters are in the Schillernationalmuseum, Marbach am Neckar; with that exception, his entire literary estate is in libraries in the United States, the two main repositories being the University of California at Los Angeles and the University of Pennsylvania. A comprehensive and detailed report on the contents and location of these and other deposits of Werfel's papers is John M. Spalek, *A Guide to the Archival Materials of the German-speaking Emigration to the United States after 1933* (Charlottesville: University Press of Virginia Press, 1978).

Stefan Zweig
(28 November 1881-23 February 1942)

Ruth V. Gross
Eastman School of Music, University of Rochester

BOOKS: *Silberne Saiten: Gedichte* (Berlin & Leipzig: Schuster & Loeffler, 1901);
Die Liebe der Erika Ewald: Novellen (Berlin: Fleischel, 1904);
Verlaine (Berlin & Leipzig: Schuster & Loeffler, 1905); translated by O. F. Theis as *Paul Verlaine* (Boston: Luce, 1913; Dublin: Maunsel, 1913);
Die frühen Kränze (Leipzig: Insel, 1906);
Tersites: Ein Trauerspiel (Leipzig: Insel, 1907); revised as *Tersites: Trauerspiel in drei Aufzügen* (Leipzig: Insel, 1919);
Émile Verhaeren (Leipzig: Insel, 1910); translated by Jethro Bithell (Boston & New York: Houghton Mifflin, 1914; London: Constable, 1914);
Erstes Erlebnis: Vier Geschichten aus Kinderland (Leipzig: Insel, 1911); republished as *Die Kette: Ein Novellenkreis*, volume 1 (Leipzig: Insel, 1923);
Der verwandelte Komödiant: Ein Spiel aus dem deutschen Rokoko (Berlin: Bloch, 1912);
Das Haus am Meer: Ein Schauspiel in zwei Teilen (Leipzig: Insel, 1912);
Brennendes Geheimnis: Eine Erzählung (Leipzig: Insel, 1913); translated by Stephen Branch (pseudonym for Zweig) as *The Burning Secret* (New York: Scott & Seltzer, 1919);
Erinnerungen an Emile Verhaeren (Vienna: Reisser, 1917);
Jeremias: Eine dramatische Dichtung in neun Bildern (Leipzig: Insel, 1917); translated by Eden and Cedar Paul as *Jeremiah: A Drama in Nine Scenes* (New York: Seltzer, 1922; new edition, with preface by Zweig, New York: Viking Press, 1929; London: Allen, 1929);
Das Herz Europas: Ein Besuch im Genfer Roten Kreuz (Zurich: Rascher, 1918);
Legende eines Lebens: Ein Kammerspiel in drei Aufzügen (Leipzig: Insel, 1919);
Fahrten: Landschaften und Städte (Leipzig: Tal, 1919);
Drei Meister: Balzac-Dickens-Dostojewski (Leipzig: Insel, 1920); translated by Eden and Cedar

(photograph Mrs. Susanne Hoeller)

Paul as *Three Masters: Balzac-Dickens-Dostoeffsky* (New York: Viking Press, 1930; London: Allen & Unwin, 1930);
Der Zwang: Eine Novelle (Leipzig: Insel, 1920);
Angst: Novelle (Berlin: Hermann, 1920);
Marceline Desbordes-Valmore: Das Lebensbild einer Dichterin (Leipzig: Insel, 1920);

Romain Rolland: Der Mann und das Werk (Frankfurt am Main: Rütten & Loening, 1921); translated by Eden and Cedar Paul as *Romain Rolland: The Man and his Work* (New York: Seltzer, 1921; London: Allen & Unwin, 1921);

Die Augen des ewigen Bruders: Eine Legende (Leipzig: Insel, 1922);

Amok: Novellen einer Leidenschaft (Leipzig: Insel, 1922);

Sainte-Beuve (Frankfurt am Main: Frankfurter Verlags-Anstalt, 1923);

Die gesammelten Gedichte (Leipzig: Insel, 1924);

Passion and Pain, translated by Eden and Cedar Paul (London: Chapman & Hall, 1924; New York: Richards, 1925)—comprises "Letter from an Unknown Woman," "The Runaway," "Transfiguration," "The Fowler Snared," "Compulsion," "The Governess," "Virata; or, The Eyes of the Undying Brother";

Der Kampf mit dem Dämon: Hölderlin-Kleist-Nietzsche (Leipzig: Insel, 1925); translated by Eden and Cedar Paul as *The Struggle with the Demon* (New York: Viking Press, 1929; London: Allen & Unwin, 1930);

Volpone: Eine lieblose Komödie in drei Akten (Berlin: Bloch, 1925); translated by Ruth Langner as *Ben Jonson's Volpone: A Loveless Comedy in Three Acts* (London: Allen & Unwin, 1928; New York: Viking Press, 1929);

Sternstunden der Menschheit: Fünf historische Miniaturen (Leipzig: Insel, 1927); edited by Felix Wittmer and Theodore Geissendoerfer (New York: Prentice-Hall, 1931); enlarged, translated by Eden and Cedar Paul as *The Tide of Fortune: Twelve Historical Miniatures* (New York: Viking Press, 1940; London: Cassell, 1955); enlarged German version published as *Sternstunden der Menschheit: Zwölf historische Miniaturen* (Stockholm: Bermann-Fischer, 1945);

Die unsichtbare Sammlung: Eine Episode aus der deutschen Inflation (Berlin: Privately printed, 1927);

Episode am Genfer See (Der Flüchtling) (Leipzig: Insel, 1927);

Verwirrung der Gefühle: Drei Novellen (Leipzig: Insel, 1927); translated by Eden and Cedar Paul as *Conflicts: Three Tales* (New York: Viking Press, 1927; London: Allen & Unwin, 1928);

Die Flucht zu Gott: Ein Epilog zu Leo Tolstois unvollendetem Drama "Das Licht scheinet in der Finsterness" (Berlin: Bloch, 1927);

Abschied von Rilke: Eine Rede (Tübingen: Wunderlich, 1927); translated by Marion Sonnenfeld as *Farewell to Rilke* (Fredonia, N.Y.: Friends of the Daniel Reed Library, State University College, 1975);

Reise nach Russland (Vienna: Österreichisches Journal, 1928);

Drei Dichter ihres Lebens: Casanova-Stendhal-Tolstoi (Leipzig: Insel, 1928); translated by Eden and Cedar Paul as *Adepts in Self-Portraiture: Casanova-Stendhal-Tolstoy* (New York: Viking Press, 1928; London: Allen & Unwin, 1929);

Thanks to Books, translated by Theodore Wesley Koch (Evanston, Ill.: Northwestern University Library, 1929);

Das Lamm des Armen: Tragikomödie in drei Akten (neun Bildern) (Leipzig: Insel, 1929);

Kleine Chronik (Leipzig: Insel, 1929);

Joseph Fouché: Bildnis eines politischen Menschen (Leipzig: Insel, 1929); translated by Eden and Cedar Paul as *Joseph Fouché: The Portrait of a Politician* (New York: Viking Press, 1930; London: Cassell, 1930);

Ausgewählte Gedichte (Leipzig: Insel, 1931);

Amok: A Story, translated by Eden and Cedar Paul (New York: Viking Press, 1931; London: Cassell, 1932);

Die Heilung durch den Geist: Franz Anton Mesmer-Mary Baker-Eddy-Sigmund Freud (Leipzig: Insel, 1931); translated by Eden and Cedar Paul as *Mental Healers: Franz Anton Mesmer, Mary Baker Eddy, Sigmund Freud* (New York: Viking Press, 1932; London: Cassell, 1933);

Marie Antoinette: Bildnis eines mittleren Charakters (Leipzig: Insel, 1932); translated by Eden and Cedar Paul as *Marie Antoinette: The Portrait of an Average Woman* (New York: Viking, Press, 1933; London: Cassell, 1933);

Triumph und Tragik des Erasmus von Rotterdam (Vienna: Reichner, 1934); translated by Eden and Cedar Paul as *Erasmus of Rotterdam* (New York: Viking Press, 1934); translation republished as *Erasmus* (London: Cassell, 1934);

Maria Stuart (Vienna, Leipzig & Zurich: Reichner, 1935); translated by Eden and Cedar Paul as *Mary, Queen of Scotland and the Isles* (New York: Viking Press, 1935); translation republished as *The Queen of Scots* (London: Cassell, 1935);

Stefan Zweig
(28 November 1881-23 February 1942)

Ruth V. Gross
Eastman School of Music, University of Rochester

BOOKS: *Silberne Saiten: Gedichte* (Berlin & Leipzig: Schuster & Loeffler, 1901);

Die Liebe der Erika Ewald: Novellen (Berlin: Fleischel, 1904);

Verlaine (Berlin & Leipzig: Schuster & Loeffler, 1905); translated by O. F. Theis as *Paul Verlaine* (Boston: Luce, 1913; Dublin: Maunsel, 1913);

Die frühen Kränze (Leipzig: Insel, 1906);

Tersites: Ein Trauerspiel (Leipzig: Insel, 1907); revised as *Tersites: Trauerspiel in drei Aufzügen* (Leipzig: Insel, 1919);

Émile Verhaeren (Leipzig: Insel, 1910); translated by Jethro Bithell (Boston & New York: Houghton Mifflin, 1914; London: Constable, 1914);

Erstes Erlebnis: Vier Geschichten aus Kinderland (Leipzig: Insel, 1911); republished as *Die Kette: Ein Novellenkreis*, volume 1 (Leipzig: Insel, 1923);

Der verwandelte Komödiant: Ein Spiel aus dem deutschen Rokoko (Berlin: Bloch, 1912);

Das Haus am Meer: Ein Schauspiel in zwei Teilen (Leipzig: Insel, 1912);

Brennendes Geheimnis: Eine Erzählung (Leipzig: Insel, 1913); translated by Stephen Branch (pseudonym for Zweig) as *The Burning Secret* (New York: Scott & Seltzer, 1919);

Erinnerungen an Emile Verhaeren (Vienna: Reisser, 1917);

Jeremias: Eine dramatische Dichtung in neun Bildern (Leipzig: Insel, 1917); translated by Eden and Cedar Paul as *Jeremiah: A Drama in Nine Scenes* (New York: Seltzer, 1922; new edition, with preface by Zweig, New York: Viking Press, 1929; London: Allen, 1929);

Das Herz Europas: Ein Besuch im Genfer Roten Kreuz (Zurich: Rascher, 1918);

Legende eines Lebens: Ein Kammerspiel in drei Aufzügen (Leipzig: Insel, 1919);

Fahrten: Landschaften und Städte (Leipzig: Tal, 1919);

Drei Meister: Balzac-Dickens-Dostojewski (Leipzig: Insel, 1920); translated by Eden and Cedar

(photograph Mrs. Susanne Hoeller)

Paul as *Three Masters: Balzac-Dickens-Dostoeffsky* (New York: Viking Press, 1930; London: Allen & Unwin, 1930);

Der Zwang: Eine Novelle (Leipzig: Insel, 1920);

Angst: Novelle (Berlin: Hermann, 1920);

Marceline Desbordes-Valmore: Das Lebensbild einer Dichterin (Leipzig: Insel, 1920);

Romain Rolland: Der Mann und das Werk (Frankfurt am Main: Rütten & Loening, 1921); translated by Eden and Cedar Paul as *Romain Rolland: The Man and his Work* (New York: Seltzer, 1921; London: Allen & Unwin, 1921);

Die Augen des ewigen Bruders: Eine Legende (Leipzig: Insel, 1922);

Amok: Novellen einer Leidenschaft (Leipzig: Insel, 1922);

Sainte-Beuve (Frankfurt am Main: Frankfurter Verlags-Anstalt, 1923);

Die gesammelten Gedichte (Leipzig: Insel, 1924);

Passion and Pain, translated by Eden and Cedar Paul (London: Chapman & Hall, 1924; New York: Richards, 1925)—comprises "Letter from an Unknown Woman," "The Runaway," "Transfiguration," "The Fowler Snared," "Compulsion," "The Governess," "Virata; or, The Eyes of the Undying Brother";

Der Kampf mit dem Dämon: Hölderlin-Kleist-Nietzsche (Leipzig: Insel, 1925); translated by Eden and Cedar Paul as *The Struggle with the Demon* (New York: Viking Press, 1929; London: Allen & Unwin, 1930);

Volpone: Eine lieblose Komödie in drei Akten (Berlin: Bloch, 1925); translated by Ruth Langner as *Ben Jonson's Volpone: A Loveless Comedy in Three Acts* (London: Allen & Unwin, 1928; New York: Viking Press, 1929);

Sternstunden der Menschheit: Fünf historische Miniaturen (Leipzig: Insel, 1927); edited by Felix Wittmer and Theodore Geissendoerfer (New York: Prentice-Hall, 1931); enlarged, translated by Eden and Cedar Paul as *The Tide of Fortune: Twelve Historical Miniatures* (New York: Viking Press, 1940; London: Cassell, 1955); enlarged German version published as *Sternstunden der Menschheit: Zwölf historische Miniaturen* (Stockholm: Bermann-Fischer, 1945);

Die unsichtbare Sammlung: Eine Episode aus der deutschen Inflation (Berlin: Privately printed, 1927);

Episode am Genfer See (Der Flüchtling) (Leipzig: Insel, 1927);

Verwirrung der Gefühle: Drei Novellen (Leipzig: Insel, 1927); translated by Eden and Cedar Paul as *Conflicts: Three Tales* (New York: Viking Press, 1927; London: Allen & Unwin, 1928);

Die Flucht zu Gott: Ein Epilog zu Leo Tolstois unvollendetem Drama "Das Licht scheinet in der Finsterness" (Berlin: Bloch, 1927);

Abschied von Rilke: Eine Rede (Tübingen: Wunderlich, 1927); translated by Marion Sonnenfeld as *Farewell to Rilke* (Fredonia, N.Y.: Friends of the Daniel Reed Library, State University College, 1975);

Reise nach Russland (Vienna: Österreichisches Journal, 1928);

Drei Dichter ihres Lebens: Casanova-Stendhal-Tolstoi (Leipzig: Insel, 1928); translated by Eden and Cedar Paul as *Adepts in Self-Portraiture: Casanova-Stendhal-Tolstoy* (New York: Viking Press, 1928; London: Allen & Unwin, 1929);

Thanks to Books, translated by Theodore Wesley Koch (Evanston, Ill.: Northwestern University Library, 1929);

Das Lamm des Armen: Tragikomödie in drei Akten (neun Bildern) (Leipzig: Insel, 1929);

Kleine Chronik (Leipzig: Insel, 1929);

Joseph Fouché: Bildnis eines politischen Menschen (Leipzig: Insel, 1929); translated by Eden and Cedar Paul as *Joseph Fouché: The Portrait of a Politician* (New York: Viking Press, 1930; London: Cassell, 1930);

Ausgewählte Gedichte (Leipzig: Insel, 1931);

Amok: A Story, translated by Eden and Cedar Paul (New York: Viking Press, 1931; London: Cassell, 1932);

Die Heilung durch den Geist: Franz Anton Mesmer-Mary Baker-Eddy-Sigmund Freud (Leipzig: Insel, 1931); translated by Eden and Cedar Paul as *Mental Healers: Franz Anton Mesmer, Mary Baker Eddy, Sigmund Freud* (New York: Viking Press, 1932; London: Cassell, 1933);

Marie Antoinette: Bildnis eines mittleren Charakters (Leipzig: Insel, 1932); translated by Eden and Cedar Paul as *Marie Antoinette: The Portrait of an Average Woman* (New York: Viking Press, 1933; London: Cassell, 1933);

Triumph und Tragik des Erasmus von Rotterdam (Vienna: Reichner, 1934); translated by Eden and Cedar Paul as *Erasmus of Rotterdam* (New York: Viking Press, 1934); translation republished as *Erasmus* (London: Cassell, 1934);

Maria Stuart (Vienna, Leipzig & Zurich: Reichner, 1935); translated by Eden and Cedar Paul as *Mary, Queen of Scotland and the Isles* (New York: Viking Press, 1935); translation republished as *The Queen of Scots* (London: Cassell, 1935);

Die schweigsame Frau: Komische Oper in drei Aufzügen frei nach Ben Jonson, music by Richard Strauss (Berlin: Fürstner, 1935);

Sinn und Schönheit der Autographen (Vienna: Reichner, 1935);

Arturo Toscanini: Ein Bildnis (Vienna: Reichner, 1935);

Die Kette (Vienna, Leipzig & Zurich: Reichner, 1936);

Kaleidoskop (Vienna, Leipzig & Zurich: Reichner, 1936);

Gesammelte Erzählungen (Vienna, Leipzig & Zurich: Reichner, 1936);

Castellio gegen Calvin oder Ein Gewissen gegen die Gewalt (Vienna, Leipzig & Zurich: Reichner, 1936); translated by Eden and Cedar Paul as *The Right to Heresy: Castellio against Calvin* (New York: Viking Press, 1936; London: Cassell, 1936);

The Old-Book Peddler and Other Tales for Bibliophiles, translated by Theodore W. Koch (Evanston, Ill.: Northwestern University, The Charles Deering Library, 1937)–comprises "Books Are the Gateway to the World," "The Old-Book Peddler: A Viennese Tale for Bibliophiles," "The Invisible Collection: An Episode from the Post-war Inflation Period," "Thanks to Books";

Georg Friedrich Händels Auferstehung: Eine historische Miniatur (Vienna, Leipzig & Zurich: Reichner, 1937); translated by Eden and Cedar Paul as *George Frederick Handel's Resurrection* (London: Corvinus Press, 1938);

Der begrabene Leuchter (Vienna: Reichner, 1937); translated by Eden and Cedar Paul as *The Buried Candelabrum* (New York: Viking Press, 1937; London: Cassell, 1937);

Begegnungen mit Menschen, Büchern, Städten (Vienna, Leipzig & Zurich: Reichner, 1937);

Magellan: Der Mann und seine Tat (Vienna, Leipzig & Zurich: Reichner, 1938); translated by Eden and Cedar Paul as *Conqueror of the Seas: The Story of Magellan* (New York: Viking Press, 1938); translation republished as *Magellan: Pioneer of the Pacific* (London: Cassell, 1938);

Ungeduld des Herzens: Roman (Stockholm: Bermann-Fischer, 1939; New York & Toronto: Longmans, Green, Alliance Book Corp., 1939); translated by Phyllis and Trevor Blewitt as *Beware of Pity* (New York: Viking Press, 1939; London: Cassell, 1939);

Worte am Grabe Sigmund Freuds (Amsterdam: De Lange, 1939);

Brasilien, ein Land der Zukunft (Stockholm: Bermann-Fischer, 1941); translated by Andrew St. James as *Brazil, Land of the Future* (New York: Viking Press, 1941; London & Toronto: Cassell, 1942);

Schachnovelle (Buenos Aires: Pigmalion, 1942);

Amerigo: A Comedy of Errors in History, translated by St. James (New York: Viking Press, 1942); German version published as *Amerigo: Die Geschichte eines historischen Irrtums* (Stockholm: Bermann-Fischer, 1944);

The World of Yesterday: An Autobiography, translated by Eden and Cedar Paul (New York: Viking Press, 1943; London: Cassell, 1943); German version published as *Die Welt von Gestern: Erinnerungen eines Europäers* (London: Hamilton/Stockholm: Bermann-Fischer, 1944);

Zeit und Welt: Gesammelte Aufsätze und Vorträge, 1904-1940, edited by Richard Friedenthal (Stockholm: Bermann-Fischer, 1943);

The Royal Game; Amok; Letter from an Unknown Woman (New York Viking Press, 1944); republished as *The Royal Game, with Letter from an Unknown Woman, and Amok* (London: Cassell, 1945)–comprises "The Royal Game" (*Schachnovelle*), translated by B. W. Huebsch, and "Amok" and "Letter from an Unknown Woman," translated by Eden and Cedar Paul;

Legenden (Stockholm: Bermann-Fischer, 1945); translated by Cedar Paul as *Jewish Legends*, edited by Jonathan D. Sarna (New York: Wiener, 1987);

Balzac: Der Roman seines Lebens, edited by Friedenthal (Stockholm: Bermann-Fischer, 1946); translated by William and Dorothy Rose as *Balzac* (New York: Viking Press, 1946; London: Cassell, 1947);

Ausgewählte Novellen (Stockholm: Bermann-Fischer, 1946);

Werke, edited by Friedenthal, 11 volumes (Frankfurt am Main: Fischer, 1954-1966);

Stories and Legends, translated by Eden and Cedar Paul and Constantine FitzGibbon (London: Cassell, 1955)–comprises "Twenty-four Hours in a Woman's Life," "A Failing Heart," "Episode in the Early Life of Privy Councillor D.," "The Buried Candelabrum," "The Legend of the Third Dove," "The Dissimilar Troubles";

Albert Schweitzer, Genie der Menschlichkeit, by Zweig, Jacques Feschotte, and Rudolf Grabs (Frankfurt am Main: Fischer, 1957);

Ausgewählte Werke, 2 volumes (Düsseldorf: Deutscher Bücherbund, 1960);

Fragment einer Novelle, edited by Erich Fitzbauer (Vienna: Verlag der Internationalen Stefan-Zweig-Gesellschaft, 1961);

Durch Zeiten und Welten, edited by Fitzbauer (Graz: Stiasny, 1961);

Im Schnee, edited by Fitzbauer (Vienna: Verlag der Internationalen Stefan-Zweig-Gesellschaft, 1963);

Der Turm zu Babel, edited by Fitzbauer (Vienna: Verlag der Internationalen Stefan-Zweig-Gesellschaft, 1964);

Frühlingsfahrt durch die Provence: Ein Essay, edited by Fitzbauer (Vienna: Verlag des Internationalen Stefan-Zweig-Gesellschaft, 1965);

Die Monotonisierung der Welt: Aufsätze und Vorträge, edited by Volker Michels (Frankfurt am Main: Suhrkamp, 1976);

Die Hochzeit von Lyon, edited by Fitzbauer (Vienna: Edition Graphischer Zirkel, 1980);

Das Stefan Zweig Buch, edited by Knut Beck (Frankfurt am Main: Fischer, 1981);

Das Geheimnis des künstlerischen Schaffens, edited by Beck (Frankfurt am Main: Fischer, 1981);

Menschen und Schicksale (Frankfurt am Main: Fischer, 1981);

Gesammelte Werke in Einzelbänden, edited by Beck, 25 volumes published (Frankfurt am Main: Fischer, 1982-).

OTHER: Paul Verlaine, *Eine Anthologie der besten Übersetzungen*, edited by Zweig (Berlin: Schuster & Loeffler, 1902);

Émile Verhaeren, *Ausgewählte Gedichte*, translated by Zweig (Berlin: Schuster & Loeffler, 1904);

Archibald B. H. Russell, *Die visionäre Kunstphilosophie des William Blake*, translated by Zweig (Leipzig: Zeitler, 1906);

Arthur Rimbaud, *Leben und Dichtung*, translated by K. L. Ammer, introduction by Zweig (Leipzig: Insel, 1907);

Honoré de Balzac, *Balzac: Sein Weltbild aus den Werken*, edited by Lothar Brieger-Wasservogel, introduction by Zweig, 2 volumes (Stuttgart: Lutz, 1908);

Verhaeren, *Ausgewählte Gedichte*, translated by Zweig (Leipzig: Insel, 1910);

Verhaeren, *Drei Dramen: Helenas Heimkehr–Phillipp II–Das Kloster*, translated by Zweig (Leipzig: Insel, 1910);

Verhaeren, *Hymnen an das Leben*, translated by Zweig (Leipzig: Insel, 1911);

Lafcadio Hearn, *Das Japanbuch: Eine Auswahl aus Lafcadio Hearns Werken*, translated by Berta Franzos, introduction by Zweig (Frankfurt am Main: Rütten & Loening, 1911);

Verhaeren, *Rembrandt*, translated by Zweig (Leipzig: Insel, 1912);

Verhaeren, *Rubens*, translated by Zweig (Leipzig: Insel, 1913);

Romain Rolland, *Den hingerichteten Völkern (Aux peuples assassinés)*, translated by Zweig (Zurich: Rascher, 1918);

Rolland, *Die Zeit wird kommen (Le Temps viendra)*, translated by Zweig (Vienna & Leipzig: Tal, 1919);

Jean-Jacques Rousseau, *Émile oder Über die Erziehung*, introduction by Zweig (Potsdam: Kiepenheuer, 1919);

Madeline Marx, *Weib: Roman*, translated by Zweig and Friderike Zweig (Basel: Rhein, 1920);

André Suarès, *Cressida*, translated by Zweig and Erwin Rieger (Vienna: Tal, 1920);

Charles Baudelaire, *Die Blumen des Bösen*, eight poems translated by Zweig (Berlin: Oesterheld, 1921);

Franz Karl Ginzkey: Dem Dichter und Freunden zum 50sten Geburtstag, epilogue by Zweig (Vienna: Wiener Literarische Anstalt, 1921);

Verlaine, *Gesammelte Werke*, edited by Zweig, 2 volumes (Leipzig: Insel, 1922);

Rolland, *Clérambault: Geschichte eines freien Gewissens im Kriege*, translated by Zweig (Frankfurt am Main: Rütten & Loening, 1922);

Charles Augustin Sainte-Beuve, *Literarische Portraits aus dem Frankreich des XVII.-XIX. Jahrhunderts*, edited by Zweig, 2 volumes (Frankfurt am Main: Frankfurter Verlags-Anstalt, 1923);

Hermann Bahr, *Die schöne Frau: Novellen*, epilogue by Zweig (Leipzig: Reclam, 1924);

François René Auguste, Vicomte de Chateaubriand, *Romantische Erzählungen*, edited by Zweig (Vienna, Leipzig & Munich: Rikola, 1924);

Franz Karl Ginzkey, *Brigitte und Regine und andere Dichtungen*, epilogue by Zweig (Leipzig: Reclam, 1924);

Max Brod, *Tycho Brahe's Weg zu Gott*, epilogue by Zweig (Berlin: Herbig, 1927);

Johann Wolfgang von Goethe, *Goethes Gedichte: Eine Auswahl*, edited by Zweig (Leipzig: Reclam, 1927);

Oskar Baum, *Nacht ist umher: Erzählung*, epilogue by Zweig (Leipzig: Reclam, 1929);

Maxim Gorki, *Erzählungen*, translated by Arthur Luther, introduction by Zweig (Leipzig: Insel, 1931);

Jean Richard Bloch, *Vom Sinn unseres Jahrhunderts*, translated by Paul Amann, introduction by Zweig (Berlin, Vienna & Leipzig: Zsolnay, 1932);

Luigi Pirandello, *Man weiß nicht wie*, translated by Zweig (Vienna: Reichner, 1935);

William Rose and G. Craig Houston, *Rainer Maria Rilke: Aspects of His Mind and Poetry*, introduction by Zweig (London: Sidgwick & Jackson, 1938);

Irwin Edman, *Ein Schimmerlicht im Dunkel*, translated by Zweig and Richard Friedenthal (Stockholm: Bermann-Fischer, 1940);

Stefan Zweig Presents the Living Thoughts of Tolstoy, essay by Zweig, translated by Barrows Mussey (Greenwich, Conn.: Fawcett, 1960).

PERIODICAL PUBLICATIONS: "Camille Lemonnier," *Neue Freie Presse*, 12 October 1902;

"Neue Lyrik," *Freistadt*, 6, no. 3 (1904): 49-51;

"Das Autographensammeln," *Vossische Zeitung*, 14 September 1913;

"An die Freunde im Fremdland," *Berliner Tageblatt*, 19 September 1914;

"Meine Autographensammlung," *Philobiblon*, 3, no. 7 (1930): 279-289;

"Der geistige Aufbau der neuen Generation," *Neue Freie Presse*, 20 November 1932.

For most people who know his name at all, Stefan Zweig is the author of the autobiography *Die Welt von Gestern* (1944; translated as *The World of Yesterday*, 1943) and several biographies written in a "faction" style that today seems much out of fashion. It is indeed difficult to believe that Zweig was one of the most widely read and translated authors of the first half of the twentieth century. His life was something of a paradox: he achieved what many writers never attain–public acknowledgment and material rewards–yet his was an unhappy existence that ended in suicide. Those acquainted with Zweig through his fiction, biographies, dramas, essays, and poetry tend to consider him a "man of yesterday," "European of yesterday," or "humanist of yesterday." "Yesterday" is the time in which Zweig lived, "yesterday" was the time for which he yearned, and "yesterday" was the time of his real fame. During the 1920s and 1930s he was the most translated German-language author. Today he is usually considered an author of the second magnitude. But a German edition of his complete works was begun in 1981 to celebrate the centenary of his birth, and it appears that a reassessment of his significance for twentieth-century German literature is taking shape among scholars.

Vienna in 1881, the year of Stefan Zweig's birth, seemed a calm and secure European metropolis. The imperial city was in those days less concerned with politics than with theater, music, opera, and the good life. Zweig's father, Moritz Zweig, had come to Vienna from his native Moravia; well educated and with a good sense for business, he had built his weaving concern into one of the great enterprises of the Austro-Hungarian Empire's textile industry. Although a millionaire, Moritz Zweig believed in living without ostentation. His Italian-born wife, Ida Brettauer Zweig, however, was given to elegant airs and ambition. Stefan Zweig, the second of two sons, disapproved of his mother's inclination toward the fashionable life, considering her self-willed and lacking in the proper concern for her family. He idolized his father, but his mother remained a dominant influence in his life until her death. Both parents became models for characters in his novella "Untergang eines Herzens" (published in *Verwirrung der Gefühle*, 1927; translated as "A Failing Heart" in *Conflicts*, 1927).

Zweig hated school; he found it boring and dreary, a place where he had to learn "die 'Wissenschaft des nicht Wissenswerten'" (the "science of the not-worth-knowing"). He generally disliked the educational system and opposed the authority represented by his teachers. Moody and rebellious, he resented the conformity to which schooling in the Austro-Hungarian Empire was directed; his desire for freedom grew into a major passion and driving force in his life. Learning from the cultural riches of Vienna was, however, another matter. In his youth he developed a great love for theater and opera, attending performances at the famed Vienna Burgtheater and State Opera whenever possible. Above all, reading became almost an obsession for Zweig and his friends and provided the basis of hours of discussion and analysis among them. Not the classics taught in school but the vital literature of the day–works by Friederich Nietzsche, August Strindberg, Rainer Maria Rilke, and Stefan George, some of which were published in the feuilleton sections of newspapers and magazines–were devoured by Zweig in the cafés he frequented. For him and the others of his generation who recognized the power of the new kind of art being produced by German and Austrian artists, there seemed to be a feeling that the turn of the century would bring with it a real change in values.

Zweig entered the University of Vienna in 1899. For the first time, he tasted a life of freedom. Choosing to live in bohemian student quarters rather than in his parents' home, Zweig began writing seriously for publication while perfunctorily pursuing his studies. In 1901 he attended the University of Berlin for a semester. There he found a greater, more complete sense of freedom than he had in Vienna. In the cafés of Berlin he encountered the vestiges of naturalism, far removed from the spirit of Jung-Wien (Young Vienna). There he could explore a darker, seamier side of life. It was during this time, at the suggestion of his friend, the poet Richard Dehmel, that he turned to translating works from other languages, leaving aside almost all original work for a while.

Also in 1901 he published his first volume of poetry, *Silberne Saiten* (Silver Strings). None of the fifty poems from this volume were included in his collected poems in 1924, perhaps because by that time he had rejected their tone of exaggerated emotionalism and flowery sweetness that was so characteristic of the poetry of the Jung-Wien writers. The early poems were, however, reprinted in a later volume of Zweig's poetry also titled *Silberne Saiten* (1961), edited by his friend Richard Friedenthal as part of Friedenthal's eleven-volume edition of Zweig's works (1954-1966).

After a favorable review of *Silberne Saiten* appeared in the *Neue Freie Presse*, one of Vienna's most prestigious daily newspapers, Zweig was asked by Theodor Herzl, the feuilleton editor, to contribute an essay on poetry. The article quickly established Zweig as a rising star in the Viennese world of letters. It also marked the beginning of a long relationship between Zweig, Herzl, and Franz Servaes, the literary critic of the *Neue Freie Presse* who did much to further Zweig's literary reputation and career.

In 1902 Zweig traveled to Belgium, chiefly to meet one of his early literary heroes, the Belgian poet and dramatist Émile Verhaeren. In his autobiography Zweig wrote that Verhaeren was among the first French-language poets to be to Europe what Walt Whitman had been to America—developer of the creed of his age of the future. Meeting Verhaeren convinced Zweig that a life devoted to literature could be a valuable one. After their first encounter, Zweig and Verhaeren met almost every year until 1914, when World War I almost ended their friendship. During these years Zweig translated many of the Belgian poet's works into German.

Zweig's poetry had found success, but he wanted to be known as something more than a young lyric poet. Several attempts at publishing short stories failed, but in 1904, his last year at the university, a volume of four novellas titled *Die Liebe der Erika Ewald* (The Love of Erika Ewald) appeared. Besides the title story, it included "Der Stern über dem Wald" (The Star over the Forest), "Die Wanderung" (The Hike), and "Das Wunder des Lebens" (The Miracle of Life).

The years following his graduation took Zweig to Paris, London, Switzerland, Spain, Norway, and Algiers, but Paris became his home away from home. He was fluent in French, and through Verhaeren he had made contact with the Parisian literary and artistic world. England, on the other hand, held little charm for him; he felt isolated and uncomfortable in London. Not until 1933, when England seemed a haven from the lunacy on the Continent, did Zweig return there and eventually become a citizen.

The year 1906 marked the appearance of another volume of Zweig's poems, *Die frühen Kränze* (Early Wreaths). These poems showed no more originality than his earlier ones had, but the book was the first of Zweig's works to be published by the Insel house, which remained his publisher until 1933. Being an "Insel author" meant that a writer had arrived.

By April 1906 Zweig had completed his first drama, *Tersites* (1907), written in iambic pentameter. Zweig turns the ugly, unloved, reviled Tersites into a kind of antihero as he confronts Achilles, king of the Myrmidons—a character who knows only success and glory and whose life has been untouched by sorrow. Tersites, who has never known the love of a woman, falls in love with Teleia, the Amazon princess captured by Achilles, and tries to free her from her heartless captor. This early drama reveals many of the themes of Zweig's later oeuvre—an antiheroic main character, suicide as an escape from an unbearable existence, woman as an object in a man's world, and pervasive loneliness. In style and structure, the work shows Zweig's talent as a dramatist, but none of the characters seems to be made of real flesh and blood.

Zweig (center) with the Belgian poet Émile Verhaeren and Verhaeren's wife (British Literary Journal)

The drama was to have its premiere at the Royal Theater in Berlin, but after several postponements and the illness and death of Adalbert Matkowsky, the famous actor who was to play Achilles, Zweig opted for simultaneous premieres of *Tersites* in Dresden and Kassel on 26 November 1908. The refusal of the Vienna Burgtheater to produce the play was one of many disappointments that Zweig would experience in his dramatic endeavors. In 1910 he wrote the one-act *Der verwandelte Komödiant* (The Transformed Actor, 1912) especially for Joseph Kainz, a Viennese actor who had tried without success to get *Tersites* performed at the Burgtheater. Before rehearsals began, Kainz was diagnosed as having cancer; he died shortly thereafter.

The unhappy fate of Zweig's play did not deter him from writing yet another work for the stage, *Das Haus am Meer* (The Seaside House, 1912). Set in a German seaport in the eighteenth century, when Germans were being forced to fight for the British in the American Revolution, Zweig's play is a dark reminder of the cost of lack of understanding between human beings. Thomas Krüger, an innkeeper, upon finding out that his wife had been a prostitute before he married her, changes places with a young seaman who has been impressed into the army. In the second part of the play Krüger returns to Germany after an absence of twenty years. His wife, believing him dead, has married a much younger man who treats her badly and who is carrying on an affair with his nineteen-year-old stepdaughter. Krüger, again unable to deal with the situation, decides to go back to America without revealing his identity; but the husband goads him into a fight, and both men die. This ending brings no catharsis, only desolation: none of the characters shows enough understanding to prevent the ultimate tragedy, and none of them grows or changes. The play attempts to educate by showing how one should *not* act: it shows what can happen

Zweig in 1912 (Stefan Zweig Estate, London)

when compassion and understanding are lacking.

At its premiere at the Burgtheater on 26 October 1912, *Das Haus am Meer* was an instant success; it was later performed in Munich, Hamburg, and Berlin. But with this play, too, there was bad fortune. Baron Alfred Berger, the manager of the Burgtheater, who had accepted the work for production and was to direct it, died suddenly two weeks before rehearsals began. Zweig's misgivings about his theatrical endeavors were reinforced, and it was five years before he would write another work for the stage.

In 1908 Zweig and Friderike Maria Burger von Winternitz saw each other for the first time at a Viennese wine garden and exchanged smiles from separate tables. Four years later, both happened to be dining at the same restaurant in Vienna, Friderike with her husband, Felix, and a friend. By chance, the friend had just given her a copy of Zweig's translation of Verhaeren's *Hymnen an das Leben* (Hymns from Life, 1911). Seeing the volume in her hand, Zweig once again smiled at her. When she returned to her country house in Lower Austria the next day, she wrote him an unsigned fan letter in which she enclosed a copy of a feuilleton she had written. They began a correspondence and then a telephone relationship. Zweig was well known for helping young authors, and it was on this basis that their relationship began. Friderike never concealed her contacts with Zweig from her husband, a civil servant from whom she had been drifting apart for many years. She confided her feelings to her father-in-law, who was the president of the Austrian Union of Writers and Journalists and had been a member of the committee that had awarded Zweig the Bauernfeld Prize for lyric poetry in 1906. He suggested that she travel to Hamburg to review a performance of *Das Haus am Meer* for the *Hamburger Fremdenblatt*. She went not only to Hamburg but also to Berlin to meet with editors and publishers about her own work, and finally met Zweig in Lübeck on 15 October 1912. They realized that their relationship had become more than an infatuation and thought it best to break it off before it took deeper root. But after months of separation, while she traveled to Italy for her daughter's health and he went to Germany and Paris, it became clear to them that there was a strong bond between them. Deciding that she could not, in fairness to her husband, return to her home in Vienna, Friderike took temporary lodgings in the nearby spa town of Baden. There Felix von Winternitz could visit his family, and Zweig, with his obsessive desire for freedom, could see Friderike whenever he chose. But after a year it was Zweig who pushed her to seek annulment, since divorce was unthinkable in Catholic Austria.

During 1912 and 1913 Zweig published many essays in newspapers and periodicals, including the *Neue Rundschau*, *Berliner Tageblatt*, and *Vossische Zeitung*. One of these articles, "Das Autographensammeln" (Collecting Manuscripts, 1913), was devoted to a hobby he had begun while still a student at the gymnasium: throughout his life, much of his income would be spent on developing his collection of literary and musical manuscripts. At this time, too, Zweig began work on an essay on Dostoyevski which would later become part of his book *Drei Meister* (1920; translated as *Three Masters*, 1930). In 1914 he returned to Paris to break off a relationship with a woman he had met the previous year. He visited Verhaeren in Belgium and returned to Austria just before the Germans invaded the country. In *Die Welt von Gestern* he remembers himself as having been too much a citizen of the world to be caught up in patriotic zeal, but in reality he came

Friderike Maria Burger von Winternitz, around the time her relationship with Zweig began (photograph by courtesy of Friderike Zweig)

back at that time to join the Austrian war effort. From his letters it is clear that he wanted to take part in the fighting; but he was declared unfit for frontline service, and his initial exuberance gave way to a more characteristic pessimism. While waiting to be given some kind of military duty he continued to write essays; in one of them, "An die Freunde im Fremdland" (To My Friends in Foreign Countries, 1914), he said goodbye to his many friends who were now in enemy lands and also explained why he would not speak up for them in his country: he felt that hatred spurred heroism, which would bring peace more quickly. A letter from the French author Romain Rolland communicating friendship and bearing news of Verhaeren, who had severed ties with Zweig as an enemy, gave Zweig hope for the future of Europe.

Encouraged by Friderike and Rolland, Zweig turned his creative efforts and his developing pacifistic views toward his next major work, *Jeremias* (1917; translated as *Jeremiah*, 1922), which he began writing in 1915 and completed in 1917. In this biblical drama, which has become his best-known original work for the stage, Zweig registers his outrage at "die Lüge des Krieges" (the lie of war). Jeremiah is summoned by God to deliver a message of peace; whatever comes his way after he has heard God's voice he accepts without question as part of his divine selection. He knows no fear and sees death as a joyous separation of the spirit from the body, the moment when life becomes eternal. In *Die Welt von Gestern* Zweig wrote that he wished to show in the play "das Problem der seelischen Superiorität des Besiegten" (the problem of the spiritual superiority of the vanquished). His Jewish identity manifested itself for the first time in this work: Jeremiah reminds his people as they are led into captivity that they are chosen by God and are beginning their journey through the world into eternity. Zweig was certain that the play would never find a publisher, since it not only prophesied defeat but even praised it; but he regarded the work as a catharsis, a personal confession. To his astonishment the Insel house published *Jeremias* at Easter 1917 and the work immediately sold twenty thousand copies. Zweig's achievement was lauded by critics and literary and political figures as diverse as Rilke, Dehmel, Thomas Mann, and Walter Rathenau.

While working on *Jeremias* Zweig, along with other Austrian writers, including Franz Theodor Csokor, Alfred Polgar, Hermann Bahr, and Rilke, fulfilled their military duties by working in the War Archive, writing and revising press releases. In 1916 he moved to Kalksburg, near Rodaun. There, two small houses sharing the same garden provided a proper solution to his and Friderike's living arrangements–she and her children living in one house, Zweig in the other. Their compound drew frequent visits from many Austrian writers, among them Rilke, Csokor, Anton Wildgans, Alfons Petzold, Felix Braun, and Hugo von Hofmannsthal.

In August 1917 Zweig purchased a dilapidated hunting lodge in Salzburg, as a home for himself and Friderike. In November, while Zweig was on leave from military service, he and Friderike traveled to Switzerland so that he could oversee rehearsals of *Jeremias* at the Zurich Stadttheater. His military discharge was arranged by the editor of the *Neue Freie Presse*, and Zweig remained in Switzerland to write monthly articles for the paper and work on his next drama, *Legende eines Lebens* (Legend of a Life, 1919).

Zweig fulfilling his military duties in the Austrian War Archive during World War I (Österreichische Nationalbibliothek, Vienna)

Jeremias was finally performed in a shortened version on 27 February 1918 and was a notable success.

Zweig and Friderike returned to Austria in March 1919 but encountered all sorts of problems in setting up house in Salzburg. Zweig, never able to cope with disorganization, fled to the security and order of his family in Vienna, returning only when Friderike had settled the problems. In Salzburg they led a happy and, for Zweig, a productive existence. He completed *Drei Meister*, essays on Balzac, Dickens, and Dostoyevski, which was published in 1920. The book was extremely well received. Thomas Mann found it brilliant and especially liked the essay on Dostoyevski; Sigmund Freud, although critical of the Dostoyevski essay, thought the work as a whole extremely insightful and compared Zweig's style of intensification through repetition to the symbols of dreams. Zweig's reduction of the three novelists to a single type was the first formulation of his concept of the "typology of the spirit" and led to two further volumes in a series he called "Baumeister der Welt" (Master Builders of the World). Finally, in late January 1920, Zweig and Friderike were married at the registry in Vienna, with Felix Braun standing in for Friderike while she remained in Salzburg.

Zweig's biography of Rolland appeared in 1921; he arranged for simultaneous publication of the book in Frankfurt am Main, Sweden, and England to ensure the book's international success and Rolland's literary fortunes east of the Rhine. It was at this time that Zweig began to think of connecting his novellas. His 1911 volume *Erstes Erlebnis* (First Experience), which comprised "Geschichte in der Dämmerung" (Story at Twilight), "Die Gouvernante" (The Governess), "Brennendes Geheimnis" (Burning Secret), and "Sommernovellette" (Summer Novellette), had conveyed the dark moods of childhood and adolescence. Zweig wished to link these novellas to a second volume that would portray adult passions. Searching for a structure to unite stories as diverse as "Die Mondscheingasse" (Moonlight Alley), "Der Amokläufer" (translated as *Amok*, 1931), "Phantastische Nacht" (Fantastic Night, translated as "Transfiguration," 1924), "Die Frau und die Landschaft" (The Woman and the Landscape), and "Brief einer Unbekannten" (translated as "Letter from an Unknown Woman," 1924), he put together the volume *Amok: Novellen einer Leidenschaft* (Amok: Novellas of a Passion, 1922). The book was Zweig's first big success, with one hundred and fifty thousand copies sold in eight years. The novellas in the second collection are among his best-known works. In each story an obsessive passion drives the main characters, often to their destruction. Even in the less tragic stories, like "Phantastische Nacht," a dark mood dominates, and the dangers of a driven psyche become evident. "Brief einer Unbekannten," which, in a much changed version, became a successful Hollywood film as *Letter from an Unknown Woman* (1948), is typical of the collection. Like many of his novellas, it is structured as a "Rahmenerzählung" (story within a story). The main character, a famous Viennese writer, reads about himself in a twenty-four-page letter from an unknown woman. The letter reveals her obsessive love for him, but it also exposes his inability to love. Without knowing it, he has encountered this woman three times, has always been intrigued by her, yet has never remembered her. In the letter she tells him that her child has just died, and that before she takes her own life she wants him to know that he was the father. She also admits that every year on his birthday, she had anonymously sent him white roses. When he

Zweig and Friderike, with her daughters Suse and Alix, at their home in Salzburg (photograph by courtesy of Friderike Zweig)

finishes reading the letter, he looks at the vase; it is empty. Although the man is a Viennese writer with a desire for freedom from personal ties, Zweig did not base the character on himself. Nevertheless, "Briefe einer Unbekannten" and many of Zweig's other novellas have been taken by his readers as personal confessions. It is this immediacy of narration that makes Zweig's fiction so involving. Also in 1922 Zweig published *Die Augen des ewigen Bruders* (Eyes of the Eternal Brother, translated as "Virata," 1924), a two-volume translation of the works of Verlaine, a translation of Rolland's *Clérambault*, and essays and book reviews in various periodicals.

In 1924 Zweig returned to Paris while Friderike stayed in Salzburg to oversee the installation of central heating in their house. On this trip he rediscovered the city he had loved in his youth. The Parisian sojourn gave him the energy to return home to complete the second volume of the "Baumeister der Welt" series, *Der Kampf mit dem Dämon* (1925; translated as *The Struggle with the Demon*, 1929)–essays on Friedrich Hölderlin, Heinrich von Kleist, and Nietzsche. Zweig was amazed at how, in contrast to the slow work on Dostoyevski, the essay on Kleist practically wrote itself. His affinity to Kleist, another au-

thor who suffered dark moods and eventually took his own life, has been noted by later critics. Zweig dedicated the book to Freud and explained in the introduction his ideas on the typology of the spirit. In Kleist, Hölderlin, and Nietzsche Zweig wished to reveal geniuses possessed and apparently defeated by their struggles with the creative demon, men who did not obey their own wills but became servants of a greater force. In Nietzsche he saw an independent spirit aspiring to the highest form of humanity. Zweig wrote Rolland that his study of Nietzsche was meant as a polemic against those who wished to claim the philosopher for Germany and the cause of war. Zweig immediately began work on the next in his "Baumeister der Welt" series, selecting Stendhal, Rousseau, and Tolstoy as three authors who had written autobiographies. This volume did not appear until 1928, with Casanova substituted for Rousseau. Zweig had many other ideas for the series, but most of the essays were never written.

Zweig's life was increasingly filled with travel throughout Europe. He now had friends, admirers, and a literary audience wherever he visited. One reason for his frequent travels was his desire to work for an intellectual unification of Europe, but because of a strong aversion to affiliat-

Woodcut by O. R. Schatz to illustrate Zweig's novella "Phantastische Nacht"

der the universal qualities of Jonson's characters accessible to twentieth-century audiences, he removed what he considered Elizabethan moralizing prologues and epilogues, some minor characters, and Jonson's topical allusions. The farce soon achieved international acclaim. An author who displayed little humor and an almost complete lack of irony in his other writing, Zweig shows himself in this work to be a master of comedy.

Verwirrung der Gefühle (translated as *Conflicts*, 1927), his third collection of novellas, was published in 1927 and sold thirty thousand copies in three months. Included in this anthology besides the title story were "Untergang eines Herzens" and "Vierundzwanzig Stunden im Leben einer Frau" (translated as "Twenty-Four Hours in a Woman's Life"). With this volume Zweig reached the apex of his mastery of the novella. Each of the three stories explores a personal relationship and reveals how strong, yet at the same time how fragile, but mostly how lonely humans are. In "Verwirrung der Gefühle" the English professor expresses Zweig's view: "Immer erkennt man ja jede Erscheinung, jeden Menschen nur in ihrer Feuerform, nur in der Leidenschaft" (You can really understand every phenomenon, every person only in their fiery state, in a state of passion): individuals realize themselves only when they live passionately.

In this novella a sixty-year-old privy councillor whose students and colleagues have just honored him with a Festschrift relates a story about himself that no one else knows: the biography put together by his admirers has left out the most essential formative experience of the councillor's life. As a young literature student, he had been ecstatically inspired by the seminars of his English professor, whom he adopted as a father figure and role model without ever suspecting that the professor's interest in him stemmed from homoerotic drives. One day the professor disappeared for several days to avoid acting upon his forbidden desires. When he returned, he cathartically revealed his secret life to his student, finally confessing his love for him. A passionate kiss passed between them, then the professor admonished the student to flee for both their sakes. The student did so, leaving behind the person in his life he loved the most. Zweig's vivid depiction of the passionate attraction not only between the two men but also between the student and the professor's young wife gives the novella an aura of intensity and nervousness. Its success

ing himself with any group he remained apart from and was sometimes critical of the pan-European organizations of the day. He believed that nothing could replace personal contact and individual persuasion. His frequent dark moods, admitted only to Friderike and his close friend Viktor Fleischer, indicated that he knew how little he was accomplishing toward his dream of a unified Europe. Another reason he traveled so widely was to find the inner freedom he so desperately desired. From his letters it appears that he was happiest when he was away from the ties of Salzburg.

To create the character of the English professor for the novella "Verwirrung der Gefühle" (1927; translated as "Confused Emotions," 1927) Zweig delved into the study of Elizabethan poetry. He discovered Ben Jonson's *Volpone* (1607), and in nine days fashioned a prose adaptation of the farce for the German stage. Zweig's *Volpone* (1925; translated, 1928) is more an adaptation than translation, for he freely changed, rearranged, and added to the original work. To ren-

Zweig in 1920 (Jewish National and University Library, Jerusalem)

can be attributed to Zweig's psychological insights into this side of human experience.

Zweig completed *Drei Dichter ihres Lebens: Casanova-Stendhal-Tolstoi* (1928; translated as *Adepts in Self-Portraiture*, 1928) in 1927. The essay on Casanova came easily; the other two, however, caused him a great deal of effort–especially the essay on Stendhal, which aroused in him feelings of inadequacy as a writer. *Drei Dichter ihres Lebens* quickly found critical favor; like his other biographical essays, these tended to be repetitious and overexplanatory, but this style accounted for much of his popular success in the genre. In 1928, a year after Zweig's complete works appeared in a Russian edition, he was invited to represent Austrian writers at the Tolstoy centenary celebrations in Moscow. After the trip he became much more skeptical of the USSR than his friend Rolland. Perhaps because of their differing views on this subject their relationship markedly cooled over the next ten years.

In his biography *Joseph Fouché* (1929; translated, 1930) Zweig wanted to portray a pure politician whose only conviction is to adapt to every change in opinion and who thus outlasts the most powerful men of his time. Zweig considered it a book directed against politics and saw it as symbolic of the Europe of his day. Since the biography had no feminine interest and an unsympathetic subject, Zweig expected it to do poorly; but to his astonishment sales of the work skyrocketed. Critics lauded it not only for its prose style– the story is told completely in the present tense– but also for its penetrating vision of the tangled world of politics. At one point Zweig compares Fouché to Lenin; at others he relates the Napoleonic age to his own time. He depicts Fouché as the builder of a totalitarian regime in miniature within his cabinet and shows that behind the extreme passions of this fanatical visionary lay the cool calculations of a clever practitioner of realpolitik. Above all, Zweig shows how quickly values can change in the world of power politics.

While writing *Joseph Fouché* Zweig simultaneously worked on a drama, in which Fouché was also a character, based on an incident during Napoleon's Egyptian campaign. *Das Lamm des Armen* (Lamb of the Poor, 1929) is extremely bitter in tone, and once again Zweig did not expect the work to achieve much success. To his surprise, both the Burgtheater and the Deutsches Volkstheater wanted to present the premiere of the play, which eventually was given several productions throughout Germany. The Burgtheater's production had to be delayed for a year because of a turnover in the directorship of the house; thus, another of Zweig's theatrical endeavors suffered bad luck.

With the sudden death in 1929 of Hofmannsthal, coming after the death of Rilke in 1926, Zweig felt that an era was ending in Austria. He immersed himself in work but left many projects unfinished. In a letter he expressed the desire to give up literature for a time, as Goethe and Schiller had, and turn to the study of science or history so that he could return renewed to his craft. He began work on a new volume of essays, *Die Heilung durch den Geist* (1931; translated as *Mental Healers*, 1932), studies of Franz Anton Mesmer, Mary Baker Eddy, and Freud. The essays on Mesmer and Eddy were written easily, but Zweig had great difficulty with the Freud essay. As with his work on Rolland, Zweig found it difficult to write about a personal acquaintance. Although open to the possibility of mental healing, Zweig was by no means uncritical of the notion. When Sybil Wilbur wrote a book about Christian Science using Zweig's essay on Eddy, taken out of context, as proof of her views, Zweig remarked ironically that business and belief went hand in hand.

Zweig's study in his home in Salzburg (photograph Mrs. Susanne Hoeller)

Freud, who read all of Zweig's works, liked the Mesmer essay the best; he was less enthusiastic about Zweig's treatment of his own theories.

Zweig worked on the biography *Marie Antoinette* (1932; translated, 1933) during travels to Hamburg, Zell am See, Frankfurt am Main, Kassel, Paris, Majorca, and finally Cap d'Antibes, where Joseph Roth joined him and Friderike to work on his novel *Radetzkymarsch* (1932; translated as *Radetzky March*, 1933). In the biography Zweig portrays the ill-fated French queen as an "average" person who was a victim of history. Although he painstakingly read all of Marie Antoinette's letters and every contemporary deposition, newspaper article, and pamphlet about her, most of that research never appears in the biography. He uses what he called "schöpferische Seelenkunde" (creative psychiatry) to create reader identification with the historical figures; he wanted to demythologize the past, not deify it. Unlike other biographers of his day, Zweig spent less time showing the rise of his subjects than the developments that led to their downfall. *Marie Antoinette* became the most popular of all his biographies. The story of her life is fascinatingly and dramatically drawn, with special suspense created in the prison and trial scenes. His interest in sexual practices at the court of Louis XVI appealed to his readers, if not to all of his critics.

The death of Hofmannsthal had prompted Richard Strauss to look for a new librettist; through their mutal friend Anton Kippenberg, director of the Insel publishing house, Strauss asked Zweig if he might be interested in working with him. Finally meeting in Munich in November 1931, they agreed to collaborate on an adaptation of Jonson's *The Silent Woman* (1610). Zweig completed a draft of "Sir Morosius," as the opera was first called, even before he finished *Marie Antoinette*. Strauss was delighted with Zweig's text, and within two months Zweig had completed the first act. The auspicious beginning of their collaboration was misleading, however; *Die schweigsame Frau* (1935), as the opera was finally titled, experienced untold difficulties during the Third Reich because Zweig was a Jew; on the other hand, some emigrés criticized Zweig harshly for his collaboration with "the enemy." Zweig repeatedly advised Strauss to get another librettist; he knew that there could be no overt relationship between Strauss and himself. But Strauss insisted on Zweig's help, and the author remained a consultant on all of Strauss's late operatic works.

As Zweig approached his fiftieth birthday he frequently expressed his fear of growing old. To avoid the visitors and the letters and telegrams of congratulation he spent his birthday in Munich with the writer Carl Zuckmayer. Adding to his dark mood at this time were worries about his income, which came largely from sources outside Austria–the family firm in Czechoslovakia, and his royalties, which were mostly from Germany. The Creditanstalt Bank in Vienna had failed in 1931, and inflation in Germany was getting worse. Zweig had never concerned himself with finances, preferring to ignore his material success; but now it seemed to him that these matters were beyond his control and might encroach on his freedom. He returned to Salzburg, stayed long enough to answer his mail, then left for Paris. As always, traveling raised his spirits. When Friderike wrote to him in early 1932 of her restlessness in Salzburg and her premonitions of future hardships, Zweig responded with assurances of his own happiness at being in Paris and selfish complaints that without secretarial help he was as productive enough as he might be.

As political events in Germany became more and more disturbing, Zweig returned home and began research for his next biography, *Triumph und Tragik des Erasmus von Rotterdam* (1934; translated as *Erasmus of Rotterdam*, 1934). Although horrified at what was taking place in Germany, Zweig remained silent. He believed that

Page of notes by Zweig for his never-completed biography of Honoré de Balzac, which he intended to be the crowning achievement of his career. His friend Richard Friedenthal revised Zweig's manuscript and published the work after Zweig's death (Archiv der Internationalen Stefan Zweig-Gesellschaft, Vienna)

German Jews had to stay out of demonstrations protesting the treatment of writers in Germany, including participation in the international P.E.N. Congress in Dubrovnik, Croatia (in what is now Yugoslavia), in 1933. Realizing that he would soon have to make important decisions, he put off confronting them by traveling. He left Salzburg in October to take up temporary residence in London to complete work on his Erasmus biography. He found the British emotional reserve a pleasant contrast to the nervousness he had left behind on the Continent. *Triumph und Tragik des Erasmus von Rotterdam* quickly took shape and became what Zweig later described as a veiled self-portrait.

Everything about the biography indicates that Zweig strongly identified with his subject; for Zweig, Erasmus was the first man conscious of being a European and the first to fight for peace. Zweig endowed his Erasmus with many of his own qualities–indecisiveness, preservation of inner freedom in spite of external pressures, love of escaping into books to avoid the danger of taking a political stance, and a fundamental belief in humankind. The more fanatical the age became in coercing people to take stands, the harder Erasmus fought to stay independent. Like Erasmus, Zweig understood that tolerance is not

Zweig (center) at a bookstore in Rio de Janeiro, 1941 (Archiv der Internationalen Stefan Zweig-Gesellschaft, Vienna)

indifference but an active decision to fight intolerance with reason, the enemy of fanaticism. Zweig was able to present the spirit of the Reformation with such vigor because he saw Erasmus's age and his own as parallel times when fanaticism reigned and people were tortured and murdered for their beliefs. Like his author, Erasmus sees his enemies multiply and his friends disappear; his solution, like his author's, is to escape into his work. Erasmus's antagonist is Martin Luther, portrayed as a fanatical man of action whose mass movement destroyed the dream of the humanists.

Zweig's strong personal involvement in his subject did not cloud his picture of history. Of all his books, *Triumph und Tragik des Erasmus von Rotterdam* was the most highly regarded by professional historians, who praised its treatment of individual personalities and its presentation of historical background. The biography was Zweig's response to Nazism: a quiet hymn of praise to the antifanatical individual for whom inner peace and artistic achievement are most important. Zweig delayed publication of the book and allowed only six hundred copies to be printed in the first edition, because, in keeping with his identification with Erasmus, he believed that the work might be taken as an active protest against contemporary politics. Just as during World War I he had valued pure pacifism because it could not be realized and thus could not be exploited, so the Erasmian ideal of tolerant detachment appealed to him now, and, he hoped, would inspire other Europeans in the future. Zweig envisaged time when reason would triumph, although he never answered how it could happen in a world which he regarded as fundamentally irrational and violent.

Zweig returned to Salzburg in December but had already planned to return to London to pursue research on Mary, Queen of Scots. While in Austria he traveled to Vienna to encourage Herbert Reichner, an acquaintance who was editor of the journal *Philobiblon*, to start his own publishing house. The Reichner Verlag was established in 1934, and before its demise in 1938 it brought

Zweig in the summer of 1941 in Ossining, New York (Susan Hoeller)

out *Marie Antoinette, Triumph und Tragik des Erasmus von Rotterdam, Maria Stuart* (1935; translated as *Mary, Queen of Scotland and the Isles*, 1935), *Castellio gegen Calvin oder Ein Gewissen gegen die Gewalt* (Castellio against Calvin; or, A Conscience against Force, 1936; translated as *The Right to Heresy*, 1936), and *Magellan* (1938; translated as *Conqueror of the Seas*, 1938), as well as some of the biographies that had already been published by Insel and several collections of Zweig's novellas. Zweig's works were so profitable that Reichner hardly found it necessary to publish books by any other writers.

Zweig's meeting with Reichner took place in February, during the Dollfuss government's attack on the workers' flats in the Floridsdorf district. Zweig left for Salzburg a day later than he had planned because of the resulting workers' strike. He was awakened one morning by the police, who had orders to search his house for hidden arms of the Schutzbund, the socialist paramilitary organization. Although there were many apologies for this intrusion in the following months, Zweig was now determined to leave Austria for good; the incident demonstrated that his personal freedom, the thing he had always valued most, was at risk. Because of Zweig's unwillingness to make a public statement about his reasons for leaving, an article in a French periodical indicated that he had left because of the "February events." An investigation by the Dollfuss government revealed that Zweig had left Austria not because of the attack on the workers, which he did not condone, but because his private world had been intruded upon. When he returned to London, he notified the Salzburg authorities that he was giving up his Austrian residence.

Friderike visited him in London, but the responsibility of winding up their affairs in Austria was left to her, and she returned there in March. Zweig needed a secretary to whom he could dictate the first draft of *Maria Stuart*; before she left Friderike found Charlotte (Lotte) Elisabeth Altmann, a twenty-six-year-old German emigré whose stenographic skills, knowledge of English, and serious demeanor made her perfectly suited for the position. Zweig could not understand his wife's hesitation about leaving Austria permanently; thus, when she went back to Salzburg, he unjustly felt that she was leaving him to face a new life alone.

His feelings about London changed radically during the next year. The British emotional reserve that he had at first welcomed he came to regard as indifference and insensitivity to the problems of the emigrés. As so often in the past, he yearned to escape his present reality by traveling, and so he accepted an invitation for a lecture tour of the United States. Before sailing, he wanted to spend a month with Friderike in Nice, France; Friderike asked Lotte to join them so that Zweig could complete *Maria Stuart*. One day Friderike walked in to find Lotte and Zweig in each other's arms. She insisted Lotte be sent away for the days remaining before Zweig's departure. He sailed from Villefranche to New York in January 1935; from America he wrote Friderike that he would give up Lotte on his return to Europe.

Zweig returned to Austria from his successful American lecture tour to see *Maria Stuart* through the press. The biography achieved instant popularity in Austria, but although Reichner's publishing house was incorporated in Leipzig as well as Vienna and Zurich, distribution of the work in Germany proved difficult because of propaganda against Zweig and other Jewish authors. In America, however, sales of *Mary, Queen of Scotland and the Isles,* whose rights Zweig had negotiated on his tour, reached two hundred thousand by the end of 1935. Meanwhile, Zweig became convinced that Friderike was purposely prolonging the process of emigration out of blind, sentimental patriotism. Because he had always been dependent on her in practical matters he did not feel free to act on the decision he had finally made to emigrate to England, and pessimism and dark moods once again beset him.

In May 1935 Zweig went to Zurich to start research for a biography of Sebastian Castellio, another European humanist in the Erasmian tradition. In July the secretary Zweig had hired in Switzerland proved unsatisfactory, and he asked Lotte to come from London to join him. He spent August with Friderike in Marienbad, but it had become clear to both of them that their life together was behind them. From Marienbad, he traveled to Vienna to visit his mother, who had been ill. She made him promise that he would never abandon Friderike.

Back in London, his outward good humor disguised the inner turmoil of being an emigré German writer in a non-German-speaking country. He felt guilt for abandoning his friends and family, longing for his homeland, and fear of having to begin anew. Although the property in Salzburg belonged to him, he gave Friderike no instructions about how to dispose of it. He increasingly placed the blame for his inability to begin a new life on her.

The P.E.N. Congress of 1936 was held in Rio de Janeiro; received by every high official, including the president and foreign minister, Zweig was overwhelmed by his popularity in Brazil, where he was considered the high priest of European letters. At the end of his stay, he knew that he would return to this new world that he found so vital and far removed from the madness of Europe.

In England, he was faced with one exasperating problem after another. With Zweig in London and his publisher in Vienna, the project of assembling new editions of his novellas proved difficult and ultimately unsatisfactory. In 1936 Reichner published a two-volume collection of old stories titled *Die Kette* (The Chain) and *Kaleidoskop*; Zweig felt that the titles would mean nothing to new readers and that his old public would buy the volumes thinking that they were collections of new stories. *Castellio gegen Calvin oder Ein Gewissen gegen die Gewalt* appeared in May 1936 with a historical error in the review copies, necessitating a quick reprinting to correct the main edition. Also, the British version of *Castellio gegen Calvin* had given prominence to Calvin, the fanatic, rather than Castellio, the humanist and true hero of Zweig's work. In its original version the biography considered the problem of uniting freedom with order. Zweig's message was that moderation outlasts fanaticism, and that to do away with dogmatism, antifanaticism had to become aggressive. Zweig had identified with Erasmus, but it is clear that although he was incapable of it, he wanted to be like Castellio. With the problem of the English edition, Zweig regretted having put Calvin in the title at all.

While sailing to South America Zweig had gotten the idea of comparing his luxurious voyage to those of early explorers. He chose Magellan because, as with Mary Stuart, many contradictory accounts had been written about him. Zweig portrays Magellan as a brave, clever, determined individual who fights for his convictions. As in his other biographies Zweig psychologizes his subject, allowing the reader to gain insight into Magellan's personality and to better comprehend the motivations for his actions. The final chapter shows Zweig's pessimistic state of mind at the time of writing the work, as well as his ideas about how history gets distorted: the surviving captains betray the now deceased Magellan and tell their versions of the voyages, which have nothing to do with the truth.

Zweig began to feel like the proverbial Wandering Jew; actually, however, he created the role for himself. For someone with Zweig's financial means and international connections, the move from Salzburg to London should have been no problem; but his inability to live in the present, to accept reality, and to take responsibility for his actions with regard to Friderike and Lotte made him feel that he was wandering and homeless. In 1937 he had written a farewell letter to Friderike, but his indecisiveness came to the fore again when he stopped to see her in Salzburg on one of his trips from Vienna to Zurich. He asked her to accompany him as far as Zell am See, where it was decided that she should come to London. When she returned to Salzburg to arrange the trip, she received a telegram asking her not to come. Zweig returned to London with Lotte and buried himself in his work. His moods became increasingly melancholy and sometimes violent. Friderike finally sold the house in Salzburg but decided not to follow Zweig to London. When the Anschluß (annexation of Austria by Germany) occurred in March 1938, she was in Paris. All of the possessions she had salvaged from the Salzburg years, including her personal library, were eventually confiscated by the Gestapo. Although Zweig had foreseen the March events, the demise of Austria was a blow to his already fragile psyche. Two weeks after the Nazis marched into Vienna Reichner fled to Switzerland, and Zweig became a German writer without a German publisher. The realization that he would now be merely a writer in translation struck him hard, and it was only after the death of his mother in Vienna in August 1938 that he decided to become a British citizen.

Throughout these turbulent years Zweig had continued work on what would become the only full-scale novel in his oeuvre. (An incomplete novel was found among his notes, was made into the movie *Das gestohlene Jahr* [The Stolen Year] in 1950, and was published in 1982 as part of Zweig's collected works under the title *Rausch der Verwandlung* [Frenzy of Change]). *Ungeduld des Herzens* (Impatience of the Heart; translated as *Beware of Pity*, 1939) appeared in 1939 and was an instant success both in German and in English; but it has always been glossed over by critics in favor of Zweig's shorter fiction, possibly because, being the only novel Zweig completed, it is considered a dilettantish effort. *Ungeduld des Herzens* is a psychological study of four characters trapped in a web of pity: Edith, the crippled daughter who becomes the object of pity; Kekesfalva, her doting father; Lieutenant Hofmiller, who learns too late to "beware of pity," and Dr. Condor, the family physician and only positive character in the work. Zweig considers the motivations and repercussions of pity and investigates from a Nietzchean perspective how dangerous it can be. His premise is that there are two kinds of pity: one is weak and sentimental, an "Ungeduld des Herzens" that simply wants to free itself from pain as quickly as possible. This is the pity of which one must beware. The other is an unsentimental and creative pity—an aggressive emotion that supports and aids the object of pity. Only Dr. Condor, who has a blind invalid wife, understands the power of this positive kind of pity and the willed self-denial necessary to achieve it.

Zweig wanted the work to be the great Austrian novel; it was written when his homesickness was greatest, and it symbolizes a leave-taking from as well as a demonstration of solidarity with his homeland. But it shows that Zweig was incapable of mastering the epic scope necessary for a successful novel; *Ungeduld des Herzens* remains a long novella. Although the story unfolds against the background of World War I, it does not, like Thomas Mann's *Der Zauberberg* (1924; translated as *The Magic Mountain*, 1927), give a broad sociological, cultural, or historical portrait of its age. As in so many of his other stories Zweig uses a first-person narrative within a frame. Here Zweig meets Lieutenant Hofmiller, and the officer tells his story to the author. As in the novellas, Zweig's strength lies in the depiction of his characters, who for the most part are motivated by drives they cannot control.

As the situation in Europe worsened in 1938 and 1939 Zweig's pacifism prevented him from issuing a clear call for resistance to the Nazis. More self-involved than ever, he felt too old and too tired to help. His aid to refugees grew less as their numbers grew; he spoke of the new waves of refugees as beggars and weak individuals "who had delayed too long." He tried to escape into his work, but most of the drafts and notes for his works in progress had been left in Salzburg and were eventually destroyed. One project, however, had been salvaged. For over thirty years he had intended to write a long biography of Honoré de Balzac, which he meant to be the crowning achievement of his life. With Lotte he moved to Bath, where his work on the Balzac biography progressed rapidly. With his mother dead he asked Friderike for a divorce, although he allowed her to keep his name; they remained good friends until his death. On 6 September 1939, Lotte and Zweig were married. Later that month Zweig, as an enemy alien, was given special dispensation to leave Bath to speak at Freud's cremation near London. On 12 March 1940 he became a British citizen.

As the war raged in Europe, Zweig's feelings of being part of a lost generation that would never again see a fairer world grew stronger. Turning from his Balzac project, which he now thought would take too long, he resolved to write an autobiography—not to tell of his own life and work but to present the story of the time through which he had lived. Differentiating three distinct periods in his life, he thought he would call it "Meine drei Leben" (My Three Lives). On a trip to Paris that Friderike, sensing his deep depression, had arranged for him, he spoke on the subject for the first time in a lecture titled "Das Wien von Gestern" (The Vienna of Yesterday). Shortly thereafter France fell to the Nazis; this news hit Zweig even harder than had the Anschluß. Feeling the need to leave Europe "temporarily," he departed with Lotte for South America by way of New York in May 1940. Although he intended to stay in New York only a short time, he felt that he had to help his friends stranded in Europe obtain entry visas to the United States. The efforts of Zweig and others were successful: President Roosevelt authorized visas for approximately one thousand "intellectuals in danger," and Friderike and her family, as well as such Austrian and German writers as Franz Werfel, Alfred Polgar, Golo Mann, and Heinrich Mann were able to leave Europe.

On 9 August Zweig and Lotte sailed to South America, where his reception, although not as grand as the first time, was once again extremely flattering. But news of the deaths of several of his close friends sent him back into deep depression, and he wrote to Friderike that he would probably never return to Europe. He was convinced that all of his possessions in England had been destroyed, and to ensure himself a place to live he applied for a permanent visa for Brazil. During this time he devoted all his concentration to completing a book on the country, putting aside his autobiography. Unable to work in the heat of the Brazilian summer, he went to New York City in January 1941. Oppressed by the vast number of refugees there, he moved to New Haven in February to complete the final draft of *Brasilien, ein Land der Zukunft* (1941; translated as *Brazil, Land of the Future*, 1941). At the Yale University library he began research on Amerigo Vespucci, completing *Amerigo: Die Geschichte eines historischen Irrtums* (1944; translated as *Amerigo: A Comedy of Errors in History*, 1942) by the end of March. Despite his distaste for New York, he moved back to that refugee capital in May.

Zuckmayer reported (in Hanns Arens, ed., *Der große Europäer Stefan Zweig*, 1956) that Zweig once said to him at dinner in New York: "Was hat es für einen Sinn, daß man als sein eigener Schatten weiterlebt? Wir sind nur Gespenster,— oder Erinnerungen" (What's the sense in continuing to live as one's own shadow? We are only ghosts—or memories). With the New York City summer heating up, Zweig and Lotte moved to Ossining, New York, where Friderike had settled some weeks before. The frenetic pace of his work frightened Friderike, who saw the deleterious effect it was having on him. At the end of August, Zweig and Lotte left for Brazil. His letters to various friends at this time reflect his confused emotions: to some he wrote that he was tired of hotels and that he hoped at some later time to return to the United States permanently; others he told that Brazil offered him the best chance of retirement and peace; and to yet others he wrote that he wanted to go back to England. In Brazil, where he took up residence in Petropolis, near Rio de Janeiro, he felt keenly the absence of friends and the lack of any real intellectual exchange or stimulus. Again the hopelessness of writing in German, far away from his European roots, struck him deeply. He was, however, finally able to complete his autobiography.

Die Welt von Gestern is Zweig's most fascinating work. It reviews the social, political, and cultural changes that had an impact on his life, yet it never touches on any details that he considered private; there is no mention of Friderike, Lotte, or of any close friends not known to a wider audience. *Die Welt von Gestern* is a biography of a generation rather than a true autobiography of Zweig. Although inaccurate in many details—Zweig wrote the book largely from memory during his wanderings—it conveys a feeling for the age that few other works can match. Zweig's aim was to capture the world he saw and experienced, not to portray himself; still, the text is so vividly evocative and the sense of loss so palpable that the persona that emerges—an Austrian who has outlived his age—became the Stefan Zweig that people remembered. In the foreword, he expresses his situation: "Von all meiner Vergangenheit habe ich also nichts mit mir, als was ich hinter der Stirne trage" (I have nothing of all my past with me, other than what I carry behind my brow.)

The last few months of his life were filled with melancholy and depression. To his acquaintances, he would always talk about his advanced age—he was only sixty—and how he would not live to see a better time. His work no longer provided the solace it had in his younger days. Preoccupied with his own misery, Zweig spent the energy he could muster studying Montaigne, especially the latter's ideas on death, and writing his last and perhaps best novella, *Schachnovelle* (1942; translated as "The Royal Game," 1944), the only really topical piece of fiction he ever created. The story takes place on an ocean liner sailing for South America. Dr. B. is a highly cultured and organized individual for whom learning chess had been salvation during a term of imprisonment by the Gestapo. He encounters a Russian chess master who is his direct opposite—dull, uncouth, and peasantlike. In prison Dr. B. had never actually played the game with another person; although he swore that he would never think of chess again, the challenge of finally playing against a real opponent becomes too great to resist, and he agrees to play a match with the master. The game, whose formal rules had been Dr. B's only hold on sanity during his incarceration, now has precisely the opposite effect on him; he begins to lose his hold on reality. The psychological perspicacity that Zweig showed so often in his other works reaches new heights in this novella, perhaps because the emigrant Dr. B. is so much a part of the author. (Zweig often played chess during his last months in Brazil, but he was never a good player.) Despite the quality of writing Zweig achieved in the work, he had no confidence in it when he had completed it; he felt that the subject was too abstruse.

In February 1942 news of the fall of Singapore and the German campaign through Libya toward the Suez Canal reached Zweig. During the last two days of his life he wrote many letters to friends explaining his state of mind. None is more revealing than his last letter to Friderike, in which he wrote: "I liked Petropolis very much, but I had not the books I wanted and the solitude which first had such a soothing effect began to become oppressive—the idea that my central work, the Balzac, could never get finished without two years of quiet life and all books was very hard and then this war which is not yet at his hight [sic]. I was too tired for all that and poor Lotte did not have a good time with me. . . . I am sure you will still see the better time and will understand why I with my 'black liver' did not wait any longer. I send you these lines in the last hours, you cannot imagine how glad I feel since I have taken the decision. . . ." He and Lotte committed suicide by taking poison on 23 February 1942. A dated and signed suicide note left on his desk expressed thanks to Brazil and included a wish that his friends might see the "dawn after the long night." The Zweigs were given a state funeral the likes of which had rarely been seen in Brazil.

The years immediately following Zweig's death produced a flood of essays and remembrances, but by the middle 1950s he no longer seemed important; to many critics Zweig's works were passé. Not until 1981, the centenary of his birth, was there a revival in Zweig scholarship which has illuminated the breadth of his humanism and literary art. The publication of his collected works in German is being accompanied by a positive reevaluation of this important Austrian writer, whose work creates a world behind which the world he lost may be fleetingly perceived.

Letters:

Briefwechsel: Stefan Zweig-Friderike Maria Zweig, 1912-1942 (Bern: Scherz, 1951; translated by Henry G. Alsberg and Erna McArthur as *Stefan Zweig and Friderike Maria Zweig: Their Correspondence* (New York: Hastings House, 1954); German edition republished as *Friderike Zweig-Stefan Zweig: Unrast der Liebe* (Bern: Scherz, 1981);

Richard Strauss-Stefan Zweig: Briefwechsel, edited by Willi Schuh (Frankfurt am Main: Fischer, 1957);

Unbekannte Briefe aus der Emigration an eine Freundin, edited by Gisella Selden-Goth (Vienna, Stuttgart & Basel: Deutsch, 1964);

Stefan Zweig: Briefe an Freunde, edited by Richard Friedenthal (Frankfurt am Main: Fischer, 1978);

The Correspondence of Stefan Zweig with Raoul Auernheimer and with Richard Beer-Hofmann, edited by Donald G. Daviau, Jorun B. Johns,

and Jeffrey B. Berlin (Columbia, S.C.: Camden House, 1983);
Stefan Zweig/Paul Zech: Briefe 1910-1942, edited by Daviau (Frankfurt am Main: Fischer, 1985);
Rilke: Briefwechsel mit Stefan Zweig, edited by Donald Prater (Frankfurt am Main: Insel, 1985).

Bibliography:
Randolph J. Klawiter, *Stefan Zweig: A Bibliography* (Chapel Hill: University of North Carolina Press, 1965).

Biographies:
Friderike Maria Zweig, *Stefan Zweig*, translated by Erna McArthur (New York: Crowell, 1946; London: Allen, 1948); German version published as *Stefan Zweig: Wie ich ihn erlebte* (Stockholm: Neuer Verlag, 1947);
Zweig, *Stefan Zweig: Eine Bildbiographie* (Munich: Kindler, 1961);
Zweig, *Spiegelungen des Lebens* (Vienna: Deutsch: 1964);
Elizabeth Allday, *Stefan Zweig: A Critical Biography* (London: Allen, 1972);
D. A. Prater, *European of Yesterday: A Biography of Stefan Zweig* (Oxford: Clarendon Press, 1972);
Prater, *Stefan Zweig: Das Leben eines Ungeduldigen* (Munich & Vienna: Hanser, 1981);
Prater and Volker Michels, eds., *Stefan Zweig: Leben und Werk im Bild* (Frankfurt am Main: Insel, 1981);
Joseph Strelka, *Stefan Zweig: Freier Geist der Menschlichkeit* (Vienna: Österreichischer Bundesverlag, 1981).

References:
Hanns Arens, ed., *Der große Europäer Stefan Zweig* (Munich: Kindler, 1956);
Arens, ed. *Stefan Zweig im Zeugnis seiner Freunde* (Munich: Langen-Müller, 1968);
Jeffrey B. Berlin, "Stefan Zweig and his American Publisher: Notes on an Unpublished Correspondence, with reference to 'Schachnovelle' and 'Die Welt von Gestern,'" *Deutsche Vierteljahresschrift für Literaturwissenschaft und Geistesgeschichte*, (1982): 259-276;
Klaus Bohnen, "Europäisches Bewußtsein in der Krise: Unveröffentlichter Briefwechsel zwischen Stefan Zweig und Georg Brandes." *Orbis Litterarum*, 33 (1978): 220-237;
Donald G. Daviau, "Stefan Zweig's Victors in Defeat," *Monatshefte*, 51 (1959): 1-12;
Daviau and Harvey I. Dunkle, "Stefan Zweig's 'Schachnovelle,'" *Monatshefte*, 65 (1973): 370-384;
Robert Dumont, *Stefan Zweig et la France* (Paris: Didier, 1967);
Dumont, *Le Théâtre de Stefan Zweig* (Paris: Presses Universitaires de France, 1976);
Erich Fitzbauer, ed., *Stefan Zweig: Spiegelungen einer schöpferischen Persönlichkeit* (Vienna: Bergland, 1959);
Marc H. Gelber, ed., *Stefan Zweig–heute: Aufsätze und Vorträge* (Frankfurt am Main: Fischer, 1983);
Pierre Grappin, ed., *Stefan Zweig: 1881-1942* (Paris: Didier, 1982);
Mimi Grossberg, "Stefan Zweig–heute," *Literatur und Kritik*, 120 (1976): 624-626;
Klaus Heydemann, "Das Beispiel des Erasmus: Stefan Zweigs Einstellung zur Politik," *Literatur und Kritik*, 169-170 (1982): 24-39;
Modern Austrian Literature, special Zweig issue, 14, no. 3/4 (1981);
Brian Murdoch, "Game, Image and Ambiguity in Stefan Zweig's 'Schachnovelle,'" *New German Studies*, 11 (Autumn 1983): 171-189;
Donald Prater, "Stefan Zweig," in *Exile: The Writer's Experience*, edited by John Spalek and Robert Bell (Chapel Hill: North Carolina University Press, 1982), pp. 311-322;
Ingrid Schwamborn, "Schachmatt im brasilianischen Paradies: Die Entstehungsgeschichte der 'Schachnovelle,'" *Germanisch-Romanische Monatsschrift*, new series 34 (1984): 404-429;
Marion Sonnenfeld, ed., *Stefan Zweig: The World of Yesterday's Humanist Today* (Albany: State University of New York Press, 1983);
Joseph P. Strelka, "Psychoanalytische Ideen in Stefan Zweigs Novellen," *Literatur und Kritik*, 169-170 (1982): 42-52;
David Turner, "The Choice and Function of Setting in the *Novellen* of Stefan Zweig," *Neophilologus*, 66 (1982): 574-588;
Turner, "The Function of the Narrative Frame in the *Novellen* of Stefan Zweig," *Modern Language Review*, 76 (1981): 116-128;
Turner, "Memory and the Humanitarian Ideal: An Interpretation of Stefan Zweig's 'Buchmendel,'" *Modern Austrian Literature*, 12 (1978): 43-62;
György M. Vajda, "Stefan Zweig: Aktueller Chronist einer vergangenen Welt," *Literatur und Kritik*, 169-170 (1982): 11-19;

Jiri Vesely, "Das Schachspiel in der 'Schachnovelle,'" *Österreich in Geschichte und Literatur,* 13 (1969): 517-523;

Klaus Zelewitz, "Geschichte erzählen: Ein Risiko? Die Biographien Stefan Zweigs," *Literatur und Kritik,* 169-170 (1982): 59-71;

Harry Zohn, "Stefan Zweig and Contemporary European Literature," *German Life and Letters,* 5 (1952): 202-212.

Papers:
The largest collection of Zweig materials in North America is at the Daniel Reed Library, State University of New York College at Fredonia.

Supplementary Reading List

Amann, Klaus. *Der Anschluß österreichischer Schriftsteller an das dritte Reich.* Frankfurt am Main: Athenäum, 1988.

Amann and Albert Berger, eds. *Österreichische Literatur der 30er Jahre: Ideologische Verhältnisse, institutionelle Voraussetzungen, Fallstudien.* Vienna: Böhlau, 1985.

Arnold, Heinz Ludwig, ed. *Kritisches Lexikon zur deutschsprachigen Gegenwartsliteratur.* Munich: Edition text + kritik, 1978ff.

Aspetsberger, Friedbert. *Literarisches Leben im Austrofaschismus: Der Staatspreis.* Königstein: Hain, 1980.

Aspetsberger, ed. *Österreichische Literatur seit den zwanziger Jahren: Beiträge zu ihrer historisch-politischen Lokalisierung.* Vienna: Österreichischer Bundesverlag, 1979.

Aspetsberger, ed. *Staat und Gesellschaft in der modernen österreichischen Literatur.* Vienna: Österreichischer Bundesverlag, 1977.

Aspetsberger, ed. *Traditionen in der neueren österreichischen Literatur: Zehn Vorträge*, edited by Hermann Möcker. Vienna: Österreichischer Bundesverlag, 1980.

Best, Alan, and Hans Wolfschütz, eds. *Modern Austrian Writing. Literature and Society after 1945.* London: Wolff, 1980; Totowa, N.J.: Barnes & Noble, 1980.

Crankshaw, Edward. *The Habsburgs: Portrait of a Dynasty.* New York: Viking, 1971.

Daviau, Donald G., ed. *Major Figures of Contemporary Austrian Literature.* New York: Lang, 1987.

Daviau, ed. *Major Figures of Modern Austrian Literature.* Riverside, Cal.: Ariadne Press, 1988.

Demetz, Peter. *After the Fires: Recent Writing in the Germanies, Austria, and Switzerland.* New York: Harcourt Brace Jovanovich, 1986.

Dimension, special dual-language issue devoted to contemporary Austrian literature, edited by A. Leslie Willson, Ernst Jandl, and Hans F. Prokop, 8, nos. 1 and 2 (1975).

Gross, Ruth V. *Plan and the Austrian Rebirth: Portrait of a Journal.* Columbia, S.C.: Camden House, 1982.

Janik, Allan, and Stephen Toulmin. *Wittgenstein's Vienna.* New York: Simon & Schuster, 1973.

Johnson, Lonnie. *Introducing Austria.* Riverside, Cal.: Ariadne Press, 1989.

Johnston, William M. *The Austrian Mind: An Intellectual and Social History, 1848-1938.* Berkeley: University of California Press, 1972.

Luft, David S. *Robert Musil and the Crisis of European Culture 1880-1942.* Berkeley: University of California Press, 1980.

McVeigh, Joseph. *Kontinuität und Vergangenheitsbewältigung in der österreichischen Literatur nach 1945.* Vienna: Braumüller, 1988.

Modern Austrian Literature, special issue: "Perspectives on the Question of Austrian Literature," 17, no. 3/4 (1984).

Nagl, Johann Willibad, Jakob Zeidler, and Eduard Castle, eds. *Deutsch-österreichische Literaturgeschichte,* volume 4. Vienna: Fromme, 1937.

Patsch, Sylvia M. *Österreichische Schriftsteller im Exil in Großbritannien.* Vienna & Munich: Brandstätter, 1985.

Pauley, Bruce F. *Hitler and the Forgotten Nazis: A History of Austrian National Socialism.* Chapel Hill: University of North Carolina Press, 1981.

Rabinbach, Anson, ed. *The Austrian Socialist Experiment. Social Democracy and Austromarxism, 1918-1934.* Boulder, Colo.: Westview Press, 1985.

Rozenblit, Marsha L. *The Jews of Vienna, 1867-1914: Assimilation and Identity.* Albany: State University of New York, 1983.

Schorske, Carl E. *Fin-de-siècle Vienna: Politics and Culture.* New York: Knopf, 1979.

Spalek, John M., Joseph Strelka, and S. H. Haurylchak. *Deutsche Exilliteratur seit 1933: Kalifornien,* 2 volumes. Bern: Francke, 1976.

Spiel, Hilde, ed. *Die zeitgenössische Literatur Österreichs.* Zurich & Munich: Kindler, 1976.

Steiner, Kurt, ed. *Modern Austria.* Palo Alto, Cal.: Society for the Promotion of Science and Scholarship, 1981.

Tuchman, Barbara W. *The Proud Tower: A Portrait of the World before the War: 1890-1914.* New York: Macmillan, 1966.

Ungar, Frederick, ed. *Handbook of Austrian Literature.* New York: Ungar, 1973.

Weinzierl, Ulrich, ed. *Österreicher im Exil: Frankreich 1938-1945. Eine Dokumentation.* Vienna: Österreichischer Bundesverlag, 1984.

Weinzierl, ed. *Österreichs Fall: Schriftsteller berichten vom Anschluß.* Vienna & Munich: Jugend und Volk, 1987.

Williams, Cedric E. *The Broken Eagle. The Politics of Austrian Literature from Empire to Anschluss.* London: Elek, 1974.

Wischenbart, Rüdiger. *Literarischer Wiederaufbau in Österreich 1945-1949.* Königstein: Hain, 1983.

Contributors

Ehrhard Bahr	*University of California, Los Angeles*
Andrew W. Barker	*University of Edinburgh*
Bettina Kluth Cothran	*Georgia State University*
Donald G. Daviau	*University of California, Riverside*
Esther N. Elstun	*George Mason University*
Ludwig Fischer	*Willamette University*
Ruth V. Gross	*Eastman School of Music, University of Rochester*
Herbert Herzmann	*University College, Dublin*
Klaus-Peter Hinze	*Cleveland State University*
Michael W. Jennings	*Princeton University*
Jorun B. Johns	*California State University, San Bernardino*
Jürgen Koppensteiner	*University of Northern Iowa*
Richard H. Lawson	*University of North Carolina at Chapel Hill*
Michael Mitchell	*University of Stirling*
Phillip H. Rhein	*Vanderbilt University*
Jens Rieckmann	*University of Washington*
Josef Schmidt	*McGill University*
Gerd K. Schneider	*Syracuse University*
George C. Schoolfield	*Yale University*
Lionel B. Steiman	*University of Manitoba*
Alfred D. White	*University of Wales College of Cardiff*

Cumulative Index

Dictionary of Literary Biography, Volumes 1-81
Dictionary of Literary Biography Yearbook, 1980-1988
Dictionary of Literary Biography Documentary Series, Volumes 1-6

Cumulative Index

DLB before number: *Dictionary of Literary Biography*, Volumes 1-81
Y before number: *Dictionary of Literary Biography Yearbook*, 1980-1988
DS before number: *Dictionary of Literary Biography Documentary Series*, Volumes 1-6

A

Abbey Press DLB-49
The Abbey Theatre and Irish
　Drama, 1900-1945 .... DLB-10
Abbot, Willis J. 1863-1934................... DLB-29
Abbott, Jacob 1803-1879 ....DLB-1
Abbott, Lyman 1835-1922................... DLB-79
Abbott, Robert S. 1868-1940 .... DLB-29
Abelard-Schuman DLB-46
Abell, Arunah S. 1806-1888 .... DLB-43
Abercrombie, Lascelles 1881-1938............ DLB-19
Abrams, M. H. 1912- DLB-67
Abse, Dannie 1923- DLB-27
Academy Chicago Publishers DLB-46
Ace Books DLB-46
Acorn, Milton 1923-1986 .... DLB-53
Actors Theatre of Louisville DLB-7
Adair, James 1709?-1783? DLB-30
Adamic, Louis 1898-1951 ....DLB-9
Adams, Alice 1926- Y-86
Adams, Brooks 1848-1927 .... DLB-47
Adams, Charles Francis, Jr. 1835-1915 .... DLB-47
Adams, Douglas 1952- Y-83
Adams, Franklin P. 1881-1960 .... DLB-29
Adams, Henry 1838-1918 ....DLB-12, 47
Adams, Herbert Baxter 1850-1901 .... DLB-47
Adams, J. S. and C. [publishing house]........ DLB-49
Adams, James Truslow 1878-1949............ DLB-17
Adams, John 1735-1826 .... DLB-31
Adams, John Quincy 1767-1848............... DLB-37
Adams, Léonie 1899-1988 .... DLB-48
Adams, Samuel 1722-1803 ....DLB-31, 43

Adams, William Taylor 1822-1897 .... DLB-42
Adcock, Fleur 1934- DLB-40
Ade, George 1866-1944 ....DLB-11, 25
Adeler, Max (see Clark, Charles Heber)
Advance Publishing Company DLB-49
AE 1867-1935 .... DLB-19
Aesthetic Poetry (1873), by Walter Pater DLB-35
Afro-American Literary Critics:
　An Introduction DLB-33
Agassiz, Jean Louis Rodolphe 1807-1873........DLB-1
Agee, James 1909-1955......................DLB-2, 26
Aiken, Conrad 1889-1973 ....DLB-9, 45
Ainsworth, William Harrison 1805-1882....... DLB-21
Aitken, Robert [publishing house]............. DLB-49
Akins, Zoë 1886-1958 .... DLB-26
Alain-Fournier 1886-1914 .... DLB-65
Alba, Nanina 1915-1968...................... DLB-41
Albee, Edward 1928- DLB-7
Alcott, Amos Bronson 1799-1888.................DLB-1
Alcott, Louisa May 1832-1888 ....DLB-1, 42, 79
Alcott, William Andrus 1798-1859.................DLB-1
Alden, Henry Mills 1836-1919................. DLB-79
Alden, Isabella 1841-1930 .... DLB-42
Alden, John B. [publishing house]............. DLB-49
Alden, Beardsley and Company DLB-49
Aldington, Richard 1892-1962..............DLB-20, 36
Aldis, Dorothy 1896-1966 .... DLB-22
Aldiss, Brian W. 1925- DLB-14
Aldrich, Thomas Bailey 1836-1907
　.........................DLB-42, 71, 74, 79
Alexander, Charles Wesley
　[publishing house] DLB-49
Alexander, James 1691-1756 .... DLB-24
Alexander, Lloyd 1924- DLB-52

343

Alger, Horatio, Jr. 1832-1899	DLB-42
Algonquin Books of Chapel Hill	DLB-46
Algren, Nelson 1909-1981	DLB-9; Y-81, 82
Allan, Ted 1916-	DLB-68
Alldritt, Keith 1935-	DLB-14
Allen, Ethan 1738-1789	DLB-31
Allen, George 1808-1876	DLB-59
Allen, Grant 1848-1899	DLB-70
Allen, Henry W. 1912-	Y-85
Allen, Hervey 1889-1949	DLB-9, 45
Allen, James 1739-1808	DLB-31
Allen, James Lane 1849-1925	DLB-71
Allen, Jay Presson 1922-	DLB-26
Allen, John, and Company	DLB-49
Allen, Samuel W. 1917-	DLB-41
Allen, Woody 1935-	DLB-44
Allingham, Margery 1904-1966	DLB-77
Allingham, William 1824-1889	DLB-35
Allison, W. L. [publishing house]	DLB-49
Allott, Kenneth 1912-1973	DLB-20
Allston, Washington 1779-1843	DLB-1
Alsop, George 1636-post 1673	DLB-24
Alsop, Richard 1761-1815	DLB-37
Altemus, Henry, and Company	DLB-49
Altenberg, Peter 1885-1919	DLB-81
Alvarez, A. 1929-	DLB-14, 40
Ambler, Eric 1909-	DLB-77
America: or, a Poem on the Settlement of the British Colonies (1780?), by Timothy Dwight	DLB-37
American Conservatory Theatre	DLB-7
American Fiction and the 1930s	DLB-9
American Humor: A Historical Survey East and Northeast South and Southwest Midwest West	DLB-11
American News Company	DLB-49
The American Poets' Corner: The First Three Years (1983-1986)	Y-86
American Publishing Company	DLB-49
American Stationers' Company	DLB-49
American Sunday-School Union	DLB-49
American Temperance Union	DLB-49
American Tract Society	DLB-49
The American Writers Congress (9-12 October 1981)	Y-81
The American Writers Congress: A Report on Continuing Business	Y-81
Ames, Fisher 1758-1808	DLB-37
Ames, Mary Clemmer 1831-1884	DLB-23
Amini, Johari M. 1935-	DLB-41
Amis, Kingsley 1922-	DLB-15, 27
Amis, Martin 1949-	DLB-14
Ammons, A. R. 1926-	DLB-5
Amory, Thomas 1691?-1788	DLB-39
Andersch, Alfred 1914-1980	DLB-69
Anderson, Margaret 1886-1973	DLB-4
Anderson, Maxwell 1888-1959	DLB-7
Anderson, Patrick 1915-1979	DLB-68
Anderson, Paul Y. 1893-1938	DLB-29
Anderson, Poul 1926-	DLB-8
Anderson, Robert 1917-	DLB-7
Anderson, Sherwood 1876-1941	DLB-4, 9; DS-1
Andreas-Salomé, Lou 1861-1937	DLB-66
Andres, Stefan 1906-1970	DLB-69
Andrews, Charles M. 1863-1943	DLB-17
Andrieux, Louis (see Aragon, Louis)	
Andrian, Leopold von 1875-1951	DLB-81
Andrus, Silas, and Son	DLB-49
Angell, James Burrill 1829-1916	DLB-64
Angelou, Maya 1928-	DLB-38
The "Angry Young Men"	DLB-15
Anhalt, Edward 1914-	DLB-26
Anners, Henry F. [publishing house]	DLB-49
Anthony, Piers 1934-	DLB-8
Anthony Burgess's *99 Novels:* An Opinion Poll	Y-84
Antin, Mary 1881-1949	Y-84
Antschel, Paul (see Celan, Paul)	
Appleton, D., and Company	DLB-49
Appleton-Century-Crofts	DLB-46
Apple-wood Books	DLB-46
Aquin, Hubert 1929-1977	DLB-53

Aragon, Louis 1897-1982 ... DLB-72
Arbor House Publishing Company ... DLB-46
Arcadia House ... DLB-46
Archer, William 1856-1924 ... DLB-10
Arden, John 1930- ... DLB-13
Arden of Faversham ... DLB-62
The Arena Publishing Company ... DLB-49
Arena Stage ... DLB-7
Arensberg, Ann 1937- ... Y-82
Arland, Marcel 1899-1986 ... DLB-72
Arlen, Michael 1895-1956 ... DLB-36, 77
Armed Services Editions ... DLB-46
Arno Press ... DLB-46
Arnold, Edwin 1832-1904 ... DLB-35
Arnold, Matthew 1822-1888 ... DLB-32, 57
Arnold, Thomas 1795-1842 ... DLB-55
Arnow, Harriette Simpson 1908-1986 ... DLB-6
Arp, Bill (see Smith, Charles Henry)
Arthur, Timothy Shay 1809-1885 ... DLB-3, 42, 79
As I See It, by Carolyn Cassady ... DLB-16
Asch, Nathan 1902-1964 ... DLB-4, 28
Ash, John 1948- ... DLB-40
Ashbery, John 1927- ... DLB-5; Y-81
Asher, Sandy 1942- ... Y-83
Ashton, Winifred (see Dane, Clemence)
Asimov, Isaac 1920- ... DLB-8
Atheneum Publishers ... DLB-46
Atherton, Gertrude 1857-1948 ... DLB-9, 78
Atkins, Josiah circa 1755-1781 ... DLB-31
Atkins, Russell 1926- ... DLB-41
The Atlantic Monthly Press ... DLB-46
Attaway, William 1911-1986 ... DLB-76
Atwood, Margaret 1939- ... DLB-53
Aubert, Alvin 1930- ... DLB-41
Aubin, Penelope 1685-circa 1731 ... DLB-39
Aubrey-Fletcher, Henry Lancelot (see Wade, Henry)
Auchincloss, Louis 1917- ... DLB-2; Y-80
Auden, W. H. 1907-1973 ... DLB-10, 20
Audio Art in America: A Personal Memoir ... Y-85

Auernheimer, Raoul 1876-1948 ... DLB-81
Austin, Alfred 1835-1913 ... DLB-35
Austin, Mary 1868-1934 ... DLB-9, 78
Austin, William 1778-1841 ... DLB-74
The Author's Apology for His Book (1684), by John Bunyan ... DLB-39
An Author's Response, by Ronald Sukenick ... Y-82
Authors and Newspapers Association ... DLB-46
Authors' Publishing Company ... DLB-49
Avalon Books ... DLB-46
Avison, Margaret 1918- ... DLB-53
Avon Books ... DLB-46
Ayckbourn, Alan 1939- ... DLB-13
Aymé, Marcel 1902-1967 ... DLB-72
Aytoun, William Edmondstoune 1813-1865 ... DLB-32

B

Babbitt, Irving 1865-1933 ... DLB-63
Babbitt, Natalie 1932- ... DLB-52
Babcock, John [publishing house] ... DLB-49
Bache, Benjamin Franklin 1769-1798 ... DLB-43
Bacon, Delia 1811-1859 ... DLB-1
Bacon, Thomas circa 1700-1768 ... DLB-31
Badger, Richard G., and Company ... DLB-49
Bage, Robert 1728-1801 ... DLB-39
Bagehot, Walter 1826-1877 ... DLB-55
Bagnold, Enid 1889-1981 ... DLB-13
Bahr, Hermann 1863-1934 ... DLB-81
Bailey, Alfred Goldsworthy 1905- ... DLB-68
Bailey, Francis [publishing house] ... DLB-49
Bailey, H. C. 1878-1961 ... DLB-77
Bailey, Paul 1937- ... DLB-14
Bailey, Philip James 1816-1902 ... DLB-32
Baillie, Hugh 1890-1966 ... DLB-29
Bailyn, Bernard 1922- ... DLB-17
Bainbridge, Beryl 1933- ... DLB-14
Baird, Irene 1901-1981 ... DLB-68
The Baker and Taylor Company ... DLB-49
Baker, Houston A., Jr. 1943- ... DLB-67

Cumulative Index

Baker, Walter H., Company
("Baker's Plays")............................ DLB-49

Bald, Wambly 1902- DLB-4

Balderston, John 1889-1954..................... DLB-26

Baldwin, James 1924-1987.......... DLB-2, 7, 33; Y-87

Baldwin, Joseph Glover 1815-1864 .... DLB-3, 11

Ballantine Books................................ DLB-46

Ballard, J. G. 1930- DLB-14

Ballou, Maturin Murray 1820-1895............ DLB-79

Ballou, Robert O. [publishing house].......... DLB-46

Bambara, Toni Cade 1939- DLB-38

Bancroft, A. L., and Company DLB-49

Bancroft, George 1800-1891............. DLB-1, 30, 59

Bancroft, Hubert Howe 1832-1918............ DLB-47

Bangs, John Kendrick 1862-1922.......... DLB-11, 79

Banks, John circa 1653-1706 .... DLB-80

Bantam Books.................................. DLB-46

Banville, John 1945- DLB-14

Baraka, Amiri 1934- DLB-5, 7, 16, 38

Barber, John Warner 1798-1885 .... DLB-30

Barbour, Ralph Henry 1870-1944............. DLB-22

Barbusse, Henri 1873-1935..................... DLB-65

Barclay, E. E., and Company DLB-49

Bardeen, C. W. [publishing house] DLB-49

Baring, Maurice 1874-1945..................... DLB-34

Barker, A. L. 1918- DLB-14

Barker, George 1913- DLB-20

Barker, Harley Granville 1877-1946........... DLB-10

Barker, Howard 1946- DLB-13

Barker, James Nelson 1784-1858 .... DLB-37

Barker, Jane 1652-1727? DLB-39

Barks, Coleman 1937- DLB-5

Barlach, Ernst 1870-1938..................... DLB-56

Barlow, Joel 1754-1812....................... DLB-37

Barnard, John 1681-1770 .... DLB-24

Barnes, A. S., and Company................... DLB-49

Barnes, Djuna 1892-1982............. DLB-4, 9, 45

Barnes, Margaret Ayer 1886-1967.............. DLB-9

Barnes, Peter 1931- DLB-13

Barnes, William 1801-1886 .... DLB-32

Barnes and Noble Books DLB-46

Barney, Natalie 1876-1972 .... DLB-4

Baron, Richard W., Publishing Company...... DLB-46

Barr, Robert 1850-1912 .... DLB-70

Barrax, Gerald William 1933- DLB-41

Barrie, James M. 1860-1937.................... DLB-10

Barry, Philip 1896-1949 .... DLB-7

Barse and Hopkins DLB-46

Barstow, Stan 1928- DLB-14

Barth, John 1930- DLB-2

Barthelme, Donald 1931- DLB-2; Y-80

Barthelme, Frederick 1943- Y-85

Bartlett, John 1820-1905 .... DLB-1

Bartol, Cyrus Augustus 1813-1900 .... DLB-1

Bartram, John 1699-1777 .... DLB-31

Bartram, William 1739-1823................... DLB-37

Basic Books................................... DLB-46

Bass, T. J. 1932- Y-81

Bassett, John Spencer 1867-1928............. DLB-17

Bassler, Thomas Joseph (see Bass, T. J.)

Bate, Walter Jackson 1918- DLB-67

Bates, Katharine Lee 1859-1929................ DLB-71

Baum, L. Frank 1856-1919.................... DLB-22

Baumbach, Jonathan 1933- Y-80

Bawden, Nina 1925- DLB-14

Bax, Clifford 1886-1962....................... DLB-10

Bayer, Eleanor (see Perry, Eleanor)

Beach, Sylvia 1887-1962....................... DLB-4

Beacon Press DLB-49

Beadle and Adams DLB-49

Beagle, Peter S. 1939- Y-80

Beal, M. F. 1937- Y-81

Beale, Howard K. 1899-1959.................. DLB-17

Beard, Charles A. 1874-1948.................. DLB-17

A Beat Chronology: The First Twenty-five
 Years, 1944-1969........................ DLB-16

Beattie, Ann 1947- Y-82

Beauchemin, Yves 1941- DLB-60

Beaulieu, Victor-Lévy 1945- DLB-53

Beaumont, Francis circa 1584-1616
 and Fletcher, John 1579-1625............. DLB-58

Beauvoir, Simone de 1908-1986	Y-86, DLB-72
Becher, Ulrich 1910-	DLB-69
Becker, Carl 1873-1945	DLB-17
Becker, Jurek 1937-	DLB-75
Becker, Jürgen 1932-	DLB-75
Beckett, Samuel 1906-	DLB-13, 15
Beckford, William 1760-1844	DLB-39
Beckham, Barry 1944-	DLB-33
Beecher, Catharine Esther 1800-1878	DLB-1
Beecher, Henry Ward 1813-1887	DLB-3, 43
Beer, George L. 1872-1920	DLB-47
Beer, Patricia 1919-	DLB-40
Beerbohm, Max 1872-1956	DLB-34
Beer-Hofmann, Richard 1866-1945	DLB-81
Beers, Henry A. 1847-1926	DLB-71
Behan, Brendan 1923-1964	DLB-13
Behn, Aphra 1640?-1689	DLB-39, 80
Behn, Harry 1898-1973	DLB-61
Behrman, S. N. 1893-1973	DLB-7, 44
Belasco, David 1853-1931	DLB-7
Belford, Clarke and Company	DLB-49
Belitt, Ben 1911-	DLB-5
Belknap, Jeremy 1744-1798	DLB-30, 37
Bell, James Madison 1826-1902	DLB-50
Bell, Marvin 1937-	DLB-5
Bell, Robert [publishing house]	DLB-49
Bellamy, Edward 1850-1898	DLB-12
Bellamy, Joseph 1719-1790	DLB-31
Belloc, Hilaire 1870-1953	DLB-19
Bellow, Saul 1915-	DLB-2, 28; Y-82; DS-3
Belmont Productions	DLB-46
Bemelmans, Ludwig 1898-1962	DLB-22
Bemis, Samuel Flagg 1891-1973	DLB-17
Benchley, Robert 1889-1945	DLB-11
Benedictus, David 1938-	DLB-14
Benedikt, Michael 1935-	DLB-5
Benét, Stephen Vincent 1898-1943	DLB-4, 48
Benét, William Rose 1886-1950	DLB-45
Benford, Gregory 1941-	Y-82
Benjamin, Park 1809-1864	DLB-3, 59, 73
Benn, Gottfried 1886-1956	DLB-56
Bennett, Arnold 1867-1931	DLB-10, 34
Bennett, Charles 1899-	DLB-44
Bennett, Gwendolyn 1902-	DLB-51
Bennett, Hal 1930-	DLB-33
Bennett, James Gordon 1795-1872	DLB-43
Bennett, James Gordon, Jr. 1841-1918	DLB-23
Bennett, John 1865-1956	DLB-42
Benoit, Jacques 1941-	DLB-60
Benson, Stella 1892-1933	DLB-36
Bentley, E. C. 1875-1956	DLB-70
Benton, Robert 1932- and Newman, David 1937-	DLB-44
Benziger Brothers	DLB-49
Beresford, Anne 1929-	DLB-40
Berford, R. G., Company	DLB-49
Berg, Stephen 1934-	DLB-5
Bergengruen, Werner 1892-1964	DLB-56
Berger, John 1926-	DLB-14
Berger, Meyer 1898-1959	DLB-29
Berger, Thomas 1924-	DLB-2; Y-80
Berkeley, Anthony 1893-1971	DLB-77
Berkeley, George 1685-1753	DLB-31
The Berkley Publishing Corporation	DLB-46
Bernanos, Georges 1888-1948	DLB-72
Bernard, John 1756-1828	DLB-37
Berrigan, Daniel 1921-	DLB-5
Berrigan, Ted 1934-1983	DLB-5
Berry, Wendell 1934-	DLB-5, 6
Berryman, John 1914-1972	DLB-48
Bersianik, Louky 1930-	DLB-60
Berton, Pierre 1920-	DLB-68
Bessette, Gerard 1920-	DLB-53
Bessie, Alvah 1904-1985	DLB-26
Bester, Alfred 1913-	DLB-8
The Bestseller Lists: An Assessment	Y-84
Betjeman, John 1906-1984	DLB-20; Y-84
Betts, Doris 1932-	Y-82
Beveridge, Albert J. 1862-1927	DLB-17
Beverley, Robert circa 1673-1722	DLB-24, 30

Bichsel, Peter 1935- DLB-75

Biddle, Drexel [publishing house] DLB-49

Bidwell, Walter Hilliard 1798-1881 .... DLB-79

Bienek, Horst 1930- DLB-75

Bierbaum, Otto Julius 1865-1910 .... DLB-66

Bierce, Ambrose 1842-1914? ... DLB-11, 12, 23, 71, 74

Biggle, Lloyd, Jr. 1923- DLB-8

Biglow, Hosea (see Lowell, James Russell)

Billings, Josh (see Shaw, Henry Wheeler)

Binding, Rudolf G. 1867-1938 .... DLB-66

Bingham, Caleb 1757-1817 .... DLB-42

Binyon, Laurence 1869-1943 .... DLB-19

Biographical Documents I Y-84

Biographical Documents II Y-85

Bioren, John [publishing house] DLB-49

Bird, William 1888-1963 .... DLB-4

Bishop, Elizabeth 1911-1979 .... DLB-5

Bishop, John Peale 1892-1944 .... DLB-4, 9, 45

Bissett, Bill 1939- DLB-53

Black, David (D. M.) 1941- DLB-40

Black, Walter J. [publishing house] DLB-46

Black, Winifred 1863-1936 .... DLB-25

The Black Arts Movement, by Larry Neal DLB-38

Black Theaters and Theater Organizations in
  America, 1961-1982: A Research List DLB-38

Black Theatre: A Forum [excerpts] DLB-38

Blackamore, Arthur 1679-? DLB-24, 39

Blackburn, Alexander L. 1929- Y-85

Blackburn, Paul 1926-1971 .... DLB-16; Y-81

Blackburn, Thomas 1916-1977 .... DLB-27

Blackmore, R. D. 1825-1900 .... DLB-18

Blackmur, R. P. 1904-1965 .... DLB-63

Blackwood, Caroline 1931- DLB-14

Blair, Eric Arthur (see Orwell, George)

Blair, Francis Preston 1791-1876 .... DLB-43

Blair, James circa 1655-1743 .... DLB-24

Blair, John Durburrow 1759-1823 .... DLB-37

Blais, Marie-Claire 1939- DLB-53

Blaise, Clark 1940- DLB-53

Blake, Nicholas 1904-1972 .... DLB-77
  (see also Day Lewis, C.)

The Blakiston Company DLB-49

Blanchot, Maurice 1907- DLB-72

Bledsoe, Albert Taylor 1809-1877 .... DLB-3, 79

Blelock and Company DLB-49

Blish, James 1921-1975 .... DLB-8

Bliss, E., and E. White [publishing house] DLB-49

Bloch, Robert 1917- DLB-44

Block, Rudolph (see Lessing, Bruno)

Bloom, Harold 1930- DLB-67

Bloomer, Amelia 1818-1894 .... DLB-79

Blume, Judy 1938- DLB-52

Blunck, Hans Friedrich 1888-1961 .... DLB-66

Blunden, Edmund 1896-1974 .... DLB-20

Blunt, Wilfrid Scawen 1840-1922 .... DLB-19

Bly, Nellie (see Cochrane, Elizabeth)

Bly, Robert 1926- DLB-5

The Bobbs-Merrill Company DLB-46

Bobrowski, Johannes 1917-1965 .... DLB-75

Bodenheim, Maxwell 1892-1954 .... DLB-9, 45

Bodkin, M. McDonnell 1850-1933 .... DLB-70

Bodsworth, Fred 1918- DLB-68

Boehm, Sydney 1908- DLB-44

Boer, Charles 1939- DLB-5

Bogan, Louise 1897-1970 .... DLB-45

Bogarde, Dirk 1921- DLB-14

Boland, Eavan 1944- DLB-40

Böll, Heinrich 1917-1985 .... Y-85, DLB-69

Bolling, Robert 1738-1775 .... DLB-31

Bolt, Carol 1941- DLB-60

Bolt, Robert 1924- DLB-13

Bolton, Herbert E. 1870-1953 .... DLB-17

Bond, Edward 1934- DLB-13

Boni, Albert and Charles [publishing house] .. DLB-46

Boni and Liveright DLB-46

Robert Bonner's Sons DLB-49

Bontemps, Arna 1902-1973 .... DLB-48, 51

The Book League of America DLB-46

Book Reviewing in America: I Y-87

Book Reviewing in America: II Y-88

Book Supply Company DLB-49

The Booker Prize
    Address by Anthony Thwaite, Chairman
    of the Booker Prize Judges
    Comments from Former Booker Prize
    Winners Y-86
Boorstin, Daniel J. 1914- DLB-17
Booth, Mary L. 1831-1889.................... DLB-79
Booth, Philip 1925- Y-82
Booth, Wayne C. 1921- DLB-67
Borchardt, Rudolf 1877-1945 .... DLB-66
Borchert, Wolfgang 1921-1947 .... DLB-69
Borges, Jorge Luis 1899-1986 .... Y-86
Borrow, George 1803-1881................ DLB-21, 55
Bosco, Henri 1888-1976...................... DLB-72
Bosco, Monique 1927- DLB-53
Botta, Anne C. Lynch 1815-1891............... DLB-3
Bottomley, Gordon 1874-1948................. DLB-10
Bottoms, David 1949- Y-83
Bottrall, Ronald 1906- DLB-20
Boucher, Anthony 1911-1968 .... DLB-8
Boucher, Jonathan 1738-1804................. DLB-31
Bourjaily, Vance Nye 1922- DLB-2
Bourne, Edward Gaylord 1860-1908 .... DLB-47
Bourne, Randolph 1886-1918 .... DLB-63
Bousquet, Joë 1897-1950 .... DLB-72
Bova, Ben 1932- Y-81
Bove, Emmanuel 1898-1945.................... DLB-72
Bovard, Oliver K. 1872-1945 .... DLB-25
Bowen, Elizabeth 1899-1973.................. DLB-15
Bowen, Francis 1811-1890................. DLB-1, 59
Bowen, John 1924- DLB-13
Bowen-Merrill Company DLB-49
Bowering, George 1935- DLB-53
Bowers, Claude G. 1878-1958 .... DLB-17
Bowers, Edgar 1924- DLB-5
Bowles, Paul 1910- DLB-5, 6
Bowles, Samuel III 1826-1878 .... DLB-43
Bowman, Louise Morey 1882-1944 .... DLB-68
Boyd, James 1888-1944....................... DLB-9
Boyd, John 1919- DLB-8
Boyd, Thomas 1898-1935 .... DLB-9

Boyesen, Hjalmar Hjorth 1848-1895 .... DLB-12, 71
Boyle, Kay 1902- DLB-4, 9, 48
Boyle, Roger, Earl of Orrery
    1621-1679................................ DLB-80
Boyle, T. Coraghessan 1948- Y-86
Brackenbury, Alison 1953- DLB-40
Brackenridge, Hugh Henry 1748-1816..... DLB-11, 37
Brackett, Charles 1892-1969................. DLB-26
Brackett, Leigh 1915-1978................... DLB-8, 26
Bradburn, John [publishing house]........... DLB-49
Bradbury, Malcolm 1932- DLB-14
Bradbury, Ray 1920- DLB-2, 8
Braddon, Mary Elizabeth 1835-1915 .... DLB-18, 70
Bradford, Andrew 1686-1742 .... DLB-43, 73
Bradford, Gamaliel 1863-1932 .... DLB-17
Bradford, John 1749-1830 .... DLB-43
Bradford, William 1590-1657.............. DLB-24, 30
Bradford, William III 1719-1791.......... DLB-43, 73
Bradlaugh, Charles 1833-1891 .... DLB-57
Bradley, David 1950- DLB-33
Bradley, Ira, and Company................... DLB-49
Bradley, J. W., and Company DLB-49
Bradley, Marion Zimmer 1930- DLB-8
Bradley, William Aspenwall 1878-1939......... DLB-4
Bradstreet, Anne 1612 or 1613-1672.......... DLB-24
Brady, Frederic A. [publishing house]....... DLB-49
Bragg, Melvyn 1939- DLB-14
Brainard, Charles H. [publishing house] DLB-49
Braine, John 1922-1986 .... DLB-15; Y-86
Braithwaite, William Stanley
    1878-1962............................. DLB-50, 54
Bramah, Ernest 1868-1942.................... DLB-70
Branagan, Thomas 1774-1843.................. DLB-37
Branch, William Blackwell 1927- DLB-76
Branden Press............................... DLB-46
Brault, Jacques 1933- DLB-53
Braun, Volker 1939- DLB-75
Brautigan, Richard 1935-1984...... DLB-2, 5; Y-80, 84
Braxton, Joanne M. 1950- DLB-41
Bray, Thomas 1656-1730...................... DLB-24
Braziller, George [publishing house] DLB-46

The Bread Loaf Writers' Conference 1983	Y-84
The Break-Up of the Novel (1922), by John Middleton Murry	DLB-36
Breasted, James Henry 1865-1935	DLB-47
Brecht, Bertolt 1898-1956	DLB-56
Bredel, Willi 1901-1964	DLB-56
Bremser, Bonnie 1939-	DLB-16
Bremser, Ray 1934-	DLB-16
Brentano, Bernard von 1901-1964	DLB-56
Brentano's	DLB-49
Brenton, Howard 1942-	DLB-13
Breton, André 1896-1966	DLB-65
Brewer, Warren and Putnam	DLB-46
Brewster, Elizabeth 1922-	DLB-60
Bridgers, Sue Ellen 1942-	DLB-52
Bridges, Robert 1844-1930	DLB-19
Bridie, James 1888-1951	DLB-10
Briggs, Charles Frederick 1804-1877	DLB-3
Brighouse, Harold 1882-1958	DLB-10
Brimmer, B. J., Company	DLB-46
Brinnin, John Malcolm 1916-	DLB-48
Brisbane, Albert 1809-1890	DLB-3
Brisbane, Arthur 1864-1936	DLB-25
Broadway Publishing Company	DLB-46
Brochu, André 1942-	DLB-53
Brock, Edwin 1927-	DLB-40
Brod, Max 1884-1968	DLB-81
Brodhead, John R. 1814-1873	DLB-30
Brome, Richard circa 1590-1652	DLB-58
Bromfield, Louis 1896-1956	DLB-4, 9
Broner, E. M. 1930-	DLB-28
Brontë, Anne 1820-1849	DLB-21
Brontë, Charlotte 1816-1855	DLB-21
Brontë, Emily 1818-1848	DLB-21, 32
Brooke, Frances 1724-1789	DLB-39
Brooke, Henry 1703?-1783	DLB-39
Brooke, Rupert 1887-1915	DLB-19
Brooke-Rose, Christine 1926-	DLB-14
Brookner, Anita 1928-	Y-87
Brooks, Charles Timothy 1813-1883	DLB-1
Brooks, Cleanth 1906-	DLB-63
Brooks, Gwendolyn 1917-	DLB-5, 76
Brooks, Jeremy 1926-	DLB-14
Brooks, Mel 1926-	DLB-26
Brooks, Noah 1830-1903	DLB-42
Brooks, Richard 1912-	DLB-44
Brooks, Van Wyck 1886-1963	DLB-45, 63
Brophy, Brigid 1929-	DLB-14
Brossard, Chandler 1922-	DLB-16
Brossard, Nicole 1943-	DLB-53
Brother Antoninus (see Everson, William)	
Brougham, John 1810-1880	DLB-11
Broughton, James 1913-	DLB-5
Broughton, Rhoda 1840-1920	DLB-18
Broun, Heywood 1888-1939	DLB-29
Brown, Alice 1856-1948	DLB-78
Brown, Bob 1886-1959	DLB-4, 45
Brown, Cecil 1943-	DLB-33
Brown, Charles Brockden 1771-1810	DLB-37, 59, 73
Brown, Christy 1932-1981	DLB-14
Brown, Dee 1908-	Y-80
Browne, Francis Fisher 1843-1913	DLB-79
Brown, Frank London 1927-1962	DLB-76
Brown, Fredric 1906-1972	DLB-8
Brown, George Mackay 1921-	DLB-14, 27
Brown, Harry 1917-1986	DLB-26
Brown, Marcia 1918-	DLB-61
Brown, Margaret Wise 1910-1952	DLB-22
Brown, Oliver Madox 1855-1874	DLB-21
Brown, Sterling 1901-	DLB-48, 51, 63
Brown, T. E. 1830-1897	DLB-35
Brown, William Hill 1765-1793	DLB-37
Brown, William Wells 1814-1884	DLB-3, 50
Browne, Charles Farrar 1834-1867	DLB-11
Browne, Michael Dennis 1940-	DLB-40
Browne, Wynyard 1911-1964	DLB-13
Brownell, W. C. 1851-1928	DLB-71
Browning, Elizabeth Barrett 1806-1861	DLB-32
Browning, Robert 1812-1889	DLB-32
Brownjohn, Allan 1931-	DLB-40

Brownson, Orestes Augustus 1803-1876..........................DLB-1, 59, 73

Bruce, Charles 1906-1971 .... DLB-68

Bruce, Leo 1903-1979 .... DLB-77

Bruce, Philip Alexander 1856-1933 .... DLB-47

Bruce Humphries [publishing house] DLB-46

Bruckman, Clyde 1894-1955 .... DLB-26

Brundage, John Herbert (see Herbert, John)

Bryant, William Cullen 1794-1878........DLB-3, 43, 59

Buchan, John 1875-1940 ....DLB-34, 70

Buchanan, Robert 1841-1901...............DLB-18, 35

Buchman, Sidney 1902-1975 .... DLB-26

Buck, Pearl S. 1892-1973......................DLB-9

Buckingham, Joseph Tinker 1779-1861 and Buckingham, Edwin 1810-1833 .... DLB-73

Buckler, Ernest 1908-1984 .... DLB-68

Buckley, William F., Jr. 1925- Y-80

Buckminster, Joseph Stevens 1784-1812....... DLB-37

Buckner, Robert 1906- DLB-26

Budd, Thomas ?-1698...................... DLB-24

Budrys, A. J. 1931- DLB-8

Buechner, Frederick 1926- Y-80

Buell, John 1927- DLB-53

Buffum, Job [publishing house] DLB-49

Bukowski, Charles 1920- DLB-5

Bullins, Ed 1935- DLB-7, 38

Bulwer-Lytton, Edward (also Edward Bulwer) 1803-1873........................ DLB-21

Bumpus, Jerry 1937- Y-81

Bunce and Brother.......................... DLB-49

Bunner, H. C. 1855-1896...................DLB-78, 79

Bunting, Basil 1900-1985..................... DLB-20

Bunyan, John 1628-1688 .... DLB-39

Burch, Robert 1925- DLB-52

Burgess, Anthony 1917- DLB-14

Burgess, Gelett 1866-1951 .... DLB-11

Burgess, John W. 1844-1931 .... DLB-47

Burgess, Thornton W. 1874-1965 .... DLB-22

Burgess, Stringer and Company............... DLB-49

Burk, John Daly circa 1772-1808 .... DLB-37

Burke, Kenneth 1897- DLB-45, 63

Burlingame, Edward Livermore 1848-1922 ... DLB-79

Burnett, Frances Hodgson 1849-1924 .... DLB-42

Burnett, W. R. 1899-1982 ....DLB-9

Burney, Fanny 1752-1840 .... DLB-39

Burns, Alan 1929- DLB-14

Burns, John Horne 1916-1953 ....Y-85

Burnshaw, Stanley 1906- DLB-48

Burr, C. Chauncey 1815?-1883................. DLB-79

Burroughs, Edgar Rice 1875-1950................DLB-8

Burroughs, John 1837-1921................... DLB-64

Burroughs, Margaret T. G. 1917- DLB-41

Burroughs, William S., Jr. 1947-1981 .... DLB-16

Burroughs, William Seward 1914-
................................DLB-2, 8, 16; Y-81

Burroway, Janet 1936- DLB-6

Burt, A. L., and Company.................... DLB-49

Burton, Miles (see Rhode, John)

Burton, Richard F. 1821-1890................. DLB-55

Burton, Virginia Lee 1909-1968............... DLB-22

Burton, William Evans 1804-1860............. DLB-73

Busch, Frederick 1941- DLB-6

Busch, Niven 1903- DLB-44

Butler, E. H., and Company................... DLB-49

Butler, Juan 1942-1981...................... DLB-53

Butler, Octavia E. 1947- DLB-33

Butler, Samuel 1835-1902 ....DLB-18, 57

Butterworth, Hezekiah 1839-1905............. DLB-42

B. V. (see Thomson, James)

Byars, Betsy 1928- DLB-52

Byatt, A. S. 1936- DLB-14

Byles, Mather 1707-1788 .... DLB-24

Bynner, Witter 1881-1968.................... DLB-54

Byrd, William II 1674-1744 .... DLB-24

Byrne, John Keyes (see Leonard, Hugh)

C

Cabell, James Branch 1879-1958 .... DLB-9, 78

Cable, George Washington 1844-1925 ...... DLB-12, 74

Cahan, Abraham 1860-1951 .... DLB-9, 25, 28

Cain, George 1943- DLB-33

Caldwell, Ben 1937- DLB-38

Caldwell, Erskine 1903-1987 .... DLB-9

Caldwell, H. M., Company DLB-49

Calhoun, John C. 1782-1850 .... DLB-3

Calisher, Hortense 1911- DLB-2

Callaghan, Morley 1903- DLB-68

Callaloo Y-87

Calmer, Edgar 1907- DLB-4

Calverley, C. S. 1831-1884 .... DLB-35

Calvert, George Henry 1803-1889 .... DLB-1, 64

Cambridge Press DLB-49

Cameron, Eleanor 1912- DLB-52

Camm, John 1718-1778 .... DLB-31

Campbell, Gabrielle Margaret Vere
    (see Shearing, Joseph)

Campbell, James Edwin 1867-1896 .... DLB-50

Campbell, John 1653-1728 .... DLB-43

Campbell, John W., Jr. 1910-1971 .... DLB-8

Campbell, Roy 1901-1957 .... DLB-20

Campion, Thomas 1567-1620 .... DLB-58

Camus, Albert 1913-1960 .... DLB-72

Candour in English Fiction (1890),
    by Thomas Hardy DLB-18

Cannan, Gilbert 1884-1955 .... DLB-10

Cannell, Kathleen 1891-1974 .... DLB-4

Cannell, Skipwith 1887-1957 .... DLB-45

Cantwell, Robert 1908-1978 .... DLB-9

Cape, Jonathan, and Harrison Smith
    [publishing house] DLB-46

Capen, Joseph 1658-1725 .... DLB-24

Capote, Truman 1924-1984 .... DLB-2; Y-80, 84

Carey, M., and Company DLB-49

Carey, Mathew 1760-1839 .... DLB-37, 73

Carey and Hart DLB-49

Carlell, Lodowick 1602-1675 .... DLB-58

Carleton, G. W. [publishing house] DLB-49

Carossa, Hans 1878-1956 .... DLB-66

Carr, Emily 1871-1945 .... DLB-68

Carrier, Roch 1937- DLB-53

Carlyle, Jane Welsh 1801-1866 .... DLB-55

Carlyle, Thomas 1795-1881 .... DLB-55

Carpenter, Stephen Cullen ?-1820? DLB-73

Carroll, Gladys Hasty 1904- DLB-9

Carroll, John 1735-1815 .... DLB-37

Carroll, Lewis 1832-1898 .... DLB-18

Carroll, Paul 1927- DLB-16

Carroll, Paul Vincent 1900-1968 .... DLB-10

Carroll and Graf Publishers DLB-46

Carruth, Hayden 1921- DLB-5

Carryl, Charles E. 1841-1920 .... DLB-42

Carswell, Catherine 1879-1946 .... DLB-36

Carter, Angela 1940- DLB-14

Carter, Henry (see Leslie, Frank)

Carter, Landon 1710-1778 .... DLB-31

Carter, Lin 1930- Y-81

Carter, Robert, and Brothers DLB-49

Carter and Hendee DLB-49

Caruthers, William Alexander 1802-1846 ...... DLB-3

Carver, Jonathan 1710-1780 .... DLB-31

Carver, Raymond 1938-1988 .... Y-84, 88

Cary, Joyce 1888-1957 .... DLB-15

Casey, Juanita 1925- DLB-14

Casey, Michael 1947- DLB-5

Cassady, Carolyn 1923- DLB-16

Cassady, Neal 1926-1968 .... DLB-16

Cassell Publishing Company DLB-49

Cassill, R. V. 1919- DLB-6

Castlemon, Harry (see Fosdick, Charles Austin)

Caswall, Edward 1814-1878 .... DLB-32

Cather, Willa 1873-1947 .... DLB-9, 54, 78; DS-1

Catherwood, Mary Hartwell 1847-1902 .... DLB-78

Catton, Bruce 1899-1978 .... DLB-17

Causley, Charles 1917- DLB-27

Caute, David 1936- DLB-14

Cawein, Madison 1865-1914 .... DLB-54

The Caxton Printers, Limited	DLB-46
Celan, Paul 1920-1970	DLB-69
Céline, Louis-Ferdinand 1894-1961	DLB-72
Center for the Book Research	Y-84
The Century Company	DLB-49
Challans, Eileen Mary (see Renault, Mary)	
Chalmers, George 1742-1825	DLB-30
Chamberlain, Samuel S. 1851-1916	DLB-25
Chamberland, Paul 1939-	DLB-60
Chamberlin, William Henry 1897-1969	DLB-29
Chambers, Charles Haddon 1860-1921	DLB-10
Chandler, Harry 1864-1944	DLB-29
Chandler, Raymond 1888-1959	DS-6
Channing, Edward 1856-1931	DLB-17
Channing, Edward Tyrrell 1790-1856	DLB-1, 59
Channing, William Ellery 1780-1842	DLB-1, 59
Channing, William Ellery II 1817-1901	DLB-1
Channing, William Henry 1810-1884	DLB-1, 59
Chaplin, Charlie 1889-1977	DLB-44
Chapman, George 1559 or 1560-1634	DLB-62
Chappell, Fred 1936-	DLB-6
Charbonneau, Robert 1911-1967	DLB-68
Charles, Gerda 1914-	DLB-14
Charles, William [publishing house]	DLB-49
The Charles Wood Affair: A Playwright Revived	Y-83
Charlotte Forten: Pages from her Diary	DLB-50
Charteris, Leslie 1907-	DLB-77
Charyn, Jerome 1937-	Y-83
Chase, Borden 1900-1971	DLB-26
Chase-Riboud, Barbara 1936-	DLB-33
Chauncy, Charles 1705-1787	DLB-24
Chayefsky, Paddy 1923-1981	DLB-7, 44; Y-81
Cheever, Ezekiel 1615-1708	DLB-24
Cheever, George Barrell 1807-1890	DLB-59
Cheever, John 1912-1982	DLB-2; Y-80, 82
Cheever, Susan 1943-	Y-82
Chelsea House	DLB-46
Cheney, Ednah Dow (Littlehale) 1824-1904	DLB-1
Cherry, Kelly 1940	Y-83
Cherryh, C. J. 1942-	Y-80
Chesnutt, Charles Waddell 1858-1932	DLB-12, 50, 78
Chester, George Randolph 1869-1924	DLB-78
Chesterton, G. K. 1874-1936	DLB-10, 19, 34, 70
Cheyney, Edward P. 1861-1947	DLB-47
Child, Francis James 1825-1896	DLB-1, 64
Child, Lydia Maria 1802-1880	DLB-1, 74
Child, Philip 1898-1978	DLB-68
Childers, Erskine 1870-1922	DLB-70
Children's Book Awards and Prizes	DLB-61
Childress, Alice 1920-	DLB-7, 38
Childs, George W. 1829-1894	DLB-23
Chilton Book Company	DLB-46
Chittenden, Hiram Martin 1858-1917	DLB-47
Chivers, Thomas Holley 1809-1858	DLB-3
Chopin, Kate 1850-1904	DLB-12, 78
Choquette, Adrienne 1915-1973	DLB-68
Choquette, Robert 1905-	DLB-68
The Christian Publishing Company	DLB-49
Christie, Agatha 1890-1976	DLB-13, 77
Church, Benjamin 1734-1778	DLB-31
Church, Francis Pharcellus 1839-1906	DLB-79
Church, William Conant 1836-1917	DLB-79
Churchill, Caryl 1938-	DLB-13
Ciardi, John 1916-1986	DLB-5; Y-86
City Lights Books	DLB-46
Clapper, Raymond 1892-1944	DLB-29
Clare, John 1793-1864	DLB-55
Clark, Alfred Alexander Gordon (see Hare, Cyril)	
Clark, Ann Nolan 1896-	DLB-52
Clark, C. M., Publishing Company	DLB-46
Clark, Catherine Anthony 1892-1977	DLB-68
Clark, Charles Heber 1841-1915	DLB-11
Clark, Davis Wasgatt 1812-1871	DLB-79
Clark, Eleanor 1913-	DLB-6
Clark, Lewis Gaylord 1808-1873	DLB-3, 64, 73
Clark, Walter Van Tilburg 1909-1971	DLB-9
Clarke, Austin 1896-1974	DLB-10, 20
Clarke, Austin C. 1934-	DLB-53
Clarke, Gillian 1937-	DLB-40

Clarke, James Freeman 1810-1888 .... DLB-1, 59

Clarke, Rebecca Sophia 1833-1906 .... DLB-42

Clarke, Robert, and Company DLB-49

Clausen, Andy 1943- DLB-16

Claxton, Remsen and Haffelfinger DLB-49

Clay, Cassius Marcellus 1810-1903 .... DLB-43

Cleary, Beverly 1916- DLB-52

Cleaver, Vera 1919- and
  Cleaver, Bill 1920-1981 .... DLB-52

Cleland, John 1710-1789 .... DLB-39

Clemens, Samuel Langhorne
  1835-1910 .... DLB-11, 12, 23, 64, 74

Clement, Hal 1922- DLB-8

Clemo, Jack 1916- DLB-27

Clifton, Lucille 1936- DLB-5, 41

Clode, Edward J. [publishing house] DLB-46

Clough, Arthur Hugh 1819-1861 .... DLB-32

Cloutier, Cécile 1930- DLB-60

Coates, Robert M. 1897-1973 .... DLB-4, 9

Coatsworth, Elizabeth 1893- DLB-22

Cobb, Jr., Charles E. 1943- DLB-41

Cobb, Frank I. 1869-1923 .... DLB-25

Cobb, Irvin S. 1876-1944 .... DLB-11, 25

Cobbett, William 1762-1835 .... DLB-43

Cochran, Thomas C. 1902- DLB-17

Cochrane, Elizabeth 1867-1922 .... DLB-25

Cockerill, John A. 1845-1896 .... DLB-23

Cocteau, Jean 1889-1963 .... DLB-65

Coffee, Lenore J. 1900?-1984 .... DLB-44

Coffin, Robert P. Tristram 1892-1955 .... DLB-45

Cogswell, Fred 1917- DLB-60

Cogswell, Mason Fitch 1761-1830 .... DLB-37

Cohen, Arthur A. 1928-1986 .... DLB-28

Cohen, Leonard 1934- DLB-53

Cohen, Matt 1942- DLB-53

Colden, Cadwallader 1688-1776 .... DLB-24, 30

Cole, Barry 1936- DLB-14

Colegate, Isabel 1931- DLB-14

Coleman, Emily Holmes 1899-1974 .... DLB-4

Coleridge, Mary 1861-1907 .... DLB-19

Colette 1873-1954 .... DLB-65

Colette, Sidonie Gabrielle (see Colette)

Collier, John 1901-1980 .... DLB-77

Collier, P. F. [publishing house] DLB-49

Collin and Small DLB-49

Collins, Isaac [publishing house] DLB-49

Collins, Mortimer 1827-1876 .... DLB-21, 35

Collins, Wilkie 1824-1889 .... DLB-18, 70

Collyer, Mary 1716?-1763? DLB-39

Colman, Benjamin 1673-1747 .... DLB-24

Colman, S. [publishing house] DLB-49

Colombo, John Robert 1936- DLB-53

Colter, Cyrus 1910- DLB-33

Colum, Padraic 1881-1972 .... DLB-19

Colwin, Laurie 1944- Y-80

Comden, Betty 1919- and Green,
  Adolph 1918- DLB-44

The Comic Tradition Continued
  [in the British Novel] DLB-15

Commager, Henry Steele 1902- DLB-17

The Commercialization of the Image of
  Revolt, by Kenneth Rexroth DLB-16

Community and Commentators: Black
  Theatre and Its Critics DLB-38

Compton-Burnett, Ivy 1884?-1969 .... DLB-36

Conference on Modern Biography Y-85

Congreve, William 1670-1729 .... DLB-39

Conkey, W. B., Company DLB-49

Connell, Evan S., Jr. 1924- DLB-2; Y-81

Connelly, Marc 1890-1980 .... DLB-7; Y-80

Connolly, James B. 1868-1957 .... DLB-78

Connor, Tony 1930- DLB-40

Conquest, Robert 1917- DLB-27

Conrad, John, and Company DLB-49

Conrad, Joseph 1857-1924 .... DLB-10, 34

Conroy, Jack 1899- Y-81

Conroy, Pat 1945- DLB-6

The Consolidation of Opinion: Critical
  Responses to the Modernists DLB-36

Constantine, David 1944- DLB-40

Contempo Caravan: Kites in a Windstorm Y-85

A Contemporary Flourescence of Chicano
  Literature Y-84

The Continental Publishing Company......... DLB-49
A Conversation with Chaim Potok.................Y-84
Conversations with Publishers I: An Interview with Patrick O'Connor Y-84
Conway, Moncure Daniel 1832-1907 ....DLB-1
Cook, David C., Publishing Company DLB-49
Cook, Ebenezer circa 1667-circa 1732 .... DLB-24
Cook, Michael 1933- DLB-53
Cooke, George Willis 1848-1923............... DLB-71
Cooke, Increase, and Company................ DLB-49
Cooke, John Esten 1830-1886 ....DLB-3
Cooke, Philip Pendleton 1816-1850 ....DLB-3, 59
Cooke, Rose Terry 1827-1892...............DLB-12, 74
Coolbrith, Ina 1841-1928...................... DLB-54
Coolidge, George [publishing house] DLB-49
Coolidge, Susan (see Woolsey, Sarah Chauncy)
Cooper, Giles 1918-1966 .... DLB-13
Cooper, James Fenimore 1789-1851..............DLB-3
Cooper, Kent 1880-1965 .... DLB-29
Coover, Robert 1932- DLB-2; Y-81
Copeland and Day............................. DLB-49
Coppel, Alfred 1921- Y-83
Coppola, Francis Ford 1939- DLB-44
Corcoran, Barbara 1911- DLB-52
Corelli, Marie 1855-1924 .... DLB-34
Corle, Edwin 1906-1956.........................Y-85
Corman, Cid 1924- DLB-5
Cormier, Robert 1925- DLB-52
Corn, Alfred 1943- Y-80
Cornish, Sam 1935- DLB-41
Corrington, John William 1932- DLB-6
Corrothers, James D. 1869-1917................ DLB-50
Corso, Gregory 1930- DLB-5, 16
Cortez, Jayne 1936- DLB-41
Corvo, Baron (see Rolfe, Frederick William)
Cory, William Johnson 1823-1892.............. DLB-35
Cosmopolitan Book Corporation DLB-46
Costain, Thomas B. 1885-1965 ....DLB-9
Cotter, Joseph Seamon, Sr. 1861-1949................................ DLB-50

Cotter, Joseph Seamon, Jr. 1895-1919................................ DLB-50
Cotton, John 1584-1652 .... DLB-24
Coulter, John 1888-1980 .... DLB-68
Cournos, John 1881-1966 .... DLB-54
Coventry, Francis 1725-1754 .... DLB-39
Coverly, N. [publishing house] DLB-49
Covici-Friede DLB-46
Coward, Noel 1899-1973 .... DLB-10
Coward, McCann and Geoghegan............. DLB-46
Cowles, Gardner 1861-1946 .... DLB-29
Cowley, Malcolm 1898- DLB-4, 48; Y-81
Cox, A. B. (see Berkeley, Anthony)
Cox, Palmer 1840-1924........................ DLB-42
Coxe, Louis 1918- DLB-5
Coxe, Tench 1755-1824 .... DLB-37
Cozzens, James Gould 1903-1978...DLB-9; Y-84; DS-2
Craddock, Charles Egbert (see Murfree, Mary N.)
Cradock, Thomas 1718-1770................... DLB-31
Craig, Daniel H. 1811-1895 .... DLB-43
Craik, Dinah Maria 1826-1887 .... DLB-35
Cranch, Christopher Pearse 1813-1892......DLB-1, 42
Crane, Hart 1899-1932.....................DLB-4, 48
Crane, R. S. 1886-1967....................... DLB-63
Crane, Stephen 1871-1900 ....DLB-12, 54, 78
Crapsey, Adelaide 1878-1914.................. DLB-54
Craven, Avery 1885-1980..................... DLB-17
Crawford, Charles 1752-circa 1815............ DLB-31
Crawford, F. Marion 1854-1909............... DLB-71
Crawley, Alan 1887-1975..................... DLB-68
Crayon, Geoffrey (see Irving, Washington)
Creasey, John 1908-1973 .... DLB-77
Creative Age Press............................ DLB-46
Creel, George 1876-1953 .... DLB-25
Creeley, Robert 1926- DLB-5, 16
Creelman, James 1859-1915................... DLB-23
Cregan, David 1931- DLB-13
Crèvecoeur, Michel Guillaume Jean de 1735-1813................................ DLB-37
Crews, Harry 1935- DLB-6
Crichton, Michael 1942- Y-81

A Crisis of Culture: The Changing Role
of Religion in the New Republic DLB-37

Cristofer, Michael 1946- DLB-7

"The Critic as Artist" (1891), by Oscar Wilde.. DLB-57

Criticism In Relation To Novels (1863),
by G. H. Lewes........................... DLB-21

Crockett, David (Davy) 1786-1836........... DLB-3, 11

Croft-Cooke, Rupert (see Bruce, Leo)

Crofts, Freeman Wills 1879-1957.............. DLB-77

Croly, Jane Cunningham 1829-1901........... DLB-23

Crosby, Caresse 1892-1970 .... DLB-48

Crosby, Caresse 1892-1970 and Crosby,
Harry 1898-1929........................... DLB-4

Crosby, Harry 1898-1929..................... DLB-48

Crossley-Holland, Kevin 1941- DLB-40

Crothers, Rachel 1878-1958 .... DLB-7

Crowell, Thomas Y., Company DLB-49

Crowley, John 1942- Y-82

Crowley, Mart 1935- DLB-7

Crown Publishers............................. DLB-46

Crowne, John 1641-1712 .... DLB-80

Croy, Homer 1883-1965........................ DLB-4

Crumley, James 1939- Y-84

Cruz, Victor Hernández 1949- DLB-41

Csokor, Franz Theodor 1885-1969 .... DLB-81

Cullen, Countee 1903-1946............. DLB-4, 48, 51

Culler, Jonathan D. 1944- DLB-67

The Cult of Biography
Excerpts from the Second Folio Debate:
"Biographies are generally a disease of
English Literature"—Germaine Greer,
Victoria Glendinning, Auberon Waugh,
and Richard Holmes Y-86

Cummings, E. E. 1894-1962............. DLB-4, 48

Cummings, Ray 1887-1957 .... DLB-8

Cummings and Hilliard DLB-49

Cummins, Maria Susanna 1827-1866......... DLB-42

Cuney, Waring 1906-1976.................... DLB-51

Cuney-Hare, Maude 1874-1936 .... DLB-52

Cunningham, J. V. 1911- DLB-5

Cunningham, Peter F. [publishing house] DLB-49

Cuomo, George 1929- Y-80

Cupples and Leon............................ DLB-46

Cupples, Upham and Company DLB-49

Cuppy, Will 1884-1949....................... DLB-11

Currie, Mary Montgomerie Lamb Singleton,
Lady Currie (see Fane, Violet)

Curti, Merle E. 1897- DLB-17

Curtis, George William 1824-1892........... DLB-1, 43

D

D. M. Thomas: The Plagiarism Controversy.......Y-82

Dabit, Eugène 1898-1936..................... DLB-65

Daborne, Robert circa 1580-1628.............. DLB-58

Daggett, Rollin M. 1831-1901 .... DLB-79

Dahlberg, Edward 1900-1977.................. DLB-48

Dale, Peter 1938- DLB-40

Dall, Caroline Wells (Healey) 1822-1912........DLB-1

Dallas, E. S. 1828-1879 .... DLB-55

The Dallas Theater Center DLB-7

D'Alton, Louis 1900-1951 .... DLB-10

Daly, T. A. 1871-1948........................ DLB-11

Damon, S. Foster 1893-1971................... DLB-45

Damrell, William S. [publishing house]........ DLB-49

Dana, Charles A. 1819-1897................DLB-3, 23

Dana, Richard Henry, Jr. 1815-1882 ....DLB-1

Dandridge, Ray Garfield..................... DLB-51

Dane, Clemence 1887-1965................... DLB-10

Danforth, John 1660-1730.................... DLB-24

Danforth, Samuel I 1626-1674 .... DLB-24

Danforth, Samuel II 1666-1727 .... DLB-24

Dangerous Years: London Theater,
1939-1945............................... DLB-10

Daniel, John M. 1825-1865................... DLB-43

Daniel, Samuel 1562 or 1563-1619 .... DLB-62

Daniells, Roy 1902-1979..................... DLB-68

Daniels, Josephus 1862-1948 .... DLB-29

Danner, Margaret Esse 1915- DLB-41

Darwin, Charles 1809-1882................... DLB-57

Daryush, Elizabeth 1887-1977 .... DLB-20

Dashwood, Edmée Elizabeth Monica
de la Pasture (see Delafield, E. M.)

d'Aulaire, Edgar Parin 1898- and
    d'Aulaire, Ingri 1904- DLB-22

Davenant, Sir William 1606-1668.............. DLB-58

Davenport, Robert ?-? DLB-58

Daves, Delmer 1904-1977 .... DLB-26

Davey, Frank 1940- DLB-53

Davidson, Avram 1923- DLB-8

Davidson, Donald 1893-1968 .... DLB-45

Davidson, John 1857-1909..................... DLB-19

Davidson, Lionel 1922- DLB-14

Davie, Donald 1922- DLB-27

Davies, Robertson 1913- DLB-68

Davies, Samuel 1723-1761..................... DLB-31

Davies, W. H. 1871-1940 .... DLB-19

Daviot, Gordon 1896?-1952 .... DLB-10
    (see also Tey, Josephine)

Davis, Charles A. 1795-1867................... DLB-11

Davis, Clyde Brion 1894-1962 ....DLB-9

Davis, Dick 1945- DLB-40

Davis, Frank Marshall 1905-?.................. DLB-51

Davis, H. L. 1894-1960 ....DLB-9

Davis, John 1774-1854........................ DLB-37

Davis, Margaret Thomson 1926- DLB-14

Davis, Ossie 1917- DLB-7, 38

Davis, Rebecca Harding 1831-1910............ DLB-74

Davis, Richard Harding 1864-1916............DLB-12, 23, 78, 79

Davis, Samuel Cole 1764-1809................. DLB-37

Davison, Peter 1928- DLB-5

Davys, Mary 1674-1732....................... DLB-39

DAW Books DLB-46

Dawson, William 1704-1752 .... DLB-31

Day, Benjamin Henry 1810-1889.............. DLB-43

Day, Clarence 1874-1935 .... DLB-11

Day, Dorothy 1897-1980 .... DLB-29

Day, John circa 1574-circa 1640 .... DLB-62

Day, The John, Company DLB-46

Day Lewis, C. 1904-1972 ....DLB-15, 20
    (see also Blake, Nicholas)

Day, Mahlon [publishing house]............... DLB-49

Day, Thomas 1748-1789...................... DLB-39

Deacon, William Arthur 1890-1977............ DLB-68

Deal, Borden 1922-1985........................DLB-6

de Angeli, Marguerite 1889-1987.............. DLB-22

De Bow, James Dunwoody Brownson
    1820-1867.............................DLB-3, 79

de Bruyn, Günter 1926- DLB-75

de Camp, L. Sprague 1907- DLB-8

The Decay of Lying (1889),
    by Oscar Wilde [excerpt].................. DLB-18

Dedication, *Ferdinand Count Fathom* (1753),
    by Tobias Smollett DLB-39

Dedication, *Lasselia* (1723), by Eliza
    Haywood [excerpt]....................... DLB-39

Dedication, *The History of Pompey the
    Little* (1751), by Francis Coventry DLB-39

Dedication, *The Wanderer* (1814),
    by Fanny Burney......................... DLB-39

Defense of *Amelia* (1752), by Henry Fielding .. DLB-39

Defoe, Daniel 1660-1731 .... DLB-39

de Fontaine, Felix Gregory 1834-1896......... DLB-43

De Forest, John William 1826-1906 .... DLB-12

de Graff, Robert 1895-1981 .... Y-81

DeJong, Meindert 1906- DLB-52

Dekker, Thomas circa 1572-1632.............. DLB-62

Delafield, E. M. 1890-1943 .... DLB-34

de la Mare, Walter 1873-1956 .... DLB-19

de la Roche, Mazo 1879-1961 .... DLB-68

Deland, Margaret 1857-1945 .... DLB-78

Delaney, Shelagh 1939- DLB-13

Delany, Martin Robinson 1812-1885........... DLB-50

Delany, Samuel R. 1942- DLB-8, 33

Delbanco, Nicholas 1942- DLB-6

DeLillo, Don 1936- DLB-6

Dell, Floyd 1887-1969 ....DLB-9

Dell Publishing Company..................... DLB-46

delle Grazie, Marie Eugene 1864-1931 .... DLB-81

del Rey, Lester 1915- DLB-8

de Man, Paul 1919-1983...................... DLB-67

Demby, William 1922- DLB-33

Deming, Philander 1829-1915................. DLB-74

Demorest, William Jennings 1822-1895........ DLB-79

Denham, Sir John 1615-1669.................. DLB-58

Denison, T. S., and Company DLB-49

Dennie, Joseph 1768-1812.......... DLB-37, 43, 59, 73

Dennis, Nigel 1912- DLB-13, 15

Dent, Tom 1932- DLB-38

Denton, Daniel circa 1626-1703 .... DLB-24

DePaola, Tomie 1934- DLB-61

Derby, George Horatio 1823-1861............. DLB-11

Derby, J. C., and Company.................... DLB-49

Derby and Miller DLB-49

Derleth, August 1909-1971.................... DLB-9

The Derrydale Press.......................... DLB-46

Desbiens, Jean-Paul 1927- DLB-53

DesRochers, Alfred 1901-1978 .... DLB-68

Desrosiers, Léo-Paul 1896-1967 .... DLB-68

Destouches, Louis-Ferdinand (see Céline, Louis-Ferdinand)

De Tabley, Lord 1835-1895 .... DLB-35

Deutsch, Babette 1895-1982................... DLB-45

Deveaux, Alexis 1948- DLB-38

The Development of Lighting in the Staging of Drama, 1900-1945 [in Great Britain]... DLB-10

de Vere, Aubrey 1814-1902 .... DLB-35

The Devin-Adair Company.................... DLB-46

De Voto, Bernard 1897-1955................... DLB-9

De Vries, Peter 1910- DLB-6; Y-82

Dewdney, Christopher 1951- DLB-60

Dewdney, Selwyn 1909-1979 .... DLB-68

DeWitt, Robert M., Publisher................. DLB-49

DeWolfe, Fiske and Company DLB-49

de Young, M. H. 1849-1925................... DLB-25

The Dial Press................................ DLB-46

Diamond, I. A. L. 1920-1988 .... DLB-26

Di Cicco, Pier Giorgio 1949- DLB-60

Dick, Philip K. 1928- DLB-8

Dick and Fitzgerald........................... DLB-49

Dickens, Charles 1812-1870 .... DLB-21, 55, 70

Dickey, James 1923- DLB-5; Y-82

Dickey, William 1928- DLB-5

Dickinson, Emily 1830-1886................... DLB-1

Dickinson, John 1732-1808.................... DLB-31

Dickinson, Jonathan 1688-1747................ DLB-24

Dickinson, Patric 1914- DLB-27

Dickson, Gordon R. 1923- DLB-8

Didion, Joan 1934- DLB-2; Y-81, 86

Di Donato, Pietro 1911- DLB-9

Dillard, Annie 1945- Y-80

Dillard, R. H. W. 1937- DLB-5

Dillingham, Charles T., Company DLB-49

The G. W. Dillingham Company DLB-49

Dintenfass, Mark 1941- Y-84

Diogenes, Jr. (see Brougham, John)

DiPrima, Diane 1934- DLB-5, 16

Disch, Thomas M. 1940- DLB-8

Disney, Walt 1901-1966 .... DLB-22

Disraeli, Benjamin 1804-1881 .... DLB-21, 55

Ditzen, Rudolf (see Fallada, Hans)

Dix, Dorothea Lynde 1802-1887................. DLB-1

Dix, Dorothy (see Gilmer, Elizabeth Meriwether)

Dix, Edwards and Company.................... DLB-49

Dixon, Paige (see Corcoran, Barbara)

Dixon, Richard Watson 1833-1900 .... DLB-19

Dobell, Sydney 1824-1874..................... DLB-32

Döblin, Alfred 1878-1957 .... DLB-66

Dobson, Austin 1840-1921..................... DLB-35

Doctorow, E. L. 1931- DLB-2, 28; Y-80

Dodd, William E. 1869-1940................... DLB-17

Dodd, Mead and Company.................... DLB-49

Dodge, B. W., and Company DLB-46

Dodge, Mary Mapes 1831?-1905............ DLB-42, 79

Dodge Publishing Company DLB-49

Dodgson, Charles Lutwidge (see Carroll, Lewis)

Dodson, Owen 1914-1983 .... DLB-76

Doesticks, Q. K. Philander, P. B. (see Thomson, Mortimer)

Donahoe, Patrick [publishing house] DLB-49

Donald, David H. 1920- DLB-17

Donleavy, J. P. 1926- DLB-6

Donnelley, R. R., and Sons Company.......... DLB-49

Donnelly, Ignatius 1831-1901 .... DLB-12

Donohue and Henneberry..................... DLB-49

Doolady, M. [publishing house]................ DLB-49

Dooley, Ebon (see Ebon)

Doolittle, Hilda 1886-1961.................DLB-4, 45

Doran, George H., Company................DLB-46

Dorgelès, Roland 1886-1973.................DLB-65

Dorn, Edward 1929- DLB-5

Dorr, Rheta Childe 1866-1948................DLB-25

Dorst, Tankred 1925- DLB-75

Dos Passos, John 1896-1970............DLB-4, 9; DS-1

Doubleday and Company....................DLB-49

Doughty, Charles M. 1843-1926..........DLB-19, 57

Douglas, Keith 1920-1944....................DLB-27

Douglas, Norman 1868-1952.................DLB-34

Douglass, Frederick 1817?-1895.....DLB-1, 43, 50, 79

Douglass, William circa 1691-1752............DLB-24

Dover Publications..........................DLB-46

Dowden, Edward 1843-1913.................DLB-35

Downing, J., Major (see Davis, Charles A.)

Downing, Major Jack (see Smith, Seba)

Dowson, Ernest 1867-1900...................DLB-19

Doxey, William [publishing house]............DLB-49

Doyle, Sir Arthur Conan 1859-1930........DLB-18, 70

Doyle, Kirby 1932- DLB-16

Drabble, Margaret 1939- DLB-14

The Dramatic Publishing Company...........DLB-49

Dramatists Play Service......................DLB-46

Draper, John W. 1811-1882..................DLB-30

Draper, Lyman C. 1815-1891.................DLB-30

Dreiser, Theodore 1871-1945........DLB-9, 12; DS-1

Drewitz, Ingeborg 1923-1986..................DLB-75

Drieu La Rochelle, Pierre 1893-1945..........DLB-72

Drinkwater, John 1882-1937.............DLB-10, 19

The Drue Heinz Literature Prize
    Excerpt from "Excerpts from a Report
      of the Commission," in David
      Bosworth's *The Death of Descartes*
    An Interview with David Bosworth...........Y-82

Dryden, John 1631-1700 .... DLB-80

Duane, William 1760-1835 .... DLB-43

Dubé, Marcel 1930- DLB-53

Dubé, Rodolphe (see Hertel, François)

Du Bois, W. E. B. 1868-1963 ....DLB-47, 50

Du Bois, William Pène 1916- DLB-61

Ducharme, Réjean 1941- DLB-60

Duell, Sloan and Pearce DLB-46

Duffield and Green........................... DLB-46

Duffy, Maureen 1933- DLB-14

Dugan, Alan 1923- DLB-5

Duhamel, Georges 1884-1966 .... DLB-65

Dukes, Ashley 1885-1959..................... DLB-10

Dumas, Henry 1934-1968 .... DLB-41

Dunbar, Paul Laurence 1872-1906 .....DLB-50, 54, 78

Duncan, Robert 1919-1988 ....DLB-5, 16

Duncan, Ronald 1914-1982................... DLB-13

Dunigan, Edward, and Brother................ DLB-49

Dunlap, John 1747-1812 .... DLB-43

Dunlap, William 1766-1839...........DLB-30, 37, 59

Dunn, Douglas 1942- DLB-40

Dunne, Finley Peter 1867-1936............DLB-11, 23

Dunne, John Gregory 1932- Y-80

Dunne, Philip 1908- DLB-26

Dunning, Ralph Cheever 1878-1930.............DLB-4

Dunning, William A. 1857-1922............... DLB-17

Plunkett, Edward John Moreton Drax,
    Lord Dunsany 1878-1957..............DLB-10, 77

Durand, Lucile (see Bersianik, Louky)

Duranty, Walter 1884-1957.................... DLB-29

Durfey, Thomas 1653-1723 .... DLB-80

Durrell, Lawrence 1912- DLB-15, 27

Durrell, William [publishing house] DLB-49

Dürrenmatt, Friedrich 1921- DLB-69

Dutton, E. P., and Company................... DLB-49

Duvoisin, Roger 1904-1980.................... DLB-61

Duyckinck, Evert Augustus 1816-1878 ......DLB-3, 64

Duyckinck, George L. 1823-1863................DLB-3

Duyckinck and Company..................... DLB-49

Dwight, John Sullivan 1813-1893.................DLB-1

Dwight, Timothy 1752-1817.................... DLB-37

Dyer, Charles 1928- DLB-13

Dylan, Bob 1941- DLB-16

Cumulative Index

E

Eager, Edward 1911-1964 .... DLB-22

Earle, James H., and Company DLB-49

Early American Book Illustration,
   by Sinclair Hamilton DLB-49

Eastlake, William 1917- DLB-6

Eastman, Carol ?- DLB-44

Eberhart, Richard 1904- DLB-48

Ebner-Eschenbach, Marie von
   1830-1916 .... DLB-81

Ebon 1942- DLB-41

Ecco Press DLB-46

Edes, Benjamin 1732-1803 .... DLB-43

Edgar, David 1948- DLB-13

The Editor Publishing Company DLB-49

Edmonds, Randolph 1900- DLB-51

Edmonds, Walter D. 1903- DLB-9

Edschmid, Kasimir 1890-1966 .... DLB-56

Edwards, Jonathan 1703-1758 .... DLB-24

Edwards, Jonathan, Jr. 1745-1801 .... DLB-37

Edwards, Junius 1929- DLB-33

Edwards, Richard 1524-1566 .... DLB-62

Effinger, George Alec 1947- DLB-8

Eggleston, Edward 1837-1902 .... DLB-12

Ehrenstein, Albert 1886-1950 .... DLB-81

Eich, Günter 1907-1972 .... DLB-69

1873 Publishers' Catalogues DLB-49

Eighteenth-Century Aesthetic Theories DLB-31

Eighteenth-Century Philosophical
   Background DLB-31

Eigner, Larry 1927- DLB-5

Eisner, Kurt 1867-1919 .... DLB-66

Eklund, Gordon 1945- Y-83

Elder, Lonne III 1931- DLB-7, 38, 44

Elder, Paul, and Company DLB-49

Elements of Rhetoric (1828; revised, 1846),
   by Richard Whately [excerpt] DLB-57

Eliot, George 1819-1880 .... DLB-21, 35, 55

Eliot, John 1604-1690 .... DLB-24

Eliot, T. S. 1888-1965 .... DLB-7, 10, 45, 63

Elkin, Stanley 1930- DLB-2, 28; Y-80

Elles, Dora Amy (see Wentworth, Patricia)

Ellet, Elizabeth F. 1818?-1877 .... DLB-30

Elliott, George 1923- DLB-68

Elliott, Janice 1931- DLB-14

Elliott, William 1788-1863 .... DLB-3

Elliott, Thomes and Talbot DLB-49

Ellis, Edward S. 1840-1916 .... DLB-42

The George H. Ellis Company DLB-49

Ellison, Harlan 1934- DLB-8

Ellison, Ralph 1914- DLB-2, 76

Ellmann, Richard 1918-1987 .... Y-87

The Elmer Holmes Bobst Awards
   in Arts and Letters Y-87

Emanuel, James Andrew 1921- DLB-41

Emerson, Ralph Waldo 1803-1882 ...... DLB-1, 59, 73

Emerson, William 1769-1811 .... DLB-37

Empson, William 1906-1984 .... DLB-20

The End of English Stage Censorship,
   1945-1968 .... DLB-13

Ende, Michael 1929- DLB-75

Engel, Marian 1933-1985 .... DLB-53

Engle, Paul 1908- DLB-48

English Composition and Rhetoric (1866),
   by Alexander Bain [excerpt] DLB-57

The English Renaissance of Art (1908),
   by Oscar Wilde DLB-35

Enright, D. J. 1920- DLB-27

Enright, Elizabeth 1909-1968 .... DLB-22

L'Envoi (1882), by Oscar Wilde DLB-35

Epps, Bernard 1936- DLB-53

Epstein, Julius 1909- and
   Epstein, Philip 1909-1952 .... DLB-26

Equiano, Olaudah circa 1745-1797 .... DLB-37, 50

Ernst, Paul 1866-1933 .... DLB-66

Erskine, John 1879-1951 .... DLB-9

Ervine, St. John Greer 1883-1971 .... DLB-10

Eshleman, Clayton 1935- DLB-5

Ess Ess Publishing Company DLB-49

Essay on Chatterton (1842),
   by Robert Browning DLB-32

Estes, Eleanor 1906-1988 .... DLB-22

360

Estes and Lauriat	DLB-49
Etherege, George 1636-circa 1692	DLB-80
Ets, Marie Hall 1893-	DLB-22
Eudora Welty: Eye of the Storyteller	Y-87
Eugene O'Neill Memorial Theater Center	DLB-7
Eugene O'Neill's Letters: A Review	Y-88
Evans, Donald 1884-1921	DLB-54
Evans, George Henry 1805-1856	DLB-43
Evans, M., and Company	DLB-46
Evans, Mari 1923-	DLB-41
Evans, Mary Ann (see Eliot, George)	
Evans, Nathaniel 1742-1767	DLB-31
Evans, Sebastian 1830-1909	DLB-35
Everett, Alexander Hill 1790-1847	DLB-59
Everett, Edward 1794-1865	DLB-1, 59
Everson, William 1912-	DLB-5, 16
Every Man His Own Poet; or, The Inspired Singer's Recipe Book (1877), by W. H. Mallock	DLB-35
Ewart, Gavin 1916-	DLB-40
Ewing, Juliana Horatia 1841-1885	DLB-21
Exley, Frederick 1929-	Y-81
Experiment in the Novel (1929), by John D. Beresford	DLB-36

F

"F. Scott Fitzgerald: St. Paul's Native Son and Distinguished American Writer": University of Minnesota Conference, 29-31 October 1982	Y-82
Faber, Frederick William 1814-1863	DLB-32
Fair, Ronald L. 1932-	DLB-33
Fairfax, Beatrice (see Manning, Marie)	
Fairlie, Gerard 1899-1983	DLB-77
Fallada, Hans 1893-1947	DLB-56
Fancher, Betsy 1928-	Y-83
Fane, Violet 1843-1905	DLB-35
Fantasy Press Publishers	DLB-46
Fante, John 1909-1983	Y-83
Farber, Norma 1909-1984	DLB-61
Farigoule, Louis (see Romains, Jules)	
Farley, Walter 1920-	DLB-22
Farmer, Philip José 1918-	DLB-8
Farquharson, Martha (see Finley, Martha)	
Farrar and Rinehart	DLB-46
Farrar, Straus and Giroux	DLB-46
Farrell, James T. 1904-1979	DLB-4, 9; DS-2
Farrell, J. G. 1935-1979	DLB-14
Fast, Howard 1914-	DLB-9
Faulkner, William 1897-1962	DLB-9, 11, 44; DS-2; Y-86
Fauset, Jessie Redmon 1882-1961	DLB-51
Faust, Irvin 1924-	DLB-2, 28; Y-80
Fawcett Books	DLB-46
Fearing, Kenneth 1902-1961	DLB-9
Federal Writers' Project	DLB-46
Federman, Raymond 1928-	Y-80
Feiffer, Jules 1929-	DLB-7, 44
Feinberg, Charles E. 1899-1988	Y-88
Feinstein, Elaine 1930-	DLB-14, 40
Fell, Frederick, Publishers	DLB-46
Fels, Ludwig 1946-	DLB-75
Felton, Cornelius Conway 1807-1862	DLB-1
Fennario, David 1947-	DLB-60
Fenno, John 1751-1798	DLB-43
Fenno, R. F., and Company	DLB-49
Fenton, James 1949-	DLB-40
Ferber, Edna 1885-1968	DLB-9, 28
Ferdinand, Vallery III (see Salaam, Kalamu ya)	
Ferguson, Sir Samuel 1810-1886	DLB-32
Ferguson, William Scott 1875-1954	DLB-47
Ferlinghetti, Lawrence 1919-	DLB-5, 16
Fern, Fanny (see Parton, Sara Payson Willis)	
Ferret, E., and Company	DLB-49
Ferrini, Vincent 1913-	DLB-48
Ferron, Jacques 1921-1985	DLB-60
Ferron, Madeleine 1922-	DLB-53
Fetridge and Company	DLB-49
Feuchtwanger, Lion 1884-1958	DLB-66
Ficke, Arthur Davison 1883-1945	DLB-54
Fiction Best-Sellers, 1910-1945	DLB-9

Fiction into Film, 1928-1975: A List of Movies
    Based on the Works of Authors in
    British Novelists, 1930-1959 .... DLB-15

Fiedler, Leslie A. 1917- DLB-28, 67

Field, Eugene 1850-1895 .... DLB-23, 42

Field, Nathan 1587-1619 or 1620 .... DLB-58

Field, Rachel 1894-1942 .... DLB-9, 22

A Field Guide to Recent Schools of
    American Poetry Y-86

Fielding, Henry 1707-1754 .... DLB-39

Fielding, Sarah 1710-1768 .... DLB-39

Fields, James Thomas 1817-1881 .... DLB-1

Fields, Julia 1938- DLB-41

Fields, W. C. 1880-1946 .... DLB-44

Fields, Osgood and Company DLB-49

Fifty Penguin Years Y-85

Figes, Eva 1932- DLB-14

Filson, John circa 1753-1788 .... DLB-37

Findley, Timothy 1930- DLB-53

Finlay, Ian Hamilton 1925- DLB-40

Finley, Martha 1828-1909 .... DLB-42

Finney, Jack 1911- DLB-8

Finney, Walter Braden (see Finney, Jack)

Firbank, Ronald 1886-1926 .... DLB-36

Firmin, Giles 1615-1697 .... DLB-24

First Strauss "Livings" Awarded to Cynthia
    Ozick and Raymond Carver
    An Interview with Cynthia Ozick
    An Interview with Raymond Carver Y-83

Fish, Stanley 1938- DLB-67

Fisher, Clay (see Allen, Henry W.)

Fisher, Dorothy Canfield 1879-1958 .... DLB-9

Fisher, Leonard Everett 1924- DLB-61

Fisher, Roy 1930- DLB-40

Fisher, Rudolph 1897-1934 .... DLB-51

Fisher, Sydney George 1856-1927 .... DLB-47

Fisher, Vardis 1895-1968 .... DLB-9

Fiske, John 1608-1677 .... DLB-24

Fiske, John 1842-1901 .... DLB-47, 64

Fitch, Thomas circa 1700-1774 .... DLB-31

Fitch, William Clyde 1865-1909 .... DLB-7

FitzGerald, Edward 1809-1883 .... DLB-32

Fitzgerald, F. Scott 1896-1940 ... DLB-4, 9; Y-81; DS-1

Fitzgerald, Penelope 1916- DLB-14

Fitzgerald, Robert 1910-1985 .... Y-80

Fitzgerald, Thomas 1819-1891 .... DLB-23

Fitzgerald, Zelda Sayre 1900-1948 .... Y-84

Fitzhugh, Louise 1928-1974 .... DLB-52

Fitzhugh, William circa 1651-1701 .... DLB-24

Flanagan, Thomas 1923- Y-80

Flanner, Hildegarde 1899-1987 .... DLB-48

Flanner, Janet 1892-1978 .... DLB-4

Flavin, Martin 1883-1967 .... DLB-9

Flecker, James Elroy 1884-1915 .... DLB-10, 19

Fleeson, Doris 1901-1970 .... DLB-29

Fleißer, Marieluise 1901-1974 .... DLB-56

The Fleshly School of Poetry and Other
    Phenomena of the Day (1872), by Robert
    Buchanan DLB-35

The Fleshly School of Poetry: Mr. D. G.
    Rossetti (1871), by Thomas Maitland
    (Robert Buchanan) DLB-35

Fletcher, J. S. 1863-1935 .... DLB-70

Fletcher, John (see Beaumont, Francis)

Fletcher, John Gould 1886-1950 .... DLB-4, 45

Flieg, Helmut (see Heym, Stefan)

Flint, F. S. 1885-1960 .... DLB-19

Flint, Timothy 1780-1840 .... DLB-73

Follen, Eliza Lee (Cabot) 1787-1860 .... DLB-1

Follett, Ken 1949- Y-81

Follett Publishing Company DLB-46

Folsom, John West [publishing house] DLB-49

Foote, Horton 1916- DLB-26

Foote, Shelby 1916- DLB-2, 17

Forbes, Calvin 1945- DLB-41

Forbes, Ester 1891-1967 .... DLB-22

Forbes and Company DLB-49

Force, Peter 1790-1868 .... DLB-30

Forché, Carolyn 1950- DLB-5

Ford, Charles Henri 1913- DLB-4, 48

Ford, Corey 1902-1969 .... DLB-11

Ford, Ford Madox 1873-1939 .... DLB-34

Ford, J. B., and Company DLB-49

Ford, Jesse Hill 1928-	DLB-6
Ford, John 1586-?	DLB-58
Ford, Worthington C. 1858-1941	DLB-47
Fords, Howard, and Hulbert	DLB-49
Foreman, Carl 1914-1984	DLB-26
Forester, Frank (see Herbert, Henry William)	
Fornés, María Irene 1930-	DLB-7
Forrest, Leon 1937-	DLB-33
Forster, E. M. 1879-1970	DLB-34
Forten, Charlotte L. 1837-1914	DLB-50
Fortune, T. Thomas 1856-1928	DLB-23
Fosdick, Charles Austin 1842-1915	DLB-42
Foster, Genevieve 1893-1979	DLB-61
Foster, Hannah Webster 1758-1840	DLB-37
Foster, John 1648-1681	DLB-24
Foster, Michael 1904-1956	DLB-9
Four Essays on the Beat Generation, by John Clellon Holmes	DLB-16
Four Seas Company	DLB-46
Four Winds Press	DLB-46
Fournier, Henri Alban (see Alain-Fournier)	
Fowler and Wells Company	DLB-49
Fowles, John 1926-	DLB-14
Fox, John, Jr. 1862 or 1863-1919	DLB-9
Fox, Paula 1923-	DLB-52
Fox, Richard K. [publishing house]	DLB-49
Fox, Richard Kyle 1846-1922	DLB-79
Fox, William Price 1926-	DLB-2; Y-81
Fraenkel, Michael 1896-1957	DLB-4
France, Richard 1938-	DLB-7
Francis, C. S. [publishing house]	DLB-49
Francis, Convers 1795-1863	DLB-1
Francke, Kuno 1855-1930	DLB-71
Frank, Leonhard 1882-1961	DLB-56
Frank, Melvin (see Panama, Norman)	
Frank, Waldo 1889-1967	DLB-9, 63
Franken, Rose 1895?-1988	Y-84
Franklin, Benjamin 1706-1790	DLB-24, 43, 73
Franklin, James 1697-1735	DLB-43
Franklin Library	DLB-46
Frantz, Ralph Jules 1902-1979	DLB-4
Fraser, G. S. 1915-1980	DLB-27
Frayn, Michael 1933-	DLB-13, 14
Frederic, Harold 1856-1898	DLB-12, 23
Freeman, Douglas Southall 1886-1953	DLB-17
Freeman, Legh Richmond 1842-1915	DLB-23
Freeman, Mary E. Wilkins 1852-1930	DLB-12, 78
Freeman, R. Austin 1862-1943	DLB-70
French, Alice 1850-1934	DLB-74
French, David 1939-	DLB-53
French, James [publishing house]	DLB-49
French, Samuel [publishing house]	DLB-49
Freneau, Philip 1752-1832	DLB-37, 43
Friedman, Bruce Jay 1930-	DLB-2, 28
Friel, Brian 1929-	DLB-13
Friend, Krebs 1895?-1967?	DLB-4
Fries, Fritz Rudolf 1935-	DLB-75
Fringe and Alternative Theater in Great Britain	DLB-13
Frisch, Max 1911-	DLB-69
Fritz, Jean 1915-	DLB-52
Frost, Robert 1874-1963	DLB-54
Frothingham, Octavius Brooks 1822-1895	DLB-1
Froude, James Anthony 1818-1894	DLB-18, 57
Fry, Christopher 1907-	DLB-13
Frye, Northrop 1912-	DLB-67, 68
Fuchs, Daniel 1909-	DLB-9, 26, 28
The Fugitives and the Agrarians: The First Exhibition	Y-85
Fuller, Charles H., Jr. 1939-	DLB-38
Fuller, Henry Blake 1857-1929	DLB-12
Fuller, John 1937-	DLB-40
Fuller, Roy 1912-	DLB-15, 20
Fuller, Samuel 1912-	DLB-26
Fuller, Sarah Margaret, Marchesa D'Ossoli 1810-1850	DLB-1, 59, 73
Fulton, Len 1934-	Y-86
Fulton, Robin 1937-	DLB-40
Furman, Laura 1945-	Y-86
Furness, Horace Howard 1833-1912	DLB-64
Furness, William Henry 1802-1896	DLB-1

Furthman, Jules 1888-1966................... DLB-26

The Future of the Novel (1899),
by Henry James......................... DLB-18

G

Gaddis, William 1922- DLB-2

Gág, Wanda 1893-1946..................... DLB-22

Gagnon, Madeleine 1938- DLB-60

Gaine, Hugh 1726-1807 .... DLB-43

Gaine, Hugh [publishing house].............. DLB-49

Gaines, Ernest J. 1933- DLB-2, 33; Y-80

Gaiser, Gerd 1908-1976 .... DLB-69

Galaxy Science Fiction Novels DLB-46

Gale, Zona 1874-1938 ....DLB-9, 78

Gallagher, William Davis 1808-1894........... DLB-73

Gallant, Mavis 1922- DLB-53

Gallico, Paul 1897-1976.....................DLB-9

Galsworthy, John 1867-1933................DLB-10, 34

Galvin, Brendan 1938- DLB-5

Gambit DLB-46

Gammer Gurton's Needle...................... DLB-62

Gannett, Frank E. 1876-1957.................. DLB-29

Gardam, Jane 1928- DLB-14

Garden, Alexander circa 1685-1756........... DLB-31

Gardner, John 1933-1982 .... DLB-2; Y-82

Garis, Howard R. 1873-1962 .... DLB-22

Garland, Hamlin 1860-1940............DLB-12, 71, 78

Garneau, Michel 1939- DLB-53

Garner, Hugh 1913-1979..................... DLB-68

Garnett, David 1892-1981 .... DLB-34

Garraty, John A. 1920- DLB-17

Garrett, George 1929- DLB-2, 5; Y-83

Garrison, William Lloyd 1805-1879..........DLB-1, 43

Gascoyne, David 1916- DLB-20

Gaskell, Elizabeth Cleghorn 1810-1865........ DLB-21

Gass, William Howard 1924- DLB-2

Gates, Doris 1901- DLB-22

Gates, Henry Louis, Jr. 1950- DLB-67

Gates, Lewis E. 1860-1924.................... DLB-71

Gay, Ebenezer 1696-1787..................... DLB-24

The Gay Science (1866),
by E. S. Dallas [excerpt].................. DLB-21

Gayarré, Charles E. A. 1805-1895 .... DLB-30

Gaylord, Charles [publishing house].......... DLB-49

Geddes, Gary 1940- DLB-60

Geddes, Virgil 1897- DLB-4

Geis, Bernard, Associates..................... DLB-46

Geisel, Theodor Seuss 1904- DLB-61

Gelber, Jack 1932- DLB-7

Gellhorn, Martha 1908- Y-82

Gems, Pam 1925- DLB-13

A General Idea of the College of Mirania (1753),
by William Smith [excerpts]............... DLB-31

Genet, Jean 1910-1986 .... Y-86, DLB-72

Genevoix, Maurice 1890-1980................. DLB-65

Genovese, Eugene D. 1930- DLB-17

Gent, Peter 1942- Y-82

George, Henry 1839-1897..................... DLB-23

George, Jean Craighead 1919- DLB-52

Gerhardie, William 1895-1977................. DLB-36

Gernsback, Hugo 1884-1967 ....DLB-8

Gerould, Katharine Fullerton 1879-1944...... DLB-78

Gerrish, Samuel [publishing house]........... DLB-49

Gerrold, David 1944- DLB-8

Geston, Mark S. 1946- DLB-8

Gibbon, Lewis Grassic (see Mitchell, James Leslie)

Gibbons, Floyd 1887-1939..................... DLB-25

Gibbons, William ?-?......................... DLB-73

Gibson, Graeme 1934- DLB-53

Gibson, Wilfrid 1878-1962.................... DLB-19

Gibson, William 1914- DLB-7

Gide, André 1869-1951....................... DLB-65

Giguère, Diane 1937- DLB-53

Giguère, Roland 1929- DLB-60

Gilbert, Anthony 1899-1973................... DLB-77

Gilder, Jeannette L. 1849-1916................ DLB-79

Gilder, Richard Watson 1844-1909.........DLB-64, 79

Gildersleeve, Basil 1831-1924.................. DLB-71

Giles, Henry 1809-1882 .... DLB-64

Gill, William F., Company DLB-49

Gillespie, A. Lincoln, Jr. 1895-1950 ....DLB-4

Gilliam, Florence ?-?	DLB-4
Gilliatt, Penelope 1932-	DLB-14
Gillott, Jacky 1939-1980	DLB-14
Gilman, Caroline H. 1794-1888	DLB-3, 73
Gilman, W. and J. [publishing house]	DLB-49
Gilmer, Elizabeth Meriwether 1861-1951	DLB-29
Gilmer, Francis Walker 1790-1826	DLB-37
Gilroy, Frank D. 1925-	DLB-7
Ginsberg, Allen 1926-	DLB-5, 16
Ginzkey, Franz Karl 1871-1963	DLB-81
Giono, Jean 1895-1970	DLB-72
Giovanni, Nikki 1943-	DLB-5, 41
Gipson, Lawrence Henry 1880-1971	DLB-17
Giraudoux, Jean 1882-1944	DLB-65
Gissing, George 1857-1903	DLB-18
Gladstone, William Ewart 1809-1898	DLB-57
Glaeser, Ernst 1902-1963	DLB-69
Glanville, Brian 1931-	DLB-15
Glapthorne, Henry 1610-1643?	DLB-58
Glasgow, Ellen 1873-1945	DLB-9, 12
Glaspell, Susan 1876-1948	DLB-7, 9, 78
Glass, Montague 1877-1934	DLB-11
Glassco, John 1909-1981	DLB-68
Glauser, Friedrich 1896-1938	DLB-56
F. Gleason's Publishing Hall	DLB-49
Glück, Louise 1943-	DLB-5
Godbout, Jacques 1933-	DLB-53
Goddard, Morrill 1865-1937	DLB-25
Goddard, William 1740-1817	DLB-43
Godey, Louis A. 1804-1878	DLB-73
Godey and McMichael	DLB-49
Godfrey, Dave 1938-	DLB-60
Godfrey, Thomas 1736-1763	DLB-31
Godine, David R., Publisher	DLB-46
Godkin, E. L. 1831-1902	DLB-79
Godwin, Gail 1937-	DLB-6
Godwin, Parke 1816-1904	DLB-3, 64
Godwin, William 1756-1836	DLB-39
Goes, Albrecht 1908-	DLB-69
Goffe, Thomas circa 1592-1629	DLB-58
Goffstein, M. B. 1940-	DLB-61
Gogarty, Oliver St. John 1878-1957	DLB-15, 19
Goines, Donald 1937-1974	DLB-33
Gold, Herbert 1924-	DLB-2; Y-81
Gold, Michael 1893-1967	DLB-9, 28
Goldberg, Dick 1947-	DLB-7
Golding, William 1911-	DLB-15
Goldman, William 1931-	DLB-44
Goldsmith, Oliver 1730 or 1731-1774	DLB-39
Goldsmith Publishing Company	DLB-46
Gomme, Laurence James [publishing house]	DLB-46
The Goodman Theatre	DLB-7
Goodrich, Frances 1891-1984 and Hackett, Albert 1900-	DLB-26
Goodrich, S. G. [publishing house]	DLB-49
Goodrich, Samuel Griswold 1793-1860	DLB-1, 42, 73
Goodspeed, C. E., and Company	DLB-49
Goodwin, Stephen 1943-	Y-82
Gookin, Daniel 1612-1687	DLB-24
Gordon, Caroline 1895-1981	DLB-4, 9; Y-81
Gordon, Giles 1940-	DLB-14
Gordon, Mary 1949-	DLB-6; Y-81
Gordone, Charles 1925-	DLB-7
Gorey, Edward 1925-	DLB-61
Gosse, Edmund 1849-1928	DLB-57
Gould, Wallace 1882-1940	DLB-54
Goyen, William 1915-1983	DLB-2; Y-83
Grady, Henry W. 1850-1889	DLB-23
Graf, Oskar Maria 1894-1967	DLB-56
Graham, George Rex 1813-1894	DLB-73
Graham, Lorenz 1902-	DLB-76
Graham, Shirley 1896-1977	DLB-76
Graham, W. S. 1918-	DLB-20
Graham, William H. [publishing house]	DLB-49
Graham, Winston 1910-	DLB-77
Grahame, Kenneth 1859-1932	DLB-34
Gramatky, Hardie 1907-1979	DLB-22
Granich, Irwin (see Gold, Michael)	
Grant, Harry J. 1881-1963	DLB-29
Grant, James Edward 1905-1966	DLB-26

Grass, Günter 1927- DLB-75

Grasty, Charles H. 1863-1924 .... DLB-25

Grau, Shirley Ann 1929- DLB-2

Graves, John 1920- Y-83

Graves, Richard 1715-1804 .... DLB-39

Graves, Robert 1895-1985 .... DLB-20; Y-85

Gray, Asa 1810-1888 .... DLB-1

Gray, David 1838-1861 .... DLB-32

Gray, Simon 1936- DLB-13

Grayson, William J. 1788-1863 .... DLB-3, 64

The Great War and the Theater, 1914-1918
  [Great Britain] DLB-10

Greeley, Horace 1811-1872 .... DLB-3, 43

Green, Adolph (see Comden, Betty)

Green, Duff 1791-1875 .... DLB-43

Green, Gerald 1922- DLB-28

Green, Henry 1905-1973 .... DLB-15

Green, Jonas 1712-1767 .... DLB-31

Green, Joseph 1706-1780 .... DLB-31

Green, Julien 1900- DLB-4, 72

Green, Paul 1894-1981 .... DLB-7, 9; Y-81

Green, T. and S. [publishing house] DLB-49

Green, Timothy [publishing house] DLB-49

Greenberg: Publisher DLB-46

Green Tiger Press DLB-46

Greene, Asa 1789-1838 .... DLB-11

Greene, Benjamin H. [publishing house] DLB-49

Greene, Graham 1904- DLB-13, 15, 77; Y-85

Greene, Robert 1558-1592 .... DLB-62

Greenhow, Robert 1800-1854 .... DLB-30

Greenough, Horatio 1805-1852 .... DLB-1

Greenwell, Dora 1821-1882 .... DLB-35

Greenwillow Books DLB-46

Greenwood, Grace (see Lippincott, Sara Jane Clarke)

Greenwood, Walter 1903-1974 .... DLB-10

Greer, Ben 1948- DLB-6

Greg, W. R. 1809-1881 .... DLB-55

Gregg Press DLB-46

Persse, Isabella Augusta,
  Lady Gregory 1852-1932 .... DLB-10

Gregory, Horace 1898-1982 .... DLB-48

Greville, Fulke, First Lord Brooke
  1554-1628 .... DLB-62

Grey, Zane 1872-1939 .... DLB-9

Grieve, C. M. (see MacDiarmid, Hugh)

Griffith, Elizabeth 1727?-1793 .... DLB-39

Griffiths, Trevor 1935- DLB-13

Griggs, S. C., and Company DLB-49

Griggs, Sutton Elbert 1872-1930 .... DLB-50

Grignon, Claude-Henri 1894-1976 .... DLB-68

Grigson, Geoffrey 1905- DLB-27

Grimké, Angelina Weld 1880-1958 .... DLB-50, 54

Grimm, Hans 1875-1959 .... DLB-66

Griswold, Rufus Wilmot 1815-1857 .... DLB-3, 59

Gross, Milt 1895-1953 .... DLB-11

Grosset and Dunlap DLB-49

Grossman Publishers DLB-46

Groulx, Lionel 1878-1967 .... DLB-68

Grove Press DLB-46

Grubb, Davis 1919-1980 .... DLB-6

Gruelle, Johnny 1880-1938 .... DLB-22

Guare, John 1938- DLB-7

Guest, Barbara 1920- DLB-5

Guèvremont, Germaine 1893-1968 .... DLB-68

Guilloux, Louis 1899-1980 .... DLB-72

Guiney, Louise Imogen 1861-1920 .... DLB-54

Guiterman, Arthur 1871-1943 .... DLB-11

Gunn, Bill 1934- DLB-38

Gunn, James E. 1923- DLB-8

Gunn, Neil M. 1891-1973 .... DLB-15

Gunn, Thom 1929- DLB-27

Gunnars, Kristjana 1948- DLB-60

Gurik, Robert 1932- DLB-60

Gütersloh, Albert Paris 1887-1973 .... DLB-81

Guthrie, A. B., Jr. 1901- DLB-6

Guthrie, Ramon 1896-1973 .... DLB-4

The Guthrie Theater DLB-7

Guy, Ray 1939- DLB-60

Guy, Rosa 1925- DLB-33

Gwynne, Erskine 1898-1948 .... DLB-4

Gysin, Brion 1916- DLB-16

H

H. D. (see Doolittle, Hilda)

Hackett, Albert (see Goodrich, Frances)

Hagelstange, Rudolf 1912-1984 .... DLB-69

Haggard, H. Rider 1856-1925................. DLB-70

Hailey, Arthur 1920- Y-82

Haines, John 1924- DLB-5

Hake, Thomas Gordon 1809-1895 .... DLB-32

Haldeman, Joe 1943- DLB-8

Haldeman-Julius Company.................... DLB-46

Hale, E. J., and Son DLB-49

Hale, Edward Everett 1822-1909........DLB-1, 42, 74

Hale, Leo Thomas (see Ebon)

Hale, Lucretia Peabody 1820-1900 .... DLB-42

Hale, Nancy 1908-1988 ....Y-80, 88

Hale, Sarah Josepha (Buell) 1788-1879..DLB-1, 42, 73

Haley, Alex 1921- DLB-38

Haliburton, Thomas Chandler 1796-1865..... DLB-11

Hall, Donald 1928- DLB-5

Hall, James 1793-1868.....................DLB-73, 74

Hall, Samuel [publishing house]............... DLB-49

Hallam, Arthur Henry 1811-1833.............. DLB-32

Halleck, Fitz-Greene 1790-1867 ....DLB-3

Hallmark Editions DLB-46

Halper, Albert 1904-1984 ....DLB-9

Halstead, Murat 1829-1908.................... DLB-23

Hamburger, Michael 1924- DLB-27

Hamilton, Alexander 1712-1756............... DLB-31

Hamilton, Alexander 1755?-1804.............. DLB-37

Hamilton, Cicely 1872-1952 .... DLB-10

Hamilton, Edmond 1904-1977 ....DLB-8

Hamilton, Gail (see Corcoran, Barbara)

Hamilton, Ian 1938- DLB-40

Hamilton, Patrick 1904-1962 .... DLB-10

Hamilton, Virginia 1936- DLB-33, 52

Hammett, Dashiell 1894-1961 ....DS-6

Hammon, Jupiter 1711-died between
    1790 and 1806........................DLB-31, 50

Hammond, John ?-1663....................... DLB-24

Hamner, Earl 1923- DLB-6

Hampton, Christopher 1946- DLB-13

Handel-Mazzetti, Enrica von
    1871-1955................................ DLB-81

Handlin, Oscar 1915- DLB-17

Hankin, St. John 1869-1909................... DLB-10

Hanley, Clifford 1922- DLB-14

Hannah, Barry 1942- DLB-6

Hannay, James 1827-1873..................... DLB-21

Hansberry, Lorraine 1930-1965 ....DLB-7, 38

Harcourt Brace Jovanovich.................... DLB-46

Hardwick, Elizabeth 1916- DLB-6

Hardy, Thomas 1840-1928.................DLB-18, 19

Hare, Cyril 1900-1958......................... DLB-77

Hare, David 1947- DLB-13

Hargrove, Marion 1919- DLB-11

Harlow, Robert 1923- DLB-60

Harness, Charles L. 1915- DLB-8

Harper, Fletcher 1806-1877 .... DLB-79

Harper, Frances Ellen Watkins
    1825-1911................................. DLB-50

Harper, Michael S. 1938- DLB-41

Harper and Brothers......................... DLB-49

Harris, Benjamin ?-circa 1720 ....DLB-42, 43

Harris, George Washington 1814-1869......DLB-3, 11

Harris, Joel Chandler 1848-1908...DLB-11, 23, 42, 78

Harris, Mark 1922- DLB-2; Y-80

Harrison, Charles Yale 1898-1954............. DLB-68

Harrison, Frederic 1831-1923 .... DLB-57

Harrison, Harry 1925- DLB-8

Harrison, James P., Company DLB-49

Harrison, Jim 1937- Y-82

Harrison, Paul Carter 1936- DLB-38

Harrison, Tony 1937- DLB-40

Harrisse, Henry 1829-1910.................... DLB-47

Harsent, David 1942- DLB-40

Hart, Albert Bushnell 1854-1943 .... DLB-17

Hart, Moss 1904-1961 ....DLB-7

Hart, Oliver 1723-1795....................... DLB-31

Harte, Bret 1836-1902.............DLB-12, 64, 74, 79

Hartlaub, Felix 1913-1945	DLB-56
Hartley, L. P. 1895-1972	DLB-15
Hartley, Marsden 1877-1943	DLB-54
Härtling, Peter 1933-	DLB-75
Hartman, Geoffrey H. 1929-	DLB-67
Hartmann, Sadakichi 1867-1944	DLB-54
Harwood, Lee 1939-	DLB-40
Harwood, Ronald 1934-	DLB-13
Haskins, Charles Homer 1870-1937	DLB-47
The Hatch-Billops Collection	DLB-76
A Haughty and Proud Generation (1922), by Ford Madox Hueffer	DLB-36
Hauptmann, Carl 1858-1921	DLB-66
Hauptmann, Gerhart 1862-1946	DLB-66
Hauser, Marianne 1910-	Y-83
Hawker, Robert Stephen 1803-1875	DLB-32
Hawkes, John 1925-	DLB-2, 7; Y-80
Hawkins, Walter Everette 1883-?	DLB-50
Hawthorne, Nathaniel 1804-1864	DLB-1, 74
Hay, John 1838-1905	DLB-12, 47
Hayden, Robert 1913-1980	DLB-5, 76
Hayes, John Michael 1919-	DLB-26
Hayne, Paul Hamilton 1830-1886	DLB-3, 64, 79
Haywood, Eliza 1693?-1756	DLB-39
Hazard, Willis P. [publishing house]	DLB-49
Hazzard, Shirley 1931-	Y-82
Headley, Joel T. 1813-1897	DLB-30
Heaney, Seamus 1939-	DLB-40
Heard, Nathan C. 1936-	DLB-33
Hearn, Lafcadio 1850-1904	DLB-12, 78
Hearst, William Randolph 1863-1951	DLB-25
Heath, Catherine 1924-	DLB-14
Heath-Stubbs, John 1918-	DLB-27
Hébert, Anne 1916-	DLB-68
Hébert, Jacques 1923-	DLB-53
Hecht, Anthony 1923-	DLB-5
Hecht, Ben 1894-1964	DLB-7, 9, 25, 26, 28
Hecker, Isaac Thomas 1819-1888	DLB-1
Hedge, Frederic Henry 1805-1890	DLB-1, 59
Heidish, Marcy 1947-	Y-82
Heinlein, Robert A. 1907-	DLB-8
Heinrich, Willi 1920-	DLB-75
Heißenbüttel 1921-	DLB-75
Heller, Joseph 1923-	DLB-2, 28; Y-80
Hellman, Lillian 1906-1984	DLB-7; Y-84
Helprin, Mark 1947-	Y-85
Helwig, David 1938-	DLB-60
Hemingway, Ernest 1899-1961	DLB-4, 9; Y-81, 87; DS-1
Hemingway: Twenty-Five Years Later	Y-85
Hemphill, Paul 1936-	Y-87
Henchman, Daniel 1689-1761	DLB-24
Henderson, Alice Corbin 1881-1949	DLB-54
Henderson, David 1942-	DLB-41
Henderson, George Wylie 1904-	DLB-51
Henderson, Zenna 1917-	DLB-8
Henley, Beth 1952-	Y-86
Henley, William Ernest 1849-1903	DLB-19
Henry, Buck 1930-	DLB-26
Henry, Marguerite 1902-	DLB-22
Henry, Robert Selph 1889-1970	DLB-17
Henry, Will (see Allen, Henry W.)	
Henschke, Alfred (see Klabund)	
Henty, G. A. 1832-1902	DLB-18
Hentz, Caroline Lee 1800-1856	DLB-3
Herbert, Alan Patrick 1890-1971	DLB-10
Herbert, Frank 1920-1986	DLB-8
Herbert, Henry William 1807-1858	DLB-3, 73
Herbert, John 1926-	DLB-53
Herbst, Josephine 1892-1969	DLB-9
Herburger, Günter 1932-	DLB-75
Hercules, Frank E. M. 1917-	DLB-33
Herder, B., Book Company	DLB-49
Hergesheimer, Joseph 1880-1954	DLB-9
Heritage Press	DLB-46
Hermlin, Stephan 1915-	DLB-69
Hernton, Calvin C. 1932-	DLB-38
"The Hero as Man of Letters: Johnson, Rousseau, Burns" (1841), by Thomas Carlyle [excerpt]	DLB-57
The Hero as Poet. Dante; Shakspeare (1841),	

by Thomas Carlyle	DLB-32
Herrick, E. R., and Company	DLB-49
Herrick, Robert 1868-1938	DLB-9, 12, 78
Herrick, William 1915-	Y-83
Herrmann, John 1900-1959	DLB-4
Hersey, John 1914-	DLB-6
Hertel, François 1905-1985	DLB-68
Herzog, Emile Salomon Wilhelm (see Maurois, André)	
Hesse, Hermann 1877-1962	DLB-66
Hewat, Alexander circa 1743-circa 1824	DLB-30
Hewitt, John 1907-	DLB-27
Hewlett, Maurice 1861-1923	DLB-34
Heyen, William 1940-	DLB-5
Heyer, Georgette 1902-1974	DLB-77
Heym, Stefan 1913-	DLB-69
Heyward, Dorothy 1890-1961 and Heyward, DuBose 1885-1940	DLB-7
Heyward, DuBose 1885-1940	DLB-7, 9, 45
Heywood, Thomas 1573 or 1574-1641	DLB-62
Hiebert, Paul 1892-1987	DLB-68
Higgins, Aidan 1927-	DLB-14
Higgins, Colin 1941-1988	DLB-26
Higgins, George V. 1939-	DLB-2; Y-81
Higginson, Thomas Wentworth 1823-1911	DLB-1, 64
Highwater, Jamake 1942?-	DLB-52; Y-85
Hildesheimer, Wolfgang 1916-	DLB-69
Hildreth, Richard 1807-1865	DLB-1, 30, 59
Hill, Geoffrey 1932-	DLB-40
Hill, George M., Company	DLB-49
Hill, "Sir" John 1714?-1775	DLB-39
Hill, Lawrence, and Company, Publishers	DLB-46
Hill, Leslie 1880-1960	DLB-51
Hill, Susan 1942-	DLB-14
Hill, Walter 1942-	DLB-44
Hill and Wang	DLB-46
Hilliard, Gray and Company	DLB-49
Hillyer, Robert 1895-1961	DLB-54
Hilton, James 1900-1954	DLB-34, 77
Hilton and Company	DLB-49
Himes, Chester 1909-1984	DLB-2, 76
Hine, Daryl 1936-	DLB-60

The History of the Adventures of Joseph Andrews (1742), by Henry Fielding [excerpt]	DLB-39
Hirsch, E. D., Jr. 1928-	DLB-67
Hoagland, Edward 1932-	DLB-6
Hoagland, Everett H. III 1942-	DLB-41
Hoban, Russell 1925-	DLB-52
Hobsbaum, Philip 1932-	DLB-40
Hobson, Laura Z. 1900-	DLB-28
Hochman, Sandra 1936-	DLB-5
Hodgins, Jack 1938-	DLB-60
Hodgman, Helen 1945-	DLB-14
Hodgson, Ralph 1871-1962	DLB-19
Hodgson, William Hope 1877-1918	DLB-70
Hoffenstein, Samuel 1890-1947	DLB-11
Hoffman, Charles Fenno 1806-1884	DLB-3
Hoffman, Daniel 1923-	DLB-5
Hofmann, Michael 1957-	DLB-40
Hofmannsthal, Hugo von 1874-1929	DLB-81
Hofstadter, Richard 1916-1970	DLB-17
Hogan, Desmond 1950-	DLB-14
Hogan and Thompson	DLB-49
Hohl, Ludwig 1904-1980	DLB-56
Holbrook, David 1923-	DLB-14, 40
Holcroft, Thomas 1745-1809	DLB-39
Holden, Molly 1927-1981	DLB-40
Holiday House	DLB-46
Holland, Norman N. 1927-	DLB-67
Hollander, John 1929-	DLB-5
Holley, Marietta 1836-1926	DLB-11
Hollingsworth, Margaret 1940-	DLB-60
Hollo, Anselm 1934-	DLB-40
Holloway, John 1920-	DLB-27
Holloway House Publishing Company	DLB-46
Holme, Constance 1880-1955	DLB-34
Holmes, Oliver Wendell 1809-1894	DLB-1
Holmes, John Clellon 1926-1988	DLB-16
Holst, Hermann E. von 1841-1904	DLB-47
Holt, Henry, and Company	DLB-49
Holt, John 1721-1784	DLB-43
Holt, Rinehart and Winston	DLB-46

Cumulative Index

Holthusen, Hans Egon 1913- DLB-69
Home, Henry, Lord Kames 1696-1782 .... DLB-31
Home Publishing Company DLB-49
Home, William Douglas 1912- DLB-13
Homes, Geoffrey (see Mainwaring, Daniel)
Honig, Edwin 1919- DLB-5
Hood, Hugh 1928- DLB-53
Hooker, Jeremy 1941- DLB-40
Hooker, Thomas 1586-1647 .... DLB-24
Hooper, Johnson Jones 1815-1862 .... DLB-3, 11
Hopkins, Gerard Manley 1844-1889 .... DLB-35, 57
Hopkins, John H., and Son DLB-46
Hopkins, Lemuel 1750-1801 .... DLB-37
Hopkins, Pauline Elizabeth 1859-1930 .... DLB-50
Hopkins, Samuel 1721-1803 .... DLB-31
Hopkinson, Francis 1737-1791 .... DLB-31
Horgan, Paul 1903- Y-85
Horizon Press DLB-46
Horne, Frank 1899-1974 .... DLB-51
Horne, Richard Henry (Hengist) 1802
    or 1803-1884........................... DLB-32
Hornung, E. W. 1866-1921 .... DLB-70
Horovitz, Israel 1939- DLB-7
Horton, George Moses 1797?-1883? DLB-50
Horwood, Harold 1923- DLB-60
Hosford, E. and E. [publishing house] DLB-49
Hotchkiss and Company DLB-49
Hough, Emerson 1857-1923 .... DLB-9
Houghton Mifflin Company DLB-49
Houghton, Stanley 1881-1913 .... DLB-10
Housman, A. E. 1859-1936 .... DLB-19
Housman, Laurence 1865-1959 .... DLB-10
Hovey, Richard 1864-1900 .... DLB-54
Howard, Maureen 1930- Y-83
Howard, Richard 1929- DLB-5
Howard, Roy W. 1883-1964 .... DLB-29
Howard, Sidney 1891-1939 .... DLB-7, 26
Howe, E. W. 1853-1937 .... DLB-12, 25
Howe, Henry 1816-1893 .... DLB-30
Howe, Irving 1920- DLB-67

Howe, Julia Ward 1819-1910 .... DLB-1
Howell, Clark, Sr. 1863-1936 .... DLB-25
Howell, Evan P. 1839-1905 .... DLB-23
Howell, Soskin and Company DLB-46
Howells, William Dean 1837-1920 .. DLB-12, 64, 74, 79
Hoyem, Andrew 1935- DLB-5
Hoyt, Henry [publishing house] DLB-49
Hubbard, Kin 1868-1930 .... DLB-11
Hubbard, William circa 1621-1704 .... DLB-24
Huch, Friedrich 1873-1913 .... DLB-66
Huch, Ricarda 1864-1947 .... DLB-66
Huck at 100: How Old Is
    Huckleberry Finn? Y-85
Hudson, Henry Norman 1814-1886 .... DLB-64
Hudson and Goodwin DLB-49
Huebsch, B. W. [publishing house] DLB-46
Hughes, David 1930- DLB-14
Hughes, Langston 1902-1967 .... DLB-4, 7, 48, 51
Hughes, Richard 1900-1976 .... DLB-15
Hughes, Ted 1930- DLB-40
Hughes, Thomas 1822-1896 .... DLB-18
Hugo, Richard 1923-1982 .... DLB-5
Hugo Awards and Nebula Awards DLB-8
Hull, Richard 1896-1973 .... DLB-77
Hulme, T. E. 1883-1917 .... DLB-19
Hume, Fergus 1859-1932 .... DLB-70
Humorous Book Illustration DLB-11
Humphrey, William 1924- DLB-6
Humphreys, David 1752-1818 .... DLB-37
Humphreys, Emyr 1919- DLB-15
Huncke, Herbert 1915- DLB-16
Huneker, James Gibbons 1857-1921 .... DLB-71
Hunt, Irene 1907- DLB-52
Hunt, William Gibbes 1791-1833 .... DLB-73
Hunter, Evan 1926- Y-82
Hunter, Jim 1939- DLB-14
Hunter, Kristin 1931- DLB-33
Hunter, N. C. 1908-1971 .... DLB-10
Hurd and Houghton DLB-49
Hurst and Company DLB-49

Hurston, Zora Neale 1891-1960 .... DLB-51

Huston, John 1906- DLB-26

Hutcheson, Francis 1694-1746................ DLB-31

Hutchinson, Thomas 1711-1780........... DLB-30, 31

Hutton, Richard Holt 1826-1897 .... DLB-57

Huxley, Aldous 1894-1963 .... DLB-36

Huxley, Elspeth Josceline 1907- DLB-77

Huxley, T. H. 1825-1895..................... DLB-57

Hyman, Trina Schart 1939- DLB-61

I

The Iconography of Science-Fiction Art.........DLB-8

Ignatow, David 1914- DLB-5

Iles, Francis (see Berkeley, Anthony)

Imbs, Bravig 1904-1946 .... DLB-4

Inchbald, Elizabeth 1753-1821................ DLB-39

Inge, William 1913-1973 .... DLB-7

Ingelow, Jean 1820-1897 .... DLB-35

The Ingersoll Prizes Y-84

Ingraham, Joseph Holt 1809-1860 .... DLB-3

Inman, John 1805-1850 .... DLB-73

International Publishers Company............ DLB-46

An Interview with Peter S. Prescott............. Y-86

An Interview with Tom Jenks Y-86

Introduction to Paul Laurence Dunbar, *Lyrics of Lowly Life* (1896), by William Dean Howells DLB-50

Introductory Essay: *Letters of Percy Bysshe Shelley* (1852), by Robert Browning........ DLB-32

Introductory Letters from the Second Edition of *Pamela* (1741), by Samuel Richardson .. DLB-39

Irving, John 1942- DLB-6; Y-82

Irving, Washington 1783-1859.............. DLB-3, 11, 30, 59, 73, 74

Irwin, Grace 1907- DLB-68

Irwin, Will 1873-1948 .... DLB-25

Isherwood, Christopher 1904-1986...... DLB-15; Y-86

The Island Trees Case: A Symposium on School Library Censorship
An Interview with Judith Krug

An Interview with Phyllis Schlafly
An Interview with Edward B. Jenkinson
An Interview with Lamarr Mooneyham
An Interview with Harriet Bernstein..........Y-82

Ivers, M. J., and Company DLB-49

J

Jackmon, Marvin E. (see Marvin X)

Jackson, Angela 1951- DLB-41

Jackson, Helen Hunt 1830-1885............DLB-42, 47

Jackson, Laura Riding 1901- DLB-48

Jackson, Shirley 1919-1965 .... DLB-6

Jacob, Piers Anthony Dillingham (see Anthony, Piers)

Jacobs, George W., and Company DLB-49

Jacobson, Dan 1929- DLB-14

Jahnn, Hans Henny 1894-1959................ DLB-56

Jakes, John 1932- Y-83

James, Henry 1843-1916 .... DLB-12, 71, 74

James, John circa 1633-1729 .... DLB-24

James Joyce Centenary: Dublin, 1982 .... Y-82

James Joyce Conference Y-85

James, U. P. [publishing house] DLB-49

Jameson, Fredric 1934- DLB-67

Jameson, J. Franklin 1859-1937 .... DLB-17

Jameson, Storm 1891-1986 .... DLB-36

Jarrell, Randall 1914-1965................DLB-48, 52

Jasmin, Claude 1930- DLB-60

Jay, John 1745-1829......................... DLB-31

Jeffers, Lance 1919-1985 .... DLB-41

Jeffers, Robinson 1887-1962................... DLB-45

Jefferson, Thomas 1743-1826 .... DLB-31

Jellicoe, Ann 1927- DLB-13

Jenkins, Robin 1912- DLB-14

Jenkins, William Fitzgerald (see Leinster, Murray)

Jennings, Elizabeth 1926- DLB-27

Jens, Walter 1923- DLB-69

Jensen, Merrill 1905-1980 .... DLB-17

Jerome, Jerome K. 1859-1927..............DLB-10, 34

Jesse, F. Tennyson 1888-1958 .... DLB-77

Jewett, John P., and Company................. DLB-49
Jewett, Sarah Orne 1849-1909..............DLB-12, 74
The Jewish Publication Society DLB-49
Jewsbury, Geraldine 1812-1880................ DLB-21
Joans, Ted 1928- DLB-16, 41
John Edward Bruce: Three Documents DLB-50
John O'Hara's Pottsville Journalism Y-88
John Steinbeck Research Center...................Y-85
John Webster: The Melbourne Manuscript........Y-86
Johnson, B. S. 1933-1973...................DLB-14, 40
Johnson, Benjamin [publishing house] DLB-49
Johnson, Benjamin, Jacob, and
 Robert [publishing house]................. DLB-49
Johnson, Charles R. 1948- DLB-33
Johnson, Charles S. 1893-1956 .... DLB-51
Johnson, Diane 1934- Y-80
Johnson, Edward 1598-1672................... DLB-24
Johnson, Fenton 1888-1958 ....DLB-45, 50
Johnson, Georgia Douglas 1886-1966 .... DLB-51
Johnson, Gerald W. 1890-1980................ DLB-29
Johnson, Helene 1907- DLB-51
Johnson, Jacob, and Company................. DLB-49
Johnson, James Weldon 1871-1938............ DLB-51
Johnson, Lionel 1867-1902 .... DLB-19
Johnson, Nunnally 1897-1977 .... DLB-26
Johnson, Owen 1878-1952.......................Y-87
Johnson, Pamela Hansford 1912- DLB-15
Johnson, Samuel 1696-1772................... DLB-24
Johnson, Samuel 1709-1784 .... DLB-39
Johnson, Samuel 1822-1882 ....DLB-1
Johnson, Uwe 1934-1984..................... DLB-75
Johnston, Annie Fellows 1863-1931 .... DLB-42
Johnston, Basil H. 1929- DLB-60
Johnston, Denis 1901-1984 .... DLB-10
Johnston, Jennifer 1930- DLB-14
Johnston, Mary 1870-1936 ....DLB-9
Johnston, Richard Malcolm 1822-1898 .... DLB-74
Johnstone, Charles 1719?-1800?.............. DLB-39
Jolas, Eugene 1894-1952 ....DLB-4, 45
Jones, Charles C., Jr. 1831-1893............... DLB-30

Jones, D. G. 1929- DLB-53
Jones, David 1895-1974 .... DLB-20
Jones, Ebenezer 1820-1860................... DLB-32
Jones, Ernest 1819-1868...................... DLB-32
Jones, Gayl 1949- DLB-33
Jones, Glyn 1905- DLB-15
Jones, Gwyn 1907- DLB-15
Jones, Henry Arthur 1851-1929................ DLB-10
Jones, Hugh circa 1692-1760.................. DLB-24
Jones, James 1921-1977 ....DLB-2
Jones, LeRoi (see Baraka, Amiri)
Jones, Lewis 1897-1939....................... DLB-15
Jones, Major Joseph (see Thompson, William
 Tappan)
Jones, Preston 1936-1979.......................DLB-7
Jones, William Alfred 1817-1900 .... DLB-59
Jones's Publishing House DLB-49
Jong, Erica 1942- DLB-2, 5, 28
Jonson, Ben 1572?-1637...................... DLB-62
Jordan, June 1936- DLB-38
Joseph, Jenny 1932- DLB-40
Josephson, Matthew 1899-1978..................DLB-4
Josiah Allen's Wife (see Holley, Marietta)
Josipovici, Gabriel 1940- DLB-14
Josselyn, John ?-1675......................... DLB-24
Joyce, Adrien (see Eastman, Carol)
Joyce, James 1882-1941 ....DLB-10, 19, 36
Judd, Orange, Publishing Company........... DLB-49
Judd, Sylvester 1813-1853......................DLB-1
June, Jennie (see Croly, Jane Cunningham)
Jünger, Ernst 1895- DLB-56
Justice, Donald 1925- Y-83

K

Kafka, Franz 1883-1924...................... DLB-81
Kalechofsky, Roberta 1931- DLB-28
Kaler, James Otis 1848-1912 .... DLB-12
Kandel, Lenore 1932- DLB-16
Kanin, Garson 1912- DLB-7

Kant, Hermann 1926-	DLB-75
Kantor, Mackinlay 1904-1977	DLB-9
Kaplan, Johanna 1942-	DLB-28
Kasack, Hermann 1896-1966	DLB-69
Kaschnitz, Marie Luise 1901-1974	DLB-69
Kästner, Erich 1899-1974	DLB-56
Kattan, Naim 1928-	DLB-53
Katz, Steve 1935-	Y-83
Kauffman, Janet 1945-	Y-86
Kaufman, Bob 1925-	DLB-16, 41
Kaufman, George S. 1889-1961	DLB-7
Kavanagh, Patrick 1904-1967	DLB-15, 20
Kavanagh, P. J. 1931-	DLB-40
Kaye-Smith, Sheila 1887-1956	DLB-36
Kazin, Alfred 1915-	DLB-67
Keane, John B. 1928-	DLB-13
Keats, Ezra Jack 1916-1983	DLB-61
Keble, John 1792-1866	DLB-32, 55
Keeble, John 1944-	Y-83
Keeffe, Barrie 1945-	DLB-13
Keeley, James 1867-1934	DLB-25
W. B. Keen, Cooke and Company	DLB-49
Keillor, Garrison 1942-	Y-87
Kelley, Edith Summers 1884-1956	DLB-9
Kelley, William Melvin 1937-	DLB-33
Kellogg, Ansel Nash 1832-1886	DLB-23
Kellogg, Steven 1941-	DLB-61
Kelly, George 1887-1974	DLB-7
Kelly, Piet and Company	DLB-49
Kelly, Robert 1935-	DLB-5
Kemble, Fanny 1809-1893	DLB-32
Kemelman, Harry 1908-	DLB-28
Kempowski, Walter 1929-	DLB-75
Kendall, Claude [publishing company]	DLB-46
Kendell, George 1809-1867	DLB-43
Kenedy, P. J., and Sons	DLB-49
Kennedy, Adrienne 1931-	DLB-38
Kennedy, John Pendleton 1795-1870	DLB-3
Kennedy, Margaret 1896-1967	DLB-36
Kennedy, William 1928-	Y-85
Kennedy, X. J. 1929-	DLB-5
Kennelly, Brendan 1936-	DLB-40
Kenner, Hugh 1923-	DLB-67
Kennerley, Mitchell [publishing house]	DLB-46
Kent, Frank R. 1877-1958	DLB-29
Keppler and Schwartzmann	DLB-49
Kerouac, Jack 1922-1969	DLB-2, 16; DS-3
Kerouac, Jan 1952-	DLB-16
Kerr, Charles H., and Company	DLB-49
Kerr, Orpheus C. (see Newell, Robert Henry)	
Kesey, Ken 1935-	DLB-2, 16
Kessel, Joseph 1898-1979	DLB-72
Kessel, Martin 1901-	DLB-56
Kesten, Hermann 1900-	DLB-56
Keun, Irmgard 1905-1982	DLB-69
Key and Biddle	DLB-49
Keyserling, Eduard von 1855-1918	DLB-66
Kiely, Benedict 1919-	DLB-15
Kiggins and Kellogg	DLB-49
Kiley, Jed 1889-1962	DLB-4
Killens, John Oliver 1916-	DLB-33
Killigrew, Thomas 1612-1683	DLB-58
Kilmer, Joyce 1886-1918	DLB-45
King, Clarence 1842-1901	DLB-12
King, Florence 1936	Y-85
King, Francis 1923-	DLB-15
King, Grace 1852-1932	DLB-12, 78
King, Solomon [publishing house]	DLB-49
King, Stephen 1947-	Y-80
King, Woodie, Jr. 1937-	DLB-38
Kinglake, Alexander William 1809-1891	DLB-55
Kingsley, Charles 1819-1875	DLB-21, 32
Kingsley, Henry 1830-1876	DLB-21
Kingsley, Sidney 1906-	DLB-7
Kingston, Maxine Hong 1940-	Y-80
Kinnell, Galway 1927-	DLB-5; Y-87
Kinsella, Thomas 1928-	DLB-27
Kipling, Rudyard 1865-1936	DLB-19, 34
Kirk, John Foster 1824-1904	DLB-79
Kirkconnell, Watson 1895-1977	DLB-68

Kirkland, Caroline M. 1801-1864 .... DLB-3, 73, 74

Kirkland, Joseph 1830-1893 .... DLB-12

Kirkup, James 1918- DLB-27

Kirsch, Sarah 1935- DLB-75

Kirst, Hans Hellmut 1914- DLB-69

Kitchin, C. H. B. 1895-1967 .... DLB-77

Kizer, Carolyn 1925- DLB-5

Klabund 1890-1928 .... DLB-66

Klappert, Peter 1942- DLB-5

Klass, Philip (see Tenn, William)

Klein, A. M. 1909-1972 .... DLB-68

Kluge, Alexander 1932- DLB-75

Knapp, Samuel Lorenzo 1783-1838 .... DLB-59

Knickerbocker, Diedrich (see Irving, Washington)

Knight, Damon 1922- DLB-8

Knight, Etheridge 1931- DLB-41

Knight, John S. 1894-1981 .... DLB-29

Knight, Sarah Kemble 1666-1727 .... DLB-24

Knister, Raymond 1899-1932 .... DLB-68

Knoblock, Edward 1874-1945 .... DLB-10

Knopf, Alfred A. 1892-1984 .... Y-84

Knopf, Alfred A. [publishing house] DLB-46

Knowles, John 1926- DLB-6

Knox, Frank 1874-1944 .... DLB-29

Knox, John Armoy 1850-1906 .... DLB-23

Knox, Ronald Arbuthnott 1888-1957 .... DLB-77

Kober, Arthur 1900-1975 .... DLB-11

Koch, Howard 1902- DLB-26

Koch, Kenneth 1925- DLB-5

Koenigsberg, Moses 1879-1945 .... DLB-25

Koeppen, Wolfgang 1906- DLB-69

Koestler, Arthur 1905-1983 .... Y-83

Kolb, Annette 1870-1967 .... DLB-66

Kolbenheyer, Erwin Guido 1878-1962 .... DLB-66

Kolodny, Annette 1941- DLB-67

Komroff, Manuel 1890-1974 .... DLB-4

Konigsburg, E. L. 1930- DLB-52

Kopit, Arthur 1937- DLB-7

Kops, Bernard 1926?- DLB-13

Kornbluth, C. M. 1923-1958 .... DLB-8

Kosinski, Jerzy 1933- DLB-2; Y-82

Kraf, Elaine 1946- Y-81

Krasna, Norman 1909-1984 .... DLB-26

Krauss, Ruth 1911- DLB-52

Kreuder, Ernst 1903-1972 .... DLB-69

Kreymborg, Alfred 1883-1966 .... DLB-4, 54

Krieger, Murray 1923- DLB-67

Krim, Seymour 1922- DLB-16

Krock, Arthur 1886-1974 .... DLB-29

Kroetsch, Robert 1927- DLB-53

Krutch, Joseph Wood 1893-1970 .... DLB-63

Kubin, Alfred 1877-1959 .... DLB-81

Kubrick, Stanley 1928- DLB-26

Kumin, Maxine 1925- DLB-5

Kunnert, Günter 1929- DLB-75

Kunitz, Stanley 1905- DLB-48

Kunjufu, Johari M. (see Amini, Johari M.)

Kunze, Reiner 1933- DLB-75

Kupferberg, Tuli 1923- DLB-16

Kurz, Isolde 1853-1944 .... DLB-66

Kusenberg, Kurt 1904-1983 .... DLB-69

Kuttner, Henry 1915-1958 .... DLB-8

Kyd, Thomas 1558-1594 .... DLB-62

Kyger, Joanne 1934- DLB-16

Kyne, Peter B. 1880-1957 .... DLB-78

L

Laberge, Albert 1871-1960 .... DLB-68

Laberge, Marie 1950- DLB-60

Lacretelle, Jacques de 1888-1985 .... DLB-65

Ladd, Joseph Brown 1764-1786 .... DLB-37

La Farge, Oliver 1901-1963 .... DLB-9

Lafferty, R. A. 1914- DLB-8

Laird, Carobeth 1895- Y-82

Laird and Lee DLB-49

Lalonde, Michèle 1937- DLB-60

Lamantia, Philip 1927- DLB-16

Lambert, Betty 1933-1983 .... DLB-60

L'Amour, Louis 1908?-	Y-80
Lamson, Wolffe and Company	DLB-49
Lancer Books	DLB-46
Landesman, Jay 1919- and Landesman, Fran 1927-	DLB-16
Lane, Charles 1800-1870	DLB-1
The John Lane Company	DLB-49
Lane, M. Travis 1934-	DLB-60
Lane, Patrick 1939-	DLB-53
Lane, Pinkie Gordon 1923-	DLB-41
Laney, Al 1896-	DLB-4
Langevin, André 1927-	DLB-60
Langgässer, Elisabeth 1899-1950	DLB-69
Lanham, Edwin 1904-1979	DLB-4
Lanier, Sidney 1842-1881	DLB-64
Lardner, Ring 1885-1933	DLB-11, 25
Lardner, Ring, Jr. 1915-	DLB-26
Lardner 100: Ring Lardner Centennial Symposium	Y-85
Larkin, Philip 1922-1985	DLB-27
La Rocque, Gilbert 1943-1984	DLB-60
Laroque de Roquebrune, Robert (see Roquebrune, Robert de)	
Larrick, Nancy 1910-	DLB-61
Larsen, Nella 1893-1964	DLB-51
Lasker-Schüler, Else 1869-1945	DLB-66
Lathrop, Dorothy P. 1891-1980	DLB-22
Lathrop, George Parsons 1851-1898	DLB-71
Lathrop, John, Jr. 1772-1820	DLB-37
Latimore, Jewel Christine McLawler (see Amini, Johari M.)	
Laughlin, James 1914-	DLB-48
Laumer, Keith 1925-	DLB-8
Laurence, Margaret 1926-1987	DLB-53
Laurents, Arthur 1918-	DLB-26
Laurie, Annie (see Black, Winifred)	
Lavin, Mary 1912-	DLB-15
Lawless, Anthony (see MacDonald, Philip)	
Lawrence, David 1888-1973	DLB-29
Lawrence, D. H. 1885-1930	DLB-10, 19, 36
Lawson, John ?-1711	DLB-24

Lawson, Robert 1892-1957	DLB-22
Lawson, Victor F. 1850-1925	DLB-25
Lea, Henry Charles 1825-1909	DLB-47
Lea, Tom 1907-	DLB-6
Leacock, John 1729-1802	DLB-31
Lear, Edward 1812-1888	DLB-32
Leary, Timothy 1920-	DLB-16
Leary, W. A., and Company	DLB-49
Léautaud, Paul 1872-1956	DLB-65
Leavitt and Allen	DLB-49
Lécavelé, Roland (see Dorgelès, Roland)	
Lechlitner, Ruth 1901-	DLB-48
Leclerc, Félix 1914-	DLB-60
Lectures on Rhetoric and Belles Lettres (1783), by Hugh Blair [excerpts]	DLB-31
Leder, Rudolf (see Hermlin, Stephan)	
Lederer, Charles 1910-1976	DLB-26
Ledwidge, Francis 1887-1917	DLB-20
Lee, Dennis 1939-	DLB-53
Lee, Don L. (see Madhubuti, Haki R.)	
Lee, George W. 1894-1976	DLB-51
Lee, Harper 1926-	DLB-6
Lee, Harriet (1757-1851) and Lee, Sophia (1750-1824)	DLB-39
Lee, Laurie 1914-	DLB-27
Lee, Nathaniel circa 1645 - 1692	DLB-80
Lee, Vernon 1856-1935	DLB-57
Lee and Shepard	DLB-49
Le Fanu, Joseph Sheridan 1814-1873	DLB-21, 70
Leffland, Ella 1931-	Y-84
le Fort, Gertrud von 1876-1971	DLB-66
Le Gallienne, Richard 1866-1947	DLB-4
Legaré, Hugh Swinton 1797-1843	DLB-3, 59, 73
Legaré, James M. 1823-1859	DLB-3
Le Guin, Ursula K. 1929-	DLB-8, 52
Lehman, Ernest 1920-	DLB-44
Lehmann, John 1907-	DLB-27
Lehmann, Rosamond 1901-	DLB-15
Lehmann, Wilhelm 1882-1968	DLB-56
Leiber, Fritz 1910-	DLB-8
Leinster, Murray 1896-1975	DLB-8

Leitch, Maurice 1933-	DLB-14
Leland, Charles G. 1824-1903	DLB-11
L'Engle, Madeleine 1918-	DLB-52
Lennart, Isobel 1915-1971	DLB-44
Lennox, Charlotte 1729 or 1730-1804	DLB-39
Lenski, Lois 1893-1974	DLB-22
Lenz, Hermann 1913-	DLB-69
Lenz, Siegfried 1926-	DLB-75
Leonard, Hugh 1926-	DLB-13
Leonard, William Ellery 1876-1944	DLB-54
Le Queux, William 1864-1927	DLB-70
Lerner, Max 1902-	DLB-29
LeSieg, Theo. (see Geisel, Theodor Seuss)	
Leslie, Frank 1821-1880	DLB-43, 79
The Frank Leslie Publishing House	DLB-49
Lessing, Bruno 1870-1940	DLB-28
Lessing, Doris 1919-	DLB-15; Y-85
Lettau, Reinhard 1929-	DLB-75
Letter to [Samuel] Richardson on *Clarissa* (1748), by Henry Fielding	DLB-39
Lever, Charles 1806-1872	DLB-21
Levertov, Denise 1923-	DLB-5
Levi, Peter 1931-	DLB-40
Levien, Sonya 1888-1960	DLB-44
Levin, Meyer 1905-1981	DLB-9, 28; Y-81
Levine, Philip 1928-	DLB-5
Levy, Benn Wolfe 1900-1973	DLB-13; Y-81
Lewes, George Henry 1817-1878	DLB-55
Lewis, Alfred H. 1857-1914	DLB-25
Lewis, Alun 1915-1944	DLB-20
Lewis, C. Day (see Day Lewis, C.)	
Lewis, Charles B. 1842-1924	DLB-11
Lewis, C. S. 1898-1963	DLB-15
Lewis, Henry Clay 1825-1850	DLB-3
Lewis, Janet 1899-	Y-87
Lewis, Matthew Gregory 1775-1818	DLB-39
Lewis, Richard circa 1700-1734	DLB-24
Lewis, Sinclair 1885-1951	DLB-9; DS-1
Lewis, Wyndham 1882-1957	DLB-15
Lewisohn, Ludwig 1882-1955	DLB-4, 9, 28
The Library of America	DLB-46
Liebling, A. J. 1904-1963	DLB-4
Lieutenant Murray (see Ballou, Maturin Murray)	
Lilly, Wait and Company	DLB-49
Limited Editions Club	DLB-46
Lincoln and Edmands	DLB-49
Lindsay, Jack 1900-	Y-84
Lindsay, Vachel 1879-1931	DLB-54
Linebarger, Paul Myron Anthony (see Smith, Cordwainer)	
Link, Arthur S. 1920-	DLB-17
Linn, John Blair 1777-1804	DLB-37
Linton, Eliza Lynn 1822-1898	DLB-18
Linton, William James 1812-1897	DLB-32
Lion Books	DLB-46
Lionni, Leo 1910-	DLB-61
Lippincott, J. B., Company	DLB-49
Lippincott, Sara Jane Clarke 1823-1904	DLB-43
Lippmann, Walter 1889-1974	DLB-29
Lipton, Lawrence 1898-1975	DLB-16
Literary Documents: William Faulkner and the People-to-People Program	Y-86
Literary Documents II: *Library Journal*— Statements and Questionnaires from First Novelists	Y-87
Literary Effects of World War II [British novel]	DLB-15
Literary Prizes [British]	DLB-15
Literary Research Archives: The Humanities Research Center, University of Texas	Y-82
Literary Research Archives II: Berg Collection of English and American Literature of the New York Public Library	Y-83
Literary Research Archives III: The Lilly Library	Y-84
Literary Research Archives IV: The John Carter Brown Library	Y-85
Literary Research Archives V: Kent State Special Collections	Y-86
Literary Research Archives VI: The Modern Literary Manuscripts Collection in the Special Collections of the Washington University Libraries	Y-87

"Literary Style" (1857), by William
    Forsyth [excerpt] DLB-57
Literature at Nurse, or Circulating Morals (1885),
    by George Moore DLB-18
Littell, Eliakim 1797-1870 .... DLB-79
Littell, Robert S. 1831-1896 .... DLB-79
Little, Brown and Company DLB-49
Littlewood, Joan 1914- DLB-13
Lively, Penelope 1933- DLB-14
Livesay, Dorothy 1909- DLB-68
Livings, Henry 1929- DLB-13
Livingston, Anne Howe 1763-1841 .... DLB-37
Livingston, Myra Cohn 1926- DLB-61
Livingston, William 1723-1790 .... DLB-31
Llewellyn, Richard 1906-1983 .... DLB-15
Lobel, Arnold 1933- DLB-61
Lochridge, Betsy Hopkins (see Fancher, Betsy)
Locke, David Ross 1833-1888 .... DLB-11, 23
Locke, John 1632-1704 .... DLB-31
Locke, Richard Adams 1800-1871 .... DLB-43
Locker-Lampson, Frederick 1821-1895 .... DLB-35
Lockridge, Ross, Jr. 1914-1948 .... Y-80
Locrine and *Selimus* DLB-62
Lodge, David 1935- DLB-14
Lodge, George Cabot 1873-1909 .... DLB-54
Lodge, Henry Cabot 1850-1924 .... DLB-47
Loeb, Harold 1891-1974 .... DLB-4
Logan, James 1674-1751 .... DLB-24
Logan, John 1923- DLB-5
Logue, Christopher 1926- DLB-27
London, Jack 1876-1916 .... DLB-8, 12, 78
Long, H., and Brother DLB-49
Long, Haniel 1888-1956 .... DLB-45
Longfellow, Henry Wadsworth 1807-1882 ... DLB-1, 59
Longfellow, Samuel 1819-1892 .... DLB-1
Longley, Michael 1939- DLB-40
Longmans, Green and Company DLB-49
Longstreet, Augustus Baldwin
    1790-1870 .... DLB-3, 11, 74
Longworth, D. [publishing house] DLB-49
Lonsdale, Frederick 1881-1954 .... DLB-10

A Look at the Cont. Black Theatre Movement..DLB-38
Loos, Anita 1893-1981 .... DLB-11, 26; Y-81
Lopate, Phillip 1943- Y-80
The Lord Chamberlain's Office and Stage
    Censorship in England DLB-10
Lorde, Audre 1934- DLB-41
Loring, A. K. [publishing house] DLB-49
Loring and Mussey DLB-46
Lossing, Benson J. 1813-1891 .... DLB-30
Lothar, Ernst 1890-1974 .... DLB-81
Lothrop, D., and Company DLB-49
Lothrop, Harriet M. 1844-1924 .... DLB-42
The Lounger, no. 20 (1785), by Henry
    Mackenzie DLB-39
Lounsbury, Thomas R. 1838-1915 .... DLB-71
Lovell, John W., Company DLB-49
Lovell, Coryell and Company DLB-49
Lovingood, Sut (see Harris, George Washington)
Low, Samuel 1765-? DLB-37
Lowell, Amy 1874-1925 .... DLB-54
Lowell, James Russell 1819-1891 .... DLB-1, 11, 64, 79
Lowell, Robert 1917-1977 .... DLB-5
Lowenfels, Walter 1897-1976 .... DLB-4
Lowndes, Marie Belloc 1868-1947 .... DLB-70
Lowry, Lois 1937- DLB-52
Lowry, Malcolm 1909-1957 .... DLB-15
Lowther, Pat 1935-1975 .... DLB-53
Loy, Mina 1882-1966 .... DLB-4, 54
Lucas, Fielding, Jr. [publishing house] DLB-49
Luce, John W., and Company DLB-46
Lucie-Smith, Edward 1933- DLB-40
Ludlum, Robert 1927- Y-82
Ludwig, Jack 1922- DLB-60
Luke, Peter 1919- DLB-13
The F. M. Lupton Publishing Company DLB-49
Lurie, Alison 1926- DLB-2
Lyly, John circa 1554-1606 .... DLB-62
Lyon, Matthew 1749-1822 .... DLB-43
Lytle, Andrew 1902- DLB-6
Lytton, Edward (see Bulwer-Lytton, Edward)
Lytton, Edward Robert Bulwer 1831-1891 .... DLB-32

Cumulative Index

M

Maass, Joachim 1901-1972.....................DLB-69

Mabie, Hamilton Wright 1845-1916...........DLB-71

Mac A'Ghobhainn, Iain (see Smith, Iain Crichton)

MacArthur, Charles 1895-1956..........DLB-7, 25, 44

Macaulay, David 1945- DLB-61

Macaulay, Rose 1881-1958.....................DLB-36

Macaulay, Thomas Babington 1800-1859...DLB-32, 55

Macaulay Company............................DLB-46

MacBeth, George 1932- DLB-40

MacCaig, Norman 1910- DLB-27

MacDiarmid, Hugh 1892-1978 ....DLB-20

MacDonald, George 1824-1905................DLB-18

MacDonald, John D. 1916-1986 ....DLB-8; Y-86

MacDonald, Philip 1899?-1980 ....DLB-77

Macdonald, Ross (see Millar, Kenneth)

MacEwen, Gwendolyn 1941- DLB-53

Macfadden, Bernarr 1868-1955 ....DLB-25

Machen, Arthur Llewelyn Jones 1863-1947 ... DLB-36

MacInnes, Colin 1914-1976....................DLB-14

MacKaye, Percy 1875-1956 ....DLB-54

Macken, Walter 1915-1967 ....DLB-13

Mackenzie, Compton 1883-1972...............DLB-34

Mackenzie, Henry 1745-1831..................DLB-39

Mackey, William Wellington 1937- DLB-38

Mackintosh, Elizabeth (see Tey, Josephine)

MacLean, Katherine Anne 1925- DLB-8

MacLeish, Archibald 1892-1982 ....DLB-4, 7, 45; Y-82

MacLennan, Hugh 1907- DLB-68

MacLeod, Alistair 1936- DLB-60

Macleod, Norman 1906- DLB-4

The Macmillan Company.....................DLB-49

MacNamara, Brinsley 1890-1963 ....DLB-10

MacNeice, Louis 1907-1963 ....DLB-10, 20

Macpherson, Jay 1931- DLB-53

Macpherson, Jeanie 1884-1946 ....DLB-44

Macrae Smith Company.......................DLB-46

Macy-Masius................................DLB-46

Madden, David 1933-........................DLB-6

Maddow, Ben 1909- DLB-44

Madgett, Naomi Long 1923- DLB-76

Madhubuti, Haki R. 1942- DLB-5, 41

Madison, James 1751-1836....................DLB-37

Mahan, Alfred Thayer 1840-1914............DLB-47

Maheux-Forcier, Louise 1929- DLB-60

Mahin, John Lee 1902-1984...................DLB-44

Mahon, Derek 1941- DLB-40

Mailer, Norman 1923-
........................DLB-2, 16, 28; Y-80, 83; DS-3

Maillet, Adrienne 1885-1963 ....DLB-68

Maillet, Antonine 1929- DLB-60

Main Selections of the Book-of-the-Month Club,
    1926-1945................................DLB-9

Main Trends in Twentieth-Century
    Book Clubs...............................DLB-46

Mainwaring, Daniel 1902-1977 ....DLB-44

Major, André 1942- DLB-60

Major, Clarence 1936- DLB-33

Major, Kevin 1949- DLB-60

Major Books................................DLB-46

Makemie, Francis circa 1658-1708............DLB-24

Malamud, Bernard 1914-1986.....DLB-2, 28; Y-80, 86

Malleson, Lucy Beatrice (see Gilbert, Anthony)

Mallock, W. H. 1849-1923..................DLB-18, 57

Malone, Dumas 1892-1986 ....DLB-17

Malraux, André 1901-1976....................DLB-72

Malzberg, Barry N. 1939- DLB-8

Mamet, David 1947- DLB-7

Mandel, Eli 1922- DLB-53

Manfred, Frederick 1912- DLB-6

Mangan, Sherry 1904-1961....................DLB-4

Mankiewicz, Herman 1897-1953...............DLB-26

Mankiewicz, Joseph L. 1909- DLB-44

Mankowitz, Wolf 1924- DLB-15

Manley, Delarivière 1672?-1724 ....DLB-39, 80

Mann, Abby 1927- DLB-44

Mann, Heinrich 1871-1950....................DLB-66

Mann, Horace 1796-1859......................DLB-1

Mann, Klaus 1906-1949 ....DLB-56

"Literary Style" (1857), by William
    Forsyth [excerpt].......................... DLB-57

Literature at Nurse, or Circulating Morals (1885),
    by George Moore DLB-18

Littell, Eliakim 1797-1870 .... DLB-79

Littell, Robert S. 1831-1896 .... DLB-79

Little, Brown and Company DLB-49

Littlewood, Joan 1914- DLB-13

Lively, Penelope 1933- DLB-14

Livesay, Dorothy 1909- DLB-68

Livings, Henry 1929- DLB-13

Livingston, Anne Howe 1763-1841 .... DLB-37

Livingston, Myra Cohn 1926- DLB-61

Livingston, William 1723-1790 .... DLB-31

Llewellyn, Richard 1906-1983 .... DLB-15

Lobel, Arnold 1933- DLB-61

Lochridge, Betsy Hopkins (see Fancher, Betsy)

Locke, David Ross 1833-1888............... DLB-11, 23

Locke, John 1632-1704 .... DLB-31

Locke, Richard Adams 1800-1871 .... DLB-43

Locker-Lampson, Frederick 1821-1895 .... DLB-35

Lockridge, Ross, Jr. 1914-1948 ....Y-80

Locrine and *Selimus*............................ DLB-62

Lodge, David 1935- DLB-14

Lodge, George Cabot 1873-1909 .... DLB-54

Lodge, Henry Cabot 1850-1924 .... DLB-47

Loeb, Harold 1891-1974....................... DLB-4

Logan, James 1674-1751 .... DLB-24

Logan, John 1923- DLB-5

Logue, Christopher 1926- DLB-27

London, Jack 1876-1916................. DLB-8, 12, 78

Long, H., and Brother DLB-49

Long, Haniel 1888-1956...................... DLB-45

Longfellow, Henry Wadsworth 1807-1882...DLB-1, 59

Longfellow, Samuel 1819-1892 ....DLB-1

Longley, Michael 1939- DLB-40

Longmans, Green and Company DLB-49

Longstreet, Augustus Baldwin
    1790-1870........................DLB-3, 11, 74

Longworth, D. [publishing house] DLB-49

Lonsdale, Frederick 1881-1954 .... DLB-10

A Look at the Cont. Black Theatre Movement..DLB-38

Loos, Anita 1893-1981............... DLB-11, 26; Y-81

Lopate, Phillip 1943- Y-80

The Lord Chamberlain's Office and Stage
    Censorship in England..................... DLB-10

Lorde, Audre 1934- DLB-41

Loring, A. K. [publishing house] DLB-49

Loring and Mussey DLB-46

Lossing, Benson J. 1813-1891 .... DLB-30

Lothar, Ernst 1890-1974....................... DLB-81

Lothrop, D., and Company.................... DLB-49

Lothrop, Harriet M. 1844-1924 .... DLB-42

The Lounger, no. 20 (1785), by Henry
    Mackenzie.................................. DLB-39

Lounsbury, Thomas R. 1838-1915.............. DLB-71

Lovell, John W., Company DLB-49

Lovell, Coryell and Company.................. DLB-49

Lovingood, Sut (see Harris, George Washington)

Low, Samuel 1765-? DLB-37

Lowell, Amy 1874-1925 .... DLB-54

Lowell, James Russell 1819-1891 .... DLB-1, 11, 64, 79

Lowell, Robert 1917-1977 ....DLB-5

Lowenfels, Walter 1897-1976...................DLB-4

Lowndes, Marie Belloc 1868-1947 .... DLB-70

Lowry, Lois 1937- DLB-52

Lowry, Malcolm 1909-1957.................... DLB-15

Lowther, Pat 1935-1975 .... DLB-53

Loy, Mina 1882-1966........................DLB-4, 54

Lucas, Fielding, Jr. [publishing house]......... DLB-49

Luce, John W., and Company DLB-46

Lucie-Smith, Edward 1933- DLB-40

Ludlum, Robert 1927- Y-82

Ludwig, Jack 1922- DLB-60

Luke, Peter 1919- DLB-13

The F. M. Lupton Publishing Company DLB-49

Lurie, Alison 1926- DLB-2

Lyly, John circa 1554-1606 .... DLB-62

Lyon, Matthew 1749-1822..................... DLB-43

Lytle, Andrew 1902- DLB-6

Lytton, Edward (see Bulwer-Lytton, Edward)

Lytton, Edward Robert Bulwer 1831-1891 .... DLB-32

M

Maass, Joachim 1901-1972.....................DLB-69

Mabie, Hamilton Wright 1845-1916...........DLB-71

Mac A'Ghobhainn, Iain (see Smith, Iain Crichton)

MacArthur, Charles 1895-1956..........DLB-7, 25, 44

Macaulay, David 1945- DLB-61

Macaulay, Rose 1881-1958.....................DLB-36

Macaulay, Thomas Babington 1800-1859...DLB-32, 55

Macaulay Company............................DLB-46

MacBeth, George 1932- DLB-40

MacCaig, Norman 1910- DLB-27

MacDiarmid, Hugh 1892-1978 ....DLB-20

MacDonald, George 1824-1905................DLB-18

MacDonald, John D. 1916-1986 .... DLB-8; Y-86

MacDonald, Philip 1899?-1980 ....DLB-77

Macdonald, Ross (see Millar, Kenneth)

MacEwen, Gwendolyn 1941- DLB-53

Macfadden, Bernarr 1868-1955 ....DLB-25

Machen, Arthur Llewelyn Jones 1863-1947 ... DLB-36

MacInnes, Colin 1914-1976....................DLB-14

MacKaye, Percy 1875-1956 ....DLB-54

Macken, Walter 1915-1967 ....DLB-13

Mackenzie, Compton 1883-1972...............DLB-34

Mackenzie, Henry 1745-1831 ....DLB-39

Mackey, William Wellington 1937- DLB-38

Mackintosh, Elizabeth (see Tey, Josephine)

MacLean, Katherine Anne 1925- DLB-8

MacLeish, Archibald 1892-1982 ....DLB-4, 7, 45; Y-82

MacLennan, Hugh 1907- DLB-68

MacLeod, Alistair 1936- DLB-60

Macleod, Norman 1906- DLB-4

The Macmillan Company......................DLB-49

MacNamara, Brinsley 1890-1963 ....DLB-10

MacNeice, Louis 1907-1963 ....DLB-10, 20

Macpherson, Jay 1931- DLB-53

Macpherson, Jeanie 1884-1946 ....DLB-44

Macrae Smith Company......................DLB-46

Macy-Masius.................................DLB-46

Madden, David 1933- DLB-6

Maddow, Ben 1909- DLB-44

Madgett, Naomi Long 1923- DLB-76

Madhubuti, Haki R. 1942- DLB-5, 41

Madison, James 1751-1836....................DLB-37

Mahan, Alfred Thayer 1840-1914.............DLB-47

Maheux-Forcier, Louise 1929- DLB-60

Mahin, John Lee 1902-1984....................DLB-44

Mahon, Derek 1941- DLB-40

Mailer, Norman 1923-
 ....DLB-2, 16, 28; Y-80, 83; DS-3

Maillet, Adrienne 1885-1963 ....DLB-68

Maillet, Antonine 1929- DLB-60

Main Selections of the Book-of-the-Month Club,
 1926-1945................................DLB-9

Main Trends in Twentieth-Century
 Book Clubs..............................DLB-46

Mainwaring, Daniel 1902-1977 ....DLB-44

Major, André 1942- DLB-60

Major, Clarence 1936- DLB-33

Major, Kevin 1949- DLB-60

Major Books..................................DLB-46

Makemie, Francis circa 1658-1708.............DLB-24

Malamud, Bernard 1914-1986.....DLB-2, 28; Y-80, 86

Malleson, Lucy Beatrice (see Gilbert, Anthony)

Mallock, W. H. 1849-1923..................DLB-18, 57

Malone, Dumas 1892-1986 ....DLB-17

Malraux, André 1901-1976....................DLB-72

Malzberg, Barry N. 1939- DLB-8

Mamet, David 1947- DLB-7

Mandel, Eli 1922- DLB-53

Manfred, Frederick 1912- DLB-6

Mangan, Sherry 1904-1961....................DLB-4

Mankiewicz, Herman 1897-1953...............DLB-26

Mankiewicz, Joseph L. 1909- DLB-44

Mankowitz, Wolf 1924- DLB-15

Manley, Delarivière 1672?-1724 ....DLB-39, 80

Mann, Abby 1927- DLB-44

Mann, Heinrich 1871-1950....................DLB-66

Mann, Horace 1796-1859......................DLB-1

Mann, Klaus 1906-1949 .... DLB-56

Mann, Thomas 1875-1955	DLB-66
Manning, Marie 1873?-1945	DLB-29
Manning and Loring	DLB-49
Mano, D. Keith 1942-	DLB-6
Manor Books	DLB-46
March, William 1893-1954	DLB-9
Marchessault, Jovette 1938-	DLB-60
Marcus, Frank 1928-	DLB-13
Marek, Richard, Books	DLB-46
Marion, Frances 1886-1973	DLB-44
Marius, Richard C. 1933-	Y-85
The Mark Taper Forum	DLB-7
Markfield, Wallace 1926-	DLB-2, 28
Markham, Edwin 1852-1940	DLB-54
Markle, Fletcher 1921-	DLB-68
Marlatt, Daphne 1942-	DLB-60
Marlowe, Christopher 1564-1593	DLB-62
Marmion, Shakerley 1603-1639	DLB-58
Marquand, John P. 1893-1960	DLB-9
Marquis, Don 1878-1937	DLB-11, 25
Marriott, Anne 1913-	DLB-68
Marryat, Frederick 1792-1848	DLB-21
Marsh, George Perkins 1801-1882	DLB-1, 64
Marsh, James 1794-1842	DLB-1, 59
Marsh, Capen, Lyon and Webb	DLB-49
Marsh, Ngaio 1899-1982	DLB-77
Marshall, Edward 1932-	DLB-16
Marshall, James 1942-	DLB-61
Marshall, Paule 1929-	DLB-33
Marshall, Tom 1938-	DLB-60
Marston, John 1576-1634	DLB-58
Marston, Philip Bourke 1850-1887	DLB-35
Martens, Kurt 1870-1945	DLB-66
Martien, William S. [publishing house]	DLB-49
Martin, Abe (see Hubbard, Kin)	
Martin, Claire 1914-	DLB-60
Martin du Gard, Roger 1881-1958	DLB-65
Martineau, Harriet 1802-1876	DLB-21, 55
Martyn, Edward 1859-1923	DLB-10
Marvin X 1944-	DLB-38
Marzials, Theo 1850-1920	DLB-35
Masefield, John 1878-1967	DLB-10, 19
Mason, A. E. W. 1865-1948	DLB-70
Mason, Bobbie Ann 1940-	Y-87
Mason Brothers	DLB-49
Massey, Gerald 1828-1907	DLB-32
Massinger, Philip 1583-1640	DLB-58
Masters, Edgar Lee 1868-1950	DLB-54
Mather, Cotton 1663-1728	DLB-24, 30
Mather, Increase 1639-1723	DLB-24
Mather, Richard 1596-1669	DLB-24
Matheson, Richard 1926-	DLB-8, 44
Matheus, John F. 1887-	DLB-51
Mathews, Cornelius 1817?-1889	DLB-3, 64
Mathias, Roland 1915-	DLB-27
Mathis, June 1892-1927	DLB-44
Mathis, Sharon Bell 1937-	DLB-33
Matthews, Brander 1852-1929	DLB-71, 78
Matthews, Jack 1925-	DLB-6
Matthews, William 1942-	DLB-5
Matthiessen, F. O. 1902-1950	DLB-63
Matthiessen, Peter 1927-	DLB-6
Maugham, W. Somerset 1874-1965	DLB-10, 36, 77
Mauriac, François 1885-1970	DLB-65
Maurice, Frederick Denison 1805-1872	DLB-55
Maurois, André 1885-1967	DLB-65
Maury, James 1718-1769	DLB-31
Mavor, Elizabeth 1927-	DLB-14
Mavor, Osborne Henry (see Bridie, James)	
Maxwell, H. [publishing house]	DLB-49
Maxwell, William 1908-	Y-80
May, Elaine 1932-	DLB-44
May, Thomas 1595 or 1596-1650	DLB-58
Mayer, Mercer 1943-	DLB-61
Mayer, O. B. 1818-1891	DLB-3
Mayes, Wendell 1919-	DLB-26
Mayfield, Julian 1928-1984	DLB-33; Y-84
Mayhew, Henry 1812-1887	DLB-18, 55
Mayhew, Jonathan 1720-1766	DLB-31
Mayne, Seymour 1944-	DLB-60

Mayor, Flora Macdonald 1872-1932	DLB-36
Mazursky, Paul 1930-	DLB-44
McAlmon, Robert 1896-1956	DLB-4, 45
McBride, Robert M., and Company	DLB-46
McCaffrey, Anne 1926-	DLB-8
McCarthy, Cormac 1933-	DLB-6
McCarthy, Mary 1912-	DLB-2; Y-81
McCay, Winsor 1871-1934	DLB-22
McClatchy, C. K. 1858-1936	DLB-25
McClellan, George Marion 1860-1934	DLB-50
McCloskey, Robert 1914-	DLB-22
McClure, Joanna 1930-	DLB-16
McClure, Michael 1932-	DLB-16
McClure, Phillips and Company	DLB-46
McClurg, A. C., and Company	DLB-49
McCluskey, John A., Jr. 1944-	DLB-33
McCollum, Michael A. 1946	Y-87
McCord, David 1897-	DLB-61
McCorkle, Jill 1958-	Y-87
McCorkle, Samuel Eusebius 1746-1811	DLB-37
McCormick, Anne O'Hare 1880-1954	DLB-29
McCormick, Robert R. 1880-1955	DLB-29
McCoy, Horace 1897-1955	DLB-9
McCullagh, Joseph B. 1842-1896	DLB-23
McCullers, Carson 1917-1967	DLB-2, 7
McDonald, Forrest 1927-	DLB-17
McDougall, Colin 1917-1984	DLB-68
McDowell, Obolensky	DLB-46
McEwan, Ian 1948-	DLB-14
McFadden, David 1940-	DLB-60
McGahern, John 1934-	DLB-14
McGeehan, W. O. 1879-1933	DLB-25
McGill, Ralph 1898-1969	DLB-29
McGinley, Phyllis 1905-1978	DLB-11, 48
McGirt, James E. 1874-1930	DLB-50
McGough, Roger 1937-	DLB-40
McGraw-Hill	DLB-46
McGuane, Thomas 1939-	DLB-2; Y-80
McGuckian, Medbh 1950-	DLB-40
McGuffey, William Holmes 1800-1873	DLB-42
McIlvanney, William 1936-	DLB-14
McIntyre, O. O. 1884-1938	DLB-25
McKay, Claude 1889-1948	DLB-4, 45, 51
The David McKay Company	DLB-49
McKean, William V. 1820-1903	DLB-23
McKinley, Robin 1952-	DLB-52
McLaren, Floris Clark 1904-1978	DLB-68
McLaverty, Michael 1907-	DLB-15
McLean, John R. 1848-1916	DLB-23
McLean, William L. 1852-1931	DLB-25
McLoughlin Brothers	DLB-49
McMaster, John Bach 1852-1932	DLB-47
McMurtry, Larry 1936-	DLB-2; Y-80, 87
McNally, Terrence 1939-	DLB-7
McNeil, Florence 1937-	DLB-60
McNeile, Herman Cyril 1888-1937	DLB-77
McPherson, James Alan 1943-	DLB-38
McPherson, Sandra 1943-	Y-86
McWhirter, George 1939-	DLB-60
Mead, Matthew 1924-	DLB-40
Mead, Taylor ?-	DLB-16
Medill, Joseph 1823-1899	DLB-43
Medoff, Mark 1940-	DLB-7
Meek, Alexander Beaufort 1814-1865	DLB-3
Meinke, Peter 1932-	DLB-5
Melançon, Robert 1947-	DLB-60
Mell, Max 1882-1971	DLB-81
Meltzer, David 1937-	DLB-16
Meltzer, Milton 1915-	DLB-61
Melville, Herman 1819-1891	DLB-3, 74
Memoirs of Life and Literature (1920), by W. H. Mallock [excerpt]	DLB-57
Mencken, H. L. 1880-1956	DLB-11, 29, 63
Mercer, Cecil William (see Yates, Dornford)	
Mercer, David 1928-1980	DLB-13
Mercer, John 1704-1768	DLB-31
Meredith, George 1828-1909	DLB-18, 35, 57
Meredith, Owen (see Lytton, Edward Robert Bulwer)	
Meredith, William 1919-	DLB-5
Meriwether, Louise 1923-	DLB-33

Merriam, Eve 1916-	DLB-61
The Merriam Company	DLB-49
Merrill, James 1926-	DLB-5; Y-85
Merrill and Baker	DLB-49
The Mershon Company	DLB-49
Merton, Thomas 1915-1968	DLB-48; Y-81
Merwin, W. S. 1927-	DLB-5
Messner, Julian [publishing house]	DLB-46
Metcalf, J. [publishing house]	DLB-49
Metcalf, John 1938-	DLB-60
The Methodist Book Concern	DLB-49
Mew, Charlotte 1869-1928	DLB-19
Mewshaw, Michael 1943-	Y-80
Meyer, E. Y. 1946-	DLB-75
Meyer, Eugene 1875-1959	DLB-29
Meynell, Alice 1847-1922	DLB-19
Meyrink, Gustav 1868-1932	DLB-81
Micheaux, Oscar 1884-1951	DLB-50
Micheline, Jack 1929-	DLB-16
Michener, James A. 1907?-	DLB-6
Micklejohn, George circa 1717-1818	DLB-31
Middleton, Christopher 1926-	DLB-40
Middleton, Stanley 1919-	DLB-14
Middleton, Thomas 1580-1627	DLB-58
Miegel, Agnes 1879-1964	DLB-56
Miles, Josephine 1911-1985	DLB-48
Milius, John 1944-	DLB-44
Mill, John Stuart 1806-1873	DLB-55
Millar, Kenneth 1915-1983	DLB-2; Y-83; DS-6
Millay, Edna St. Vincent 1892-1950	DLB-45
Miller, Arthur 1915-	DLB-7
Miller, Caroline 1903-	DLB-9
Miller, Eugene Ethelbert 1950-	DLB-41
Miller, Henry 1891-1980	DLB-4, 9; Y-80
Miller, J. Hillis 1928-	DLB-67
Miller, James [publishing house]	DLB-49
Miller, Jason 1939-	DLB-7
Miller, May 1899-	DLB-41
Miller, Perry 1905-1963	DLB-17, 63
Miller, Walter M., Jr. 1923-	DLB-8
Miller, Webb 1892-1940	DLB-29
Millhauser, Steven 1943-	DLB-2
Millican, Arthenia J. Bates 1920-	DLB-38
Milne, A. A. 1882-1956	DLB-10, 77
Milner, Ron 1938-	DLB-38
Milnes, Richard Monckton (Lord Houghton) 1809-1885	DLB-32
Minton, Balch and Company	DLB-46
Miron, Gaston 1928-	DLB-60
Mitchel, Jonathan 1624-1668	DLB-24
Mitchell, Adrian 1932-	DLB-40
Mitchell, Donald Grant 1822-1908	DLB-1
Mitchell, Gladys 1901-1983	DLB-77
Mitchell, James Leslie 1901-1935	DLB-15
Mitchell, John (see Slater, Patrick)	
Mitchell, John Ames 1845-1918	DLB-79
Mitchell, Julian 1935-	DLB-14
Mitchell, Ken 1940-	DLB-60
Mitchell, Langdon 1862-1935	DLB-7
Mitchell, Loften 1919-	DLB-38
Mitchell, Margaret 1900-1949	DLB-9
Modern Age Books	DLB-46
"Modern English Prose" (1876), by George Saintsbury	DLB-57
The Modern Language Association of America Celebrates Its Centennial	Y-84
The Modern Library	DLB-46
Modern Novelists—Great and Small (1855), by Margaret Oliphant	DLB-21
"Modern Style" (1857), by Cockburn Thomson [excerpt]	DLB-57
The Modernists (1932), by Joseph Warren Beach	DLB-36
Moffat, Yard and Company	DLB-46
Monkhouse, Allan 1858-1936	DLB-10
Monro, Harold 1879-1932	DLB-19
Monroe, Harriet 1860-1936	DLB-54
Monsarrat, Nicholas 1910-1979	DLB-15
Montague, John 1929-	DLB-40
Montgomery, John 1919-	DLB-16
Montgomery, Marion 1925-	DLB-6
Montherlant, Henry de 1896-1972	DLB-72

Cumulative Index

Moody, Joshua circa 1633-1697 .... DLB-24

Moody, William Vaughn 1869-1910 .... DLB-7, 54

Moorcock, Michael 1939- DLB-14

Moore, Catherine L. 1911- DLB-8

Moore, Clement Clarke 1779-1863 .... DLB-42

Moore, George 1852-1933 .... DLB-10, 18, 57

Moore, Marianne 1887-1972 .... DLB-45

Moore, T. Sturge 1870-1944 .... DLB-19

Moore, Ward 1903-1978 .... DLB-8

Moore, Wilstach, Keys and Company DLB-49

The Moorland-Spingarn
  Research Center DLB-76

Morency, Pierre 1942- DLB-60

Morgan, Berry 1919- DLB-6

Morgan, Charles 1894-1958 .... DLB-34

Morgan, Edmund S. 1916- DLB-17

Morgan, Edwin 1920- DLB-27

Morgner, Irmtraud 1933- DLB-75

Morison, Samuel Eliot 1887-1976 .... DLB-17

Morley, Christopher 1890-1957 .... DLB-9

Morley, John 1838-1923 .... DLB-57

Morris, George Pope 1802-1864 .... DLB-73

Morris, Lewis 1833-1907 .... DLB-35

Morris, Richard B. 1904- DLB-17

Morris, William 1834-1896 .... DLB-18, 35, 57

Morris, Willie 1934- Y-80

Morris, Wright 1910- DLB-2; Y-81

Morrison, Arthur 1863-1945 .... DLB-70

Morrison, Toni 1931- DLB-6, 33; Y-81

Morrow, William, and Company DLB-46

Morse, James Herbert 1841-1923 .... DLB-71

Morse, Jedidiah 1761-1826 .... DLB-37

Morse, John T., Jr. 1840-1937 .... DLB-47

Mortimer, John 1923- DLB-13

Morton, John P., and Company DLB-49

Morton, Nathaniel 1613-1685 .... DLB-24

Morton, Sarah Wentworth 1759-1846 .... DLB-37

Morton, Thomas circa 1579-circa 1647 ...... DLB-24

Mosley, Nicholas 1923- DLB-14

Moss, Arthur 1889-1969 .... DLB-4

Moss, Howard 1922- DLB-5

The Most Powerful Book Review in America
  [*New York Times Book Review*] Y-82

Motion, Andrew 1952- DLB-40

Motley, John Lothrop 1814-1877 .... DLB-1, 30, 59

Motley, Willard 1909-1965 .... DLB-76

Motteux, Peter Anthony 1663-1718 .... DLB-80

Mottram, R. H. 1883-1971 .... DLB-36

Mouré, Erin 1955- DLB-60

Movies from Books, 1920-1974 .... DLB-9

Mowat, Farley 1921- DLB-68

Mowrer, Edgar Ansel 1892-1977 .... DLB-29

Mowrer, Paul Scott 1887-1971 .... DLB-29

Mucedorus DLB-62

Muhajir, El (see Marvin X)

Muhajir, Nazzam Al Fitnah (see Marvin X)

Muir, Edwin 1887-1959 .... DLB-20

Muir, Helen 1937- DLB-14

Mukherjee, Bharati 1940- DLB-60

Muldoon, Paul 1951- DLB-40

Mumford, Lewis 1895- DLB-63

Munby, Arthur Joseph 1828-1910 .... DLB-35

Munday, Anthony 1560-1633 .... DLB-62

Munford, Robert circa 1737-1783 .... DLB-31

Munro, Alice 1931- DLB-53

Munro, George [publishing house] DLB-49

Munro, H. H. 1870-1916 .... DLB-34

Munro, Norman L. [publishing house] DLB-49

Munroe, James, and Company DLB-49

Munroe, Kirk 1850-1930 .... DLB-42

Munroe and Francis DLB-49

Munsell, Joel [publishing house] DLB-49

Munsey, Frank A. 1854-1925 .... DLB-25

Munsey, Frank A., and Company DLB-49

Murdoch, Iris 1919- DLB-14

Murfree, Mary N. 1850-1922 .... DLB-12, 74

Murphy, Beatrice M. 1908- DLB-76

Murphy, John, and Company DLB-49

Murphy, Richard 1927- DLB-40

Murray, Albert L. 1916- DLB-38

Murray, Gilbert 1866-1957 .... DLB-10

Murray, Judith Sargent 1751-1820 .... DLB-37

Murray, Pauli 1910-1985 .... DLB-41

Muschg, Adolf 1934- DLB-75

Musil, Robert 1880-1942 .... DLB-81

Mussey, Benjamin B., and Company DLB-49

Myers, Gustavus 1872-1942 .... DLB-47

Myers, L. H. 1881-1944 .... DLB-15

Myers, Walter Dean 1937- DLB-33

N

Nabbes, Thomas circa 1605-1641 .... DLB-58

Nabl, Franz 1883-1974 .... DLB-81

Nabokov, Vladimir 1899-1977 ...... DLB-2; Y-80; DS-3

Nabokov Festival at Cornell Y-83

Nafis and Cornish DLB-49

Naipaul, Shiva 1945-1985 .... Y-85

Naipaul, V. S. 1932- Y-85

Nancrede, Joseph [publishing house] DLB-49

Nasby, Petroleum Vesuvius (see Locke, David Ross)

Nash, Ogden 1902-1971 .... DLB-11

Nathan, Robert 1894-1985 .... DLB-9

The National Jewish Book Awards Y-85

The National Theatre and the Royal Shakespeare Company: The National Companies DLB-13

Naughton, Bill 1910- DLB-13

Neagoe, Peter 1881-1960 .... DLB-4

Neal, John 1793-1876 .... DLB-1, 59

Neal, Joseph C. 1807-1847 .... DLB-11

Neal, Larry 1937-1981 .... DLB-38

The Neale Publishing Company DLB-49

Neely, F. Tennyson [publishing house] DLB-49

"The Negro as a Writer," by G. M. McClellan DLB-50

"Negro Poets and Their Poetry," by Wallace Thurman DLB-50

Neihardt, John G. 1881-1973 .... DLB-9, 54

Nelson, Alice Moore Dunbar 1875-1935 .... DLB-50

Nelson, Thomas, and Sons DLB-49

Nelson, William Rockhill 1841-1915 .... DLB-23

Nemerov, Howard 1920- DLB-5, 6; Y-83

Ness, Evaline 1911-1986 .... DLB-61

Neugeboren, Jay 1938- DLB-28

Neumann, Alfred 1895-1952 .... DLB-56

Nevins, Allan 1890-1971 .... DLB-17

The New American Library DLB-46

New Directions Publishing Corporation DLB-46

A New Edition of *Huck Finn* Y-85

New Forces at Work in the American Theatre: 1915-1925 .... DLB-7

New Literary Periodicals: A Report for 1987 .... Y-87

New Literary Periodicals: A Report for 1988 .... Y-88

The New *Ulysses* Y-84

The New Variorum Shakespeare Y-85

A New Voice: The Center for the Book's First Five Years Y-83

The New Wave [Science Fiction] DLB-8

Newbolt, Henry 1862-1938 .... DLB-19

Newbound, Bernard Slade (see Slade, Bernard)

Newby, P. H. 1918- DLB-15

Newcomb, Charles King 1820-1894 .... DLB-1

Newell, Peter 1862-1924 .... DLB-42

Newell, Robert Henry 1836-1901 .... DLB-11

Newman, David (see Benton, Robert)

Newman, Frances 1883-1928 .... Y-80

Newman, John Henry 1801-1890 .... DLB-18, 32, 55

Newman, Mark [publishing house] DLB-49

Newsome, Effie Lee 1885-1979 .... DLB-76

Newspaper Syndication of American Humor .. DLB-11

Nichol, B. P. 1944- DLB-53

Nichols, Dudley 1895-1960 .... DLB-26

Nichols, John 1940- Y-82

Nichols, Mary Sargeant (Neal) Gove 1810-1884 .... DLB-1

Nichols, Peter 1927- DLB-13

Nichols, Roy F. 1896-1973 .... DLB-17

Nichols, Ruth 1948- DLB-60

Nicholson, Norman 1914- DLB-27

Cumulative Index

Ní Chuilleanáin, Eiléan 1942- DLB-40

Nicol, Eric 1919- DLB-68

Nicolay, John G. 1832-1901 and
   Hay, John 1838-1905 .... DLB-47

Niebuhr, Reinhold 1892-1971 .... DLB-17

Niedecker, Lorine 1903-1970................. DLB-48

Nieman, Lucius W. 1857-1935................ DLB-25

Niggli, Josefina 1910- Y-80

Niles, Hezekiah 1777-1839 .... DLB-43

Nims, John Frederick 1913- DLB-5

Nin, Anaïs 1903-1977 .... DLB-2, 4

1985: The Year of the Mystery:
   A Symposium Y-85

Nissenson, Hugh 1933- DLB-28

Niven, Larry 1938- DLB-8

Nizan, Paul 1905-1940....................... DLB-72

Nobel Peace Prize
   The 1986 Nobel Peace Prize
      Nobel Lecture 1986: Hope, Despair
         and Memory
      Tributes from Abraham Bernstein,
         Norman Lamm, and John R. Silber Y-86

The Nobel Prize and Literary
   Politics Y-88

Nobel Prize in Literature
   The 1982 Nobel Prize in Literature
      Announcement by the Swedish Academy
         of the Nobel Prize
      Nobel Lecture 1982: The Solitude of Latin
         America
      Excerpt from *One Hundred Years
         of Solitude*
      The Magical World of Macondo
      A Tribute to Gabriel García Márquez Y-82
   The 1983 Nobel Prize in Literature
      Announcement by the Swedish
         Academy
      Nobel Lecture 1983
      The Stature of William Golding Y-83
   The 1984 Nobel Prize in Literature
      Announcement by the Swedish
         Academy
      Jaroslav Seifert Through the Eyes of the
         English-Speaking Reader
         Three Poems by Jaroslav Seifert Y-84
   The 1985 Nobel Prize in Literature
      Announcement by the Swedish
         Academy

   Nobel Lecture 1985 ....Y-85
   The 1986 Nobel Prize in Literature
      Nobel Lecture 1986: This Past Must
         Address Its Present....................Y-86
   The 1987 Nobel Prize in Literature
      Nobel Lecture 1987 ....Y-87
   The 1988 Nobel Prize in Literature
      Nobel Lecture 1988 ....Y-88

Noel, Roden 1834-1894 .... DLB-35

Nolan, William F. 1928- DLB-8

Noland, C. F. M. 1810?-1858 .... DLB-11

Noonday Press............................... DLB-46

Noone, John 1936- DLB-14

Nordhoff, Charles 1887-1947 ....DLB-9

Norman, Marsha 1947- Y-84

Norris, Charles G. 1881-1945...................DLB-9

Norris, Frank 1870-1902 .... DLB-12

Norris, Leslie 1921- DLB-27

Norse, Harold 1916- DLB-16

North Point Press............................ DLB-46

Norton, Alice Mary (see Norton, Andre)

Norton, Andre 1912- DLB-8, 52

Norton, Andrews 1786-1853 ....DLB-1

Norton, Caroline 1808-1877................... DLB-21

Norton, Charles Eliot 1827-1908 ....DLB-1, 64

Norton, John 1606-1663..................... DLB-24

Norton, Thomas (see Sackville, Thomas)

Norton, W. W., and Company................. DLB-46

Nossack, Hans Erich 1901-1977 .... DLB-69

A Note on Technique (1926), by Elizabeth
   A. Drew [excerpts] DLB-36

Nourse, Alan E. 1928- DLB-8

The Novel in [Robert Browning's] "The Ring
   and the Book" (1912), by Henry James ... DLB-32

Novel-Reading: *The Works of Charles Dickens,
   The Works of W. Makepeace Thackeray* (1879),
   by Anthony Trollope..................... DLB-21

The Novels of Dorothy Richardson (1918), by
   May Sinclair............................. DLB-36

Novels with a Purpose (1864),
   by Justin M'Carthy...................... DLB-21

Nowlan, Alden 1933-1983.................... DLB-53

Noyes, Alfred 1880-1958 .... DLB-20

Noyes, Crosby S. 1825-1908 .... DLB-23

Noyes, Nicholas 1647-1717	DLB-24
Noyes, Theodore W. 1858-1946	DLB-29
Nugent, Frank 1908-1965	DLB-44
Nye, Edgar Wilson (Bill) 1850-1896	DLB-11, 23
Nye, Robert 1939-	DLB-14

O

Oakes, Urian circa 1631-1681	DLB-24
Oates, Joyce Carol 1938-	DLB-2, 5; Y-81
Oberholtzer, Ellis Paxson 1868-1936	DLB-47
O'Brien, Edna 1932-	DLB-14
O'Brien, Fitz-James 1828-1862	DLB-74
O'Brien, Kate 1897-1974	DLB-15
O'Brien, Tim 1946-	Y-80
O'Casey, Sean 1880-1964	DLB-10
Ochs, Adolph S. 1858-1935	DLB-25
O'Connor, Flannery 1925-1964	DLB-2; Y-80
O'Dell, Scott 1903-	DLB-52
Odell, Jonathan 1737-1818	DLB-31
Odets, Clifford 1906-1963	DLB-7, 26
O'Faolain, Julia 1932-	DLB-14
O'Faolain, Sean 1900-	DLB-15
O'Flaherty, Liam 1896-1984	DLB-36; Y-84
Off Broadway and Off-Off-Broadway	DLB-7
Off-Loop Theatres	DLB-7
Offord, Carl Ruthven 1910-	DLB-76
Ogilvie, J. S., and Company	DLB-49
O'Grady, Desmond 1935-	DLB-40
O'Hagan, Howard 1902-1982	DLB-68
O'Hara, Frank 1926-1966	DLB-5, 16
O'Hara, John 1905-1970	DLB-9; DS-2
O. Henry (see Porter, William Sydney)	
Old Franklin Publishing House	DLB-49
Older, Fremont 1856-1935	DLB-25
Oliphant, Laurence 1829?-1888	DLB-18
Oliphant, Margaret 1828-1897	DLB-18
Oliver, Chad 1928-	DLB-8
Oliver, Mary 1935-	DLB-5
Olsen, Tillie 1913?-	DLB-28; Y-80
Olson, Charles 1910-1970	DLB-5, 16
Olson, Elder 1909-	DLB-48, 63
On Art in Fiction (1838), by Edward Bulwer	DLB-21
On Learning to Write	Y-88
On Some of the Characteristics of Modern Poetry and On the Lyrical Poems of Alfred Tennyson (1831), by Arthur Henry Hallam	DLB-32
"On Style in English Prose" (1898), by Frederic Harrison	DLB-57
"On Style in Literature: Its Technical Elements" (1885), by Robert Louis Stevenson	DLB-57
"On the Writing of Essays" (1862), by Alexander Smith	DLB-57
Ondaatje, Michael 1943-	DLB-60
O'Neill, Eugene 1888-1953	DLB-7
Oppen, George 1908-1984	DLB-5
Oppenheim, E. Phillips 1866-1946	DLB-70
Oppenheim, James 1882-1932	DLB-28
Oppenheimer, Joel 1930-	DLB-5
Optic, Oliver (see Adams, William Taylor)	
Orczy, Emma, Baroness 1865-1947	DLB-70
Orlovitz, Gil 1918-1973	DLB-2, 5
Orlovsky, Peter 1933-	DLB-16
Ormond, John 1923-	DLB-27
Ornitz, Samuel 1890-1957	DLB-28, 44
Orton, Joe 1933-1967	DLB-13
Orwell, George 1903-1950	DLB-15
The Orwell Year	Y-84
Osbon, B. S. 1827-1912	DLB-43
Osborne, John 1929-	DLB-13
Osgood, Herbert L. 1855-1918	DLB-47
Osgood, James R., and Company	DLB-49
O'Shaughnessy, Arthur 1844-1881	DLB-35
O'Shea, Patrick [publishing house]	DLB-49
Oswald, Eleazer 1755-1795	DLB-43
Otis, James (see Kaler, James Otis)	
Otis, James, Jr. 1725-1783	DLB-31
Otis, Broaders and Company	DLB-49
Ottendorfer, Oswald 1826-1900	DLB-23
Otway, Thomas 1652-1685	DLB-80

Ouellette, Fernand 1930- DLB-60
Ouida 1839-1908 .... DLB-18
Outing Publishing Company................... DLB-46
Outlaw Days, by Joyce Johnson............... DLB-16
The Overlook Press DLB-46
Overview of U.S. Book Publishing, 1910-1945...DLB-9
Owen, Guy 1925- DLB-5
Owen, John [publishing house]............... DLB-49
Owen, Wilfred 1893-1918 .... DLB-20
Owsley, Frank L. 1890-1956................... DLB-17
Ozick, Cynthia 1928- DLB-28; Y-82

P

Pack, Robert 1929- DLB-5
Packaging Papa: *The Garden of Eden* Y-86
Padell Publishing Company.................... DLB-46
Padgett, Ron 1942- DLB-5
Page, L. C., and Company.................... DLB-49
Page, P. K. 1916- DLB-68
Page, Thomas Nelson 1853-1922........... DLB-12, 78
Page, Walter Hines 1855-1918................ DLB-71
Paget, Violet (see Lee, Vernon)
Pain, Philip ?-circa 1666 .... DLB-24
Paine, Robert Treat, Jr. 1773-1811........... DLB-37
Paine, Thomas 1737-1809 .... DLB-31, 43, 73
Paley, Grace 1922- DLB-28
Palfrey, John Gorham 1796-1881............ DLB-1, 30
Palgrave, Francis Turner 1824-1897........... DLB-35
Paltock, Robert 1697-1767.................... DLB-39
Panama, Norman 1914- and
  Frank, Melvin 1913-1988 .... DLB-26
Pangborn, Edgar 1909-1976.................... DLB-8
"Panic Among the Philistines": A Postscript,
  An Interview with Bryan Griffin............ Y-81
Panneton, Philippe (see Ringuet)
Panshin, Alexei 1940- DLB-8
Pansy (see Alden, Isabella)
Pantheon Books DLB-46
Paperback Library............................ DLB-46

Paperback Science Fiction DLB-8
Paquet, Alfons 1881-1944 .... DLB-66
Paradis, Suzanne 1936- DLB-53
Parents' Magazine Press DLB-46
Parisian Theater, Fall 1984: Toward
  A New Baroque............................. Y-85
Parizeau, Alice 1930- DLB-60
Parke, John 1754-1789 .... DLB-31
Parker, Dorothy 1893-1967................ DLB-11, 45
Parker, James 1714-1770 .... DLB-43
Parker, Theodore 1810-1860................... DLB-1
Parkman, Francis, Jr. 1823-1893 .... DLB-1, 30
Parks, Gordon 1912- DLB-33
Parks, William 1698-1750..................... DLB-43
Parks, William [publishing house] DLB-49
Parley, Peter (see Goodrich, Samuel Griswold)
Parrington, Vernon L. 1871-1929 .... DLB-17, 63
Parton, James 1822-1891 .... DLB-30
Parton, Sara Payson Willis 1811-1872 ..... DLB-43, 74
Pastan, Linda 1932- DLB-5
Pastorius, Francis Daniel 1651-circa 1720...... DLB-24
Patchen, Kenneth 1911-1972 .... DLB-16, 48
Pater, Walter 1839-1894...................... DLB-57
Paterson, Katherine 1932- DLB-52
Patmore, Coventry 1823-1896................. DLB-35
Paton, Joseph Noel 1821-1901................. DLB-35
Patrick, John 1906- DLB-7
Pattee, Fred Lewis 1863-1950 .... DLB-71
Patterson, Eleanor Medill 1881-1948 .... DLB-29
Patterson, Joseph Medill 1879-1946 .... DLB-29
Pattillo, Henry 1726-1801 .... DLB-37
Paul, Elliot 1891-1958....................... DLB-4
Paul, Peter, Book Company DLB-49
Paulding, James Kirke 1778-1860 .... DLB-3, 59, 74
Paulin, Tom 1949- DLB-40
Pauper, Peter, Press DLB-46
Paxton, John 1911-1985 .... DLB-44
Payn, James 1830-1898........................ DLB-18
Payne, John 1842-1916 .... DLB-35
Payne, John Howard 1791-1852................. DLB-37

Payson and Clarke	DLB-46
Peabody, Elizabeth Palmer 1804-1894	DLB-1
Peabody, Elizabeth Palmer [publishing house]	DLB-49
Peabody, Oliver William Bourn 1799-1848	DLB-59
Peachtree Publishers, Limited	DLB-46
Pead, Deuel ?-1727	DLB-24
Peake, Mervyn 1911-1968	DLB-15
Pearson, H. B. [publishing house]	DLB-49
Peck, George W. 1840-1916	DLB-23, 42
Peck, H. C., and Theo. Bliss [publishing house]	DLB-49
Peck, Harry Thurston 1856-1914	DLB-71
Peele, George 1556-1596	DLB-62
Pellegrini and Cudahy	DLB-46
Pemberton, Sir Max 1863-1950	DLB-70
Penguin Books	DLB-46
Penn Publishing Company	DLB-49
Penn, William 1644-1718	DLB-24
Penner, Jonathan 1940-	Y-83
Pennington, Lee 1939-	Y-82
Percy, Walker 1916-	DLB-2; Y-80
Perelman, S. J. 1904-1979	DLB-11, 44
Periodicals of the Beat Generation	DLB-16
Perkins, Eugene 1932-	DLB-41
Perkoff, Stuart Z. 1930-1974	DLB-16
Permabooks	DLB-46
Perry, Bliss 1860-1954	DLB-71
Perry, Eleanor 1915-1981	DLB-44
"Personal Style" (1890), by John Addington Symonds	DLB-57
Perutz, Leo 1882-1957	DLB-81
Peter, Laurence J. 1919-	DLB-53
Peterkin, Julia 1880-1961	DLB-9
Petersham, Maud 1889-1971 and Petersham, Miska 1888-1960	DLB-22
Peterson, Charles Jacobs 1819-1887	DLB-79
Peterson, Louis 1922-	DLB-76
Peterson, T. B., and Brothers	DLB-49
Petry, Ann 1908-	DLB-76
Pharr, Robert Deane 1916-	DLB-33
Phelps, Elizabeth Stuart 1844-1911	DLB-74
Philippe, Charles-Louis 1874-1909	DLB-65
Phillips, David Graham 1867-1911	DLB-9, 12
Phillips, Jayne Anne 1952-	Y-80
Phillips, Stephen 1864-1915	DLB-10
Phillips, Ulrich B. 1877-1934	DLB-17
Phillips, Willard 1784-1873	DLB-59
Phillips, Sampson and Company	DLB-49
Phillpotts, Eden 1862-1960	DLB-10, 70
Philosophical Library	DLB-46
"The Philosophy of Style" (1852), by Herbert Spencer	DLB-57
Phinney, Elihu [publishing house]	DLB-49
Phoenix, John (see Derby, George Horatio)	
PHYLON (Fourth Quarter, 1950), The Negro in Literature: The Current Scene	DLB-76
Pickard, Tom 1946-	DLB-40
Pictorial Printing Company	DLB-49
Pike, Albert 1809-1891	DLB-74
Pilon, Jean-Guy 1930-	DLB-60
Pinckney, Josephine 1895-1957	DLB-6
Pinero, Arthur Wing 1855-1934	DLB-10
Pinnacle Books	DLB-46
Pinsky, Robert 1940-	Y-82
Pinter, Harold 1930-	DLB-13
Piontek, Heinz 1925-	DLB-75
Piper, H. Beam 1904-1964	DLB-8
Piper, Watty	DLB-22
Pisar, Samuel 1929-	Y-83
Pitkin, Timothy 1766-1847	DLB-30
The Pitt Poetry Series: Poetry Publishing Today	Y-85
Pitter, Ruth 1897-	DLB-20
Pix, Mary 1666-1709	DLB-80
The Place of Realism in Fiction (1895), by George Gissing	DLB-18
Plante, David 1940-	Y-83
Plath, Sylvia 1932-1963	DLB-5, 6
Platt and Munk Company	DLB-46
Playboy Press	DLB-46

Cumulative Index

Playwrights and Professors, by Tom Stoppard.................................. DLB-13

Playwrights on the Theater.................... DLB-80

Plenzdorf, Ulrich 1934- DLB-75

Plessen, Elizabeth 1944- DLB-75

Plievier, Theodor 1892-1955 .... DLB-69

Plomer, William 1903-1973.................... DLB-20

Plumly, Stanley 1939- DLB-5

Plumpp, Sterling D. 1940- DLB-41

Plunkett, James 1920- DLB-14

Plymell, Charles 1935- DLB-16

Pocket Books DLB-46

Poe, Edgar Allan 1809-1849......... DLB-3, 59, 73, 74

Poe, James 1921-1980 .... DLB-44

The Poet Laureate of the United States Statements from Former Consultants in Poetry Y-86

Pohl, Frederik 1919- DLB-8

Poliakoff, Stephen 1952- DLB-13

Polite, Carlene Hatcher 1932- DLB-33

Pollard, Edward A. 1832-1872................. DLB-30

Pollard, Percival 1869-1911.................. DLB-71

Pollard and Moss DLB-49

Pollock, Sharon 1936- DLB-60

Polonsky, Abraham 1910- DLB-26

Poole, Ernest 1880-1950.......................DLB-9

Poore, Benjamin Perley 1820-1887 .... DLB-23

Popular Library DLB-46

Porlock, Martin (see MacDonald, Philip)

Porter, Eleanor H. 1868-1920 ....DLB-9

Porter, Henry ?-? DLB-62

Porter, Katherine Anne 1890-1980.....DLB-4, 9; Y-80

Porter, Peter 1929- DLB-40

Porter, William Sydney 1862-1910......DLB-12, 78, 79

Porter, William T. 1809-1858..............DLB-3, 43

Porter and Coates DLB-49

Portis, Charles 1933- DLB-6

Poston, Ted 1906-1974....................... DLB-51

Postscript to [the Third Edition of] *Clarissa* (1751), by Samuel Richardson............ DLB-39

Potok, Chaim 1929- DLB-28; Y-84

Potter, David M. 1910-1971 .... DLB-17

Potter, John E., and Company................. DLB-49

Pottle, Frederick A. 1897-1987 ....Y-87

Poulin, Jacques 1937- DLB-60

Pound, Ezra 1885-1972.................DLB-4, 45, 63

Powell, Anthony 1905- DLB-15

Pownall, David 1938- DLB-14

Powys, John Cowper 1872-1963 .... DLB-15

Powys, T. F. 1875-1953....................... DLB-36

The Practice of Biography: An Interview with Stanley Weintraub Y-82

The Practice of Biography II: An Interview with B. L. Reid.....................................Y-83

The Practice of Biography III: An Interview with Humphrey Carpenter........................Y-84

The Practice of Biography IV: An Interview with William Manchester........................Y-85

The Practice of Biography V: An Interview with Justin Kaplan Y-86

The Practice of Biography VI: An Interview with David Herbert Donald Y-87

Praeger Publishers........................... DLB-46

Pratt, Samuel Jackson 1749-1814.............. DLB-39

Preface to *Alwyn* (1780), by Thomas Holcroft................................. DLB-39

Preface to *Colonel Jack* (1722), by Daniel Defoe DLB-39

Preface to *Evelina* (1778), by Fanny Burney ... DLB-39

Preface to *Ferdinand Count Fathom* (1753), by Tobias Smollett DLB-39

Preface to *Incognita* (1692), by William Congreve.................................. DLB-39

Preface to *Joseph Andrews* (1742), by Henry Fielding............................ DLB-39

Preface to *Moll Flanders* (1722), by Daniel Defoe DLB-39

Preface to *Poems* (1853), by Matthew Arnold.................................... DLB-32

Preface to *Robinson Crusoe* (1719), by Daniel Defoe DLB-39

Preface to *Roderick Random* (1748), by Tobias Smollett................................... DLB-39

Preface to *Roxana* (1724), by Daniel Defoe DLB-39

Preface to *St. Leon* (1799),
    by William Godwin...................... DLB-39

Preface to Sarah Fielding's *Familiar Letters*
    (1747), by Henry Fielding [excerpt]....... DLB-39

Preface to Sarah Fielding's *The Adventures of
    David Simple* (1744), by Henry Fielding ... DLB-39

Preface to *The Cry* (1754), by Sarah Fielding... DLB-39

Preface to *The Delicate Distress* (1769), by
    Elizabeth Griffin DLB-39

Preface to *The Disguis'd Prince* (1733), by Eliza
    Haywood [excerpt]........................ DLB-39

Preface to *The Farther Adventures of Robinson
    Crusoe* (1719), by Daniel Defoe............ DLB-39

Preface to the First Edition of *Pamela* (1740), by
    Samuel Richardson....................... DLB-39

Preface to the First Edition of *The Castle of
    Otranto* (1764), by Horace Walpole........ DLB-39

Preface to *The History of Romances* (1715), by
    Pierre Daniel Huet [excerpts]............. DLB-39

Preface to *The Life of Charlotta du Pont* (1723),
    by Penelope Aubin....................... DLB-39

Preface to *The Old English Baron* (1778), by
    Clara Reeve.............................. DLB-39

Preface to the Second Edition of *The Castle of
    Otranto* (1765), by Horace Walpole........ DLB-39

Preface to *The Secret History, of Queen Zarah, and
    the Zarazians* (1705), by Delarivière
    Manley................................... DLB-39

Preface to the Third Edition of *Clarissa* (1751),
    by Samuel Richardson [excerpt]........... DLB-39

Preface to *The Works of Mrs. Davys* (1725), by
    Mary Davys DLB-39

Preface to Volume 1 of *Clarissa* (1747), by
    Samuel Richardson....................... DLB-39

Preface to Volume 3 of *Clarissa* (1748), by
    Samuel Richardson....................... DLB-39

Préfontaine, Yves 1937- DLB-53

Prelutsky, Jack 1940- DLB-61

Prentice, George D. 1802-1870 .... DLB-43

Prentice-Hall DLB-46

Prescott, William Hickling 1796-1859....DLB-1, 30, 59

The Present State of the English Novel (1892),
    by George Saintsbury DLB-18

Preston, Thomas 1537-1598.................. DLB-62

Price, Reynolds 1933- DLB-2

Price, Richard 1949- Y-81

Priest, Christopher 1943- DLB-14

Priestley, J. B. 1894-1984........ DLB-10, 34, 77; Y-84

Prime, Benjamin Young 1733-1791 .... DLB-31

Prince, F. T. 1912- DLB-20

Prince, Thomas 1687-1758 .... DLB-24

The Principles of Success in Literature (1865), by
    George Henry Lewes [excerpt]............ DLB-57

Pritchett, V. S. 1900- DLB-15

Procter, Adelaide Anne 1825-1864............ DLB-32

The Progress of Romance (1785), by Clara Reeve
    [excerpt] DLB-39

Prokosch, Frederic 1906- DLB-48

The Proletarian Novel........................DLB-9

Propper, Dan 1937- DLB-16

The Prospect of Peace (1778), by Joel Barlow.... DLB-37

Proud, Robert 1728-1813..................... DLB-30

Proust, Marcel 1871-1922 .... DLB-65

Prynne, J. H. 1936- DLB-40

Przybyszewski, Stanislaw 1868-1927 .... DLB-66

The Public Lending Right in America
    Statement by Sen. Charles McC. Mathias, Jr.
    PLR and the Meaning of Literary Property
    Statements on PLR by American Writers Y-83

The Public Lending Right in the United Kingdom
    Public Lending Right: The First Year in the
    United Kingdom..........................Y-83

The Publication of English Renaissance
    Plays DLB-62

Publications and Social Movements
    [Transcendentalism] DLB-1

Publishers and Agents: The Columbia
    Connection................................Y-87

Publishing Fiction at LSU Press Y-87

Pugin, A. Welby 1812-1852.................... DLB-55

Pulitzer, Joseph 1847-1911 .... DLB-23

Pulitzer, Joseph, Jr. 1885-1955 .... DLB-29

Pulitzer Prizes for the Novel, 1917-1945.........DLB-9

Purdy, James 1923- DLB-2

Pusey, Edward Bouverie 1800-1882 .... DLB-55

Putnam, George Palmer 1814-1872.........DLB-3, 79

Putnam, Samuel 1892-1950.....................DLB-4

G. P. Putnam's Sons DLB-49

Puzo, Mario 1920- DLB-6

Pyle, Ernie 1900-1945 .... DLB-29

Pyle, Howard 1853-1911 .... DLB-42

Pym, Barbara 1913-1980 .... DLB-14; Y-87

Pynchon, Thomas 1937- DLB-2

Pyramid Books DLB-46

Pyrnelle, Louise-Clarke 1850-1907 .... DLB-42

Q

Quad, M. (see Lewis, Charles B.)

The Queen City Publishing House DLB-49

Queneau, Raymond 1903-1976 .... DLB-72

The Question of American Copyright
 in the Nineteenth Century
  Headnote
  Preface, by George Haven Putnam
  The Evolution of Copyright, by Brander
   Matthews
  Summary of Copyright Legislation in the
   United States, by R. R. Bowker
  Analysis of the Provisions of the Copyright
   Law of 1891, by George Haven Putnam
  The Contest for International Copyright,
   by George Haven Putnam
  Cheap Books and Good Books,
   by Brander Matthews DLB-49

Quin, Ann 1936-1973 .... DLB-14

Quincy, Samuel of Georgia ?-? DLB-31

Quincy, Samuel of Massachusetts 1734-1789 .. DLB-31

Quist, Harlin, Books DLB-46

R

Rabe, David 1940- DLB-7

Radcliffe, Ann 1764-1823 .... DLB-39

Raddall, Thomas 1903- DLB-68

Radiguet, Raymond 1903-1923 .... DLB-65

Radványi, Netty Reiling (see Seghers, Anna)

Raine, Craig 1944- DLB-40

Raine, Kathleen 1908- DLB-20

Ralph, Julian 1853-1903 .... DLB-23

Ralph Waldo Emerson in 1982 .... Y-82

Rambler, no. 4 (1750), by Samuel Johnson
 [excerpt] DLB-39

Ramée, Marie Louise de la (see Ouida)

Ramsay, David 1749-1815 .... DLB-30

Rand, Avery and Company DLB-49

Rand McNally and Company DLB-49

Randall, Dudley 1914- DLB-41

Randall, Henry S. 1811-1876 .... DLB-30

Randall, James G. 1881-1953 .... DLB-17

The Randall Jarrell Symposium: A Small
 Collection of Randall Jarrells
 Excerpts From Papers Delivered at
  the Randall Jarrell Symposium Y-86

Randolph, Anson D. F. [publishing house] DLB-49

Randolph, Thomas 1605-1635 .... DLB-58

Random House DLB-46

Ranlet, Henry [publishing house] DLB-49

Ransom, John Crowe 1888-1974 .... DLB-45, 63

Raphael, Frederic 1931- DLB-14

Raphaelson, Samson 1896-1983 .... DLB-44

Raskin, Ellen 1928-1984 .... DLB-52

Rattigan, Terence 1911-1977 .... DLB-13

Rawlings, Marjorie Kinnan 1896-1953 .... DLB-9, 22

Raworth, Tom 1938- DLB-40

Ray, David 1932- DLB-5

Ray, Henrietta Cordelia 1849-1916 .... DLB-50

Raymond, Henry J. 1820-1869 .... DLB-43, 79

Raymond Chandler Centenary Tributes
 from Michael Avallone, James Elroy, Joe Gores,
 and William F. Nolan Y-88

Reach, Angus 1821-1856 .... DLB-70

Read, Herbert 1893-1968 .... DLB-20

Read, Opie 1852-1939 .... DLB-23

Read, Piers Paul 1941- DLB-14

Reade, Charles 1814-1884 .... DLB-21

Reader's Digest Condensed Books DLB-46

Reading, Peter 1946- DLB-40

Reaney, James 1926- DLB-68

Rechy, John 1934- Y-82

Redding, J. Saunders 1906-1988 .... DLB-63, 76

Redfield, J. S. [publishing house] DLB-49

Redgrove, Peter 1932-	DLB-40
Redmon, Anne 1943-	Y-86
Redmond, Eugene B. 1937-	DLB-41
Redpath, James [publishing house]	DLB-49
Reed, Henry 1808-1854	DLB-59
Reed, Henry 1914-	DLB-27
Reed, Ishmael 1938-	DLB-2, 5, 33
Reed, Sampson 1800-1880	DLB-1
Reese, Lizette Woodworth 1856-1935	DLB-54
Reese, Thomas 1742-1796	DLB-37
Reeve, Clara 1729-1807	DLB-39
Regnery, Henry, Company	DLB-46
Reid, Alastair 1926-	DLB-27
Reid, Christopher 1949-	DLB-40
Reid, Helen Rogers 1882-1970	DLB-29
Reid, James ?-?	DLB-31
Reid, Mayne 1818-1883	DLB-21
Reid, Thomas 1710-1796	DLB-31
Reid, Whitelaw 1837-1912	DLB-23
Reilly and Lee Publishing Company	DLB-46
Reimann, Brigitte 1933-1973	DLB-75
Reisch, Walter 1903-1983	DLB-44
Remarque, Erich Maria 1898-1970	DLB-56
"Re-meeting of Old Friends": The Jack Kerouac Conference	Y-82
Remington, Frederic 1861-1909	DLB-12
Renaud, Jacques 1943-	DLB-60
Renault, Mary 1905-1983	Y-83
Representative Men and Women: A Historical Perspective on the British Novel, 1930-1960	DLB-15
(Re-)Publishing Orwell	Y-86
Reuter, Gabriele 1859-1941	DLB-66
Revell, Fleming H., Company	DLB-49
Reventlow, Franziska Gräfin zu 1871-1918	DLB-66
Review of [Samuel Richardson's] *Clarissa* (1748), by Henry Fielding	DLB-39
The Revolt (1937), by Mary Colum [excerpts]	DLB-36
Rexroth, Kenneth 1905-1982	DLB-16, 48; Y-82
Rey, H. A. 1898-1977	DLB-22
Reynal and Hitchcock	DLB-46
Reynolds, G. W. M. 1814-1879	DLB-21
Reynolds, Mack 1917-	DLB-8
Reznikoff, Charles 1894-1976	DLB-28, 45
"Rhetoric" (1828; revised, 1859), by Thomas de Quincey [excerpt]	DLB-57
Rhett, Robert Barnwell 1800-1876	DLB-43
Rhode, John 1884-1964	DLB-77
Rhodes, James Ford 1848-1927	DLB-47
Rhys, Jean 1890-1979	DLB-36
Rice, Elmer 1892-1967	DLB-4, 7
Rice, Grantland 1880-1954	DLB-29
Rich, Adrienne 1929-	DLB-5, 67
Richards, David Adams 1950-	DLB-53
Richards, George circa 1760-1814	DLB-37
Richards, I. A. 1893-1979	DLB-27
Richards, Laura E. 1850-1943	DLB-42
Richards, William Carey 1818-1892	DLB-73
Richardson, Charles F. 1851-1913	DLB-71
Richardson, Dorothy M. 1873-1957	DLB-36
Richardson, Jack 1935-	DLB-7
Richardson, Samuel 1689-1761	DLB-39
Richardson, Willis 1889-1977	DLB-51
Richler, Mordecai 1931-	DLB-53
Richter, Conrad 1890-1968	DLB-9
Richter, Hans Werner 1908-	DLB-69
Rickword, Edgell 1898-1982	DLB-20
Riddell, John (see Ford, Corey)	
Ridge, Lola 1873-1941	DLB-54
Ridler, Anne 1912-	DLB-27
Riffaterre, Michael 1924-	DLB-67
Riis, Jacob 1849-1914	DLB-23
Riker, John C. [publishing house]	DLB-49
Riley, John 1938-1978	DLB-40
Rilke, Rainer Maria 1875-1926	DLB-81
Rinehart and Company	DLB-46
Ringuet 1895-1960	DLB-68
Rinser, Luise 1911-	DLB-69
Ripley, Arthur 1895-1961	DLB-44
Ripley, George 1802-1880	DLB-1, 64, 73

The Rising Glory of America: Three Poems... DLB-37

The Rising Glory of America: Written in 1771 (1786), by Hugh Henry Brackenridge and Philip Freneau DLB-37

Riskin, Robert 1897-1955..................... DLB-26

Risse, Heinz 1898- DLB-69

Ritchie, Anna Mowatt 1819-1870............... DLB-3

Ritchie, Anne Thackeray 1837-1919.......... DLB-18

Ritchie, Thomas 1778-1854................... DLB-43

Rites of Passage [on William Saroyan]............ Y-83

The Ritz Paris Hemingway Award................ Y-85

Rivers, Conrad Kent 1933-1968 .... DLB-41

Riverside Press DLB-49

Rivington, James circa 1724-1802 .... DLB-43

Rivkin, Allen 1903- DLB-26

Robbins, Tom 1936- Y-80

Roberts, Elizabeth Madox 1881-1941........ DLB-9, 54

Roberts, Kenneth 1885-1957 .... DLB-9

Roberts Brothers DLB-49

Robertson, A. M., and Company DLB-49

Robinson, Casey 1903-1979.................... DLB-44

Robinson, Edwin Arlington 1869-1935 .... DLB-54

Robinson, James Harvey 1863-1936.......... DLB-47

Robinson, Lennox 1886-1958.................. DLB-10

Robinson, Mabel Louise 1874-1962........... DLB-22

Robinson, Therese 1797-1870 .... DLB-59

Rodgers, Carolyn M. 1945- DLB-41

Rodgers, W. R. 1909-1969.................... DLB-20

Roethke, Theodore 1908-1963 ....DLB-5

Rogers, Will 1879-1935....................... DLB-11

Rohmer, Sax 1883-1959 .... DLB-70

Roiphe, Anne 1935- Y-80

Rolfe, Frederick William 1860-1913 .... DLB-34

Rolland, Romain 1866-1944 .... DLB-65

Rolvaag, O. E. 1876-1931..................... DLB-9

Romains, Jules 1885-1972 .... DLB-65

Roman, A., and Company..................... DLB-49

Roosevelt, Theodore 1858-1919 .... DLB-47

Root, Waverley 1903-1982..................... DLB-4

Roquebrune, Robert de 1889-1978 .... DLB-68

Rose, Reginald 1920- DLB-26

Rosen, Norma 1925- DLB-28

Rosenberg, Isaac 1890-1918.................. DLB-20

Rosenfeld, Isaac 1918-1956................... DLB-28

Rosenthal, M. L. 1917- DLB-5

Ross, Leonard Q. (see Rosten, Leo)

Rossen, Robert 1908-1966.................... DLB-26

Rossetti, Christina 1830-1894................. DLB-35

Rossetti, Dante Gabriel 1828-1882............ DLB-35

Rossner, Judith 1935- DLB-6

Rosten, Leo 1908- DLB-11

Roth, Henry 1906?- DLB-28

Roth, Philip 1933- DLB-2, 28; Y-82

Rothenberg, Jerome 1931- DLB-5

Rowe, Elizabeth 1674-1737 .... DLB-39

Rowlandson, Mary circa 1635-circa 1678 ...... DLB-24

Rowley, William circa 1585-1626 .... DLB-58

Rowson, Susanna Haswell circa 1762-1824 .... DLB-37

Roy, Gabrielle 1909-1983..................... DLB-68

The Royal Court Theatre and the English Stage Company DLB-13

The Royal Court Theatre and the New Drama DLB-10

The Royal Shakespeare Company at the Swan Y-88

Royall, Anne 1769-1854 .... DLB-43

The Roycroft Printing Shop................... DLB-49

Rubens, Bernice 1928- DLB-14

Rudd and Carleton........................... DLB-49

Rudkin, David 1936- DLB-13

Ruffin, Josephine St. Pierre 1842-1924........ DLB-79

Ruggles, Henry Joseph 1813-1906............. DLB-64

Rukeyser, Muriel 1913-1980................... DLB-48

Rule, Jane 1931- DLB-60

Rumaker, Michael 1932- DLB-16

Rumens, Carol 1944- DLB-40

Runyon, Damon 1880-1946 .... DLB-11

Rush, Benjamin 1746-1813................... DLB-37

Ruskin, John 1819-1900...................... DLB-55

Russ, Joanna 1937- DLB-8

Russell, B. B., and Company DLB-49

Russell, Benjamin 1761-1845 .... DLB-43

Russell, Charles Edward 1860-1941 .... DLB-25
Russell, George William (see AE)
Russell, R. H., and Son DLB-49
Rutherford, Mark 1831-1913 .... DLB-18
Ryan, Michael 1946- Y-82
Ryan, Oscar 1904- DLB-68
Ryga, George 1932- DLB-60
Ryskind, Morrie 1895-1985................... DLB-26

S

The Saalfield Publishing Company DLB-46
Saberhagen, Fred 1930- DLB-8
Sackler, Howard 1929-1982 ....DLB-7
Sackville, Thomas 1536-1608
    and Norton, Thomas 1532-1584 .... DLB-62
Sackville-West, V. 1892-1962 .... DLB-34
Sadlier, D. and J., and Company DLB-49
Saffin, John circa 1626-1710.................. DLB-24
Sage, Robert 1899-1962 ....DLB-4
Sahkomaapii, Piitai (see Highwater, Jamake)
Sahl, Hans 1902- DLB-69
Said, Edward W. 1935- DLB-67
St. Johns, Adela Rogers 1894-1988 .... DLB-29
St. Martin's Press DLB-46
Saint-Exupéry, Antoine de 1900-1944 .... DLB-72
Saintsbury, George 1845-1933................ DLB-57
Saki (see Munro, H. H.)
Salaam, Kalamu ya 1947- DLB-38
Salemson, Harold J. 1910-1988................DLB-4
Salinger, J. D. 1919- DLB-2
Salt, Waldo 1914- DLB-44
Sampson, Richard Henry (see Hull, Richard)
Sanborn, Franklin Benjamin 1831-1917 ....DLB-1
Sanchez, Sonia 1934- DLB-41
Sandburg, Carl 1878-1967...................DLB-17, 54
Sanders, Ed 1939- DLB-16
Sandoz, Mari 1896-1966......................DLB-9
Sandys, George 1578-1644 .... DLB-24
Santayana, George 1863-1952 ....DLB-54, 71

Santmyer, Helen Hooven 1895-1986 ....Y-84
Sapper (see McNeile, Herman Cyril)
Sargent, Pamela 1948- DLB-8
Saroyan, William 1908-1981............DLB-7, 9; Y-81
Sarton, May 1912- DLB-48; Y-81
Sartre, Jean-Paul 1905-1980................... DLB-72
Sassoon, Siegfried 1886-1967................ DLB-20
Saturday Review Press........................ DLB-46
Saunders, James 1925- DLB-13
Saunders, John Monk 1897-1940............. DLB-26
Savage, James 1784-1873..................... DLB-30
Savage, Marmion W. 1803?-1872.............. DLB-21
Savard, Félix-Antoine 1896-1982 .... DLB-68
Sawyer, Ruth 1880-1970..................... DLB-22
Sayers, Dorothy L. 1893-1957 ....DLB-10, 36, 77
Sayles, John Thomas 1950- DLB-44
Scannell, Vernon 1922- DLB-27
Scarry, Richard 1919- DLB-61
Schaeffer, Albrecht 1885-1950 .... DLB-66
Schaeffer, Susan Fromberg 1941- DLB-28
Schaper, Edzard 1908-1984 .... DLB-69
Scharf, J. Thomas 1843-1898.................. DLB-47
Schickele, René 1883-1940 .... DLB-66
Schlesinger, Arthur M., Jr. 1917- DLB-17
Schlumberger, Jean 1877-1968 .... DLB-65
Schmid, Eduard Hermann Wilhelm
    (see Edschmid, Kasimir)
Schmidt, Arno 1914-1979 .... DLB-69
Schmidt, Michael 1947- DLB-40
Schmitz, James H. 1911- DLB-8
Schnitzler, Arthur 1862-1931.................. DLB-81
Schnurre, Wolfdietrich 1920- DLB-69
Schocken Books DLB-46
The Schomburg Center for Research
    in Black Culture DLB-76
Schouler, James 1839-1920................... DLB-47
Schrader, Paul 1946- DLB-44
Schreiner, Olive 1855-1920................... DLB-18
Schroeder, Andreas 1946- DLB-53
Schulberg, Budd 1914- DLB-6, 26, 28; Y-81
Schulte, F. J., and Company.................. DLB-49

Schurz, Carl 1829-1906..................... DLB-23

Schuyler, George S. 1895-1977 ....DLB-29, 51

Schuyler, James 1923- DLB-5

Schwartz, Delmore 1913-1966..............DLB-28, 48

Schwartz, Jonathan 1938- Y-82

Science Fantasy................................DLB-8

Science-Fiction Fandom and Conventions DLB-8

Science-Fiction Fanzines: The Time Binders DLB-8

Science-Fiction Films DLB-8

Science Fiction Writers of America and the
    Nebula Awards...........................DLB-8

Scott, Evelyn 1893-1963 ....DLB-9, 48

Scott, Harvey W. 1838-1910.................. DLB-23

Scott, Paul 1920-1978........................ DLB-14

Scott, Sarah 1723-1795 .... DLB-39

Scott, Tom 1918- DLB-27

Scott, William Bell 1811-1890 .... DLB-32

Scott, William R. [publishing house]........... DLB-46

Scott-Heron, Gil 1949- DLB-41

Charles Scribner's Sons...................... DLB-49

Scripps, E. W. 1854-1926.................... DLB-25

Scudder, Horace Elisha 1838-1902 ....DLB-42, 71

Scudder, Vida Dutton 1861-1954.............. DLB-71

Scupham, Peter 1933- DLB-40

Seabrook, William 1886-1945................DLB-4

Seabury, Samuel 1729-1796 .... DLB-31

Sears, Edward I. 1819?-1876 .... DLB-79

Sears Publishing Company DLB-46

Seaton, George 1911-1979.................... DLB-44

Seaton, William Winston 1785-1866........... DLB-43

Sedgwick, Arthur George 1844-1915 .... DLB-64

Sedgwick, Catharine Maria 1789-1867.......DLB-1, 74

Seeger, Alan 1888-1916 .... DLB-45

Segal, Erich 1937- Y-86

Seghers, Anna 1900-1983 .... DLB-69

Seid, Ruth (see Sinclair, Jo)

Seidel, Frederick Lewis 1936- Y-84

Seidel, Ina 1885-1974 .... DLB-56

Séjour, Victor 1817-1874 .... DLB-50

Séjour Marcou et Ferrand,
    Juan Victor (see Séjour, Victor)

Selby, Hubert, Jr. 1928- DLB-2

Selden, George 1929- DLB-52

Selected English-Language Little Magazines and
    Newspapers [France, 1920-1939]...........DLB-4

Selected Humorous Magazines (1820-1950) ... DLB-11

Selected Science-Fiction Magazines and
    Anthologies DLB-8

Seligman, Edwin R. A. 1861-1939 .... DLB-47

Seltzer, Thomas [publishing house]............ DLB-46

Sendak, Maurice 1928- DLB-61

Sensation Novels (1863), by H. L. Manse...... DLB-21

Seredy, Kate 1899-1975 .... DLB-22

Serling, Rod 1924-1975...................... DLB-26

Settle, Mary Lee 1918- DLB-6

Seuss, Dr. (see Geisel, Theodor Seuss)

Sewall, Joseph 1688-1769..................... DLB-24

Sewell, Samuel 1652-1730 .... DLB-24

Sex, Class, Politics, and Religion [in the British
    Novel, 1930-1959]...................... DLB-15

Sexton, Anne 1928-1974 ....DLB-5

Shaara, Michael 1929-1988 ....Y-83

Shadwell, Thomas 1641?-1692................. DLB-80

Shaffer, Anthony 1926- DLB-13

Shaffer, Peter 1926- DLB-13

Shairp, Mordaunt 1887-1939................. DLB-10

Shakespeare, William 1564-1616 .... DLB-62

Shange, Ntozake 1948- DLB-38

Shapiro, Karl 1913- DLB-48

Sharon Publications........................... DLB-46

Sharpe, Tom 1928- DLB-14

Shaw, Bernard 1856-1950 ....DLB-10, 57

Shaw, Henry Wheeler 1818-1885.............. DLB-11

Shaw, Irwin 1913-1984 .... DLB-6; Y-84

Shaw, Robert 1927-1978....................DLB-13, 14

Shay, Frank [publishing house]................ DLB-46

Shea, John Gilmary 1824-1892 .... DLB-30

Shearing, Joseph 1886-1952................... DLB-70

Shebbeare, John 1709-1788 .... DLB-39

Sheckley, Robert 1928- DLB-8

Shedd, William G. T. 1820-1894 .... DLB-64

Sheed, Wilfred 1930- DLB-6

Sheed and Ward.................................. DLB-46

Sheldon, Alice B. (see Tiptree, James, Jr.)

Sheldon, Edward 1886-1946..................... DLB-7

Sheldon and Company DLB-49

Shepard, Sam 1943- DLB-7

Shepard, Thomas I 1604 or 1605-1649........ DLB-24

Shepard, Thomas II 1635-1677 .... DLB-24

Shepard, Clark and Brown DLB-49

Sheridan, Frances 1724-1766.................. DLB-39

Sherriff, R. C. 1896-1975...................... DLB-10

Sherwood, Robert 1896-1955................DLB-7, 26

Shiels, George 1886-1949...................... DLB-10

Shillaber, B.[enjamin] P.[enhallow]
  1814-1890..............................DLB-1, 11

Shine, Ted 1931- DLB-38

Shirer, William L. 1904- DLB-4

Shirley, James 1596-1666...................... DLB-58

Shockley, Ann Allen 1927- DLB-33

Shorthouse, Joseph Henry 1834-1903 .... DLB-18

Showalter, Elaine 1941- DLB-67

Shulevitz, Uri 1935- DLB-61

Shulman, Max 1919-1988 .... DLB-11

Shute, Henry A. 1856-1943 .... DLB-9

Shuttle, Penelope 1947- DLB-14, 40

Sidney, Margaret (see Lothrop, Harriet M.)

Sidney's Press.................................. DLB-49

Siegfried Loraine Sassoon: A Centenary Essay
  Tributes from Vivien F. Clarke and
  Michael Thorpe..........................Y-86

Sierra Club Books DLB-49

Sigourney, Lydia Howard (Huntley)
  1791-1865..........................DLB-1, 42, 73

Silkin, Jon 1930- DLB-27

Silliphant, Stirling 1918- DLB-26

Sillitoe, Alan 1928- DLB-14

Silman, Roberta 1934- DLB-28

Silverberg, Robert 1935- DLB-8

Simak, Clifford D. 1904-1988 .... DLB-8

Simcox, George Augustus 1841-1905......... DLB-35

Simenon, Georges 1903- DLB-72

Simmel, Johannes Mario 1924- DLB-69

Simmons, Herbert Alfred 1930- DLB-33

Simmons, James 1933- DLB-40

Simms, William Gilmore 1806-
  1870 ....DLB-3, 30, 59, 73

Simon, Neil 1927- DLB-7

Simon and Schuster DLB-46

Simons, Katherine Drayton Mayrant 1890-1969...Y-83

Simpson, Helen 1897-1940.................... DLB-77

Simpson, Louis 1923- DLB-5

Simpson, N. F. 1919- DLB-13

Sims, George R. 1847-1922..................DLB-35, 70

Sinclair, Andrew 1935- DLB-14

Sinclair, Jo 1913- DLB-28

Sinclair Lewis Centennial Conference Y-85

Sinclair, May 1863-1946 .... DLB-36

Sinclair, Upton 1878-1968..................... DLB-9

Sinclair, Upton [publishing house]............ DLB-46

Singer, Isaac Bashevis 1904- DLB-6, 28, 52

Singmaster, Elsie 1879-1958................... DLB-9

Siodmak, Curt 1902- DLB-44

Sissman, L. E. 1928-1976...................... DLB-5

Sisson, C. H. 1914- DLB-27

Sitwell, Edith 1887-1964...................... DLB-20

Skelton, Robin 1925- DLB-27, 53

Skinner, John Stuart 1788-1851 .... DLB-73

Skipsey, Joseph 1832-1903 .... DLB-35

Slade, Bernard 1930- DLB-53

Slater, Patrick 1880-1951 .... DLB-68

Slavitt, David 1935- DLB-5, 6

A Slender Thread of Hope: The Kennedy
  Center Black Theatre Project DLB-38

Slick, Sam (see Haliburton, Thomas Chandler)

Sloane, William, Associates DLB-46

Small, Maynard and Company DLB-49

Small Presses in Great Britain and Ireland,
  1960-1985................................ DLB-40

Small Presses I: Jargon Society Y-84

Small Presses II: The Spirit That
  Moves Us Press Y-85

Small Presses III: Pushcart Press Y-87

Smiles, Samuel 1812-1904 .... DLB-55

Smith, Alexander 1829-1867	DLB-32, 55
Smith, Betty 1896-1972	Y-82
Smith, Carol Sturm 1938-	Y-81
Smith, Charles Henry 1826-1903	DLB-11
Smith, Charlotte 1749-1806	DLB-39
Smith, Cordwainer 1913-1966	DLB-8
Smith, Dave 1942-	DLB-5
Smith, Dodie 1896-	DLB-10
Smith, Doris Buchanan 1934-	DLB-52
Smith, E. E. 1890-1965	DLB-8
Smith, Elihu Hubbard 1771-1798	DLB-37
Smith, Elizabeth Oakes (Prince) 1806-1893	DLB-1
Smith, George O. 1911-1981	DLB-8
Smith, H. Allen 1907-1976	DLB-11, 29
Smith, Harrison, and Robert Haas [publishing house]	DLB-46
Smith, Iain Crichten 1928-	DLB-40
Smith, J. Allen 1860-1924	DLB-47
Smith, J. Stilman, and Company	DLB-49
Smith, John 1580-1631	DLB-24, 30
Smith, Josiah 1704-1781	DLB-24
Smith, Ken 1938-	DLB-40
Smith, Lee 1944-	Y-83
Smith, Mark 1935-	Y-82
Smith, Michael 1698-circa 1771	DLB-31
Smith, Red 1905-1982	DLB-29
Smith, Roswell 1829-1892	DLB-79
Smith, Samuel Harrison 1772-1845	DLB-43
Smith, Samuel Stanhope 1751-1819	DLB-37
Smith, Seba 1792-1868	DLB-1, 11
Smith, Stevie 1902-1971	DLB-20
Smith, Sydney Goodsir 1915-1975	DLB-27
Smith, W. B., and Company	DLB-49
Smith, William 1727-1803	DLB-31
Smith, William 1728-1793	DLB-30
Smith, William Gardner 1927-1974	DLB-76
Smith, William Jay 1918-	DLB-5
Smollett, Tobias 1721-1771	DLB-39
Snellings, Rolland (see Touré, Askia Muhammad)	
Snodgrass, W. D. 1926-	DLB-5
Snow, C. P. 1905-1980	DLB-15, 77
Snyder, Gary 1930-	DLB-5, 16
Sobiloff, Hy 1912-1970	DLB-48
The Society for Textual Scholarship and *TEXT*	Y-87
Solano, Solita 1888-1975	DLB-4
Solomon, Carl 1928-	DLB-16
Solway, David 1941-	DLB-53
Solzhenitsyn and America	Y-85
Sontag, Susan 1933-	DLB-2, 67
Sorrentino, Gilbert 1929-	DLB-5; Y-80
Sources for the Study of Tudor and Stuart Drama	DLB-62
Southerland, Ellease 1943-	DLB-33
Southern, Terry 1924-	DLB-2
Southern Writers Between the Wars	DLB-9
Southerne, Thomas 1659-1746	DLB-80
Spark, Muriel 1918-	DLB-15
Sparks, Jared 1789-1866	DLB-1, 30
Sparshott, Francis 1926-	DLB-60
Späth, Gerold 1939-	DLB-75
Spellman, A. B. 1935-	DLB-41
Spencer, Anne 1882-1975	DLB-51, 54
Spencer, Elizabeth 1921-	DLB-6
Spencer, Herbert 1820-1903	DLB-57
Spencer, Scott 1945-	Y-86
Spender, Stephen 1909-	DLB-20
Spicer, Jack 1925-1965	DLB-5, 16
Spielberg, Peter 1929-	Y-81
Spier, Peter 1927-	DLB-61
Spinrad, Norman 1940-	DLB-8
Spofford, Harriet Prescott 1835-1921	DLB-74
Squibob (see Derby, George Horatio)	
Stafford, Jean 1915-1979	DLB-2
Stafford, William 1914-	DLB-5
Stage Censorship: "The Rejected Statement" (1911), by Bernard Shaw [excerpts]	DLB-10
Stallings, Laurence 1894-1968	DLB-7, 44
Stallworthy, Jon 1935-	DLB-40
Stampp, Kenneth M. 1912-	DLB-17
Stanford, Ann 1916-	DLB-5

Stanton, Elizabeth Cady 1815-1902	DLB-79
Stanton, Frank L. 1857-1927	DLB-25
Stapledon, Olaf 1886-1950	DLB-15
Star Spangled Banner Office	DLB-49
Starkweather, David 1935-	DLB-7
Statements on the Art of Poetry	DLB-54
Steadman, Mark 1930-	DLB-6
The Stealthy School of Criticism (1871), by Dante Gabriel Rossetti	DLB-35
Stearns, Harold E. 1891-1943	DLB-4
Stedman, Edmund Clarence 1833-1908	DLB-64
Steele, Max 1922-	Y-80
Steere, Richard circa 1643-1721	DLB-24
Stegner, Wallace 1909-	DLB-9
Stehr, Hermann 1864-1940	DLB-66
Steig, William 1907-	DLB-61
Stein, Gertrude 1874-1946	DLB-4, 54
Stein, Leo 1872-1947	DLB-4
Stein and Day Publishers	DLB-46
Steinbeck, John 1902-1968	DLB-7, 9; DS-2
Steiner, George 1929-	DLB-67
Stephen, Leslie 1832-1904	DLB-57
Stephens, Alexander H. 1812-1883	DLB-47
Stephens, Ann 1810-1886	DLB-3, 73
Stephens, Charles Asbury 1844?-1931	DLB-42
Stephens, James 1882?-1950	DLB-19
Sterling, George 1869-1926	DLB-54
Sterling, James 1701-1763	DLB-24
Stern, Richard 1928-	Y-87
Stern, Stewart 1922-	DLB-26
Sterne, Laurence 1713-1768	DLB-39
Sternheim, Carl 1878-1942	DLB-56
Stevens, Wallace 1879-1955	DLB-54
Stevenson, Anne 1933-	DLB-40
Stevenson, Robert Louis 1850-1894	DLB-18, 57
Stewart, Donald Ogden 1894-1980	DLB-4, 11, 26
Stewart, Dugald 1753-1828	DLB-31
Stewart, George R. 1895-1980	DLB-8
Stewart and Kidd Company	DLB-46
Stickney, Trumbull 1874-1904	DLB-54
Stiles, Ezra 1727-1795	DLB-31
Still, James 1906-	DLB-9
Stith, William 1707-1755	DLB-31
Stockton, Frank R. 1834-1902	DLB-42, 74
Stoddard, Ashbel [publishing house]	DLB-49
Stoddard, Richard Henry 1825-1903	DLB-3, 64
Stoddard, Solomon 1643-1729	DLB-24
Stoker, Bram 1847-1912	DLB-36, 70
Stokes, Frederick A., Company	DLB-49
Stokes, Thomas L. 1898-1958	DLB-29
Stone, Herbert S., and Company	DLB-49
Stone, Lucy 1818-1893	DLB-79
Stone, Melville 1848-1929	DLB-25
Stone, Samuel 1602-1663	DLB-24
Stone and Kimball	DLB-49
Stoppard, Tom 1937-	DLB-13; Y-85
Storey, Anthony 1928-	DLB-14
Storey, David 1933-	DLB-13, 14
Story, Thomas circa 1670-1742	DLB-31
Story, William Wetmore 1819-1895	DLB-1
Storytelling: A Contemporary Renaissance	Y-84
Stoughton, William 1631-1701	DLB-24
Stowe, Harriet Beecher 1811-1896	DLB-1, 12, 42, 74
Stowe, Leland 1899-	DLB-29
Strand, Mark 1934-	DLB-5
Stratemeyer, Edward 1862-1930	DLB-42
Stratton and Barnard	DLB-49
Straub, Peter 1943-	Y-84
Street, Cecil John Charles (see Rhode, John)	
Street and Smith	DLB-49
Streeter, Edward 1891-1976	DLB-11
Stribling, T. S. 1881-1965	DLB-9
Stringer and Townsend	DLB-49
Strittmatter, Erwin 1912-	DLB-69
Strother, David Hunter 1816-1888	DLB-3
Stuart, Jesse 1906-1984	DLB-9, 48; Y-84
Stuart, Lyle [publishing house]	DLB-46
Stubbs, Harry Clement (see Clement, Hal)	
The Study of Poetry (1880), by Matthew Arnold	DLB-35

Sturgeon, Theodore 1918-1985 .... DLB-8; Y-85

Sturges, Preston 1898-1959.................... DLB-26

"Style" (1840; revised, 1859), by Thomas
  de Quincey [excerpt]...................... DLB-57

"Style" (1888), by Walter Pater DLB-57

Style (1897), by Walter Raleigh [excerpt]....... DLB-57

"Style" (1877), by T. H. Wright [excerpt]...... DLB-57

"Le Style c'est l'homme" (1892),
  by W. H. Mallock DLB-57

Styron, William 1925- DLB-2; Y-80

Such, Peter 1939- DLB-60

Suckling, Sir John 1609-1642................. DLB-58

Suckow, Ruth 1892-1960 .... DLB-9

Suggs, Simon (see Hooper, Johnson Jones)

Sukenick, Ronald 1932- Y-81

Suknaski, Andrew 1942- DLB-53

Sullivan, C. Gardner 1886-1965 .... DLB-26

Sullivan, Frank 1892-1976.................... DLB-11

Summers, Hollis 1916- DLB-6

Sumner, Henry A. [publishing house]......... DLB-49

Surtees, Robert Smith 1803-1864.............. DLB-21

A Survey of Poetry
  Anthologies, 1879-1960 .... DLB-54

Surveys of the Year's Biography
  A Transit of Poets and Others: American
    Biography in 1982 ....Y-82
  The Year in Literary Biography Y-83
  The Year in Literary Biography Y-84
  The Year in Literary Biography Y-85
  The Year in Literary Biography Y-86
  The Year in Literary Biography Y-87
  The Year in Literary Biography Y-88

Surveys of the Year's Book Publishing
  The Year in Book Publishing................Y-86

Surveys of the Year's Drama
  The Year in Drama Y-82
  The Year in Drama Y-83
  The Year in Drama Y-84
  The Year in Drama Y-85
  The Year in Drama Y-87
  The Year in Drama Y-88

Surveys of the Year's Fiction
  The Year's Work in Fiction: A Survey Y-82
  The Year in Fiction: A Biased View Y-83
  The Year in Fiction Y-84
  The Year in Fiction Y-85

  The Year in Fiction Y-86
  The Year in the Novel Y-87
  The Year in Short Stories...................Y-87
  The Year in the Novel Y-88
  The Year in Short Stories...................Y-88

Surveys of the Year's Poetry
  The Year's Work in American Poetry.........Y-82
  The Year in Poetry Y-83
  The Year in Poetry Y-84
  The Year in Poetry Y-85
  The Year in Poetry Y-86
  The Year in Poetry Y-87
  The Year in Poetry Y-88

Sutherland, John 1919-1956................... DLB-68

Sutro, Alfred 1863-1933...................... DLB-10

Swados, Harvey 1920-1972 ....DLB-2

Swain, Charles 1801-1874 .... DLB-32

Swallow Press................................ DLB-46

Swenson, May 1919- DLB-5

Swerling, Jo 1897- DLB-44

Swift, Jonathan 1667-1745.................... DLB-39

Swinburne, A. C. 1837-1909................DLB-35, 57

Swinnerton, Frank 1884-1982 .... DLB-34

Swisshelm, Jane Grey 1815-1884 .... DLB-43

Swope, Herbert Bayard 1882-1958 .... DLB-25

Swords, T. and J., and Company.............. DLB-49

Swords, Thomas 1763-1843 and
  Swords, James ?-1844 .... DLB-73

Symonds, John Addington 1840-1893 .... DLB-57

Symons, Arthur 1865-1945.................DLB-19, 57

Symons, Scott 1933- DLB-53

Synge, John Millington 1871-1909..........DLB-10, 19

T

Taggard, Genevieve 1894-1948................ DLB-45

Tait, J. Selwin, and Sons..................... DLB-49

Talvj or Talvi (see Robinson, Therese)

Taradash, Daniel 1913- DLB-44

Tarbell, Ida M. 1857-1944.................... DLB-47

Tarkington, Booth 1869-1946 ....DLB-9

Tashlin, Frank 1913-1972 .... DLB-44

Tate, Allen 1899-1979.................DLB-4, 45, 63

Tate, James 1943-	DLB-5
Tate, Nahum circa 1652-1715	DLB-80
Taylor, Bayard 1825-1878	DLB-3
Taylor, Bert Leston 1866-1921	DLB-25
Taylor, Charles H. 1846-1921	DLB-25
Taylor, Edward circa 1642-1729	DLB-24
Taylor, Henry 1942-	DLB-5
Taylor, Sir Henry 1800-1886	DLB-32
Taylor, Mildred D. ?-	DLB-52
Taylor, Peter 1917-	Y-81
Taylor, William, and Company	DLB-49
Taylor-Made Shakespeare? Or Is "Shall I Die?" the Long-Lost Text of Bottom's Dream?	Y-85
Teasdale, Sara 1884-1933	DLB-45
The Tea-Table (1725), by Eliza Haywood [excerpt]	DLB-39
Tenn, William 1919-	DLB-8
Tennant, Emma 1937-	DLB-14
Tenney, Tabitha Gilman 1762-1837	DLB-37
Tennyson, Alfred 1809-1892	DLB-32
Tennyson, Frederick 1807-1898	DLB-32
Terhune, Albert Payson 1872-1942	DLB-9
Terry, Megan 1932-	DLB-7
Terson, Peter 1932-	DLB-13
Tesich, Steve 1943-	Y-83
Tey, Josephine 1896?-1952	DLB-77
Thacher, James 1754-1844	DLB-37
Thackeray, William Makepeace 1811-1863	DLB-21, 55
Thanet, Octave (see French, Alice)	
The Theater in Shakespeare's Time	DLB-62
The Theatre Guild	DLB-7
Thério, Adrien 1925-	DLB-53
Theroux, Paul 1941-	DLB-2
Thoma, Ludwig 1867-1921	DLB-66
Thoma, Richard 1902-	DLB-4
Thomas, Audrey 1935-	DLB-60
Thomas, D. M. 1935-	DLB-40
Thomas, Dylan 1914-1953	DLB-13, 20
Thomas, Edward 1878-1917	DLB-19
Thomas, Gwyn 1913-1981	DLB-15
Thomas, Isaiah 1750-1831	DLB-43, 73
Thomas, Isaiah [publishing house]	DLB-49
Thomas, John 1900-1932	DLB-4
Thomas, Joyce Carol 1938-	DLB-33
Thomas, Lorenzo 1944-	DLB-41
Thomas, R. S. 1915-	DLB-27
Thompson, Dorothy 1893-1961	DLB-29
Thompson, Francis 1859-1907	DLB-19
Thompson, George Selden (see Selden, George)	
Thompson, John 1938-1976	DLB-60
Thompson, John R. 1823-1873	DLB-3, 73
Thompson, Maurice 1844-1901	DLB-71, 74
Thompson, Ruth Plumly 1891-1976	DLB-22
Thompson, William Tappan 1812-1882	DLB-3, 11
Thomson, James 1834-1882	DLB-35
Thomson, Mortimer 1831-1875	DLB-11
Thoreau, Henry David 1817-1862	DLB-1
Thorpe, Thomas Bangs 1815-1878	DLB-3, 11
Thoughts on Poetry and Its Varieties (1833), by John Stuart Mill	DLB-32
Thurber, James 1894-1961	DLB-4, 11, 22
Thurman, Wallace 1902-1934	DLB-51
Thwaite, Anthony 1930-	DLB-40
Thwaites, Reuben Gold 1853-1913	DLB-47
Ticknor, George 1791-1871	DLB-1, 59
Ticknor and Fields	DLB-49
Ticknor and Fields (revived)	DLB-46
Tietjens, Eunice 1884-1944	DLB-54
Tilton, J. E., and Company	DLB-49
Time and Western Man (1927), by Wyndham Lewis [excerpts]	DLB-36
Time-Life Books	DLB-46
Times Books	DLB-46
Timothy, Peter circa 1725-1782	DLB-43
Timrod, Henry 1828-1867	DLB-3
Tiptree, James, Jr. 1915-	DLB-8
Titus, Edward William 1870-1952	DLB-4
Toklas, Alice B. 1877-1967	DLB-4
Tolkien, J. R. R. 1892-1973	DLB-15
Tolson, Melvin B. 1898-1966	DLB-48, 76

Tom Jones (1749), by Henry
 Fielding [excerpt] DLB-39

Tomlinson, Charles 1927- DLB-40

Tomlinson, Henry Major 1873-1958 ....DLB-36

Tompkins, Abel [publishing house]...........DLB-49

Tompson, Benjamin 1642-1714 ....DLB-24

Tonks, Rosemary 1932- DLB-14

Toole, John Kennedy 1937-1969................Y-81

Toomer, Jean 1894-1967 ....DLB-45, 51

Tor Books....................................DLB-46

Torrence, Ridgely 1874-1950.................DLB-54

Toth, Susan Allen 1940- Y-86

Tough-Guy Literature........................DLB-9

Touré, Askia Muhammad 1938- DLB-41

Tourgée, Albion W. 1838-1905...............DLB-79

Tourneur, Cyril circa 1580-1626 ....DLB-58

Tousey, Frank [publishing house] DLB-49

Tower Publications DLB-46

Towne, Benjamin circa 1740-1793...........DLB-43

Towne, Robert 1936- DLB-44

Tracy, Honor 1913- DLB-15

The Transatlantic Publishing Company DLB-49

Transcendentalists, American DS-5

Traven, B. 1882? or 1890?-1969?...........DLB-9, 56

Travers, Ben 1886-1980 ....DLB-10

Tremain, Rose 1943- DLB-14

Tremblay, Michel 1942- DLB-60

Trends in Twentieth-Century
 Mass Market Publishing...................DLB-46

Trent, William P. 1862-1939 ....DLB-47

Trescot, William Henry 1822-1898...........DLB-30

Trevor, William 1928- DLB-14

Trilling, Lionel 1905-1975.................DLB-28, 63

Triolet, Elsa 1896-1970 ....DLB-72

Tripp, John 1927- DLB-40

Trocchi, Alexander 1925- DLB-15

Trollope, Anthony 1815-1882 ....DLB-21, 57

Trollope, Frances 1779-1863 ....DLB-21

Troop, Elizabeth 1931- DLB-14

Trotti, Lamar 1898-1952 ....DLB-44

Trottier, Pierre 1925- DLB-60

Troupe, Quincy Thomas, Jr. 1943- DLB-41

Trow, John F., and Company DLB-49

Trumbo, Dalton 1905-1976...................DLB-26

Trumbull, Benjamin 1735-1820 ....DLB-30

Trumbull, John 1750-1831 ....DLB-31

T. S. Eliot Centennial........................Y-88

Tucholsky, Kurt 1890-1935...................DLB-56

Tucker, George 1775-1861 ....DLB-3, 30

Tucker, Nathaniel Beverley 1784-1851.........DLB-3

Tucker, St. George 1752-1827................DLB-37

Tuckerman, Henry Theodore 1813-1871 .....DLB-64

Tunis, John R. 1889-1975 ....DLB-22

Tuohy, Frank 1925- DLB-14

Tupper, Martin F. 1810-1889 ....DLB-32

Turbyfill, Mark 1896- DLB-45

Turco, Lewis 1934- Y-84

Turnbull, Gael 1928- DLB-40

Turner, Charles (Tennyson) 1808-1879 ....DLB-32

Turner, Frederick 1943- DLB-40

Turner, Frederick Jackson 1861-1932.........DLB-17

Turner, Joseph Addison 1826-1868...........DLB-79

Turpin, Waters Edward 1910-1968............DLB-51

Twain, Mark (see Clemens, Samuel Langhorne)

Tyler, Anne 1941- DLB-6; Y-82

Tyler, Moses Coit 1835-1900 ....DLB-47, 64

Tyler, Royall 1757-1826 ....DLB-37

Tylor, Edward Burnett 1832-1917............DLB-57

U

Udall, Nicholas 1504-1556....................DLB-62

Uhse, Bodo 1904-1963 ....DLB-69

Under the Microscope (1872), by A. C.
 Swinburne DLB-35

United States Book Company DLB-49

Universal Publishing and Distributing
 Corporation..............................DLB-46

The University of Iowa Writers'
 Workshop Golden Jubilee....................Y-86

"The Unknown Public" (1858), by
 Wilkie Collins [excerpt] DLB-57

Unruh, Fritz von 1885-1970................... DLB-56

Upchurch, Boyd B. (see Boyd, John)

Updike, John 1932- DLB-2, 5; Y-80, 82; DS-3

Upton, Charles 1948- DLB-16

Upward, Allen 1863-1926................... DLB-36

Ustinov, Peter 1921- DLB-13

V

Vail, Laurence 1891-1968 ....DLB-4

Vajda, Ernest 1887-1954 .... DLB-44

Valgardson, W. D. 1939- DLB-60

Van Allsburg, Chris 1949- DLB-61

Van Anda, Carr 1864-1945................. DLB-25

Vanbrugh, Sir John 1664-1726............... DLB-80

Vance, Jack 1916?- DLB-8

Van Doren, Mark 1894-1972................. DLB-45

van Druten, John 1901-1957 .... DLB-10

Van Duyn, Mona 1921- DLB-5

Van Dyke, Henry 1852-1933 .... DLB-71

Van Dyke, Henry 1928- DLB-33

Vane, Sutton 1888-1963..................... DLB-10

Vanguard Press............................ DLB-46

van Itallie, Jean-Claude 1936- DLB-7

Vann, Robert L. 1879-1940.................. DLB-29

Van Rensselaer, Mariana Griswold
  1851-1934............................ DLB-47

Van Rensselaer, Mrs. Schuyler (see Van
  Rensselaer, Mariana Griswold)

Van Vechten, Carl 1880-1964 .... DLB-4, 9

van Vogt, A. E. 1912- DLB-8

Varley, John 1947- Y-81

Vassa, Gustavus (see Equiano, Olaudah)

Vega, Janine Pommy 1942- DLB-16

Veiller, Anthony 1903-1965 .... DLB-44

Verplanck, Gulian C. 1786-1870............... DLB-59

Very, Jones 1813-1880 ....DLB-1

Vian, Boris 1920-1959...................... DLB-72

Vickers, Roy 1888?-1965 .... DLB-77

Victoria 1819-1901 .... DLB-55

Vidal, Gore 1925- DLB-6

Viebig, Clara 1860-1952....................... DLB-66

Viereck, George Sylvester 1884-1962.......... DLB-54

Viereck, Peter 1916- DLB-5

Viewpoint: Politics and Performance, by David
  Edgar..................................... DLB-13

Vigneault, Gilles 1928- DLB-60

The Viking Press.............................. DLB-46

Villard, Henry 1835-1900 .... DLB-23

Villard, Oswald Garrison 1872-1949........... DLB-25

Villemaire, Yolande 1949- DLB-60

Villiers, George, Second Duke
  of Buckingham 1628-1687 .... DLB-80

Viorst, Judith ?- DLB-52

Volland, P. F., Company DLB-46

von der Grün, Max 1926- DLB-75

Vonnegut, Kurt 1922- DLB-2, 8; Y-80; DS-3

Vroman, Mary Elizabeth circa 1924-1967...... DLB-33

W

Waddington, Miriam 1917- DLB-68

Wade, Henry 1887-1969...................... DLB-77

Wagoner, David 1926- DLB-5

Wah, Fred 1939- DLB-60

Wain, John 1925- DLB-15, 27

Wainwright, Jeffrey 1944- DLB-40

Waite, Peirce and Company DLB-49

Wakoski, Diane 1937- DLB-5

Walck, Henry Z............................. DLB-46

Walcott, Derek 1930- Y-81

Waldman, Anne 1945- DLB-16

Walker, Alice 1944- DLB-6, 33

Walker, George F. 1947- DLB-60

Walker, Joseph A. 1935- DLB-38

Walker, Margaret 1915- DLB-76

Walker, Ted 1934- DLB-40

Walker and Company DLB-49

Walker, Evans and Cogswell Company DLB-49

Walker, John Brisben 1847-1931 .... DLB-79

Cumulative Index

Wallace, Edgar 1875-1932 .... DLB-70

Wallant, Edward Lewis 1926-1962 .... DLB-2, 28

Walpole, Horace 1717-1797 .... DLB-39

Walpole, Hugh 1884-1941 .... DLB-34

Walrond, Eric 1898-1966 .... DLB-51

Walser, Martin 1927- DLB-75

Walser, Robert 1878-1956 .... DLB-66

Walsh, Ernest 1895-1926 .... DLB-4, 45

Walsh, Robert 1784-1859 .... DLB-59

Wambaugh, Joseph 1937- DLB-6; Y-83

Ward, Artemus (see Browne, Charles Farrar)

Ward, Arthur Henry Sarsfield
 (see Rohmer, Sax)

Ward, Douglas Turner 1930- DLB-7, 38

Ward, Lynd 1905-1985 .... DLB-22

Ward, Mrs. Humphry 1851-1920 .... DLB-18

Ward, Nathaniel circa 1578-1652 .... DLB-24

Ward, Theodore 1902-1983 .... DLB-76

Ware, William 1797-1852 .... DLB-1

Warne, Frederick, and Company DLB-49

Warner, Charles Dudley 1829-1900 .... DLB-64

Warner, Rex 1905- DLB-15

Warner, Susan Bogert 1819-1885 .... DLB-3, 42

Warner, Sylvia Townsend 1893-1978 .... DLB-34

Warner Books DLB-46

Warren, John Byrne Leicester (see De Tabley, Lord)

Warren, Lella 1899-1982 .... Y-83

Warren, Mercy Otis 1728-1814 .... DLB-31

Warren, Robert Penn 1905- DLB-2, 48; Y-80

Washington, George 1732-1799 .... DLB-31

Wassermann, Jakob 1873-1934 .... DLB-66

Wasson, David Atwood 1823-1887 .... DLB-1

Waterhouse, Keith 1929- DLB-13, 15

Waterman, Andrew 1940- DLB-40

Waters, Frank 1902- Y-86

Watkins, Tobias 1780-1855 .... DLB-73

Watkins, Vernon 1906-1967 .... DLB-20

Watmough, David 1926- DLB-53

Watson, Sheila 1909- DLB-60

Watson, Wilfred 1911- DLB-60

Watt, W. J., and Company DLB-46

Watterson, Henry 1840-1921 .... DLB-25

Watts, Alan 1915-1973 .... DLB-16

Watts, Franklin [publishing house] DLB-46

Waugh, Auberon 1939- DLB-14

Waugh, Evelyn 1903-1966 .... DLB-15

Way and Williams DLB-49

Wayman, Tom 1945- DLB-53

Weatherly, Tom 1942- DLB-41

Webb, Frank J. ?-? DLB-50

Webb, James Watson 1802-1884 .... DLB-43

Webb, Mary 1881-1927 .... DLB-34

Webb, Phyllis 1927- DLB-53

Webb, Walter Prescott 1888-1963 .... DLB-17

Webster, Augusta 1837-1894 .... DLB-35

Webster, Charles L., and Company DLB-49

Webster, John 1579 or 1580-1634? DLB-58

Webster, Noah 1758-1843 .... DLB-1, 37, 42, 43, 73

Weems, Mason Locke 1759-1825 .... DLB-30, 37, 42

Weidman, Jerome 1913- DLB-28

Weinbaum, Stanley Grauman 1902-1935 .... DLB-8

Weisenborn, Günther 1902-1969 .... DLB-69

Weiß, Ernst 1882-1940 .... DLB-81

Weiss, John 1818-1879 .... DLB-1

Weiss, Peter 1916-1982 .... DLB-69

Weiss, Theodore 1916- DLB-5

Welch, Lew 1926-1971? DLB-16

Weldon, Fay 1931- DLB-14

Wellek, René 1903- DLB-63

Wells, Carolyn 1862-1942 .... DLB-11

Wells, Charles Jeremiah circa 1800-1879 ...... DLB-32

Wells, H. G. 1866-1946 .... DLB-34, 70

Wells, Robert 1947- DLB-40

Wells-Barnett, Ida B. 1862-1931 .... DLB-23

Welty, Eudora 1909- DLB-2; Y-87

Wendell, Barrett 1855-1921 .... DLB-71

Wentworth, Patricia 1878-1961 .... DLB-77

Werfel, Franz 1890-1945 .... DLB-81

The Werner Company DLB-49

Wersba, Barbara 1932- DLB-52

Wescott, Glenway 1901- DLB-4, 9
Wesker, Arnold 1932- DLB-13
Wesley, Richard 1945- DLB-38
Wessels, A., and Company DLB-46
West, Anthony 1914-1988 .... DLB-15
West, Dorothy 1907- DLB-76
West, Jessamyn 1902-1984 .... DLB-6; Y-84
West, Mae 1892-1980 .... DLB-44
West, Nathanael 1903-1940 .... DLB-4, 9, 28
West, Paul 1930- DLB-14
West, Rebecca 1892-1983 .... DLB-36; Y-83
West and Johnson DLB-49
Western Publishing Company DLB-46
Wetherell, Elizabeth (see Warner, Susan Bogert)
Whalen, Philip 1923- DLB-16
Wharton, Edith 1862-1937 .... DLB-4, 9, 12, 78
Wharton, William 1920s?- Y-80
What's Really Wrong With Bestseller Lists Y-84
Wheatley, Dennis Yates 1897-1977 .... DLB-77
Wheatley, Phillis circa 1754-1784 .... DLB-31, 50
Wheeler, Charles Stearns 1816-1843 .... DLB-1
Wheeler, Monroe 1900-1988 .... DLB-4
Wheelock, John Hall 1886-1978 .... DLB-45
Wheelwright, John circa 1592-1679 .... DLB-24
Wheelwright, J. B. 1897-1940 .... DLB-45
Whetstone, Colonel Pete (see Noland, C. F. M.)
Whipple, Edwin Percy 1819-1886 .... DLB-1, 64
Whitaker, Alexander 1585-1617 .... DLB-24
Whitaker, Daniel K. 1801-1881 .... DLB-73
Whitcher, Frances Miriam 1814-1852 .... DLB-11
White, Andrew 1579-1656 .... DLB-24
White, Andrew Dickson 1832-1918 .... DLB-47
White, E. B. 1899-1985 .... DLB-11, 22
White, Edgar B. 1947- DLB-38
White, Ethel Lina 1887-1944 .... DLB-77
White, Horace 1834-1916 .... DLB-23
White, Richard Grant 1821-1885 .... DLB-64
White, Walter 1893-1955 .... DLB-51
White, William, and Company DLB-49
White, William Allen 1868-1944 .... DLB-9, 25

White, William Anthony Parker (see Boucher, Anthony)
White, William Hale (see Rutherford, Mark)
Whitechurch, Victor L. 1868-1933 .... DLB-70
Whitehead, James 1936- Y-81
Whitfield, James Monroe 1822-1871 .... DLB-50
Whiting, John 1917-1963 .... DLB-13
Whiting, Samuel 1597-1679 .... DLB-24
Whitlock, Brand 1869-1934 .... DLB-12
Whitman, Albert, and Company DLB-46
Whitman, Albery Allson 1851-1901 .... DLB-50
Whitman, Sarah Helen (Power) 1803-1878 ...... DLB-1
Whitman, Walt 1819-1892 .... DLB-3, 64
Whitman Publishing Company DLB-46
Whittemore, Reed 1919- DLB-5
Whittier, John Greenleaf 1807-1892 .... DLB-1
Whittlesey House DLB-46
Wideman, John Edgar 1941- DLB-33
Wiebe, Rudy 1934- DLB-60
Wiechert, Ernst 1887-1950 .... DLB-56
Wieners, John 1934- DLB-16
Wier, Ester 1910- DLB-52
Wiesel, Elie 1928- Y-87
Wiggin, Kate Douglas 1856-1923 .... DLB-42
Wigglesworth, Michael 1631-1705 .... DLB-24
Wilbur, Richard 1921- DLB-5
Wild, Peter 1940- DLB-5
Wilde, Oscar 1854-1900 .... DLB-10, 19, 34, 57
Wilde, Richard Henry 1789-1847 .... DLB-3, 59
Wilde, W. A., Company DLB-49
Wilder, Billy 1906- DLB-26
Wilder, Laura Ingalls 1867-1957 .... DLB-22
Wilder, Thornton 1897-1975 .... DLB-4, 7, 9
Wiley, Bell Irvin 1906-1980 .... DLB-17
Wiley, John, and Sons DLB-49
Wilhelm, Kate 1928- DLB-8
Wilkes, George 1817-1885 .... DLB-79
Wilkinson, Sylvia 1940- Y-86
Wilkinson, William Cleaver 1833-1920 .... DLB-71
Willard, L. [publishing house] DLB-49
Willard, Nancy 1936- DLB-5, 52

Willard, Samuel 1640-1707	DLB-24
Williams, A., and Company	DLB-49
Williams, C. K. 1936-	DLB-5
Williams, Chancellor 1905-	DLB-76
Williams, Emlyn 1905-	DLB-10, 77
Williams, Garth 1912-	DLB-22
Williams, George Washington 1849-1891	DLB-47
Williams, Heathcote 1941-	DLB-13
Williams, Hugo 1942-	DLB-40
Williams, Isaac 1802-1865	DLB-32
Williams, Joan 1928-	DLB-6
Williams, John A. 1925-	DLB-2, 33
Williams, John E. 1922-	DLB-6
Williams, Jonathan 1929-	DLB-5
Williams, Raymond 1921-	DLB-14
Williams, Roger circa 1603-1683	DLB-24
Williams, Samm-Art 1946-	DLB-38
Williams, Sherley Anne 1944-	DLB-41
Williams, T. Harry 1909-1979	DLB-17
Williams, Tennessee 1911-1983	DLB-7; Y-83; DS-4
Williams, Valentine 1883-1946	DLB-77
Williams, William Appleman 1921-	DLB-17
Williams, William Carlos 1883-1963	DLB-4, 16, 54
Williams, Wirt 1921-	DLB-6
Williams Brothers	DLB-49
Williamson, Jack 1908-	DLB-8
Willingham, Calder Baynard, Jr. 1922-	DLB-2, 44
Willis, Nathaniel Parker 1806-1867	DLB-3, 59, 73, 74
Wilmer, Clive 1945-	DLB-40
Wilson, A. N. 1950-	DLB-14
Wilson, Angus 1913-	DLB-15
Wilson, Arthur 1595-1652	DLB-58
Wilson, Augusta Jane Evans 1835-1909	DLB-42
Wilson, Colin 1931-	DLB-14
Wilson, Edmund 1895-1972	DLB-63
Wilson, Ethel 1888-1980	DLB-68
Wilson, Harriet E. Adams 1828?-1863?	DLB-50
Wilson, Harry Leon 1867-1939	DLB-9
Wilson, John 1588-1667	DLB-24
Wilson, Lanford 1937-	DLB-7
Wilson, Margaret 1882-1973	DLB-9
Wilson, Michael 1914-1978	DLB-44
Wilson, Woodrow 1856-1924	DLB-47
Wimsatt, William K., Jr. 1907-1975	DLB-63
Winchell, Walter 1897-1972	DLB-29
Winchester, J. [publishing house]	DLB-49
Windham, Donald 1920-	DLB-6
Winsor, Justin 1831-1897	DLB-47
John C. Winston Company	DLB-49
Winters, Yvor 1900-1968	DLB-48
Winthrop, John 1588-1649	DLB-24, 30
Winthrop, John, Jr. 1606-1676	DLB-24
Wirt, William 1772-1834	DLB-37
Wise, John 1652-1725	DLB-24
Wisner, George 1812-1849	DLB-43
Wister, Owen 1860-1938	DLB-9, 78
Witherspoon, John 1723-1794	DLB-31
Wodehouse, P. G. 1881-1975	DLB-34
Wohmann, Gabriele 1932-	DLB-75
Woiwode, Larry 1941-	DLB-6
Wolcott, Roger 1679-1767	DLB-24
Wolf, Christa 1929-	DLB-75
Wolfe, Gene 1931-	DLB-8
Wolfe, Thomas 1900-1938	DLB-9; DS-2; Y-85
Wollstonecraft, Mary 1759-1797	DLB-39
Wondratschek, Wolf 1943-	DLB-75
Wood, Benjamin 1820-1900	DLB-23
Wood, Charles 1932-	DLB-13
Wood, Mrs. Henry 1814-1887	DLB-18
Wood, Samuel [publishing house]	DLB-49
Wood, William ?-?	DLB-24
Woodberry, George Edward 1855-1930	DLB-71
Woodbridge, Benjamin 1622-1684	DLB-24
Woodhull, Victoria C. 1838-1927	DLB-79
Woodmason, Charles circa 1720-?	DLB-31
Woodson, Carter G. 1875-1950	DLB-17
Woodward, C. Vann 1908-	DLB-17
Woolf, David (see Maddow, Ben)	
Woolf, Virginia 1882-1941	DLB-36
Woollcott, Alexander 1887-1943	DLB-29

Woolman, John 1720-1772 ... DLB-31
Woolner, Thomas 1825-1892 ... DLB-35
Woolsey, Sarah Chauncy 1835-1905 ... DLB-42
Woolson, Constance Fenimore 1840-1894 .. DLB-12, 74
Worcester, Joseph Emerson 1784-1865 ... DLB-1
The Works of the Rev. John Witherspoon (1800-1801) [excerpts] ... DLB-31
A World Chronology of Important Science Fiction Works (1818-1979) ... DLB-8
World Publishing Company ... DLB-46
Worthington, R., and Company ... DLB-49
Wouk, Herman 1915- ... Y-82
Wright, Charles 1935- ... Y-82
Wright, Charles Stevenson 1932- ... DLB-33
Wright, Frances 1795-1852 ... DLB-73
Wright, Harold Bell 1872-1944 ... DLB-9
Wright, James 1927-1980 ... DLB-5
Wright, Jay 1935- ... DLB-41
Wright, Louis B. 1899-1984 ... DLB-17
Wright, Richard 1908-1960 ... DS-2, DLB-76
Wright, Richard B. 1937- ... DLB-53
Wright, Sarah Elizabeth 1928- ... DLB-33
Writers' Forum ... Y-85
Writing for the Theatre, by Harold Pinter ... DLB-13
Wycherley, William 1641-1715 ... DLB-80
Wylie, Elinor 1885-1928 ... DLB-9, 45
Wylie, Philip 1902-1971 ... DLB-9

Y

Yates, Dornford 1885-1960 ... DLB-77
Yates, J. Michael 1938- ... DLB-60
Yates, Richard 1926- ... DLB-2; Y-81
Yeats, William Butler 1865-1939 ... DLB-10, 19
Yep, Laurence 1948- ... DLB-52

Yerby, Frank 1916- ... DLB-76
Yezierska, Anzia 1885-1970 ... DLB-28
Yolen, Jane 1939- ... DLB-52
Yonge, Charlotte Mary 1823-1901 ... DLB-18
A Yorkshire Tragedy ... DLB-58
Yoseloff, Thomas [publishing house] ... DLB-46
Young, Al 1939- ... DLB-33
Young, Stark 1881-1963 ... DLB-9
Young, Waldeman 1880-1938 ... DLB-26
Young, William [publishing house] ... DLB-49
Yourcenar, Marguerite 1903-1987 ... DLB-72; Y-88
"You've Never Had It So Good," Gusted by "Winds of Change": British Fiction in the 1950s, 1960s, and After ... DLB-14

Z

Zangwill, Israel 1864-1926 ... DLB-10
Zebra Books ... DLB-46
Zebrowski, George 1945- ... DLB-8
Zech, Paul 1881-1946 ... DLB-56
Zelazny, Roger 1937- ... DLB-8
Zenger, John Peter 1697-1746 ... DLB-24, 43
Zieber, G. B., and Company ... DLB-49
Zieroth, Dale 1946- ... DLB-60
Zimmer, Paul 1934- ... DLB-5
Zindel, Paul 1936- ... DLB-7, 52
Zolotow, Charlotte 1915- ... DLB-52
Zubly, John Joachim 1724-1781 ... DLB-31
Zu-Bolton II, Ahmos 1936- ... DLB-41
Zuckmayer, Carl 1896-1977 ... DLB-56
Zukofsky, Louis 1904-1978 ... DLB-5
zur Mühlen, Hermynia 1883-1951 ... DLB-56
Zweig, Arnold 1887-1968 ... DLB-66
Zweig, Stefan 1881-1942 ... DLB-81